Classical Music
on CD

THE ROUGH GUIDE

KT-237-302

NAFL

NORWICH CITY COLLEGE LIBRARY

Stock No	789.912016
Class	145258
Cat.	Proc.

FOR
REFERENCE ONLY

Also available in Rough Guides music reference series:
The Rough Guide to World Music

Forthcoming:
The Rough Guide to Jazz
The Rough Guide to Opera

145 258

Acknowledgements:
Thanks to: Mark Ellingham and Martin Dunford for deciding to go ahead; Henry Iles for designing the book and providing technical back-up; Andy Hilliard for typesetting; Alan Spicer for computer trickery; Vanessa Kelly for picture research; Alan Jefferson; Vivien Antwi; and Ian Mulvey of Barrett Berkeley. Special thanks to two people who shouldered vastly more than their fair share of the load: Abendroth Minor (who in turn thanks Victoria Osterman) and Susanne Hillen.

Thanks also to all those at the record companies who have supported this book, in particular: Michael Deacon at RCA/BMG; Marius Carboni and Lucy Colyer at EMI; Sarah Herdson at Virgin; Lucy Maxwell-Stewart and Sophie Beck at Deutsche Grammophon; Kate Jones at Philips; Carol Lowry at Decca; Terri Robson at Polygram; Katherine Howard at Sony; Celia Ballantyne at Hyperion; David Blake at Harmonia Mundi; Rona Harrison and David Denton at Naxos; Harriet Capaldi at Warner; Anne Hyde Crofts at Conifer; Paul Westcott at Chandos; Alf Goodrich at Nimbus; John Jones at Collins. Finally, thanks to Susan Stevens at Stockhausen-Verlag, and to Stockhausen himself.

In memory of Neil Vint (1970–1994).

This first edition published 1994 by Rough Guides Ltd, 1 Mercer Street, London WC2H 9QJ.
Distributed by The Penguin Group:

Penguin Books Ltd, 27 Wrights Lane, London W8 5TZ
Penguin Books USA Inc., 375 Hudson Street, New York 10014, USA
Penguin Books Australia Ltd, 487 Maroondah Highway, PO Box 257, Ringwood, Victoria 3134, Australia
Penguin Books Canada Ltd, 10 Alcorn Avenue, Toronto, Ontario, Canada M4V 1E4
Penguin Books (NZ) Ltd, 182–190 Wairau Road, Auckland 10, New Zealand

Typeset in Bodoni and Gill Sans to an original design by Henry Iles.
Printed in the UK by The Bath Press, Avon.

All drawings © Guus Ong.

No part of this book may be reproduced in any form without permission from the publisher except for the quotation of brief passages in reviews.

© Rough Guides Ltd 1994.

480pp. includes index

A catalogue record for this book is available from the British Library.
ISBN 1-85828-113-X

Classical Music
on CD

THE ROUGH GUIDE

Written by

Matthew Boyden, Matthew Rye, Simon Broughton,
Joe Staines, Gavin Thomas, Jonathan Webster,
Sophie Fuller, Stephen Jackson, Mark Prendergast, David
Doughty, Jonathan Buckley and Kim Burton

Edited by

Jonathan Buckley

THE ROUGH GUIDES

CONTENTS

INTRODUCTION

The compact disc format has released a flood of classical music. The catalogue of current classical CDs runs to some fourteen hundred tightly packed triple-column pages, and lists some eighty composers before reaching the second letter of the alphabet. An average month sees some four hundred recordings added to the pile. THE ROUGH GUIDE TO CLASSICAL MUSIC ON CD attempts to make sense of this over-whelming volume of music, giving you the information that's essential whether you're starting from the beginning or have already begun exploring.

As well as being a buyer's guide to CDs, this book is a Who's Who of classical music, ranging from Hildegard of Bingen, one of the great figures of eleventh-century European culture, to George Benjamin, born in 1960. Of course we've been selective, and any selection is bound to be controversial. Not everyone would allow Philip Glass into the same club as Johann Sebastian Bach, for example, while others might wonder why some names are missing. A few composers have been omitted because we think they are primarily of historical importance, and a few interesting characters are not included because you can't get decent recordings of their music. On the other hand, you'll find a lot of unjustly neglected composers alongside the big names, and some we think you should keep an eye on.

With each composer's output we've been similarly choosy. Domenico Scarlatti was a fascinating musician, but no book of this scope could do justice to each of his five hundred keyboard sonatas. Gaetano Donizetti wrote more than seventy operas, but you wouldn't want to listen to all of them. We've gone for what we think are the best, some-times adding pieces that should be better known, sometimes relegating work we think is overrated. When it comes to CDs the situation requires even greater ruthlessness. Beethoven may have written only nine symphonies, but there are more than one hundred versions of the fifth in the catalogue, and scores of recordings of all the others. Many of these CDs should never have been issued – they are there simply because any up-and-coming conductor has to make a Beethoven recording as a kind of calling card, regardless of any aptitude for the music. However, a fair proportion of the Beethoven CDs are worth listening to, because a piece of music as complex as a Beethoven symphony will bear as many different readings as a Shakespeare play.

Although there are recordings that stand head and shoulders above the competition, no performance can be described as definitive, which is one reason why we have often recommended more than one account of a work. Whereas all our first-choice CDs make persuasive cases for the music, some of the additional recommendations are included because they make provocative counter-arguments. Where price is a consideration, we've also listed a lower-cost alternative whenever feasible – thus we might suggest a mid-price boxed set of symphonies as an alternative to buying them as full-price indi-vidual CDs. Finally, in many instances we've picked an outstanding pre-stereo perfor-mance as a complement to a modern recording.

These "historic" reissues are a big growth area, and their success is not due to mere nostalgia. There are some genuinely great musicians around today: the conductor Carlos Kleiber, the pianist Maurizio Pollini, the singer Cecilia Bartoli, or the violinist

Maxim Vengerov would have been remarkable in any era. Yet there's also a lot of hype in the modern music business. There are soloists who owe their success more to the way they look than to the way they play – and conversely, many superlative musicians who remain obscure because they don't project the requisite glamour. But it's in the area of orchestral music and opera that the situation is especially bad. Orchestral musicians are now trained to a very high standard, but they rarely enjoy the sort of long-term relationship with an individual conductor that used to give each orchestra its distinctive sound. The same goes for opera companies, which used to have a stable core of singers and musicians working under the same conductor for years. Now we have a system of jet-setting stars, who might be singing or conducting in London one night, New York the next, then in the recording studio for a few days to record something with people they hadn't met until the day the session started. You don't necessarily get a good football team by paying millions for a miscellaneous batch of top-flight players, and you don't build a good musical team that way either.

Musically, then, new is not always best. And don't assume that a recording made more than thirty years ago will sound terrible. Sound quality won't match that of digital CDs, but you'll be surprised at how good it can be – indeed, many people prefer the warmth of the old vinyl sound to the often chilly precision produced by modern studios. (We've warned you if surface noise or tinny quality might be a hindrance to enjoyment.) In short, you'll be missing a lot if you insist on hi-tech – no recent releases can match Horowitz's 1940 account of Tchaikovsky's *Piano Concerto No. 1*, or Josef Hofmann's versions of the Chopin piano concertos from the 1930s, or Rachmaninov playing his own music.

How this book works

Immediately after this introduction you'll find a list of all the composers covered in the guide, arranged chronologically, so you can see at a glance who fits where. If you find you like the music of Palestrina, you could check the list and decide to listen to Byrd, his contemporary, or if you like Xenakis you might want to try Ligeti. At the end of the book there's a directory of major performers, giving cross-references to the main part of the guide, and recommended recital and compilation recordings. After that comes a detailed glossary, defining all the technical terms we've used.

Between lies the bulk of the guide, an A to Z of composers from John Adams to Alexander Zemlinsky. Each entry starts with an introduction to the composer's music, usually with an outline biography. (Many composers were too busy writing music to lead interesting lives, but if there's a story to tell, we tell it.) That's followed by a run-through of the main compositions, with subheadings for individual works that need detailed discussion. These subheadings follow the same basic order, moving from largest-scale works down to the smallest: thus operas precede symphonies and concertos, which in turn precede chamber works and solo instrumental music. With the most important figures – such as Haydn, Mozart and Beethoven – we've grouped the music under generic headings (eg "Symphonies"), giving an introduction to each composer's work in that genre before going on to the individual pieces, which are then arranged chronologically.

Under each heading you'll find a short discussion of the piece or pieces to which the heading refers, followed by recommended recordings of those pieces, and a review of each CD. The CD details conform to a regular format: soloist first, then orchestra (and/or choir), then conductor, with the record company and serial number in parenthesis. (The serial number is generally the same in Europe as in North America, except that the -2 suffix is usually dropped in North America.) You'll have to get your store to order many of the CDs we've recommended, as most stores stock just the best-sellers and the new releases. Ordering is no problem, however – you should be able to get hold of ninety-five percent of our recommendations within a week of asking for them. Should you find that a listed CD is not in your store's catalogue, get them to check that the performance has not been repackaged under a different serial number – if a new classical recording doesn't meet its quota in its first two months on sale, it will usually be allowed to drift out of stock and then reissued, either at a lower price band, or combined with different music. Each listing is preceded by a symbol indicating the price of the CD, as in the following examples:

⊙	Schubert Songs: Fischer-Dieskau (DG etc)	= under £7 or $8;
◑	Schubert Songs: Souzay (Philips etc)	= £7–10 or $8–13;
●	Schubert Songs: Fassbaender (Hyperion etc)	= over £10 or $13.

The pricing of CDs is a contentious subject. The difference between prices in North America and Britain is explained by differences in taxation and mark-up margins, but you'll come across the argument that top-price CDs are overpriced in both markets. Certainly some CDs are too expensive – there are plenty of cases of major labels recycling a best-selling vinyl disc as a full-price CD with little more than half an hour's music on it. That said, the vast majority of CDs are good value. The catalogues of the multinationals are bursting with CDs that pack the contents of two former LPs onto a single eighty-minute disc, often at mid-price or lower. As a broad rule, the more specialized the music the more the disc will cost, as the recondite areas of the repertoire tend to be the preserve of smaller, independent labels, who need to recoup their costs on discs that won't sell in vast numbers. But even here you'll find that big stores often have special promotions, while many smaller outlets can beat the average prices of the megastores, and there are plenty of mail-order companies selling CDs at a discount.

On top of all this, in recent years there's been an explosion of budget labels, led by Naxos. Don't think that a CD can't be any good if it hasn't got a famous face on the cover – the commitment you get on many of the budget-label performances outweighs the professionalism of the major league players, and in several instances they win on all fronts. The success of these relative newcomers has spurred the big companies to put more effort into their own budget-price series – every big company now has a range of CDs costing less than half the top price, and two-for-the-price-of-one packages are becoming increasingly popular. There's never been a better time to assemble a classical music collection.

CHRONOLOGY OF COMPOSERS

Born before 1400
Hildegard of Bingen 1098–1179
Pérotin 1160–1225
Guillaume de Machaut 1300–77

Born 1400–1500
Guillaume Dufay 1400–74
Johannes Ockeghem 1410–97
Josquin Desprez 1440–1521
Antoine Brumel c. 1460–1515
John Taverner 1490–1545

Born 1500–1600
Thomas Tallis 1505–85
Giovanni Palestrina 1526–94
Roland Lassus 1532–94
William Byrd 1543–1623
Tomás Luis de Victoria 1548–1661
Giovanni Gabrieli 1557–1612
Carlo Gesualdo 1561–1613
John Dowland 1563–1626
Claudio Monteverdi 1567–1643
Orlando Gibbons 1583–1625
Heinrich Schütz 1585–1672

Born 1600–1700
Giacomo Carissimi 1605–74
Jean-Baptiste Lully 1632–87
Alessandro Stradella 1644–82
Marc-Antoine Charpentier 1645–1704
Arcangelo Corelli 1653–1713
Henry Purcell 1659–1695
Alessandro Scarlatti 1660–1725
François Couperin 1668–1733
Tomaso Albinoni 1671–1750
Antonio Vivaldi 1678–1741
Georg-Philipp Telemann 1681–1767
Jean-Philippe Rameau 1683–1764
George Frideric Handel 1685–1759
Domenico Scarlatti 1685–1757
J.S. Bach 1685–1750

Born 1700–1800
Giovanni Pergolesi 1710–36
C.P.E. Bach 1714–88
Christoph Gluck 1714–87

Joseph Haydn 1732–1809
Luigi Boccherini 1743–1805
Muzio Clementi 1752–1832
Wolfgang Amadeus Mozart 1756–91
Ludwig van Beethoven 1770–1827
Johann Hummel 1778–1837
Nicolò Paganini 1782–1840
Carl Maria von Weber 1786–1826
Giacomo Meyerbeer 1791–1864
Gioachino Rossini 1792–1868
Franz Schubert 1797–1828
Gaetano Donizetti 1797–1848

Born 1800–1825
Vincenzo Bellini 1801–35
Hector Berlioz 1803–69
Johann Strauss the Elder 1804–49
Mikhail Glinka 1805–57
Felix Mendelssohn 1809–47
Frédéric Chopin 1810–49
Robert Schumann 1810–56
Ferenc Liszt 1811–86
Giuseppe Verdi 1813–1901
Richard Wagner 1813–83
Charles François Gounod 1818–93
Jacques Offenbach 1819–80
César Franck 1822–90
Anton Bruckner 1824–96
Bedrich Smetana 1824–84

Born 1825–1850
Johann Strauss the Younger 1825–99
Alexander Borodin 1833–87
Johannes Brahms 1833–97
Camille Saint-Saëns 1835–1921
Leo Delibes 1836–91
Georges Bizet 1838–75
Max Bruch 1838–1920
Modest Mussorgsky 1839–81
Pyotr Il'yich Tchaikovsky 1840–93
Antonin Dvořák 1841–1904
Jules Massenet 1842–1912
Arthur Sullivan 1842–1900
Edvard Grieg 1843–1907
Nicolai Rimsky-Korsakov 1844–1908
Gabriel Fauré 1845–1924
Hubert Parry 1848–1918

Born 1850–1875

Engelbert Humperdinck 1854–1921
Leoš Janáček 1854–1928
Edward Elgar 1857–1934
Ruggero Leoncavallo 1857–1919
Giacomo Puccini 1858–1924
Ethel Smyth 1858–1944
Isaac Albéniz 1860–1909
Gustav Mahler 1860–1911
Hugo Wolf 1860–1903
Claude Debussy 1862–1918
Frederick Delius 1862–1934
Pietro Mascagni 1863–1945
Richard Strauss 1864–1949
Alexander Glazunov 1865–1936
Carl Nielsen 1865–1931
Jean Sibelius 1865–1957
Ferruccio Busoni 1866–1924
Erik Satie 1866–1925
Enrique Granados 1867–1916
Umberto Giordano 1867–1948
Hans Pfitzner 1869–1949
Franz Lehár 1870–1948
Alexander Zemlinsky 1871–1942
Alexander Scriabin 1872–1915
Ralph Vaughan Williams 1872–1958
Sergey Rachmaninov 1873–1943
Max Reger 1873–1916
Gustav Holst 1874–1934
Josef Suk 1874–1935
Charles Ives 1874–1954
Arnold Schoenberg 1874–1951

Born 1875–1900

Maurice Ravel 1875–1937
Manuel de Falla 1876–1946
Franz Schreker 1878–1934
Ottorino Respighi 1879–1936
Béla Bartók 1881–1945
Zoltán Kodály 1882–1967
Igor Stravinsky 1882–1971
Karol Szymanowski 1882–1937
Arnold Bax 1883–1953
Edgard Varèse 1883–1965
Anton Webern 1883–1945
Alban Berg 1885–1935
Lili Boulanger 1893–1918
Heitor Villa-Lobos 1887–1959
Frank Martin 1890–1974
Bohuslav Martinů 1890–1959
Sergey Prokofiev 1891–1953
Arthur Honegger 1892–1955
Darius Milhaud 1892–1974

Paul Hindemith 1895–1963
Carl Orff 1895–1982
Erich Wolfgang Korngold 1897–1957
Viktor Ullmann 1898–1944
Hanns Eisler 1898–1962
George Gershwin 1898–1937
Francis Poulenc 1899–1963

Born 1900–1925

Aaron Copland 1900–90
Kurt Weill 1900–50
Joaquín Rodrigo 1901–
William Walton 1902–83
Aram Khachaturian 1903–78
Michael Tippett 1905–
Elisabeth Lutyens 1906–83
Dmitri Shostakovich 1906–75
Elizabeth Maconchy 1907–90
Elliott Carter 1908–
Olivier Messiaen 1908–92
Grazyna Bacewicz 1909–67
Samuel Barber 1910–81
John Cage 1912–92
Benjamin Britten 1913–76
Witold Lutosławski 1913–94
Leonard Bernstein 1918–90
Malcolm Arnold 1921–
Robert Simpson 1921–
Iannis Xenakis 1922–
György Ligeti 1923–

Born 1925–present

Luciano Berio 1925–
Pierre Boulez 1925–
Morton Feldman 1926–87
Hans Werner Henze 1926–
Karlheinz Stockhausen 1928–
Sofia Gubaidulina 1931–
Henryk Górecki 1933–
Krzysztof Penderecki 1933–
Harrison Birtwistle 1934–
Peter Maxwell Davies 1934–
Alfred Schnittke 1934–
Nicholas Maw 1935–
Arvo Pärt 1935–
Steve Reich 1936–
Philip Glass 1937–
Michael Nyman 1944–
John Tavener 1944–
John Adams 1947–
Judith Weir 1954–
James Macmillan 1959–
George Benjamin 1960–

JOHN ADAMS

(1947–   )

Like Philip Glass and the other Minimalists with whom he is often bracketed, John Adams has set out to reverse the influence of modernist cerebralism, to make it okay for composers to write unashamedly tonal music again. For Adams, "tonality is not just a cultural invention, but a natural force, like gravity". But unlike any thoroughgoing Minimalist, Adams writes fairly eventful music which in a way is reminiscent of Charles Ives: never coy about using vernacular and "banal" elements, he is a crusading synthesist who is quite happy to openly borrow from sources as wide-ranging as jazz, Arabian music, church music and folk tunes.

Adams' father was a dance-band saxophonist and, as a boy, he was encouraged by both parents to listen to a huge variety of music, ranging from Mozart to Duke Ellington. (Adams has always considered Ellington to be a great composer, and one of his most cherished boyhood memories was of being taken to an Ellington concert and put up on the piano stool next to the jazz maestro.) When Adams arrived at Harvard in the late 1960s he was swept up by the radicalism of the times, and was particularly fascinated by William Burroughs' use of "vernacular, junkie language", which directly inspired him to develop a musical language that "didn't make a distinction between high art and low art, highbrow and middlebrow and lowbrow". An even greater influence in those years was the composer John Cage (see p.89), whose *Silence*, a delightfully eccentric Zen-like collection of essays, gave Adams the courage to find his own voice as a composer.

After graduation, he headed west to San Francisco, where he encountered the Minimalist works of Steve Reich, Terry Riley and Philip Glass for the first time. Adams was immediately drawn to Minimalism's resolute reliance on tonality, its insistent, hypnotic rhythms, and its absorption of Balinese, African, Indian and other non-Western musics. Yet, while Adams still stands by the view that Minimalism is "the most important stylistic development in Western art music since the Fifties", he soon saw the limitations of a technique that placed so much emphasis upon repetition. With *Shaker Loops* (1978) he heralded what he termed "post-minimalism", a style characterized by a more fluid and layered sound, and greater dynamic contrasts.

With his three-act opera *Nixon in China*, premiered at Houston in 1985, Adams really hit his stride. The choice of subject – Nixon's groundbreaking visit to Peking in 1972 – was a daring departure for a genre that tends to fall back on ancient history or mythology for its plots, and Adams' music showed the potential of a style that amalgamated Minimalist procedures with more dramatic forms of writing. Sections of *Nixon* display the same sort of highly kinetic repetitive rhythms as you'll hear in Philip Glass, but it also has stretches of witty pastiche and parody, and the coloratura role of Madame Mao is perhaps modern opera's most vivid caricature.

BETTY FREEMAN/LEBRECHT COLLECTION

Audience response to *Nixon in China* was very positive, and the work has played in several major opera houses and festivals worldwide. The critics, however, were sharply divided, some declaring *Nixon* the most accomplished new opera since *Peter Grimes*, others condemning it for relying too heavily on mere spectacle. European critics were notably less enthusiastic than their US counterparts, but with his second opera, *The Death of Klinghoffer* (see below), Adams has started to get a more respectful press on both sides of the Atlantic.

THE DEATH OF KLINGHOFFER

The Death of Klinghoffer (premiered in March 1991), is similar to *Nixon in China* in that it tackles an event from very recent political history – the hijacking by Palestinian terrorists of the ocean liner *Achille Lauro*, and their murder of one of the passengers, Leon Klinghofer. Adams created it in partnership with the librettist Alice Goodman and the director Peter Sellars, the team responsible for *Nixon*, but there the similarities between the two operas end. While *Nixon in China* was essentially a comedy, albeit one of "very serious jests", as Goethe said of his own *Faust*, *Klinghoffer* is preoccupied with the deep religious and economic conflicts that drove the terrible events of October 1985. Whereas *Nixon in China* is for the most part naturalistic in pace and setting, the dramaturgy of *Klinghoffer* is based, according to Adams, on largely static models, encompassing Bach's Passion settings, Greek tragedy, and Persian and Japanese drama. *Klinghoffer* is too raw to make for a comfortable night at the theatre, but it is an emotionally riveting experience, and Adams' most impressive achievement to date.

⦿ Maddalena, Felty, Hammons, Young, Perry, Sylvan, Friedman, Nadler; Lyon Opera Chorus & Orchestra; Nagano (Elektra Nonesuch 7559-79281-2; 2 CDs).

It's clear right from the opening orchestral F minor chords that Kent Nagano has a tight grip on this piece, and the entire performance turns out to be deep and searching. The expressiveness of the Lyon Opera Orchestra is remarkable, while the soloists give performances of real stature, with James Maddalena, as the ship's philosophical captain, and Sanford Sylvan, as Klinghofer, particularly outstanding.

ISAAC ALBÉNIZ
(1860–1909)

Isaac Albéniz, a crucial figure in the creation of a distinctively Spanish classical musical idiom, is associated primarily with works for the piano, and above all with *Iberia*, a suite of twelve piano pieces composed between 1906 and 1909. It's hardly surprising that the majority of his pieces were written for that instrument, given Albéniz's extraordinary gifts as a performer.

Born into a musical family (his sister Clementine was also a talented pianist), Isaac made his public debut at Barcelona's Teatro Romea at the age of four, where some members of the incredulous audience supected that some kind of fraud was being perpetrated. When he was seven his mother took him to audition at the Paris Conservatoire, where he was praised by Professor Marmontel – the man who had taught both Bizet and Debussy the piano – but was considered too young to become a student. In 1869 the Albéniz family moved to Madrid, where Isaac was enrolled at the conservatory, and it was about this time that his fiercely independent spirit began to manifest itself. When he was ten he suddenly ran away from home and supported himself by giving concerts in various cities of Castile, but the unpleasant experience of losing his luggage to bandits drove him back to his parents. A couple of years later he topped that escapade by stowing away on a ship to

South America, travelling to the USA via Argentina, Uruguay, Brazil, Cuba and Puerto Rico, supporting himself by playing piano in so-called "places of entertainment".

Although to his family's immense relief he returned to Spain, settled down and became a diligent student, Albéniz never fully exorcized his wanderlust and spent much of the rest of his life moving between Barcelona, Madrid, Paris and London, as much to perfect his pianistic and compositional technique as to earn a living. On one trip in 1880 he followed his idol Liszt through Weimar, Prague, Vienna and Budapest, gaining invaluable instruction along the way. The fulcrum of his nomadic existence for much of the 1890s was Paris, where he taught piano and struck up friendships with, among others, Debussy. His encounters with the new wave of French composers, headed by Debussy and Ravel, were immensely productive – and the relationship was not the one-way process it's sometimes depicted as having been, as Albéniz contributed much to the emergence of impressionist music.

One other person was to have a profound influence upon Albéniz and his two most illustrious Spanish contemporaries, Falla (see p.130) and Granados (see p.152), and that was the musicologist and folk song collector Felipe Pedrell. Albéniz's earliest compositions were overblown Lisztian waltzes, mazurkas and marches, but after his encounter with Pedrell he began to explore and experiment with Spanish folk idioms. Inspired by Pedrell he tried to make it as a writer of zarzuelas, Spain's equivalent of operetta, and made several efforts to compose large-scale orchestral works that incorporated folk elements, but time and again his abilities as a pianist brought him back to the solo piano as his natural mode of expression. As the nineteenth century came to a close, it was Albéniz's music above all that defined everything that was exciting about modern Spanish piano writing. Pieces like *La Vega*, the *Cantos de España* and *Suite española* are bursting with national colour, evoking the sound of guitars, flamenco rhythms, and dances like the Sevillana and Corranda.

Although enough survives of Albéniz's output to get a good overview of his achieve-

GUUS ONG

ments, biographers have been thwarted in their attempts to devise a definitive catalogue of his works owing to the fact that his manuscripts were so widely dispersed during his lifetime, with the result that many pieces have gone missing. Equally unfortunate is the fact that there are no recordings of Albéniz playing the piano – his death at the early age of 49 just preceded the spread of the earliest gramophones.

IBERIA

Everything in Albéniz's life had been building up to his twelve-part *Iberia* suite, and the last three years of his life he obsessively worked on this music to get it just right. *Iberia* was immediately recognized as the most important Spanish work for solo piano, a status it still retains, and its bold sonorities and harmonies were an inspiration for that country's young composers. In this single work Albéniz conjures up the presence of a whole array of different regions, ranging from Seville to Cadiz and Madrid, capturing the musical essence of each local culture not by merely aping and embellishing its tunes, but through a subtle snatch of rhythm here and the faintest outline of a melodic refrain there.

○ de Larrocha (EMI CMS 7 64504 2; with various other Albéniz piano works; 2 CDs).
○ de Larrocha (DECCA 417 887-2; with *Navarra & Suite española*).

Although we have no recordings of Albéniz playing his own music, we have the next best thing: Alicia de Larrocha performing *Iberia*. Larrocha learnt piano from Frank Marshall, a collaborator and disciple of Enrique Granados, and thus with her performances you are in touch with a performing tradition stretching back to Pedrell and Albéniz himself. The EMI set – which offers a substantial overview of the rest of Albéniz's output – was made in 1962, when de Larrocha was full of youthful ardour and prepared to take risks. On the other hand, the level of hiss on the record makes some people prefer the digital performance she made for Decca twenty-five years later – a fine CD, if not quite as volatile as its predecessor.

TOMASO ALBINONI

(1671–1751)

Albinoni is almost entirely known for a piece of music he didn't actually write. The famous *Adagio in G minor* was not merely reconstructed by the Italian musicologist Remo Giazotto, as is usually acknowledged after Albinoni's name – it was pretty well written by him in its entirety. Giazotto came across the manuscript in a library in Dresden just after World War II. The music consisted of a bass line, a few bars of the violin part, and nothing more. Deciding that what he'd found was a church sonata, Giazotti scored the piece for organ and strings. The result is a work of solemnity and affecting simplicity, which has proved an astonishingly durable favourite, almost on a par with Vivaldi's *Four Seasons* (which was rediscovered around the same time, but is entirely genuine). If, as is rumoured, Giazotto owns the copyright to the *Adagio*, he must by now be very rich indeed.

Approaching Albinoni's genuine compositions after the lushness of the *Adagio* can come as a shock. On the whole it is bright, lively and melodious music, with more than a passing resemblance to that of Vivaldi, his great contemporary and fellow-Venetian. Unlike Vivaldi, Albinoni didn't have to compose to earn his living. As the eldest son of a highly prosperous paper merchant, he approached music as a committed amateur, but soon made his mark as an opera composer, writing over fifty works (of which few have survived intact). In 1721 the family business, part of which he had inherited in 1709, was successfully claimed by one of his father's many creditors, but this loss of income coincided with the most successful period of Albinoni's career. His operas were being performed outside Italy, and he was invited to supervise one of them, *I Veri Amici* (The True Friends) at the Bavarian court in Munich. He even received the accolade of having three themes used as the subjects for fugues by J. S. Bach – perhaps the pinnacle of his reputation until the resurrection of the *Adagio*.

> ◗ **Adagio in G minor**: I Musici (Philips 410 606-2; with Pachelbel's *Canon* etc).
> ◗ **Albinoni and Vivaldi Wind Concertos**: Goodwin; The King's Consort; King (Hyperion CDA 66383).

Performances of the *Adagio* range from the overblown (Herbert von Karajan's high kitsch version being the most notorious) to the briskly efficient versions from early music groups, who often sound as if they are ashamed to be doing it in the first place. The recording by the Italian string orchestra I Musici makes a satisfying compromise. The pace is slow without being ponderous, the string sound is generous but not too big, and the vibrato is never overdone. As is usually the case, the *Adagio* is coupled with a selection of Baroque and Classical favourites, including Pachelbel's *Canon* and Boccherini's *Minuet*.

After the spurious *Adagio*, the most recorded of Albinoni's works are the two sets of oboe concertos opus 7 and opus 9. The King's Consort recording combines three of the concertos from opus 9 and a concerto for trumpet, three oboes and bassoon by Albinoni with three wind concertos by Vivaldi. It makes for a well-balanced programme, both in terms of the different combinations of instruments and in the contrasts between the two composers. Vivaldi is clearly the more brilliant of the two, with his characteristically hard-driven rhythms, but Albinoni excels in the slow movements which are consistently lyrical and – in the D minor oboe concerto and the G major concerto for two oboes – outstandingly beautiful. Paul Goodwin, a Baroque oboe specialist, combines a fine tone with a marvellously assured sense of phrasing.

MALCOLM ARNOLD

(1921–)

Like George Lloyd and Robert Simpson (see p.342), Malcom Arnold is one of the last staunchly traditional, quintessentially English composers. Although there are traces of jazz in some of his music, his output is based almost exclusively on straightforward melody and diatonic harmony, and it has found a stable if static audience. Still writing well into his seventies, Arnold has produced a vast amount of orchestral music, including dozens of concertos, overtures, film scores, dances and suites in which he displays a greater mastery of orchestration than Simpson or Lloyd. (Of his eighty or so film commissions, most famous is the score for *The Bridge on the River Kwai* which took him only ten days to compose and won him an Oscar.) But on the other hand, where Simpson and Lloyd have developed intricate personal styles, Arnold's musical personality has remained somewhat vague – he has stated that his greatest influence has been Berlioz, but you won't find much of the Berlioz temperament in Arnold's professionally crafted music. Consciously designed for popularity, Arnold's music can be rather short-winded, but he has consistently refused to compromise with fashion and he remains a composer of enjoyable music that wallows in its association with the English tradition.

THE MUSIC

Some of Arnold's most appealing music is to be found in his series of national dances, a continuing sequence of pieces derived from the folk songs of various countries. These are tuneful orchestral showpieces, designed to entertain the player as much as the listener, and are, perhaps, the most immediate introduction to Arnold's music. Of his symphonies, the second is similarly beguiling. A sunny and high-spirited work, it flagrantly uses devices that are, in Malcolm's own words, "emotional cliches", which sometimes obscures the genuine drama and warmth of the piece. Some may find its "Englishness" a bit twee but there's nonetheless a lot of fresh and brilliantly orchestrated music here.

⦿ English, Scottish, Cornish and Irish Dances: Philharmonia Orchestra; Thomson (Chandos CHAN 8867).
◗ Symphonies Nos. 2 & 5: City of Birmingham Symphony Orchestra; Groves, Arnold (EMI 7 63368-2; with Peterloo Overture).

Bryden Thomson's recording of the English, Scottish, Cornish and Irish Dances is spontaneous and brimming with life. The recording is clear and well-focused and the playing of the Philharmonia is very light and responsive. This is a slightly short disc, but worth the money. If it gives you a taste for Arnold's music, you could explore other parts of the Chandos catalogue, as the company has embarked on a vast retrospective of Arnold's career.

Charles Groves's conducting of the *Symphony No. 2* occasionally adopts slow tempi that tend to sap the music's energy, but this is a clear and unpretentious account of this fine work. It's coupled with the more sombre Symphony No. 5 and one of Arnold's most rousing overtures.

ROSS STUDIOS

Bryden Thomson

GRAZYNA BACEWICZ

(1909–1969)

Poland's most important woman composer, Grazyna Bacewicz was born in Lodz into a musical family – her brother Kiejstut was a fine pianist with whom she frequently performed – and began studying at the Warsaw conservatory in 1928. She continued her musical education in Paris with two of the most influential teachers of the period, Carl Flesch for violin and Nadia Boulanger for composition. She was unfortunate to be entered for the Wieniawski violin competition in 1935, the same year as David Oistrakh and Ginette Neveu, two of the greatest violinists of the century. She did well enough, however, to gain a first-class distinction and went on to have an outstanding career as a soloist, being especially noted as an interpreter of the first violin concerto of her fellow countryman and mentor Karol Syzmanowski (see p.367).

Unsurprisingly much of her best writing is for the violin. She wrote no fewer than seven violin concertos and five sonatas for violin and piano, but even her orchestral writing tends to locate the dynamic drive in the string section. The music composed before 1960 is often described as neoclassical and, though she disliked the term, it adequately summarizes her emphasis on clear contrapuntal lines, the general brightness of her sound-world, and her avoidance of sentimentality. That is not to say her work lacks emotion – for example, the slow movement of the concerto for string orchestra,

one of her best works, contains a sensuous and haunting cello part set against soft but rhythmically insistent high strings. Occasionally the momentum flags and the writing can sometimes seem a rather schematic interchange of voices, but on the whole she maintains a firm grip on the proceedings. From 1960 her work is marked by an attempt to assimilate some of the sonorities of the avant-garde, particularly those techniques, such as glissandi and clusters, often associated with her younger compatriot Penderecki (see p.264). The CD reviewed below introduces the best of Bacewicz.

◉ **Sonata No. 4 for violin and piano; Piano Sonata No. 2; Concerto for String Orchestra; Violin Concerto No. 7:** Statkiewicz; Utrecht; Zimerman; Janowski; Polish Chamber Orchestra; National Philharmonic Orchestra Warsaw; Maksymiuk; Markowski (Olympia OCD 392).

There is a wide variety of music on this disc, ranging from an electrifying account of the brilliant *Concerto for String Orchestra* (1948) to a live performance of the *Violin Concerto No. 7* (1965), a work high on atmospheric effects if rather lower on coherence. In general the earlier works are the most memorable, with an infectious wit and vitality. The *Piano Sonata No. 2*, here given a bravura performance by Krystian Zimerman, is a virtuosic catalogue of pianistic tricks, at times reminiscent of Ravel but with a rather more restrained harmonic language. Better still is the *Violin Sonata No. 4* (1949), a work similar to Bartók in its abrasive energy, but in no way derivative. It has an unnervingly edgy slow movement in which a lilting but anguished lullaby is framed by defiant-sounding broken chords on the piano.

CARL PHILIPP EMANUEL BACH

(1714–1788)

Of Johann Sebastian Bach's twenty children, three were outstanding musicians in their own right. Of these three – Wilhelm Friedmann, Johann Christian and Carl Philipp Emanuel – the last was the

most influential as a composer, creating a bridge between the exuberant Baroque style of his father and the Classical style of Haydn and Mozart. While always acknowledging a great debt to his father (his only teacher), he came to reject the complexity of polyphonic music, preferring a much more subjective and dramatic approach, full of unexpected and odd shifts in harmony, and with an emphasis on melody – a style known as *empfindsamer Stil* (expressive style).

Although C.P.E. Bach's educational background was broader than his father's – he trained as a lawyer and preferred the company of writers and intellectuals to that of musicians – he suffered a similar hard grind as a musician: in his case nearly thirty badly paid years as a keyboard player at the court of Frederick the Great at Potsdam. Frederick's taste was conservative, and the experimental nature of much of C.P.E. Bach's music meant that he never won preferment – indeed his principal duty seems to have been to accompany Frederick, a keen amateur flautist, on the harpsichord. Perhaps it was to widen his fame outside the narrow confines of Potsdam that he published his *Essay on the True Art of Playing Keyboard Instruments*, a highly influential treatise which was used as a teaching aid by both Mozart and Beethoven. In 1767, upon the death of his godfather, Georg-Philipp Telemann, the restless C.P.E. Bach succeeded him as music director of the five principal churches in Hamburg. His work load was enormous but, away from his church duties, the freer atmosphere of the commercial city-state made the last twenty years of his life much more stimulating.

KEYBOARD MUSIC

C.P.E. Bach's favourite keyboard instrument was the clavichord, a soft and delicate-sounding instrument whose strings were struck like those of the piano, rather than plucked like the harsichord, and whose dynamics could therefore be controlled by touch. He was an immensely sensitive performer, famed above all for the emotional intensity of his improvisations, a quality most evident in his fantasias and the slow movements of his sonatas, which are more harmonically quirky and unconventional than those of his great successors Haydn and Mozart.

🔘 **A Wayward Genius, Sonatas and Rondos of C.P.E. Bach**: Bartschi (Jecklin-Disco JD 683-2).

Surprisingly, C.P.E. Bach's keyboard music has not been taken up by pianists in the same way as his father's or Domenico Scarlatti's. That it can sound equally convincing on the piano is proved by this fine recital by Werner Bartschi, who plays four sonatas, two rondos and a fantasia from various stages in C.P.E. Bach's career. Bartschi's playing is cleanly articulated and he possesses a sufficiently delicate touch to do justice to the evasive, will-o'-the-wisp nature of this subtle and beautiful music. He's at his most sensitive in the first piece on the disc, the G minor sonata of 1746, in which the sudden changes of mood and speed are very deftly handled.

CHORAL MUSIC

The sheer volume of music that C.P.E. Bach had to provide for the Hamburg churches inevitably had a deleterious effect on its quality – as well as composing in a hurry, he also was obliged to knock together composite works using music by his relations and by Telemann. Of his later works the oratorio *Die Isrealiten in der Wuste* (1769) is worth hearing, but his undoubted choral masterpiece is an earlier work, the *Magnificat* of 1749. The opening words of praise of the Virgin Mary are set with a thrilling energy that looks back to the Baroque, especially to the setting of the same words by his father. However, apart from a fugal final chorus, this is not a contrapuntal work but one whose impact derives from its operatic arias and its vigorous choruses.

🔘 **Magnificat**: Gachinger Kantorei Stuttgart; Bach-Collegium Stuttgart; Rilling (Hanssler-Verlag 98.970; with J.N. Bach, *Missa Brevis*)

Rilling is a veteran conductor of Baroque choral music, and this recording from the mid-1970s still sounds fresh and lively, with clear and incisive singing from the chorus. The soloists are extremely fine, with the soprano Arleen Auger excelling in her long and tender aria *Quia respexit humilitatem*, while the alto, Helen Watts, and tenor, Kurt Equiluz, provide one of the work's highlights in their dynamic duet *Deposuit potentes* (He has put down the mighty). The *Magnificat* is coupled with an interesting but considerably less exciting *Missa Brevis* by Johann Nikolaus Bach, J.S. Bach's second cousin.

SYMPHONIES

With their emphasis on the emotional manipulation of the listener, the symphonies of C.P.E. Bach exemplify the *empfindsamer Stil* just as much as his keyboard pieces. They are intense, compact works whose three movements tend to follow a pattern: fast and agitated, followed by slow and sorrowful, and concluding fast and cheerful. The best and most adventurous of them, the six *Hamburg Symphonies* were commissioned by Baron van Swieten (later a patron of Mozart), who allowed the composer a completely free hand. The result is startlingly original: audacious changes of key, sudden contrasts in dynamics and complete breaks in the musical flow all contribute to the music's restless excitement.

◉ **The Six Hamburg Symphonies**: C.P.E. Bach Chamber Orchestra; Haenchen (Capriccio 10 106).

The volatility of these symphonies makes them difficult to perform without sounding incoherent or capricious, but Haenchen and the C.P.E. Bach Chamber Orchestra avoid the pitfalls by taking the mood-swings completely seriously: their fast movements really rattle along, while their slow movements have a languidness that seems entirely authentic. Occasionally they get over-enthusiastic and the ensemble playing becomes a little ragged, but this is a small price to pay for performances of such energy and commitment.

JOHANN SEBASTIAN BACH
(1685–1750)

Johann Sebastian Bach is unquestionably the greatest composer before Mozart, and arguably the greatest ever. On one level, his music is an example of supreme craftsmanship, mastering with mathematical precision the formal problems of counterpoint, producing keyboard music in which as many as five separate lines of argument are simultaneously sustained. Yet this is also music of the deepest humanity, and not just in the most overtly dramatic of Bach's works, such as his depiction of Christ's suffer-

ROYAL COLLEGE OF MUSIC

ing in the *St Matthew Passion*. To listen to a complete performance of the *Goldberg Variations* – as purely abstract as anything he wrote – is to participate in a journey of extraordinary transformations, in which the final return of the original theme is a deeply moving and satisfying experience.

Bach came not so much from a musical family as from a musical dynasty: the line of musical Bachs begins all the way back in the sixteenth century and extends to the middle of the nineteenth, when it finally comes to an end. And to a large extent, despite his superior talent, Johann Sebastian's career was no more distinguished than those of several of his forbears. For Bach there was to be none of the international experience and renown of his great contemporary Handel.

After spells as church organist at Arnstadt and Mulhausen, Bach's first important position was at Weimar, where in 1708 he became the court organist and a chamber musician to the duke, Wilhelm Ernst. When eight years later a disgruntled Bach overinsistently applied for permission to leave, having been passed over for the senior post of Kapellmeister, the duke's response was to jail him for one month for his impertinence. (Disagreements with employers were to occur throughout his career.) The position he was attempting to leave for, and which he took up in 1718, was Kapellmeister at the small court of Prince Leopold of Anhalt-Cothen. Here he composed most of his instrumental and orchestral music, since the prince belonged to the Calvinist church, whose austere services employed little music beside psalm singing. When the prince married, his enthusiasm for music waned and in 1722 Bach applied to be cantor at the Thomasschule (the school of St Thomas) in Leipzig – rather reluctantly, since it seemed like a demotion. He got the position, but only after Telemann (see p.381), among others, had turned the job down.

Bach was to spend the last 27 years of his life dealing with the gruelling workload at Leipzig, where his duties were almost impossibly demanding. As well as teaching at the Thomasschule (his primary task), he was also responsible for the music for the church of St Thomas and three other of the town's churches, and on top of that was expected to provide music for important civic occasions. In his first six years there he composed a staggering amount of music, including five cycles of cantatas for the main services in the Lutheran church calendar, and his two magnificent settings of the Passion.

Even so, by 1729 there was sufficient friction between Bach and his employers for him to consider moving on once again. Among the problems, according to Bach, was the fact that "the place is very expensive and the authorities are hard to please and care little for music". In the end he stayed put, but he diversified his compositional activities, most significantly by writing for the Collegium Musicum of Leipzig, a musical society of students and professionals which met in Zimmermann's coffee house – which must have provided Bach with a much more sympathetic working environment than that which he was used to.

He died in July 1750, leaving unfinished his last extended project, a complex and theoretical exploration of counterpoint called *The Art of Fugue*. By the time of his death he was regarded as hopelessly old-fashioned, and his work remained under-performed until well into the nineteenth century. The most creative of Bach's sons, Carl Philip Emmanuel (see p.6), was to develop a style markedly different from that of his father.

CHORAL MUSIC

The Lutheran church had always regarded music as an integral component of its liturgy, with a strong emphasis on congregational participation in the form of hymns or chorales, often to words and music by Luther himself. The music for the main Sunday service, which could last as long as five hours, consisted of a motet, the Lutheran Mass, several chorales (a type of hymn) and a cantata (see below). Then there was the music for special occasions, like the settings of the Passion for Easter. In Leipzig, where the bulk of his choral music was written, Bach was responsible for providing the music (though not necessarily writing it all) for four churches, of which St Thomas and St Nicholas were the most important. Most of his singers and some of the instrumentalists required would have come from the Thomasschule, with the rest recruited from the town. Standards would thus have been variable but this did not prevent Bach from writing consistently rich and exhilarating works that often make great demands on the singers.

MAGNIFICAT

A Magnificat is a musical setting of the Virgin Mary's words of joy ("My soul doth magnify the Lord") to her cousin Elizabeth, after she has conceived. Bach's first setting, his only surviving one, was written for the Christmas celebrations of 1723, and is one of the most Italianate of all his choral works, with a splendid Vivaldi-like blast of rippling semi-quavers in the opening chorus. It is broken up into sections like a cantata, and involves soloists as well as a chorus, providing them with some melodies that are disarmingly simple and direct by Bach's normally complex standards.

⦿ Nederlands Kamerkoor; Kuijken (Virgin VC 7 59528 2; with *Cantata BWV 21*).

Above all it is the commitment of the choral singing that impresses here – this might not be the slickest perfromance, but it is always fervently alive. Perfectly controlling the balance between voices and instruments, Kuijken treats the joyous opening in a more dignified way than is often the case, but the result extends rather than subdues the mood, and you couldn't wish for anything more animated then the bouncy rendition of the chorus *Omnes generationes*. By contrast the cantata on this disc is a mournful one, with a text that elicts some of Bach's most expressive writing.

THE CANTATAS

Chorales and the setting of biblical texts were the dominant musical forms in the Lutheran church until about 1700, when the theologian-poet Neumeister published a collection of religious verses that were intended to be sung. Unlike oratorios, these so-called cantatas were not narrative pieces, but rather commentaries on the biblical texts used in the service – most importantly on the gospel reading. All the major German composers wrote them – Telemann almost as many as Bach – but no-one wrote music as ambitious or as lavish as Bach's, in which recitatives and arias, dramatic choruses and chorales were often combined together in one dramatic whole. About three-fifths of Bach's cantata output, over two hundred works, has survived.

⊙ **Cantatas BWV 140 and 147**: Monteverdi Choir; Gardiner (Deutsche Grammophon Archiv 431 809-2) .
⊙ **Cantatas BWV 39, 93 and 107**: Collegium Vocale, Ghent; Herreweghe (Virgin VC 7 59320 2).
⊙ **Cantatas BWV 82, 49 and 58**: Argenta, Mertens; La Petite Bande; Kuijken (Accent ACC 9395).

Two of the most famous cantatas are given performances of real verve by Gardiner and his Monteverdi Choir. *Wachet auf* (Sleepers' Wake) begins with a marvellous chorale tune by Philipp Nicolai rising up over Bach's orchestral embellishments. *Herz und Mund* (Heart and Mouth) uses a similar device in the chorale that closes each of its two sections, a tune popularly known as *Jesu, joy of man's desiring*. Herreweghe's fine choir, the Collegium Vocale, is less hard-driven than Gardiner's but no less effective, giving radiant performances of three rather more reflective works than cantatas 140 and 147. A warm but resonant acoustic and outstanding orchestral playing augment this perfect introduction to the less well-known cantatas.

Not all Bach's cantatas are large-scale works. The Kuijken disc presents the most famous of the solo cantatas – the intensely meditative BWV 82 (*Ich habe genug*) – and two cantatas for soprano and bass, which function as a kind of musical conversation. All three are given powerfully concentrated performances by the well-matched soloists.

THE CHRISTMAS ORATORIO

Though there is a narrative to the *Weichnachts-Oratorium* or Christmas Oratorio, this is not really an oratorio at all, but more a series of cantatas to be performed at the six services that begin with Christmas day and end with Epiphany (January 6). In Bach's time it would never have been performed as a single work. The author of the text is unknown, but the joyfulness of its theme is perfectly evoked by some of the most thrillingly exuberant music that Bach ever wrote. Nowhere is this more evident than in the work's brilliant opening, which combines kettle-drums, a fanfare and a rousing chorus to the words "Jauchzet, frohlocket!" (Rejoice, Exult!).

⊙ Schlick, Chance, Crook, Kooy; Collegium Vocale; Herreweghe (Virgin VCD 7 59530 2; 2CDs).

Herreweghe instantly captures the prevailing festive mood of the work with a sparkling opening, in which the instrumentalists acquit themselves brilliantly. Howard Crook makes a strong and sympathetic Evangelist, and there are no weak links among the other soloists. The dramatic elements are never overplayed, in keeping with the innocent world of the story.

B MINOR MASS

The *B minor Mass* is a composite work, most of it put together over two decades from cantata movements, and it was possibly intended as a compendium to show off Bach's skill as a choral composer, rather than as a piece for a specific occasion. Bach sent the Kyrie and the Gloria to the Catholic Elector of Saxony in 1733, along with a letter complaining about his Leipzig employers, and asking for a job, which he did not get. From such unpromising beginnings emerged one of his greatest works. Its first chorus, a stately fugue, establishes the sense of solid and unshakeable faith with which the work is imbued. Not all the music is so solemn, however. The glorious Sanctus is an animated rush of energy for six-part choir and high trumpets, with rhythms that suggest dancing rather than worship.

⊙ Argenta, Denley, Tucker, Varcoe; Collegium Musicum 90; Hickox (Chandos CHAN 0533/4; 2 CDs).

Hickox doesn't follow recent tendencies to scale the choral forces right down (sometimes to one voice per part), instead using a medium-sized choir that's able to provide clear and bright textures in the Kyrie, but can also pile on the power where necessary, for instance at the beginning of the Gloria. The Kyrie's fugue, which can sound dull and meandering if badly phrased, is here built and shaped with real attention to detail. Similarly the Sanctus, which can be made to swing too much, is here given a controlled but radiant treatment.

THE PASSIONS

Among Bach's most celebrated choral works are his two settings of the Passion, taken from the gospels of Saint Matthew and Saint John. As in the cantatas, Bach took an already existing form – in this case musical settings of the suffering and death of Christ, a genre that had existed since the Middle Ages – and turned it into an epic drama which, above all, emphasized the human dimension of the story. To the basic gospel narratives were added new texts by Picander (the author of many of the Bach cantatas) for the *St Matthew Passion*, and by a variety of authors for the *St John*. As in the cantatas, the additional words function largely as meditations and commentaries on the proceedings.

The *St John* is on a smaller scale, more concise and concentrated, and with the gospel text dwelling in greater detail on the cruelty of the crowd and the dilemma of Pilate. The *St Matthew*, scored for a double choir and orchestra, is a greater work in every sense: its prevailing mood is less dramatic and more contemplative, and though a terrible feeling of tragedy pervades the music, there is an even stronger sense of the humanity that binds all the participants together.

> ◗ **St Matthew Passion**: Pears, Fischer-Dieskau, Schwarzkopf, Ludwig, Gedda, Berry; Philharmonia Choir and Orchestra; Klemperer (EMI CMS 7 63058 2; 3 CDs).
> ◉ **St John Passion**: Argenta, Holton, Rolfe Johnson, Varcoe, Hauptmann, Chance; Monteverdi Choir; Gardiner (Deutsche Grammophon Archiv 419 324-2; 2 CDs).

Klemperer's St Matthew Passion is one of the great Bach recordings of the last forty years. By the standards of "authentic" performances his forces might be big and his speeds slow to the point of stateliness, but his ability to control a large chorus, and his unfailing sense of the shape and direction of a phrase, makes this account unrivalled in its grandeur and solemnity. A devotional intensity is sustained through the whole work, making the final chorus *Wir setzen uns mit Tränen nieder* (We sit down in tears) almost unbearably powerful. The choice of soloists is inspired, with Peter Pears a model of clarity and restraint as the Evangelist and Fischer-Dieskau a noble Christ.

EMI

Otto Klemperer – conductor of a classic Matthew Passion

Gardiner's constrastingly bright, forceful style is admirably suited to the *St John Passion*. His speeds are consistently fast, but this only serves to increase the almost theatrical drive of the work. As usual the Monteverdi Choir are superbly flexible and versatile: sinister and aggressive in the choruses at the Crucifixion, powerful but tender in the chorales. They are matched by the fine solists, with Anthony Rolfe Johnson immensely authoritative as the Evangelist and a pure-toned Nancy Argenta outstanding in the soprano arias.

CONCERTOS

It was at Weimar that Bach first came into contact with the Italian style of concerto in which a large instrumental ensemble played in alternation with a smaller group of soloists. It was exemplified by the concertos of Vivaldi several of which Bach arranged for solo keyboard and as concertos. However, it was at Cothen that he composed his first original concertos, though these were still largely based on the Vivaldian model. This consisted of three movements (fast-slow-fast): an aria-like slow movement, and outer movements that were characterized by vigourous forward-driven rhythms in which thematic material (the ritornello) repeatedly returned. As well as the concertos mentioned below, he also wrote several that survive only in part – mostly for oboe, some of which have been reconstructed for performance.

BRANDENBURG CONCERTOS

First printed in 1721, the six *Brandenburg Concertos* were dedicated to the Margrave of Brandenburg, who had commissioned them after hearing Bach play two years earlier. All but the first, and possibly the third, were written at Cothen, and they were undoubtedly conceived primarily for the court orchestra since the unusual orchestration of several of them is known to have matched the players at Bach's disposal there. Largely assembled from other compositions, some of them written around the same time, others earlier, the *Brandenburgs* were probably intended to demonstrate the potential of the concerto form. From the jubilant first to the intimate sixth concerto, Bach develops his thematic material in a more complex and extended fashion than Vivaldi does, and the relationship between the soloist and the orchestra

similarly breaks new ground – the harpsichord part in the fifth sounds in places like an anticipation of Mozart's piano concertos.

⊙ Amsterdam Baroque Orchestra; Koopman (Erato 4509-91935-2; 2 CDs).

Koopman is one of the most interesting present-day Bach interpreters. Although his approach is essentially an "authentic" one, nearly all his recordings are primarily concerned with communicating the sheer excitement of these pieces. Koopman tends to favour quite snappy tempos, especially in the fifth, but the flair of his soloists means that there is never any sense of rush.

VIOLIN CONCERTOS

The two *Violin Concertos*, in A minor and E major, and the marvellous *Double Violin Concerto in D minor*, also probably date from Bach's Cothen period, although it is by no means certain. The E major concerto, which opens with three bold chords (a classic Vivaldian device), comes close to the bouyant mood of the Brandenburgs, and also contains one of Bach's most inspired and poignant slow movements, in which the delicate solo melody is framed by slow and sombre music in the lower strings. Best of all is the *Double Concerto*, a marvel of contrapuntal inventiveness, with the imitative solo lines weaving in and out of each other with a playful brilliance in the outer movements, and with a fulsome lyricism in the slow movement.

⊙ Perlman, Zuckerman; English Chamber Orchestra; Barenboim (EMI CDC 7 47856 2).

This recording dates from the late 1960s when Perlman, Zuckerman and Barenboim frequently played together, and there is a rapport and a freshness to this music-making which is genuinely thrilling. Perlman plays the solo concertos with his characteristic sweetness and fullness of tone, which is especially telling in the wonderfully vocal slow movements, and there is a competitive edge to the swagger that both soloists bring to the double concerto.

HARPSICHORD CONCERTOS

Most of Bach's harpsichord concertos started life in another form, usually as concertos for different instruments, and in one case – the *Concerto for four harpsichords* – as a concerto by Vivaldi. Transcribing them from a single-line instrument (or intruments) to one capable of playing polyphonically, meant that their textures became denser and the elaboration of their thematic ideas more complicated, so that the piece often undergoes a complete change of character. Several of these harpsichord concertos were written for the Collegium Musicum of Leipzig, and would have been performed with Bach himself at the keyboard.

🔵 Amsterdam Baroque Orchestra; Koopman (Erato 4509 91930-2; 2 CDs).

As in the *Brandenburgs*, the most impressive aspect of these performances is their energy and lightness. Koopman takes a refreshingly flexible attitude to his solo part, treating ornamentation in a way that sounds both idiomatic and spontaneous. The balance between soloist and orchestra is near perfect, with the harpsichord seeming to move effortlessly in and out of the orchestral fabric.

INSTRUMENTAL MUSIC

Bach's renown in his own lifetime was less as a composer than as a keyboard player, both at the harpsichord and at the organ. His great ability was summarized in his obituary: "How strange, how new, how beautiful were his ideas in improvising. How perfectly he realized them! All his fingers were equally skillful; all were capable of the most perfect accuracy in performance." Such skill and knowledge could be put to a variety of uses. Not only did Bach write music in every known form of his time (both for performance and for education), he was also known for his ability as a designer of organs, and at Cothen was expected to carry out all the repairs on the court harpsichords.

Cothen possessed a wealth of talented instrumental players, with Prince Leopold himself a gifted amateur who played the harpsichord, the violin, and the viola da gamba. Oddly enough there is not a great deal of chamber music from this, or any other, period of Bach's career, and much of what has survived is of dubious authorship. Undoubtedly his greatest achievements in the sphere of instrumental music are his three partitas and three sonatas for unaccompanied violin, his six suites for unaccompanied cello, and the *Well-Tempered Clavier*, a piece that epitomizes Bach's blend of the pedagogical and the expressive.

THE WELL-TEMPERED CLAVIER

The Well-Tempered Clavier consists of two books of twenty-four preludes and fugues, each book working through the twelve major and twelve minor keys. Intended for as a sort of manual of keyboard playing and composition, the *Well-Tempered Clavier* is western music's first systematic exploration of harmony, and remains unequalled in the profligacy of its inventiveness. The fugues, written in as many as five voices, use devices such as inversion (turning the melody upside down) and augmentation (lengthening the duration of notes) to produce a texture so dense that in places it is difficult to discern the melodic pattern that's common to these individual voices. Yet these are not desiccated academic studies. They are full of sprightly dance-like passages and strong, concise melodies, and the preludes that introduce each fugue can be seen as prototypes for the poetic distillations of Chopin's *Préludes* and *Études* – indeed, Chopin revered the "48", as it's often known. Of the two books, the slightly earlier first book is marginally more playful and inventive. (And "Well-Tempered", by the way, refers to the method of tuning the instrument so that the twelve semi-tones of the chromatic scale are an equal distance apart in terms of pitch. If you tune a keyboard using strict mathematical principles rather than the evidence of your ears, you end up with scales that sound out of tune.)

The Well-Tempered Clavier Book I:
🔵 Nikolayeva (Mezhdunarodnaya Kniga MK 418042; 2 CDs).
🔵 Gould (Sony SM2K 52600; 2 CDs).
The Well-Tempered Clavier Book II:
🔵 Nikolayeva (Mezhdunarodnaya Kniga MK 418043; 2 CDs).
🔵 Gould (Sony SM2K 52603; 2 CDs).

Among performers of Baroque music there's a continuing controversy as to whether Bach's keyboard music sounds better played on the harpsichord or the modern piano. It sounds good on both, but certainly the piano, with its greater responsiveness to touch, allows a performer a wider range of sounds with which to explore the intricacies of Bach's contrapuntal style. Tatiana Nikoleyeva exploits the full range of the piano's sonorities: a crisp, hard touch is used for the more rhythmically motorized preludes, like the C minor from Book I, yet when necessary there are no qualms about using the

Gould's Well-Tempered Clavier – one of his great Bach recordings

sustaining pedal to add colour and warmth to the sound (though never with any loss to contrapuntal clarity). Her speeds can be slow, especially in some of the fugues, but the shape and direction of a piece is never in any doubt.

Glenn Gould's account could hardly be more different. As with all his Bach performances he goes nowhere near the pedal, preferring a shallow sound that emphasizes line above tone. And as with all his performances of anything, he has some weird ideas about tempo – some fugues are played so slowly they almost fall apart, others are taken at a speed your ears can only just keep up with. This set was hailed as "one of the greatest piano recordings of the century"; for Bach authenticists it's one of the most maddening. Incidentally, a recording of Gould's version of the first prelude of Book I was placed on board the Voyager space-shot, in order that any alien civilization intercepting the machine would gain some idea of the capabilities of the human species.

GOLDBERG VARIATIONS

This set of thirty variations on a theme were supposedly commissioned by Baron von Kayserling – the Russian Ambassador to the Dresden court – in order to relieve the wearisome hours of his insomnia, and were named after the baron's harpsichordist, who was to play them. The work begins with a highly ornamented but rather demure theme, around whose bass line Bach proceeds to fashion an astonishing series of transformations, from the ebullient to the introspective. The variations are grouped in threes, each group ending with a canon, except for the very last variation which is a quodlibet – a rousing piece which

combines two popular songs. The epic scope of the piece is due not simply to its length, but to its enormous variety – both stylistically and in terms of mood – and the way the whole work is held together by the constant underlying presence of the original thematic material.

> ○ Gould (Sony SMK 52619).
> ◉ Cole (Virgin VC 791444-2).

Glenn Gould's 1955 recording of the *Goldberg Variations*, his debut release, revolutionized people's perception of how Bach should be played, and established the pianist's reputation as one of the great Bach interpreters. His 1982 recording, released shortly before his death, is even more remarkable for the vivid precision of his touch, and the way that each line of the music is so clearly articulated. Speeds are sometimes idiosyncratic, but you'll be swept along by Gould's verve and enthusiasm. A possible drawback (though one you get used to) is his habit of quietly singing along, rather tunelessly, as he plays. Harpsichord enthusiasts are well served by Maggie Cole's intense and concentrated performance.

THE ENGLISH AND FRENCH SUITES

The titles of the *English Suites* and *French Suites* were not chosen by Bach, and their significance is unclear, as they do not define any substantial differences between these two sets of dance movements. Written purely for enjoyment rather than for instruction, they follow approximately the same format, with a steady allemande followed by a more rapid courante, a stately sarabande and an extremely lively gigue, sometimes with additional short movements – such as a bourrée – inserted between the sarabande and gigue. The *English Suites*, however, begin with a prelude which is often, as in the third suite, a large-scale concerto-like movement. The *French Suites* are less grandiose: the sarabandes and briefer additional movements are less contrapuntal than the equivalents in the *English Suites*, and bear a slight resemblance to the easy-going and flowery style of Couperin, with whom Bach is known to have corresponded.

> ○ **English Suites**: Gould (Sony SM2K 52606; 2 CDs).
> ○ **French Suites**: Gould (Sony SM2K 52609; with *Overture in the French Style*; 2 CDs).

Though there was no shortage of objectors to Glenn Gould's cavalier treatment of the printed page, nobody could match the clarity that he brought to Bach's multi-stranded keyboard music. These two sets show Gould at his most enjoyable – astonishingly fleet-fingered and full of argumentative intelligence.

ORGAN MUSIC

While organist at Arnstadt, Bach requested four weeks leave to walk to Lübeck (some two hundred miles away) in order to hear Diderik Buxtehude, then the greatest organist in Germany. Much of Bach's early organ works show the influence of the older man, but a more dynamic style, and one with a greater sense of continuity, was forged, once again, as a result of Bach's contact with the music of Vivaldi. Bach composed a wide range of organ works, of which the best known and most exciting are the spectacular fugues, often preceded by a short prelude or a more virtuosic toccata. Closer to the heart of the Lutheran church tradition are the chorales and chorale preludes, works based on the unaccompanied hymns sung by the congregation and played as introductions to them. Bach's ability to create florid improvisations on these simple tunes drew complaints from his congregation on more than one occasion.

⦿ **Organ Works** vol. I: Koopman (Novalis 150 005-2).

Ton Koopman's characteristic flair and panache are much in evidence on his series of discs of Bach's organ works. The series is especially attractive because Koopman presents a selection of different types of pieces – chorale-preludes, preludes and fugues and so forth – on each disc. Volume 1 contains the famous *D minor Toccata and Fugue* (not by Bach according to some scholars) and a sparkling account of the equally famous *G minor Fantasia*. Bach's organ music invariably sounds better on smaller organs, and this one – at Amsterdam's Waalse-Kerk – has a particularly bright and cheerful sound.

VIOLIN SONATAS AND PARTITAS

Although a stringed instrument is capable of playing two notes at the same time, one expects a work for a solo stringed instrument to produce a single line of music, without harmony and without counterpoint. The extraordinary achievement of Bach's violin sonatas and partitas (a collection of dance movements) is that harmony and counterpoint

are implied by the device of frequently spreading the component notes of a chord – and for the second movement of each sonata Bach provides a fully realized fugue. Listening to these works for the first time it is difficult to believe that you are only hearing just one instrument. At the same time this is not simply intellectual wizardry: these works abound with vivid melodies and, in the famous chaconne from the *D minor Partita*, some of the most deeply emotional moments in all of Bach's music.

⦿ **Complete Sonatas and Partitas for Solo Violin**: Grumiaux (438 736-2; 2CDs).

These pieces are the Everest of the violin repertoire, extremely difficult to play and of course utterly exposed, with no orchestra or piano to cover mistakes. Grumiaux makes it all sound terribly easy: his playing is clean and above all incisive with a stylish sense of line, and double-stopping (the playing of chords) that is boldly and clearly articulated. By employing an occasionally springier touch he also suggests the dance origins of many of the movements – the gigue from the second *Partita* is especially lively.

CELLO SUITES

There is no fugal writing in the *Cello Suites* but they share with the unaccompanied violin works the same capacity to create a multi-textured sound from a single voiced instrument. A spectacular example of this is the prelude of the first suite, in which succeeding chords are separated out into their individual notes – what you hear is both the gently rocking, forward momentum of the separated notes, and the underlying harmonic structure. Like the violin works, these are virtuosic pieces – the first ever written for cello – and may have been composed for one of the most talented of the Cothen players, the cellist and viola da gamba player Christian Ferdinand Abel.

⦿ Bylsma (RCA RD 70950; 2 CDs).

Bylsma has recorded the cello suites twice, both times on Baroque instruments that employ gut rather than metal strings, thus making for a warmer and more diffuse sound. This suits his style of playing, which tends to stress the delicacy and intimacy of these pieces, rather than their difficulty. He is a master of phrasing and of touch, with subtle shifts of emphasis that can refashion a phrase in a bold but utterly convincing manner.

FLUTE SONATAS

By the early eighteenth century the transverse flute (as opposed to the recorder) had become hugely popular, and there was a continuous demand for new music for it. Of the six flute sonatas traditionally ascribed to Bach, two are now thought to be highly doubtful though both are delightful works. The genuine ones are marked by the intricacy of the writing, in which the equal importance of each line (the flute part, and the bass and right-hand harpsichord lines) make them closer to trio sonatas than to solo ones. They are generally charac-terized by cool restraint, rarely matching the energy or dynamism of the unaccompanied violin or cello pieces, yet there is much of great beauty in this tightly reined music, notably the *B minor Sonata* where flute and keyboard function as equals.

⊙ Bennett; Malcolm (ASV CD QS 6108).

William Bennett possesses a full and controlled tone, and makes an eloquent and refined soloist, especially impressive in the long elegant phrases of the *E minor Sonata*. The dynamic control of these performances make them livelier than most – a fine example is the way the emphasis shifts from instrument to instrument in the first movement of the *B minor Sonata*.

SAMUEL BARBER
(1910–1981)

Right back in the 1930s, when Samuel Barber was being lauded in some quarters as one of the most talented American composers of his generation, his music was being labelled as utterly anachronistic by the modernist factions. Totally unperturbed, Barber went on writing in his neo-Romantic vein, turning out essentially dramatic and lyrical works in a tonal language rooted in the late nineteenth century. In the 1970s, with a large and varied body of work behind him, Barber was able to state with a certain satisfaction: "it is said that I have no style at all but that doesn't matter. I just go on doing, as they say, my thing. I believe this takes a certain courage."

It's hardly surprising that many of Barber's compositions are vocal settings – he was an excellent baritone and as a young student at the Curtis Institute he entertained notions of becoming a professional singer. By the time Barber graduated in 1932 he was already a confident composer with several highly accomplished works under his belt, including *Dover Beach* (a song singled out for praise by Vaughan Williams) and the *Serenade for String Quartet*. From the start his music exhibited many of the Barber hallmarks, notably extended lyrical lines and a remarkable facility for instrumental colour and text-setting. Barber was never coy about wearing his heart on his sleeve – his music was always first and foremost to do with the expression of profound personal emotion, a quality which soon got him noticed, not least by Toscanini. Once Toscanini had performed the *Adagio for Strings* in 1938, Barber never looked back. Numerous awards came his way, including Pulitzer prizes for the opera *Vanessa* (1958) and for his *Piano Concerto* (1962), and it must have seemed as though his star would never stop rising.

The bubble was to burst, however, with the failure of Barber's biggest work of the 1960s, the full-scale Shakespearean opera *Antony and Cleopatra*. Franco Zeffirelli's libretto was decidedly over the top, as was his production for the 1966 premiere, which with all its live animals and hundreds of extras looked like a second-rate Cecil B. de Mille movie. The opera was revised by his lifelong companion Gian Carlo Menotti, and restaged in 1975 at the Juilliard School in New York, but never found many admirers. Although Barber had a spate of commissions in the early 1970s, his writing tailed off at the close of the decade, due in no small part to his losing fight with cancer.

THE MUSIC

Barber's name is synonymous with one composition, the undeniably beautiful *Adagio for Strings*. With its intense, slow, long melodic lines and anguished climax it is not difficult to see why it has taken on the status of a twentieth-century classic and a movie soundtrack favourite (eg *Platoon*). Unfortunately the *Adagio* has overshadowed all his other immensely fine work, but fortunately there is now a healthy cross-section of his music appearing on CD.

Perhaps the most attractive pieces are his songs, in even the earliest of which – such as *Slumber Song of the Madonna* (1925) – Barber shows an impressive facility with vocal colour and word-setting. By the time of *Dover Beach*, for string quartet and baritone, he was completely in control of the medium, exploring rich harmonic textures and complicated polyphony. His range of expression is unrivalled among modern songwriters, encompassing every mood from Schubertian tenderness and simplicity (as in *A Nun Takes the Veil*, 1937) to the artfully decadent (as in the café-style *Solitary Hotel*, 1968–69).

DG's survey of Barber's songs – the best available

⚫ **The Complete Songs**: Hampson, Studer; Browning; Emerson Quartet (Deutsche Grammophon DG 435 867-2; 2 CDs).

This account of the *Adagio* is powerfully atmospheric, fluid and spacious, with a lovely rich orchestral sound giving maximum expressive weight to the work's climax. The strings of the Detroit Symphony play beautifully, as do the massed orchestral forces in Barber's undeservedly neglected *Symphony no. 2*. As a complement to Barber's music, you get Bristow's *Symphony in F sharp minor*, a fascinating antecedent to Barber's Romanticism.

The DG set of Barber's songs is a splendid chronological survey, excellently performed by all involved. Thomas Hampson is especially fine, effortless in Barber's protracted lyrical melodies yet intensely dramatic where necessary.

⚫ **Adagio for Strings; Symphony No. 2**: Detroit Symphony Orchestra; Järvi (Chandos CHAN 9169; with Bristow's Symphony in F sharp minor).

⸙

BÉLA BARTÓK

(1881–1945)

During the first two decades of the twentieth century, the tonal basis of classical music – the tyranny of major and minor keys, as Stravinsky termed it – finally collapsed. For Schoenberg and his Viennese cohorts, the logical progression from the lush ambiguities of Wagner was the development of serialism, replacing the exhausted principles of tonality with the rigours of the twelve-tone system. Béla

Bartók, however, found another way out of the impasse, producing music in which the Germanic tradition was given new life by incorporating it into a strongly nationalist style. In this he was of course not unique. Nationalism had been an increasingly powerful force since the European wave of revolutions in 1848, and received crucial impetus with the outbreak of world-wide conflict in the 1910s, as can be heard in the work of

MARY EVANS PICTURE LIBRARY

in Hungarian folk traditions – and his discovery of Debussy's impressionism – encouraged him to look beyond the confines of purely tonal expression and he developed a fascination with dissonance, a feature of nearly all his music written after his extraordinary opera *Duke Bluebeard's Castle* (1911).

Bartók was not the first composer to write "Hungarian" classical music, but whereas Brahms and Liszt had written pieces in a style that was Hungarian in atmosphere rather than substance, Bartók marked a clear break with tradition by treating his folk melodies and rhythms as truly raw material, emphasizing their "primitive" elements. On the other hand, though his music was often aggressive and harsh, its essential language never diverged from tonality, and the structural principles of his greatest compositions – such as the astringent string quartets – justify the description of Bartók as one of the last and most original Romantic composers. His ardent nationalism and his refusal to adopt the methods of the Second Viennese School placed him outside the mainstream of the European avant-garde, and Bartók's name did not feature prominently on concert programmes during his lifetime. His successes in the USA, where he spent the last five unhappy yet productive years of his life, were engineered by extremely prominent performers whose advocacy did more to persuade the promoters and press than did than the music itself. He remains a slightly eccentric figure in the history of modern music – his music is now featured widely in concert halls and record catalogues, but he's the least influential of this century's indisputably great composers. There is no school of Bartók.

DUKE BLUEBEARD'S CASTLE

Bartók composed only three stage works: the ballets *The Wooden Prince* and *The Miraculous Mandarin*, and the one-act opera *Duke Bluebeard's Castle*, and they are all masterpieces. *Bluebeard's Castle*, the finest of the three, is a disturbing, static drama with just two characters – Bluebeard himself (bass/baritone) and his new wife, Judith (soprano). The opera represents Bartók's

such diverse figures as Dvořák, Prokofiev, Janáček, Grieg, Sibelius and Vaughan Williams. But no other composer managed to produce work in which folk elements were absorbed into music of such power and modernity.

Bartók's early music was the product of years of studying the German tradition at the Budapest Academy. Bearing the imprint of Wagner, Brahms, Liszt and Strauss, it was traditional, slightly old-fashioned and full of unfettered melodic expression. In 1902 Bartók was inspired by a performance of Strauss's *Also Sprach Zarathustra* to write his own tone poem (*Kossuth*) but for all his composing ambitions, he spent the next five years pursuing the career of a travelling piano virtuoso, specializing in the music of Liszt. The partial exorcism of these Romantic influences began in 1905, when he interrupted his touring to begin an exploration of Hungarian peasant music; the following year, he and his friend Kodály published a collection of twenty Magyar songs. However, his own music was persistently rejected and in 1907, recognizing the futility of life as a composer, he took a position as head of piano studies at the Budapest Academy, where he continued his ethnological studies. Bartók's immersion departure from his intoxication with German music in general and Richard Strauss in particular, though his debt to Strauss's chromatic indulgence is revealed in the Romantic grandeur of the music he assigns to Judith. Her sinister husband sings in contrastingly dour and stark tones, setting up a tension that is quintessentially Bartók.

The action of this deeply disturbing tale is simple. Against his wishes, Bluebeard allows his wife to open the seven doors that open onto the hall of his castle. Behind each door she discovers something terrible – from a torture chamber to a magic garden where the roses are spotted with blood – until finally she realizes that she is to be imprisoned forever, along with his three other wives, behind the seventh door. The opening of the fifth door is an awesome moment: as it opens, Judith is confronted by a blinding ray of sunshine, an event for which Bartók found one of his greatest inspirations – a simple but amazingly effective C-major chord, from which develops some of the opera's most stunning music. This scene is a staggering visual coup, but Bluebeard's general lack of narrative incident makes it one of the few operas that's as effective on disc as it is on stage.

⦿ Ramey; Marton; Hungarian State Orchestra; Fischer (CBS CD44523).

This graphic, intense music makes enormous demands on its performers, but as it has a cast of just two and can be fitted on a single CD, *Bluebeard* is comparatively inexpensive to record – which is why there are more than ten versions available, some with very starry casts. The CBS recording is perhaps the best of these. Eva Marton, not the most reliable of voices, on this occasion delivers a rainbow of vocal colours, and Sam Ramey similarly makes the most of his role's potential, while their few ensembles are as convincing as possible – this is one of the finest recordings either singer has made. Adam Fischer directs the whole thing with a sometimes overwhelming passion; especially in the finale, he manufactures a translucent sound that highlights the mastery of Bartók's orchestrations and chillingly conveys the horror of the story.

THE PIANO CONCERTOS

Bartók was an excellent pianist and his first two piano concertos, dating from 1926 and 1931, were clearly written to suit his own particular style of playing. In both concertos, Bartók treats the piano as a percussion instrument, and their raw ferocity can still shock listeners as much as they did on their first performances. Unlike his other concertos, there is no lyricism or Romantic lilt here – you might be seduced by the music of these other works, the first two piano concertos batter you into submission.

The third piano concerto was one of Bartók's final pieces and was left incomplete at his death – after the final seventeen bars had been completed by a former student the work was first performed on February 8, 1946. Written for Bartók's wife Ditta, the third concerto is considerably less aggressive and more classical in form – indeed it is one of the most conventionally constructed works he wrote. The music reflects the composer's contentment at the very end of his life: America may not have turned out to be the land of milk and honey, but the Nazis had been defeated and he had been restored to all his official musical posts in his absence, encouraging him to consider a return to his native Hungary.

⦿ **Piano Concertos Nos. 1 & 2**: Pollini; Chicago Symphony Orchestra; Abbado (Deutsche Grammophon DG 415 371-2GH)
◗ **Concerto No. 3**: Anda; Berlin RIAS Orchestra; Fricsay (Deutsche Grammophon DG 427 410-2GDO2; 2 CDs; with Concerto for Orchestra).

For performances of the first two concertos, Pollini's marvellous, punchy accounts are unbeatable, with his dynamic virtuosity well matched by Abbado and the Chicago orchestra. For the third concerto pick the version conducted by Ferenc Fricsay, a brilliantly original conductor who studied with Bartók and Kodály in Hungary; Geza Anda, the soloist here, was best known for his readings of Mozart and Liszt, and he brings both the Classical and Romantic sides of his character to this exciting recording.

THE VIOLIN CONCERTOS

Bartók wrote his two-movement first violin concerto in 1908, soon after returning from his first folk-song collecting expedition to Transylvania. This headily Romantic piece was written for the young violinist Stefie Geyer, but sadly she did not reciprocate the emotion so clearly expressed in the lovely first movement, and she left the composer shortly after the work's completion. Bartók duly shelved the concerto, which remained unperformed until two years after Geyer's death and fifty years after it was written.

Thirty years after the troubled inception of this first concerto, the Hungarian violinist Zoltán Székely asked Bartók to have another go. The composer preferred to write an extended set of variations but Székely maintained that, as he was paying for the work, he should get what he asked for. Not wishing to be defeated, Bartók then cheated by writing a three-movement concerto which is, in fact, an extended set of variations – though it requires close analysis to find the relation between the opening pizzicati and the finale. It has its moments of dissonance, but predominently this concerto is as melodic as the earlier one, and repeated listening reveals a flood of ideas that seem to tumble over each other.

○ **Violin Concertos Nos. 1 & 2**: Midori; Berlin Philharmonic Orchestra; Mehta (Sony CD45941).
◐ **Violin Concerto No. 2**: Menuhin; Dallas Symphony Orchestra; Dorati (RCA 09026 61395-2; with Lâlo, *Symphonie espagnole*).

Midori's recording of the Bartók concertos was the one that showed that the Japanese-American whizzkid amounted to a lot more than just an amazing technique: this disc is a marvel, its interpretations well measured, understated and deeply thought-out. Menuhin's 1946 recording of the second concerto is less intimidating than Midori's high-octane performance: it's a profoundly lyrical reading, with Menuhin producing an astonishingly sweet tone.

CONCERTO FOR ORCHESTRA

The genre of the "concerto for orchestra" was a twentieth-century invention inspired by the rapidly increasing technical abilities of American orchestras in the period after World War I. Kodály and Lutosławski both wrote pieces in this format, but neither quite matches Bartók's intricately constructed show-piece, which gloriously displays the virtuoso talents of each of the orchestral sections.

One of the composer's last works, the *Concerto for Orchestra* was commissioned by the pioneering conductor Serge Koussevitzky in 1943, whose Boston Symphony Orchestra gave the first performance at the end of the following year, an event received with great acclaim. The five movements present a gradual transition from the severity of the first to a life-affirming finale, with interruptions along the way – thus the satirical and light-hearted second movement is followed by a *Song of Death*, which in turn gives way to an Intermezzo that pulls Shostakovich's leg by quoting his seventh symphony.

○ London Symphony Orchestra; Dorati (Mercury 432 017-2MM; with *Dance Suite, Two Portraits* and excerpts from *Mikrokosmos*).

Unsurprisingly, the *Concerto for Orchestra* is very popular with orchestras and ambitious conductors, but even with over thirty different recordings available, it's relatively easy to single out the finest. Antal Dorati was a friend and student of Bartók's for over fifteen years, and recorded the Concerto several times. His best version, made in 1962, is incomparable, combining fierce energy and rhythmic momentum with extremes of colour – the savagery of the first movement is indicative of Dorati's uncompromising nature, a quality he shared with the composer. The LSO, with whom Dorati had a long partnership, play with great virtuosity, especially in the daunting finale. Coupled with the Concerto is a shuddering account of the *Dance Suite* and *Two Portraits*, the latter an early work that Bartók derived from the first movement of his first violin concerto.

MUSIC FOR STRINGS, PERCUSSION AND CELESTA

Commissioned by one of this century's most important patrons, Paul Sacher, and first performed by him and his Basle Chamber Orchestra in 1937, *Music for Strings, Percussion and Celesta* is one of Bartók's most unorthodox, complicated and demanding works. It's written in four continuous movements, lasts around thirty minutes, and is scored for a unique ensemble: two groups of strings, a phalanx of percussion instruments including cymbals, drums, tam-tam, timpani and xylophone, plus piano, harp and celesta, a piano-like instrument with metal bars instead of strings. It's an extremely eerie piece of music (Kubrick used it on the soundtrack of *The Shining*), and a seminal one, too – its monothematicism (ie the whole thing is generated from a single theme) and its emphasis on rhythmic power rather than on melody, established a mature style from which Bartók did not stray until his last five years.

○ Oslo Philharmonic Orchestra; Jansons (EMI CDC7 54070-2; with *Concerto for Orchestra*).

Mariss Jansons

In the early phase of his career Mariss Jansons built up a strong rapport with the Oslo orchestra, with whom he gave some memorable concerts and made many excellent records. One of his finest of these recordings was this performance *Music for Strings, Percussion and Celesta*, where he brilliantly conjures the translucent texture demanded by Bartók. More importantly, Jansons doesn't labour the work's thematic re-inventions, instead allowing the ear to filter sounds that other conductors frenetically accentuate. The coupled performance of the *Concerto for Orchestra* is too slick and drilled to bear comparison with the Dorati version.

THE STRING QUARTETS

Bartók's six string quartets are his greatest achievement and span his entire creative life: the first was completed in 1908, the second in 1917, the third in 1927, the fourth in 1928, the fifth in 1934 and the last in 1938. As with Beethoven and Shostakovich, Bartók translated his deepest and most personal thoughts into his quartets, and each of the six is the purest distillation of his immersion in Magyar folk song – a source that's audible no matter how extreme and difficult some of the music may initially sound. If you come to these quartets straight from the quartets of Mozart and Haydn you'll undoubtedly find them abrasive and uncomfortable, but don't give up – these pieces are among the most rewarding experiences in twentieth-century music.

⊙ Emerson Quartet (Deutsche Grammophon DG 423 657 2GH2; 2 CDs).
⊙ Lindsay Quartet (ASV CD DCS 301; 3 CDs).

On a technical level the Emerson Quartet's award-winning recording of the complete quartet cycle is unrivalled. However, these quartets require a lot more than concentration on precision, and you can't help feeling – especially in the last two works – that the Emersons are sometimes preoccupied with accuracy at the expense of expression. The Lindsay Quartet, on the other hand, take risks in the service of the music's spirit rather than subject each bar to excessive analysis and rehearsal; not everything is exactly in its place, but this doesn't really matter, as you're left marvelling at what Bartók wrote rather than at the prowess of the performers. The only problem with this set is an economic one, as it spreads onto one more CD than the Emersons' recording.

VIOLIN SONATA

After the string quartets, Bartók's most important chamber music is his *Violin Sonata*, Opus 117, one of the greatest works ever written for unaccompanied violin. It was commissioned by Yehudi Menuhin in 1944, the year after Bartók had praised Menuhin's performance of the composer's first sonata for violin and piano. Although it was written in America, a period of almost unrelieved unhappiness for Bartók, the sonata is an incredibly positive piece of music, showing an understanding of the violin's capabilities that's extraordinary for a composer who didn't play this difficult instrument. With the exception of Ysaye's six sonatas, Bartók's was the first sonata for solo violin to be written since Bach's, and the example of Bach's compositions is never far away in this neoclassically structured piece. Bartók's imagination was inspired by these self-imposed restraints – with its strange cross-rhythms and harmonics, the sonata gives the violin a wholly original voice.

◗ Menuhin (EMI CDH7 69804-2; with *Violin Concerto No. 2*).
⊙ Nikkanen (Collins CD1203-2; with *Sonata No. 1 for Violin and Piano & Romanian Folk Dances*).

Menuhin's premiere recording of the sonata – made two years after the composer's death – has obvious historic value, but it doesn't show him at his best, and his approach is far more angular than the music warrants. Musically superior is the CD from the young Kurt Nikkanen, a fabulous performance, technically so secure that the sonata's demands are taken for granted, allowing his vision of the piece to surface unhindered.

ARNOLD BAX

(1883–1953)

Arnold Bax's generation of British composers – unlike its predecessors (Holst and Vaughan Williams) and its successors (Walton, Tippett, Britten) – was particularly outward-looking. Several of them, such as Cyril Scott (1879–1970) and Roger Quilter (1877–1953), formed the so-called Frankfurt school, after the place of their musical education, but most of them, including also the more familiar Frank Bridge (1879–1941) and John Ireland (1879–1962), were primarily influenced by French impressionism. (One can include the English-born, German-taught and French-settled Delius among this group because, although born some twenty years earlier, his most characteristic works are contemporary with those of his younger compatriots.) Bax's own music often displays elements of the Romantic strength of Richard Strauss and the pictorial moods of Debussy, but his main extra-musical inspiration came from Celtic folklore, a fascination that sprang from his reading of Yeats and subsequently developed into an obsession with the culture of Ireland. He frequently visited the island and even had some novels published in Dublin under the pseudonym Dermot O'Byrne.

Bax developed relatively late as a composer. He failed to finish his course at the Royal Academy of Music and was in his mid-thirties before he produced works of lasting stature, in particular the evocative tone poems *The Garden of Fand* (1916), *November Woods* (1917) and *Tintagel* (1919). In the 1920s he began his series of seven symphonies, which occupied him until the outbreak of World War II, a sequence interspersed with concertos, more tone poems and a vast quantity of chamber and instrumental works. His compositional activities tailed off during and after the war, but he found a new interest in writing for films, most notably with the score for David Lean's *Oliver Twist* in 1948.

Sometimes Bax's music gives a sense of his compositional facility out-performing his technical competence, with the occasionally prosaic melodic line and abrupt change of gear in his larger-scale works, but what never fails to impress is the sumptuousness of his orchestration, his engaging harmonic writing, and his ability to create atmosphere. His style of overt late-Romanticism fell out of favour with audiences and concert promoters after his death, but there has recently been a resurgence of interest in his music thanks chiefly to the proselytizing zeal of a few record companies.

THE SYMPHONIES

Bax's orchestral music is the most rewarding part of his output, but it has to be admitted that the symphonies are variable in quality and are prone to rhapsodizing. At their best, however, they rival those of Vaughan Williams. The first of the seven (1922) emerged as an orchestral enlargement and development of his *Piano Sonata No. 1* (1910, revised 1921). It is a dramatic work that led its audiences, ignorant of its early origins, to hear it as Bax's response to the losses of friends in the Easter Uprising in Ireland; it's perhaps more a response to the beautiful but terrifying power of nature, a theme that dominated Bax's creative thinking. The same dichotomy continued in *Symphony No. 2* (1926), but a kind of peace was established in the incandescent finale of *Symphony No. 3* (1929), arguably the best of the lot. The fourth (1931) is more uneven, with a sporadic power that cannot completely transcend some of the music's commonplace episodes. The same could be said of *Symphony No. 5* (1932), which was dedicated to Sibelius (an admirer of Bax's music) but does not really live up to its association in its control of form. *Symphony No. 6* (1934), his least successful essay in the form, was followed five years later by one of his most successful – the seventh has all the grandeur of the earlier works but more integrity in its use of material, and it never fails to be affecting in its sense of nostalgia and world-weariness.

● **Symphonies Nos. 1–7**: London Philharmonic
Orchestra, Ulster Orchestra; Thomson (Chandos CHAN
8906/10; 5 CDs).
● **Symphonies Nos. 1 & 7**: London Philharmonic
Orchestra; Fredman, Leppard (Lyrita SRCD 232).

Perhaps the greatest service ever done to Bax's music was the resurrection of his orchestral music by Bryden Thomson during the 1980s. In his hands even the crassest writing in the symphonies is made to sound alive – the crudities in the fourth, for example, are forgivable when performed with such zest, and the award-winning engineering is breathtakingly full and vivid. All seven works are now packaged together, but are also still available on single discs with their original couplings of symphonic poems and other works (see below). From a slightly earlier generation (the early 1970s), but no less recommendable, comes the coupling of the first and the last symphonies on Lyrita, a superb transfer of classic recordings to CD.

THE SYMPHONIC POEMS

The symphonic poems show Bax at his most imaginative and luxuriant, and are probably the best way into his music. One of the earliest is *The Garden of Fand*, based on an Irish legend about the attempted seduction of a ship's crew by a fairy-like figure, for which Bax conjures up a magical watery world. In a similarly maritime vein is *Tintagel*, perhaps his masterpiece – it's a stunning evocation of the eponymous Cornish castle, home in legend to Tristan and Isolde's illicit lovemaking (hence Bax's quotation from Wagner's opera). While these two works have their roots firmly in Celtic folklore, other Bax tone poems are more generally pictorial and are occasionally reminiscent of Delius. *November Woods*, for example, was probably inspired by the beech woodland of the Chiltern Hills, while *Summer Music*, in Bax's words, depicts "a hot, windless June midday in some woodland place of Southern England".

● **Festival Overture; Christmas Eve; Orchestral
Sketches; Paean; Nympholet; Tintagel**: London
Philharmonic Orchestra, Ulster Orchestra; Thomson
(Chandos CHAN 9168).
● **November Woods; The Happy Forest; The
Garden of Fand; Summer Music**: Ulster Orchestra;
Thomson (Chandos CHAN 8307).

The first of these discs is a compilation of the fillers for the original Bryden Thomson symphony cycle; these works do not come better played or better recorded than this, with *Tintagel* in particular sounding extraordinarily rich. The other disc is the issue that launched the Thomson/Chandos partnership in Bax, and it set especially high standards – the sound has a richness few other companies have ever equalled and the performances put the Ulster Orchestra on the map in the early 1980s. The highlights are the two best-known works, *November Woods* and *The Garden of Fand*.

LUDWIG VAN BEETHOVEN

(1770–1827)

Beethoven the demi-god, the tragic yet otherworldly genius, scornful of society and oblivious of life's trivialities, is the product of almost two centuries of mythologizing. Dubious biographies with titles such as *Beethoven the Creator*, *Beethoven, the Man who Freed Music* and *Beethoven, Life of a Conqueror* are typical of the awestruck image-creation that has been going on since the composer's day, extrapolating an astounding character from the astounding music. Yet the facts of Beethoven's life – such as are known for certain – are fairly humdrum, and they do not paint a particularly attractive picture. The most revealing reflection on what he must have been like comes not from his own words or from those of the people who knew him, but from Alexander Thayer, who immersed himself in researching his hero's life sixty years after Beethoven's death. He soon began to realize that his conception of the composer had been completely without foundation, and, unable to reconcile what he discovered with his Victorian moral code, abandoned his project to another writer.

Beethoven has been exalted as the ultimate product of German idealism and the very

POPPERFOTO

His sense of morality was packed with contradictions. He believed that Don Giovanni was an immoral subject for an opera and yet openly conducted affairs with married women. He probably fathered children but there is no record of his supporting a family, and he battled five years with his dead brother's wife for custody of their son Karl. Having been appointed guardian, he then mistreated the boy, chastising him harshly for his untidiness, yet living in squalor himself, leaving unemptied chamber pots and uneaten food lying around his apartment for weeks on end. Eventually, aged twenty, Karl attempted to blow his brains out rather than put up with his uncle's irrational behaviour. In essence, Beethoven's principles came down to the brutal formulation he once wrote in a letter to a friend: "I don't want to know anything about your system of ethics. Strength is the morality of the man who stands out from the rest, and it is mine." And there is no question that Beethoven, by virtue of his music, stands out from the rest.

From the time of its composition, his music has been celebrated as western civilization's most powerful expression of its innermost experiences. In 1791 the critic Carl Junker heard the twenty-one-year-old Beethoven play Beethoven: "His style of treating the instrument is so different from that usually heard that it gives one the idea the he has attained that height of excellence . . . by a path of his own discovery." So it was throughout his career. If a rule was accepted, Beethoven would work at disproving it. In one of his notebooks he recorded seventeen different attempts at proving that a certain rule of harmony was wrong; when asked, on one occasion, who had admitted his use of a universally proscribed combination of notes, he replied "I admit them!" Never doubting the validity of his ground-breaking departures from convention, he overcame poverty, unpopularity and, finally, deafness to forge a musical language that encompassed an unprecedented range of feeling, from the heights of religious serenity to the depths of solitary anguish.

personification of an age of revolution; yet in 1803, when French troops entered Vienna, he hid under his kitchen table, with a towel over his head. Works such as *Fidelio* and the ninth symphony declare Beethoven's love of humanity in the abstract, but he hated most people – especially the aristocracy, which made his relationship with his patrons rather turbulent. Beethoven endured the upper classes solely to have them pay his way, and his determination to get what he saw as his due was often ugly – when Prince Kinsky, a kind and decent man, went bankrupt, Beethoven took him to court to extract the sums he had been promised. He was capable of selling the same score to six or seven different publishers simultaneously, and would demand unreasonably large fees for the simplest of pieces. Whereas Mozart and his predecessors were craftsmen who supplied a commodity to a paying master, Beethoven asserted his independence and the absolute importance of self-expression: "What is in my heart must come out and so I write it down."

Beethoven was the greatest, most respected pianist of the day, able to improvise at length upon any theme and capable of technical feats that, even today, many trained musicians find impossible to duplicate. When he moved from Bonn to Vienna in 1792, Mozart had been dead for just over a year and the public was conditioned to the smooth and fluent Mozartian use of the instrument. Beethoven's technique came as a shock: raising his hands above his head, he smashed the keys with such force that he regularly broke the strings. Unable to reproduce the sounds he could hear in his head, he punished the keyboard for not allowing him greater freedom, and begged the city's keyboard makers to devise an instrument of the necessary strength and range – but the piano capable of playing Beethoven's music to its full potential remained a fantasy until the 1840s, when the American John Hawkins produced the first iron-framed piano.

The piano was central to his career. His public contests with rival virtuosos propelled him to the centre of Vienna's musical culture and into the arms of the aristocracy, many of whom regarded him as something of a freak. In fairness, he did not cut the most prepossessing figure in high society: short, stocky and swarthy, he dressed badly, held no affection for bathing, and was fond of crude language. Notwithstanding his lack of graces, by the turn of the century Beethoven had conquered Vienna, giving increasingly frequent concerts and regularly receiving commissions. However, by 1801 he had begun to notice a change in his hearing. At first, he suffered from a terrible buzzing which continued day and night, but before long his ability to distinguish pitch was disappearing rapidly. By 1803 he was virtually stone deaf.

His correspondence and notebooks are full of complaints about the social consequences of this affliction, but his greatest deprivation was that he could no longer play the piano properly – there are many sad tales of his disastrous, cacophonic attempts to hammer out something he could hear. Yet nowhere did he complain that his deafness had in any way impaired his creativity – indeed, he went on to compose the most adventurous piano music ever written, and it was at the onset of total deafness that he completed his third symphony, the *Eroica*, arguably the most significant single work of his entire life. As a broad generalization, Beethoven prior to the *Eroica* had been a composer of the eighteenth century; with this symphony music entered the age of Romantic complexity.

The post-*Eroica* decade produced a succession of masterpieces including the opera *Fidelio*, the *Rasumovsky* string quartets, the *Violin Concerto*, the fourth and fifth piano concertos, symphonies four to eight, and some magnificent works for solo piano – notably the *Waldstein* and *Appassionata* sonatas. These "middle period" works, containing most of Beethoven's great melodic writing, have remained the most popular, but in terms of intensity and originality the finest was yet to come. Around the middle of the 1810s, his retreat from the outside world almost complete, Beethoven commenced perhaps the greatest continuous cycle of composition in history: the last five piano sonatas, the last five string quartets, the *Diabelli Variations*, the *Missa Solemnis* and, most famous of all, the gargantuan *Symphony No. 9*, all come from this, his so-called "late period". This is music with no precedent, characterized by ever greater abstraction and contrast, by the proximity of episodes of stridency and violence with lyrical passages that seem to melt into silence, by a sense of unbearable self-revelation.

As Beethoven plumbed the depths of introspection, his fame grew so far that by 1824, when his final symphony was given its first performance, his name and music were international in a way that not even Mozart's had been. When he died, aged 57, obituarists recorded that a terrible storm had raged in Vienna, and that the dying man had shaken his fist at the heavens as thunder and lightning struck the town.

OPERA – FIDELIO

Although Beethoven dallied with numerous operatic plans from 1800 to 1815, he completed only one opera – *Fidelio*. It is, however, one of the greatest of all German operas and, in its mastery of Mozartian "realism", it can be seen as the apotheosis of eighteenth-century operatic style. With its themes of unselfish love, loyalty, courage, sacrifice and heroic endurance, *Fidelio* is furthermore the nearest thing Beethoven ever produced to an explicit political-philosophical creed.

The plot, said to be based upon an event during the French Revolution, concerns the unjust imprisonment of Florestan, husband of Leonore, who attempts to free him by disguising herself as a man and entering the service of Pizarro, the prison governer. Pizarro, a veritable emblem of ancien régime repression, tries to have Florestan executed before the arrival of Don Fernando, the minister of state, but his plot is thwarted by Leonore. Don Fernando arrives at the prison, sets Florestan free and duly punishes Pizarro. This simple narrative gives rise to some astonishing moments, perhaps the most powerful being the prisoners' chorus, a slow and deeply moving song of solidarity that opens with a simple set of shifting chords quite unlike anything ever written before.

The first performance in 1805 was not a success, owing partly to the simple fact that many people found the opera too long and too demanding. Even the subsequent heavy revisions did not give *Fidelio* the popularity of Mozart's more ingratiating operas, and it remains a woefully under-staged masterpiece. If you ever get the chance to see it in the opera house, you should jump at the chance – few other operas can match its sustained seriousness and intensity.

◗ Ludwig, Vickers, Frick, Berry, Crass; Hallstein; Philharmonia Orchestra and Chorus; Klemperer (EMI CMS 769324-2 ; 2 CDs).

Klemperer's 1961 performance for EMI is a very fine achievement, with Jon Vickers a splendid Florestan and Christa Ludwig unrivalled in the role of Leonore. Throughout his long career Klemperer had a profound affinity with this opera and although at the time of this recording he was old, semi-paralysed and bearing the scars of sixty percent burns , his resolve and integrity produced an awe-inspiring performance.

SACRED MUSIC

Beethoven's distinctly personal Christian faith, a faith that denied conventional observances and public display, was sorely tested throughout the years of his deafness, but two Masses came out of this period. The first of these, the *Mass in C*, is a fine work; the second, known as the *Missa Solemnis*, is the nineteenth century's finest.

Early in June 1819 Beethoven wrote to his pupil Rudolph, the Archduke of Austria: "The day on which a High Mass composed by me will be performed during the ceremonies solemnized by Your Imperial Highness will be the most glorious day of my life". Soon afterwards he began work on his D major Mass, the *Missa Solemnis*, but this mighty, uncompromising work was not finally completed until 1823.

There's no piece of religious music to compare with the *Missa Solemnis*, for this is a composition that externalises its creator's struggle to achieve inner peace, with extraordinary dynamic contrasts and passages that make enormous demands of the soloists. Perhaps the most remarkable section is the Benedictus, a huge, Gothic conception culminating in a ten-minute violin solo of extreme beauty that leads, like some massive papal procession, into the Agnus Dei, a section that incorporates an episode of brash, almost militaristic declamation. The polar opposite of most Masses, it's a disconcertingly exposed work, sometimes tranquil, sometimes strenuous, but always profoundly spiritual.

◗ **Missa Solemnis**: Janowitz, Ludwig, Wunderlich, Berry; Berlin Philharmonic Orchestra; Karajan (Deutsche Grammophon DG 423 913-2; 2 CDs; with Mozart, *Mass in C*).

Among the many recordings of the *Missa Solemnis* there is no serious rival to this, one of Karajan's best recordings, featuring one of the finest vocal quartets of the century. It's not perfect – the tempi are sometimes too slow, the balance is odd in places, and the solo violin tends to wander out of tune – but the pathos and weight of the performance are desperately moving. The singing is magnificent (Janowitz and Wunderlich in particular), and Karajan's direction is consistently expressive.

THE SYMPHONIES

With a mere nine symphonies, Beethoven revolutionised the orchestra and overturned all previous attitudes to symphonic form. The first two, completed in 1800 and 1802 respectively, are openly based upon the examples of Mozart and Haydn, but the third – the *Eroica* – heralded an entirely new concept of scale. Numbers five through to nine increasingly free the structure from classical restraints and moved swiftly towards the more Romantic, subjective approach that prevailed in mid-nineteenth century Europe. Beethoven completed his Ninth Symphony in 1824; just six years later, Berlioz completed his first symphonic work, the *Symphonie Fantastique*.

Symphonies 1–9
- ◉ Cleveland Orchestra; Maazel (CBS M5K 45532; 5 CDs).
- ◉ Vienna Philharmonic Orchestra; Furtwängler (EMI CHS7 63606-2; 5 CDs).
- ◉ Philharmonia; Karajan (EMI CMS 7 63310-2; 5 CDs).
- ◎ London Symphony Orchestra; Morris (PickwickPCD911; 5 CDs).

Since Felix Weingartner recorded the first complete Beethoven cycle in the 1930s, over fifty conductors have recorded these immense works, and frankly some of them should not have bothered. There are, however, a few whose overview justifies the cost of buying the full set of nine symphonies. Best overall is the first of Karajan's four cycles, recorded with the Philharmonia in the 1950s – this is Karajan at his best and is his only set to bear repeated listening. If you want a more modern sound, then Maazel's set is the one to go for, though none of his interpretations would be a first choice for individual symphonies, and some might find the recordings a bit too glassy. If, on the other hand, pristine technology doesn't rate highly on your list of requirements, then Furtwängler's post-war cycle will offer genuine insights, though the playing is variable – as you might expect from a "cycle" that was put together from performances given over quite a long spread of time. At budget price, Wyn Morris's recordings for Pickwick are excellent value: some of the tempi are erratic, but this set has some fabulous playing from the LSO, and the recording of the Ninth is especially fine.

SYMPHONY NO. 1

Though neither of Beethoven's first two symphonies is comparable to the majesty and innovation of the Eroica, it is a mistake to look upon them as mere preludes to that amazing piece – by the time Beethoven came to write the first symphony he was already thrty and had a considerable body of music to his name. *Symphony No. 1* clearly reflects Haydn's towering presence in late eighteenth-century Vienna, but Beethoven brought his own, rough-edged manner to the old master's style – Beethoven's fingerprints are especially in evidence in his reworking of Haydn's trick of slow introductions to the outer movements.

- ◗ Malboro Festival Orchestra; Casals (Sony CD45891; with *Symphony No. 6*).

Pablo Casals – unbeatable in the early symphonies

Although famed primarily as a cellist, by the 1960s Pablo Casals had established himself as a master of small-scale orchestral music. This particularly imaginative performance – which dates from that decade – revels in the intimacy of the chamber orchestra, bringing a sense of freedom to the music that many grander performances overlook.

SYMPHONY NO. 2

The *Symphony No. 2* grew out of a period of intense despair as Beethoven struggled to come to terms with his increasing deafness. Amazingly, it's a work that bears little sign of this torment – rather, it bubbles with life and optimism. This is more obviously a piece by Beethoven than is the first symphony – the leg-pulling Scherzo, for example, is unmistakeably his, with its innovative scoring and its unexpected exchanges, stops and starts. On the other hand, the finale – while maintaining the mood of the preceding movement – plainly looks to the eighteenth century as it slips into a polyphonic style that owes considerably more to Bach than to Mozart or Haydn.

- ◗ Malboro Festival Orchestra; Casals (Sony CD46247; with *Egmont Overture* and Brahms' *Haydn Variations*).

Again, Casals' liberating influence flows through this performance, generating a warmth and affection that most conductors are unable to extract from their Beethoven-weary orchestras. The playing is, at times, not exactly polished, but its flaws merely add to the sense of spontaneity and exploration. A fine testament to a great musican.

SYMPHONY NO. 3

Beethoven's *Symphony No. 3* is better known as the *Eroica*, a title thoroughly befitting what many people consider the greatest symphony ever written. Completed in the spring of 1804, this amazing score contains the very foundations of Romanticism in its grandiose gestures and burgeoning themes, and in its unprecedented scale – the outer movements are enormous structures that virtually ignore the accepted conventions of sonata form.

The thunderous opening chords – like those launching the fifth symphony – are some of the most recognizable in all music and the last movement is the most exciting and thrilling of all his symphonies. On the way to this finale one crosses extremes of exultation and misery that belong to a world unknown to the music of the eighteenth century. Another crucial characteristic of the *Eroica* is its anticipation of programme music – i.e. music with a narrative. That said, the extra-musical references are more elusive than those to be found in Berlioz or Strauss, for example. Some have suggested that the second movement's funeral march was inspired by a real-life cortège or by a poem describing one, while others – on slightly surer ground – have inferred that the references to English and Hungarian music in the last movement were intended as tributes to the nations uniting to defeat Napoleon (the symphony's dedicatee until he went and crowned himself Emperor, whereupon Beethoven tore the title page in half and re-dedicated it to Prince Lobkowitz).

⦿ San Francisco Symphony Orchestra; Blomstedt (Decca 430 515-2DH; with *Symphony No. 1*).

Blomstedt's performance of the *Eroica* is at times over-cautious, but it has an impressively purposeful clear-sightedness, especially in the opening two movements. Where other conductors have swamped the music beneath aggression and bombast, his unerring sense of structure and steady tempi imbue the performance with true dignity.

SYMPHONY NO. 4

Beethoven's fourth symphony, completed in 1806 and performed the following year, is often dismissed – along with the other even-numbered symphonies – as one of his "lighter", unclouded pieces. The categorisation is hard to fathom, as the symphony shares its mysterious key of B flat with some of Beethoven's most profound music – the *"Archduke" Piano Trio*, the *Piano Sonata No. 29* and the *String Quartet No. 13*. This neglected symphony is a witty yet often disturbing creation, with an opening movement that recalls the titanic strength of the first movement of the *Eroica* and an Adagio not far removed from the *Eroica*'s funeral march.

⦿ Bavarian State Orchestra; Kleiber (Orfeo C100841H).

This Orfeo CD, recorded live with the Bavarian State Orchestra, is a truly remarkable performance. Kleiber's rhythmic flexibility verges on the extreme, but he maintains a flowing, uninterrupted sense of line that holds the music together no matter what his chosen pulse. Though it contains just over half an hour's music, this CD is special enough to justify the full price.

The greatest living conductor tackles Beethoven's Fourth

SYMPHONY NO. 5

The first five bars of the fifth symphony – perhaps the most famous musical motif ever written – are so terrifyingly direct that commentators have been unable to resist attributing some autobiographical "meaning" to them. "Fate knocking at the door" is a more noble interpretation than the one that links the orchestral hammering to the arrival of Beethoven's bad-tempered cleaner, but this exceptional work really doesn't benefit from any narrative additions. Those opening beats provide the impetus for a first movement that is as concentrated as anything in symphonic literature, and the unrelenting forward motion is maintained right through the whole symphony. The impact of the finale – again announced by united chords – is heightened by the addition of trombones, piccolo and contra-bassoon, instruments that heralded enormous advances in orchestration. The headlong rush into C major at the close is almost as euphoric as in the *Eroica*, concluding with emphatic chordal repetitions that still sound shocking.

● Vienna Philharmonic Orchestra; Kleiber (Deutsche Grammophon DG 415 861-2GH).
● New York Philharmonic Orchestra; de Sabata (Nuova Era NUOV 0136338; with Brahms, *Violin Concerto*).

There are numerous good fifths – among them those by Karajan, Klemperer, Furtwängler and Jochum – but two really stand out. Carlos Kleiber's version is one of the most celebrated recordings since the war, and much of the praise is justified. The last movement may be slightly under-charged, but the drive that Kleiber imparts to the first movement and the Scherzo are unequalled by any other conductor in the studio – this is one of the very few performances that doesn't make this symphony sound hackneyed music. It's a reflection on Kleiber's reputation that DG can get away with issuing this fifth at full price with no coupling. Victor de Sabata's live recording, made in 1950 with the New York Philharmonic, does not have good recorded sound, but the incandescent performance goes a long way to justify some critics' description of him as the twentieth century's most exciting conductor.

SYMPHONY NO. 6 – THE PASTORAL

It is remarkable that the fifth and sixth symphonies were both written in 1808 and were performed on the same evening shortly before Christmas the same year. Subtitled the "Pastoral" in response to its obvious representation of the countryside, the *Symphony No. 6* is replete with characteristic Beethoven touches, with a profusion of contrasting ideas following hard on each other's heels, but is completely unlike its

Promethean predecessor in atmosphere. Its five highly melodic movements are predominantly sunny, and Beethoven attached unambiguously bucolic titles to each of them – "Awakening of joyful feelings on arrival in the country", "Merry-making of the country folk" and so on. He was anxious, though, that the symphony should not be taken as a sequence of naïvely descriptive episodes – as he wrote in his notebook, "the meaning of the work is obvious without verbal description". Of all Beethoven's symphonies, the sixth is the one that most clearly looks forward to the tone-poems of the late nineteenth century.

● NDR Sinfonieorchester; Wand (RCA 61930-2; with *Symphony No. 5*).

This CD came as a surprise when it was released late in 1993. Günther Wand was eighty when he made this live recording but this performance is bursting with energy. Some of Wand's earlier work was excessively concerned with fidelity to the score, but here he delivers a fresh and personal view of a piece that can too often sound hackneyed.

SYMPHONY NO. 7

The seventh symphony, composed during 1812, plainly reflects the terrible circumstances in which it was written. The Napoleonic wars were wreaking havoc across Europe, Beethoven's deafness was far advanced and, to make things worse, he was in love with a woman who was already married – recognizing the futility of his affections, he wrote letters to her which he never sent. Amongst this anguish he created the gigantic *Symphony No. 7*, a work that was one of Beethoven's notable financial successes.

It opens – as does the first – with a slow introduction, but this one leads into a thrilling Vivace, in which Beethoven juxtaposes rhythms derived from Sicilian dance music with a cleverly syncopated theme. The following Allegretto is an almost unrelievedly doom-laden episode, with its relentlessly repeated statements of grief and mourning. An austere Presto then precedes an Allegro of manic fury, which is dominated by monumentally grand themes, the orchestral texture being dominated by the timpani and horns.

● Vienna Philharmonic Orchestra; Kleiber (Deutsche Grammophon DG 415 862-2GH).

Carlos Kleiber's astounding vision of the seventh is the most thrilling performance of this symphony on disc. As with most of his work, there is a tautness to his conducting that keeps the tension running high, but never out of control. His is one of the few performances that takes the Allegretto at the tempo Beethoven intended, keeping the tension high rather than milking the pathos with a slow-paced approach.

SYMPHONY NO. 8

The eighth symphony – often disparagingly known as the "Little" Symphony – was written at the same time as the heroic seventh, though you'd never guess it. This is a much lighter piece, with a vein of humour that's apparent from the start. The polite-toned first movement, which at first hearing might seem something of a regression into nostalgia, is a self-consciously slight piece of music in which Beethoven makes fun of the recently invented metronome, a mechanism recently devised by his friend Johann Maelzel. The sense of fun continues throughout the Scherzo (for once a genuinely jokey movement), the Trio and, finally, into a bizarrely constructed Finale, in which Beethoven plays one last trick by beginning the coda extremely early, and using it to create entirely new themes rather than bring the music to a swift conclusion. Formally, this is Beethoven's oddest symphonic creation; its also his most entertaining.

> ◗ Royal Philharmonic Orchestra; Beecham (EMI CDM7 63398-2).

Thomas Beecham, perhaps the wittiest man ever to wield a baton, was a natural for this remarkable work. It's a typically enthusiastic performance, encouraging his players to relax into the music to produce an account that contains nothing pompous or heavy-handed.

SYMPHONY NO. 9

The idea of setting Schiller's *Ode to Joy* came to Beethoven as early as 1793, but it was not until the winter of 1823–24 that he completed the work for which that poem provided the climax – the *Symphony No. 9*, or *Choral Symphony*. Beethoven's most grandiose work, it heralded the epics of Wagner and Berlioz, and has entered the western consciousness to such an extent that, over a century and a half later, it was the obvious choice as the anthem of the European Community – a tepid political approximation to the universal community celebrated in Schiller's text and Beethoven's triumphant music. It's a work so stupendous that later composers felt a superstitious dread of completing their ninth symphony, as if it were tempting fate to attempt to venture beyond the number marked by Beethoven's final work in the genre. For others, however, the ninth symphony was a catalyst. Beethoven's fusion of poetry and orchestral music was the starting point for Wagner's obsession with the development of an art form that would make possible the expression of unbounded feeling, and when he laid the foundation stone of his theatre at Bayreuth, Wagner celebrated the occasion with a performance of the *Symphony No. 9*, paying homage to a score that was the foundation stone of his own life's work.

Lasting over an hour, the four movements of the ninth symphony are extraordinarily diverse and can be a desperately draining experience. The long opening movement – combining innovative orchestration with formal restraint – leads to a fiery Scherzo, an amazing piece of music that seems to be on the brink of being forced apart under its own head of steam. Nothing in these two movements prepares one for the massive spirituality of the Adagio – almost unbearably moving in its troubled tranquillity, this one section of the ninth can lay claim to being the most influential forerunner of Romantic expressionism. The finale, a colossal conceit for four soloists, a chorus and full orchestra, is the symphony's centre of gravity – indeed, it quite explicitly declares its primacy, summoning quotes from the previous movements only to reject them in favour of the titanic outburst of the *Ode to Joy*. Beethoven's concept of the symphony as a cogent unit with an overriding dynamic that propels the audience towards the climactic last movement here reaches its glorious fruition.

> ◗ Curtin, Kopleff, McCollum, Gramm; Chicago Symphony Orchestra and Chorus; Reiner (RCA 61795-2).
> ◉ Briem, Hongen, Anders, Watzke; Bruno Kittel Choir; Berlin Philharmonic Orchestra; Furtwängler (Music & Arts CD 653).

Fritz Reiner's marvellous, deeply emotional performance was made two years before his death in 1963, and carries an overwhelming sense of reconciliation to mortality. If you're not

Furtwängler in typically intense mode

fussy about sound quality, then listen to Wilhelm Furtwängler's March 1942 performance, live from Berlin: this is the greatest of his ten recordings of the symphony, and probably the greatest performance ever recorded by any one. This is a reading unlike any other, imbued with religious devotion and yet wrought with anguish and torment – his vision of the last two movements is terrifying, with no sacrifices to pedantic accuracy.

THE CONCERTOS

Beethoven's first concerto was composed for the piano in 1795 and his last, again for piano, in 1809. In between he composed a further three concertos for piano, one for violin and one for piano trio – one of the very few ever written for violin, cello and piano, and the only Beethoven concerto to fall short of greatness. The concerto for solo violin, on the other hand, is a highly melodic masterpiece with a sense of cohesion and an understanding of the instrument that has remained unequalled. Each of the piano concertos is a microcosm of the composer's style at the time of its composition, and show the evolution in his conception of the relative roles of orchestra and soloist. The piano finally triumphs in the opening bars of the fifth, the *Emperor Concerto*, a work written for an ideal instrument that would not become a physical reality until the time of Brahms' *Piano Concerto No. 1*.

THE PIANO CONCERTOS

Beethoven's piano concertos were the first to challenge the formula of the eighteenth century. Until Beethoven's emergence, the piano repeated or developed an opening theme played by the orchestra, and sometimes took over the material on its own – but never did it battle openly with the "accompaniment". Beethoven recognized the form's potential for dramatic conflict and gave the protagonists material to be played independently of each other, but working towards a common goal. With Beethoven the concerto ceased to be a series of delicate exchanges between soloist and orchestra.

All five concertos are in three movements, with a slow and intense central movement being followed by a finale of generally boisterous, upbeat temperament. All five are splendid creations, but the *Emperor* stands clear of the others – Beethoven would not have approved of the title, but it does justice to the stature of the piece. The piano can now more than stand up to the orchestra, which here, with a few chords, does little more than make a harmonic statement of key to announce the soloist's entry. The piano then lets loose a flood of sound that washes over the orchestra before attacking a cadenza of great difficulty which, eventually, allows the orchestra back in to pursue a standard sonata-form exposition. The slow movement is the most touching and beautiful of all those to be found in the piano concertos (though the fourth concerto runs it close), and leads into the animated Rondo finale by a "bridge" of mystical, lightly touched chords.

> **Piano Concertos Nos. 1–5**: Backhaus; Vienna Philharmonic Orchestra; Schmidt-Isserstedt (Decca 433 891-2; 3 CDs).
> **Piano Concertos Nos. 1–5**: Pollini; Vienna Philharmonic Orchestra; Böhm & Jochum (Deutsche Grammophon DG 419 793-2GH3; 3 CDs).
> **Piano Concertos Nos. 1–5**: Pollini; Berlin Philharmonic Orchestra; Abbado (Deutsche Grammophon DG 439 770-2; 3 CDs).
> **Piano Concertos Nos. 3 & 5**: Kempff, Berlin Philharmonic Orchestra; Leitner (Deutsche Grammophon DG 419 468-2GGA).

Wilhelm Backhaus played his first tour as a boy of sixteen in 1899; his complete set of the Beethoven concertos for Decca was made towards the end of his life, but is remarkable for the youthful freshness of the playing. The sound quality is a bit dated and some of Backhaus's slow tempi may be slightly frustrating but this is a brilliantly thought-through cycle, full of personality. For more dynamic – if less idiomatic – playing, Maurizio Pollini's first cycle is consistently stimulating and, unlike the Backhaus, is available on separate discs. Pollini's more recent cycle is a live set made with his friend and compatriot Claudio Abbado, and it sounds more like a real partnership than did the first. These are not perfect performances – they have been over-edited, the miking is too close, and the orchestral playing is often anonymous. But then, Pollini's technique is so fine that problems of execution never get in the way of his interpretation, and this set is the product of a pianist who has spent a long time journeying towards a mature understanding of the music. Some might find Pollini's obsession with accuracy occasionally offputting, but on balance this is the best cycle of recent years.

Perhaps the best single CD of the *Emperor* is the one from Wilhelm Kempff, no showstopping virtuoso but a musician with a deep affinity with Beethoven's music. Eschewing the overblown gestures that some pianists resort to in the *Emperor*, he is strong without being over-assertive, and in the slow movement he achieves a liquid sonority which, with Leitner's beautifully phrased accompaniment, is headily affecting.

THE VIOLIN CONCERTO

Beethoven's *Violin Concerto* was first performed on December 23, 1806 by Franz Clement, who hadn't seen the piece before the night of its premiere, let alone rehearsed it. This was surely for this reason that the press found little to praise in the work – except Clement's "entertainment" between the first and second movements, when he played a sonata of his own composition on only one string, with the violin held upside down. The concerto remained lost in obscurity until Joseph Joachim rescued it as a child and gave a series of memorable performances with Mendelssohn conducting.

The first movement – based upon a series of four crotchets first tapped out on the timpani – is a grand construction lasting over twenty minutes alone, but it contains music of such beauty that you might wish it lasted twice as long. The Adagio is even more exquisite, featuring one of the composer's most inspired tunes, and the finale offers superb counterplay between orchestra and soloist – a sparring relationship that, in essence, makes this the first Romantic violin concerto.

Jascha Heifetz – setting the standard as usual

⦿ Heifetz; Philharmonic Symphony Orchestra; Rodzinski (Music and Arts CD 3873; with concertos by Korngold, Brahms, Mendelssohn and Sibelius; 2 CDs).
⦿ Perlman; Berlin Philharmonic Orchestra; Barenboim (EMI CDC7 49567-2; with *Two Romances*).

Heifetz's live recording, made on January 14, 1945, is the stuff of dreams. His tone and delivery are light and unfussy, yet Heifetz's prodigious technical proficiency never dominates the performance – it's the music one remembers. Like Heifetz, Itzhak Perlman has recorded this work more than once; his 1986 CD – a "live" version edited from a several concerts with studio patching – is one of his very best performances on record, if slightly dry in comparison to Heifetz. It's particularly notable for Perlman's brilliantly lyrical playing of Kreisler's imaginative cadenza to the first movement.

CHAMBER MUSIC

Some of Beethoven's most beguiling music is to be found in his piano trios (for piano, cello and violin) and in the violin sonatas (for piano and violin), but to get right to the core of Beethoven's mind you need to immerse yourself in his string quartets, the most revolutionary compositions in the history of chamber music.

The string quartet had come to prominence during the latter half of the eighteenth century, when Mozart and Haydn between them produced over a hundred quartets of exceptional quality. Beethoven's first set of six quartets, (op. 18), begun when the composer was twenty-eight, bear his individual stamp but are clearly written in the shadows of his great predecessors. His seventh quartet, Op. 59 No. 1 (1806) – first of three quartets named after Count Rasumovsky, their dedicatee – is the turning point in the development of the genre, initiating a departure from the accepted rules as radical as that brought about by the *Eroica* symphony. The subsequent middle-period quartets are characterized by slow introductions, lengthy four-movement structures, complicated dramatic counterpoint and the development of an elaborate sonority far removed from the decorous formality of Haydn and Mozart. Even more startling are the last five quartets. As spare and intense as the last five piano sonatas, these astonishing compositions are marked by an increasing predilection for a polyphonic style, evident not only in movements that are overtly fugal but also in episodes where the four separate parts finally become thematically indivisible, creating a sense of four minds combining for the perfect expression of a single idea. The emotional and intellectual range of these last quartets proved too much for contemporary audiences and musicians alike (some thought he'd gone mad), and every succeeding composer of chamber music has had to struggle with their intimidating presence. Quite simply, they are the greatest body of string quartets ever written.

PIANO TRIOS

Beethoven's first published works – his Opus 1 – were three trios for piano, cello and violin, and already they show a marked advance on Haydn's trios in the comparative independence of the three parts. Their freedom from Haydn's frequently oppressive formality looks forward to the first mature trios, the pair that comprises Op. 70: displaying all sorts of harmonic twists, thematic innovations and structural idiosyncracies, these trios make much of the piano part and contain plenty of those dramatic outbursts that are typical of Beethoven's middle period. Even more arresting is first of the two Op. 70 trios (1808), nicknamed the *Ghost* because of its mysterious and haunting Largo; its sibling boasts a cheerful, bombastic finale that's the most entertaining music Beethoven composed for this combination of intruments.

The so-called *Archduke Trio*, Op. 97 (1811), was Beethoven's last full-scale work for piano trio, and is typically conclusive. The third movement is its centre of gravity: a highly moving set of variations, with the cello dominating the thematic content, it opens with a hymn-like theme and progresses to a coda which magnificently sums up the movement's ideas. The finale might be less powerful than that of Op. 70 No. 2, but it nevertheless has a sweeping rhythmic power.

● Complete Piano Trios: Trio Zingara (Collins COLL 7004-2; 3 CDs).

These recordings were made late in the 1980s, and as an overview of the complete trios there is no finer set. It is usually the case in chamber music that drama is conveyed by the adoption of lunatic speeds and constant loudness – fortunately, the Trio Zingara understand the power of understated but varied phrasing. What's more, these spontaneous and entertaining performances really convince you that the musicians are enjoying themselves.

VIOLIN SONATAS

Beethoven was the first composer to write sonatas for "Piano and . . ." as opposed to the classical norm of sonatas for ". . . and Piano", an arrangement that had subjugated the keyboard to the role of accompanying instrument. In Beethoven's violin sonatas the piano carries as much responsibility for the musical argument as the violin, and many of his violin sonatas are fearsomely difficult for the pianist.

Of the ten violin sonatas, *Sonata No. 5*, subtitled the *Spring*, and *Sonata No. 9*, known as the *Kreutzer*, are recorded and performed almost to the exclusion of the remaining eight. They do indeed warrant the attention, yet they are very different pieces indeed. As you might guess, the *Spring* sonata is a light-hearted work, demanding beauty of tone rather than trail-blazing virtuosity; the *Kreutzer*, on the other hand, might initially seem to require nothing but virtuosity. Both parts are fiendishly difficult, although the piano is very much the dominant party and carries most of the weight – especially in the first movement. The aggressive exchanges and heavy counterpoint are particularly dramatic if played well, but – being long and full of repeated motifs – the *Kreuzer* can be a struggle to begin with. It is best to hear the *Spring* sonata first.

⦿ **Complete Sonatas for Piano and Violin**:
Oistrakh, Oborin (Philips 412 570-2PH4; 4 CDs).
◉ **Violin Sonatas Nos. 5 & 9**: McAslan, Blakely
(Pickwick PCD 833).
⦿ **Sonata No. 9**: Vengerov; Markovich (Teldec 9031-
74001-2; with sonatas by Brahms and Mendelssohn).

If you're looking for a complete set of the sonatas, go for the cycle recorded by David Oistrakh and Lev Oborin – it's a magnificent achievement, uncompromising and noble from beginning to end.

Lorraine McAslan has nothing like the reputation of David Oistrakh, but her performances of the *Spring* and the *Kreutzer* are superb, pulse-quickening interpretations that throw caution to the wind. A complete contrasts to McAslan's wildness is offered by the *Kreutzer* of Maxim Vengerov, a violinist now spoken of in the same breath as Heifetz. He was just seventeen when he made this recording, and some people think he has since lost some of the unaffected purity of technique he shows here. This is a perfectionist performance of controlled brilliance, adopting brisk tempi and producing a rich, tightly knit and varied sound.

STRING QUARTETS

Although there is, of course, a lot of fine music in Beethoven's early quartets, the best place for the newcomer to start is the *Quartet No. 7*, the first of the quartets dedicated to Count Rasumovsky, written when Mozart and Haydn's influences were completely assimilated. The *Quartet No. 7* still respects the classical forms, but employs such idiosyncratic harmonic and melodic devices that, at the first performance, the instrumentalists laughed at what they were expected to play and the audience launched an angry protest. The middle two movements epitomize Beethoven's innovative writing: the Scherzo juggles numerous ideas, each passing within sight of the others but never uniting, while in the impassioned, poignant third movement, Beethoven reverses the accepted hierarchy of the opening motifs – the first being lithe and elegant, with the second taking on the punchy, dominant role normally given to the opening statement. Apart from the second and third *Rasumovsky* quartets, the other middle-period pieces are the tenth, known as the *Harp* (1809) because of the pizzicato exchanges in the first movement, and the eleventh, the *Serioso* (1810) – unlike most, a title ascribed by Beethoven – which is the last and most powerful quartet before the final five.

Each of these late quartets is a titanic piece, but the supreme achievement is the six-movement *Quartet No. 13* (op. 130). The Schuppanzigh Quartet, who gave the first performances, were quite unable to understand this music, and refused to play the awesome last movement, the *Grosse Fuge* – their protests over its impossible technical demands allegedly prompted Beethoven to remark "what do I care about you and your fucking fiddles." In the Schuppanzigh's defence, the fugue is a terrifying piece. Running to 745 bars and lasting over twenty minutes, it reaches new extremities of anguish and violence, making terrible demands of the four performers. Beethoven was begged to write an alternative ending for the quartet and, for the first and only time in his life, gave in. In revenge, he gave the musicians a feeble replacement finale that bore no relation to the remainder of his late music, and published the *Grosse Fuge* separately as Op. 133. Beethoven wrote that this was the "the high point to my entire chamber music"; more than that, this single movement represents the greatest of Beethoven.

⦿ **Complete String Quartets**: Lindsay String Quartet (ASV ALHB304 [3 CDs], ALHB307 [2 CDs] & DDCS403 [4 CDs]).
⦿ **String Quartet No. 13**: Lindsay String Quartet (ASV CDDCA 602).
⦿ **String Quartet Nos. 7 & 13**: Busch Quartet (CBS CD47687).

The peerless Busch Quartet

There are numerous complete sets of the quartets, many of them very good, some simply fantastic. Perhaps the most searching and original performances cycle is the one from the Lindsay Quartet – these recordings are at times eccentric, but they have an electric sense of occasion normally found only in the concert hall. Leaving little to editing or post-production, the Lindsays sacrifice precision to an urgency that touches every movement – even the earliest quartets are given a new lease of life by their sense of discovery. Their devotion to this music reaches its apogee with their interpretation of *Quartet No. 13* (available separately), one of the greatest recordings of the last thirty years. No other quartet has dredged such pathos from the slow movement nor confronted the fury of the Grosse Fuge with such a lack of compromise. This is an essential CD, as is the completely different version from the Busch Quartet, one of the last quartets to play in a style that had its foundations in the nineteenth century. Using vibrato only when the music demands a sweetening of the texture, they produce a tone quite unlike modern quartets, and their way of playing together is a bracing contrast to today's "follow-my-leader" orthodoxy, creating an invigorating sense of spontaneity and struggle within the group.

PIANO MUSIC

Just as Beethoven's string quartets are the finest body of quartets created by one person, so his piano sonatas are the summit of that instrument's repertoire. All thirty-two sonatas are masterpieces, while his final major work for solo piano, the *Diabelli Variations*, is western music's most profound summation of a lifetime's work.

The crucial thing to remember when listening to these works is that every note that Beethoven wrote for the piano was written solely with himself in mind. Beethoven's independence and self-reliance colour each of the thirty-two sonatas, from the three pieces that comprise Op. 2, begun when Beethoven was only 23, to the final Opus 111, a composition so extraordinary that Thomas Mann devoted part of his *Doctor Faustus* to an exposition on its form. His attitude towards the piano was typical of his attitude towards all instruments, in that everything he wrote posed a challenge to the piano's resources – only Liszt contributed as much to the development of technique. With the last five sonatas he went as far as the instrument could possibly take him, and then looked towards the quartet as the ultimate means of expression.

As with the symphonies and the quartets, you should really listen to the whole lot, and the easiest way to do that is to buy one of the cycles listed below. However, if want to get to know the sonatas slowly, begin with the ones we've singled out – they are not necessarily the greatest, but each one vividly characterizes certain crucial aspects of Beethoven's approach to the form.

⊙ **Complete Piano Sonatas**: Lill (ASV CDQS 6055–6064; 10 CDs).
◉ **Complete Piano Sonatas** Goode (Elektra Nonesuch 7559-79328-2; 10 CDs).
◗ **Twenty-One Sonatas**: Gould (Sony SMK 52645; SM3K 52638 [3 CDs]; SM3K 52642 [3 CDs]).

There is no better overview of the sonatas than John Lill's retrospective for ASV – available as ten separate CDs at bargain price (there's no boxed set). Don't think that the price tag means you're getting cheap performances – Lill might not possess the breathtaking technique of a Maurizio Pollini or Emil Gilels, but he has a powerful grip on these noble pieces, especially the middle-period sonatas. Lill's performances are instantly recognizable, chiefly because of the definition he brings to the rhythmic idiosyncrasies that may pianists simply gloss over. He might also claim to be the ultimate "authenticist" – Lill believes that Beethoven advises him on how to play his music and that, on certain occasions, the composer stands behind him during his performances.

Richard Goode's recent cycle is at its best with the last five sonatas, which are available in a separate box (the rest of the cycle is divided into two four-CD sets). The middle-period sonatas sometimes suffer from a percussive and over-weighted strength, while his playing of the early sonatas suggests that Goode is happier with profound introspection than with humour. Despite these limitations, this is a personal and very revealing cycle that can stand up to any of the existing competition – it's also well recorded and superbly annotated.

Glenn Gould was renowned above all for his playing of Bach, and notoriously had little time for any piano music that smacked of Romanticism. It's scarcely surprising, then, that his recordings of twenty-one of Beethoven's sonatas are the most eccentric ever made – in the *Moonlight* sonata, for example, he perversely plays the first movement fast and the second slow (the opposite of Beethoven's intentions), while in the last sonata he seems determined to make Beethoven sound like an eighteenth-century musician. That said, Gould was a phenomenally intelligent and technically dazzling pianist, and his playing possesses an unflagging improvisatory quality of which Beethoven would certainly have approved. These interpretations unearth layers of meaning that nobody else ever suspected were there – and in some cases they weren't. In short, Gould's are endlessly stimulating and aggravating performances, only to be bought after hearing "straight" versions.

SONATA NO. 8 – THE PATHÉTIQUE

The *Pathétique*, the most important of Beethoven's early sonatas, was written in 1798–89 during his "C minor period", when this was almost the only minor key he used for important works – other examples being the *Piano Concerto No. 3*, *String Quartet No. 4* and the third of the Op. 1 piano trios. It's a key well-suited to the expression of pathos – hence one element on the title that Beethoven gave to this work – *Grand sonata pathétique*. The other component of the title – the sonata's scale – has less to do with mere length than with the size of the sound, for the orchestral sonority of the *Pathétique* must have placed a great deal of strain on the instruments of the day. Showing obvious signs of Beethoven's dissatisfaction with the rigidities of classical form, this is a mighty, sometimes desperate work, reflecting Beethoven's awareness of the deterioration in his hearing. There's a terrible sense of loneliness in the weightily solemn central movement, a section which – as in the *Appassionata* – is framed by contrastingly dramatic outer movements.

⏺ Gilels (Deutsche Grammophon DG 439 426-2 with *Sonatas Nos. 23 & 31*).

The Russian pianist Emil Gilels was revered for his granite-like performances of Beethoven's music, and he was never more impressive than on this Deutsche Grammophon recording of the *Pathétique*. He adopts slower than average tempi but the playing never drags, such is his grasp of the music's structure. His tone is expressive and resonant throughout, notably in the central Adagio, where his massive, weighted sound produces such an atmosphere of terrible oppression that the finale comes as a welcome relief. Coupled with an equally brilliant *Appassionata*, this CD is exceptional value.

SONATAS NOS. 13 & 14 – THE MOONLIGHT

By the end of 1801 Beethoven had completed a further seven sonatas, including the two sonatas of Op. 27. The second of these, the so-called *Moonlight Sonata*, opens with Beethoven's most famous piano passage, a dreamy, melancholic movement that's now too well-known to be heard as the revolutionary idea it was. By labelling this sonata and its twin as "Quasi una fantasia" (Like a Fantasy), Beethoven was explicitly differentiating his

work from the weighted, formal structures of his predecessors, and by opening the *Moonlight* with a slow movement he was instantly establishing a sound-world in which the certainties of classical form no longer applied. The second movement, an Allegretto, was described by Liszt as a "flower between two abysses" and it really is little more than an interlude before the stormy finale – a movement built upon a rhythmic idea rather than a melody.

The other Op. 27 sonata is also a marvellous work, but has never achieved the same popularity, perhaps through the lack of so memorable an opening. Comprising four movements that are unbroken in performance, it's a strangely prophetic work – with its inward-looking freedom of construction, and its alternating moments of unannounced restfulness and sudden near-dementia, it looks forward to the late sonatas.

⏺ Sonatas Nos. 13, 14 & 15: Pollini (Deutsche Grammophon DG 427 770-2GH).

There are over one hundred recordings of the *Moonlight* in the current catalogue, and many of them just run through the music as if it were little more than a Romantic scribble. With Pollini you certainly don't get anything wishy-washy: this performance is well thought out and fanatically secure in its technique. The other two sonatas on the CD are similarly serious and thoughtful, but his performance of Op. 27 No. 1. has an extra degree of warmth and emotional involvement.

SONATA NO. 21 – THE WALDSTEIN

In 1804, Beethoven generously repaid the support he'd received from Count Ferdinand von Waldstein by dedicating a piano sonata to him. Written a year after the *Eroica*, the *Waldstein* is a similar landmark in the evolution of its genre, accelerating the dissolution of conventional cyclic forms and pushing towards a great expansion in scale. The *Waldstein* had begun as a relatively normal three-movement sonata, albeit one with a monumental opening movement constructed from an audaciously simple rhythmic conceit – the whole movement is generated by just two bars of chopping quavers. The masterstroke of Beethoven's rewriting was to remove the central movement and replace it with a slow and haunting section which is little more than an introduction to the Rondo finale.

Where an eighteenth-century sonata would pause for contented reflection, the Waldstein merely halts long enough to catch its breath before hurrying onward.

◉ Kovacevich (EMI 7 54896-2; with Sonatas Nos. 24 & 31).

The weight and tension of Kovacevich's playing is the product of many years' experience, and there is nothing flashily impressive about this performance – though his uninhibited prestissimo ending to the finale is as thrilling as any crowd-pleasing virtuoso could muster. The accompanying performance of the Op. 110 sonata is stupendous (see below), and the recorded sound is faultless.

SONATA NO. 23 – THE APPASSIONATA

In the opinion of Beethoven his greatest sonata was the *Sonata No. 23* (1804), a titanic four-movement work of unprecedently extreme emotional and technical challenges. The initial Allegro and the succeeding Andante (a huge set of variations) are magnificent creations, but it is the last movement that justifies the name *Appassionata*, which was bestowed on it a few years after Beethoven's death. This tempestuous finale is introduced by crashing, repeated chords which are followed by a simple series of semiquavers, in turn punctuated by shockingly violent outbursts. After a number of unexpected pauses, introduced by aggressive high-speed octave passages, comes the coda – one minute of uninterrupted, surging mayhem. This final section is extraordinarily difficult to play and is always disturbing, no matter how often you listen to it. Its first audience must have been utterly perplexed.

⊙ Ogdon (Pickwick PCD828; with Sonatas Nos. 8 & 14).
☽ Gilels (Deutsche Grammophon DG 439 426-2; with Sonatas Nos. 8 & 31).

John Ogdon's *Appassionata* is error-strewn and imprecise, but this is the only sort of playing that does justice to the music's terrifying demands. Creating a sense of furious tension through his barely perceptible gradations of dynamics, he over-pedals and smashes the keys with such anger that, quite simply, there is probably no more exciting performance of Beethoven's piano music on record. Emil Gilels' 1974 version is the perfect foil to Ogdon's maniacal ravings. Where Ogdon is wild Gilels is incisive, producing sharply distinguished rhythmic punctuation and a biting, metallic piano sound.

THE LATE SONATAS

With his last five sonatas, Beethoven took keyboard writing into a new realm, and at their completion he almost decided to finish with the piano for good, declaring that it was an "unsatisfactory instrument" – though he went on to compose the *Diabelli Variations*. A brief glance at some of the movement headings gives a good idea of what the composer was looking for in his music – the words *appassionato*, *molto sentimento*, *espressivo* and *dolente* litter the scores. Striving for absolute expression, Beethoven ventured into a complex revaluation of tradition, in which the standard forms of classical music were invested with extraordinary emotional potency. The impetus of each sonata's musical argument propels one on to the final movement, and the finales of Op. 109 and Op. 111 are in variation form, while the finales of Op. 106 and Op. 110 are fugal. Beethoven had, in effect, come full circle: tormented by the most unclassical of feelings, he followed the old paths in search of new freedoms.

Beethoven's longest and most difficult sonata is the twenty-ninth, Op. 106, subtitled the *Hammerklavier* – technically a pointless title, since *Hammerklavier* is German for "pianoforte", but one that has appropriately aggressive connotations. No other sonata covers as vast a terrain as this one. Once you've recovered from the percussive opening movement, you find yourself in a strange lopsided march that is then hammered by petulant chords before expiring mid-phrase. After that comes a slow movement of heartwrenching intensity, in which the music persistently ebbs away to the verge of silence; the desperate conclusion is a colossal fugue, an almost unmanageably complex construction which is attacked by Beethoven almost as if he wants to beat it into submission.

The last sonata, Op. 111, is the most mysterious. It contains only two movements, a disconcertingly unclassical structure that has prompted much speculation. In Thomas Mann's *Doctor Faustus*, one of the characters gives a lecture entitled "Why did Beethoven write no third movement to Op. 111?" – and the answer, in a nutshell, was that the second movement had effectively nailed the sonata form into its coffin. This second movement is a monumental set of variations based upon a beguilingly simple "Arietta" theme that becomes the basis for some of Beethoven's most agonized, most serene and most eccentric writing – including one heavily syncopated section which sounds like a jazz break. As the piece comes to a close, the exhausted pianist is required to play a huge series of trills, turning a device that in the eighteenth century was merely a decorative convention into a devastatingly moving episode, a suggestion of refuge after the preceding storms.

🅞 **The Late Sonatas**: Pollini (Deutsche Grammophon DG 419 199-2GH2; 2 CDs).
🅞 **The Late Sonatas**: Goode (Elektra Nonesuch 7559-79211-2; 2 CDs).
🅞 **Sonatas Nos. 30–32**: Papadopoulos (Pickwick PCD 1009).
🅞 **Sonata No. 31**: Kovacevich EMI 7 5489620; with *Sonatas Nos. 21 & 24*).

Maurizio Pollini's technically overwhelming set of the last five sonatas is rightly famous, winning admirers even among those who generally find his perfectionism a touch too clinical. The performance of Op. 101 is unimprovably delicate, and the *Hammerklavier* gets the full powerhouse treatment – it might seem overdone, but is probably exactly how the composer imagined the music would sound on a piano more muscular

LUDWIG VAN BEETHOVEN
Die späten Klaviersonaten
The Late Piano Sonatas · Les dernières Sonates pour Piano · Le ultime Sonate per Pianoforte
MAURIZIO POLLINI

Maurizio Pollini's awesome set of the late sonatas

than the ones at his disposal. Richard Goode is a less exciting musician, but he is stronger when it comes to the contemplative element of these sonatas. It would be best to own both versions, simply to see how this inexhaustible music can be read so differently.

Marios Papadopoulos is not exactly a household name, but his bargain-price recording of the last three sonatas is one of the finest. The weight and sobriety of his playing reaches a depth that only a very few have managed on disc, and the recorded sound is unsurpassed. Finally, Kovacevich's performance of Op. 110 is incredible, with an awesome, spiritualized reading of the fugal last movement.

THE DIABELLI VARIATIONS

Beethoven's *Thirty-Three Variations on a Theme by Diabelli* were completed in 1823 in response to a commission from publisher and composer Anton Diabelli. Thinking he'd hit upon a way to make a fast buck, Diabelli asked fifty composers to submit a variation on a theme that Diabelli had written, with a view to publishing the results as a composite creation. He received one from Schubert, one from the eleven-year-old Liszt, and thirty-three from the insulted Beethoven. Diabelli had never seen the like of them before, but immediately recognizing their greatness he published them as a separate album. In this incredible work, Beethoven realized a new mode of variation in which each variation radically reinterpreted the original theme, instead of merely parodying it or playing upon its basic framework. At the end of the *Diabelli*'s colossal trajectory, in which a host of musical forms has been quoted and transformed, Beethoven comes up with an astonishing gesture of reconciliation – a Haydnesque theme ending in a simple C major chord.

🅒 Kovacevich (Philips 422 969-2PCC).

Stephen Kovacevich's recording of the *Diabelli* is a classic, as free-flowing as Beethoven's approach to the variation form. His playing is muscular yet supple, accentuating the integrity of each variation without sacrificing the sense of overall structure. That final chord, which can make or break a performance of the *Diabelli*, is like a goal reached at the end of a long, long journey.

VINCENZO BELLINI
(1801–1835)

It can be difficult to appreciate what it was that made Vincenzo Bellini so remarkable, as modern audiences tend to have a problem with his abundance of oom-pah-pah orchestral passages, bombastic choruses and solo histrionics. But it's worth persevering, for there's more to Bellini than first meets the ear. Italian opera composers immediately prior to Bellini saw themselves primarily as creators of melodies, and those melodies had little or no connection with the words that the singers were singing. Effectively, the libretto and the orchestra were operating independently of each other. Bellini set about writing intense yet melodic music which related closely to the attitudes and sentiments of his characters, thus laying the foundations for the dramatic masterpieces of Donizetti, Verdi and Puccini. Whereas Rossini and his predecessors had relied on formula, enabling them to dash off an opera in seven days, Bellini took time and effort over his work, struggling towards a poised and well-proportioned form that appealed to the emotions as well as to the ear. He was, as Wagner wrote after Bellini's death, "all heart".

Born two years before Beethoven wrote the *Eroica*, Bellini lived for only 34 years, leaving his eleventh opera incomplete. His first great success was *Il Pirata*, commissioned by La Scala in 1827 and written (as were *I Puritani* and *La Sonnambula*) for the expressively lyrical voice of Giovanni Rubini, a man famous all over Europe as "the King of Tenors". Bellini's music is the summit of the bel canto style, requiring voices of massive flexibility and range – and, as far as the lead roles are concerned, enormous stamina. Even though the tenor parts are now transposed downwards, as they were written for falsetto voices rather than the full chest voice of the present day, Bellini's male leads are among the most demanding in the repertoire.

In 1831 he wrote his masterpiece, *Norma*, which ever since has been the vehicle for some of the world's greatest sopranos – Maria Callas, Montserrat Caballé and Joan Sutherland have all excelled in the title role. This fabulously emotive score, in which the words carry as much of the meaning as does the music, and the pace of the action is dictated by dramatic necessity, clearly represented a turning point in the development of Italian opera. The passionate ecstasy and elegiac melancholy of Bellini's music, allied with his fragile good looks, led to his idolization as the very personification of Romanticism, though not everyone was susceptible to his charm. The German poet Heinrich Heine wrote of him acidly: "he was coquettish, ever looking as though just removed from a bandbox . . . his features had something vague in them, a want of character, something milk-like; and in this milk-like face flittered sometimes a painful-pleasing expression of sorrow. The whole man looked like a sigh in pumps and silk stockings".

Bellini's early death compounded the Romantic myth. Exhausted by the effort of composing *I Puritani*, he fell ill and died, alone, in a dreary house in a suburb of Paris, where his last opera had just had its premiere. Rossini was among the bearers of the funeral shroud at the Requiem Mass; Bellini was later buried in the cathedral of his native Catania.

LA SONNAMBULA

As its title suggests, the plot of *La Sonnambula* (The Sleepwalker) is not exactly a model of plausibility. Amina is to marry Elvino. Lisa also loves Elvino but agrees to entertain Count Rodolfo, a handsome lord recently returned from abroad. Unknown to everyone, Amina is a sleepwalker, and she winds up, all unwitting, in the bed of Rodolfo. Elvino then agrees to marry Lisa, but Rodolfo attempts to explain the mistake. Everyone scoffs at his story, but as they do, Amina is seen walking along the roof of a mill, which collapses as soon as she is safely across. Elvino and Amina duly marry. Bellini's essentially simple music transforms this tale into a touching rustic idyll. *La Sonnambula* contains a substantial amount of beautifully expressive writing for soprano and tenor, especially in the second act, and the role of Amina features some real show-stopping coloratura singing.

⊙ Sutherland, Pavarotti, Ghiaurov, Buchanan, Jones, Tomlinson, de Palma; London Opera Chorus; National Philharmonic Orchestra; Bonynge (Decca 417 424-2DH2; 2 CDs).

Richard Bonynge's recording is low on atmosphere but blessed with the incredible voice of the young Luciano Pavarotti as Elvino. His voice has the texture and confidence of a singer at the height of his powers, and his phrasing is pure and enthrallingly musical. Pavarotti's pairing with Joan Sutherland works wonderfully – her singing might occasionally be over-stylized but she revels in Bellini's expressive artistry. Even if Bonynge's direction is fairly uninspired and allows his wife too much rhythmic freedom, this recording is a winner for the freshness of Pavarotti and Sutherland's partnership and for the former's magnificent presence.

I PURITANI

The excessively complicated plot of *I Puritani* is set in England at the time of the civil war, the action revolving around two rival families, one Roundhead, the other Cavalier. Yet for all its complexity, the libretto provided Bellini with considerably more substantial characters than *La Sonnambula*, and it inspired him to create some of his most perfect and demanding music for the tenor voice. The first act's *A te, o cara* is one of his most beautiful solo arias, while the final act's *Vienni, fra queste braccia* demands two high D naturals – two full notes higher than the penultimate note of *Nessun Dorma*. Elvira, the soprano lead, is less involving than Amina or Norma but suffers no dearth of lyrical music, and the concluding *Credeasi, misera!* is one of the saddest, most affecting tenor/soprano duets ever written.

⊙ Sutherland, Pavarotti, Ghiaurov, Cappucilli, Luccardi; Royal Opera House Chorus; London Symphony Orchestra; Bonynge (Decca 417 588-2DH3; 3 CDs).

This recording boasts four of the protagonists featured in Decca's *La Sonnambula* and they are similarly effective here. Pavarotti steals the show with an awesome performance of seemingly effortless flair – in fact, this is some of the greatest bel canto tenor singing on record. Sutherland is slightly self-conscious at times, as if in awe of her partner's abilities, but she produces some wonderful moments, not least when singing of her supposed betrayal. Again, Bonynge encourages her to take all sorts of liberties with the tempo and pulse, which is

not in itself a bad thing, but it does tend to make the slow sections too slow. With that proviso, Sutherland and Pavarotti work well together, and the recording is slightly more atmospheric than their *Sonnambula*.

NORMA

Norma is Bellini's greatest opera, its glorious music triumphing in the face of a plot that degenerates into near farce. The action takes place in Gaul during the Roman occupation. Pollione, a Roman, has abandoned the Gaul high priestess Norma and their two children in favour of another priestess, Adalgisa. Discovering Pollione's infidelity, Norma moves to kill her children but is unable to go ahead with the terrible deed. Adalgisa implores Pollione to return to Norma but fails. Norma then incites war between the Gauls and Romans, a conflict which leads to Pollione's capture and death sentence. Norma, still in love with her husband, offers her life in exchange for his, and mounts the funeral pyre, where Pollione joins her.

From this raw material Bellini creates a lyric drama which, in the last act, takes on a true tragic grandeur. Bellini's mastery of long and deeply expressive melodies is at its most sublime in *Casta Diva*, the ultimate bel canto soprano aria, and in the soberly moving soprano/tenor duets *In mia man* and *Qual cor tradisti*. It's no overstatement to say that the final act is the greatest example of dramatic bel canto ever written.

Serafin's version of Norma – Callas at her peak

) Callas, Corelli, Ludwig, Zaccaria, de Palma, Vincenzi; La Scala Orchestra & Chorus; Serafin (EMI CMS7 63000-2; 3 CDs).
) Callas, Filippeschi, Stignani, Rossi-Lemeni, Caroli, Cavallari; La Scala Orchestra & Chorus; Serafin (EMI CDS7 47304-8; 3 CDs).

Norma is the most recorded of Bellini's operas and there are presently over ten versions of it on CD. The title role is also one of the most difficult to bring to life, as it demands a soprano who can act as well as she can sing. Maria Callas possessed this combination of qualities, and dominated the role during the late Fifties and Sixties. She recorded *Norma* twice for EMI, both times conducted by Tullio Serafin with La Scala's forces, but the later performance (1960) boasts the amazing Pollione of Franco Corelli – this is some of the most impressive Bellini tenor singing on record. Callas's earlier recording (1954) shows her in purer and more secure voice, but her later version is blessed with genuine pathos and greater interpretative depth. Another plus for the 1960 set is the presence of Christa Ludwig, whose full and well-projected voice makes her extremely convincing as the troubled Adalgisa.

GEORGE BENJAMIN

(1960–)

All the world loves a prodigy, and all the world takes a perverse satisfaction in seeing yesterday's wonderkids fizzle out. George Benjamin, perhaps the most naturally gifted British composer since Benjamin Britten, has known both the pleasures of instant success and the subsequent trials of living with high expectations.

By the age of fourteen he was flying to Paris for weekly composition lessons with the great Olivier Messiaen (see p.231), with whose music and personality he had an immediate and strong sympathy. For a year his studies consisted of doing nothing but writing thousands of chords, discovering the subtle nuances and infinite possibilities of harmony, and the first major work produced under Messiaen's tutelage, the piano sonata of 1978, duly displays an affinity with the colourful world of Debussy and Ravel rather than with the austerities of the postwar avant-garde. Within three years of the sonata Benjamin had produced *Ringed by the flat horizon*, which was played at the London Promenade concerts in 1980 (making him the youngest composer ever to have a work performed at the Proms), and had followed this success with *At first light* and *A mind of winter*, two of the most magical works of the 1980s.

There then followed the inevitable post-prodigal phase of critical self-examination and reassessment. Having reached a venerable 22, Benjamin was no longer happy with the essentially intuitive and improvisatory nature of his music – all those chords, however beautiful and finely judged, had become something of a straitjacket. A long period of creative near-silence ensued, during which Benjamin returned to Paris to work at Pierre Boulez's gargantuan music research centre, IRCAM (see p.63). The result of this second Parisian sojourn, *Antara*, was finally unveiled in 1989, and marked a new departure in its adroit electronic manipulation of the sound of the Peruvian panpipes (*antara*) played by buskers outside the Pompidou centre.

Benjamin's next work, *Upon silence* (1990), was a complete contrast to the futuristic sonorities of *Antara* – written for the unusual combination of soprano and viol consort, it's a piece whose period instruments and harmonies suggest a composer grappling with the lessons of the past rather than with the uncharted territories of the future. What *is* new in this work is its play on musical time, the way in which its progress constantly fluctuates, passing through sudden eddies of time in which different parts simultaneously accelerate, decelerate or remain constant. It's an interest which resurfaces in Benjamin's most recent major work, *Sudden time* (1993), an orchestral piece which explores the elasticity of time and the contrasts between the extended spaces of "dream time" and the more rapid and mechanical motion of "real time". With *Sudden time* Benjamin seems to have completed his transformation from an instinctive prodigy into a composer whose abstract speculations on the nature of time, harmony and rhythm are leading him into ever-more complex territory – though, paradoxically, the results are as seductive and as apparently spontaneous as ever.

At the time of going to press, CD recordings of *Upon silence* and *Sudden time* are being prepared by Nimbus, one of Britain's most enterprising small companies; two of their current CDs of Benjamin's music are reviewed below.

THE MUSIC

The three major works of Benjamin's youth – *Ringed by the flat horizon, At first light* and *A mind of winter* – all show his acute feeling for harmonic and instrumental colours, a fluid approach to form and a sensual delight in sounds for their own sakes. What's more, they demonstrate an amazing ability to translate visual or poetic images into vivid music, whether in the atmospheric evocations of *At first light*, matching the luminous early morning colours of a Turner painting, or in the snow-filled landscapes of *A mind of winter*, where swirls of string harmonics and distant horns echo the voice of the Wallace Stevens poem that inspired it.

Only time will tell if *Antara* was a detour on Benjamin's creative highroad or a prophetic excursion into the world of electronics and innovative tuning systems, but it's indisputable that Benjamin's creative hiatus produced fascinating results. Here he uses IRCAM's computer to simulate the tones of the pan

George Benjamin presents the music of George Benjamin

pipes, a sound mirrored by two flutes and backed by a string octet, and later interrupted by the "dirty" sounds of trombones, anvils and electronics. Gone are the luscious waves of orchestral sound and those ravishing harmonies – instead the music shows a leanness, a new-found feeling for counterpoint and a remarkable rhythmic poise.

◐ At first light; A mind of winter; Ringed by the flat horizon: Walmsley-Clark; London Sinfonietta, BBC Symphony Orchestra; Benjamin, Elder (Nimbus NI 5075).
◐ Antara: London Sinfonietta; Benjamin (Nimbus NI 5167; with Harvey, *Song offerings*; Boulez, *Dérive & Memoriale*).

These performances are all excellent, with Mark Elder and the composer providing taut control, and Penelope Walmsley-Clarke a splendid soloist in *A mind of winter*. The delicious Boulez pieces on the award-winning recording of *Antara* make interesting comparisons.

𝕭𝕲

ALBAN BERG

(1885–1935)

Alban Berg is the most accessible composer of the triumvirate known as the Second Viennese School. Though he shared Schoenberg's and Webern's dissatisfaction with conventional harmony, and wrote music that was similarly astringent, Berg was never quite as puritanical in his application of atonal principles. In most of his compositions you can hear traces of the sound worlds of Richard Strauss and Gustav Mahler,

LEBRECHT COLLECTION

Alban Berg (left) with Anton Webern (see p.413)

the dominant influences on Arnold Schoenberg when Berg began studying with him in 1904.

As was the case with his teacher, Berg's move to atonality was gradual and it was not until 1910, with the last of his *Four Songs*, that he finally broke with the Romantic tradition. With the *String Quartet* of that year, the last score to be written under Schoenberg's guidance, Berg definitively became a colleague rather than a student, bringing an immediately identifiable approach to the creation of a newly expressive musical language. Even though a performance of two of his *Altenberg Lieder* in 1913 was brought to a close by the audience's rioting, Berg's flexible, expansive interpretation of atonality was soon attracting critical praise.

In May 1914, Berg attended a performance of Georg Büchner's *Woyzeck* and was so taken by it that he instantly determined to make the play the subject of his first opera. His efforts were interrupted by military service but in 1920 he finally completed *Wozzeck*, generally believed to be his greatest score. Its premiere in 1925 generated a fair amount of hostility,

but ushered in a decade during which he wrote a string of magnificent pieces that sealed his reputation – the *Chamber Concerto*, the *Lyric Suite for String Quartet*, the *Violin Concerto*, and the unfinished opera *Lulu*, which Berg dedicated to Schoenberg. The two men had become estranged, largely because of Schoenberg's inability to accept Berg's undogmatic independence, but at the end Schoenberg paid his former pupil the greatest compliment he could. When he heard of Berg's death, he wrote to Webern that the greatest of their number had gone.

Berg died before the Nazis' persecution of the Jews could place him in danger. Even so, his music was swiftly labelled "degenerate" and was hardly played until after the war, when a resurgence of interest from various prominent conductors led to regular performances. His essential lyricism and open emotionality has ensured that of the three pioneering atonalists, Berg is today the one likeliest to feature on concert programmes.

WOZZECK

Wozzeck is based on the famous play by Georg Büchner, a fragmentary proto-expressionist drama in turn based on a true story. Its eponymous hero is a hapless army private who supplements his pay by allowing a doctor to use him as a research animal in order to prove his lunatic theories. His slovenly mistress, Marie, goes off with a drum major, a swaggering brute of a man who assaults Wozzeck. Finally, pushed over the edge by jealousy and despair, Wozzeck murders Marie and drowns himself. *Wozzeck*'s jagged music and its libretto pull no punches, but it definitely rewards persistence – if you find it hard going at first, bear in mind that Erich Kleiber, who conducted the first perfromance, required over a hundred rehearsals to get it right.

Berg telescopes the action into fifteen fast-moving cinematic scenes, with often just seconds of music joining them – a problem for scene changes. In place of melodic reference points, Berg makes use of certain musical forms, such as a sonata or a fugue, to unify each component of the individual scenes. Just as Wagner does, Berg employs certain leitmotifs to tie the whole work together, the most prominent of which is associated with Wozzeck's predicament as a poor man who cannot afford morality – the motif appears in the final interlude as a luscious post-Romantic summary of the tragedy. But don't think that *Wozzeck* makes no sense if you can't conduct a musical analysis of it – above all else, this is a shockingly visceral experience.

◉ Waechter; Silja; Winkler; Vienna Philharmonic Orchestra; Dohnányi (Decca 417 348-2; with Schoenberg, *Erwartung*; 2 CDs).
◗ Fischer-Dieskau; Lear; Stolze; Wunderlich; Deutsche Oper Berlin; Böhm (Deutsche Grammophon DG 435 705-2; with *Lulu*; 3 CDs).

Neither of these two recordings is fully satisfactory, but each offers insights into this miraculous score. Waechter is slightly too bland in comparison to Fischer-Dieskau's intense portrayal for Böhm, though the latter is at times rather too aristocratic for the part of the ignorant soldier. Both sopranos are good, despite a bit of a wobble in Silja's voice, and both conductors lavish loving care on the orchestral sound – Dohnányi having the rather better sound. The main problem with the Böhm set is that it is coupled with a second-class performance of the unfinished *Lulu*, whereas Dohnányi has an excellent account of Schoenberg's monodrama, *Erwartung*.

LULU

Berg's second opera was left incomplete at his death and his sketches for the third act were kept hidden, almost as a sacred relic, by his widow Hélène. *Lulu* was thus performed incomplete at its premiere in Zurich in 1937, and for many years after, despite rumours in certain circles that the final act, contrary to Hélène's assertions, was in an advanced state; this two-act version was usually supplemented by pieces extracted from the symphony that Berg made from the opera (see below). It was not until 1976, when the composer's widow died, that the third act could be completed. As was suspected, the necessary work was minimal, but more importantly, the last act turned out to be crucial to Berg's plan – *Lulu* was to form a musical and dramatic arch, with characters and music from the earlier parts of the opera returning at the close, where Lulu's final three customers were to be played by the same singers as her earlier lovers. The completion was made by a disciple of Berg,

Friedrich Cerha, and first performed in Paris by Pierre Boulez.

Derived from two plays by Austrian expressionist playwright Frank Wedekind, *Lulu* is the tale of the rise and fall of its amoral heroine, a character who brings sexual obsession and destruction in her wake. She causes the suicide of her painter husband, murders her protector, Doctor Schön, seduces Schön's son, infects her lesbian lover with cholera, and finally ends up working as a prostitute in London, where she is slaughtered by Jack the Ripper. Schoenberg's discomfiting twelve-tone system is ideally suited to this gruesome story, and *Lulu* is more thoroughgoing in its use of the system than is *Wozzeck*. Yet *Lulu* is as seductive as it is violent. The harmonies here are richer than in *Wozzeck*, and the musical shape of the opera is more readily discernible, thanks in large part to the theme associated with Lulu herself, which serves as a point of reference throughout the score.

◉ **Lulu**: Wise, Fassbaender, Schöne, Straka; Orchestre Nationale de France; Tate (EMI CDS 7 54622-2; 3 CDs).
◗ **Lulu Symphony**: Pilarczyk; London Symphony Orchestra; Dorati (Mercury 432 006-2; with *Three Orchestral Pieces*).
◗ **Lulu Symphony**: Price; London Symphony Orchestra; Abbado (Deutsche Grammophon DG 423 238-2; with *Altenberg Lieder & Three Orchestral Pieces*).

It is a great pity that Dohnányi's radiant performance of the opera, with Anja Silja, uses the two-act version – *Lulu* is only a shadow of its true greatness without that crucial finale. Boulez recorded the initial performances of the "complete" opera for Deutsche Grammophon, and that set is something of a landmark. Jeffrey Tate's live performance has many more slips but there is much more emotion and theatricality here than in Boulez's rather dry reading. Patricia Wise is immersed in the lead role and Tate has the incomparable Brigitte Fassbaender as Geschwitz, Lulu's traduced lesbian lover – her final lament is heartbreaking.

Berg composed suites from both his operas, partly in fear that the works might not otherwise reach his intended public. The *Lulu Symphony* makes an especially good introduction to the work: the lengthy opening movement is a sort of fantasy on themes from the opera; the following movements are mostly lifted straight from the full-length work, including the tragic lament of the dying Geschwitz. There are two fine recordings of it: the combination of Abbado and Margaret Price make the DG recording a sumptuous wallow, bringing out the lush eroticism of the piece, while Dorati's classic 1962 performance is almost worth the money just for Helga Pilarczyk's death scream in the final movement.

THE VIOLIN CONCERTO

Of all of Berg's orchestral works, none is so moving as his violin concerto. Berg contemplated writing a violin concerto for the American violinist Louis Krasner for some time, but the final impetus came in April 1925, when Manon Gropius, the daughter of Alma Mahler (the composer's widow) and the architect Walter Gropius, died of polio at the age of eighteen. Berg wrote the concerto as a requiem for the girl, which is dedicated to "the memory of an angel", although recent research into Berg's preoccupation with numerology leads to an interpretation that much of the work is a coded message to Berg's mistress Hanna Fuchs, the wife of a Czech industrialist whom he first met in 1925. (The same is true of the *Lyric Suite*.)

Whatever the truth of the inspiration, the *Violin Concerto* is Berg's final masterpiece, reconciling the twelve-note system with the classical tradition by including quotations from distinctly tonal pieces – a Carinthian folksong (in the opening movement) and a chorale from a Bach cantata (in the second). The concerto begins as if the soloist is tuning the violin against the orchestra; thereafter the tension mounts throughout the first movement, as the music increases in speed and volume. As in *Lulu*, Berg then reverses the process in the second half, where the music slows and quietens until the Bach chorale steals in, and the violin and orchestra sink into a final feeling of loss and resignation.

> ● Krasner; BBC Symphony Orchestra; Webern (Testament SBT1004; with *Lyric Suite*).
> ◐ Chung; Chicago Symphony Orchestra; Solti (Decca 430 349-2; with *Chamber Concerto*).

These two CDs are the pick of a fine crop. Krasner's version, accompanied by Webern, is the first recording ever made of this work and despite the inevitable crackle on the transfer from 78s, this is a deeply moving performance. Kyung Wha Chung's eloquent performance with Solti and the virtuosic Chicago players makes an excellent modern alternative, and has the advantage of being coupled with an excellent account of the Chamber Concerto, directed by David Atherton.

LYRIC SUITE

Berg's music for chamber groups and solo instruments generally does not have the appeal of the bold larger-scale works, but one exception is the *Lyric Suite*, which was composed as a six-movement piece for string quartet in 1925–26. This original version was first performed in 1927, and Berg was sufficiently impressed with their reception to arrange the second, third and fourth movements for string orchestra the following year. This orchestrated form was premiered in 1929 and has proved more durable than the quartet.

The *Lyric Suite* contains quotations from Wagner's *Tristan und Isolde*, Zemlinsky's *Lyric Suite* and his own *Wozzeck*, but its basic idea again comes from Berg's love for Hanna Fuchs – he incorporated his own and Hanna's initials in the twelve-note row from which the piece is constructed ("H" is the German equivalent to "B", whereas the German "B" equals the English B flat).

> ● Balleys; Deutsches Symphony Orchestra; Ashkenazy (Decca 436 567-2; with songs & orchestral pieces).

Herbert von Karajan's three-CD set of music by Schoenberg, Berg and Webern (DG 427 424-2GC3) includes a fine performance of the *Lyric Suite*, but if you don't want to plunge in that far, Ashkenazy's excellent disc of major vocal and orchestral pieces is first recommendation (see below also for Lieder).

SONGS

As you might expect of one of the greatest opera composers, Berg also wrote some extremely fine songs. The very earliest pieces – those with no opus numbers – are unremarkable examples of late nineteenth-century Romanticism, but with the set known as *Seven Early Songs* (1908–10) a more distinctive voice emerges. Originally written for piano accompaniment, they were orchestrated by Berg in 1928, and these new versions are an improvement, as they accentuate the lush sensuality of the vocal part.

Most amazing of all Berg's songs are the *Altenberg Lieder*, using texts by the poet Peter Altenberg which were sent to Berg on postcards from the Alps. The first performance of the songs in 1913 caused consternation – it was shocking enough to use such epigrammatic texts as the basis for a song cycle, and the audience was baffled by Berg's use of a large orchestra to produce such quiet, chamber-like textures. Today, the songs can be heard as successors to Strauss's *Four Last*

Last Songs, with which they share a certain heavily laden lyricism.

Margaret Price's version of the Altenberg songs is something of a classic – marvellous rich and lush vocal tone, accompanied by Abbado at his most eloquent; the songs come as fill-up to a fine *Lulu Symphony* (see above). Brigitte Baileys cannot match the purity of Price's voice, but the slight edge to her tone is quite well suited to the Altenberg songs. Including the best available version of the orchestrated *Seven Early Songs*, as well as a couple of fine purely orchestral performances, this CD makes this disc as good an introduction to Berg as any.

LUCIANO BERIO
(1925–   )

Of all the leading figures of his generation, Luciano Berio is the most prodigal and encyclopedic, drawing on a range of influences that reaches from the poetry of Dante to the politics of Martin Luther King and from the operas of Monteverdi to the riffs of modern jazz. His output includes beautiful settings of traditional folk songs, yet has also embraced all the major musical developments of its time, including electronic music, music theatre, and works using quotation and collage – hence one critic's description of him as an "omnivore". Above all his music possesses a dynamic lyricism which links him to the great Italian tradition of Verdi and Puccini.

Berio's formative years, the 1950s, were spent as much in the studio as in the concert hall, and in early works such as *Omaggio a Joyce* and *Visage* he produced some of the seminal electronic music of the period. Both these pieces incorporate the recorded voice of Berio's then wife, Cathy Berberian, a mezzo-soprano whose vocal gifts were matched by a vivid stage presence which was exploited to the full in other works Berio wrote for her – *Recital*, for instance, in which the performer is asked to enact the nervous breakdown of a neurotic concert singer. But Berio's vocal music is not just concerned with theatrical role-playing or with recreating the beauties of Italian bel canto for the twentieth century. It's also interested in the very nature of language and speech, as in *Circles* (another piece written for Berberian), in which the singer's movement in a circle around the stage is mirrored

by a musical circle in which three poems by e.e.cummings are progressively deconstructed into their constituent phonetic parts and then reconstructed. A similar idea underpins the beautiful *O King* (1967) for mezzo and five instruments, in which the words "O Martin Luther King" are gradually constructed out of their vowel sounds.

O King was later incorporated into *Sinfonia* (1969), one of three major vocal and orchestral works from the 1960s – with *Epiphanie* (1962) and *Laborintus 2* (1965) – that perfectly demonstrate the omnivorousness of Berio's music. *Epiphanie* sets words by Proust and Brecht (among others) in a variety of vocal styles ranging from the extravagantly ornamented to the monotonously spoken, interleaved with orchestral movements, while *Laborintus 2* uses speaker, singers, orchestra and jazz musicians to explore a welter of texts organized around the poetry of Dante. Most extraordinary of all is the third movement of *Sinfonia*, where a musical and verbal labyrinth is built around the third movement of Mahler's Symphony no. 2 and passages from Samuel Beckett's *The Unnameable*. Berio's appropriation of other people's words and music hasn't always aspired to the complexity found in *Sinfonia*, however. *Folk Songs* (1964), his transcriptions for soprano and ensemble of folk songs from around the world (including one by Berio himself), has proved one of his most popular and accessible works, and was followed, in the 1980s, by transcriptions of works by de Falla, Mahler and

Brahms – and, in *Rendering*, by the completion of unfinished symphonic sketches by Schubert. Folk music has become an important source of material in more recent works such as *Voci* (1984), a haunting recomposition of Sicilian folk melodies for viola and orchestra, and, more elaborately, in *Ritorno degli snovidenia* (1977), for cello and orchestra.

Berio's taste for recomposition and collage runs throughout his work, as does his love of the theatrical. This theatrical element looms large in the *Sequenza* cycle, a series of solo pieces which launch an innovative and sometimes zany investigation into the virtuosic and dramatic possibilities of musical performance, ranging from the vocal extravangazas of *Sequenza III* for voice to the instrumental bufoonery of *Sequenza V* for trombone. Later, some of these pieces were themselves recomposed in yet another cycle of works, called *Chemins*, in which new layers of musical "commentary" are added to the original *Sequenza*.

Such "commentary" techniques, both literary and musical, also appear in the first of Berio's three "operas", baldly entitled *Opera* (1970), which uses the techniques developed in *Epiphanie*, *Laborintus II* and *Sinfonia* to interweave three distinct narratives drawn from the sinking of the Titanic, Monteverdi's *Orfeo* and a contemporary American drama about the care of the dying. *Opera* suffers from a certain musical and dramatic incoherence, but in his two later operas, *La vera storia* ("The true story"; 1981) and *Un re in ascolto* ("A king listens"; 1984) Berio has achieved a remarkable synthesis of extended theatrical techniques and large-scale musical means,

albeit one which owes little to traditional operatic models. These works show Berio transforming the experimental fervour of his earlier work into a musical language of greater restraint and consistency, a process that can be charted through works such as the dazzling piano concerto . . . *points on the curve to find* . . . (1974), the magnificent orchestral piece *Formazione* (1987), or the exquisitely drifting sonorities of *Requies* (1985).

THE MUSIC

With much of Berio's music the staging of the piece is an inseparable part of the experience, so it's hardly surprising that there's only a small portion of his work available on disc. None of the operas has been recorded, for example, and his output from the 1950s and 1960s remains under-represented in the catalogues – a situation that to an extent reflects the unevenness of his output. However, the two CDs listed below, covering works from the mid-1960s to mid-1980s, will give you a good grasp of Berio's scope.

◉ **Sinfonia; Formazione; Folk songs**: Electric Phoenix; Concertgebouw; van Nes; Chailly (Decca 425 832-2).

◉ **Ritorno degli snovidenia; Corale; Chemins II & IV; . . . points on the curve to find . . .** : Ensemble InterContemporain; Boulez (Sony SK 45 862).

The Chailly CD is the perfect introduction to Berio's world, including the labyrinthine *Sinfonia*, the limpidly beautiful *Folk songs* and the tautly dramatic *Formazione*. The Boulez recording features astonishing performances of the brilliant piano and violin "concertos", . . . *points on the curve to find* . . . and *Corale*, plus the exquisite *Ritorno degli snovidenia*, the frenzied *Chemins II* for viola and ensemble, and *Chemins IV*, for oboe and strings.

HECTOR BERLIOZ
(1803–1869)

The life of Hector Berlioz – as related in his dazzling if over-imaginative memoirs – is classical music's Byronic epic. Yet this quintessential Romantic began rather inauspiciously, in the backwater

of Grenoble. Whereas most musical giants displayed prodigious gifts in childhood, Berlioz learned neither the piano nor the violin, though he did develop an enthusiasm for the flute and, later, the guitar.

HULTON DEUTSCH

Notwithstanding his lack of practical musical ability, he wanted to pursue a career in music, but his father insisted that he enter the medical profession. Berlioz did as he was told, but in 1822, while studying at the Paris medical school, he began to take serious music lessons for the first time.

Owing to the fact that his father's allowance was forthcoming only for as long as he remained at school, Berlioz hesitated over making a serious break until 1826, when he mustered the courage to leave the medical school and enter the music conservatory. His subsequent development was bewilderingly fast, and was actually aided by his inability to play the piano well – other composers tended to work out their ideas at the piano, but Berlioz found himself free of such creative limitations and soon realized that the orchestra and large ensembles were his true métier.

In 1827 he experienced one of many life-changing events when he went to see a performance of *Hamlet*. Even though his English was far from fluent, the play hit him "like a thunderbolt", as did the beauty of the leading lady, Harriet Smithson. It was to be the start of a lifelong addiction to the Bard and an equally intense, if less durable, passion for Miss Smithson (they married in 1833 and separated nine years later). During the first five months of 1830 – having in the interim immersed himself in Goethe's poetry and attended a revelatory series of Beethoven concerts in Paris – he composed his *Symphonie Fantastique*, a huge orchestral piece in which he attempted to sublimate his passion for the actress; its subtitle, "Episodes in the life of an artist" betrays an autobiographical element that was never far below the surface of Berlioz's music.

Not long after, Berlioz finally succeeded in winning the *Prix de Rome*, a scholarship given to artists to enable them to study at the Villa Medici in Rome – and Italy was duly to become another of his great inspirations. Berlioz proceeded to produce a string of similarly colossal and innovative works that secured the admiration of composers such as Liszt, Paganini and Chopin, but had difficulty obtaining a wider audience, not least because his music usually demanded very large and expensive forces.

The work that posed the greatest problems in this respect was his penultimate opera, *Les Troyens*, a five-act, four-hour monster which the Paris Opéra refused to produce in its entirety. Berlioz then divided the work into two parts and, eventually, he saw the second of these, *Les Troyens à Carthage*, staged at the Théatre-Lyrique in 1863. As with so many of his works, the performance was a grand failure, but this failure hit him harder than any.

He found occasional solace through conducting, but his last seven years were overshadowed by illness, despair and resentment at his country's inability or unwillingness to recognize his talent – a situation that has not really changed, for Berlioz is far more widely respected abroad than he is at home. His music was doubtless very strange for its time, with its irregular rhythms and almost boastfully complicated orchestration, and certainly it can be pompous and overblown. However, Berlioz is one of music's great originals, spurning traditional formulas to blend literary, pictorial and musical elements into highly energetic and highly personal creations.

STAGE WORKS

Of Berlioz's five stage works, two are master-pieces – the classically inspired *Les Troyens*, and his homage to Goethe, *La Damnation de Faust*. The early *Les Francs Juges* is lost apart from a lengthy overture which is sometimes programmed in orchestral concerts. *Benvenuto Cellini*, the story of the intrigues surrounding the Renaissance sculptor and his rivals, gets an occasional performance and recording, but is too lengthy for its content, although Berlioz created one of his best overtures – *Le Carnaval Romain* – out of its carnival scene. His late Shakespearian comedy, *Béatrice et Bénédict*, a hotch-potch of styles with heavy reliance on spoken scenes, has never been a success, despite containing one or two musical highlights and an attractive overture.

LA DAMNATION DE FAUST

Berlioz read a translation of the first part of Goethe's *Faust* in 1828 and fell under its spell at once. He immediately set to work on eight *Scenes from Faust*, which he sent to the poet for approval – a bad move, as it turned out. Goethe showed the score to a composer friend who was appalled by Berlioz's outra-geous music, and the result was that Berlioz withdrew the work. Many years later, he reworked the scenes into *La Damnation de Faust*, a hybrid work, more closely resem-bling an oratorio for concert performance than an opera – Berlioz himself called it a "dramatic legend". It was produced at the Opéra-Comique in 1846, then in Drury Lane two years later, after which Berlioz planned a further revision to make the work a true opera – it's almost impossible, for example, to stage the *Ride to Hell* and *Pandemonium*. However, the Drury Lane opera company for which the opera was to be written soon went bankrupt, and so *La Damnation* remained as it was.

Berlioz sticks much closer to his source than many composers have – Gounod, for example, concentrated merely on the Faust and Gretchen scenes in his *Faust*. Not only does he retain the narrative scope of the origi-nal text, he tackles its supernatural and philo-sophical apsects too, and in this respect *La Damnation* resembles Busoni's version of the

legend (see p.86). Temperamentally, however, there's a world of difference between Busoni's cerebral opera and Berlioz's kaleidoscopic work, which crams an extraordinary range of music into its two-hour span. Between the crashing Hungarian March of the opening scene and the climactic ride to hell, there's a rowdy tavern scene, a supernatural ballet as Faust dreams of Marguerite (Gretchen in the original), a love scene, a mad aria and a great pantheistic invocation of nature, one of the most advanced parts of this amazingly vivid score. No previous work for the stage had risked such violent contrasts, and few subse-quent composers could bring them off so successfully.

◉ Veasey, Gedda, Bastin; Ambrosian Singers; London Symphony Orchestra; Davis (Philips 416 395-2; 2 CDs).

Despite being recorded over twenty years ago, this Philips set is wonderfully vivid. Colin Davis is masterful in portraying the tender moments of Marguerite's despair as well as the vast climaxes of the Hungarian March and the ride to hell. Josephine Veasey is a poignant heroine, Nicolai Gedda a magnificent Faust, and Jules Bastin a suitably evil Mephistopheles.

LES TROYENS

Berlioz's epic tale of the Trojan war was writ-ten in the late 1850s but brought together the obsessions of several decades – primarily the poetry of Shakespeare and Virgil, and the operas of Gluck, whose finely structured libretti provided a model for the text of this most un-Gluck-like extravaganza. Berlioz never lived to see *Les Troyens* performed complete: after five years of waiting for the Paris Opéra to agree to a production, he split the opera in two and let the second section, *Les Troyens à Carthage*, be performed at the smaller Théatre Lyrique. The first part, *La prise de Troie*, wasn't performed until 1890, by which time *Les Troyens* had pretty well fallen into oblivion as a unified work. It wasn't until 1957 that a nearly uncut version was played in one evening at Covent Garden, a premiere that put paid to the notion that the piece was even more unwieldy than Wagner's later operas. *Les Troyens* is nonetheless too expensive to be performed regularly – you're more likely to see semi-staged concert performances than full-dress opera house productions.

The opera begins in war-ravaged Troy, quickly introducing the prophetess Cassandra, the pivotal figure of the first two acts (ie *La prise de Troie*), and the role with perhaps the noblest music in the entire score. The whole of this first part of *Les Troyens* is full of grandiose and doomstruck music, its highlights being Cassandra's aria, the procession of the widowed Andromache, the entry of the wooden horse, the ghost scene in Aeneas's tent and finally the mass suicide of Cassandra and the Trojan women.

Berlioz creates a wholly different sound world for the sensuality of the court of Queen Dido at Carthage, where Aeneas and his party arrive after fleeing the conflagration of Troy. These final three acts progress at a slower and more luxuriant pace. After the celebratory first act comes the best known music of the opera, the symphonic interlude known as *The Royal Hunt and Storm*, commencing a succession of beautiful set pieces that culminates in a great love duet for Aeneas and Dido, set to words from Shakespeare. The final act brings the Aeneas' desertion of Dido and her suicide, a scene redolent of the majesty of Gluck.

⦿ Veasey, Vickers, Lindholm; Royal Opera House Orchestra and Chorus; Davis (Philips 416 432-2; 4 CDs).

This set, featuring the cast of the 1969 Covent Garden performances, demonstrates Davis' unrivalled ability to project Berlioz's wonderful melodies, often quirky rhythms and rich orchestral colours. Josephine Veasey is a full-sounding Dido, Berit Lindholm a powerful Cassandra and Jon Vickers is simply the perfect Aeneas – no-one since has brought the sheer power and nobility to this most difficult of roles.

CHORAL AND VOCAL WORKS

Berlioz wrote a considerable amount of vocal music apart from the operas, including a number of cantatas (several of which are lost), some lovely orchestral songs and two large-scale religious works – the *Grand Messe des Morts* and *L'Enfance du Christ* (The Childhood of Christ). Written in 1837 and 1850–54 respectively, they are total opposites in style – the *Grand Messe* is a hyperbolically massive affair, *L'Enfance* a gentle series of musical tableaux.

GRAND MESSE DES MORTS

The *Grand Messe des Morts* (1837) is unique in being a Requiem created by a man of no real religious belief. It is doubly strange in that it is written almost entirely for chorus and orchestra – there's just one soloist, a tenor, and he appears in one movement only. Comparable to Beethoven's *Missa Solemnis* in its dynamic extremes, the *Grand Messe* is famed primarily for its use of four brass bands in the *Tuba Mirum* movement, placed at the four compass points to conjure the Day of Judgement in an ear-splitting display. Certainly nothing else in the work matches the theatricality of this moment, but there is much to admire in this austerely grand and sometimes lurid composition.

◔ Burrows; Orchestre National de France; Bernstein (Sony M2YK 46461; with *Te Deum*).

No recording is able to fully capture the impact of those brass bands, but this well-produced performance, suitably intense and romantic, is the best compromise. The coupling is a none too impressive version of the *Te Deum* under the direction of Barenboim.

L'ENFANCE DU CHRIST

L'Enfance du Christ is so distinctly archaic in style that it hardly seems possible that it's written by the composer of the *Grand Messe*. A self-confessed agnostic, Berlioz presents the story of the young Christ as a legendary narrative rather than as an uplifting religious experience. The work is in three sections: the first centring on the birth of Christ and the predicament of King Herod; the second is a pastoral interlude in which the Holy Family flee into Egypt, a scene containing some of the composer's most placid music; and the final part depicts the hospitality given to them in Egypt, an episode featuring some fairly crass scene-painting but a serene choral ending.

⦿ Murray, Tear, Allen; Royal Philharmonic Orchestra; King's College Choir; Cleobury (EMI CDS 7 49935-2; 2 CDs).

The King's College choir makes this a very special recording and the soloists too are excellent, especially Anne Murray as Mary. The recorded sound is good, and the only complaint is the lack of a fill-up on these two full-priced CDs.

LES NUITS D'ÉTÉ

Les Nuits d'été, a cycle of songs to words by Théophile Gautier, was first written in 1841 as a composition for voice and piano. A couple of years later Berlioz orchestrated the third song, *Absence*, and in 1856 he decided to make orchestral versions of the other five. It is impossible to overstate the importance of this piece to French music: whereas Beethoven, Schubert and Schumann had already established the concept of the song cycle in Germany, it was Berlioz who single-handedly introduced the form to France. Yet its novelty is but a small part of the appeal of *Les Nuits d'été*, for these are among the loveliest songs of the nineteenth century, thanks to music that's completely attuned to the melancholic languor of Gautier's poems.

⊙ Crespin; Orchestre de la Suisse Romande; Ansermet (Decca 417 813-2; with other French songs).
⊙ Armstrong, Veasey, Patterson, Shirley-Quirk; London Symphony Orchestra; Davis (Philips 438 307-2; with *Lélio*).

Berlioz originally wrote the songs for different voice types but nowadays they are usually sung by a soprano – and it's difficult to find a voice that's exactly right for all these songs, as the opening and concluding songs are of a lightness that contrasts with deep sorrow expressed in the longer central pieces. Most successful of all the solo versions is that of Régine Crespin, who is as close to ideal as any one singer could be. Colin Davis reverts to the concept of four different singers, with variable results: Frank Patterson is excellently light in the style of the true French tenor, Josephine Veasey is rich and profound, but John Shirley-Quirk gives a rather laboured performance. Davis conducts Berlioz with his customary flair, and there's an imaginative fill-up in the shape of *Lélio*, Berlioz's rather incoherent sequel to the *Symphonie Fantastique*.

ORCHESTRAL WORKS

Berlioz's early overtures – especially *Le Corsair* and *Le Carnaval Romain* – generate a certain fidgety excitement, but there's no disputing which two compositions stand out as the best of his small output of orchestral work: the *Symphonie Fantastique*, the first and greatest Romantic symphony, and *Harold en Italie*, a sort of travelogue for viola and orchestra.

SYMPHONIE FANTASTIQUE

Both as a first symphony and as a work by a twenty-seven-year old, the *Symphonie Fantastique* is a staggering achievement. Written just three years after Beethoven's death, at a time when he was still regarded as a radical, this hour-long and five-movement work took several steps beyond Beethoven's symphonic structures. For one thing, this is the first symphony to make thorough use of the *idée fixe*, a single melody that reappears in different guises throughout the work – a concept that is the forerunner of the leitmotifs in Wagner and Richard Strauss. Furthermore, although composers had written scenic music before the *Symphonie Fantastique* (eg Beethoven's *Symphony No. 6*) and simple musical onomatopoeia had been common for centuries (eg Vivaldi's *Four Seasons*), no composer had used instrumental music to present so specific a narrative drama. In short, this symphony is an opera without words.

Mythologizing Berlioz's neurotic obsession with Harriet Smithson, the "plot" of the *Symphonie Fantastique* is an opium-induced phantasmagoria, in which the hero imagines the torrid progress of a love affair that ends ultimately in his execution for the murder of his lover. Berlioz supplies sub-titles to explain events: *Reveries – Passions*; *A Ball*; *Scene in the Country*; *March to the Scaffold* and *Dream of a Witches' Sabbath*. The *idée fixe* runs chillingly through each movement and reaches its gruesome climax when it is coupled with the terrifying Dies Irae plainchant – Romanticism's ultimate musical theme.

⊙ Vienna Philharmonic Orchestra; Davis (Philips 432 151-2).

The symphony, with its vast forces, wild rhythms and extremes of loudness and softness, is a tour de force of orchestral writing and no-one knows it better than Sir Colin Davis. His third recording of it, with the Vienna Philharmonic has the advantage of superb sound and excellent playing.

HAROLD EN ITALIE

Although it was composed in 1834, the gestation of *Harold en Italie* began three years earlier, when Berlioz was travelling through Italy after winning the Prix de Rome. While crossing from Marseilles to Leghorn, he had met a sea captain who claimed to have ferried Byron – author of the immensely popular *Childe Harold's Pilgrimage* – around the Greek islands. That gave Berlioz his initial ideas for the piece, but the catalyst was Paganini, who approached him for a viola concerto; Berlioz accepted the commission, then promptly abandoned the idea of a strict concerto in favour of what amounted to a symphony with obbligato viola.

The work was based, as Berlioz wrote, upon his "impressions recollected from . . . wanderings in the Abruzzi mountains", and the solo viola was conceived as a portrayal of "a kind of melancholy dreamer in the style of Byron's *Childe Harolde*". Paganini was unimpressed. He had asked for a concerto and expected something to display his notorious abilities: when he realized that there was nothing even vaguely difficult in the score he refused to play it. The two duly fell out, but when Paganini heard the work performed he threw himself at Berlioz's feet to beg forgiveness and later sent the composer a note comparing him to Beethoven – enclosed was a gift of 20,000 francs. Berlioz needed the money and they became friends once again, but Paganini never played his commission.

Again, the work is in five movements and is dominated by a central thematic idea (Harold's theme), but Berlioz now takes the *idée fixe* a stage farther – whereas in the *Symphonie Fantastique* the *idée fixe* recurs unchanged, here the "Harold" idea appears in every movement but serves as the basis for thematic development. The rhythmic pungency of *Harold en Italie* is even more engaging than the symphony, and the melodies – especially in the adrenalin-pumping finale – are much more immediate. In effect Berlioz's second symphony, it has proved less popular than the first, but is musically its superior, for whereas the drama of the *Symphonie Fantastique* can sound close to orchestral gimmicry, here everything takes second place to the thematic content, and it is Berlioz's genius for melody and harmony that remains uppermost.

Imai; London Symphony Orchestra; Davis (Philips 416 431-2; with *Tristia*).

Davis correctly sees the piece as more a symphony than a concerto and Nobuko Imai is an excellent partner, always playing the viola as part of the integral musical soundscape, never clamouring for the limelight. Excellently recorded, the disc also has a fascinating fill-up in the little-known *Tristia* pieces.

LEONARD BERNSTEIN

(1918–1990)

Leonard Bernstein's big break is the stuff of legend – substituting for the sick maestro Bruno Walter for a New York Philharmonic concert on November 14, 1943, he became famous overnight, launching a meteoric and controversial career as a conductor. For some, Bernstein got right to the heart of Beethoven, Mahler and the other great symphonists, giving himself unreservedly to the music's emotional pulse; for others, he was a self-indulgent showman, besotted with himself and with audience's applause. Yet conducting was but one strand of a career that was remarkably varied but at the same time consistent.

From the mid-1950s Bernstein presented dozens of TV programmes – most famous being the *Young People's Concerts* (1958–73) – in which he played and brilliantly explicated the works that he so manifestly loved. The basis for Bernstein's lectures was his belief, very similar in its thrust to Noam Chomsky's theories of speech structure, that all music is rooted in a universal language that is basically tonal. This belief was fundamental to his own compositions, in which Bernstein strove to forge a connection between art music and the music of the American people. More specifically, he felt that jazz was the essential sound of the USA – though the jazz you hear

SONY

Leonard Bernstein – twentieth-century Renaissance man ?

in Bernstein's music is not so much a direct legacy of Duke Ellington or Jelly Roll Morton, but jazz as reworked by Aaron Copland.

As a composer his greatest successes were in music for the stage, and he created a string of hit shows that culminated in *West Side Story* (1957), a classic of American musical theatre. His theatrical instincts frequently spilled over into his concert works, Bernstein himself admitting to "a deep suspicion that every work I write, for whatever medium, is really theatre music in some way". Such compositions as his three symphonies, *Jeremiah*, *The Age of Anxiety* and *Kaddish*, are indeed profoundly dramatic, but they also draw sustenance from Bernstein's Jewish heritage, with its basis in synagogue chant.

As the 1960s progressed, Bernstein came under increasing fire from radical young musicians, for whom the serialist principles of Schoenberg, Berg and Webern, and their hardline successors Boulez and Stockhausen, were the new orthodoxy. Although Bernstein fought a vigorous rearguard action against the dogmatic rejection of the general public's taste, he began to lose his confidence as a composer, preferring instead to develop his role as the guardian of what he felt was best in music. Bernstein's liberal humanism, sincere though it was, didn't always endear him to the younger generation either. Most notoriously, his fundraising evening for the Black Panther movement backfired calamitously when Tom Wolfe made it the subject of his most celebrated article, *Radical Chic*.

Yet even in the face of vilification Bernstein never relinquished his musical values, and his principles have come to be more relevant now than they were at the time. There may be some truth in the accusation that Bernstein's own music is often nothing more than immensely skilled pastiche, but it's equally true that he could be seen as the precursor of a generation of American composers – Adams, Glass, Reich and so on – who are are as effusively theatrical, eclectic and tonal in their leanings as Bernstein was.

WEST SIDE STORY

Of all Bernstein's music, it's the stage works that sum up best what he was all about, and of these *West Side Story* is the most consistently tuneful. Transposing Romeo and Juliet to the gangland of New York's West Side in the 1950s, it was not a huge success at its premiere – its reputation soared after the release of the film version in 1961. Though

West Side Story is full of great songs, including *America*, *Maria* and *Tonight*, it's equally remarkable for the quality of its dance music (which Bernstein later rearranged as a concert suite) and for its decidedly downbeat ending, breaking one of the cardinal rules of music theatre.

● Te Kanawa, Carreras, Troyanos, Horne, Ollman; chorus and orchestra; Bernstein (Deustche Grammophon G 415 253-2; with *On The Waterfront, Symphonic Suite*; 2 CDs).

This award-winning recording is a controversial one. The recording made by the original cast featured gritty, full-blooded performances, but didn't contain the complete score. This newer version is complete, but gives the piece the full-blown operatic treatment, and it has to be said that some ears find the voices of Kiri Te Kanawa and José Carreras rather lifeless and overpolished. On the other hand, there's no doubt that Bernstein taps his soloists' ability to elicit more subtle vocal effects than would be possible from Broadway singers, while the orchestral players – drawn from on and off Broadway – inject the piece with a jazzy rhythmic exuberance. Bernstein's exciting symphonic suite from *On the Waterfront* is thrown in for good measure.

HARRISON BIRTWISTLE
(1934–)

Despite acknowledged debts to Stravinsky and Varèse (see p.360 & p.387), Harrison Birtwistle's music sounds as if it has sprung into being from a point outside the mainstream of European music, evoking the stylized ceremonies of Greek tragedy, the ritual violence of ancient myths, the bleak and depopulated landscapes of rural England. Many of Birtwistle's compositions have the massive, rough-hewn quality of a prehistoric monument, but he can also produce music of spare lyrical beauty and, on occasion, haunting delicacy.

During the 1950s, when Birtwistle began his musical studies, the English scene was dominated by the shadow of Vaughan Williams (see p.388) and other such pastoral composers, while recent events in European music were generally regarded with reactionary disdain. It was in this claustrophobic environment that the "Manchester School", consisting of composers Birtwistle, Alexander Goehr and Peter Maxwell Davies (see p.226z), plus conductor Elgar Howarth and pianist John Ogdon, began their careers, looking to the latest developments on the continent for inspiration. Birtwistle bided his time, studying clarinet and keeping his ambitions as a composer to himself until 1957 when, with the wind quintet *Refrains and choruses*,

he launched himself as the most distinctive voice among his illustrious contemporaries. Here, immediately, is a fully formed style. It's strikingly raw and hard-edged music, and it unfolds not by any conventional development but as a series of static blocks, evoking a kind of imaginary rite.

Birtwistle scored his first major critical success with the ensemble piece *Tragœdia* (1965) – the title, meaning "goat dance", is drawn from Greek drama, one of the principal influences on Birtwistle during this period. Birtwistle's works of the 1960s culminated in the notorious chamber opera *Punch and Judy*, which was premiered at the Aldeburgh Festival in 1968, when Benjamin Britten – guiding light of the festival – was among those who walked out in disgust or incomprehension. Here the ritual violence of purely instrumental works such as *Tragœdia* is transferred to an explicitly theatrical context, depicting the gruesome encounters of Punch and Judy. What is typical of this and subsequent works for the stage is the lack of progressive narrative: the story is not told in sequence from beginning to end, but re-enacted over and over again, each time from a slightly different angle (Punch commits no fewer than four murders), creating a tension between the heated, murderous subject matter and its cool, rather distanced presentation.

The work that really signalled the arrival of Birtwistle as one of the major composers of his generation was *The Triumph of Time* (1972), a monumental orchestral procession inspired by Brueghel's depiction of the remorseless progress of Time and Death. After this came a series of masterful works such as *Silbury Air*, *Secret Theatre*, *The Fields of Sorrow* and, in 1983, *The Mask of Orpheus*, an opera which, with its mythologized, masked characters, represents the summation of Birtwistle's love of hieratic structures and repetitive narratives. Since the long-postponed premiere of *The Mask of Orpheus* in 1986, Birtwistle has increasingly turned his attention to opera. In 1988 came the "mechanical pastoral" *Yan tan tethera*, a supernatural tale of two shepherds, their sheep and the devil, followed in 1991 by the monumental opera *Gawain*, in which he counterpoints the Arthurian hero's trials against the remorseless cycles of nature. A further opera, *The Second Mrs Kong*, was completed in 1994. Other recent compositions have included the massive orchestral *Earth dances*, the brilliant trumpet concerto *Endless parade* and a piano concerto, *Antiphonies*, premiered in 1993.

If the savagery of Birtwistle's earlier work was its most immediately striking feature, the lyrical qualities of his music have come to the fore as his career has progressed, along with a new richness and spontaneity of texture. Indeed, the longer you listen to Birtwistle's music, the more you tend to appreciate the particularly "English" qualities of his work, so that it now seems possible to place him in the very same tradition as Vaughan Williams, unlikely as it would have seemed twenty years ago, when he was regarded as epitomizing all that was most dangerous in musical modernism.

THE MUSIC

Marshalling huge orchestral forces in a work lasting over half an hour, *The Triumph of Time* represents the classic instance of how Birtwistle was able to achieve a structure that has nothing to do with traditional ways of sustaining an extended piece of music. Birtwistle often describes his works as "imaginary landscapes", and the description is particularly apt here – listening to *The Triumph of Time* is rather like moving through a landscape and viewing the same landmarks from ever-changing perspectives.

If *The Triumph of Time* is the apotheosis of the processional, ritualistic side of Birtwistle's music, *Secret Theatre* – perhaps his finest work to date – represents the summit of its equally characteristic lyrical and more intimate aspects. Birtwistle's preoccupation with the whole nature of song and singing is exemplified by the story of *The Mask of Orpheus*, but *Secret Theatre*, a half-hour work for fourteen players, is its most eloquent musical demonstration, being composed entirely out of long-spun melodic lines set against a ticking, clockwork accompaniment.

The other piece you should get to know is *Earth Dances*, an overwhelming forty-minute orchestral work evoking the predatory natural world in dense, unremitting music.

> ◉ **The Triumph of Time**; **Gawain's Journey**: Philharmonia; Howarth (Collins Classics 13872).
> ◉ **Secret Theatre**; **Silbury Air**; **Carmen arcadiae mechanicae perpetuum**: London Sinfonietta; Howarth (Etcetera KTC 1052).
> ◉ **Earth Dances**: BBC Symphony Orchestra; E,tv,s (Collins Classics 20012).

This fine recording of the *Triumph of Time*, conducted by Birtwistle's student colleague Elgar Howarth, is coupled with *Gawain's Journey*, Howarth's orchestral arrangement of excerpts from the opera Gawain – a bit of a pot-pourri, but with some memorable moments. *Secret Theatre* is the definitive Birtwistle recording, performed by the excellent London Sinfonietta, who commissioned all three works on the CD – the others are *Silbury Air*, one of Birtwistle's most memorable "landscape" pieces, and *Carmen arcadiae*, a brief but brilliant jigsaw puzzle of brightly coloured fragments. The Collins CD single recording of *Earth Dances* is in an accomplished performance, recorded live at the 1991 Proms.

GEORGES BIZET

(1838–1875)

Like so many nineteenth-century opera composers, Bizet attained immortality through a single score – *Carmen*. He completed its fourth and final act in 1874; a year later he was dead.

Bizet packed a lot into his short life. By the age of nine he had entered the Paris Conservatoire and within months was winning every major prize for piano, organ and composition. In 1857, aged nineteen, he won the coveted Prix de Rome, which set him on a steady course to security and fame. An example of his abilities at this time can be found in his *Symphony in C major*, an astonishing work which reflects the influence of Gounod, whom Bizet had befriended in 1856.

His first major opera, *Les Pêcheurs des Perles* (The Pearl Fishers), was produced at the Opéra Comique in 1863. It was written to an appalling libretto whose authors later admitted that, had they been aware of Bizet's talents, they would not have saddled him with such a "white elephant". However, the public warmed to Bizet's sensual and melodic music, and *Les Pêcheurs des Perles* became one of

Bizet's very few immediate successes – though its continued survival is primarily due to one lovely duet for tenor and baritone. He went on to compose a number of comic and dramatic operas, many of which were left incomplete, and none of which suggested anything more remarkable than proficiency. Then in 1872 Bizet began to take an interest in Prosper Merimée's short novel *Carmen*; the Opéra Comique, however, was far from enthusiastic – they didn't want death on their stage, and neither were they keen on a project dominated by thieves, gypsies and cigar-makers. Despite these misgivings, the manager finally committed himself to a production and on March 3, 1875, *Carmen* was given its premiere.

Bizet described the result as "a definite and hopeless flop" (an exaggeration) and, ever prone to psychosomatic illness, took to his bed. Four hours after the curtain had fallen on the 33rd performance, he died from the second of two major heart attacks.

CARMEN

Carmen is the first "realistic" French opera, and its merging of intense local colour with well-crafted tragic drama attracted praise from influential quarters: Wagner wrote of it, "Here thank God . . . is somebody with ideas in his head"; both Brahms and Tchaikovsky adored it; and Nietzsche used the opera as a stick with which to beat Wagner, suggesting that he adopt some of Bizet's healthy Mediterranean philosophies. However, the hot-blooded characterization of Carmen, and of her rival lovers Don José and Escamillo, scandalized the first audiences, as did the tragic ending, in which Don José murders the heroine.

Bizet's evocation of the opera's Spanish locales displays amazing abilities as an orchestrator, while the plentiful magnificent arias are so adroitly and economically woven into the plot that you come away with the sense that nothing could possibly be added or taken away. It is hard to imagine how critics could have attacked *Carmen* for being

LEBRECHT COLLECTION

Bizet

tuneless – it boasts more memorable tunes than any other French opera except Gounod's *Faust*, which remains the only French opera more popular than *Carmen*.

⊙ Price, Corelli, Freni, Merrill, Linval, Macaux; Vienna Boys Choir, Vienna State Opera Chorus, Vienna Philharmonic Orchestra; Karajan (RCA GD86199; 3 CDs).

Though he's less comfortable with the French language than is Placido Domingo, Franco Corelli is the greatest Don José on record. His massive voice is incomparably thrilling, and he produces an outstandingly tragic portrayal that remains unequalled. He sings opposite Leontyne Price, with whom he made his New York debut two years before this 1963 recording was made; she may not be the most characterful recorded Carmen, but she brings an effective sense of malice to the part, and is perfectly attuned to Corelli's style. They are also at one with Karajan's exciting if unsubtle approach to Bizet's score, and with Mirella Freni in exquisite voice and Merrill in marvellously declamatory form, this set is the most entertaining introduction to Bizet.

SYMPHONY IN C MAJOR

Bizet's finest orchestral score, the *Symphony in C major*, was composed in 1855, when he had only recently turned seventeen – though it was not performed until 1935 when the conductor Felix Weingartner discovered the manuscript in Paris. Like its model, Gounod's *Symphony No. 1*, Bizet's work makes no claims to originality, but it's a fresh, ingenious and uninhibited piece, something like a French version of Schubert in its beautiful melodic writing (though Bizet could not have known Schubert's large-scale works). Like Mendelssohn's early music, this is more than mere juvenilia.

⊙ Beecham; Royal Philharmonic Orchestra (EMI CDC 7 47794-2; with *L'Arlésienne Suites*).

Beecham's charming and light-footed account of the symphony is full of wit and colour. His moulding of Bizet's intricate architecture is unfailingly sure and the orchestra responds to his demands with engaging immediacy. The recording is well produced and comes coupled with a marvellous performance of the two suites from Bizet's incidental music to Alphonse Daudet's tragedy of Provencal life, *L'Arlésienne*. Although the music is available complete, it is best known and most successful in the form of these suites, which were made by Bizet after the unsuccessful premiere.

LUIGI BOCCHERINI

(1743–1805)

Though Boccherini was a highly successful cellist and a prolific composer – especially of chamber music – he is largely known today for just one work, the Minuet from his *String Quintet in E*, a piece that gained a new lease of life when it was used on the soundtrack of the classic comedy film *The Ladykillers*. He was almost an exact contemporary of Haydn, and his music possesses a similar classical elegance and charm – indeed, the Minuet bears a marked resemblance to Haydn's equally popular Serenade. It is true that he rarely matches the depth or passion of the older composer, but to dismiss him, as the violinist Giuseppe Pupo did, as "Haydn's wife" is grossly unfair. His music might occasionally be insipid, but it's full of good tunes, always pleasant, and sometimes startlingly original.

Boccherini was born in Lucca, the son of a double-bass player and cellist, who gave him his first lessons. His early career was spent as a cello virtuoso, and he took part in the first ever public string quartet concerts in Milan in 1765, at the same time forming a friendship with one of the violinists, Filippo Manfredi. The two decided to tour together, travelling to Paris in 1767, and then onto Madrid a year later, where Boccherini gained the patronage of the Infante Don Luis, the king's younger brother. He was to remain in Madrid for the rest of his life, serving Don Luis until 1785, and then the Benavente-Osuna family until 1798, while at the same time providing music for Prince Frederick-William of Prussia.

His final years were full of misfortune. The Parisian music publisher Pleyel took advantage of Boccherini's good humour and generosity, refusing to return manuscripts, and demanding changes in his style to match public taste. Two daughters died in 1802, and his wife and another daughter in 1805 – events that almost certainly contributed to his mental decline. He died in poverty, although ironically his music was to enjoy a real vogue almost immediately after his death.

CHAMBER MUSIC

"There is perhaps no instrumental music more ingenious, elegant and pleasing, than his quintets," wrote Charles Burney in 1770. Boccherini went on to write over a hundred of them plus nearly as many string quartets, so it is unsurprising that a lot of his chamber music is bland and repetitive. That said, several of his chamber pieces involve the interesting imitation of non-musical sounds, like bird-song, in his quintet *L'Ucelliera*, or – even more strikingly – street sounds in the quintet entitled *Night music in the streets of Madrid*. Unfortunately, these pieces are available only on CDs that are largely devoted to fairly uninteresting music; for a decent recording of the famous Minuet from the *String Quintet in E*, you're best advised to buy the Baroque compilation CD recommended on p.4.

You can, however, buy a fine CD of the delightful guitar quintets, which were arranged for the Marquis of Benavente, a talented amateur guitarist, and evoke the sunny, easy-going atmosphere of the early paintings of Goya. One remarkable aspect of these quintets is the variety of effects that Boccherini spins out of this combination of instruments. In some pieces the guitar is clearly the dominant voice, in others, like the boldly dramatic first movement of the first quintet, it is the violin that prevails. The most extraordinary single piece though, is the last movement from the fourth quintet where, after a slow introduction, a full-blooded fandango lets rip, complete with strumming guitar, insistent rhythmic repetitions and even castanets.

◗ The Guitar Quintets: Romero; Academy of St Martin in the Fields Chamber Ensemble (Philips 438 769-2; 2 CDs).

This is a fine introduction to Boccherini's music. Delicacy and wit predominate, but Pepe Romero and the Academy chamber players are not afraid to let go where necessary – the performance of the *Fandango Quintet* is particularly thrilling.

CELLO CONCERTOS

Boccherini wrote at least eleven cello concertos, and all of them were written for himself to perform – thus they often make difficult technical demands on the soloist, with much of the solo writing not just richly ornamented but also placed consistently high in the register. As with most of his music, the prevailing mood of these works is of an easy gracefulness and poise. In the nineteenth century a cellist named Grutzmacher took movements from two of the best concertos and arranged them into a single work, a romanticized hybrid that is still, after the Minuet, Boccherini's best-known work.

◉ Three Cello Concertos; Aria Accademica: Coin; Almajano; Ensemble Baroque de Limoges (Astreé E8517).

The cello concertos on this disc include the two tampered with by Grutzmacher, here performed in their original versions. The B flat major concerto is a lightly scored work and in this recording the cello sound has been carefully integrated with the ensemble, making for some wonderfully airy and delicate textures. The highpoint of the G major concerto, the other concerto of the pair, is the lugubrious but lyrical slow movement, the long phrases of which are shaped and controlled by Coin with a beguiling restraint. The third concerto, in D major, has some wonderfully ornate passage work in its slow movement, while the disc's fill-up is a brilliant concert aria for soprano, full of virtuosic runs, in which the cello part dominates the orchestral writing.

ALEXANDER BORODIN

(1833–1887)

Like many of his Russian contemporaries, Borodin was essentially an amateur composer, in the sense that he had a flourishing career in a completely different field and composed in his spare time – which accounts for both his relatively small output and the high proportion of works that he never found time to finish. Yet Borodin made a distinctive contribution to the Russian musical nationalist cause in the 1870s and 1880s. In addition to his fertile melodic talent, he had a good ear for exotic orchestral sounds, and created some pungent harmonic writing that gives his music a real strength and originality.

He was the illegitimate son of a Georgian prince and by the tradition of such things was given the name of one of the prince's serfs. Despite displaying a childhood passion for music, he trained as a chemist and physician and it was as an academic chemist that he first made his name, engaging in important research as a professor at the Academy of Medico-Surgery in St Petersburg.

Although he had been attempting to compose since his teens, he began to exploit his compositional skills only when, as a young man, he came under the influence of Mily Balakirev (1837–1910), the figurehead of a group of radical musicians based in St Petersburg (the others were César Cui, Modest Mussorgsky and Nikolai Rimsky-Korsakov). He refused to contemplate cutting down on his scientific responsibilities, and the five years it took for him to complete his first work, his *Symphony No. 1*, set the pattern for his rate of composition. Characteristically, he worked on the opera *Prince Igor* for some eighteen years, from penning the first ideas in 1869 to his death in 1887, when it was still not complete. In the meantime, he did manage to finish one of his most popular works, his *Symphony No. 2* (after nearly seven years' work), though its successor, begun in 1885, also remained incomplete on his death and, like much of the opera, was made performable by Alexander Glazunov (see p.145).

GUUS ONG

PRINCE IGOR

Borodin's first and only complete opera, *The Bogatyrs* (1867), was an unsuccessful comic parody of grand opera and was followed by an equally futile bid to write a serious opera, *The Tsar's Bride*. But in *Prince Igor*, rambling though some of it may be, he created a worthy counterpart to Russian opera's greatest historical tragedy, Mussorgsky's *Boris Godunov* (see p.250). It is more an opera of tableaux than of forward-moving action, and gave Borodin the chance to demonstrate his flair for oriental imagery and orchestral colour, best demonstrated in the orchestral highlights that, despite the opera's rarity on stage, have always been popular in the concert hall and on record. The overture, reputedly written by Glazunov from memories of Borodin's piano improvisations, is a vivid foretaste of what's to come; the other famous excerpts – a *Polovtsian March*, the *Dance of the Polovtsian Maidens* and the choral *Polovtsian Dances* – all come from the scene set in the encampment of Igor's enemies.

> ◉ **Prince Igor**: Martinovich, Ghiuselev, Ghiaurov, Kaludov, Milcheva; Sofia Festival Orchestra & National Opera Chorus; Tchakarov (Sony SK44878; 3 CDs).
> ◗ **Prince Igor**: Cherkerliiski, Christoff, Wiener, Todorov, Penkova; Sofia National Opera Chorus & Orchestra; Semkow (EMI CMS 7 63386 2; 3 CDs).
> ◗ **Overture & Polovtsian Dances**: Royal Liverpool Philharmonic Orchestra & Chorus; Mackerras (Virgin VC 5 61135-2; with Mussorgsky, *Pictures at an Exhibition* & *Night on the Bare Mountain*).

The only complete recording, featuring all four acts, is a Bulgarian one with only one or two familiar names among the cast, including Nicolai Ghiaurov as the Khan – but the result is more than simply worthy under Emil Tchakarov's inspired direction. Otherwise there is the rather aged recording featuring Boris Christoff singing the roles of both the Khan and Prince Galitzky, but the performance omits Act III. The orchestral excerpts can be found on any number of Russian orchestral collections, but good accounts of the overture and *Dances* come from Charles Mackerras.

SYMPHONIES AND ORCHESTRAL WORKS

Although Borodin in effect wrote only two and a half symphonies, they represent a significant contribution to the history of the form in Russia. Like Tchaikovsky's earlier symphonies, Borodin's employ typically Russian harmonies, melodies and rhythms against a fairly conventional Germanic formal background. *Symphony No. 1*, in particular, looks back to Schumann, one of Borodin's prime influences at the time, yet is a distinctly Russian work, particularly in the use of a folk song in the Scherzo and the oriental lyricism of the slow movement. *Symphony No. 2* represents his first fully mature work and demonstrates all his most characterful features: rhythmic drive, grandeur, nostalgia and exuberance. From reminiscences by his colleagues Borodin clearly had the whole of his *Symphony No. 3* in his head, but only completed the spellbinding second movement and sketched the first.

Of Borodin's other orchestral works only one is a self-contained original work in that form – *In the Steppes of Central Asia*, a tone poem depicting an oriental caravan (evocatively suggested by a cor anglais melody) crossing the central Asian plains with an escort of Russian soldiers. The *Petite Suite*, originally composed for piano in 1885, is not so petite – it lasts for nearly half an hour and has seven movements, alternating tone paintings and dances. It's become best known in Glazunov's orchestration.

> ◎ **Symphonies Nos. 1–3**: CSR Symphony Orchestra Bratislava; Gunzenhauser (Naxos 8.550238).
> ◉ **In the Steppes of Central Asia; Petite Suite**: Gothenburg Symphony Orchestra; Järvi (Deutsche Grammophon DG 435 757-2; with *Prince Igor Overture, Dance of Polovtsian Maidens, Polovtsian Dances* & *Nocturne*; 2 CDs).
> ◉ **In the Steppes of Central Asia; Petite Suite**: USSR Symphony Orchestra; Svetlanov (Melodiya SUCD 10-00155; with *Symphony No. 3 & Prince Igor Overture*).

The budget-price CD from Stephen Gunzenhauser and the authentically Slav-sounding Czechoslovak Radio Symphony Orchestra of Bratislava is among the most successful in the Naxos catalogue, with brilliant performances and a vivid recording quality that puts several bigger-name companies to shame. Slightly more full-blooded and refined performances can be found on Neeme Järvi's set of virtually the complete orchestral music, more extravagantly spread across two full-priced discs. Svetlanov's slightly less comprehensive survey, from the 1960s, features glowing playing from the USSR Symphony Orchestra and, despite a couple of imperfections in the master tape, it sounds surprisingly up-to-date.

THE STRING QUARTETS

Borodin's mature chamber music comprises just two string quartets. The second (1881) is by far the more popular, largely because of its slow movement, a ravishing, orientally flavoured Nocturne that has gained a separate life of its own in versions for string orchestra as well as in its original scoring. Its other three movements are no less striking, particularly the amiable Scherzo.

> ◉ Borodin Quartet (EMI Melodiya CDC 7 47795 2).

The suitably named Borodin Quartet has recorded the second quartet several times, but the most successful is on this 1980 disc of both quartets, recorded in Russia and issued by EMI. This is a delightful, exciting performance, with a warm sound quality.

LILI BOULANGER

(1893–1918)

Lili Boulanger has been eclipsed by the reputation of her younger sister Nadia, one of the most influential teachers and musicologists of her time. Yet in her tragically short life Lili produced music that can stand comparison with virtually anything written at that time in France, and had she lived longer it's almost certain that she would have become one of the century's greats. Despite the advocacy of her sister and a phalanx of other musicians, she remains shamefully neglected.

The sisters came from a long line of musicians, including a cellist grandfather, a soprano grandmother and a father who managed to win the coveted Prix de Rome, a scholarship whose previous winners included Hector Berlioz. (Lili herself became the first woman ever to take the prize when in 1913 she was awarded it for her dramatic cantata *Faust et Hélène*, her most substantial work.) They were educated by their aristocratic Russian mother, establishing a cultural cross-connection that was strengthened by the Parisian vogue for all things Russian, such as the ballets of Diaghilev and Stravinsky – though Lili's music bears stronger traces of her teacher and mentor Gabriel Fauré.

From the age of two Lili suffered worsening pain from bronchopneumonia, the disease that was to kill her, and as a young adult she had to face the additional struggle of resisting the establishment prejudice against women composers. In view of this, and the social context of a country mired in the hell of World War I, it's scarcely surprising that much of her small output is tinged with desolation.

THE MUSIC

Boulanger loved the music of Fauré, and like Fauré's work most of her best compositions are melancholic pieces that are principally for the voice. The finest of them all is *Du fond de l'abîme*, a setting of the De Profundis composed between 1914 and 1917. It's a massive work of great solemnity, thickly written but subtle in its handling of the combination of large forces and solo voice. The occasionally routine chromaticism and laboured counterpoint betray a composer still finding her feet but, even so, *Du fond de l'abîme* is a deeply felt and highly personal creation that accentuates the tragedy of her premature death.

> ❿ **Du fond de l'abîme and other works**: Dominguez, Amade, Menuhin, Curzon; Concerts Lamoureux; Markevitch (EMI CDM 7 64281-2).

Of the few discs of Boulanger's music in the catalogue, EMI's historic survey serves as the most complete introduction. As well as an intensely moving version of *Du fond de l'abîme*, it contains the lovely *Pie Jesu*, her magnificent settings of Psalms 24 and 129, and some violin and piano pieces excellently played by Yehudi Menuhin and Clifford Curzon. The only drawback is the rather dated sound.

PIERRE BOULEZ

(1925–)

The figure of Pierre Boulez has dominated the avant-garde of western music since 1950. One of the century's finest composers, Boulez has also been one of its great conductors and most outspoken ideologists, whose ideas and polemics have alternately captivated and infuriated successive generations of musicians. Born in Montbrison in southeastern France, Boulez studied composition with Messiaen in Paris before

POLYGRAM

bursting into spectacular compositional life in the late 1940s with works such as the first two piano sonatas and the cantatas *Le visage nuptial* and *Le soleil des eaux*. Marrying the rhythmic complexities of Stravinsky and Messiaen with the atonal vocabulary of Schoenberg and, particularly, Webern, Boulez achieved a distinctive new synthesis to which he added something completely his own – a sense of unbridled violence, as typified by the second piano sonata.

Thus established as the *enfant terrible* of French music, Boulez then embarked on a period of research into ways of writing music that would eradicate all traces of tradition, an enterprise he shared with other young Turks such as Stockhausen and Nono – the so-called "Darmstadt School", named after the German town which hosted a summer school devoted to their ideals. It was Messiaen's uncharacteristically austere *Mode de valeurs et d'intensités* which showed them how, by systematically ordering pitch, rhythm and dynamics in strict numerical sequences, one could write "automatic" and almost completely impersonal music. And it was Boulez who produced – in *Structures I* for two

pianos – the classic work of what has come to be known as total serialism.

Boulez, the figurehead of the hyper-modernist cause, promulgated the doctrine loudly not only in his own music but also in his denunciations of Schoenberg and Stravinsky, in both of whose later works he had come to see signs of a fatal compromise with tradition. However, it's impossible to ignore the suspicion that Boulez was always preaching what he would rather not practise. Ever since *Structures*, his music has been characterized by the way in which his natural gifts, which link him to Debussy rather than Webern, have increasingly succeeded in transcending his self-imposed ideological limits. Indeed his next major work, *Le marteau sans maître*, already suggests the conflict between the hermetic demands of total serialism and a love of colour that's typical of French music.

Yet as the 1950s and 1960s progressed, Boulez's effortless creative confidence seemed to evaporate, though there was no slackening in his protean intellectual speculations. He flirted with electronics in *Poésie pour pouvoir*, with open-ended form in *Figures, doubles, prismes*, and with indeterminacy, in the *Piano Sonata No. 3* – all backed up by elaborate theorizing but subsequently withdrawn, revised or left unfinished. The one project which seemed to sustain him during this stage of his life was the monumental vocal cycle, *Pli selon pli*.

It was at this time that Boulez emerged as a conductor of international standing, and although he has always denied any connection, one can hardly escape the conclusion that conducting has been at least partly a means of avoiding his creative impasse. By 1970 he was holding prestigious but onerous positions as chief conductor to both the BBC Symphony Orchestra and the New York Philharmonic, and his composing had virtually dried up – the monumental orchestral work *Rituel* was the only finished work to emerge during the entire 1970s. History seemed to have marginalized the modernist cause and to have robbed Boulez of the revolutionary fervour which had fuelled his earlier achievements.

Then, in 1977, came the greatest public challenge of his career, when he secured a colossal government grant for the establishment of the Institut de Recherche et Coordination Acoustique/Musique (IRCAM), a futuristic musical laboratory buried under the Pompidou Centre in the heart of Paris. Overseen by Boulez, IRCAM would provide a hi-tech venue in which leading composers and scientists would work together to investigate the possibilities of technology in music, educating musicians and public in a set-up complete with its own resident ensemble, the matchless Ensemble InterContemporain. In the history of music only Wagner previously had been able to command patronage on this scale, and expectations were high, the greatest one being of course that Boulez himself would use the resources of IRCAM to produce the masterpiece which seemed to be demanded by investment on such a massive scale. Boulez's response, *Répons*, premiered in 1981 and constantly revised since, seemed set to meet the demands of producing a huge public statement using the latest computerized gadgetry, but like so many of Boulez's works it remains under a cloud, unfinished and unrecorded. Since the massive undertaking of *Répons*, Boulez seems once more to have lost the ability to tackle fresh major projects. The works which have appeared include exquisite miniatures such as *Dérive* and *Memoriale* and further revisions and recompositions of earlier works, notably a sumptuous new version of *Le visage nuptial*.

Assessing Boulez's achievement is complicated not only by his status as the firebrand of modernism and by his manifold musical activities, but also by the chaotic state of his output. Some pieces have been temporarily or permanently withdrawn by him, others have been left unfinished (and perhaps unfinishable), or reissued in versions entirely different from the form in which they first appeared, or are still "in progress" half a century after they were begun. The most talented of all postwar composers has, it seems, been silenced by the contradiction between Boulez the uncompromising evangelist of hardline modernism, and Boulez the musician, whose extraordinary gifts – untrammelled by doctrine – could have produced work as seductive and evocative as anything in this century's music.

THE MUSIC

If you want to chart Boulez's development from the beginning, the best place to start is the *Piano Sonata No. 2*, a furious assault on the keyboard, with jagged lines and unremitting rhythmic pile-ups that were something quite new to European music.

The violence of the sonata is subsumed in *Le marteau sans maître* into something more subtle, in which you are aware of the music itself far more than of the complex procedures that lie behind it. Scored for the exotically original ensemble of soprano, alto flute, viola, guitar, xylophone) vibraphone and percussion, *Le marteau* sets three surreal poems by René Char in nine interlocked movements that often – with their insistent drum beats and incantatory flute lines – owe as much to Africa as to Europe.

The slightly later *Pli selon pli* is in many ways the summation of everything Boulez had achieved to date, and it's one of his most immediately attractive pieces; it exudes a quality of hypnotic stasis, with its fantastically sculpted vocal lines saturated with brittle percussion sonorities. After that, you could move on to *Rituel*, the major Boulez work from the 1970s, and finally to the intoxicatingly beautiful *Le visage nuptial*, a piece that took over forty years to emerge in its final version.

The orchestral works are all available in performances conducted by the composer, while the sonata is featured on one of the most astounding CDs of modern piano music currently available.

○ **Piano Sonata No. 2**: Pollini (DG 419 202-2GH; with Prokofiev, *Sonata No. 7*; Stravinsky, *Three Pieces from Petrushka*; Webern *Variations*).
○ **Le marteau sans maître; Notations pour Piano; Structures pour deux Pianos; Livre II**: Chen; Wambach; Laurence; Ensemble InterContemporain; Boulez (CBS MK 42619).
○ **Pli selon pli**: Bryn-Julson; BBC Symphony Orchestra; Boulez (Erato 2292-45376-2).
○ **Rituel; Eclat; Multiples**: BBC Symphony Orchestra; Ensemble InterContemporain; Boulez (Sony SMK 45839).
○ **Le visage nuptial; Le soleil des eaus; Figures, doubles, prismes**: BBC Symphony Orchestra & Singers; Bryn-Julson; Laurence; Boulez (Erato 2292-45494-2).

The fearsomely demanding second sonata is the Everest of the twentieth-century piano repertoire, and Pollini's taut, vehement performance has yet to be bettered. Equally taxing is *Le marteau*, a piece that required fifty rehearsals before its first performance; the composer is one of the very few conductors able to meet its demands, and this is his most recent, and most laid-back, recording of the work. Boulez's favourite soprano, Phyllis Bryn-Julson, sings memorably under his characteristically immaculate direction on *Pli selon pli* – this CD makes possibly the best introduction to Boulez. The

massed orchestral groups of *Rituel*, his most austere work, make a bracing contrast with *Eclat*, a brief but dazzling jewel of scintillating percussion sonorities, later developed – with additional instruments – into *Multiples*. *Le visage*, Boulez's most irresistible score, is given a lavish performance on the last CD with another of his finest works, *Le soleil des eaux*, and the patchy orchestral piece *Figures, doubles, prismes*.

JOHANNES BRAHMS

(1833–1897)

In the face of Liszt, Wagner and the "New German School" of music, it was Brahms who upheld the long-established ideals of the German tradition. He was not, however, the reactionary figure he's sometimes portrayed as being. No less a revolutionary than Arnold Schoenberg praised Brahms's combination of "economy and riches", and his best music (of which there's a great deal) generates a remarkable power from the tension between its seething emotions and the propriety of its classical structures.

As in the case with so many composers, Brahms's life lacked much in the way of incident. His childhood in Hamburg was devoted

MANSELL COLLECTION

to study and it was not until he was fifteen that he began to play in public. In order to make himself some money, he often played in brothels, a fact which various biographers have linked to Brahms's precarious later relationships with women. Whatever the cause of his notorious reticence and boorishness, Brahms always felt uncomfortable with women, but was able to see the positive side to his awkwardness – it saved him, he said, from "both opera and marriage".

One of the greatest influences on his life and music was the great violinist Joseph Joachim, whom he met in Hanover in 1853 while touring with another Hungarian violinist, the self-styled "gypsy" musician Eduard Reményi. Upon hearing the young Brahms perform some of his own work, Joachim gave him written introductions to Liszt and Schumann; when Schumann in turn heard Brahms play, he hailed the young man as a genius – not the first time he'd become overexcited by a new young artist, but on this occasion he was right. The ensuing friendship with Schumann and with Schumann's wife, the pianist Clara Wieck, did much to nurture Brahms's talent, but it was not until after Schumann's death, in 1856, that Brahms began to devote much time to composing.

In 1860 he put his name to a declaration – also signed by Joachim – that disassociated the signatories from the new trends championed by Liszt and his circle. This professed conservatism meant that success remained elusive for years, and it was not until 1869, when his *Deutsches Requiem* was first performed, that he was recognized as a major creative force. In 1872, having moved to Vienna, he succeeded Rubinstein as artistic director of the *Gesellschaft der Musikfreunde*, a post he held onto for only three years. From 1875 until his death his time was dominated by composition, and by occasional engagements as a conductor or pianist.

The symphonies, all but one of the concertos and most of the chamber music for which he is now remembered were composed during this extraordinarily fertile quarter-century, years which saw Brahms drift ever further away from public life. He was happiest on his own. In 1885 Clara Schumann, his friend and rumoured lover, said of him "To me he is as much a riddle – I might almost say as much a stranger – as he was twenty-five years ago". There is, however, little sense of distance in his work, which is some of the most profound, elegiac and unsentimental music of his century.

THE SYMPHONIES

Brahms's four symphonies are unique in that they are all products of the composer's maturity. The fear of comparison with Beethoven inhibited him so much that he struggled for decades with the idea of writing his first symphony, which finally saw the light only in 1876. Within a decade he'd completed his second, third and fourth, a sequence of greatly different compositions that encompass a vast range of styles, forms and emotional states. In the opinion of many, it's the most important body of symphonic music after Beethoven's. Hans von Bülow, conductor of the premiere of *Symphony No. 4*, declared that his favourite key was E flat, for its three flat notes (signified by the letter b in German) symbolized for him the trinity of Bach, Beethoven and Brahms.

Complete symphonies:
⊙ Royal Liverpool Philharmonic Orchestra; Janowski (ASV CDQS6 101–104; with overtures; 4 CDs).
◗ Berlin Philharmonic Orchestra; Karajan (Deutsche Grammophon DG 429 644-2; 3 CDs).

It would be pointless to buy a full-price cycle of the Brahms symphonies as there is none available that boasts the qualities of the individual performances recommended below. If, however, you want to get to know the symphonies for minimum outlay the ASV budget-price set (not available as a box)

has a lot to commend it – Janowski is an honest and clear-sighted conductor whose performances are full of enthusiasm. Alternatively, Karajan's 1978 DG cycle offers loving performances and fine recorded sound at mid-price.

SYMPHONY NO. 1

Although the first symphony was only received politely at its premiere in Karlsruhe, by the time it reached Vienna it was being nicknamed "Beethoven's Tenth", affirming Brahms's arrival in the ranks of the symphonic masters. The first movement does indeed owe something to Beethoven but it is in the last movement's second principal theme, announced in unison by the violins after the dark and ominous introduction, that the influence is clearest, in its allusion to the main theme from the last movement of Beethoven's ninth. The joyful thrill of this movement is unmatched by any of the other symphonies, as Brahms's relief at having finally managed to embark upon his first symphony finds outlet in a finale of awesome scale.

⊙ Bavarian Radio Symphony Orchestra; Böhm (Orfeo C 263 921-B; with Mozart, *Piano Concerto No. 9*)
◗ Philharmonia; Klemperer (EMI CDM 7 69651-2; with overtures).

Böhm's performance, recorded live in 1969, is quite simply the most exciting and moving account ever captured on record. Böhm may slow down slightly at the last movement's final chorale, but otherwise this is as muscular as this music can get. The sound is marvellous – only Böhm's sporadic grunting and stamping betrays the fact that it was not made in the studio.

Klemperer's reading of the first symphony is extraordinarily slow-paced in comparison to Böhm's, but it's a majestic account, with grandeur and warmth going hand in hand.

SYMPHONY NO. 2

When Brahms set about writing his second symphony he had the confidence to relax, and this work is a much more amiable piece than its predecessor. It repeated the success of the first in Vienna, and duly attracted more comparisons to Beethoven, acquiring the nickname "The Pastoral" in reference to Beethoven's sixth. The Symphony No. 2 marked a crucial point in Brahms's career – on the back of its reception both his first and second symphonies were published, and he embarked on a series of triumphant European concert tours.

○ Vienna Philharmonic Orchestra; Furtwängler
(Deutsche Grammophon DG 435 324-2GWP; with
Beethoven, *Leonore No.3* and *Grosse Fuge*).
○ Columbia Symphony Orchestra; Walter (Sony MYK
44870; with *Academic Festival Overture*).

The searing energy of the Furtwängler performance almost defies description – the finale will have your heart in your mouth. The accompanying *Leonore No. 3* (one of Beethoven's three alternative overtures for *Fidelio*) is just as fine. This is what great conducting and great symphonic music are all about, but if you think you'll have problems with the dodgy sound quality, go for the Bruno Walter recording – he was one of the great conductors of the standard repertory, and this is a particularly warm rendition of the Brahms's second. However, if one record is going to convince you that pristine digital sound is sometimes of secondary importance, the Furtwängler is it.

SYMPHONY NO. 3

The Viennese public had to wait another six years for the third symphony, and when it finally arrived it was received with even more enthusiasm than the first two. Eduard Hanslick, the vociferous anti-Wagner and pro-Brahms music critic, declared that it united the titanism of the first symphony with the untroubled charm of the second. It's certainly a magnificent achievement (some would say Brahms's greatest symphony), but it's not the most ingratiating composition. The third symphony is a tightly wrought piece and its drama is generally low-key – there are no firecrackers here, but rather a mood of subdued confession. With this symphony it's essential to give the music time to work on you.

● Berlin Philharmonic Orchestra; Abbado (Deutsche
Grammophon DG 429 765-2; with *Schicksalslied & Tragic
Overture*).

Abbado's excellently recorded performance emphasizes the lyrical and melodic aspects of the symphony. Some people find it a bit woolly in its execution, but at the moment there's not a lot of competition around – if Guido Cantelli's EMI recording is ever reissued, snap it up.

SYMPHONY NO. 4

With the *Symphony No. 4* Brahms reached the culmination of his symphonic style – the outer movements are virtually symphonies in themselves, containing ideas that are almost too grand to be fully worked through. The vast

opening movement is packed with huge and intoxicating melodic ideas, while the momentous finale, a Passacaglia built upon a simple harmonic idea, has the same air of finality as the conclusion of Beethoven's ninth.

● Vienna Philharmonic Orchestra; Kleiber (Deutsche
Grammophon DG 400 037-2).

From the evidence of this recording it's a fair bet that Kleiber heard Furtwängler conduct this symphony, for this is a performance characterized by the same command of orchestral colour and electrifying dynamism. There is no serious competition.

CONCERTOS

Brahms wrote four concertos – two for piano, one for violin and one for violin and cello (the so-called *Double Concerto*) – and all except the last have become regular fixtures in the concert halls. Though each is quite distinct in character, they are united by Brahms's conception of the concerto as a symphonic form, in which the soloist becomes at times subservient to the independent-minded orchestra. Thus in the *Violin Concerto* the second movement is introduced by a theme that the soloist never gets to play, while in the *Piano Concerto No. 2* the third movement is dominated not by the pianist but by the principal cellist, whose long and beautiful theme is taken up by the rest of the orchestra. As in Beethoven's concertos, there are moments of antagonistic drama as the soloist and orchestra contend supremacy, but in Brahms the sense of unity prevails.

○ Complete Concertos: Kremer, Maisky, Zimmerman;
Vienna Philharmonic; Bernstein (Deutsche Grammophon
DG 431 207-2GX3; 3 CDs).

This set is the only available overview of all four concertos in one boxed set. Naturally, it has its weaknesses – not least Bernstein's emotional hand-wringing – but his soloists are all in fine form. Good sound and orchestral playing all round, and good value.

PIANO CONCERTOS

Brahms began his first piano concerto at the age of twenty-one, shortly after Robert Schumann's attempted suicide, as a tribute to Robert and to Clara, who had given the first performance of Schumann's piano concerto.

Eventually the work was premiered by Brahms in 1859, three years after Schumann's death, and it was a disaster. Soon, however, with Clara's help, the work's quality was recognized and, even now, it remains the more popular of the piano concertos. Though it begins with an orchestral introduction that keeps the soloist out of the picture for some four minutes, it's a more flamboyant and virtuosic piece than the second concerto, building to a wonderful finale with a momentous and percussive principal theme that dominates from beginning to end.

The second concerto – one of the longest ever written – was composed some twenty years later, while Brahms was basking in the acclaim for his third symphony. Like that work, it shows the mellower aspects of the composer, particularly in the slow movement, with its innovative use of a second solo instrument (the cello) to carry the main theme. It's by no means a placid piece of music, however – the tussle between piano and orchestra in the second movement is one of the most exhilarating episodes in the entire concerto repertoire.

> **Piano Concertos Nos. 1 & 2**: Gilels; Berlin Philharmonic Orchestra; Jochum (Deutsche Grammophon DG 419 158-2; with Op. 116 piano works; 2 CDs).
> **Piano Concerto No. 1**: Kovacevich; London Philharmonic Orchestra; Sawallisch (EMI CDC7 54578-2; with Lieder Op. 91).
> **Piano Concerto No. 1**: Barenboim; Philharmonia; Barbirolli (EMI CDM 7 63536-2; with *Haydn Variations*).
> **Piano Concerto No. 2**: Barenboim; Philharmonia; Barbirolli (EMI CDM 7 63537-2; with overtures).

Most of the great pianists of this century have recorded these concertos, but nobody has quite the authority that Gilels brings to both works – these are grand, romantic and enthralling performances. The Gilels recordings are never out of the catalogue but they are sometimes repackaged as two separate CDs with different couplings, so check the shelves carefully. The Barenboim-Barbirolli performances are almost as fine, but are considerably slower and more expansive, an approach that some people find immensely rewarding. Stephen Kovacevich's recent performance of the first concerto with Sawallisch is passionate and declamatory, with an acute sense of architecture and real strength of purpose. Sawallisch allows his orchestra more freedom than most conductors – their last movement is just about the most exciting on record.

VIOLIN CONCERTO

For years Brahms promised to write a concerto for Joseph Joachim, but as with so many of his major projects he kept putting it off. Finally, spurred by the success of the second symphony, he set to work on the piece, taking guidance from Joachim as to what was possible for the instrument. Although it was originally conceived in four movements, Brahms was persuaded to drop one of the central movements to keep the concerto down to a more conventional length – the excised portion later reappeared as part of the second piano concerto. Essentially lyrical, the final version shares much of the second symphony's mood – the key of D major is common to both works, as it is to the Beethoven concerto which Brahms so admired. By the time of its premiere, on New Year's Day 1879, Brahms had become somewhat eccentric in his mode of dress, and the staid Leipzig audience watched in horror as the composer-conductor's trousers, tied up with an old necktie, began to slip. Fortunately the trousers remained on, but the verdict on the concerto was lukewarm. Its breakthrough came shortly afterwards, when Joachim introduced the work to England, and since then it's been one of the most popular concertos in the violin repertory.

> Neveu; Philharmonia; Dobrowen (EMI CDH 7 61011-2; with Sibelius, *Violin Concerto*).
> Heifetz; Chicago Symphony Orchestra; Munch (RCA RD 85402; with Beethoven, *Violin Concerto*).
> Heifetz; Philharmonic Symphony Orchestra; Szell (Music & Arts CD-766; with Beethoven, Mendelssohn, Sibelius & Korngold violin concertos; 2 CDs).

Ginette Neveu, who died in a plane crash in 1949 at the age of only thirty, left what is perhaps the finest recorded version of this concerto. This is a marvellously poetic and dramatic performance, and it has been well transferred from original 78s – though inevitably the sound lacks the subtleties of modern engineering. There are also two brilliant Heifetz recordings of the concerto, one a studio version with Charles Munch, the other a live recording made in 1951. In both performances the fervour of Heifetz's playing is almost overwhelming, but the latter is perhaps marginally the more intense, while the former has the better sound quality.

DOUBLE CONCERTO

The *Double Concerto*, like the *Violin Concerto*, owes its creation to Joachim, whom

The best Brahms Double, coupled with Beethoven's Triple

Brahms had alienated by supporting Joachim's wife during their unpleasant divorce. He conceived this concerto as a gesture of reconciliation, but it has to be said that another violin concerto might have been a more appropriate gift – in some ways, it is almost as if Brahms were baiting the violinist, as he gives nothing of great importance to the solo violin. Written after the symphonies and piano concertos, it's a particularly angular and aggressive piece, and in places is too thickly orchestrated. Yet, while this might not be his greatest work, it does feature some wonderful interplay between cello and violin.

> ◗ Oistrakh, Rostropovich; Cleveland Orchestra; Szell (EMI CDM 7 64744-2; with Beethoven, *Triple Concerto*).

There is no better case to be made for the concerto than this CD – Rostropovich and Oistrakh knew each other's style so well that they move through the music with a single mind. Their pugnacity might take some getting used to, but the bluster is mixed with lyricism of great beauty. It's coupled with a 1969 recording of the rather superior Beethoven *Triple Concerto*.

CHORAL WORKS

Brahms wrote many unaccompanied choral pieces for women's choral societies as well as a huge output of songs for solo voice, duet and other combinations. Much of this output was for amateur musicians and is of mixed quality, so very little of it is now recorded or performed except by amateur groups. Two

works stand out from the rest: the *Deutsches Requiem* – his greatest vocal work and his first orchestral score to receive widespread praise – and the *Alto Rhapsody*, one of his most moving creations.

EIN DEUTSCHES REQUIEM

The idea of writing a Requiem Mass first came to Brahms after the death of Schumann in 1856, but for various reasons – not least of them his lack of true faith – the intention lapsed until 1865, when the death of his mother plunged him into inconsolable grief. Four years later he completed his tribute to her, *Ein deutsches Requiem* (A German Requiem), a Mass quite unlike any previous Requiem. Spurning the conventional Latin texts, Brahms set sections of Luther's translation of the Bible in a composition that was primarily intended to reconcile the living to their loss, and dwelt more on the hope of the Resurrection than on the fear of Judgement Day. It first appeared without its central and most beautiful section, the soprano solo which makes up the fifth movement.

> ◗ Janowitz, Waechter; Berlin Philharmonic Orchestra; Karajan (Deutsche Grammophon DG 427 252-2).
> ◗ Schwarzkopf, Fischer-Dieskau; Philharmonia; Klemperer (EMI CDC 7 47238-2).
> ◗ Margiono, Gilfry; Orchestre Révolutionaire et Romantique; Gardiner (Philips 432 140-2).

Best bet for a conventional reading is Karajan's performance from 1964, with a soaringly beautiful soprano solo from Gundula Janowitz. Klemperer's 1961 recording is a reverential account with excellent solos from Fischer-Dieskau and Schwarzkopf and fine choral singing, but is too slow and dense for most tastes. John Eliot Gardiner's more recent recording uses period instruments and produces amazingly clear sound and textures; the soloists hardly match up to their rivals on the other two sets, but this is a thrilling and revealing performance.

ALTO RHAPSODY

The *Rhapsody for Alto, Chorus and Orchestra* – to give the *Alto Rhapsody* its full name – was written in a fit of despair. Brahms' feelings for Clara Schumann had subsided after her husband's death and he had transferred his affection to her daughter Julie – one of many such futile infatuations. Julie, oblivious to Brahms's motives, saw him merely as a benevolent uncle figure, and in 1869 she got married. As a wedding gift Brahms presented her with the *Rhapsody*, a setting of Goethe's poem *A Winter Journey in the Harz Mountains* – a thunderous example of Brahms's gift for self-pity, as Clara noticed, even if her daughter did not. The mood of the piece is decidedly unmatrimonial, but the despairing bleakness of its opening is soon left behind – the point at which the chorus finally joins the soloist is one of the most heartwarming moments in all Brahms's output.

> ♪ Ludwig; Philharmonia; Klemperer (EMI CDM 7 69650-2; with *Symphony No. 2*).
> ♪ Ferrier; London Philharmonic Orchestra; Krauss (Decca 433 477-2 with Lieder by Brahms & Mahler).

The Klemperer-Ludwig performance is essential to any Brahms collection; Christa Ludwig, one of the century's greatest German altos, gets marvellously restrained orchestral accompaniment from the Philharmonia at its peak. Ludwig's only rival is Kathleen Ferrier, whose plangent tones impart a profound sense of loss to this historic recording on Decca.

CHAMBER MUSIC

Brahms was happiest at the piano, and was somewhat reluctant to explore the unknown territory of chamber music. His first ventures into the genre were undertaken partly to perfect his technique and partly as preparation for orchestral composition – they have not survived, as Brahms had a habit of destroying music of which he did not approve. It's remarkable then that his mature chamber music is among the greatest of the nineteenth century. Only Beethoven wrote so successfully for so many different ensembles: Brahms's output includes sonatas for violin, viola, cello and clarinet, trios for clarinet, horn and piano, sextets, string quartets, quartets for piano, string quintets, a piano quintet and – perhaps his masterpiece in this field – a quintet for clarinet and strings. There are no duds among this group, but the pieces we've singled out will take you to the heart of things.

> ♪ Sextets; Piano Quintet; String Quintets; Clarinet Quintet: Amadeus Quartet; Leister; Aronowitz; Pleeth; Eschenbach (Deutsche Grammophon DG 419 875-2).

This three-disc set is an ideal introduction to Brahms's chamber works. This music needs to be played with an airy consistency to keep the density of the writing from obscuring the beautiful harmony and melody – these generally quick-paced, elegant and strong performances do just that.

STRING SEXTETS

Brahms's two sextets, both scored for two violins, two violas and two cellos, are among his finest works. The first, composed in 1858, is fairly straightforward in its construction, with an almost complacent feel that contrasts starkly with the deliberate contrapuntal introspection of the second, written six years later in absolute privacy – almost certainly in response to the failure of a friendship with one of his lady friends, Agathe von Siebold. Both works share a similarly constructed opening movement but it is in the finales that Brahms's expression most obviously differs. The first ends with cheerful exuberance while the second concludes with a turbulent and complex re-working of a single idea that, in well disguised form, reappears throughout the other movements. In short, the second sextet is Brahms at his most engagingly melancholy.

> ⊙ Raphael Ensemble (Hyperion CDA 66276).

The Raphael Ensemble really warm to Brahms's typically independent part-writing – each of the players shines in these rich and enthusiastic performances, assisted throughout by a clear and spacious recorded sound.

QUINTET FOR CLARINET AND STRINGS

The astonishing *Quintet for Clarinet and Strings* is the finest of four clarinet pieces written for Richard Mühlfeld, a dazzling instrumentalist who also inspired Mendelssohn. Composed in the calming atmosphere of the Alpine resort of Bad Ischl in 1891, the quintet seems to show that its morose and difficult creator had found peace in his final years – only Mozart's clarinet quintet can strike quite as deeply as this resonant masterpiece. The unprecedented range of expression and unrivalled understanding of the solo instrument's capabilities give this piece a sense of completeness that few of Brahms's other chamber works can boast.

⦿ Busch Quartet; Kell (Testament SBT 1001; with *Horn Trio*).

⦿ Gabrieli Quartet; King (Hyperion CDA 66107; with *Clarinet Trio*).

The playing of the Busch Quartet and Reginald Kell is the closest thing you'll hear to the sort of playing that Brahms would have heard. Giving the music's weighted counterpoint a rare freedom and sense of direction, this is one of the most moving Brahms recordings ever made. A modern alternative is Thea King's recording with the Gabrieli Quartet – it can't match the glowing humanity of the Busch and Kell version, but a strong point in its favour is that it's coupled with a fine performance of the genial clarinet trio.

VIOLIN SONATAS

The three violin sonatas, written between 1878 and 1886, epitomize Brahms's remarkable ability to reconcile heartfelt expression with classical discipline. The first – in fact his fourth, as three earlier ones were destroyed – is the perhaps the most lyrical and is an outstanding example of his use of cyclic form: the whole work is unified by a single idea, three repeated notes that are first heard at the work's beginning. The second sonata exudes an optimistic and confident atmosphere, but the third – also written in the summer of 1886 – is a bleak, melancholic and introspective piece. Unlike its predecessors, the third sonata is in four movements, and whereas the outer movements dominate the earlier sonatas, here it is the central movements that form the crux.

⦿ Perlman; Ashkenazy (EMI CDC 7 47403-2).

Perlman and Ashkenazy give outstanding, mellow performances, complemented by the recording's rich and warm sound. This is some of the most contented music-making on any chamber music disc.

PIANO WORKS

Brahms was a formidable pianist and he wrote a large amount of music for the instrument throughout his creative life. Though there is more virtuoso display in his early piano works and more of an emphasis on chordal writing in the later ones, Brahms's piano style evolved only slightly once he had achieved maturity – there is not, as there is with Beethoven, a sense that this piano music

traces the course of a long journey. You'll find some lovely melodies here, but an equally important aspect of most of the works listed below is their quasi-orchestral texture, a quality that again allies Brahms with Schumann. Brahms thought with all ten fingers, and the resulting music can sometimes seem laboured, but when played by a pianist with the requisite sensitivity to tone, Brahms's piano works are revealed as masterpieces of condensed writing.

As is the case with Schumann, Brahms's sonatas are relatively neglected, and his reputation as a composer for the piano rests almost exclusively upon a group of short, condensed pieces – the *Ballades* Op. 10, the two *Rhapsodies* Op. 79, and the piano pieces of Op. 117, Op. 118 and Op. 119.

Listening to the four *Ballades*, which were composed in 1854 when Brahms was only 21, you can hear why Schumann so readily proclaimed him a genius. They share a basic ternary structure, and the first three *Ballades* are almost demonic in character (as Schumann remarked at the time), but the last and longest of the four is something quite different. A sighing Adagio of immense beauty, it encapsulates an innocence that you won't find in any of Brahms's later music.

The two *Rhapsodies* (1879), are closer in spirit to the first three Ballades – marked "agitato" and "passionata", these are thrilling pieces, full of basic energy.

Most intense and personal of all Brahms's piano compositions are the pieces gathered under the titles Op. 117, Op. 118 and Op. 119. These miscellanies of ballades, romances, rhapsodies and intermezzos (terms with no precise denotation), offer a kaleidoscopic image of the composer, compacting an extraordinary range of emotion into a brief space. Each of these miniatures is a marvel of immediacy, making Op. 117, Op. 118 and Op. 119 the best place to start an exploration of Brahms's piano music.

◗ Complete Piano Works: Katchen (Decca 430 053-2; 6 CDs).

⦿ Ballades: Brendel (Philips PHIL 426 439-2; with Weber, *Sonata in A flat*).

◗ Rhapsodies and piano pieces Op. 117–119: Lupu (Decca 417 599-2DH).

If you want to tackle all of Brahms's piano music, pick Julius Katchen's mid-price set from the mid-1960s – something of a heyday for Decca recordings. Avoiding any tendency to heaviness, his playing has invigorating refinement and spirit.

There are some excellent Brahms recitals in the catalogue from the likes of Arturo Benedetti Michelangeli and Stephen Kovacevich, but perhaps the two best are these from Alfred Brendel and Radu Lupu. Brendel is sometimes accused of excessive introspection, but his recording of the *Ballades* is deeply emotional. Avoiding over-reverence, he moulds the music strongly and eloquently – an approach typified by the final *Ballade*, where he adopts an unusually slow tempo for the outer episodes. Radu Lupu is a master of Brahms's late style, allowing each detail room to breathe, and defining all the varied inner voices that are so important to the Op. 117–119 pieces. He may not be the most exciting pianist to have recorded these works, but his unshowy approach makes him one of the most revealing. An excellent choice as your first Brahms CD.

PHILIPS — *Digital Classics*

BRAHMS
Ballades Op. 10
WEBER
Sonata in A Flat, Op. 39
ALFRED
BRENDEL

Brendel turns his attention to Brahms

BENJAMIN BRITTEN
(1913–1976)

Benjamin Britten was simply the most prolific and most significant British composer since Purcell, with almost one hundred major compositions to his credit, ranging from full-scale operas to accessible but unpatronizing music for schoolchildren.

He was born in Lowestoft on Saint Cecilia's day (November 22) – appropriately, as she is the patron saint of music. His mother, a keen amateur musician and singer, was the formative influence in his early years, and by the age of five he was already writing. Britten went on to take lessons from the composer Frank Bridge, who introduced him to the music of progressive European composers such as Bartók, Berg and Schoenberg. After studying at the Royal College of Music, Britten got a job with the Post Office film unit and wrote music for a number of innovative documentary films, a crucial experience in refining his technique as a dramatic composer. He also met and collaborated with the poet W. H. Auden, who was to be one of the most important influences of his life, reinforcing Britten's pacifism and

providing the text for his first important song cycle, *Our Hunting Fathers* (1936).

Discontented with life in England, Auden emigrated to America in 1939, followed a few months later by Britten and Peter Pears, the tenor who was to be Britten's partner for almost forty years – it's hard to find a partnership that so dominated the creative output of a composer as did this one. Britten and Pears spent nearly three years in America, where Britten wrote his first big orchestral work, the *Sinfonia da Requiem* (1940) and his first dramatic work, the operetta *Paul Bunyan* (1941), to a libretto by Auden. This period in the States was crucial in bringing out Britten's profound attachment to his English heritage, and his feelings for his native East Anglia were heightened by an article he read on the Suffolk poet George Crabbe. He determined to go back to England and to set Crabbe's work as an opera.

Britten returned home in 1942 and had soon written some of his very best music – *A Ceremony of Carols* and a song cycle for Pears titled *Serenade for Tenor, Horn and Strings.*

HULTON DEUTSCH

But it was the opera *Peter Grimes* (1945), based on a story by Crabbe, that put him firmly on the map, establishing him not just as a brilliant composer but also a sincere commentator on social and political events, something that runs through most of his output. At the time of *Peter Grimes* there were only two established opera companies in Britain, so Britten turned to the medium of chamber opera and created his own company, the English Opera Group, to perform these small-scale pieces. They became the centre-piece of the annual Aldeburgh Festival, which Britten started in 1948 in the Suffolk seaside town he had made his home.

Throughout the rest of his life, in addition to writing works for Aldeburgh and for amateur groups and schoolchildren (*Noye's Fludde*, 1957, is the best of these), Britten received several major commissions, the greatest of which was the *War Requiem* (1961), composed for the consecration of Coventry Cathedral after its post-war reconstruction. Britten had been a conscientious objector during the war, and several of his works carry a pacifict message, the *War Requiem* foremost among them. A few years later the opening of the Snape Maltings just outside Aldeburgh allowed for larger-scale

opera productions, and *Death in Venice*, the last of Britten's fifteen operas, was produced there in 1973. Giving Pears his most demanding stage role, *Death in Venice* was Britten's most public statement about his long-standing relationship with the singer.

Britten accepted a life peerage – the first musician to be so honoured – in 1976. He died in December of that year, of the heart disease that had weakened him in his last few years.

PETER GRIMES

Peter Grimes, which reopened Sadler's Wells theatre after the war in June 1945, marked a watershed for Britten and a rebirth for British opera. It was so widely publicized and well received that a bus conductor on the route to the theatre is reported to have announced "Sadler's Wells! Any more for *Peter Grimes*, the sadistic fisherman?"

The story is a grim one and reflects themes which frequently recur in Britten's music – innocence as a prey to violence and the outsider as prey to society. Grimes is a fisherman whose temperament and conduct have put him at odds with the Aldeburgh community in which the opera is set. At the outset he is acquitted of the murder of his young apprentice, who has died at sea. Here Grimes has music of great beauty and vulnerability that is sharply contrasted with the gossips and busybodies of The Borough. But we see his darker side as he bullies his new apprentice, who then accidentally falls to his death. Grimes sets sail in his ship and sinks it out at sea.

Though the action of *Peter Grimes* is focused on the ambiguous fisherman and his finely drawn social background, its magnificent orchestral score evokes another principal character, the sea itself. The opera's four vivid *Sea Interludes*, which allow for scene changes, have become concert pieces in their own right, and the music conjures up tempests throughout the piece. It's the sea that closes the opera as Grimes' boat disappears and the community resumes its daily routine, already forgetting its outcast.

> ◉ Pears, Watson, Pease; Chorus & Orchestra of the Royal Opera House; Britten (Decca 414 577-2; 2 CDs).
> ◉ Rolfe Johnson, Lott, Allen; Chorus & Orchestra of the Royal Opera House; Haitink (EMI 7 54832 2; 2 CDs).

Most of Britten's recordings of his own operas stand as classics, and nowhere is that truer than with *Peter Grimes*, recorded complete for the first time in 1958, with Peter Pears superb in the title role and Britten bringing a pacy energy to the score. Pears' singing of *Now the Great Bear and Pleiades* in Scene Two evokes poignantly the loneliness of the fisherman at the mercy of fate and the elements.

Anthony Rolfe Johnson, in the EMI recording of 1993, is almost as good at the poetic side of Grimes and brings out more of his ambiguities in his brutal treatment of the boy. Felicity Lott is a glorious Ellen Orford, the one person in the community sympathetic to Grimes, and the orchestral score comes across brilliantly.

THE RAPE OF LUCRETIA

Britten's next operatic venture, *The Rape of Lucretia*, was the first of his chamber operas, a form he was to make very much his own. Premiered at Glyndebourne in 1946, it inhabits a more abstract world than the realistic Suffolk of *Grimes*, although once again it concerns a lone individual standing apart from the crowd – in this case the virtuous Lucretia, who commits suicide after being raped by Tarquinius (another ambiguous character, part thug, part welcomed seducer).

Cast for eight singers and twelve instrumentalists with a prominent part for piano, it's a less sumptuous and more hard-edged piece than *Grimes*: when Tarquinius steals into Lucretia's bedroom, for instance, he's accompanied only by drums. However, there are also moments of great beauty, notably the Female Chorus depicting Lucretia's sleep, Lucretia's plangent aria on the day after the rape, and the music as she approaches her husband – a glorious instrumental section on cor anglais and low strings.

> ◉ Pears, Harper, Baker, Shirley-Quirk, Luxon; English Chamber Orchestra; Britten (Decca 425 666-2; 2 CDs).

Unlike many of Britten's recordings this is not an "original cast" version, but it certainly has a starry cast and they all have an affinity with Britten's music. Peter Pears as the Male Chorus and Janet Baker as Lucretia sound excellent.

BILLY BUDD

Britten's next large-scale opera was *Billy Budd*, composed for the Festival of Britain in 1951. Based on a story by Herman Melville, it recapitulates the maritime setting and several of the themes of *Peter Grimes*. Billy Budd, a sailor unjustly accused of murder, is driven to his execution by the vindictive Claggart and by Captain Vere, a decent man forced by circumstance to sacrifice him. The dual aspects of Grimes – the brutal and poetic – reappear in these latter characters, and again there is a sexual undercurrent to the action, with the suggestion of Claggart's stifled homosexual desire for Billy. *Billy Budd* was highly acclaimed at its first performances – some proclaiming it greater than *Grimes* – although it hasn't enjoyed the same popularity since.

> ◉ Glossop, Pears, Langdon; London Symphony Orchestra; Britten (Decca 417 428-2; 3 CDs).

This recording is unchallenged. The three principal singers are perfectly cast, the orchestral sound is suitably dark and violent, and the final scene of Billy's hanging is intensely powerful.

GLORIANA

Gloriana, Britten's "national" opera, was premiered a week after the coronation of Queen Elizabeth II in June 1953, and a dismal occasion it turned out to be. The audience of dignitaries and diplomats were expecting a glorification of Elizabeth I that would serve as a glorification of the new queen; what they got instead was a tragic portrayal of a woman torn between her illicit love for Essex and her duty to have him executed as a traitor – a dilemma that echoes that of Captain Vere in *Billy Budd*.

Divorced from the expectations of those first performances, the piece has recently been reassessed as a very fine and idiosyncratic dramatic work. Its distinctive musical character comes from its evocation of the Elizabethan world through re-creation of that era rather than mere imitation, a technique similar to that used by Stravinsky in his mock-Pergolesi piece, *Pulcinella* (see p.363) Gloriana's various public scenes – a masque and various courtly and choral dances – are among Britten's finest set-pieces, and the whole score has a pleasantly accessible tone thanks to its Elizabethan models.

● Barstow, Langridge; Welsh National Opera Chorus & Orchestra; Mackerras (Decca Argo 440 213-2; 2 CDs).

After its troubled inception *Gloriana* had to wait until 1993 for this premiere recording from Charles Mackerras, long an admirer of this piece. The rhythmic fanfares at the opening are bold and punchy with a brassy glow that sets the required mood of pageantry. Josephine Barstow is excellent as the troubled Queen and Philip Langridge brings a gentle lyricism to the role of Essex.

THE TURN OF THE SCREW

Britten's next opera, *The Turn of the Screw* (1954), inhabits a totally different world. Written for Britten's English Opera Group and premiered at La Fenice in Venice, it's the finest of his chamber operas, tailor-made for six singers and thirteen instrumentalists whose musical abilities Britten knew intimately. The libretto was written by Myfanwy Piper (wife of the painter John Piper, who designed the sets for many of Britten's operas), based closely on the story by Henry James. It tells of Miles and Flora, two children in a remote country house haunted by the ghost of Peter Quint, the man who may have sexually corrupted them. The exact nature of what went on between Quint and the children is unclear, as is the contribution made by the imagination of the children's governess. Britten described the opera's

subject as the "nearest to me of any I have chosen (although what that indicates of my own character I shouldn't like to say!).''

Britten composed the opera at lightning speed, yet it is one of his most brilliant scores. It is very tightly constructed as a sequence of variations on a theme using all twelve notes of the chromatic scale, yet because it requires two child performers the music also has a wonderful simplicity and transparency – indeed, some nursery rhymes are cunningly woven into the score. The sheer range and delicacy of the sounds Britten gets from the chamber orchestra is quite remarkable.

● Lott, Langridge; Aldeburgh Festival Ensemble; Bedford (Collins 70302; 2 CDs).

This 1994 recording is so wonderful it even supercedes the version made under the direction of Britten himself. Felicity Lott is perfectly heroic yet vulnerable as the Governess and Philip Langridge menacing and seductive as Quint. The two children, Sam Pay and Eileen Hulse, are good too. Much of the special atmosphere of this piece is created by the orchestral textures, which have never sounded as luminous as here.

A MIDSUMMER NIGHT'S DREAM

A Midsummer Night's Dream, composed for Aldeburgh in 1960, is probably Britten's most immediately attractive major operatic score. The libretto is a drastically reduced version of Shakespeare's play, but it retains the plays three distinct groups of characters – the fairies, the rude mechanicals and the Athenian lovers who enter the wood – and gives each group its own distinctive musical characteristics. The most startlingly original music is that associated with the fairies, who have ethereal sliding strings, harps, tuned percussion and celesta; Oberon, the fairy king, is a counter-tenor while Titania, the fairy queen, is a coloratura soprano, so they both have an otherworldly quality to their voices.

The rude mechanicals (or "rustics" as Britten calls them) are depicted in a much more basic way, with an emphasis on instruments such as the bassoon and trombone. Their performance of *Pyramus and Thisbe* is a crude but hilarious pastiche of nineteenth-century grand opera: it was a topical joke aimed at Zeffirelli's production of Donizetti's *Lucia di Lammermoor* at Covent Garden –

Peter Pears took the part of Flute/Thisbe and did a devastating imitation of Joan Sutherland, the star of the Zeffirelli show.

The Athenian lovers are portrayed in a more conventional musical language, although it is never pedestrian – the highlight is the four lovers' reconciliation at the beginning of Act Three, a simple but astonishingly beautiful quartet.

◉ Deller, Harwood, Harper, Veasey, Pears, Hemsley, Watts, Shirley-Quirk; London Symphony Orchestra; Britten (Decca 425 663-2; 2 CDs).

Despite very strong competition from Richard Hickox, the Britten recording is still supreme. It was made in 1966 and contains several of the original singers, notably Alfred Deller, for whom the part of Oberon was created. This is pretty much an all-star cast and the orchestral textures sound marvellous, with Britten bringing out a sinister underside to the magical realm.

CURLEW RIVER

After *A Midsummer Night's Dream* and the *War Requiem* (see below) Britten's musical language underwent a paring-down process, and this more ascetic and concentrated later style is exemplified by *Curlew River* (1964), the first of three so-called Church Parables (*The Burning Fiery Furnace* and *The Prodigal Son* were to follow). Deploying even sparser resources than any of the chamber operas (its ensemble comprises just flute, horn, viola, double bass, harp, percussion and organ), *Curlew River* is derived from the ritual and simplicity of Noh drama, which Britten saw on a trip to Tokyo in 1956. For years afterwards he wanted to translate this experience into a work of his own, but his fear of creating a mere pastiche meant it took a long time for him to find the right form.

The story takes place in the English fens, where a Madwoman comes to the Ferryman of the Curlew River, searching for her son. The Ferryman tells her of a boy who had died there a year before. She realizes this was her son, has a vision of him by his grave, and receives his blessing. The piece is intensely ritualized and intensely moving, fusing medieval church music with oriental elements to create a wonderful sound world of sliding strings (the fairies' music from *A Midsummer Night's Dream* taken a stage

Britten conducts Britten – usually the best combination

further) and dramatic percussive effects. The singers are all male, as they are in the Noh theatre, and some of the sounds are obviously suggested by the flute and drum accompaniment to Noh drama, but Britten extends the extremely austere sound of Noh into an incredibly inventive and colourful score.

◖ Pears, Shirley-Quirk; English Opera Group; Britten (Decca 421 858-2).

This recording, made in Orford church a year after the premiere there, is an historic document and is unlikely to be bettered. Pears and John Shirley-Quirk, the original exponents of the Madwoman and Ferryman, are superb, and the entire project is extremely atmospheric.

DEATH IN VENICE

Britten's last opera, *Death in Venice* (1973), is a heavily symbolic adaptation of Thomas Mann's great novella, in which the writer Aschenbach is led to his fate by a number of sinister characters representing Death – all played by one singer. The most striking music in the opera is associated with Tadzio (the young boy who is the object of Aschenbach's doomed infatuation) and his friends, who dance to seductive gamelan-like music played on timpani and tuned percussion. Attractive as they are, these sections can seem over-long, and the same is true of the opera as a whole.

While he was working on *Death in Venice* Britten's heart condition became extremely serious, and he knew this was likely to be his last major composition. Accordingly there's a strong autobiographical and valedictory feeling about the work: moments like *The Games of Apollo*, where Tadzio and the dancers perform athletics while Apollo sings of male beauty, are barely sublimated expressions of Britten's erotic impulses. If the work is confessional about Britten's attraction to boys, it is also a statement about his constraint in acting upon it.

◉ Pears, Shirley-Quirk, Bowman; English Chamber Orchestra; Bedford (Decca 425 669-2; 2 CDs).

With Britten in ill-health, it was Steuart Bedford who conducted the original performances, and this recording, made in the Snape Maltings in 1974, is a definitive one. Anyone who saw Pears in the role of Aschenbach is unlikely to forget it and it is hard for anyone to match the intensity of his performance, with all its personal resonances.

SONGS

Britten composed his precocious *Quatre Chansons Français* for soprano and orchestra at the age of fifteen, and song cycles were to form a prominent part of his output from then onwards.

His first major cycle was *Our Hunting Fathers* (1936), which shows him as something of an *enfant terrible*, with its wild orchestral writing, strenuous vocal line and political message. W. H. Auden's text ostensibly deals with humanity's cruelty to animals, but the real subject is anxiety at the current situation in Europe – the *Dance of Death* specifically alludes to German persecution of the Jews.

More oblique is *Les Illuminations* (1939), a tightly structured setting of eight verses by Arthur Rimbaud, featuring some glorious effects from the strings – evoking the sound of bells, for instance, in *Phrase*. The cycle incorporates a nightmarish evocation of city life, a love song dedicated to a close friend and another dedicated to Peter Pears, but the precise meaning is elusive. The line that frames the cycle, "J'ai seul la clef de cette parade sauvage" (I alone hold the key to this savage parade) suggests that it is probably autobiographical. It is certainly one of Britten's most attractive and inspired scores.

Perhaps Britten's finest cycle, the *Serenade for Tenor, Horn and Strings*, was written for

Pears in 1943 and takes the night as its subject. Its unusual instrumentation was the result of Britten's admiration for the horn playing of Dennis Brain, who demonstrated the possibilities of using the instrument's natural harmonics rather than the valves for the mysterious scene-setting prologue. The technique gives the music an eerie, slightly "out of tune" sound which is highly effective.

Another important cycle, with a similar subject but a more expressionist mood, is the *Nocturne* of 1958. The work is related in theme and style to *A Midsummer Night's Dream* and begins with a Shelley poem about the creative power of dreams. Each of the songs is given a distinctive character by an instrument that's unique to it within the cycle, ranging from the dramatic timpani to the elegiac cor anglais.

◗ **Our Hunting Fathers; Serenade; Folksongs**: Söderström, Tear; Welsh National Opera Orchestra, Northern Sinfonia; Armstrong, Marriner (EMI CDM 7 69522 2).
◗ **Les Illuminations; Serenade; Nocturne**: Pears, Tuckwell; English Chamber Orchestra; Britten (Decca London 436 395-2).
◉ **Les Illuminations, Serenade, Quatre Chansons Français**: Lott, Rolfe Johnson; Scottish National Orchestra; Thompson (Chandos CHAN 8657).

Elizabeth Söderström's 1982 recording of *Our Hunting Fathers* was the work's first and it confirms it as one of Britten's most remarkable and uncompromising works. Robert Tear and Alan Civil, on the horn, are first-class soloists in this CD's idiomatic performance of *Serenade*, but the folksong settings are slighter and rather mannered.

The reissue of Pears' recordings of these major song cycles represents the essential disc of Britten's vocal music and not just for historical reasons. Of course Pears brings a special quality to this repertoire, but the technical and artistic quality of the whole disc is unbeatable.

On the Chandos disc a beautifully understated performance of the *Serenade* by Anthony Rolfe Johnson, with Michael Thompson on horn, is combined with Felicity Lott singing *Les Illuminations* – it was originally intended for a soprano. The youthful *Quatre Chansons Français* are also very beautiful.

CHORAL MUSIC

Britten's choral writing, another crucial part of his output, ranges from small-scale pieces for boys' choir to massive works like the *Spring Symphony* and the *War Requiem*.

The Hymn to St Cecilia (1942) for unaccompanied five-part chorus is quintessential Britten, with text (by Auden) and setting that emphasize not just the emotional and aesthetic power of music, but its erotic power as well. He followed it with one of his freshest pieces, *A Ceremony of Carols* (1942), for the economical combination of boys' voices and harp. A series of nine medieval lyrics, it's a simple, tuneful and inventive celebration of innocence.

The *Spring Symphony* (1949), commissioned by Serge Koussevitsky for the Boston Symphony Orchestra, is like the *Ceremony of Carols* writ large. Inspired directly by the experience of the Suffolk countryside, it sets a series of fourteen poems for soloists and chorus, evoking the progress of winter to spring and the onset of summer. Given the nature of the poems, it is a testament to Britten's ingenuity that the music steers well away from the hackneyed English pastoral tradition. The orchestra is large, but he scores the music for small and contrasted instrumental groups.

Britten's choral masterpiece is the *War Requiem* (1961), an altogether deeper and more complex structure than any of its predecessors, interweaving the Latin Mass (for soprano, chorus and orchestra) with nine poems by Wilfred Owen (for tenor and baritone soloists with chamber orchestra), with a third element in the form of a distant choir of boys' voices accompanied by an organ. Britten had a strong message and he wanted to tell it as strongly as possible: "My subject is War, and the Pity of War. The Poetry is in the pity . . . All a poet can do today is warn" is the Owen inscription on the title page. Owen himself is a symbol of the pity of war, as he was killed in the last days of World War I, and Britten chose some of his most powerful verses to set, culminating in *Strange Meeting*, in which a soldier encounters the enemy he has killed. Fundamentally this is a work of reconciliation, and Britten wanted this fact to be represented by the three soloists in the first performance: Peter Pears, Dietrich Fischer-Dieskau and Galina Vishnevskaya, from Britain, Germany and Russia respectively. In the event the Soviets wouldn't give Vishnevskaya a visa and the part was taken at short notice by Heather Harper, although the intended soloists recorded it the following year.

◉ **A Ceremony of Carols; Missa Brevis; A Hymn to the Virgin and other works**: Choir of Westminster Cathedral; Hill (Hyperion CDA66220).

◗ **A Ceremony of Carols; Missa Brevis; Hymn to St Cecilia; Rejoice in the Lamb and other works**: Kings College Choir; Willcocks, Ledger (EMI CDC 7 47709 2).

◗ **Spring Symphony; Cantata Academica; Hymn to St Cecilia**: Vyvyan, Procter, Pears; Orchestra & Chorus of the Royal Opera House, London Symphony Orchestra & Chorus; Britten, Malcolm (Decca 436 396-2).

◉ **War Requiem; Ballad of Heroes**; Sinfonia da Requiem: Harper, Langridge, Shirley-Quirk; London Symphony Orchestra & Chorus; Hickox (Chandos CHAN8983/4; 2 CDs).

The best all-round recording of Britten's smaller-scale choral music is by David Hill and the Westminster Cathedral Choir. The voices are clear and pure and the acoustic gives the music just the right bloom. The King's College Choir recording has better fill-up items, but the performances don't have quite the magic of the Hyperion disc.

The 1960 Britten recording of the *Spring Symphony* is tremendously vivid and comes with a performance of the *Cantata Academica*, a very high-spirited and ebullient piece written for Basle University in 1959. The performance of the *Hymn to St Cecilia* is rather over-rich, however.

There are currently five performances of the *War Requiem* and they are all good. The original Britten recording is a classic, featuring as it does the trio of Pears, Fischer-Dieskau and Vishnevskaya, but top of the highly competitive market is the 1991 recording conducted by Richard Hickox. A work of this size and complexity really benefits from a clean modern recording, and it comes with soloists deeply rooted in the music. Heather Harper was soprano soloist for the premiere and Philip Langridge and John Shirley-Quirk are seasoned Britten performers. The set has generous fill-ups too.

ORCHESTRAL MUSIC

Britten wrote relatively little purely orchestral music, but some of it ranks amongst his best work.

The *Variations on a Theme of Frank Bridge* (1937) is a tribute to his teacher – Britten said that each of the movements portrayed a different aspect of Bridge's character. It is a tremendously confident and extrovert work, including affectionate pastiches of classical forms and a Viennese waltz, although it has its darker moments as well. It has deservedly become one of the composer's most popular works, as has the *Young Person's Guide to the Orchestra* (1946), a tribute to Henry Purcell, whom Britten always cited as his prime example in setting the English language – scores like *A Midsummer Night's Dream* resonate with the spirit of Purcell. The *Young Person's Guide* was written as the soundtrack for an educational film and is made up of a series of variations on a Purcell theme, presented by the different sections of the orchestra and culminating in an exuberant fugue.

In sharp contrast to the carefree mood of the *Young Person's Guide* is the *Sinfonia da Requiem* (1940), the closest Britten came to writing an orchestral symphony; written while he was in America, it is a mournful three-movement requiem for his parents and for the war dead of Europe. Outstanding amongst

Britten's other orchestral scores are various suites extracted from his operas, especially the *Four Sea Interludes from Peter Grimes.*

◉ Young Person's Guide to the Orchestra; Variations on a Theme of Frank Bridge; Simple Symphony: English Chamber Orchestra; Britten (Decca 417 509-2).

◉ Sinfonia da Requiem; Four Sea Interludes & Passacaglia from Peter Grimes; Young Person's Guide to the Orchestra: Royal Liverpool Philharmonic; Pešek (Virgin VC 7 90834-2).

Britten's recording of his most popular orchestral scores is bright and vivacious, making a good introduction to the lighter side of his music. The Pešek recording of the *Sinfonia da Requiem* is powerfully conceived and extremely well played, and the same goes for the *Sea Interludes and Passacaglia*, which form a wonderful symphonic evocation of the world of Grimes. Including the *Young Person's Guide*, this is a very good cross-section of Britten's orchestral music.

MAX BRUCH

(1838–1920)

B ruch is widely known just for his first violin concerto, which is perhaps unfair and certainly misleading. One of the late nineteenth century's most prominent German composers, he produced a large amount of tuneful, lush music that was completely out of step with the expressive innovations of Gustav Mahler, let alone the

radical experiments of Schoenberg. His career was something of a procession along the establishment path, winning competitions, studying with well-respected figures, composing for the theatre, concert hall and church, and accepting various short-term positions until, in 1891, he was made Professor at the Berlin Academy, where he taught composition until 1910. Like Pfitzner (see p.267), he lived out of academia's palm, producing music that was designed first and foremost to appease the institutions that supported him, and, secondarily, to entertain the public in the least demanding fashion.

His music made something of a comeback in the decade after his death, but with the Nazis rise to power his work was suppressed, along with all other Jewish music. Though the bulk of his output remains in limbo, there's been something of a mini-revival of late: his symphonies and concertos are now well represented on record, and the most successful of his three operas, *Die Loreley*, has even been staged by at least three different companies.

GUUS ONG

Bruch's symphonic style owes much to Mendelssohn and Schumann, and even more to Brahms, whose influence is clear in Bruch's *Symphony No. 3* – the last and best of his symphonies, it was written in 1887, two years after Brahms' fourth. That said, the symphony displays more complicated orchestration and a less rigid structure than you'll find in Brahms, and you'd have to have a hard heart not to find something intoxicating in the sweep of its old-fashioned melodies.

If you don't know the *Violin Concerto No. 1* by name you're almost certain to recognize it in performance. This is the quintessential Romantic showpiece, full of engaging themes and bravura writing that makes this concerto as exciting as anything in the repertoire, when played well. The remaining concertos are less memorable but are still highly entertaining, as is the silly but tuneful *Scottish Fantasy*.

○ **Symphonies Nos. 1–3**: Leipzig Gewandhaus; Masur (Philips PHIL 420 932-2PH2; with *Swedish Dances*; 2 CDs).

○ **Violin Concerto No. 1**: Heifetz; New Symphony Orchestra; Sargent (RCA RD86214; with *Scottish Fantasy and Vieuxtemps, Concerto No. 2*).
○ **Violin Concerto No. 1**: Lin; Chicago Symphony Orchestra; Slatkin (Sony MDK 44902; with Mendelssohn's *Violin Concerto*).
○ **Violin Concerto No. 1**: Accardo; Leipzig Gewandhaus; Masur (Philips 432 282-2; with other works for violin and orchestra; 3 CDs).

Kurt Masur's set of the symphonies is the best – he indulges Bruch's sweeping (sometimes rambling) lyricism, and brings a rewarding flexibility to the music. The sound is superb and the playing enthusiastic.

The finest version of Bruch's *Violin Concerto No. 1* is the historic account from Jascha Heifetz – the quality of his sound and his response to the music's inflections are stunning, and his phrasing encourages Sargent and the orchestra to wallow in the score's sensual beauty. Similarly magnificent is the playing of the *Scottish Fantasy*, in which Heifetz gives a performance that throbs with energy. For the classic coupling of the Bruch and Mendelssohn concertos, there is no finer modern recording than the one from Cho-Liang Lin and Leonard Slatkin, a performance that's particularly beautiful and intense in the slow movement of the Bruch. Good value, if considerable less engaging, is Salvatore Accardo's version with Masur – it's chief merit is that it comes coupled with performances of Bruch's second and third violin concertos and a good portion of Bruch's other works for violin.

ANTON BRUCKNER
(1824–1896)

For much of the earlier part of this century, Bruckner's name was routinely paired with that of Mahler: both were Austrian, both wrote vast symphonies and both have needed many years of proselytizing for their music to be truly appreciated. Apart from these similarities, however, they were very dissimilar people. Mahler the neurotic and adventurous composer-conductor has little fundamentally in common with Bruckner the pious church organist, who wrote his massively simple music to the glory of God.

Bruckner's grandfather and father were both village teachers. As the position traditionally went hand in hand with that of church organist, young Anton was surrounded by the worlds of the schoolroom and the church from an early age, and by the age of ten he was deputizing for his father at the organ. He began receiving formal music education the following year, and in 1836 he was accepted as a choirboy at the monastery of St Florian near Linz in Upper Austria.

He spent 1840–41 in Linz itself, training to be a teacher, and landed his first position in a small village on the Bohemian border. But his true ambition was achieved when he gained a teaching post at St Florian, where he remained for ten years. During all this time he continued his musical education and composed his first works, mainly liturgical

MANSELL COLLECTION

series of truly original scores, including the *Symphony in D minor* (1863–64), which he later numbered No. 0, the three mature Masses (1864, 1865–66 and 1867–68), and his acknowledged *Symphony No. 1* (1865–66), all of them recognizably Brucknerian in scale and content. In the middle of this period, he suffered a mental breakdown and a bout of numeromania (an obsession with counting), and spent the spring and summer of 1867 in a sanatorium until he was fully recovered. The following year he moved to Vienna to succeed his old teacher Sechter at the city's music conservatory, where he taught theory and the organ, and later became a lecturer at the University.

Here, between 1871 and 1876, he composed his next four symphonies, beginning each one as soon as he had finished its predecessor. He then spent the next three years making revisions to these, before embarking on his next great creative surge, writing his *String Quintet* (1879), *Symphonies No. 6* (1879–81), *No. 7* (1881–83) and *No. 8* (1884–87) and the *Te Deum* (1881–84). A further period of revisions followed – largely spurred on by friends seeking ways of making his music more successful – and was the main reason behind his inability to complete his last symphony, *No. 9* (1891–96). He died in Vienna in October 1896 and in accordance with his wishes was buried beneath the organ at St Florian.

Throughout all his years in Vienna, Bruckner had to put up with continual barracking from the anti-Wagnerites and in particular the critic Eduard Hanslick, who wielded far-reaching powers in Viennese musical life. Only *Symphony No. 7* brought him unchallenged success and led to international recognition during his last decade. Some still carp at the crudities and naiveties that many of Bruckner's works display, yet there was arguably no other composer who spent so many years studying his art before establishing his unique voice. He remained a devout Catholic for the whole of his life and his faith pervades all his music, though it was with the traditionally secular symphony – Gothic cathedrals in sound, as they have often been described – that his originality was established.

pieces. In 1855 he moved back to Linz to take up the position of cathedral organist and soon established himself as one of the greatest exponents of the instrument. His studies still continued, this time with the Viennese theoretician Simon Sechter, and he later took lessons in formal composition and orchestration with a teacher ten years his junior, Otto Kitzler.

It was through Kitzler that Bruckner found his true musical vocation, when the former gave a performance of Wagner's *Tannhäuser* in Linz. It proved a revelation. Bruckner had spent nearly forty years of his life learning all the theoretical rules of composition; his exposure to Wagner made him realize that his way forward was to break these rules, as Wagner had done, and to create in the symphony what Wagner had achieved in music drama. (He and Wagner subsequently became firm friends, something that the pro-Brahms Viennese faction used against him.)

Until this point, none of Bruckner's compositions had really stood out from the run-of-the-mill music written for day-to-day use in the Catholic church. Now, as if to make up for lost time, he immediately began a

CHORAL MUSIC

Before Bruckner had any idea about how to write for an orchestra, he had excelled in his writing for choir with basic instrumental accompaniment. Indeed, his liturgical output exceeds his symphonic, though many of these early works are best left to the dedicated. Much more worthwhile are the mature Masses, which bring to the Mass tradition of Mozart and Haydn both the lyricism of Schubert and the austerity of Bach. On a grander scale is the *Te Deum*, a work Bruckner felt to be one his best. "When God finally calls me," he once said, "and asks 'What have you done with the talent I gave you, my boy?', I will present him with the score of my *Te Deum* and hope he will judge me mercifully."

MASSES NOS. 1–3

Bruckner wrote as many as seven Masses, but only the last three, dating from the 1860s and known confusingly as numbers 1, 2 and 3, are performed with any regularity. These works were no more immune from Bruckner's revisionary practices than were his symphonies and the third, in F minor, was reworked at least four times before he arrived at a definitive version. The first (D minor) and last have orchestral accompaniment, but the middle work (E minor) has only an accompaniment of wind instruments in response to the more austere sect for whom he wrote the work.

○ **Mass No. 1**: Rodgers, Wyn-Rogers, Lewis, Miles; Corydon Singers & Orchestra; Best (Hyperion CDA 66650; with *Te Deum*).
○ **Mass No. 2**: English Chamber Orchestra Wind Ensemble; Corydon Singers; Best (Hyperion CDA 66177; with *Libera me & Aequali*).
○ **Mass No. 3**: Booth, Rigby, Ainsley; Corydon Singers & Orchestra; Best (Hyperion CDA 66599; with *Psalm 150*).

Matthew Best and the Corydon Singers have made their name in this music and these Hyperion discs provide some of the most intensely moving Bruckner available, sensitively performed and recorded.

TE DEUM

Bruckner's setting of the great hymn of praise to God, the Te Deum, was written between the seventh and eighth symphonies and is thus his most mature vocal composition. It is on the same scale as his symphonies, requiring four soloists, a choir, organ and orchestra, and, despite its key of C major, it has even been used, following Bruckner's own misguided suggestion, as a choral finale to the ninth symphony, which is in D minor.

○ Norman, Minton, Rendall, Ramey; Chicago Symphony Orchestra; Barenboim (Deutsche Grammophon DG 435 068-2; with *Symphony No. 1*).

Daniel Barenboim gets the measure of this great affirmation of faith, with a top team of soloists, including Jessye Norman and Samuel Ramey, and the brilliant, incisive playing of the Chicago Symphony Orchestra. The spacious recording does full justice to the occasion.

THE SYMPHONIES

Bruckner was forty before he found his symphonic vocation, then went on to write ten symphonies on a scale not heard before. While his contemporary Brahms was happy to follow the example of Beethoven's classicism, Bruckner sought a much more modern and novel development of the form, an enterprise in which he was immensely influenced by the operas of Wagner. Bruckner's orchestral forces are on a truly Wagnerian scale – the late symphonies, for example, call for a quartet of Wagner tubas in addition to the already substantial brass section, and the music cries out for vast numbers of string and woodwind instruments.

Yet the music itself often betrays Bruckner's background as an organist. Huge sections of the symphonies concentrate exclusively on a particular combination of instruments, as if a particular selection of organ stops had been chosen; these blocks of sound often change abruptly, sometimes with a naïve pause to divide them; themes are presented and developed in long strands that are often achieved by simply repeating phrases before moving on; climactic sections often find the full orchestra reiterating a single chord; and, at his most basic, Bruckner has the whole orchestra playing in unison – a dramatic stroke, but one which often sounds coarse and unsophisticated. So Bruckner is not the most subtle or natural of symphonists, but there is so much in the way of harmonic ingenuity, melodic sweep and sheer orchestral magnificence in his music that, despite its scale, diffuseness and clumsiness, it invariably repays your patience. The best works for a first try are symphonies *No. 4* and *No. 7*.

All of the symphonies except numbers 0, 5, 6 and 7 were subjected to revisions of varying degrees in an attempt to make them more acceptable to audience and critics, and this has resulted in the survival of several different versions of many of them. To make things worse, most were first published with further "improvements" by his followers and pupils. Their motives were good – they wanted to increase the symphonies' chances of performance – but their cuts and additions often harmed Bruckner's overall plan. Between the 1930s and 1950s two musicologists, Robert Haas and Leopold Nowak, each brought out a complete edition of Bruckner's scores, as far as possible restoring them to their original form, though each editor often had his own interpretation of that original state. It's recently been revealed that Haas was encouraged in his editorial policy by the Nazis, who urged him to go for more monumental readings; in a sense, Nowak's subtler and more refined versions can be seen as a de-Nazification of the texts. Both versions are still very much in circulation.

> ◗ Symphonies Nos. 0–9: Chicago Symphony Orchestra; Barenboim (Deutsche Grammophon DG 429025-2; with *Te Deum, Psalm 150 & Helgoland*; 10 CDs).

A recording of the complete symphonies won't necessarily provide you with the best performance of each work, but has the advantage in terms of convenience and cost, since all available sets are at reduced price, and make the best use of disc space. The choice of cycles lies between Jochum (twice), Karajan (1974–81) and Barenboim, who is already into his second cycle. His first, for Deutsche Grammophon, has recently been reissued and provides perhaps the most consis-. tent pleasure – it's also the only cycle that includes *No. 0*, and the set includes Barenboim's fine *Te Deum* (see above).

SYMPHONIES NOS. 0–2

Though less distinguished than the later symphonies, the first three nevertheless established many of Bruckner's most distinctive characteristics, from the sense of scale to the organ-like washes of orchestral sound and the construction of long expanses from short, repeated phrases. Bruckner's stylistic devel-

opment was very much a gradual process, however, so there is often little to distinguish one symphony from the next.

Much of the music of *No. 0* postdates *No. 1*: Bruckner at first abandoned it then revised it before embarking on *No. 2*, but felt that the work now known as *Symphony No. 1* was worthier of the title, so relegated *No. 0* to its zero status. *No. 1* was the first to be performed, at a concert in Linz in 1868 conducted by the composer. Shortly afterwards, he moved to Vienna and from time to time over the next twenty or more years tinkered with the score of the work, finally producing a complete revision in 1891 (the so-called Vienna version) that left hardly a bar untouched. The second symphony was the first to be completed after his move to Vienna and before the anti-Wagner claque began directing its venom towards him. It had a successful first performance in 1873, but his friend Johann Herbeck encouraged him to makes changes and cuts, resulting in the 1877 version, though Robert Haas restored the cuts in his edition and it is this version that is invariably played today.

> ◉ **Symphony No. 0**: Berlin Radio Symphony Orchestra; Chailly (Decca 421 593-2; with *Overture in G*).
> ◉ **Symphony No. 1**: Berlin Philharmonic Orchestra; Karajan (Deutsche Grammophon DG 415 985-2; with *Symphony No. 5*; 2 CDs). 3x
> ◉ **Symphony No. 2** (1877 version – ed. Haas): Concertgebouw Orchestra; Chailly (Decca 436 154-2).

POLYGRAM

Riccardo Chailly

Riccardo Chailly is the most persuasive conductor of the early symphonies, and in this performance of No. 0 it emerges as not perceivably a lesser work than its companions. With Chailly's fine account of No. I currently out of the catalogue, Karajan's 1981 recording regains its supremacy. Moving from the Berlin Radio Symphony Orchestra to Amsterdam, Chailly continues his survey with a thoroughly convincing account of the second.

SYMPHONY NO. 3

In September 1873, Bruckner took an incomplete symphonic score to Richard Wagner at Bayreuth, along with the score of *Symphony No. 2*, to ask Wagner which one he would like to have dedicated to him. He chose the unfinished piece, and from then on, Bruckner always referred to his *Symphony No. 3* as the "Wagner Symphony". Its first version contained a string of quotations from Wagner's operas, but these were eradicated before the premiere in 1877, and Bruckner made a further revision in 1889. It is one of his most enjoyable early symphonies, full of original harmonic and melodic touches, and with a concluding section that, more than any of his other works, looks forward to the grandeur of Mahler.

● **Symphony No. 3** (1874 version): Frankfurt Radio Symphony Orchestra; Inbal (Teldec 2292-42961-2).
◉ **Symphony No. 3** (1889 version – ed. Nowak): Berlin Philharmonic Orchestra; Karajan (Deutsche Grammophon DG 413 362-2).

Iliahu Inbal's richly rewarding recording with the Frankfurt Radio Symphony Orchestra uses the original 1874 version of the symphony, complete with Wagner quotations. When it comes to the 1889 version, which has superceded that of 1877, it's a choice between the more-or-less equal virtues of Karajan, Haitink and Böhm, though on balance it is Karajan who makes the most of its qualities.

SYMPHONY NO. 4 – THE ROMANTIC

Bruckner himself referred to his fourth symphony as the "Romantic", but when Bruckner uses the term he's not thinking of any Byronic human drama, but rather of the romanticism of nature. This symphony is in essence an allegorical representation of the Austrian countryside. Following the example of Weber's *Der Freischütz* (see p.412), in which the sound of the horn first acquired

romantic connotations, Bruckner makes the instrument dominate this symphony: the opening movement features avalanches of brass tones, but the horn really comes into its own in the Scherzo, an evocation of a hunting scene that alludes to the rustic Austrian dance known as the *Ländler*. This movement first introduces a characteristic triplet rhythm which became known as the "Bruckner rhythm", so often did he use it subsequently.

There were as many as four versions of this symphony, though only three survive: the first from 1874, a revised one from 1878–80, when he added the "hunting-horn" Scherzo, and an unauthorized, bastardized version by his pupil Ferdinand Löwe, made in 1888 but long since superceded by the Haas edition of the 1878–80 (though there are still recordings available of this version).

● **Symphony No. 4** (1878–80 version): Berlin Philharmonic Orchestra; Jochum (Deutsche Grammophon DG 427 200-2).
● **Symphony No. 4** (1888 version): Vienna Philharmonic Orchestra; Böhm (Decca 425 036-2).

Although it uses the 1888 version, Böhm's recording is nevertheless a classic, with the Vienna horns making the most of the Scherzo. For a more "authentic" account, Jochum's is a fine example of his personal yet faithful way with Bruckner.

SYMPHONY NO. 5

This was the first of Bruckner's mature symphonies to survive in a single version and was his most monumental to date, being both longer and more finely worked-out than its predecessors. It has a sense of solemnity not found in the earlier symphonies, with a dramatic sense of conflict generated by the suggestion that passion is always being kept in check. Bruckner's characteristic use of rich brass chorales is here becoming an increasingly prominent feature, while the finale is a marvellously constructed amalgam of fugue and chorale.

◉ Berlin Philharmonic Orchestra; Karajan (Deutsche Grammophon DG 415 985-2; with *Symphony No. 1*; 2 CDs).

Karajan is at his best in the more spacious Bruckner symphonies, and this is one of his finest recordings; his grasp of the structure of No. 5 gives the work a powerful feeling of inevitable flow.

SYMPHONY NO. 6

Bruckner's next symphony proved to be a lighter, more congenial work than its predecessor – the equivalent, say, of Beethoven's eighth or Brahms's second. This is not one of his most frequently performed symphonies, perhaps because of its relative coolness and detachment, but it is typical Bruckner to the core, and again it required no revision on Bruckner's part.

◗ New Philharmonia; Klemperer (EMI Studio CDM 7 63351-2).

This has long been regarded a classic among Bruckner recordings and wears its three decades well, with Klemperer revelling in the symphony's joyous climaxes.

SYMPHONY NO. 7

Symphony No. 7 is the work that brought Bruckner most success in his lifetime, and has always been his best-loved symphony. After *No. 6* the expansiveness is back, and the symphony begins with his broadest theme yet, a wonderful, noble, arching E major melody on the cellos, variously coloured by other instruments – Bruckner is supposed to have heard it in a dream, though it quotes from his *Mas No. 1*, which he was revising at the time. The work as a whole is intimately connected with Wagner, who died while Bruckner was working on the already funereal Adagio. As a tribute, he introduced the mellow sound of a quartet of Wagner tubas into this movement, and the heartrending coda was written as a direct response to the news of his mentor's death in 1883.

◉ Cleveland Orchestra; Dohnányi (Decca 430 841-2).

Together with *No. 4*, this is the most frequently recorded of the symphonies, with some forty versions in the catalogue; Christoph von Dohnányi's is the finest of the lot.

SYMPHONY NO. 8

The *Symphony No. 8* is Bruckner at his grandest, most uplifting and most religious. At around eighty minutes long, with a slow movement lasting up to half an hour, it can seem daunting and diffuse on first hearing, but it repays repeated acquaintance for the sumptuousness of its orchestral sound and grandeur of its themes. Like nearly all his symphonies, Bruckner opens with pianissimo tremolo strings, an allusion to the opening of Beethoven's ninth, where similarly the music seems to emerge from nothingness – and the theme the strings accompany even matches the rhythm of Beethoven's at the same point. Bruckner completed his symphony in 1887 but then bowed to the inevitable pressure to make cuts, and a new version was completed in 1890.

◉ Vienna Philharmonic Orchestra; Karajan (Deutsche Grammophon DG 427 611-2; 2 CDs).

Karajan recorded the symphony a number of times, always opting for the Haas version of the fuller 1887 text. His last account, with the Vienna Philharmonic Orchestra and issued posthumously, is the most powerful of them, with an unparalleled sense of communion between conductor, orchestra and music. However, coming in at only three minutes beyond the capacity of a single disc and with no coupling, it is a money-grabbing issue, sadly characteristic of the Karajan/Deutsche Grammophon combine.

SYMPHONY NO. 9

So preoccupied was Bruckner with making needless revisions of his earlier symphonies that he never managed to complete his last work in the form. Attempts have been made to furnish it with a finale from Bruckner's sketches, but it has long been accepted in the form of a three-movement torso. More approachable than *No. 8* (and if completed it would probably have been even longer), it is a musical summation of his life: the great Adagio subtly alludes to earlier works, while the symphony's drama expresses the resolution of his self-doubts in the solace of overpowering religious faith.

◉ Berlin Philharmonic Orchestra; Karajan (Deutsche Grammophon DG 419 083-2).

Few conductors have excelled in these late symphonies as Karajan did. His 1976 Berlin recording improved upon his performance of a decade earlier, reaching new heights of expression and ethereal drama – but it's still inexplicably at full price.

ANTOINE BRUMEL

(c.1460–c.1520)

Antoine Brumel, born near Chartres around the middle of the fifteenth century, was one of the most respected musicians and composers of his time. Josquin's *Deploration sur la morte d'Ockeghem* mentions Brumel as one of four followers of Ockeghem who should "weep great tears of grief" at the loss of their "good father" (the others are Josquin himself, Pierre de la Rue and Loyset Compère), and although the theorist Glareanus sourly notes that Brumel excelled through his industry rather than his natural gifts, most writers of his period showered him with praise.

Like many of his contemporaries he travelled widely: probably beginning his career in the choir of Chartres cathedral, he was last heard of in Italy, where he settled in Rome for some time. Brumel had a reputation as a difficult man to deal with, and this may be borne out by the rapidity with which he moved from job to job – for example, he held a post at Notre Dame in Paris for no more than a year before leaving in some haste. Nonetheless, he was sufficiently valued for Alphonso I of Ferrara, an important patron, to make more than one attempt to hire him. The duke finally succeeded in enticing him to his court in 1505 with the offer of a large salary augmented by a travel allowance. He remained there for five years before his move to Rome. Neither the date nor the place of his death are known.

THE MUSIC

Although we know of over fifty *chansons*, Brumel's greatest works are religious. Of his sixteen surviving settings of the mass, which include one of the earliest Requiems, the late *Missa de Beata Virgine* is probably his masterpiece. It may well have been written in competition with Josquin's setting, and suffers little in comparison, showing an easy control of counterpoint with a sometimes insouciant approach to dissonance, daring melodic and rhythmic invention and an immaculate sense of pacing. Brumel's particular gift for raising the tension towards the end of a movement as the voices chase each other in a flurry of cross-rhythms and ever-decreasing note-values before coming to satisfying rest is especially notable here. Unfortunately, at the time of writing there's no CD of this mass, but there is a recording of the astonishingly assured and flamboyant *Missa Et Ecce Terrae Motus* for twelve voices, which mixes strict canonic techniques with free invention, contrasts of timbre and impressively full textures when all twelve voices are singing at once.

 Missa "Et Ecce Terrae Motus"; Sequentia "Dies Irae": Huelgas Ensemble; van Nevel (Sony Vivarte SK 46 384).

The massive sonorities of this mass are well served here by an acoustic that suits the grandeur of Brumel's conception without obscuring the complex interweave of the twelve voices. The energy of the writing and the powerful ostinati that are such a feature of his work are joyfully brought out by van Nevel's ensemble, who also convey the sense of awe at the mystery of the Incarnation, the very heart of the mass. The inclusion of the solemn setting (the earliest known) of the Dies Irae from his *Requiem* is an extra treat.

VIVARTE

Antoine Brumel
Missa "Et ecce terrae motus" a 12 voci
Sequentia "Dies irae"
Huelgas Ensemble
Paul van Nevel

The best Brumel recording in the catalogue

FERRUCCIO BUSONI

(1866–1924)

Ferruccio Busoni is the forgotten man of twentieth-century music, a situation partly due to the fact that he can't be classified neatly. He was born in Tuscany but his father was German; he grew up regarding German culture as the apex of western civilization, and was to spend most of his professional life in Germany. Classically trained (he developed into an astounding pianist), he came to feel that his mission was to merge the conflicting philosophies of Brahms and Wagner, the one standing for the authority of tradition, the other representing the challenge of progress.

Busoni's theoretical writings soon established him as one of the leading figures of the avant-garde, espousing such outrageous ideas as microtonal music (ie music with 36 notes to an octave) and the development of electronic music. However, he was unable to sacrifice the traditions most sacred to him and incorporate any of his daring notions into his own compositions, preferring to write music that looked back to the eighteenth century for inspiration. Proclaiming the merits of what he termed "Young Classicism", he championed the *Magic Flute* as the greatest of all operas, deplored the unseemly representation of passion on stage, and devoted much of his time to the rearrangement of other composers' music – his piano transcriptions of Bach are brilliant achievements, and have been played by virtuosos ever since.

Ultimately Busoni was hamstrung by his own analytical intelligence and by his reverence for the past, and is probably most likely to be remembered as a formidable pianist. There are, however, a few works in which Busoni manages to struggle free of the weight of history, and these are his gargantuan piano concerto and his operas. The stage works are not ingratiating pieces – Busoni hated the exciting realism of verismo opera, aspiring instead to create a hieratic music drama in which a perfect fusion of music and text would facilitate the spiritual elevation of the audience. The results can be turgid in places, but

Turandot and *Doktor Faust* in particular have moments of great power, and each of the operas is clearly the product of an interesting mind.

ARLECCHINO AND TURANDOT

Busoni's *Turandot* (based on the same source as Puccini's) was composed as a companion piece for his earlier one-act opera *Arlecchino*, and the two works were first performed together in 1917 under the heading *La nuova commedia dell'arte*. Brilliant examples of Busoni's eclectic but highly individual style, they are scored for modest forces which Busoni uses with great economy and wit. The better of the pair is *Turandot*, with its thickly layered oriental melodies and general air of chinoiserie – though somewhat enigmatically Busoni breaks the oriental mood at the beginning of Act Two, when he incorporates, of all things, the music of *Greensleeves*. The music for this neo-classical *Turandot* shows a complete mastery of the human voice; Busoni's vocal writing may be less memorable than Puccini's, but it's more effective as a component of a coherent theatrical experience.

⊙ **Arlecchino; Turandot**: Gessendorf, Selig, Dahlberg, Schafer, Kraus, Holzmair; Choir & Orchestra of the Lyon Opera; Nagano (Virgin VIRG 7777 593132-7; 2 CDs).

Kent Nagano's performances of Busoni's two comic operas are characterful and highly charged, even if much of the singing is not exceptional – Mechthild Gessendorf is a good Turandot, but Stefan Dahlberg's one-dimensional Kalaf is unable to convey much beyond the words. The recording is clear and well defined, although the chorus is allowed an overbearing prominence.

DOKTOR FAUST

Busoni began the libretto of *Doktor Faust* in 1914, basing it not on Goethe's poem but on an old German puppet-play and on Marlowe's *Doctor Faustus*. The finished article, however, is a metaphysical drama that bears little resemblance – beyond its sixteenth-century setting – to Marlowe's semi-farcical creation. The barest outline is as follows. Having invoked Mephistopheles to help him gain "riches, power, fame" et cetera, Busoni's Faust runs away with the recently married Duchess of Parma, whom he abandons when she becomes pregnant. Later he meets the Duchess, now destitute, carrying the body of their child. Stricken by the scene, Faust offers his own life that the child might live; as Faust dies, defiant of God and the Devil alike, a young man rises from his child's corpse.

Completed after Busoni's death by Philip Jarnach (Puccini, who also died in 1924, similarly didn't complete his final opera), *Doktor Faust* a work of immense power that confronts the complexities of the Faust legend more completely than any other operatic treatment of it. Though written in strict classical form, its orchestration is lush and inventive, and the heavily chromatic vocal parts infuse the rigid structure with a sweeping sensuousness not found in Busoni's other work for the stage. The text is difficult and the opera does demand repeated listening for its ideas and leitmotifs to have any effect, but as with any twentieth-century progressive opera, a little effort reaps very great rewards.

◗ Fischer-Dieskau, Cochran, de Ridder, Hildebrecht; Bavarian Radio Orchestra & Chorus; Leitner (Deutsche Grammophon 427 413-2GC3; 3 CDs).

This is the only available recording of *Doktor Faust*, and it's so fine that it has probably dissuaded record companies from attempting to compete. Fischer-Dieskau's Faust and William Cochran's Mephistopheles are especially good – Cochran's purposeful and ringing tenor voice well balanced by Fischer-Dieskau's smooth but highly coloured baritone. Busoni makes less of the Duchess than the text might suggest but Hildegard Hillebrecht sings the part with conviction and considered characterization. However, it is Fischer-Diskau's astonishing portrayal of Faust's final failure to find Christian redemption that steals the show. Keep the libretto in sight at all times – without it, the work makes almost no sense.

CONCERTO FOR PIANO AND ORCHESTRA

Busoni's *Concerto for Piano and Orchestra* is a massive creation, requiring the pianist to play almost continually for over an hour and – come the last movement – to do battle with a male chorus as well as a hundred-strong orchestra. It shows Busoni as a consummate synthesist: there is a great deal of Brahms' influence here (especially the opening theme) and a constant recourse to traditional Italian rhythms and melodies – each of the first three movements is built around folksongs, while the fourth is a highly developed quasi-Neapolitan song. The work contains perhaps Busoni's most accessible and memorable writing, with grand melodies that surge through the piano part and some fine passages of orchestration. The last ten minutes of the fifth and final movement are particularly beautiful, and the music's transformation into its conclusive glowing resolution is a remarkable achievement.

◗ Ogdon; John Alldis Choir; Royal Philharmonic Orchestra; Revenaugh (EMI CDM7 69850-2).

Ogdon's legendary recording for EMI is still unrivalled, although the same label's live performance with Donahoe is better recorded. Both pianists do the work justice, but Ogdon – who studied with Egon Petri, Busoni's favourite pupil and the pianist for the work's British premiere – has an unmatched grasp of the colossal structure. Ogdon's mighty technique is remarkable throughout, with some of his playing in the outer movements being almost beyond belief.

WILLIAM BYRD

(1542–1623)

William Byrd was called by his contemporaries "Britanniae Musicae Parens", the father of British music. It was a title he fully deserved: though writing in the Golden Age of English music, he stands out for his combination of sensuousness and formal precision. It was an achievement all the more remarkable since

Byrd was a lifelong Catholic at a time when anti-Catholic feeling was at its height. What saw him through was probably a combination of shrewdness, friends in high places (the Earl of Worcester, a leading Catholic, was a patron), and his outstanding musical ability.

Little is known about his family background. He may have been the son of Thomas Byrd, a gentleman of the Chapel Royal and a colleague of Thomas Tallis (see p.370), with whom the younger Byrd is said to have studied, or he may have been a chorister at St Paul's Cathedral and studied under the Catholic Sebastian Westcote. In 1563 he was appointed organist of Lincoln Cathedral, a post he held until 1572 when he moved to London to become joint organist at the Chapel Royal with Tallis. The two men also held the exclusive right to print and publish music and in 1575 they published *Cantiones Sacrae*, a collection dedicated to Queen Elizabeth and containing seventeen motets by each composer. After the enterprise's financial failure the pair petitioned the Queen and were granted the lease of the manor of Longney in Gloucestershire. In his later years he became more and more uncompromising about his religious beliefs and on several occasions he and his wife were fined for recusancy. In 1593 he moved to a large property at Stondon Massey in Essex, possibly to be near the Catholic Petre family, in whose chapel one of the three Latin Masses, his greatest music, was almost certainly first performed.

SACRED MUSIC

Byrd was a prolific composer of church music. As well as the *Cantiones Sacrae* of 1575 he published two more collections with the same title in 1598 and 1591, and two sets of *Gradualia* (cycles of music for the Catholic liturgical year) in 1605 and 1607. These last two publications had Byrd's name printed on every page, even though, as Catholic works, they were illegal. In the first volume he wrote of the effect the scriptural texts had upon him: "I have found that there is such a power hidden away and stored up in those words that . . . all the most fitting melodies come as it were of themselves, and freely present themselves when the mind is alert and eager."

● **The Great Service and Anthems**: The Tallis Scholars; Phillips (Gimell CDGIM 011).
● **The Three Masses**: The Choir of Winchester Cathedral; Hill (Argo 430 164-2).

The *Great Service* is Byrd's finest music for the Anglican church and his most substantial work, being scored for a ten-part choir divided into two semi-choirs. Byrd uses the size of the choir not so much for volume or declamatory effects, but for a marvellously rich variety of vocal textures and sonorities, which are particularly evident in the *Te Deum*. This is measured and unruffled music, which particularly suits the Tallis Scholars with their well-balanced voices and emotionally controlled sound.

It is scarcely surprising that Byrd, a persecuted Catholic, should have produced such concentrated and intense settings of the Mass. Each of the *Three Masses* is written for a different voice combination – for three parts, four parts and five parts – but they share a similar clarity and directness, with the vigorous counterpoint never obscuring the audibility of the words. These works demand an altogether more expressive approach than Byrd's Anglican music, and Winchester Cathedral choir responds to this austere but powerful music with clear and measured phrasing, and with real sensitivity to the subtlety of Byrd's word setting.

INSTRUMENTAL MUSIC

Byrd is equally important as a composer of secular music – with the exception of lute music, there are surviving examples of virtually every musical form current during his lifetime. He revolutionized the writing of keyboard music, creating complex and inventive pieces which sound surprisingly modern. Mostly contained in two collections, *My Ladye*

Ursula Deutschler plays Byrd

Nevells Virginal Booke and the *Fitzwilliam Virginal Book*, they include several sets of variations based on popular English airs, like *The Carman's Whistle* – a relatively banal tune which Byrd brilliantly transforms into ever more elaborate figurations.

⊙ **Pieces from The Fitzwilliam Virginal Book:**
Duetschler (Claves CD 50-9001).

Ursula Deutschler plays a seventeenth-century Italian harpsichord which has a warm but assertive tone, well-suited to the liveliness of this music. As with so much of Byrd, there is a vigorous, no-nonsense quality to these pieces: elaboration never overwhelms the overall shape, with the theme (or "ground") always remaining clear throughout its various transformations – as can be heard even in the two most ambitious pieces, *The Bells* (based on a three-note "peal" motif) and the long *Walsingham Variations*. Deutschler's strong and unfussy playing is well recorded in a spacious acoustic.

JOHN CAGE
(1912–1992)

Guru to some, charlatan to others, John Cage constantly challenged the very idea of music, using randomness as a basis for composition, doctoring instruments to produce new sonorities, and including the widest array of sounds in his works. He wanted to break down the barrier between art and life, "not to bring order out of chaos . . . but simply to wake up to the very life we're living." His most famous work, *4'33"* (1952), requires a pianist to lift the lid of a piano and then not play it for four minutes and thirty-three seconds – the point was to reveal to the audience the impossibility of total silence and to focus their attention on the wealth of sounds that surround them. This blurring of the conventional separation of real life and the concert hall reached its extreme in certain notorious performances in which Cage would sit on stage frying mushrooms – he was a notable expert on fungi, and in 1958 he won $6000 on an Italian TV quiz show answering questions on the subject.

In his twenties Cage studied with the composer Henry Cowell, who had already written pieces for piano in which the performer plucked and beat the strings directly. He also studied with Schoenberg, and their arguments about harmony (Cage thought it unimportant) led Schoenberg to say of him: "He's not a composer, he's an inventor – of genius." Cage's works of the 1930s, mainly for percussion, are based around numerically ordered rhythmic patterns, and are more akin to eastern than western music – another aspect of Cowell's influence. In 1938, developing Cowell's ideas, he started inserting objects like screws, wood, or paper onto the strings of a piano in order to produce a wide range of percussive sounds. Much of his most expressive music was written for what Cage called the "prepared piano".

In the late 1940s Cage's attitude to music underwent a profound change as a result of his study of Zen Buddhism. In an attempt to rid his music of all vestiges of self-expression and intentionality he started to introduce chance as a guiding principle. In *Music of Changes* (1951) for solo piano, the performer decides what to play and how to play by tossing a coin – a method inspired by the Chinese book of divination the *I Ching*. Most of his chance works were written out, not in conventional notation, but as visually startling and often ambiguous graphic designs. As these became increasingly irrational and anarchic, Cage developed a cult following during the 1960s, though many fellow musicians, such as Pierre Boulez, believed that his emphasis on randomness was a conceptual blind-alley. In the last twenty years of his life he returned to more organizational methods of composing.

THE MUSIC

Cage's major contribution to the music of the twentieth century is his "prepared piano", an instrument he invented out of necessity:

unable to fit a percussion ensemble onstage to accompany a dance performance, he modified a piano to produce "a percussion ensemble controllable by one player." The potential of this clattering construction is best shown in his *Sonatas and Interludes*, a cycle of pieces written between 1946 and 1948, in which he exploits a wide range of sonorities, some bright and bell-like others more delicate and subdued. Rhythmic motifs and patterns recur, producing an incantatory and hypnotic quality close to that produced by the gamelan, the percussion orchestras of Java and Bali. Less well-known are Cage's works for the voice, but they are equally inventive in their treatment of the singer as an instrument of endless possibilities.

⊙ **Sonatas and Interludes for Prepared Piano**: Fremy (Etcetera KTC 2001).
⊙ **Singing Through: Vocal Compositions by John Cage**: La Barbara; Stein; Winant (New Albion NA 035 CD).

Gerard Fremy's CD is the best introduction to Cage – his sympathetic and sensitive playing sustains an atmosphere of enraptured contemplation. After that, move on to Joan La Barbara's selection of vocal music from right across Cage's career, ranging from the lyrical (if unconventional) to the difficult and disturbing – featuring grunts, squeaks, moans and all. *The Wonderful Widow of Eighteen Springs* (1942), one of Cage's most recorded songs, matches the poetic words of James Joyce to a simple almost folk-like melody, mostly using just three notes, while a restless drum rhythm scurries underneath. Rather more bizarre is the *Solo for Voice 52* which employs a fragmentary text of vowels, consonants and words from five languages, all rendered at odd and unpredictable pitches.

GIACOMO CARISSIMI
(1605–1674)

The oratorio – the musical setting of a religious text in the form of a dramatic narrative – emerged as a distinct form at the same time as opera, at the end of the sixteenth century. Like opera, it employed solo singers, recitative, a chorus and instrumentalists, but unlike opera it usually employed a narrator and was rarely intended for staging. It developed in Rome, out of an initiative by Filippo Neri to provide a more accessible and emotionally direct form of worship for Catholics in the wake of the Reformation, and was performed at informal gatherings in which readings and a sermon were combined with the musical performance. The venue for these gatherings was not the church itself but a nearby hall called an oratory – hence the name of the new genre.

Giacomo Carissimi, a name now almost forgotten, was the leading oratorio composer of the mid-seventeenth century. Despite several prestigious job offers, including that of successor to Monteverdi at St Mark's in Venice, Carissimi spent almost his entire professional life as *maestro di cappella* at the

powerful Jesuit centre, the Collegio Germanico. His numerous oratorios were not composed for the Collegio however, but for the upper-crust confraternity of the Most Holy Crucifix, who every Lent celebrated the miraculous survival of a crucifix from the fire that destroyed the church of San Marcello in Rome.

Carissimi's most celebrated work, *Jepthe*, so impressed Handel that he borrowed its final chorus for his own oratorio *Samson*, and has continued to be performed since it was written. The overt emotionalism of the music, largely conveyed through an aria-like style of recitative that gives a melodic tenderness to the rhythms of speech, makes it the most appealing of his compositions.

JEPTHE

The text of *Jepthe*, taken from the Book of Judges, tells of the dilemma of Jepthah (Jepthe in Italian): having promised to sacrifice the first person to greet him when he returns home, if God will grant him victory over the Ammonites, he is met by his beloved daughter. The story is short and intense, and contains striking contrasts of feeling, as when the daughter's joyous praises to God at her father's homecoming are followed by a touching and intimate dialogue between them as he explains her fate. Most famous of all is her final lament, an extended recitative which achieves its emotional impact largely through dissonances in the accompaniment. Even more beautiful is the ensuing grieving chorus, in which, according to a contemporary, "you would swear that you hear the sobs and moans of the weeping girls".

◉ **Jepthe; Judicium Salomonis; Jonas**: Gabrieli Consort and Players; McCreesh (Meridian CDE 84132).

There is no shortage of recordings of *Jepthe*, but this one is the best currently available simply because it is the most heart-felt and the most dramatic. Contrasts of mood are pointed up by quite extreme changes of speed – the slowness of the final chorus, for instance, draws out the emotion ever more painfully. The decision to use a light accompaniment – no original details of the scoring have survived – also enhances the immediacy of the characters' predicament, with the lament merely using a marvellously resonant chittarone (a large lute) to offset the declamatory voice. Of the other two oratorios on this CD, *Jonas* (Jonah) is the more dramatically varied and contains one exceptional moment – a marvellously energetic evocation of a storm at sea sung by an eight-part chorus.

ELLIOTT CARTER

(1908–   )

Elliott Carter belongs to that great line of American musical pioneers, stretching from Charles Ives to Steve Reich (see p.180 & p.292), whose radical achievements have been based largely on their independence from the traditions of Europe. Evoking the windswept plains in the *Concerto for Orchestra*, or a seagull wheeling above New York at the beginning of the *Symphony of Three Orchestras*, his music describes a very American world, but above all it's urban music, reflecting the density of life in great cities – music which, as Carter puts it, attempts to "make sense of the mess". It's tough and challenging work, and at its finest it has an exhilarating sweep and a feeling of cyclonic energy which no other composer of the century has been able to emulate.

Carter came late to serious composition, despite early encouragement from Charles Ives, who sold insurance to Carter's parents until they discovered the subversive influence he was having on their son. He first studied English and mathematics at Harvard before, in the face of determined parental opposition, going to Paris to study with the celebrated teacher and Stravinsky disciple Nadia Boulanger. Returning to America, Carter

BETTY FREEMAN/LEBRECHT COLLECTION

began to compose works combining elements of Boulanger's neo-classicism (a style he later characterized, in the advent of World War II, as "a masquerade in a bomb shelter") with a more populist, American voice. With the *Piano Sonata* of 1946 he exhausted the possibilities of this neo-classical style, and in the *Cello Sonata* of 1940 began to evolve a startlingly original language. This reached fruition with the *String Quartet No. 1* of 1951, the work that shot him to international prominence – paradoxically, as he wrote it entirely for his own satisfaction, doubting it would ever be played. Like all Carter's subsequent works, it owes much to cinematic and collage techniques in the way material is cross-cut and superimposed, blurring conventional formal divisions as different streams of music move in and out of focus.

Encouraged by the success of the quartet, Carter launched into a series of increasingly innovative works in which he gave highly contrasted material to each instrument or group of instruments, achieving a structure he compared to Mozart's operatic ensembles, in which groups of characters express their differing thoughts within a complex musical fabric. But whereas the ensembles of Mozart produce a unified overall texture, Carter's music stresses the disunity and irreconcilabilty of opposite forces – a tendency most strikingly shown in the *String Quartet No. 2* of 1959.

During the 1960s he produced just three works, all concertos: the *Piano Concerto*, the *Double Concerto for Piano and Harpsichord* (neither available on CD) and the *Concerto for Orchestra* – arguably his masterpiece. The last two are both parables of the movement from chaos to order and back into chaos, and found their inspiration in literary parables of birth, growth and decay – for the *Double Concerto* the source was Lucretius's *De rerum natura*, with its description of the creation of matter from a chaos of spinning atoms, while the *Concerto for Orchestra* sprang from St John Perse's poem *Vents*, in which the winds blowing over America destroy and re-form everything in their path.

Carter's quartet cycle continued in 1971 with his formidable *String Quartet No. 3*, which, with the subsequent *Symphony of three orchestras*, marks the outer limits of his strenuous technical experiments. The appearance four years later of *A mirror on which to dwell*, his first vocal work for thirty years, ushered in a new period of creative ease – at the age of almost seventy Carter seemed finally to have established his definitive style and the music suddenly began to pour forth. *A mirror* was rapidly followed by further vocal works – *In sleep, in thunder* and the curious *Syringa*, juxtaposing settings of ancient Greek with John Ashbery's deadpan poem of the same title. Other notable recent works include *Triple duo*, premiered in 1983, *Three*

occasions for orchestra, and further concertos for oboe and violin. Approaching ninety, Elliott Carter is still in full creative flow.

THE QUARTETS

Complexes of simultaneous musical events are the most original and challenging feature of Carter's music – one instrument may accelerate to vanishing point while another slows to immobility; heady romantic lyricism may be set against metronomic pulses; often there may be as many as four completely independent streams of music running in parallel. Perhaps the best introduction to Carter's sound-world is the *String Quartet No. 2*, in which the music is composed out of the confrontations and collisions between the differentiated instrumental characters – the headstrong, virtuoso first violin, the precise, mechanical second, the melancholy viola and the lyrically effusive cello. The *String Quartet No. 3* shows his style at its most technically complex – the instruments are divided into two duos, each playing in different tempos and with different music throughout, so that you are, in effect, listening simultaneously to two completely different pieces. A fourth quartet – one of Carter's less memorable works – followed in 1986.

> ❍ **String Quartets Nos. 1–4**: Juilliard Quartet; Mann, Oldfather (Sony S2K 47229; 2 CDs; with *Duo for Violin and Piano*).

Both the Arditti and Juilliard quartets have recorded all four Carter quartets on CD. The Juilliard, with their warmer sound and greater emphasis on the music's lyrical aspects, just shade it as first choice.

CONCERTO FOR ORCHESTRA

Carter's *Concerto for Orchestra* was to have the same resounding effect on a generation of composers that Stravinsky's *The Rite of Spring* had fifty years previously, and like *The Rite* it's a work with the titanic impetuosity of a thunderstorm, unleashing elemental forces to devastating effect. Conjuring a world where nothing is stable, the music constantly transforms itself until the material of the entire concerto is swept up in the final movement before finally disintegrating back into the silence from which it emerged.

Concerto for Orchestra; Three Occasions; Violin Concerto: Böhn; London Sinfonietta; Knussen (Virgin VC 7 91503-2)

This breathtaking performance of the *Concerto* is the perfect introduction to Carter's work. Two recent pieces, the lyrical *Violin Concerto* and scintillating *Three Occasions*, make an accessible coupling.

MARC-ANTOINE CHARPENTIER

(1643–1704)

Neglected for centuries, Charpentier has recently emerged as one of the greatest French composers of sacred music in the seventeenth century, arguably superior to his more successful contemporary, Lully (see p.202). His music shows more diversity than Lully's, ranging – often within the same work – from the stately to the intimate. The key to this achievement was his adoption of a style, based on the new Italian concerto, which employed dramatically telling contrasts between different groupings of voices throughout a work. Moreover, Charpentier softened the predominantly formal and grandiose style of French music, introducing a more Italianate sensuousness and a greater sensitivity to word-setting.

Little is certain about Charpentier's early life. He was born in Paris, and is known to have been in Rome in the mid-1660s, where he studied with the leading oratorio composer Carissimi (see p.90). Back in Paris he served a series of aristocratic patrons, beginning with the Duchess of Guise, noted for her piety and for the excellence of her musical establishment, which Charpentier directed and sang in as a counter-tenor. He succeeded Lully as the playwright Molière's collaborator, writing the music for his last play, *Le Malade Imaginaire*, in 1673. In the 1680s he was on the fringes of the court, serving the Dauphin as music director and acting as teacher to the Duke of Chartres, but illness intervened when he seemed close to an appointment at the Royal Chapel. It was also in the 1680s that Charpentier gained the position of composer and *maître de musique* of the principal Jesuit church of St Paul, a position he held until 1698, when he moved to the even more prestigious post of *maître de musique* at Sainte-Chapelle du Palais. He wrote just one opera, *Medée* (1693), but the taste for Lully was strong enough to eclipse all rivals, even after his death, and Charpentier's work ran for only ten performances.

SACRED MUSIC

The most striking aspects of Charpentier's choral music are the refined elegance of the melodies, and its rich and expressive harmonies. Though religious sobriety characterizes the overall tone, this is lush music, with subtle underlining of key moments in the text, and marked contrasts between succeeding episodes. Even a large-scale, celebratory work like the D major *Te Deum*, written for the church of St Paul, is broken up into distinct sections with clearly distinguished moods – thus it begins with kettle drums and trumpets, but contains moments of quiet devotional intensity, like the soprano solo to the words "Te ergo quaesumus" (Therefore we beseech thee). Similarly in the greatest of his Masses, the *Missa Assumpta est Maria*, the prevailing mood is sombre but there are subtle shifts of emphasis achieved by various combinations of the eight soloists.

Te Deum; Missa Assumpta est Maria; Litanie de la Vierge: Les Arts Florissants; Christie (Harmonia Mundi HMC 901298).

Christie is a Charpentier specialist, and it would be hard to find a better way of getting to know this great composer than through this CD. The balancing and control is exemplary, with the switches from full chorus to small vocal groupings never sounding abrupt. There are many outstanding moments: in the *Te Deum* the magnificently triumphant orchestral prelude and refulgent opening chorus both stand out; in the Mass, an even more beautiful work, the sprightly Sanctus is followed by a meltingly tender setting of the *Agnus Dei*.

FRÉDÉRIC CHOPIN

(1810–1849)

ROYAL COLLEGE OF MUSIC

Frédéric (or Fryderyk) Chopin, the only son of a French father and a Polish mother, was born near Warsaw, and his Polishness always remained immensely important to him, even though most of the latter half of his life was spent in Paris. The music of Poland permeates his compositions, which were written almost exclusively for the piano, an instrument that by then had become the supreme means of Romantic self-expression. But whereas his great contemporary Liszt used the piano to create heroic self-portraits and vast panoramas, Chopin was an introvert and a miniaturist, infusing conventional forms such as the sonata and the prelude with an intimacy and an emotional intensity which the poet Heine described as the "poetry of feeling".

Chopin was essentially an experimental composer, exploiting the potential of the recent developments in piano construction, like the increase of their range to a full seven octaves and the use of heavily felted hammers which could produce a more refined tone. But although his works are often extremely difficult to play, they are rarely – unlike much of Liszt – virtuosic for virtuosity's sake. Another feature that crucially distinguishes Chopin from Liszt, Schumann and most Romantic composers, is that he did not write music that carried literary, pictorial or biographical significance – his works are to be understood in purely musical terms. Not that this has stopped people from finding non-musical meanings in his music. And in fact the concentrated and volatile nature of his imagination does invite such speculation. Though Chopin found the process of composition extremely arduous, his solo pieces in particular often sound like spontaneous improvisations that have been forced from the unconscious by overwhelming emotion.

When Chopin arrived in Paris in 1831 he was simply one virtuoso pianist among many. His concert debut early the next year was on a bill which included Kalkbrenner, the most celebrated pianist of the day – who had earlier rather patronizingly offered to give Chopin lessons. Chopin, playing his F minor piano concerto and *Mozart Variations*, was a huge success. Liszt and Mendelssohn were present, and both were greatly impressed by him, despite their own utterly different styles. Chopin's playing was particularly admired for the variety of his touch, and for the singing quality (or *cantabile*) of his right hand – though later critics were to suggest that many of Chopin's piano works relegated the left hand to a merely accompanying role. He also employed a distinctive interpretative device called rubato (literally "robbed"), whereby rhythm, instead of being applied in strict time, was expressively distorted by shortening some notes and lengthening others, an effect likened by Liszt to the movement of a tree's leaves in the breeze. However, neither physically nor temperamentally was he suited for a career as a virtuoso, and he only performed on a mere thirty occasions, many of which were private recitals in the salons of the aristocracy.

The dominant influence of Chopin's adult life was the free-thinking novelist Aurore Dudevant, better known as George Sand. Their affair began in the summer of 1838 and they spent the winter of the same year

94 CHOPIN

together in Majorca, where, because of Chopin's tuberculosis, they were made to occupy a deserted monastery – a situation that considerably worsened his condition. Back in Paris they lived in nearby apartments and spent each summer at Sand's country house at Nohant, where many of Chopin's greatest works were composed. Their relationship was turbulent, and Sand became increasingly irritated by what she saw as his excessive demands on her affections. In 1847 they finally separated, and Chopin composed very little after that date. After undergoing a purgatorial concert tour of Britain in 1848, he finally succumbed in October of the following year to the tuberculosis which had dogged him for most of his life.

CONCERTOS

Of the several works for piano and orchestra that Chopin wrote, the two concertos are the most significant. Both were written shortly before Chopin finally left Poland, and both show the influence of Hummel and the Irish composer Field in their emphasis on long unbroken lines in the right hand – especially in the two highly poetic slow movements. The orchestra's role is strictly subordinate (for which Chopin has been criticized), either simply accompanying the piano, or providing long introductions that create a sense of expectation before the piano's entrance.

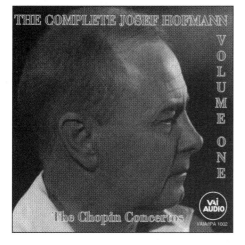

Hofmann's historic Chopin recording

◉ Hofmann (VAI IPA 1002).
◗ Vasary; Berlin Philharmonic; Semkow, Kulka (Deutsche Grammophon DG 4 515-2).

Josef Hofmann was one of the supreme interpreters of these works. He possessed an extraordinary touch – delicate but at the same time strong– and used a rubato so spontaneous and unsentimental that it sounds as if he is making the music up as he goes along. These radio performances date from the 1930s (the orchestra is unknown), and the sound is necessarily quite rough, but the intensity of the playing still shines through. One of the best modern recordings is Tamas Vasary's – these are understated performances, with a crystalline touch which brings out the slightly rarified refinement of the concertos.

SONATAS

Structure and thematic development have long been held up as the weak areas of Chopin's work, particularly in longer pieces such as the three piano sonatas. One contemporary critic went so far as to dismiss the third sonata because " . . . the entire work is not a consequence of the first idea." But these are Romantic sonatas that should not be strait-jacketed by the rigours of sonata form. The best of them, the second in B flat minor (1839) and the third in B minor (1844), are tumultuous displays of sustained energy: the second fast and furious (apart from its famous funeral march), the third more epic in scope and more lyrical, and with a huge sweep of shifting moods and ideas.

◗ **Sonatas Nos. 2 & 3**: Argerich (Deutsche Grammophon DG 419 055-2).

Marta Argerich is one of the great Chopin interpreters of the last thirty years, famed for the sheer daring and power of her performances. Her playing always stresses the restlessness of Chopin's imagination, nowhere more dramatically than in these two sonatas. The second seems to go at a breakneck pace (even the funeral march is faster than usual), but with a sense of urgency rather than rush; the third has a nobility and grandeur which is largely generated by her brilliant range and control of dynamics.

PRELUDES

The twenty-four *Preludes* (Op. 2) were written on the island of Majorca during the winter of 1838. They have been compared to the similarly concise preludes of Bach's *Well-Tempered Clavie*r, which work through every major and minor key in the same way. The comparison is reasonable enough, as Chopin took a copy of that score with him to Majorca, but whereas each of the Bach preludes prepares the way for a fugue, there is nothing remotely introductory about Chopin's. These are highly concentrated poetic miniatures, and the most atmospheric works he ever wrote. George Sand's account of their stay at the old monastery tells of Chopin's ". . . morbid anxiety created by his own imagination"; her version of events might be slightly romanticized, but the *Preludes* certainly fluctuate wildly between euphoria and despair.

◗ **26 Preludes**: Argerich (Deutsche Grammophon DG 415 836-2; with *Barcarolle, Polonaise in A flat major, Scherzo No. 2*).

This is the most celebrated of all Argerich's recordings, and deservedly so – every note sounds fresh and alive, as if conceived at the moment of its playing. The rich variety of her touch perfectly matches the mood of each piece the restrained melancholy of No. 6, the delicate capriciousness of No. 11, the passionate drive of No. 24 – all are conjured with spontaneity and a sense of elation. The CD also includes two posthumous preludes, a wonderfully warm performance of the *Barcarolle* and scintillating accounts of the sixth *Polonaise* and the second *Scherzo*.

ÉTUDES

Piano studies were something of a growth industry in the early nineteenth century – practically every virtuoso, from Clementi to Kalkbrenner, was prepared to impart the method behind his prowess via a book of études or studies. Chopin's two collections of twelve études, Op. 10 and Op. 25, are something rather different, however. Although individual pieces are concerned with conventional technical problems, Chopin transforms them into music of real depth and feeling, while at the same time exploring the boundaries of the technically possible and the harmonically acceptable.

◎ **Études Op. 10 & Op. 25**: Pollini (Deutsche Grammophon DG 413 794-2).

Like Argerich, Pollini is a former winner of Warsaw's Chopin Piano Competition, but his approach to the composer could hardly be more different. Where she is all quicksilver and passion, he is calm and precise, though not as glacial as some critics have suggested. In the *Études* his more measured style and near flawless technique produce brilliant results. The abundant rapid cascades of notes, as in the eleventh étude

from Op. 25, are managed with an almost imperious ease, but in the quieter and warmer moments, like the gently wistful third from Op. 1, he is no less convincing.

POLONAISES

The polonaise is a Polish national dance of a rather stiff and stately nature, written in triple time – it had much the same status in Polish culture as the waltz did in the Austro-Hungarian empire. Chopin's polonaises, as one might expect, greatly transcend the formal restraints of the genre, which in his hands becomes a vehicle for his impassioned feelings about his native land – a land that in his lifetime was partitioned between the great powers of Europe, then invaded by Russia. There is a bold and defiant character to these pieces even when, as in the *C minor Polonaise*, they are shot through with a melancholy anxiety.

◉ **Polonaises; Polonaise-Fantasie**: Pollini (Deutsche Grammophon DG 413 795-2).

Chopin wrote a total of sixteen polonaises, of which only the seven later ones are regularly performed. They are all on this CD, along with the *Polonaise-Fantasie*, a remarkable piece that commences with one of Chopin's most arresting ideas then continues into what sounds like an extended improvisation. Again Pollini's unshowy strength makes these accounts utterly compelling. His articulation of the polonaise's martial rhythms is superbly crisp and arrogant, an effect assisted by the way Pollini builds slowly to the climax of each big tune without ever quite reaching it, enabling the tune to retain all its vigour each time it returns. This works as effectively in the sombre *C minor Polonaise* as it does in the so-called "Heroic" Polonaise, a piece that shows Chopin at his most fiery. Pollini's *Polonaises* are also available in the mid-price box of 3 CDs, with his recordings of the *Études* (see above) and the *Preludes* – so if you're contemplating getting both the first two sets, you may as well buy this box and get his *Preludes* for next to nothing.

MAZURKAS

The mazurka is another Polish dance form in triple time, but with a dotted rhythm that makes it resemble a kind of lurching waltz; it was usually danced slightly faster than the polonaise but not as fast as the waltz. Chopin clearly did not intend his mazurkas to be danced to, but rather to evoke a more elusive, bitter-sweet image of Poland than was projected by the more forthright *Polonaises*. The moods of the *Mazurkas* are more varied than the *Polonaises*, ranging from the sparklingly energetic first mazurka of Op. 7 to the quiet despair of the fourth from Op. 17.

● Rubinstein (RCA RD 5171; 2 CDs).

Artur Rubinstein is another really great Chopin interpreter, who by his direct and unfussy performances did much to dispel the image of the composer as a sentimental lightweight. The *Mazurkas* reveal him at his best, with a light and subtle touch, completely attuned to the music's quiet charm and the quirky ebb and flow of its rhythms.

WALTZES

The craze for waltzes began in the late eighteenth century and by Chopin's time was in full stride. Though he began writing them himself when he was just sixteen, a trip to Vienna in 1830 left him markedly unimpressed by the popular waltzes of Lanner and the older Johann Strauss. A greater influence was Weber's *Invitation to the Dance*: a brilliant and sophisticated showpiece that had enjoyed huge popularity since its appearance in 1819. Chopin's *Waltzes* are a similarly personal response to the dance form, an imaginative evocation of the gaiety and abandon, and sometimes the sadness, of the ballroom.

◗ 14 Valses: Lipatti (EMI C 769 802-2; with *Barcarolle, Nocturne Op. 27 No. 2, Mazurka Op. 50 No.3*).

Dinu Lipatti recorded the *Waltzes* in 1950, the year he died aged only 33, and the recording has remained a benchmark for this music ever since. His delicacy of touch and elegance of conception were matchless: the shimmering passage work and his unforced rubato effortlessly convey the music's evanescent brilliance. The mono sound is a little bit boxy but more than acceptable.

NOCTURNES

John Field invented the piano nocturne as a lyrical and dreamy short piece (not necessarily indicative of night-time), in which an expressive melody in the right hand was gently supported by broken chords in the left hand. Their singing quality was partly derived from the bel canto arias of Bellini's operas. Field's charming but essentially langorous creation was transformed and extended by Chopin into something with a greater emotional range, though a sense of wistfulness generally prevails. These are the pieces that established Chopin's reputation in the aristocratic salons of Paris, and their absolute simplicity and directness of expression has made them the most popular of all his works.

● Rubinstein (RCA D 89563; 2 CDs).

The gentle lyricism of the *Nocturnes* is perfectly suited to Rubinstein's unassertive style and limpid tone. But his readings stand out, above all, for the way the long, meandering right-hand phrases, with their finely spun ornamentation, are delicately shaped through subtle shifts of emphasis that bring out every nuance.

SCHERZI

A scherzo was originally a light-hearted piece which had taken over from the minuet and trio as a short animated movement within a symphony or sonata. Beethoven developed it into an even livelier component of a large-scale composition, but in Chopin's hands the form achieved complete independence and, while Chopin retained the mercurial nature of the scherzo, he almost emptied it of any humour. Like the *Ballades* (see below), the *Scherzi* are extended pianistic tone poems, into which Chopin pours some of his most tempestuous writing.

● Richter (Olympia OC 338; with Schumann, *Bunte Blätter*).

Sviatoslav Richter plays these pieces like a man inspired, with such presence and seriousness that every moment sounds as though it has been carefully weighed up. Yet there is no sense of calculation or strain, and you would be hard pressed to find playing of greater immediacy. Highpoints include his handling, in *Scherzo No. 1*, of the transition from its frantic opening to the lullaby of its middle section, which is played with a rapt tenderness.

BALLADES

The four *Ballades* are among Chopin's most extraordinary and powerful works, abounding in quite startlingly dramatic contrasts, with moments of lyric tenderness being followed by passages of tumultuous energy. The narrative implications of the name "ballade" (here applied to music for the first time) have led many commentators to link these pieces with the longer poems of Chopin's Polish contemporary Adam Mickiewicz, several of whose works Chopin set to music as songs. However, though the poems and the music share a certain volatile and episodic quality, there is no evidence that the composer had any specific programme in mind when writing the *Ballades*.

⊙ Idil Biret (Naxos 8 55050; with *Fantasie in F minor* and other works).

The complete Chopin edition on Naxos has rightly been praised for its superb value and, more importantly, for the wonderful playing of Idil Biret. Fro her, Chopin is primarily about bringing out the richness and complexity of the music's texture, and her accounts of the *Ballades* reveal the works' subtle gradations of mood and colour, without recourse to melodrama. Even better is her reading of the magnificent *Fantasie in F minor*, which is wonderfully spontaneous and full of steely intensity.

CHAMBER MUSIC

Of the little chamber music that Chopin wrote, the outstanding item is the grave and autumnal *Sonata for Cello and Piano in G minor*, his last composition of any importance. He had written for the cello before, but the inspiration behind the sonata was his friendship and admiration for the cellist Auguste Franchomme, who helped him with the technical aspects of the work and to whom it is dedicated.

◗ **Sonata for Cello and Piano**: Argerich, Rostropovich (Deutsche Grammophon DG 419 86-2; with Polonaise brilliante and Schumann's *Adagio and Allegro for Cello and Piano*).

Chopin's sonata for cello and piano stresses the differences between the two instruments – the piano part full of agitated passage work, the cello calmer, with longer and more subdued phrases. This is a near-perfect pairing of musicians, with Argerich's passion tempered by the insinuating warmth of Rostropovich's tone. Even the rather rambling first movement sounds compelling, but most moving is the third movement, which contains one of Chopin's most poignantly elegiac melodies.

MUZIO CLEMENTI
(1752–1832)

If it were not for the affection with which Vladimir Horowitz regarded his music, Muzio Clementi's prolific contribution to piano literature would by now have faded to the edge of oblivion. As it is, he's known more as a pianist, scholar, theorist, teacher, piano manufacturer and as Beethoven's friend and publisher than as a composer. However, as a child Clementi was paraded as a prodigy of Mozartian abilities, and for most of his eighty years he was one of the most famous and highly respected muscans in Europe.

Italian born, Clementi was entrusted by his father to the care of Peter Beckford MP, and in 1767 the fifteen-year-old was moved to England, where he made his home, with Beckford, in Dorset. In 1774 he was freed of his obligations to his mentor and went to London where, from 1777, he conducted Italian opera. Four years later he began to tour Europe, engaging rival pianists in public battles of improvisation and sight-reading –

the young Mozart was one of his opponents. In 1810 he made a semi-permanent return to London, where he settled down to composing symphonies, concertos, piano sonatas and the famous *Gradus ad Parnassum*, a series of one hundred keyboard studies which remains a foundation of piano technique.

After 1810 Clementi made sporadic trips into Europe – two of them extended – with the intention of impressing his symphonic music upon audiences in Paris and Leipzig. These efforts were mostly wasted for, by 1824, his music had all but disappeared from concert programmes, due principally to the increasing fame and popularity of Beethoven's work. Some time after 1830 Clementi retired from professional life and moved to Lichfield and, soon after, to Evesham. Such was his reputation that his funeral was held at Westminster Abbey, and so many people turned up that mourners were obliged to stand; Clementi was then buried in the abbey cloisters, where his tombstone describes him as "The Father of the Pianoforte".

THE PIANO SONATAS

Clementi composed over one hundred piano sonatas, and their influence is hard to overestimate – many of them were highly regarded by Beethoven, for example, and by Clementi's pupil John Field, the creator of the nocturne (see p.97). The early sonatas are little more than homages to Domenico Scarlatti, but between the Op. 10 and Op. 14 sonatas a distinctive Clementi style comes to the fore. Rejecting the conventional Italianate two-movement form, these sonatas inaugurated the three-movement structure, and in their use of thematic development and generally more abrasive melodic style they anticipated Beethoven's keyboard writing. However, Clementi's music has none of Beethoven's heroics or purposeful self-scrutiny – it's predominantly light in nature, and most of the sonatas up to the end of the century have the feel of harpsichord pieces. Come the advent of the full grown piano, his style had advanced harmonically to such an extent that some of his late music foreshadows the early work of Field and Chopin. If Clementi never fulfilled the promise of his youth, he nonetheless developed a solid personal style that is instantly recognizable and immediately charming.

> ◗ **Piano sonatas Op. 33 No. 3; Op. 34 No. 2; Op. 14 No. 3; Op. 26 No. 2; Op. 47 No. 2**: Horowitz (RCA GD87753).

Horowitz's interest in Clementi ensured that the composer's name was preserved outside the rarefied world of musicology, but there is only one Horowitz CD entirely devoted to Clementi's sonatas. One of his principal reasons for playing them was evidently that they offered such scope for personal expression, and it has to be said that Horowitz's interpretations sometimes take liberties. But even if these performances have as much to do with Horowitz as with Clementi, that is all part of their appeal – these are delightful displays of two prodigious musical imaginations at work.

Horowitz's Clementi – a highlight of a long career

AARON COPLAND
(1900–1990)

Aaron Copland is best known for his morale-boosting ballets and patriotic pieces of the 1930s and 1940s, and these are certainly among the most remarkable compositions of their time, particularly when you bear in mind that their cowboy hoedowns and jigs were written by a sassy New Yorker of Russian-Jewish background. It would be wrong, however, to view scores like *Billy the Kid*, *Rodeo* and *Appalachian Spring* in isolation. Masterpieces though they undoubtedly are, they are only one side of the work of a highly inquisitive and analytical artist who was always on the lookout for a new challenge.

The seeds of Copland's remarkable independence were sown way back in his student years, a period when American music was squarely provincial. To show just how entrenched things then were, Copland was

HULTON DEUTSCH

fond of telling how Rubin Goldmark, his highly conservative music teacher, once caught him looking at the score of Ives' *Concord Sonata* and warned him not to contaminate himself with such things. It is lucky for posterity that he followed the advice of a friend, gathered together his hard-earned savings, and headed for Paris, the lair of every artistic revolutionary from Joyce to Hemingway and Picasso to Stravinsky.

When Copland arrived he set about enrolling at the New School for Americans at Fontainbleau, where he was taught by Nadia Boulanger, the remarkable woman who coached an entire generation of budding American composers between the wars. The four years with Boulanger (1921–25) were the most important musical experience of his life: she opened him up to a huge variety of musical influences and taught him all about the virtues of clarity and restraint, as well as giving him a solid technical grounding and a thorough knowledge of orchestration. Stravinsky's neo-classicism made a particularly strong impact on him, as did the music of Les Six (see p.268) and the exciting new

sound of jazz, then sweeping Europe. Copland never looked back. On returning to New York in 1925 he resolved to be as distinctively American-sounding as Mussorgsky and Stravinsky were Russian, and now, thanks to Boulanger, he had the courage and the technical means to achieve his ambitions.

In a long and fruitful career Copland went through no fewer than four highly distinct phases: an exuberant jazzy first phase from 1925 to 1929 (as typified by *Music for The Theatre* and the *Piano Concerto*); a severe avant-garde period from 1930 to 1936 (eg the *Piano Variations*); the hugely popular "Americana" phase of 1936–49 (see below); and a final return to difficult serial territory (eg the *Piano Fantasy* and *Inscape*). Yet despite these abrupt stylistic shifts, there is a distinctive Copland sound, a sound largely determined by his brilliant abilities as an orchestrator. The American composer Virgil Thomson described Copland's orchestration as "plain, clean-coloured, deeply imaginative . . . theatrically functional", and its transparency is the key factor – even in the midst of the busiest textures everything is lucid and opaque. Boulanger had taught him the knack of "keeping instruments out of each other's way", a skill to which he allied a knack of making each part of the orchestra carry its own "expressive idea", bringing a specific emotional connotation to the unfolding drama of a piece.

Copland was also a master of rhythm. The nervous energy of his orchestral music relies heavily on dance and march rhythms, spiced with the displaced accents of jazz, but at the other end of the spectrum he could achieve very complex trance-like effects, as in the slow finale of the *Piano Sonata*. His harmonies were no less expressive and elegant. Time and again Copland found new contexts for conventional intervals and familiar chords, dropping them unexpectedly into very dissonant passages, making them sound fresh and new.

THE BALLETS

The spaciousness of Copland's musical textures has often been compared to America's open landscapes, and nowhere is the comparison more apt than in the ballets of his so-called "Americana" period.

With its sinewy orchestration, jaunty dance rhythms and use of folk tunes, *El Salon Mexico* (1936) was indicative of what was to come. *Billy the Kid* (1938) continued the pattern with a vivid depiction of the Wild West, right down to the obligatory shoot-outs. With *Appalachian Spring* (1944), written at the behest of Martha Graham for her dance company, he reached the summit of his achievements in this form. It's a simple story of love and marriage, in which Copland excels himself in music that is by turns poignantly quiet and spiritual one moment, then exultantly joyous the next. *Appalachian Spring* is typical of Copland's ability to wear his sophis-tication lightly – making ample use of a simple Shaker tune, he evokes emotion in a way that is charmingly straight and accessible, without ever talking down to his audience.

> **⏵ Appalachian Spring; Billy the Kid; Rodeo; Dance Panels**: St Louis Symphony Orchestra, New York Chamber Symphony Orchestra; Slatkin, Schwarz (EMI CMS7 64315-2; 2 CDs).

This two-disc set offers no fewer than three major Copland ballets in their complete orchestral versions. Slatkin is a most persuasive advocate, and the St Louis Symphony Orchestra handle Copland's biting rhythms with real flair, at the same time extracting all the sweetness of Copland's many memorable lyrical passages. An added bonus is the bracing and vivid performance of Copland's rarely heard orchestral work, *Dance Panels*, by Gerald Schwarz and the NY Chamber Symphony Orchestra.

ARCANGELO CORELLI

(1653–1713)

Though instrumental music was becoming increasingly important by the middle of the seventeenth century, Corelli is still unusual in that he wrote absolutely no music for the voice. Instead he worked exclusively in the three genres which he helped to establish and refine: the concerto grosso, the trio sonata, and the solo sonata. His published output was small but his influence was enormous. All subsequent composers who worked in these genres, up until the last quarter of the eighteenth century, used Corelli's work as a model and some – like Couperin in his *L'Apotheose de Corelli* – paid open homage to him.

Corelli was born in Fusignano, between Bologna and Ravenna, into a family of well-to-do landowners with no history of musical talent. He reputedly studied with a local priest but his main musical education took place at Bologna, then an important centre for instrumentalists. From 1675 he was based in Rome, where he gradually established himself as one of the city's leading violinists, playing in theatres and in church ensembles. As a performer Corelli was renowned for the elegance and pathos of his playing, "I never met with any man" wrote a contemporary "that suffered his passions to hurry him away so much whilst he was playing on the violin." However, occasionally his technique let him down – indeed, during a visit to Naples in 1701 he had the embarrassing experience, while leading the orchestra in an opera by Alessandro Scarlatti, of being unable to play a high note which the Neapolitans could manage with ease. Among his patrons were Queen Christina, Cardinal Pamphili, whose music master he became in 1687, and Cardinal Ottoboni, in whose palace he lived from 1689 almost until his death. He died a rich man, leaving not just the predictable pile of instruments and manuscripts, but also a fine collection of paintings.

CONCERTI GROSSI

The concerto grosso, a form of orchestral music that appeared towards the end of the seventeenth century, was like most other instrumental music of the time, in that it consisted of a series of contrasting quick/slow movements based on dance forms. What was new about it was the way that the orchestra was organized into two different groups: a small group called the concertino and a larger group called the concerto grosso (later known as the ripieno or tutti). These two groups played in alternation, with the concerto grosso for the most part simply echoing the material of the concertino, creating a contrast between loud and soft passages. Corelli's concerti grossi have a prevailing mood of balance and control: even in their exuberant fast movements these concertos are quite different from Vivaldi's, which are full of unbridled energy and unpredictability.

⬤ **Six Concerti Grossi**: The English Concert; Pinnock (Archiv 431 706-2).

This CD contains half the concerti grossi that Corelli published, though he evidently wrote many more. All these pieces are easy-going and graceful, and there's much of great beauty here, particularly in concerto No. 8 (Christmas Concerto) with its dramatic opening, its varied and inventive melodies and its grave and sonorous slow movements.

TRIO SONATAS

By Corelli's time the term "sonata" – which had originally meant any piece of music that was played rather than sung – normally referred to a piece played by a small ensemble, in four alternately slow and fast movements. A trio sonata – the most important chamber music genre of the Baroque period – consisted of three parts played by four instruments: two upper parts, usually violins, plus a bass part (called a continuo) played by a keyboard and a low stringed instrument. Generally a distinction was made between the chamber sonata, which employed dance forms, and the more serious church sonata, which usually did not, but in Corelli's hands the difference between the two forms became increasingly blurred. All his trio sonatas are refined and elegant works in which the violin

parts, especially in the slower movements, have a lyrical quality akin to the human voice. This is enjoyable but undemanding music, which avoids extremes of register and of emotion.

⬤ Trio Sonatas: Pinnock; Standage; Comberti; Pleeth; North (Archiv 419 614-2).

Of the ten sonatas on this disc, the six from Opus 1 are church sonatas while the four from Opus 2 are chamber sonatas. The playing is consistently warm-toned and graceful in the two violin parts parts but, as if aware of a certain risk of monotony, Pinnock has effectively varied the use of instruments in the continuo part.

SOLO SONATAS

The twelve sonatas that make up Corelli's opus 5 are called solo sonatas but in fact are for solo violin and continuo – so at least three instruments are heard. Formally they resemble the trio sonatas but include an additional fast movement. Corelli was as influential a performer and teacher of the violin as he was a composer, and these works can be seen as summarizing his understanding of the best qualities of the instrument. Though considerably more virtuosic in the violin part than the trio sonatas, they possess the same classic qualities of tastefulness and easy lyricism. Even in the most technically difficult moments the brilliance of the passage work serves the music rather than the performer.

⬤ **Sonate a Violino e Violone o Cimbalo Op. 5**: Banchini (Harmonia Mundi HMC 901307).

The enriched continuo part (harpsichord, cello and archlute) make these first six sonatas from Opus 5 seem even more like ensemble works in which the violin has the dominant voice. Chiara Banchini's playing is marvellously full, and she brings a spontaneous and improvisatory quality to the music through small surges of volume and the delicacy of her rapid ornamentation. As in all Corelli's work it is the melting intensity of the slow movements that provide the best movements, notably in the richly ornamented Grave of the sonata that opens the disc.

FRANÇOIS COUPERIN

(1668–1733)

François Couperin, known as Couperin le Grand to distinguish him from his various musical relations, was the outstanding French composer of the period between Lully (see p.202) and Rameau (see p.285). In his music he succeeded in reconciling the graceful lyric qualities of the French style with the energy of the Italian, as exemplified by Corelli – a composer he very much admired. He is mainly known for his four books of harpsichord pieces (*Pièces de Clavecin*): some 220 brilliantly crafted miniatures, whose mysterious titles and delicate wit have frequently been compared to the enigmatic paintings of his contemporary Antoine Watteau.

The Couperins were a musical dynasty to rival that of the Bachs. Indeed François Couperin's first job, as organist at the Paris church of St Gervais, had been held by his father and uncle before him, and was to remain in the family until 1826. At the age of twenty-five he succeeded his teacher, Jacques Thomelin, as organist to the king, and a few years later consolidated his position at court when he became harpsichord teacher to several of the royal children. Few other details are known about his life. He acquired a coat of arms shortly after arriving at court, and in 1702 was made a Chevalier of the Order of Latran. None of his correspondence with J.S. Bach has survived (it is thought to have finished up as jam-pot covers), but from the tone of his surviving letters and of his famous keyboard treatise *L'Art de toucher le clavecin* (The Art of Playing the Harpsichord), he seems to have possessed a sardonic sense of humour. Perhaps it was this that kept him from any further appointments at court until 1717, when he took over from d'Anglebert as the king's harpsichordist, a position he retained until his death.

VOCAL MUSIC

The wit and inventiveness which is a characteristic of much of Couperin's music gives way in his sacred vocal pieces to something much more simple and direct, though still with an emphasis on melody. These works tend to be small-scale and intimate, following the model of Carissimi and his French pupil Charpentier, and none of them is more beautiful than the *Leçons de ténèbres*, settings of the Lamentations of Jeremiah to be performed on the three days before Easter. The name, which means "lessons of shadows", refers to the fact that during the services held on those three days all the church candles were gradually extinguished to symbolize the sufferings of Christ. Couperin wrote the full quota of nine lessons (three for each day) but only the first three (for Maundy Thursday) have survived. Each lesson opens with a Hebrew letter sung to an exquisitely sensuous and fluid vocal line: thereafter the vocal style is a fusion between the declamatory and the lyrical, giving a restrained anguish to Jeremiah's lament at the fall of Jerusalem.

○ **Leçons de Ténèbres; Motet pour le jour de Pâques; Magnificat**: Boulay; van der Sluis; Laurens (Erato 2292-45012-2).

The Leçons were written for a convent, so it's more appropriate to have them sung by two sopranos rather than, as is often the case, two counter-tenors. Both sopranos on this CD have a dark and slightly exotic timbre to their voices, which highlights the passionate nature of the music, and they blend together extremely well. The third lesson is the definite highlight of this disc (though inexplicably it has been placed first), which also includes Couperin's exuberant Easter motet and a Magnificat, both for two voices.

INSTRUMENTAL MUSIC

Couperin's four books of harpsichord pieces are organized into twenty-seven suites which he called *Ordres*. Though based on dance forms, most of the individual pieces within these suites have fanciful titles such as *Les Baricades Misterieuses* or *L'Arlequin*, some of which are evidently descriptive while others may have had some private significance. The music's expressiveness is enhanced by rich ornamentation, which – unusually for the time – is never left to the discretion of the performer, but always precisely specified. Though lacking the formal fascination of Bach's keyboard works, Couperin's are more personal and idiosyncratic works, with an emphasis on melody and a wide variety of moods, from the light and elegant to the sombre and subdued.

The outstanding item from Couperin's other solo instrumental music is a late work, the *Pièces de violes*. It was written in 1728, the year after the death of Marin Marais, the great viol master of the period (and the subject of the film *Tous les Matins du Monde*), so perhaps Couperin's pieces are a tribute to him – and to an art form that was already in decline. This is certainly some of the finest and most difficult music ever written for the instrument.

⦿ **Pièces de Clavecin**: Sempé (Deutsche Harmonia Mundi RD 77219).

⦿ **Pièces de Violes; Suites from Les Gouts Réunis**: Kuijken; Uemura; Kohnen (Accent ACC 9288).

Skip Sempé's personal selection makes the perfect introduction to Couperin's harpsichord music. He includes two complete *Ordres* (the third and eighth), five of the eight preludes written for L'Art de toucher le clavecin, while the rest is his own ordering of miscellaneous works, largely by key. The tone of the instrument (a modern copy of the type that Couperin would have played) is exceptionally bright, but it is Sempé's free and expansive playing that brings the music so convincingly to life.

From the opening wistful prelude of the first suite to the scurrying activity of the second suite's concluding movement, the Pièces de violes is music of rare inventiveness and charm. It needs technically brilliant playing, and it gets from Kuijken, although the rather resonant church acoustic puts a little distance on the sound. The bass viol (or viola da gamba) does not have the same incisiveness as the modern cello, but the quality of its string tone gives it a mellowness and a vulnerability that is very appealing. The CD is filled by two suites from *Les Gouts Réunis* (The Styles Reunited), simple and elegant music here played by two viola da gambas.

CLAUDE DEBUSSY
(1862–1918)

Claude Debussy was a radical from the outset. As a student, he continually failed his harmony exams because, like Beethoven over a century before him, he refused to accept the totalitarianism of the text book. A brilliant pianist, he would irritate and shock his contemporaries by inventing harmonies and chords that effectively were re-interpreting tonality – already he was moving towards the creation of musical Impressionism. In 1882 he he failed to win the Prix de Rome, just as the previous great French musical revolutionary, Hector Berlioz, had done, but two years later he took the coveted prize and moved to Rome. He spent the next two years there, meeting Liszt and Verdi, among others, and hearing dozens of contemporary works, including Wagner's *Lohengrin*.

His attendance at the 1888 and 1889 Bayreuth festivals deepened his understanding of Wagner's operas, but although he recognized the importance of *Tristan und Isolde* and *Parsifal* he also saw that these gargantuan, mythic works were something of a dead end. While other French composers such as Chabrier and Chausson responded to Wagnerism by composing their own grand Norse dramas, Debussy looked beyond the mainstream western traditions as a way of expanding the vocabulary of music. A Javanese gamelan performance at the Paris Exposition of 1889 had a profound effect, overwhelming him with the elemental beauty of its indeterminate harmonies. However, it was within Russian music that Debussy found the clearest guidance as to how he might create a musical aesthetic as distinctly French as the art of the Impressionist painters and Symbolist poets with whom he was so close. For Debussy, Russian music was primarily suggestive and evocative, a corrective to Wagner's sternly philosophical and self-consciously profound dramas.

ROYAL COLLEGE OF MUSIC

Debussy began to explore a compositional process that avoided conventional thematic development, instead moving its material through constantly shifting harmonic and orchestral backgrounds – impression mattered more than direction. The first great example of this carefully crafted vagueness was his only opera *Pelléas et Mélisande* (1892), followed two years later by his orchestral *Prélude à l'après-midi d'un faune*, an apparently free-floating composition that was attacked for formlessness but turned out to be one the most influential pieces of music ever written.

His three *Nocturnes*, performed in 1900 and 1901, marked an increasing sophistication of technique, and four years later Debussy produced what many regard as his masterpiece, the symphonic sketches *La Mer*. At the same time he wrote one of the finest of his many piano works, the *Images*, evocative music in which he came close to realizing his ideal of the "hammerless piano". His remaining orchestral works, among them the ballet *Jeux*, were received with great enthusiasm in more adventurous circles, but his final years, during which he produced mainly chamber and piano pieces, were clouded by illness and World War I.

By reason of his influence, Debussy could be classed as perhaps the most important composer of the twentieth century – figures as diverse as Stravinsky, Bartók, Ravel, Webern, Messiaen and Boulez all admitted a debt to him. He is also one of the most approachable. However abstract and ambiguous his work may seem, Debussy believed fervently that music should be communicative. As he once wrote: "Love of art does not depend on explanations, or on experience as in the case of those who say 'I need to hear that several times'. Utter rubbish! When we really listen to music, we hear immediately what we need to hear."

PELLÉAS ET MÉLISANDE

Debussy had a clear idea of what he required from opera: "I wanted from music a freedom which it possesses perhaps to a greater degree than any other art, not being tied to a more or less exact reproduction of Nature but to the mysterious correspondences between Nature and Imagination". With Maurice Maeterlinck's play, *Pelléas et Mélisande*, he found his perfect libretto, a misty tale of doomed love that proceeded by hint and implication rather than by dramatic incident. He began setting the play, virtually uncut, in 1893 and proceeded to revise it obsessively until the first performance at the Opéra Comique on April 30, 1902. It was immediately recognized as a watershed in the history of opera and classical music.

The influence of Wagner's *Parsifal* is clear in Debussy's orchestration, as it is in some of his melodic lines and in his emphasis on the metaphysical dimension of the medieval world in which *Pelléas* is set. Yet this dramatically static work is the very antithesis of Wagnerian heroics. Debussy once remarked that "music in opera is far too predominant", and here he created an opera in which music doesn't so much emphasize the meaning of the text as complement or revise it. In a letter to Chausson he wrote of *Pelléas*: "I have found . . . a technique which strikes me as fairly new, that is silence as a means of expression and perhaps the only way to give the emotion of a phrase its full power". Debussy's conception of silence as a dramatic device is one of his most lasting innovations, while the interaction between his exquisitely delicate music and Maeterlink's nebulous text produces tensions unimaginable in through-composed operas.

There are no big tunes in *Pelléas*, and it contains few moments of traditional lyricism – on the whole, Debussy's writes vocal parts that correspond to the patterns of French speech. Some people find it boring, others regard it as the greatest of all French operas, but there's no disputing its status as a ground-breaker. Moreover, it is one of the few stageworks to thrive on record.

◉ Shirely, Soderstrom, McIntyre, Ward, Minton, Britten, Wick; Royal Opera House Chorus, Royal Opera House Orchestra; Boulez (Sony CD47265; 3 CDs).

Pierre Boulez's recording of Debussy's opera is a brilliant and rare example of one composer expressing his total sympathy for the work of another. He clarifies the complex orchestral colours and shapes each of the brief scenes as part of the over-all structure. Soderstrom is glowing as Mélisande, while Shirely conveys Pelléas's confusion without resorting to over-emphasis. Perhaps there are moments of indulgence and the final act conveys less emotional turmoil than it might, but all in all this is a very sensitive production, and is well recorded – even if it is unnecessarily spread onto three CDs.

PRÉLUDE À L'APRÈS-MIDI D'UN FAUNE

Pierre Boulez once remarked that "just as modern poetry surely took root in certain of Baudelaire's poems, so one is justified in saying that modern music was awakened by *L'après-midi d'un faune*". Saint-Saëns's took a rather less positive approach – "It's as much a piece of music as the palette a painter has worked from is a painting" – but he comes close to capturing the essence of this amazing tone poem. Debussy based his composition upon the poem of the same name by Mallarmé and, like the poem, the music works by suggestion rather than statement. A trance-like flute theme opens the work, establishing a uniquely hedonistic and languid atmosphere that is then extended by some marvellously deft and harmonically innovative writing for woodwind.

◗ Orchestre de la Suisse Romande; Ansermet (Decca 433 712-2DMG; with *Nocturnes & Jeux*).
◉ Philharmonia Orchestra; Cantelli (Testament SBT 10046; with *La Mer* and excerpts from *Le Martyre de Saint Sébastien*).

These two fine performances, each forming part of a stunning Debussy concert disc, reveal different aspects of the score: Ansermet best captures the sensuality of Debussy's orchestral sounds, whereas Cantelli makes it into a less evanescent piece of music, highlighting its structural cohension. Ansermet is more obedient to the composer's spirit, but Cantelli's reading is a memorable and legitimate one.

NOCTURNES

The three *Nocturnes* feature some of Debussy's most imaginative orchestral writing. Untypically, he provided an explanatory note to the set, providing as fine an introduction as could be wished for. "The title *Nocturnes* is . . . not meant to designate the usual form of a nocturne, but rather all the various impressions and the special effects of light that the word suggests. *Nuages* renders the immutable aspect to the sky and the slow, solemn motion of the clouds, fading away in grey tones lightly tinged with white. *Fêtes* gives us the vibrating atmosphere with sudden flashes of light. The background remains persistently the same: a festival, with its blending of music and luminous dust, participating in the cosmic rhythm. *Sirènes* depicts the sea and its countless rhythms and presently, among the waves silvered by the moonlight, is heard the mysterious song of the sirens as they laugh and pass on."

◗ Orchestre de la Suisse Romande; Ansermet (Decca 433 712-2DM; with *L'après-midi d'un faune & Jeux*).

Ansermet is the ideal conductor for this music, as he always gives preference to the transient atmospherics of a piece rather than to its architecture. There are few pieces of orchestral music in which less seems to happen than in the first movement of *Nocturnes*, but in Ansermet's hands the work comes to life, producing the sort of sounds that might have been heard on Prospero's island.

LA MER

In the summer of 1904 Debussy left his wife for another woman, provoking his wife into a suicide attempt. Debussy fled, mistress in hand, to Eastbourne in Sussex, and there he composed his finest orchestral work, *La Mer*. The first performance in 1905 excited hostility in some quarters that seems scarcely credible today, with the critic from *The Times* remarking – "As long as actual sleep can be

Toscanini's protégé conducts Debussy

avoided, the hearer can derive great pleasure from the strange sounds that enter his ears if he will only put away all ideas of definite construction or logical development".

The piece is in three movements titled "From dawn to mid-day on the sea", "Play of the waves'"and "Dialogue of the wind and the sea" – at the first rehearsal, Eric Satie facetiously commented that he "particularly liked the bit around half-past ten". While the music is not as programmatic as anything by Strauss, it still conveys clear images of the sea through flickering, fragmentary themes and some of Debussy's finest orchestrations – notable among which is a section in the first movement when the sixteen cellos are divided into four groups of four.

◉ Philharmonia Orchestra; Cantelli (Testament SBT 10046; with *L'après-midi* and excerpts from *Le Martyre*).

This performance is the highlight of Guido Cantelli's famed "Debussy sessions", recorded in London with what was then one of the world's finest orchestras. Cantelli's worship of his mentor Toscanini is clear from the opening bars – every nuance and colour is achieved with startling immediacy, giving Debussy's instrumental textures a wonderful freshness and vitality. Overall, there is no finer introduction to Debussy than this disc.

JEUX

Debussy's last three orchestral works were all ballets. The first and finest of them, *Jeux* (Games), was composed in 1912 and premiered in 1913 by Diaghilev's Ballet Russes. Debussy based the work's construction upon a basic, undulating phrase which is then developed into a wild variety of musical gestures, vaguely corresponding to the strokes of a tennis game. Stravinsky hailed the work as a masterpiece, with the reservation that he found some of the ideas over-kind on the ear – though Stravinsky was probably alone in this reaction to a score which, in its emphasis on percussive orchestration, prefigures much of this century's avant-garde music.

◗ Orchestre de la Suisse Romande; Ansermet (Decca 433 711-2DM; with *Nocturnes* & *L'après-midi d'un faune*).

Ernst Ansermet became conductor of the Ballet Russes in 1915, two years after the first performance of *Jeux* and his recordings of Debussy's music have unique authority and insight. His elegant sense of line and his overall attention to the formal cohesion of *Jeux* is unrivalled; the Suisse Romande is a little unsure of itself at times, but plays with delicacy and wit.

STRING QUARTET

In the early 1880s Debussy was adopted by Tchaikovsky's patron Madame von Meck, for whom he wrote his rarely heard *Piano Trio* and the *Nocturne and Scherzo* for cello and piano. These early forays into chamber music are not particularly successful but by the time he got round to writing his *String Quartet* in 1893 he had achieved complete mastery of the medium. The first movement's opening theme provides the basic material for all four movements of a work in which rhythm prevails over harmonic and melodic considerations. This quality is particularly remarkable in the Scherzo, where the disruptive combination of plucking and bowing creates a confusion that forces you to concentrate on the textures rather than the linear form.

◉ Hagen Quartet (Deutsche Grammophon DG 437 836-2; with quartets by Ravel and Webern).

The Hagen Quartet recording of this wonderful work is beautifully judged – their playing of the opening movement is thrilling, while the Andante has a hallucinatory feel that has never been bettered in the studio.

VIOLIN SONATA

Written in the year the Great War finally ended, the *Violin Sonata* is a bleak, acerbic score except for its final movement – unable to finish the work to his satisfaction, Debussy tacked on a facile finale that isn't really worthy of the preceding movements. In common with a lot of European chamber music written at this time, the violin writing is indebted to gypsy folk music (or what was perceived as gypsy music), a connection that's unmistakeable in the sonata's assertive melodies.

⚫ Heifetz; Bay (RCA GD8787-1; with works by Ravel, Respighi and Martinů).

⚫ Mintz; Bronfman (Deutsche Grammophon DG 415 683-2GH; with sonatas by Franck and Ravel).

Jascha Heifetz's account, recorded in 1950, is a remarkably intense performance, though the unrelenting tension does bypass some of the gentler aspects of the piece. Unlike Heifetz, Mintz guides and entices the melodic lines out of their shells, so that one hears the music rather than the musician, but neither violinist has all the answers – try to hear both.

CHILDREN'S CORNER

Of all Debussy's piano compositions, the most transparent is the *Children's Corner* suite, written for his daughter in 1906. These are sprightly and good-humoured pieces, some of them satirical – such as *Doctor Gradus ad Parnassum*, a joke at the expense of Clementi's finger exercises (see p.98) – others brilliantly pictorial – such as the delicious *The snow is dancing*. Inspired by his daughter's governess, Debussy gave English titles to each of these six miniatures, but his English wasn't quite as perfect as his piano writing, which is how one piece came to be called *Jimbo's Lullaby* – Debussy meant it as a lullaby for a baby elephant.

⚫ Michelangeli (Deutsche Grammophon DG 415 372-2GH; with *Images*).

⚫ Michelangeli (Memories HR4368/9; 2 CDs; with Beethoven, *Piano Concerto No. 5 & Sonata No. 32*; Grieg *Piano Concerto*; Ravel, *Gaspard de la nuit*).

Arturo Benedetti Michelangeli has made two dazzling recordings of *Children's Corner*. The DG studio recording is a showcase for Michelangeli's astonishing control of tone and weight, drawing out nuances that scarcely any other pianist is equipped to discover. The live performance on Memories' two-CD set is a lighter, more ingenuous and child-like reading. In short, the DG version is perfect Michelangeli, whereas the other is perfect Debussy. The DG recording is coupled with

the best *Images* (see below); the live recording is coupled with great performances of the Emperor and Grieg concertos, and a sensational account of Ravel's *Gaspard de la nuit*.

IMAGES

Debussy's two sets of *Images* (1905 and 1907) are musical homages to pure sensation, conjuring the sound of bells through leaves, sunlight reflected from the scales of goldfish, and a multitude of other transient moments. The opening piece, *Reflets dans l'eau*, straight away establishes Debussy's unique understanding of the keyboard's potential, translating the rhythms of water into hypnotic, refreshing music that's as vividly pictorial as anything Liszt could have created. However, the *Images* require a degree of patience if you're coming to them from the incident-packed music of the nineteenth century, for their dynamic levels are generally very low, and the sense of silence, so mastered in *Pelléas*, is again a central feature of these aural landscapes. Whatever you do, don't reject them on first hearing – these miniatures are among the richest of all piano works.

⚫ Michelangeli (Deutsche Grammophon DG 415 372-2GH; with *Children's Corner*).

Michelangeli's performances of these works are astonishing, creating an ever-shifting and constantly fascinating world of sound. This is one of the greatest Debussy recordings ever made – buy it.

PRÉLUDES

Debussy's two books of *Préludes* (1910 and 1913) are the last of his descriptive piano works. Titles such as *La cathédrale engloutie* (The Drowned Cathedral) indicate an affinity with the allusive world of the *Images*, but others, such as *Feux d'artifice* (Fireworks) and *La danse de Puck*, are indicative of a more outgoing element to the *Préludes* – indeed several of the Préludes make use of popular musical influences, including Neapolitan songs and music-hall numbers. They might be slightly more accessible than the *Images* (though bear in mind that Debussy did not intend all 24 to be heard in one session), but if anything they are technically even more demanding – only the Études require more of the pianist.

● **Books 1 & 2**: Gieseking (EMI CDH7 61004-2).
● **Book 1**: Michelangeli (Deutsche Grammophon DG 413 450-2).
● **Book 2**: Michelangeli (Deutsche Grammophon DG 427 391-2).

Walter Gieseking's recording of the *Préludes*, made in 1953–54, late in the pianist's life, is a legendary set. The sound is not digital-pure, but this playing transcends any such considerations. For panache and range of colour, only one pianist could be said to match Gieseking in playing Debussy, and that's Arturo Benedetti Michelangeli. Some critics find Michelangeli a cold-hearted musician, preoccupied with the creation of wonderful sounds at the expense of musical depth, but his

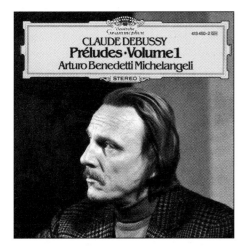

One of Benedetti Michelangeli's great Debussy recordings

epicurean style, with its infinite gradations of dynamics and timbre, is perfectly suited to Debussy. As the DG set is spread out over two CDs, your best bet is to go for Gieseking first, and if you like what you hear, add Michelangeli to your collection.

ÉTUDES

The *Études*, Debussy's last major works for piano, were written in 1915 yet they reflect nothing of his depression during the war years. Early in that year, Debussy had edited the complete piano works of Chopin and he duly dedicated his own two books of studies to the memory of his great precursor. Like Chopin's *Études*, these pieces explore different aspects of piano technique, but are far more than mere technical exercises – though extremely difficult, the twelve *Études* are among the most entertaining of all his piano works. The first book is the more traditional, experimenting with problems of overall dexterity, whereas the second is concerned with the very vocabulary of music, and displays some typically advanced harmonic and melodic ideas.

● Uchida (Philips 422 412-2PH).

Mitsuko Uchida is on top of even the most demanding studies, playing with a crispness, style and sophistication that mark her out as a brilliant Debussy pianist. On top of this, the recorded sound is one of the finest ever engineered.

LEO DELIBES

(1836–1891)

Friedrich Nietzsche said he liked Leo Delibes because he made "no pretensions to depth", which just about summarizes the accepted view of a composer whose music can seem to be made up entirely of the echoes of Meyerbeer, Gounod, Bizet and countless other French composers. He may have possessed no strong identity of his own, yet Delibes achieved considerable fame during his lifetime, and can be regarded as the father of the modern, symphonic ballet.

After having worked for some time as a chorister and later as a chorus master (assisting Gounod, Bizet and Berlioz), Delibes composed a string of enormously successful comic operas and operettas, most of which were written in the style of Offenbach. However, he was driven by a desire to compose for the ballet and in 1866 the success of *La source* (co-written with Louis Minkus) convinced him that his talents were indeed best suited to dance. In 1869 he composed his last operetta and the following year he completed his ballet *Coppélia*, which was a huge hit. Delibes pursued his métier with renewed enthusiasm, but he did not neglect the opera, and in 1883 (a year after the first performance of Wagner's *Parsifal*), *Lakmé* was first performed at the Opéra Comique. It too was an immense success, and his reputation has rested securely upon it – and *Coppélia* – ever since.

LAKMÉ

Lakmé is a particularly egregious example of European exoticism, set in mid-nineteenth-century India. An English lieutenant named Gerald is smitten by Lakmé, the daughter of a Brahmin priest, who eventually stabs Gerald upon discovering his identity. Lakmé tends Gerald's wounds in her forest hut, but he is unable to decide between his love for her and his responsibility to his regiment. Lakmé decides for him by eating a poisonous leaf.

Delibes' deliciously light melodic writing saves the day – the first act's beautiful *Flower Duet* for two sopranos is one of the best-known moments in opera, though that's largely due to the fact that British Airways used it as their theme tune for a while. Lakmé's show-stopping *Bell Song* is the opera's other high spot, but this is not just a virtuoso showpiece for soprano. The male lead role is well drawn and theatrically compulsive, and the music's oriental inflections are consistently entertaining, for all *Lakmé*'s conservatism.

Sutherland, Vanzo, Bacquier, Sinclair; Orchestre

National de l'Opéra de Monte Carlo; Bonynge (Decca 425 485-2; 2 CDs).

Bonynge's recording stars his wife, Joan Sutherland, as a technically superb heroine – none of the difficulties of the *Bell Song* pose any problems for her. She is admirably partnered by the sweet-toned tenor of Alain Vanzo, and the supporting cast is good too, with a delightful plummy English lady from Monica Sinclair.

COPPÉLIA

Coppélia prompted Tchaikovsky to remark that he preferred Delibes to Brahms. Admittedly, Tchaikovsky had a special love of ballet and a special hatred of Brahms ("that talentless bastard", as he once called him), but there can be little doubt that, together with Tchaikovsky's dance music, *Coppélia* is one of the seminal nineteenth-century works in this genre. Based upon E.T.A. Hoffmann's short story *The Sandman*, which concerns the toymaker Doctor Coppelius and his dancing doll (a story Offenbach used in his *Tales of Hoffmann*), the music is full of fine melodies, vivid characterization and brilliantly conceived dances. It is not a sophisticated score, but this is one of the few classical ballets that will bear close attention away from the stage.

Rotterdam Philharmonic Orchestra; Zinman (Philips 438 763-2; with Chopin, *Les Sylphides*; Gounod, *Faust ballet music*).

David Zinman conducts an excellent version of the complete ballet, with an alert and theatrical sounding Rotterdam Philharmonic. The fine sound, the generous fill-ups and the price all make this a number one choice.

FREDERICK DELIUS
(1862–1934)

Born in England to a German father, Fredrick Delius turned to composing while in Florida, then spent most of his working life in rural France. His music is similarly cosmopolitan and difficult to classify, but it was largely inspired by a mystical response to nature, whose beauty and imper-manence Delius evoked in rich, diaphanous orchestral textures, full of shifting chromatic harmonies. A late Romantic composer, he regarded his music as a means of expressing his spiritual values, which were largely an amalgam of the philosophy of Nietzsche and the pantheistic writings of Walt Whitman.

ROYAL COLLEGE OF MUSIC

In contrast to roistering years in Paris, Delius's life at Grez was deliberately reclusive, and it was here that he gradually developed his individual impressionistic style. His music gained its initial success in Germany, but its biggest following was in England (a country he claimed to loathe), principally through the advocacy of his greatest interpreter, Sir Thomas Beecham, who organized major Delius festivals in 1929 and 1946. The latter stage of his life, however, was marked by increasing ill-health, which eventually left him blind and paralysed – the result of syphilis contracted in his youth.

CHORAL MUSIC

The orchestral miniatures may be the most popular of Delius's compositions, but it is the orchestral songs for soloists and chorus that are his greatest achievement, and all of them combine, to varying degrees, a sense of the thrilling vitality of life with a sadness at its transience.

Sea Drift (1903–04), a setting of a Whitman poem, tells of a sea-bird that has lost its mate and waits faithfully, but in vain, for her return. The *Songs of Sunset* (1906–07) are even more melancholic, setting poems that are permeated by the evanescence of happiness and love. In both works there are no breaks in the music, and Delius employs an idiosyncratic and informal style of vocal writing – part recitative part arioso – that gives each work a sense of an unfolding awareness.

By contrast the *Mass of Life* (1904–05) is a rapturous celebration of the life force (though even here there are moments of despair), taken from Nietzsche's *Also Sprach Zarathustra* – also the inspiration for one of Richard Strauss's most popular works (see p.359). Zarathustra is Nietzsche's idea of the Superman, a man disdainful of weakness and conventional morality, and the *Mass of Life* is a fittingly huge and powerful work, full of sinewy and vigorous choral writing, and – especially in the night-time music – some remarkable orchestration. In scope and ambition it stands alongside Mahler's *Symphony No. 2* (see p.212) and Schoenberg's *Gurrelieder* (see p.310).

Delius was brought up in Bradford, the son of a prosperous wool-merchant who at first insisted that the boy join the family business. But it had no appeal for him, and in 1884 he left for Florida in order to run an orange plantation. It was here, on hearing the workers' songs wafting across the St John river, that he decided to become a composer. He took some lessons with a local organist named Thomas Ward, a course of instruction he later claimed taught him more than his eighteen months at the Leipzig Conservatorium between 1886 and 1888.

One thing he did gain from Leipzig was the friendship and support of Edvard Grieg, who persuaded Delius's father that Frederick's future was as a composer. Delius came to regard Norway as his spiritual home, and his Bohemian spell in Paris, in the early 1890s, was largely spent in the company of Scandinavian artists, including the painter Edvard Munch and the playwright August Strindberg. Paris was also where he met Jelka Rosen, a painter whom he later married. In 1897 the couple moved to the village of Grez-sur-Loing near the forest of Fointainebleau; it was to be their home for the rest of his life, with the exception of the war years, which were spent in England and Norway.

◉ **Sea Drift**: Hampson; Welsh National Opera Choir & Orchestra; Mackerras (Argo 430 206-2; with Florida Suite).

◑ **A Mass of Life; Songs of Sunset**: Harper, Watts, Tear, Luxon, Baker, Shirley-Quirk; Liverpool Philharmonic Choir & Orchestra, London Philharmonic Choir & Orchestra; Groves (EMI CMS 764 218-2; with An Arabesque; 2 CDs).

The strength of Mackerras's conducting is the way he controls his forces so that the sound emerges both lush and lucid. The orchestral introduction and opening chorus of *Sea Drift* convey a real sense of the immensity and beauty of the sea. Thomas Hampson is a controlled soloist, never forcing the emotion but allowing the clear words and expressive music to work their spell.

The set from Charles Groves begins with a wonderfully moving performance of the *Songs of Sunset*, in which both soloists are superior even to those on the classic Beecham compilation (reviewed below), bringing an unequalled intimacy and intensity to the words. The *Mass of Life* has been called a pagan oratorio, and Groves manages to whip up the right mood of frenzy and abandonment, especially in the blazing first chorus *O du mein Wille!* (O thou my Will!) and the opening of the second half *Herauf du grosser Mittag* (Arise, thou glorious noontide) – a splendidly Wagnerian chorus of ecstacy. Groves handles these moments brilliantly but he is also good when the excitement subsides and a more contemplative music prevails.

ORCHESTRAL MUSIC

Delius's most immediately accessible music is found in short orchestral pieces such as *Brigg Fair* (1907), *Summer Night on the River* (1911) and *On hearing the first Cuckoo in Spring* (1912) – works whose very titles evoke a benign, pastoralist image of nature. He is not a composer whose strength comes from melodic inventiveness (though he does have some good tunes) or from tightly structured forms; rather it is the orchestration and harmony that make his sound-world unique. Subtle combinations of instruments (including beautifully evocative woodwind writing), gently lilting rhythms, chromaticism that is hazy yet coherent – these are the things that create the overwhelming sense of tranquillity and spaciousness that colours so much of his orchestral work.

◉ **Beecham conducts Delius**: Royal Philharmonic Orchestra; Beecham (EMI CDS 747 5098; 2 CDs).

Delius's music is difficult to play really well, in such a way that the textures of the scoring are clearly heard. Throughout his life Beecham was the supreme interpreter of Delius, with an ability to bring his music to life like no-one else, and these recordings of the bulk of Delius's orchestral music are the legacy of his achievement. Despite their age (late 1950s – early 1960s), the sound is remarkably fresh and bright, with the conductor's attention to phrasing and the detailing of dynamics producing spectacular results – nowhere more hauntingly than in *Brigg Fair*, a work which in terms of sumptuousness and delicacy of colouring matches the best of Debussy or Ravel.

VIOLIN CONCERTO

Of the four concertos Delius wrote, for piano, violin, cello, and for violin and cello together, it is the *Violin Concerto* (1916) that is the most satisfying work. Though Delius was himself a talented violinist and the work was written for the brilliant English violinist Albert Sammons, it is markedly not a virtuosic showpiece. The solo part might often soar and glide rhapsodically over the orchestral texture, but it is always connected harmonically with the orchestral writing and seems to grow from out of it. The work is in one long movement divided into three clear sections, and abounds in moments of passionate spontaneity, sometimes dreamlike, sometimes fervent.

◉ Little; Welsh National Opera Orchestra; Mackerras (Argo 433 704-2; with *On hearing the First Cuckoo in Spring*, *Summer Night on the River*, *Dance Rhapsodies*).

Mackerras is an ideal Delius conductor, unerringly judging the music's shape and direction, while Tasmin Little is an inspired soloist, bringing to the work an ardour which is utterly compelling. Balance between soloist and orchestra is perfect, with the musical momentum seeming to pass effortlessly from one to the other.

JOSQUIN DESPREZ

(c.1440–1521)

Josquin Desprez (usually referred to simply as Josquin) dominated western Europe's musical landscape at the end of the fifteenth century in much the same way as Dufay had dominated it at the middle. Like Dufay he came from northern Europe, almost certainly from the Picardy region of France, but worked for much of his life in Italy where he established, if anything, an even greater reputation than Dufay. Contemporaries compared him to Michelangelo, and Luther memorably said of him "Josquin is master of the notes, which do what he wants, while other composers must do what the notes want." Polyphony came of age with Josquin: he consolidated the achievements of his great predecessors, Dufay and Ockeghem, turning their essentially linear style into something more harmonically complex and expressive. For the first time, real attention was paid to conveying the meaning of words, but it is the sheer beauty of the sound which is most striking. It was Josquin who established the pattern for Renaissance sacred music, creating rich vocal textures made up of long arching phrases, in which consistent imitation between the voices creates a sense both of unity and of progression.

Very little is known about Josquin's early years, but from 1459 he was in Milan, firstly as a singer at the cathedral, next at the Chapel of the Duke of Milan from 1473, then in the service of the duke's brother, Ascanio Sforza, after the duke was assassinated. When Ascanio became a cardinal in 1484, Josquin accompanied him to Rome, where he continued to serve him but also became a member of the Papal Choir in the new Sistine Chapel. In the early 1500s Josquin briefly returned to France and may have been connected to the court of Louis XII, but by the end of 1502 he had returned south, this time to the court of Duke Ercole of Ferrara. He had been recommended by one of the duke's talent scouts, although another scout had suggested a different composer, Isaac, on the grounds that Josquin was irascible, composed when he wanted to, and charged too much. The duke chose Josquin and was rewarded with a Mass setting based on his name. When the plague hit Ferrara a year later, Josquin sensibly left the court and returned north (his successor, Obrecht, died of the plague in 1505), where he became provost of the collegiate church of Notre Dame at Condé-sur-l'Escaut, a position he held until his death.

SACRED MUSIC

Though Josquin wrote a substantial amount of courtly songs, it is as a composer of motets and Masses that he exerted the widest influence. In much of Josquin's sacred music the technique of imitation, whereby one voice repeats part or more of what another voice has just sung, becomes increasingly apparent. Another device which he exploits is that of suspension, in which a note in one voice is held while the other voices move onto a new chord – the resulting discord sets up a tension which is only resolved when the held note moves on to the correct note. Josquin also makes plentiful use of the old technique of basing music on an already existing tune, called the cantus firmus: he based his Mass *"Ave Maris Stella"* (Hail Star of the Sea) on a plainsong hymn to the Virgin, and wrote Masses that employ a secular cantus firmus, two of them using the popular song *L'homme armé* (The armed man).

⦿ **Missa "Ave Maris Stella", Motets and Chansons**: Taverner Consort and Choir; Parrott (EMI CDC 7 54659 2).
⦿ **L'homme armé Masses**: The Tallis Scholars; Phillips (Gimell CDGIM 019).

The Taverner Consort's CD is a well-balanced and generous disc, including six chansons and three motets as well as the "Ave Maris Stella" Mass. The all-male Taverner choir (nuns were the only women allowed to sing sacred music at this time) might not have such a homogenous and pure style as some of their early music rivals but their feel for the flexibility of the vocal lines is outstanding. The disc's highlight is the vigorous and joyful motet *Gaude Virgo* (Rejoice Virgin), here given a bright and energetic performance.

Though probably written around the same time, the two *L'homme armé* Masses sound very different: the first has a medieval feel, possibly due to the four voices' overlapping in pitch, while the later work spreads the voices wider, creating a more spacious feel. As well as using women to sing the highest part, the Tallis Scholars adopt a different approach to the Taverner Consort, bringing out the long seamless lines of the music and stressing its serenity, despite its frequent rhythmic adventurousness. The clarity of the singing makes the rich and elaborate canonical writing in the *Agnus Dei* particularly memorable. The disc includes the anonymous chanson on which both works are based.

GAETANO DONIZETTI
(1797–1848)

It is hard to understand how two adjacent European countries could produce such disparate musical styles as did nineteenth-century Italy and Austria. Gaetano Donizetti and Franz Schubert were born in 1797, the former in Bergamo, the latter in Vienna, and yet there have surely never been two less similar neighbours. Whereas Schubert's music trawled the deepest recesses of the mind, Donizetti's exhibitionistic operas required no-one to think too deeply. "Music for the Italians", noted Berlioz, "is a sensual pleasure and nothing more. For this noble expression of the mind they have hardly more respect than for the art of cooking. They want a score that,

like a plate of macaroni, can be assimilated immediately without having to think about it." And yet, though it's true that Donizetti's crowd-pleasers won't bear examination by the rigorous standards of contemporaries such as Beethoven, Schubert, Schumann or Chopin, he nonetheless had a genuine artistic vision. Like Bellini – the other master of bel canto opera – he wanted to bring music and drama into a "closer, more direct conjunction", to quote the composer himself.

In all, he wrote some seventy-three operas, and the majority of them are populated either with historical personalities (eg *Lucrezia Borgia*, *Anna Bolena* and *Maria Stuarda*) or with characters lifted from writers such as Schiller, Hugo and Walter Scott. It was the last of this trio who provided him with the material for his finest opera, *Lucia di Lammermoor* (1835), a daring attempt to reconcile his post-Rossinian devotion to exquisite vocal line with the need for real character development. Like Bellini and Rossini before him, Donizetti was more than happy to accommodate the bravura talents of his star singers (many of whom had worked closely with Bellini), but his career showed an increasing willingness to subordinate display to the needs of the drama. His move away from the strict framework of "aria-recitative-chorus" was gradual, but by the end of his life he was writing through-form operas, in which the action remained constant without interruptions for set-piece singing.

Donizetti undoubtedly wrote too much too quickly, but it should be remembered that the conditions in which he worked were hardly conducive to the creation of profound or

HULTON DEUTSCH

sophisticated art. To get further work, the opera composer had to complete his current commission quickly, and when confronted by an impatient, fee-paying impresario, Germanic concepts of self-expression mattered for nothing. For all his "commercialism", Donizetti is, with Bellini, nineteenth-century Italy's most important composer of opera before Verdi, a composer who wrote pastiche Donizetti for his first twenty years – then paid his precursor the compliment of stealing one of his tunes for the Grand Chorus of *Aïda*.

L'ELISIR D'AMORE

In 1832, Donizetti completed his first great comic opera, *L'Elisir d'amore* (The Elixir of Love), a tongue-in-cheek re-interpretation of the Tristan and Isolde myth. A "love potion" is bought from a quack doctor by Nemorino, in the hope of winning the love of Adina. She chooses to marry another man but, before doing so, is forced to realize that she loves Nemorino after all, and they finally marry. The quack then does a roaring trade.

L'Elisir d'amore is a great sentimental-pastoral comedy, and it features some of the composer's finest music, with Nemorino's second-act *Una furtiva lagrima* standing out as one of the most affecting bel canto tenor arias ever written. Adina, the soprano lead, has plenty of beautiful writing, including a first-act duet with Nemorino and a solo in the second act, *Prendi, prendi per me sei libero*.

⊙ Sutherland, Pavarotti, Cossa, Mala, Casula; Ambrosian Singers; English Chamber Orchestra; Bonynge (Decca 414 461-2DH2; 2 CDs).

Luciano Pavarotti's early recording with Joan Sutherland and Dominic Cossa, conducted by Bonynge, is the most rewarding of the many versions in the current catalogue. (The best *Elisir* of all, Carlo Bergonzi's live 1967 version, is not available at the moment.) Pavarotti's voice might not quite catch Nemorino's naïve innocence, but he and Sutherland establish a genuine relationship, and Cossa is endearingly convincing as the roguish charlatan Dulcamara.

LUCIA DI LAMMERMOOR

Sir Walter Scott's *The Bride of Lammermoor* afforded Donizetti with a perfect vehicle for intensely emotional writing. Basically, the tale recounts the long-standing feud between the families of Lammermoor and Ravenswood and the love between Lucia and Edgardo – Lucia being the sister of the head of Lammermoor and Edgardo the head of Ravenswood. Lucia dies after killing her enforced husband-to-be and, upon seeing her coffin carried towards burial, Edgardo kills himself in desperation.

The superb characterizations of *Lucia di Lammermoor* and its string of glorious melodies – at once fresh and sentimental – make this his most successful opera, and it received frequent productions when bel canto enjoyed a vogue back in the 1950s. The archetypal Romantic Italian opera, *Lucia* is renowned for the extraordinary soprano pyrotechnics of the "Mad Scene" in Act Three, but it contains some magnificent tenor passages as well – in fact, the male role attracted more attention from Donizetti's first audiences.

⊙ Moffo, Bergonzi, Sereni, Flagello, Vozza, Duval, Pandano; RCA Italian Opera Orchestra & Choir; Prêtre (RCA GD86504; 2 CDs).

The cascading difficulty of Lucia's vocal writing demands fabulous singers and there have been none finer in the two lead roles than Carlo Bergonzi and Anna Moffo. Bergonzi may not have had the ringing "top" of Pavarotti, but his beautiful phrasing is unparalleled, while Moffo's bright, thrilling and absolutely steady voice is perfect for the contrary aspects to Lucia's character. Prêtre's exciting direction serves this amazing partnership well.

LA FILLE DU RÉGIMENT

One of Donizetti's most light-hearted operas, *La Fille du régiment* (1840) was also one of his most successful, receiving forty-four performances in its first year in Paris. A tale of love triumphant against the odds, it is famous for two episodes, one for the soprano lead, the other for the tenor. The former, Marie's *Song of the Regiment*, is full of flowing ideas that will stick in your mind for days after you first hear it. However, it is her suitor Tonio's *Ah mes amis* that is the show-stopping tour de force, requiring the tenor to sing for upwards of five minutes before a terrifically demanding sequence of nine consecutive high Cs. Few singers have been able to manage such acrobatics, which is why this greatly enjoyable opera rarely reaches the stage.

◉ Sutherland, Pavarotti, Sinclair, Bruyere, Mala, Garrett, Coates, Jones; Royal Opera House Orchestra & Chorus Bonynge (Decca 414 520-2DH2; 2 CDs).

In the 1960s, when this record was made, Luciano Pavarotti was unrivalled in bel canto roles, and it was his New York Met appearance as Tonio that made him a superstar. This is a really remarkable performance, powerful, accurate and bursting with character. Joan Sutherland is extremely fine if a bit precious, and Richard Bonynge binds the whole together with his brisk and enthusiastic accompaniment.

DON PASQUALE

In *Don Pasquale* (1843), his late comic masterpiece, Donizetti plundered the classical heritage of Mozart to create a sort of operatic *commedia dell'arte*. Centering on an old man's attempt to find himself a young wife, the opera is remarkable for its free-flowing conversational recitative and the lightness of its orchestration and vocal writing. The small cast, headed by nineteenth-century opera's most perfect soubrette role, make *Don Pasquale* ideally suited to small opera houses, yet it's infrequently performed, perhaps because it doesn't deliver the heart-stopping vocal tricks that people have come to expect from Italian opera. Fortunately, it works extremely well on record, where the quality of its tightly written libretto come to the fore.

◗ Corena, Sciutti, Oncina, Krause, Mercuriali; Vienna State Opera Orchestra & Chorus; Kertesz (Decca 433 036 2DM2; 2 CDs).

The Piccola Scala staged a famous prodution of Don Pasquale in 1959, almost exclusively for the talents of Graziella Sciutti, who was by then one of the world's greatest soubrettes. Decca recorded her in the role of Norina not long after and her perfomance sets the mark against which all others have to be measured – her voice is light, brilliantly flexible and shimmering with personality. Similarly outstanding are Fernando Corena and Tom Krause as the gullible Don and the scheming Doctor Malatesta. István Kertesz, in one of his few operatic recordings, strongly suggests he should have made more.

JOHN DOWLAND
(1563–1626)

The lute was the most popular solo instrument in Europe at the end of the sixteenth century and John Dowland was one of its most skilful practitioners. Nevertheless he repeatedly failed to gain the position he so coveted at the English court, a failure he felt strongly in spite of his highly successful career abroad. Perhaps his Catholicism, to which he had converted while resident in France in the 1580s, had hindered him. At any rate he gave up the faith in 1597 prior to returning briefly to England from Italy where, as an itinerant performer, he had fallen in with a group of disaffected English Catholics whose treasonable plans had considerably alarmed him. The following year he obtained an extremely lucrative position as lutenist to King Christian IV of Denmark, remaining there until 1606 but making several lengthy trips to London to visit his wife and son – and, almost certainly, to apply again for a post at the English court. Ironically, when he was finally appointed as one of the King's lutenists in 1612, his inspiration – at least as a composer – seems to have deserted him.

Dowland was greatly admired in his lifetime by fellow-musicians as well as by writers: the poet Richard Barnfield, in his sonnet in *Praise of Music and Poetry* wrote that his "heavenly touch upon the lute doth ravish human sense". Yet despite this esteem he appears to have been a profoundly discontented and melancholic man, a fact reflected in his music, which dwells almost obsessively on sadness and death.

THE MUSIC

Apart from his lute music, which displays a contrapuntal sophistication far in excess of most of his contemporaries, Dowland also wrote for viols and, perhaps most inventively of all, for the human voice. His most famous work is a collection of pieces for viol consort and lute entitled *Lachrimae, or Seaven Teares figured in Seaven Passionate Pavans*, a series of subtle variants on a slow and sombre melody that had previously existed as both a lute solo and as a song titled *Flow My Tears*. This song had originally appeared in 1600 in the second of the four books of songs that Dowland published, most of which consistently display his customary melancholy. His greatness as a song-writer lies in his ability to match exactly the music to the feeling of the words, a preoccupation that places him closer to his Italian contemporaries, like Monteverdi, than to his English ones.

> ◉ **Lachrimae**: Hesperion XX (Astree E 8701).
> ◉ **The First Booke of Songs**: Muller; Wilson (ASV CD GAU 135).

The seven pavans of *Lachrimae* are effectively a set of subtle variations on the first one, with the opening motif of a falling fourth recurring throughout the sequence. There is no getting away from the fact that these are profoundly gloomy pieces, but Hesperion XX combat the prevailing darkness by alternating each pavan with a contrasting galiard, rather than playing these more sprightly pieces at the end, as printed by Dowland. They also employ a warm tone and expressive dynamics which considerably enliven the music, even though their speeds are markedly slower than most rival recordings. Purists have criticized their approach, but the result is the most compelling account of this music currently available.

The First Booke of Songs, the least morose of Dowland's song compilations, has a simplicity and a directness which is well served by Rufus Muller's clear and firm-toned voice. The meaning of the sometimes complex texts is on the whole nicely conveyed, although he sometimes succumbs to the precious English habit of over-enunciating consonants at the beginning of words. He is at his best in the slower more introsective songs like *Go Crystal Tears* or *Come, Heavy Sleep*, where he allows himself a greater degree of expressiveness and a more intimate tone quality.

GUILLAUME DUFAY

(c.1400–1474)

Guillaume Dufay is one of an outstanding group of Franco-Flemish composers that emerged from the Dukedom of Burgundy, the most opulent and artistically fertile of the courts of fifteenth-century northern Europe. Dufay was connected to the Burgundian court but never formally attached to it, instead spending much of his working life in Italy, where his reputation grew so high that he was described by Piero de' Medici as "the greatest ornament of our age". Like Machaut, Dufay was a priest and he received a substantial part of his income from largely honorary church appointments, but unlike Machaut much of his music was written for the church. He is a seminal figure in the field of sacred music, helping to establish the Mass as a coherent and unified whole, a development that made it the principal vehicle of elaborate polyphony for the next century and a half.

Dufay was born in or near Cambrai, an important centre of religious music, and he began his career there in 1409 as a chorister at the cathedral. While still a young man he went to Italy to work for the Malatesta family at Pésaro before joining the Papal Chapel in 1428. Apart from two years as maestro di cappella to the Duke of Savoy, he remained a member of the papal choir until 1437, based firstly at Rome, then at Bologna and Florence. It was at Florence that he composed a motet, *Nuper Rosarum Flores*, for the consecration of the cathedral after the completion of Brunelleschi's stupendous dome – basing the form of the motet on the mathematical proportions of the cathedral. From 1440 until his death he was back at Cambrai, apart from one more spell with the Duke of Savoy between 1452 and 1458.

SACRED MUSIC

Polyphonic music – which in Dufay's time was reserved for occasions of great importance – was transformed by Dufay into a clearer, richer and more sonorous musical language, with harmonies and carefully placed dissonances that gave the music a feeling of forward progress. In his later Masses, his finest works, he employs the cantus firmus method, in which the musical material is built around an already existing melody, usually a section of plainchant. One of the best of these late Masses is the *Missa Ecce Ancilla Domine* (Behold the handmaid of the Lord), its name taken from the plainsong chant that forms its cantus firmus. It is written for four voices but at least half the Mass, as a means of contrast, uses just two voices in different combinations. It's a remarkably powerful and attractive piece, in which slow, reverent passages are balanced by more rhythmically lively sections in the two-part writing.

⊙ Missa Ecce Ancilla Domini: Ensemble Gilles Binchois; Vellard (Virgin VC 545 050-2).

The Ensemble Binchois is one of the most exciting early-music groups around, with a wonderfully unforced style. In keeping with increasingly common practice, the *Missa Ecce Ancilla Domine* is here placed within a liturgical context which includes the various chants and hymns appropriate to the service for which it was written (the Feast of the Annunciation), thus helping to create a sense of occasion. The voices, which are all male, have a warmth and a suppleness which brings out the zest of the music without recourse to overt expressiveness. This is a performance which, though solemn, still feels like a celebration.

SECULAR MUSIC

Dufay wrote many secular songs (or *chansons*), and although he rarely set words as refined as Machaut's they mostly deal with the same theme of unrequited courtly love. Most of the songs are *rondeaux*, with sections of words and music recurring throughout, and many of them are polyphonic, employing three and sometimes four voices. Although he composed *chansons* throughout his career there is no obviously discernible change of style between the early and the late songs. All are characterized by a refined and lyrical quality, with memorable melodies that are often tinged with a hint of melancholy.

⊙ Dufay and Binchois: Ballades, Rondeaus, Lamentation: Ensemble Gilles Binchois; Vellard (Harmonic Records H/CD 8719).

Eleven of the eighteen works on this disc are by Dufay – the rest are by Binchois, a colleague of Dufay's and his equal as a songwriter. Vellard adopts a flexible approach: some songs are performed by voices, some by instruments, and some by both. As in their recording of *Missa Ecce Ancilla Domine* there is a delightful lightness and purity to the singing of the Ensemble Gilles Binchois, with the plaintive tones of Brigitte Lesne making an outstanding contribution. The disc's one drawback is that though the sleeve-notes tell you what microphones were used, they don't provide translations of any of the songs.

ANTONIN DVOŘÁK
(1841–1904)

With the tide of revolutions that swept across the continent during the 1840s, nationalism became a dominating factor in European art. Nowhere was this process more important than in Czechoslovakia, and no composer was more prominently nationalistic than Antonin Dvořák. Of the three great Czech composers – Smetana (see p.343) and Janáček (see p.182) are the others – Dvořák was the one whose influence upon the development of a national voice was the most original and lasting, and it was Dvořák who was most successful in recon-

ciling folk traditions with symphonic music. Few composers of his time could match his flair for infectious melody or his ability to orchestrate with kaleidoscopic colour and nuance.

Born in Bohemia, Dvořák spent his uneventful early life in study and practice, then in 1863 played in a concert of Wagner excerpts, conducted by the composer himself – an experience that had a significant impact on his approach to opera. From 1864 he played viola in the Prague National Theatre Orchestra, where from 1866 the chief

MARY EVANS PICTURE LIBRARY

ship of the National Conservatory of Music in New York, with an annual salary of $15,000. In October 1892, after a five-month farewell tour of Bohemia and Moravia, Dvořák finally moved to the US, where he remained for three years. This period was not especially happy but it was very fruitful, as Dvořák's discovery of America's folk heritage combined with his aching homesickness to produce a string of masterpieces, including the violin concerto and the *New World Symphony*.

In 1895 he returned to teach at the Prague conservatory, becoming its director in 1901 – the year of his sixtieth birthday, which was celebrated in Prague by performances of his work. His final years were extremely contented, and most of his time was spent working on tone poems and operas. Unfortunately, though Dvořák produced a total of ten operas, only one of them, *Rusalka*, has achieved any popularity, and that's largely down to one extremely famous soprano aria (*O Silver Moon*). His reputation continues to rest primarily on his orchestral music.

conductor was Smetana, the fountainhead of Czech musical nationalism. In 1873 Dvořák left the orchestra to devote himself to composition, and within a year his *Symphony No. 3* had won him an Austrian national prize as well as the respect of Brahms, who was on the jury. Two years later, Dvořák's *Moravian Duets* brought him the same prize, and again Brahms was delighted by the young man's progress, going so far as to recommend his music to a publisher.

With the appearance of such distinctively Czech works as the *Slavonic Rhapsodies* (1878) Dvořák was soon gaining ever widening recognition: Brahms's friend Joachim commissioned a violin concerto from him (but had to wait years for it); Richter, Elgar's friend, commissioned a symphony; while von Bülow, Wagner's friend, promoted Dvořák's work through concerts and tours. Numerous trips to England, where he was championed for his conducting as much as his composition, extended his fame, brought him money and produced several of his greatest works, including the *Symphony No. 7*.

Dvořák's success reached one of its peaks in 1891, when he was appointed professor of composition at the Prague conservatory, awarded an honorary doctorate by Cambridge University and invited to take up the director-

ORCHESTRAL MUSIC

Admiration for the music of Beethoven and Schubert was what first led Dvořák to consider writing symphonic music, and his early symphonies (the first, *Bells of Zlonice*, was completed in 1865) betray these Viennese influences quite strongly, as well as the influence of Brahms. It was not until his wholehearted commitment to Czech nationalism in the mid-1870s that Dvořák's voice began to be heard properly, and though there's a strong Czech element to his fourth symphony (1874), the sequence improves markedly with *Symphony No. 6*. Even stronger expressions of nationalist feeling are to be found in Dvořák's late symphonic poems, a genre in which he could transform the material of Czech folklore freed from the constrictions of classical form.

SYMPHONY NO. 6

The marvellous *Symphony No. 6* (1880) owes much to Brahms's second symphony, which is also in D major and in places displays somewhat over-weighted orchestration, but at the same time it's unmistakeably a Dvořák symphony. Typical of Dvořák's mature style are the frequent, quasi-romantic key modulations within the determinedly classical structure, and the use of the Scherzo for fervently nationalist sentiments. This movement, a *Furiant* (a Czech dance), was the first to establish him as a Slavonic composer, and it clearly distanced him from the plethora of German symphonists (most now forgotten) who were then jostling for attention.

⊙ Dohnányi; Cleveland Orchestra (Decca 430 204-2).

The recording of the sixth stands out as the finest of Dohnányi's cycle of Dvořák's later symphonies. In general tempi are slow, but Dohnányi establishes an enthralling sense of momentum and prevents the music from appearing cumbersome.

SYMPHONY NO. 7

A stark contrast to the well-being of the sixth symphony, the *Symphony No. 7* is overshadowed by intimations of tragedy, and in this respect, as in its sense of retrospection, it is not unlike Brahms's third symphony, of which Dvořák was almost certainly aware – they were written in the same year (1885), and it is surely no accident that this symphony is in the bleak relative minor key to the F major of Brahms's third. The Scherzo and finale contain some of Dvořák's most remarkable musical ideas, and their combination of rhythmic vitality and free-form melody make these movements two of the finest of the late nineteenth century. The emotional gravity of this mighty work gives this symphony a claim to be Dvořák's greatest.

⊙ Scottish National Orchestra; Järvi (Chandos CHAN 8501; with *Golden Spinning Wheel*).

Neeme Järvi's recording of the seventh is the best of his complete cycle, keen and energetic, with a good sense of scale and revealing attention to detail. The orchestra play with real enthusiasm, and the fill-up performance of one of the late symphonic poems is excellent. There is a better seventh in the catalogue – the Kubelik version – but that's available only as part of a complete symphony set.

SYMPHONY NO. 8

Dvořák's *Symphony No. 8* (1889) again stands in complete contrast to the preceding symphony. In many ways it harks back to the exuberant cheerfulness and Czech feeling of *No. 6*, and only in the first movement's introduction is there any sign of the seventh's sobriety. Although the main theme from this opening is repeated later in the movement, the bulk of it is dominated by one of Dvořák's most inspired melodies. The Adagio, almost a tone poem of bird-song and country life, is similarly melodic, while the third movement is a rustic dance of infectious good humour. The finale is a set of variations (rare for Dvořák) that builds towards a rousing and suitably conclusive climax.

⊙ Kubelik; Berlin Philharmonic (Deutsche Grammophon DG 429 518-2; with *Carnaval Overture* & *The Wood Dove*).

Kubelik's is an intense and exciting account, but it's let down slightly by the Berlin Philharmonic, who were hardly suited to music that requires as much flexibility as tonal richness and instrumental cohesion. A less regimented band would have better suited Kubelik's balletic direction but he nonetheless extracts a performance of engaging warmth and enthusiasm.

SYMPHONY NO. 9

The best-known tune in all Dvořák is the main theme from the third movement of the *Symphony No. 9* (1893), a mournfully nostalgic piece of music that has been appropriated by countless TV producers and advertising types – it was the music from the old Hovis ads, with the cloth-capped little lad pushing his bike up the cobblestoned road past the coal pits. The symphony was intended to celebrate the fourth centennial of Columbus's "discovery" of America, and its title, *From the New World*, might lead you to expect a more upbeat tone. Dvořák wrote of it that "the influence of America can be felt by anyone who has a nose", but the symphony's American-influenced rhythmic patterns and tunes are turned into an expression of acute homesickness and thus of Czech identity – similar to his *American Quartet* (see below). The music is tirelessly melodic and brilliantly scored for a large orchestra, but be warned that it is very long and in the wrong hands can become tedious.

⊙ Berlin Philharmonic Orchestra; Kubelik (Deutsche Grammophon DG 427 202-2GR; with *Scherzo Capriccioso*).

◗ Vienna Philharmonic Orchestra; Kondrashin (Decca 430 702-2; with *American Suite*).

For all its pathos, the *New World Symphony* is not a sentimental piece, but most conductors choose to make it one, and good performances are rare indeed. Kubelik's dry-eyed Berlin recording is a reliable, quick and tightly executed account that spurns cheap effects in favour of hard-etched feeling. There is also something special about Kondrashin's performance, an early digital CD with demonstration-standard sound; it's coupled with the composer's rather less inspired *American Suite*.

THE SYMPHONIC POEMS

Dvořák's four symphonic poems – *The Water Goblin*, *The Noonday Witch*, *The Golden Spinning Wheel* and *The Wild Dove* – were written in 1896, and were based upon some gruesome folk ballads by the nationalist writer Erben. Following the examples of Liszt, Smetana and Richard Strauss, Dvořák here uses a single theme for each central character and transforms it as the situation demands, thereby creating musical continuity while projecting a sense of narrative development. If he is less successful than Strauss, it is because he follows the very specific source material too closely but, despite this, Dvořák's masterly orchestration brings considerable life and colour to these Grimm-like creations.

◗ Bavarian Radio Symphony Orchestra; Kubelik (DG 435 074-2; with overtures; 2 CDs).

Again, Kubelik is highly sympathetic to Dvořák's fruity orchestral style and he allows the music to follow its natural course without straining to score interpretive points. He brings entertaining flair to these pieces, and the Bavarian Radio Symphony Orchestra respond with perfect spontaneity.

CONCERTOS

Dvořák wrote four concertos, but the piano concerto is a Beethoven-ish hybrid that never really gets off the ground, while the first of the two cello concertos is a fairly insubstantial work which was only discovered seventy years ago in sketch form, and needed to be orchestrated by a third party. The latter is of interest chiefly as a preparation for the second cello concerto, a piece that ranks alongside the majestic concerto for violin.

CELLO CONCERTO NO. 2

The second cello concerto, the last major composition that Dvořák composed during his stay in America, has become one of the most popular of all his works and perhaps the most popular concerto ever written for the instrument. Dvořák was asked to write the piece by a friend of Wagner, the cellist Hanus Wihan, who gave the first performance of Strauss's cello sonata as well as this concerto. The music that Dvořák composed is richly inventive, full of deep feeling (the final movement was revised after the death of his wife), and perfectly fitted to the cello – Dvořák's experience as an orchestral player enabled him to appreciate the problems of balance and blending that arise when orchestrating for a solo instrument with such a low tonal register. Dvořák's understanding of orchestral sonority and of the cello's distinct textural qualities make this grand and emotionally intense piece one of his finest achievements.

● Rostropovich; Berlin Philharmonic Orchestra; Karajan (Deutsche Grammophon DG 413 819-2; with Tchaikovsky, *Rococo Variations*).

Modern orchestras tend to distort the concerto's intricately studied proportions, but Karajan was aware of this potential for imbalance and he controls the Berlin Philharmonic with uncommon clarity. Of Rostropovich's many recordings of this score this one, made in 1969, is the best, bursting with energy and fresh ideas. It's coupled with a beautifully paced account of Tchaikovsky's *Rococo Variations*.

VIOLIN CONCERTO

Like Brahms's concerto, the *Violin Concerto* was dedicated to and written with the help of Joachim, but unlike the Brahms this is an under-explored work. Certainly it has its weaknesses. The first movement is a truncated affair that finishes before all its thematic ideas have been fully explored, and the finale is an annoyingly irregular movement that never quite grips your attention. The reason for hearing this work is its slow movement, which contains some of Dvořák's most haunting melodies. The central theme, when repeated near the movement's end by the full orchestra, is one of the finest creations in the concerto repertoire.

● Mintz; Berlin Philharmonic Orchestra; Levine
(Deutsche Grammophon 419 618-2GH; with Sibelius,
Violin Concerto).

Shlomo Mintz's characterful and intensely beautiful sound wins
the day in the face of Levine's excessively prominent accompaniment. This is a profoundly lyrical performance that makes
much of the sweeping central movement.

CHAMBER MUSIC

Dvořák composed a large amount of chamber
music, which is hardly surprising for a viola
player who greatly admired the chamber work
of the classical masters. His Op. 1 and Op. 2
were both for string quartet, an ensemble for
which he wrote some fourteen of his forty
chamber pieces, one of which – the *String
Quartet No. 12.* – is one of three masterpieces
in this broad category. Like the other two
outstanding works, the *Piano Trio No. 3* and
the *String Quintet No. 2*, this quartet
resembles Brahms's music in its contrapuntal
weight, but his style is invariably lighter,
more sweetly melodic and more freely
inventive.

PIANO TRIO NO. 3

The third piano trio (1883) is perhaps
Dvořák's greatest chamber composition,
containing almost every distinctive feature of
Dvořák's music within its four movements.
Characterized by an unprecedented seriousness of purpose, it marked a decisive step
forward in his career and foreshadowed the
epic expression of the seventh symphony,
which came two years later. The Allegretto
grazioso contains music of haunting pathos
but this tendency towards sadness is
restrained by some entrancing, disruptive
cross-rhythms.

● Suk Piano Trio (Denon CO1410; with *Piano Trio No. 4*).

This is wonderful, incisive playing that drives the music on without excessive aggression. Especially in the Allegretto, the trio

achieve a balance that accentuates the novelty of Dvořák's light
textures. The coupling contains one of the composer's most
beautiful Adagios – all in all, this recording is a gem.

STRING QUARTET NO. 12

Subtitled the "American", the *String Quartet
No. 12* was the first of three chamber works
composed in 1893 while Dvořák was living in
the US, and it was soon established as his
best-loved quartet. Although its opening was
modelled on the introduction to Smetana's
Quartet No. 1, there is little of Smetana's raw
misery here – frustrated energy and nostalgia
are the prevailing moods, the latter element
typified by the Lento, with its plaintive, soaring violin melody.

● Hagen Quartet (Deutsche Grammophon DG 419 601-
2; with *Cypresses & Kodály, String Quartet No. 2*)

The intonation, style and recorded sound of the Hagen
Quartet are faultless, and it's greatly to their credit that they
refuse to sentimentalize Dvořák's music. As a bonus, the quartet is coupled with elegant performances of Dvořák's lovely
transcriptions of his bittersweet songs, *Cypresses*.

STRING QUINTET NO. 2

The second of the three chamber works
composed in America, Dvořák's second
quintet is scored for unconventional forces –
string quartet plus double bass. The music is
disarmingly original as well, merging Czech
and North American Indian melodies, and, in
the Larghetto, following Haydn's example of
composing a set of variations with a double
theme. It's full of incredibly difficult music,
but Dvořák's propensity for instrumental
colour and independence makes this one of
the most entertaining of all quintets.

◗ Serenata of London (Collins COLL 3007-2; with
Britten, *Simple Symphony*; Strauss, *Till Eulenspiegl*).

This CD contains some remarkable, spontaneous playing –
the Serenata really do seem to be enjoying the melodies and
rhythmic elan of the *Quintet*. The sound might be a little too
close, but it does highlight the vibrant textures of the music.

HANNS EISLER

(1898–1962)

The reason that Hanns Eisler remains confined to the ranks of cult musicians is political – he was one of the few decent composers who took readily to the new political system in post-war East Germany, and his loyalty to that discredited regime is unlikely to make record companies rush to his aid. Though a convinced communist, Eisler was not a socialist-realist hack. He was a pupil of Arnold Schoenberg in the early 1920s, then felt that he had to break with a teacher whose ideals were irreconcilable with Eisler's desire to make serious music a part of the daily lives of ordinary people. This mission to create radically politicized art led him from Vienna to Berlin and into collaboration with Bertolt Brecht, and then into problems with the Nazis – a sequence of events similar to the career of Kurt Weill (see p.415). Like so many of his generation, he eventually fled to the United States, where he worked for the film studios (he wrote the score for Fritz Lang's *Hangmen Also Die*) and renewed his partnership with Brecht. In 1947 he fell victim to the McCarthy witch-hunts and appeared before the infamous Un-American Activities committee. Despite the intercession of a group of intellectuals including Einstein and Thomas Mann, in 1950 Eisler was deported to East Germany, where he spent the rest of his life.

THE MUSIC

Eisler wrote little music specifically for the concert hall – he wanted his music to have a social function, and thus devoted much of his energy to composing strongly political songs, many of them to texts by Bertolt Brecht. Like Weill's songs, these pieces often skirt the boundaries of jazz and classical music, and are good enough to survive separation from their theatre or cabaret context, even if the lyrics sometimes show their age. The best of the songs date from the years in the USA, where Brecht supplied him with lyrics that are intensely committed without lapsing into propaganda. Eisler's instrumental music may have to wait a while longer for rehabilitation; only a small portion of his output has been recorded, but it shows Eisler to have been at the very least a highly competent composer of orchestral scores.

⦿ **Songs**: Fischer-Dieskau; Reimann (Teldec 2292 43676-2).
⦿ **Tank Battles – The Songs of Hanns Eisler**: Krause (Antilles ANCD 8739).
⦿ **Kammersinfonie; Kleine Sinfonie; Orchesterstücke; Ouvertüre zu einem Lustspiel**; Magdeburg Philharmonic Orchestra; Husmann (CPO 999 071-2).

Dietrich Fischer-Dieskau's recording is the most comprehensive survey of Eisler's songs, though at times he's too well-bred to catch the edge of this music. Hamburg-born Dagmar Krause, who began her singing career in the nightclubs of the notorious Reeperbahn, gives a sassier account, and is particularly strong on more militant pieces like *Ballad of the Sackslingers* and *Song of the Whitewash*.

Mathias Husmann's selection of Eisler's orchestral music is well played and excellently recorded. The *Kleine Sinfonie* (Small Symphony), shows Eisler's mastery of twelve-tone technique, while *Kammersinfonie* (Chamber Symphony) is a fascinating experiment in cinematic-symphonic writing, including musical pictures of snowstorms and icebergs.

Dagmar Krause sings Eisler

EDWARD ELGAR

(1857–1934)

The so-called English musical renaissance really got going in the years immediately following World War I, as Vaughan Williams and his contemporaries began to write pieces that reflected their researches into English folk music. Edward Elgar, on the other hand, though he was the progenitor of this renaissance in the sense that he gave international stature to British music, was a more purely European composer, with a musical language derived more from Wagner and Brahms than from anything native. In his own day his older contemporaries Stanford and Parry were equally well respected, but history has established him as the greater original – and arguably the first great English composer since Purcell.

Despite his haughty aristocratic appearance and later recognition by the Edwardian social establishment, Elgar was always a provincial, countryman at heart – although he

ROYAL COLLEGE OF MUSIC

lived in London during the early years of the twentieth century, he found refuge from city life in the Sussex hills. He was born in a village outside Worcester, where his father served as organist at the Catholic church and ran a music shop and piano-tuning business. Edward never received much in the way of formal musical education. Initially he picked up his skills from the environment in which he lived, helping his father by playing the organ in church and teaching himself the violin in order to play in the local orchestra. His compositional technique was acquired by similar means, trying out his early works with the help of his siblings.

His ambitions grew when in 1889 he married one of his piano pupils, Caroline Alice Roberts, the daughter of a retired army general. The combination of the warmth of this relationship and his acceptance into upper middle-class circles seems to have inspired him, and the 1890s saw a great increase in his prowess. The *Serenade for Strings* (1892) was his first work to be published, though international fame eluded him until the first performances of the *Enigma Variations* in 1899. His greatest choral work, *The Dream of Gerontius*, was premiered the following year, but to little acclaim at the time, though the succeeding years were to be his most successful. He became a household name following the appearance of his *Pomp and Circumstance March No. 1* in 1901, was knighted in 1904 and in 1911 was awarded the Order of Merit. In the intervening years he composed some of his largest works, among them *The Apostles* (1903), the *Introduction and Allegro for Strings* (1905), *The Kingdom* (1906), *Symphony No. 1* (1908), the *Violin Concerto* (1910), *Symphony No. 2* (1911) and the symphonic study *Falstaff* (1913).

Just a few patriotic works emerged during the war years, but the end of the war brought forth perhaps his greatest work, the *Cello Concerto* (1919). Three major chamber works composed at the same time, a *Violin Sonata*, a

String Quartet and a *Piano Quintet* share its valedictory, autumnal mood, as if Elgar were pouring out his disillusionment with the changes the war had brought. The death of his wife in 1920 put a virtual stop to his creativity, and for the fourteen years that remained to him he composed little, concentrating instead on conducting and making recordings of his music.

Elgar was one of this century's consummate masters of orchestral writing – his scores are almost mosaic-like in their selective, ever-changing use of instrumental sounds. Moreover, he was one of the least parochial English composers – Wagner's *Parsifal* pervades the music of *Gerontius*, while the melodic lines and harmonic idiom of Brahms are particularly noticeable in the late chamber works. Yet the grandeur and nostalgia of Elgar, his pastoralism and occasional pomposity, makes him the epitome of a particularly Edwardian English style.

CHORAL MUSIC

Though choral music was a preoccupation of Elgar's early years, nothing of lasting value emerged until *The Light of Life* (1896) and the historical oratorios of the late 1890s, *King Olaf* and *Caractacus*. Most rewarding of his choral compositions is the series of works from the turn of the century, beginning with *The Dream of Gerontius*.

Elgar had been brought up a Roman Catholic, but his faith had never been particularly strong. *The Dream of Gerontius*, a setting of Cardinal Newman's poem dealing with the soul's passage from life into death, can be seen as Elgar's attempt to establish his faith more fully – and indeed, he followed it up with two Biblical oratorios. This is one of his most deeply felt works, a sensitive yet stirring setting of a text that tackles the most fundamental concepts, as Gerontius moves through his final illness and is led on his journey to heaven by the figure of an angel. Elgar's dramatic imagination lifts *Gerontius* clear of the morass of forgettable Victorian oratorios.

From the success of Gerontius emerged a plan to compose a trilogy of oratorios detail-

ing the founding of the Christian Church, a project sadly abandoned when the first two – *The Apostles* and *The Kingdom* – failed to achieve a positive response from their audiences. *The Apostles* is sometimes too dogged in its adherence to the Biblical text, falling short of Elgar's professed intention to make these oratorios work as unstaged music dramas rather than static choral music. Yet, for all its over-piousness, there is enough music of real originality here to make *The Apostles* worth investigating. *The Kingdom*, which narrates the events leading up to the Last Supper, in places suffers from the same Victorian solemnity as *The Apostles*, but its music is as fine as the more widely known *Gerontius*, and a couple of recent recordings have led to a reappraisal of its dramatic values.

> ⦿ **The Dream of Gerontius**: Watts, Gedda, Lloyd; London Philharmonic Orchestra; Boult (EMI CDS 7 47208 2; with *The Music Makers*; 2 CDs).
> ◗ **The Dream of Gerontius**: Wyn-Rogers, Rolfe Johnson, George; Royal Liverpool Philharmonic Orchestra; Handley (EMI CD-EMDX2500; with *Organ Sonata*; 2 CDs).
> ⦿ **The Apostles**: Hargan, Hodgson, Rendall, Terfel, Roberts, Lloyd; London Symphony Orchestra & Chorus; Hickox (Chandos CHAN 8875/6; 2 CDs).
> ⦿ **The Kingdom**: Kenny, Hodgson, Gillett, Luxon; London Philharmonic Orchestra; Slatkin (RCA RD87862; 2 CDs).

Adrian Boult's classic 1970s version of *Gerontius* is a refined, intense reading, well-recorded and with fervent orchestral playing; only the unidiomatic tenor of Nicolai Gedda is something of a let-down. The more recent recording from Vernon Handley is in the Boult tradition and makes a viable mid-price alternative.

Among a distinguished series of British choral works recorded for Chandos, Richard Hickox's performance of the rarely performed *Apostles* is one of his finest, going some way to revive what can seem a forbidding piece. The most successful recording of *The Kingdom* is that by Leonard Slatkin, who emphasizes the dramatic modernity of Elgar's conception more than its antiquated elements.

ORCHESTRAL MUSIC

"Gentlemen, let us now rehearse the greatest symphony of modern times, written by the greatest modern composer, and not only in this country." Thus the conductor Hans Richter greeted the London Symphony

Orchestra when preparing Elgar's first symphony for its London premiere. Not unlike his mentor Brahms, Elgar struggled long and hard for many years before embarking on this most exacting of instrumental forms, and he managed to complete only two, though fine works they are. Compared with the contemporary symphonies of Mahler they are traditional works, but these are arguably the first great British symphonies, revealing often highly original solutions to form and structure.

Some of Elgar's finest music is to be found in his other pieces for full orchestra – the outstanding works being the famous *Enigma Variations* and the rich orchestral tapestry of *Falstaff*.

Just as Elgar wrote only two symphonies, so he only turned to the concerto form twice in his life, with a violin concerto and a cello concerto. And in the same way that the two symphonies have quite distinct characters, so these works also show widely different approaches to the form and its traditions.

SYMPHONY NO. 1

As early as 1898 Elgar had contemplated a symphony in memory of General Gordon, the British governor of Sudan who had been killed at Khartoum in 1885. Elgar wrote to a friend that "the thing possesses me, but I can't write it down yet", but when he did come to compose his *Symphony No. 1*, in 1907–08, it seemed to have lost its specific historical reference – as Elgar again wrote, "There is no programme beyond a wide experience of human life with a great charity (love) and a massive hope in the future." It was first performed to great acclaim in Manchester in December 1908, conducted by its dedicatee, Hans Richter. The symphony is dominated by a melody that's given Elgar's characteristic expressive marking of *nobilmente* (nobly); returning at salient points throughout the four movements, this melody encapsulates the mood of this grand, optimistic and distinctly Germanic work.

◗ London Philharmonic Orchestra; Boult (EMI CDM 7 64013-2; with *Serenade for Strings*, *Chanson de matin*, *Chanson de nuit*).

Though conductors such as Handley, Slatkin and Haitink have recently tackled the first symphony with great success, it was for years the preserve of old-school British conductors such as Barbirolli and Boult. For a performance of real majesty and sweep, without interpretative quirks but with plenty of bite and character, Boult's last recording of the work for EMI is unbeatable, with the London Philharmonic Orchestra, which has probably recorded the work more times than any other orchestra, in superb form.

SYMPHONY NO. 2

His confidence boosted by the reception of his *Symphony No. 1*, Elgar soon began a second, completing it in 1911. He dedicated it to the memory of the late King Edward VII, but despite a funereal element in the slow movement, Elgar intended no programmatic link to be made. Indeed, its mood is generally cheerful, though its finale is rather understated and its argumentative structure is more complex and subtle than the first symphony, which may well account for the less than overwhelming reception it received in its early years.

◉ London Philharmonic Orchestra; Handley (Classics for Pleasure CD-CFP4544).
❶ BBC Symphony Orchestra; Davis (Teldec 9031-74888-2; with *In the South*).

The symphony's more enigmatic nature has led to a greater number of failed recordings than other Elgar works have received, though there are still some very fine accounts available. Two of the best are Vernon Handley's highly recommendable bargain account, and the more recent recording from Andrew Davis and the BBC SO, one of the finest entries in his on-going "British Line" series. The Davis account is coupled with a splendid version of *In the South (Alassio)*, one of Elgar's most exuberant orchestral works, paradoxically inspired by a rather damp winter holiday on the Italian Riviera in 1903. Elgar must have known his Richard Strauss, since the score is full of allusions (probably unconscious) to Strauss's *Don Juan* and other tone poems, and his orchestration is reminiscent of the German composer's.

ENIGMA VARIATIONS

The true title of this work is *Variations on an Original Theme*, as the "Enigma" is strictly speaking only the title of the section that introduces the theme. Ever since the work first appeared, musicologists have tried to unravel what this enigma might be: the consensus has long been that the theme was composed as harmony and counterpoint to another theme that is never itself heard, so the crux of the argument is over the identity of that implied theme. The conundrum is irrelevant to the glorious music of the variations themselves, which were all given cryptic titles referring to Elgar's "friends pictured within", as his dedication has it. These friends have long been identified, as Elgar often tagged their initials and nicknames onto the music. Thus the first variation, *CAE* is a portrait of his wife Caroline Alice Elgar, while the well-known *Nimrod* – long a favourite of the ad agencies – a tribute to his publisher friend A.E. Jaeger, whose surname is German for "huntsman", hence the allusion to the Old Testament figure of Nimrod the hunter.

◗ Philharmonia; Barbirolli (EMI CDM7 69185 2; with *Falstaff*).
◗ London Philharmonic Orchestra; Boult (EMI CDM7 64015-2; with *Pomp & Circumstance Marches 1–5*).

Few conductors have equalled John Barbirolli in the *Enigma Variations*, and his 1962 performance with the Philharmonia is a classic. The recorded sound is admittedly somewhat dated, but the nobility and finesse of the interpretation easily outweigh such a drawback.

Adrian Boult provides a more aristocratic but equally enjoyable reading of the *Enigma*. It comes coupled with lively but earnest accounts of Elgar's celebrated *Pomp and Circumstance* marches – these may not constitute his greatest music, but there is no denying the panache that he brought to the concept of the military march. Incidentally, it was at King Edward VII's suggestion that the trio melody of the best known, No. 1, should be set to words – the infamous "Land of Hope and Glory"; Elgar did not approve of its triumphalist sentiments.

John Barbirolli

EMI

SERENADE FOR STRINGS & INTRODUCTION AND ALLEGRO

Composed in 1892, the *Serenade for Strings* is the first recognizably Elgarian work – "I like 'em," he later wrote of the *Serenade*'s three movements, "(The first thing I ever did)." But the second of his two major works for strings, the *Introduction and Allegro* was undoubtedly more influential. With its juxtaposition of a string quartet against a full string orchestra he sparked off a succession of English string works that have their roots in the Baroque concerto grosso idea of "competing" string ensembles, the most notable subsequent examples coming in the works of Vaughan Williams and Tippett.

⊙ Serenade for Strings; Introduction and Allegro: London Chamber Orchestra; Warren-Green (Virgin VCX7 59095-2; with Vaughan Williams, *The Lark Ascending*; *Greensleeves*; *Tallis Fantasia*).

In the tradition of violinist-led string ensembles, the London Chamber Orchestra's performances under Christopher Warren-Green are suitably vigorous yet refined. The Serenade is especially excellent – too many performances over-indulge in the slow movement – and forms part of a superb programme of Elgar and Vaughan Williams string works.

FALSTAFF

Elgar's penultimate orchestral work (the *Cello Concerto* came later) is arguably his finest. Unlike Verdi's opera, which concentrates on the womanizing side of Falstaff's character as portrayed in Shakespeare's *Merry Wives of Windsor*, Elgar's "symphonic study" dwells on his relationship with Prince Hal in *Henry IV* and *Henry V*, culminating in the newly crowned king's rejection of his old friend, and Falstaff's death – perhaps symbolic of the passing of the age in which Elgar had grown up and felt secure. The score is marvellously detailed and reveals a sense of humour not heard so openly in any of Elgar's music, though the grandiose and melancholy elements play equally important roles.

⊙ Falstaff: Handley; London Philharmonic Orchestra (Classics for Pleasure CD-CFP4617; with *Cockaigne Overture* and *Introduction and Allegro*).

Vernon Handley's recording for the bargain-price Classics for Pleasure label in 1978 first revealed him as the successor to

Barbirolli and Boult, combining attention to the symphonic scale and structure of the work with ripe characterization and a superb performance from those experienced Elgarians of the London Philharmonic Orchestra.

VIOLIN CONCERTO

The *Violin Concerto* displays the characteristic Elgarian mixture of wistfulness, grandeur and lyricism, but it is immensely virtuosic as well – indeed, some rate it as the most difficult violin concerto in the repertory, and many a fine violinist has been scared off attempting what is a most rewarding piece. This concerto marks a real development from its predecessors in the repertory, most in the notably extended and highly original accompanied cadenza in the last movement, an episode in which the soloist mulls over themes from the whole work.

⊙ Menuhin; London Symphony Orchestra; Elgar (EMI CDH7 69786-2; with *Cello Concerto*).
⊙ Kang; Polish National Radio Symphony Orchestra; Leaper (Naxos 8 550489; with *Cockaigne Overture*).

The concerto has a distinguished recording history, stretching back to the classic account from the young Yehudi Menuhin made in 1932, with the 75-year-old composer himself conducting. The best modern account comes from Naxos's

The young Yehudi

budget-price recording with the resplendent Poland National Radio SO and the superb Korean violinist Dong-Suk Kang, for whom Elgar's formidable writing holds no fears. It's coupled with the *Cockaigne Overture*, a swaggering portrait of London in 1901.

CELLO CONCERTO

World War I took its toll on Elgar. Although he was not directly involved in any participatory way, he saw in it the destruction of the world he had known since childhood, and there is a tangible sense of regret and dejection in his last major works. Along with three important chamber works (see below), the most famous of these is the *Cello Concerto*, a work that conveys the impression, in the words of the Elgar scholar Michael Kennedy, of "a man wearied with the world . . . finding solace in the beauty of music". The texture has something of the transparency of chamber music, and the form of the concerto reflects a state of emotional flux – it's divided into four movements which further divide into sections with quite contrasting moods, though mournfulness is the dominant tone. Resonant cello chords frame the whole piece, opening the concerto with buttonholing immediacy, and making a poignant comeback towards the end.

⊙ Du Pré; London Symphony Orchestra; Barbirolli (EMI CDC7 47329 2; with *Sea Pictures*).

The *Cello Concerto* was not too well received at first and it could be argued that it was the young Jacqueline du Pré who made the piece popular with her ecstatic performances. Her magnificent recording with John Barbirolli has dominated the catalogue since it was issued in the mid-1960s, even though not a year goes by without the release of a new attempt from the latest star soloist. Few cellists have penetrated the concerto's inner recesses so deeply, or produced a performance of such burning intensity. This is the place to begin any Elgar collection.

Jacqueline du Pré – nobody has ever played Elgar better

CHAMBER MUSIC

Elgar wrote a lot of chamber music in his youth, notably the series of so-called "shed music" he wrote for himself and his young wind-playing friends to play in his garden. But his only works of significance, apart from the various salon pieces for violin, date from the end of World War I, when he rented a quiet cottage in the wooded uplands of Sussex and composed his *Violin Sonata*, *String Quartet* and *Piano Quintet*, works expressing with deep seriousness his disillusionment with post-war life, yet also conveying some of the "wood magic", as Elgar's wife called it, of their surroundings.

The three-movement *Violin Sonata* is Elgar at his most openly, gushingly Romantic, the very antithesis of straitlaced Englishness; the theme of the opening movement is the most arresting idea in all Elgar's chamber music. The *Piano Quintet* is Elgar's most overtly Brahmsian work, but is dominated as much by Elgar's highly personal way of creating a sense of atmosphere with ghostly undertones. The *String Quartet* is more intimate in style; it's a wistful and melancholic piece, but there's plenty of power in it too.

> ◉ **Piano Quintet; String Quartet**: Bingham, Medici Quartet (Medici-Whitehall MQCD7002).
> ◗ **Violin Sonata; Piano Quintet**: Bean, Parkhouse (EMI CDM7 69889-2; with piano works).

John Bingham and the Medici Quartet catch the *Quintet's* dignified and resigned mood perfectly; it's coupled with an equally successful account of the *Quartet*. For the *Violin Sonata* there's nothing to match the account from Hugh Bean, a pupil of Elgar's great friend Albert Sammons and a musician associated particularly with this work. Suitably sweeping and intense, he generates enormous energy without resorting to crude display.

---

§

MANUEL DE FALLA
(1876–1946)

Glimpses of Manuel de Falla's personality, as seen by his contemporaries, are tantalisingly rare, but two images of him are well known: one is Picasso's melancholy drawing of 1920, the other is Stravinsky's remark that he was "the most unpityingly religious person I have ever known – and the least sensible to manifestations of humour." Yet this austere man, a lifelong bachelor, wrote some of the most sensuous and alluring music to have come out of Spain.

Born into a prosperous family in the seaport of Cadiz, Falla had every encouragement to immerse himself in music, receiving piano lessons first from from his mother and then from an array of eminent teachers. Yet for several years he could not decide between a musical or a literary career. He was about seventeen when he finally committed himself to becoming a composer, around the time that he encountered the music of Grieg.

Immediately impressed by Grieg's strong national character and his rejection of Teutonic notions of musical structure, Falla conceived "an intense desire to create one day something similar with Spanish music".

After a distinguished spell at the Madrid Conservatory (1898–99), when he took top marks and prizes in all his classes, Falla persuaded Felipe Pedrell, the seminal figure of Spanish musical nationalism, to take him on as a pupil. Pedrell's influence on budding Spanish composers of the day was profound, as important as that which the Russian teacher-composer Rimsky-Korsakov had over the young Stravinsky. Pedrell exhorted Falla, as he had Albéniz and Granados before him, to develop a style based on folk music, and showed him how to achieve this within a wider European framework. Although Falla took many of his teacher's ideas to heart, his own style differed from Pedrell's in two fundamental ways. Firstly, his inclination throughout his life was to write sparely, and he had an abhorrence of music with too many notes – Pedrell's own compositions and those of his other students (eg Albeniz's *Iberia* and Granados' *Goyescas*) are decidedly expansive. Secondly, Falla chose not to quote folk tunes directly as Pedrell would do, but to extract the essence of the music, to build something new from this raw material. As he put it in an essay of 1917, "I think that in popular song the spirit is more important than the letter."

In 1907, two years after winning a prestigious competition for his opera *La Vida Breve*, Falla bought a one-week return train ticket to Paris, and ended up staying seven years. Soon after arriving he was befriended by Debussy, Ravel and Dukas, and got caught up in the anti-Wagnerianism sweeping French musical circles. Even though he was never particularly successful financially, Paris was the making of him as a composer, enabling him to reassess the musical heritage of his homeland in the context of the impressionist masterpieces of the French innovators. The first fruit of this process was *Noches en los jardines de España* (1911–15), a lush composition for piano and orchestra.

At the outbreak of World War I Falla returned to Spain. Many of the compositions of this period, including the two ballet scores *El amor brujo* (1915) and *El sombrero de tres picos* (1917–19), derive their character from the *cante jondo*, the highly evocative song style of Andalusia, of which Falla had been making a thorough study. These ballets were highly popular, and suites of dances from *El sombrero* soon became international concert favourites. Falla could have gone on profitably mining the rich orchestral style of his ballets but, inspired by the neo-classicism of his friend Stravinsky, he set off on a new phase, working to condense and distill his style.

In 1919 he moved to Granada, where he gathered around him a circle of intellectuals, the most notable of whom was the writer and poet Lorca. Though each new work took ever longer to write, with Falla poring over every note and phrase, the music of Falla's neo-classical phase attained a lapidary perfection, for example in the small-scale theatre piece *El retablo de maese Pedro* and the *Concerto for harpsichord* (1923–26).

Never a man to repeat himself, Falla then embarked on *Atlantida*, a huge oratorio for soloists, chorus and orchestra. This was the most ambitious work he had ever undertaken and he was to devote the rest of his life to it, but it remained unfinished and was not performed until 1962. Falla's last years were lived out in self-imposed exile in Argentina, where the composer had moved to escape the regime of General Franco.

THE MUSIC

For better or worse, Falla is best known for a trio of works: the dazzling ballets *El amor brujo* (Love the Sorcerer) and *El sombrero de tre picos* (The Three-Cornered Hat) and *Noches en los jardines de España* (Nights in the Gardens of Spain). With their rich, colourful orchestration and their vivid use of folk materials, these pieces have plenty of immediate attractions – so many, in fact, that you can easily overlook Falla's consummate skill as a composer, in the way he gets unexpected sonorities from such modest instrumental forces. As he once remarked – "I can make as much noise with twenty instruments as with a hundred." Falla was an adventuous composer, but this music, although harmonically very bold, is firmly tonal; Falla was well aware of Schoenberg's atonal compositions, but referred to them as an "extremely grave mistake".

> ☽ **El sombrero de tre picos; El amor brujo; Noches en los jardines de España**; de los Angeles; Soriano; Philharmonia Orchestra, Orchestre de la Société des Concerts du Conservatoire; Giulini, de Burgos (EMI CDM 7 64746 2).
> ◐ **El amor brujo (original version); El corregidor y la molinara**: Powell, Gomez; Aquarius; Cleobury (Virgin VC7 90790-2).

EMI have amalgamated two very fine sets of performances from conductors and soloists who excel in Latin repertoire, to bring seventy minutes of brilliantly atmospheric music. The highlight is *El amor brujo*, with Giulini's masterly conducting exactly matching the characterfulness of Victoria de los Angeles, who is in ravishing voice.

In the Virgin recording Nicholas Cleobury directs the original chamber versions of *El amor brujo* and *El sombrero de tres picos*, the latter titled *El corregidor y la molinara*. These performances are particularly strong on spontaneity, and the vocal soloists – Claire Powell in *El amor* and Jill Gomez in *El corregidor* – beautifully recreate the throaty vigour of flamenco.

GABRIEL FAURÉ
(1845–1924)

Like Delius, Fauré is a composer whose music does not seem to travel well: revered in his native France, he is known elsewhere almost solely for his *Requiem* and perhaps a few of his songs. Unfortunately this excludes a wealth of highly refined and beautiful music. Fauré's style displays a Romantic sensibility held in check by a classical sense of form and decorum – it is music of feeling, sometimes of passion, but it never aspires to the epic or the transcendent, preferring a more discreet and intimate means of expression.

Fauré was the youngest of six children, possibly an unplanned addition to the family, and was a precocious talent. When he was nine he was sent to the École Niedermeyer, a Paris music school with a bias towards ecclesiastical music. In 1861 the twenty-five year old Saint-Saëns arrived at the school to teach piano, and proceeded to introduce his students to the music of Lizst and Wagner – and formed a friendship with Fauré which was to last until Saint-Saëns's death.

Fauré's career began as an organist, firstly at Rennes and then, after serving in the Franco-Prussian war of 1870, at the Paris church of St Honoré d'Eylau. In 1879 he heard the whole of Wagner's *Ring* cycle in Munich, and although he later acknowledged its effect on him ("Such things seep into you just like water seeps through sand") he was not swept up in the Wagner mania that hit Paris a few years later, unlike many other French composers. In 1896 he won two major appointments, as organist at the church of La Madeleine and professor of composition at the Paris Conservatoire where he exerted a strong influence on a succession of pupils, including Ravel and Nadia Boulanger, the twentieth-century's most important composition teacher. Even though he gave up the Madeleine job in 1905 when he was appointed Director of the Conservatoire, the time he could set aside for writing music decreased substantially, a problem exacerbated by his growing deafness. Fauré's later work is characterized by a paring down of his musical language, an unfashionable restraint that probably accounts for the relative failure of his only opera, *Pénélope* (1913).

CHORAL MUSIC

Of the great Requiems of the nineteenth century, Verdi's sounds as if it was written for the opera house and Brahms's for the concert hall – Fauré's alone has the odour of incense, doubtless thanks to his career as an organist and his familiarity with church music. The Fauré *Requiem* is music to comfort and to reassure the faithful in the face of death, rather than to overwhelm them with the finality of judgement – significantly it omits the full, fearsome text of the Dies irae (Day of Wrath), allowing only a passing reference to it in the Libera me (Deliver me) section. The overwhelming impression is one of peace and serenity which, in the Agnus Dei, is transformed into an almost joyous resignation.

Fauré wrote several other liturgical works, of which the short *Messe Basse* (Low Mass) for high voices is the best known. Originally written in collaboration with Messager, when it was known as the *Messe des Pêcheurs de Villerville*, it was revised by Fauré in 1906 to make it entirely his own, creating a work that's striking for the clarity and simplicity of its religious sentiment.

> ◉ **Requiem (1894 version); Messe des Pêcheurs de Villerville**: Mellon, Kooy, Van Doeselaar; Petits Chanteurs de Saint-Louis, Paris Chapelle Royale; Musique Oblique Ensemble; Herreweghe (Harmonia Mundi HMC 90 1292).
>
> ◗ **Requiem (1900 version); Messe Basse**: Auger, Luxon, Smy; Choir of King's College Cambridge; English Chamber Orchestra, Ledger (EMI CD-EMX 2166).
>
> Herreweghe's recording is unusual for giving us the original version of the *Messe Basse* and an earlier and simpler version of the *Requiem*. His decision is fully justified by performances in which the closer balance between orchestra and choir creates a wonderful sense of intimacy. For the *Requiem's* more full-blooded version, the performance by King's College is particularly good value, with an outstanding soprano soloist, Arléen Auger, in the haunting Pie Jesu.

Faure wrote nearly one hundred songs throughout his career, and they show off his lyric gift at its subtle and eloquent best. They include settings of poems by Baudelaire, Gautier and Victor Hugo, but the poet with whom he seems to have the strongest sympathy was Paul Verlaine, who inspired some of his most sensuous and concentrated writing. Both poet and composer are concerned with atmosphere more than description, and the instrumental part in these songs never acts just as accompaniment but rather shapes and directs the vocal line in ways that delicately alter the mood. *La Bonne Chanson* (1892–94), the finest of his song-cycles, possesses a fresh and heart-felt ardour that reflects Fauré's feeling towards the work's first performer, his mistress Emma Bardac.

⦿ **La Bonne Chanson**: Walker; Nash Ensemble (CRD CRD3389; with *Piano Trio*).
◗ **L'Horizon chimérique and other songs**: Souzay; Bonneau (Philips 425 975-2; with Chausson songs).

The English mezzo Sarah Walker, performing *La Bonne Chanson* in Fauré's arrangement for singer and string quintet, has a darkness and sensuality to her voice that feels absolutely appropriate to this music. This disc also contains a fine account of the spare and enigmatic *Piano Trio*, a late work.

Gerard Souzay is one of the greatest of all interpreters of French song, possessing a warm and sweet-toned baritone which at the same time is always clear and incisive – the perfect combination for Fauré's elusive bitter-sweet songs. The seven songs by Chausson make an interesting foil to the Fauré pieces – Chausson's gift for melody is clear, but he has less depth and creates less of a sense of the gradual emergence of each song's meaning.

Fauré was unduly self-critical and nervous about writing orchestral works, but in chamber music he had no such inhibitions, producing an array of works of a consistently high standard that is unrivalled in French music at that period. Much of it, particularly the two piano quartets, has the breadth and energy that you associate with orchestral music, and nearly all of it includes a piano part. Of his early chamber music, the two most celebrated works are the *Violin Sonata No. 1* and the *Piano Quartet No. 1*, both written in the mid-1870s and both characterized by an underlying melancholy that is offset by sparkling Scherzo-like movements. Both the *Piano Quartet No. 2* (1886) and the *Violin Sonata No. 2* (1917) are darker, less effusive works, in which thematic material from their first movements are skilfully developed in subsequent sections.

⦿ **Piano Quartets Nos. 1 & 2**: Domus (Hyperion CDA 66166).
◗ **Violin Sonatas Nos. 1 & 2**: Grumiaux; Crossley (Philips 426 384-2; with Franck, *Violin Sonata*).

Domus have all the qualities required for a perfect chamber group: distinctive instrumental voices that can shine individually when necessary, but above all a strong sense of common cause. Both piano quartets are held together by some brilliantly nimble piano playing, and there is an emotional depth to the slow movements which is utterly compelling.

Grumiaux and Crossley respond warmly and imaginatively to the violin sonatas, treating their rhythmic ebb and flow with a flexibility that brings out their quicksilver charm. Grumiaux's variety of tone and touch is particularly apparent in the slow movements, where his highlighting of details heightens the sense of personal utterance. The addition of Franck's delightful sonata makes this disc exceptionally good value.

MORTON FELDMAN

(1926–1987)

As a broad generalization, the music of the American avant-garde differs from its European counterpart in being primarily concerned with the sensual qualities of sounds themselves rather than the shaping and ordering of those sounds. Morton

Feldman is typical of this tendency: his sound-world, especially in his later works, consists of small, soft and unhurried musical gestures which emphasize the physical detail of instrumental timbre. With this comes a fondness for repetition and an absence of rhythmic momentum which is, in Feldman's own words, ". . . a conscious attempt at formalising a disorientation of memory". The cumulative effect is of an hallucinatory stasis, not dissimilar to the large canvases of Mark Rothko, a painter Feldman knew and admired. It is a music where little happens – very beautifully.

Feldman was born in New York and studied composition, unsatisfactorily, with Stefan Wolpe and then Wallingford Riegger. The catalyst for his attempts to liberate sound from structure came when he met John Cage in 1949. *Projections* (1950–51) was a Cage-influenced work, written on squared paper with fairly general instructions, allowing the performer almost limitless freedom of choice over pitch and note duration. This was fairly rapidly replaced as a working method by more precise notation, but with note duration still left relatively free. The effect, in works like *Piece for Four Pianos* (1957) or *The Swallows of Salangan* (1960), is of a kind of anarchic counterpoint in which material disconcertingly overlaps and shifts. In Feldman's later work the emphasis changes again, from a preoccupation with the exploration of timbre to a fascination with time – a fascination exemplified by the *Piano and String Quartet* of 1985.

PIANO AND STRING QUARTET

In the *Piano and String Quartet* the piano, with the sustaining pedal held down, plays an arpeggiated chord as the string quartet plays a sustained chord. Notes change, harmonies shift, individual notes are sounded, but the essential pattern of broken chord plus sustained chord continues, to increasingly mesmerizing effect, for the eighty-minute duration of the work. The piece seems to have no beginning or end, no intention or direction, and yet listening to it heightens aural awareness to such a degree that the smallest modification of the chords possess a resonance and an intensity that is startling.

Kronos Quartet with Aki Takahashi (Elektra Nonesuch 7559-79320-2).

The Quartet was written for these specific players, and their performance is characterized by a steady and unruffled calm: Takahashi's piano sound is cool but never hard, while the Kronos Quartet bring an extraordinary precision to their playing, almost as if they were controlled by just one person. This is music that you don't so much listen to, as allow to envelop you .

CÉSAR FRANCK
(1822–1890)

Although Belgian, César Franck became the figurehead for a generation of French composers who had little interest in the predominantly operatic fare on offer in France, being instead attracted to Germanic ideas of symphonic form and musical abstraction. Acclaim for his work was meagre in his lifetime, but Franck brought a new seriousness to French music that ultimately would resonate in the compositions of later figures like Debussy and Honegger.

He was born in the Walloon city of Liège to a Flemish family, hence the mixture of French and Flemish in his name. At the age of eleven he made his first tour as a virtuoso pianist and two years later the whole family moved to Paris so he could study there. His earliest compositions were chiefly vehicles for his piano tours, followed by a series of religious works, then by pieces for the organ – at which he showed stunning prowess after the move to Paris – and for full orchestra. For many of his middle years his energies were given over to teaching and disseminating a musical philosophy that wanted to take French music away from its perceived frivolity and mediocrity. Nearly all his finest and best-known works were crammed into his last decade: the *Piano Quintet* (1879), the symphonic poem *Le chasseur maudit* (1882), the *Prelude, Chorale and Fugue* for solo piano (1884), the *Symphonic Variations* for piano and orchestra (1885), the *Violin Sonata* (1886), the *Symphony in D minor* (1888), the *String Quartet* (1889) and the three *Chorales* for organ (1890), as well as two long-forgotten operas, *Hulda* (1885) and *Ghisèle* (1890) – the last unfinished when Franck died after being knocked down by a bus.

Franck's first-rate orchestral works amount to just a single symphony, one concertante work for piano and orchestra and a handful of symphonic poems. His reputation rests primarily on his instrumental pieces, the best of which are his *Piano Quintet*, *Violin Sonata* and organ music, most of which comes from the years of his maturity, whereas the piano pieces are mainly the product of his years as a touring virtuoso, when his compositional technique lagged some way behind his dexterity.

THE ORCHESTRAL WORKS

When Franck began his *Symphony in D minor* in 1886, he had few French examples except Berlioz to follow – his most obvious influences were Liszt's symphonic poems, in which a rigid structure is combined with the inventive transformation of themes that metamorphose as their harmonies and contexts change. Franck's symphony marks a development of the concept of cyclic form, in which music from one movement reappears later on, providing unity and coherence – thus ideas from the symphony's first two movements are recalled in the third. The slow movement is famous for its cor anglais solo, an instrument French critics of the time thought unsuitable for a major role in a serious symphony.

Often regarded as Franck's masterpiece, the *Symphonic Variations* for piano and orchestra is an irresistibly engaging show-piece that shows him again using Liszt's principle of thematic metamorphosis, this time to develop two main themes in a miraculous series of transformations, culminating in an extended final section that is more a full symphonic movement than a mere coda.

Franck's best symphonic poem, *Le Chasseur Maudit* (The Accursed Hunter) is about a count who dares to go hunting on the

Sabbath and pays the consequences when he is consigned to being eternally chased by a pack of demons. For all his adherence to musical abstraction elsewhere, Franck conjures up the action vividly.

◉ **Symphony in D minor**: Dutoit; Montréal Symphony Orchestra (Decca 430 278-2; with d'Indy, *Symphonie sur un chant montagnard français*).

◗ **Symphony in D minor**: Monteux; Chicago Symphony Orchestra (RCA 09026 61967-2 with d'Indy, *Symphonic Variations*).

◗ **Symphonic Variations**: Curzon; London Symphony Orchestra; Boult (Decca 433 628-2; with Grieg & Schumann piano concertos).

◗ **Le Chasseur Maudit**: Paris Orchestra; Barenboim (Deutsche Grammophon DG 437 244-2; with *Nocturne*, *Rédemption*, Berlioz: *Romeo et Juliette*; 2 discs).

◗ **Le Chasseur Maudit**: Philadelphia Orchestra; Muti (EMI CDM7 64747 2; with *Symphony & Symphonic Variations*).

For all its dynamism and Wagnerian harmonies, the Symphony can often sound stolid in performance due to Franck's conception of orchestral sound, which relies on organ-like blocks of sound. Charles Dutoit and his sleek Montréal Symphony avoid such pitfalls, producing a performance of great sweep and majesty. Similarly light-footed is Monteux's 1961 account for RCA, recently re-released as part of a splendid fifteen-disc Monteux Edition, but available as a single CD. This clear-sighted and unfussy account does justice to a work that has suffered at the hands of conductors straining for interpretative novelty.

Clifford Curzon's romantic account of the *Symphonic Variations* is a bargain, coupled with fine performances of the Grieg and Schumann concertos (the latter with Friedrich Gulda as soloist).

Monteux, doyen of French conductors

The best account of *Le Chasseur Maudit*, by Daniel Barenboim and the Paris Orchestra, is now harnessed to his (admittedly superb) account of Berlioz's *Romeo and Juliet* symphony, which spreads on to two discs. The best single-disc recommendation goes to Riccardo Muti's performance, coupled on a mid-price EMI disc with Karajan's slightly over-weight recordings of the *Symphony* and *Symphonic Variations*.

CHAMBER WORKS

The *Piano Quintet*, written at the beginning of Franck's productive final decade, is one of his most passionate and personal works and may well have been inspired by an extra-marital affair with one of his students. It has been said to contain more fortissimos and pianissimos than any other chamber work.

His other main chamber piece, the melodious *Violin Sonata*, was written as a wedding present for his fellow Liègeois, the great violinist Eugène Ysaÿe. A triumphant example of cyclic form, it has four movements: a languid Allegretto, which was changed from being an Adagio after Ysaÿe convinced Franck it worked better at a faster tempo; a fiery Allegro, a recitative-fantasia recalling earlier themes; and a gentle finale.

> ◗ **Piano Quintet**: Curzon, Vienna Philharmonic Quartet (Decca 421 153-2; with Dvořák, *Piano Quintet*).
> ◗ **Violin Sonata**: Chung, Lupu (Decca 421 154-2; with Debussy, *Violin Sonata & Sonata for Flute, Viola and Harp*; Ravel, *Introduction* and *Allegro*).

The *Quintet* is less popular today than it once was and for a really fine account of the work you have to go back three decades to Clifford Curzon's passionate version with the Vienna Philharmonic Quartet. Kyung Wha Chung's classic account of the *Violin Sonata*, coupled with some fine Debussy and Ravel, is an essential mid-price CD. Chung has the poise for this music, not swooning over the main theme like some of her competitors, and she has a sympathetic partner in the pianist Radu Lupu.

ORGAN WORKS

Franck's reputation as a composer for the organ rests on the masterful series of about a dozen works written in the early 1860s and during the last ten years of his life, most notably the *Prélude, fugue et variation* (1862) and the three magisterial *Chorales* (1890). For all the grandeur of his orchestral works, it is perhaps in this medium that he felt most at home, even if the organ pieces do not represent him at his most adventurous and forward-looking.

> ◗ **Prélude, fugue et variation**; Chorales Nos. 1–3, and other works: Murray (Telarc CD80234; 2 CDs).
> ◗ **Chorales Nos. 1–3; Pièce héroïque**: Dupré (Mercury 434 311-2).

Michael Murray's two-disc set contains all twelve major works in faithful performances using a Toulouse organ little changed since Franck's day. Marcel Dupré's more imaginatively played single disc of highlights is sonically impressive, giving little sign that it was recorded as long ago as 1959.

GIOVANNI GABRIELI
(c.1553–1612)

Towards the end of the sixteenth century many composers were looking for alternatives to the polyphony that had dominated church music for the last one hundred and fifty years. Among the new styles to appear was one that was peculiar to the state of Venice, a style that had developed out of the lavish ceremonial music performed at the city's magnificent church of St Mark. This Venetian style was called polychoralism because it employed no fewer than two, and sometimes as many as five, separated choirs (*chori spezzati*), which were placed in different locations around the high altar, including the galleries on each side of it.

Much of the most sumptuous music written for St Mark's in the polychoral style was by Andrea Gabrieli and his nephew Giovanni, both of whom served as organists there. The music itself was homophonic, that is made up of chords rather than the independent lines of polyphony. Great blocks of sound, with an emphasis on sonorous textures and dramatically varied dynamics, acted as the aural equivalent of the sumptuous but hieratic splendour of St Mark's itself, the most Byzantine of all great European churches. In Giovanni's music the textures were further enriched by the use of instrumental music, especially violins, cornetts (an early wooden version of the trumpet) and sackbuts (close to the modern trombone).

Not much is known about Giovanni Gabrieli's life: he studied with his uncle Andrea, and like him spent some time at the at the Munich court of Albrecht V where he would have worked with Lassus (see p.191). He succeeded Merulo as organist at St Mark's in 1585, and when his uncle died the following year he became the church's principal composer of ceremonial music. He was also an organist at the Scuola di San Rocco, a confraternity given to lavish celebration on its patron saint's day. Much of Gabrieli's music was published in 1597 in a collection titled *Sacrae Symphoniae*, and his subsequent fame led to him being sought out as a teacher, especially by pupils from Germany. The greatest of these was Schütz (see p.330), who assimilated Gabrieli's style and perpetuated it in Germany long after it had been forgotten in Venice. He was obviously a favourite pupil of Gabrieli's, since he received a ring from him on his deathbed.

Polychoralism was replaced in Venice by the more eclectic and expressive style of Monteverdi (see p.236) who became maestro di cappella at St Mark's a year after Gabrieli's death.

CEREMONIAL MUSIC

Gabrieli's career coincides with one of the most opulent periods of Venetian history, presided over by one of its most lavish doges, Marino Grimani, who spent colossal amounts on state occasions. Obviously such occasions involved the church, but it was Venice rather than God that was being celebrated, and at St Mark's priests could actually be fined if they interrupted the music. Gabrieli clearly revelled in the musical extravagance that was expected of him, and he was one of the first composers to make highly specific instructions about dynamics: one piece is actually entitled *Sonata pian e forte* (loud and soft sonata). Instrumental music was as important as choral for creating the right atmosphere of solemnity, and some of Gabrieli's finest works are his *canzoni*, in which the instruments are treated with all the sensitivity usually accorded to voices alone.

⊙ **A Venetian Coronation 1595 – music by Andrea and Giovanni Gabrieli**: Gabrieli Consort and Players; McCreesh (Virgin VC 759 006 2).

This disc is a reconstruction of the music that might have been performed at the coronation of Marino Grimani in 1595. Slightly less than half the music is by Giovanni Gabrieli, while the rest is a setting of the Mass by Andrea Gabrieli, plus some fanfares and a small amount of plainsong. Far from being an empty academic exercise this is a wonderfully exciting and evocative recording which really conveys the splendour and solemnity of the occasion – a fifteen-part canzona sounds all the more splendid if it has been preceded by a minute of plainsong. The performances are wonderfully vigorous, and the engineers have really captured a spatially convincing sound, even though it was recorded in a Northumberland Priory rather than in St Mark's.

GEORGE GERSHWIN
(1898–1937)

Like many other songwriters who held sway over American popular music in the 1920s and 1930s, George Gershwin was a New Yorker of European-Jewish extraction. During his boyhood his family was constantly on the move from one Manhattan tenement to another, and his parents were far too busy trying to support their children to have much time for any cultural pursuits. The young George, however, had a homegrown

HULTON DEUTSCH

piano part himself at the premiere on February 12, 1924. Attended by the likes of Toscanini, Stravinsky and Rachmaninov, the concert was a sensation, and it made Gershwin famous overnight.

From that time on his reputation was sealed, although he occasionally had periods of insecurity that drove him to snatch lessons wherever he could. On a trip to Paris he even approached Ravel for tuition. Ravel's answer was "Why do you want to become a second-rate Ravel when you're already a first-class Gershwin?" Legend has it that he also asked Stravinsky for compositional guidance, but that the latter, upon hearing what the young man earned in one year ("About 250,000 dollars"), asked him for lessons instead.

Apart from Stravinsky, the classical composers who most fascinated Gershwin in the mid-1920s were Schoenberg and Berg, yet it was the music produced by the group of French composers known as Les Six which directly inspired the half-jazzy, half-classical *An American in Paris* (1928). His final "serious" work, the jazz-oriented folk opera *Porgy and Bess* (premiered in Boston on September 30, 1935), was not universally popular at first – some eminent black composers, including Duke Ellington, were less than complimentary – but its array of wonderful songs has ensured its place on the stage ever since.

With *Porgy* he had gone further than ever in fusing popular and classical styles, and at no cost to his mass audience appeal. But at this peak in his career Gershwin was cut down with a brain tumour while working on his third Hollywood film score, *The Goldwyn Follies*. Among those who most keenly felt the loss was his friend Arnold Schoenberg, who said of Gershwin: "Music was what made him feel, and music was the feeling he expressed. Directness of this kind is given only to great men, and there is no doubt that he was a great composer."

PORGY AND BESS

It would have been easy for Gershwin to go on repeating the formula that had made his musical comedies such successes, but in 1926 he came across a novel called *Porgy and Bess* by Dubose Heyward, and the book

artistic collaborator in the shape of his older brother Ira, who in later years was to write the lyrics to most of his classic songs. The purchase by the Gershwins of their first piano in 1910 was to change George's life. Originally intended for Ira, the instrument was soon monopolized by George, who quickly went through a variety of neighbourhood piano teachers, rapidly outgrowing what each one had to offer.

By the age of sixteen Gershwin had dropped out of business school and was working on Tin Pan Alley as a plugger of other people's songs. In 1919 he had his first hit with *Swannee*, taken from his comedy *La La Lucille*. It was the start of an unending stream of hit shows, peppered with songs that are a roll-call of twentieth-century popular music's highpoints, including *Fascinatin' Rhythm, Someone To Watch Over Me* and *Lady Be Good*.

But despite the money and fame, Gershwin was not satisfied. Fascinated since childhood by classical music, he started to entertain the idea of writing extended instrumental works that would use American musical forms, like ragtime, blues and jazz to convey the vibrant everyday life of the American people. The catalyst for this new departure was provided by the band leader Paul Whiteman, who invited Gershwin to contribute a piece to a concert advertised as "An Experiment in Modern Music". In under a month Gershwin wrote his *Rhapsody in Blue*, and he played the immediately fired his imagination. He soon determined to turn this story of a South Carolina black community into an opera – "If I am successful" he wrote, "it will resemble a combination of the drama and romance of *Carmen* and the beauty of *Meistersinger*". He succeeded beyond all expectations: just as in *Carmen* there are plenty of beautiful songs, effortlessly woven into the score; and like *Meistersinger* it displays a highly skillful use of leitmotifs and large choral numbers, creating a sense of tight community in Catfish Row similar to that in Wagner's Nuremberg.

⦿ Carey, Haymon, Blackwell, Evans, White; Glyndebourne Chorus; London Philharmonic Orchestra; Rattle (EMI CDS 749568-2; 3 CDs).

Based closely on the Glyndebourne production that marked *Porgy*'s breakthrough into the opera-house repertoire, this is a highly spontaneous performance with an exhilarating atmosphere. Under Rattle's exuberant direction the LPO inject just the right rhythmic fluidity into their playing, giving a jazzy swing to the proceedings when called for. The characterization on the part of all the singers is of so high a standard that it would be invidious to select anyone for particular praise.

ORCHESTRAL & CONCERT WORKS

Although "jazzy" is the word that immediately springs to mind when looking for a term to sum up Gershwin's concert works, they were in fact drawn from a whole mix of traditions. Listen carefully to *Rhapsody in Blue*, *An American in Paris* and the *Piano Concerto in F* and one catches strains of fully blown Romantic piano virtuosity, New York Yiddisher melancholy, Dixieland, a Stravinskian use of tonality and a lot more. But what marks these works out more than

anything else are their soaring melodies. As with many of his popular songs, Gershwin had a simple device for imprinting his melodies on the listener's subconscious: he would repeat the opening material of a piece several times before moving onto a contrasting section. What gave his music its special melodic grit was the use of so-called blue notes, those flattened thirds and sevenths which are the staple diet of popular Afro-American music. Another legacy of the blues, the ubiquitous twelve-bar progression, provided Gershwin with a ready made harmonic framework: one that he used to great effect both in the *Piano Concerto*'s second movement, and in *An American in Paris*.

◗ **An American in Paris; Rhapsody in Blue**: Bernstein; New York Philharmonic Orchestra (Sony SMK 47529; with pieces by Bernstein).
◉ **An American in Paris; Catfish Row; Piano Concerto in F; Cuban Overture; "I got rhythm" variations; Lullaby for string orchestra; Promenade; Rhapsody in blue; Second Rhapsody for piano and orchestra**: Siegel; St Louis Symphony Orchestra; Slatkin (Voxbox 1154832; 2CDs).

In the symphonic jazz repertoire there were few interpreters to touch Leonard Bernstein, and this reissue from the late 1950s features the conductor at the very height of his powers. Bernstein brings out all the pazzazz, energy and warmth of Gershwin's two masterpieces, not only directing the NYPO but performing the Rhapsody's piano part himself. Those who want a hefty slice of the Bernstein canon with their Gershwin need look no further than this recording, which includes superb renditions of the *Symphonic Dances* from *West Side Story* as well as the overture to *Candide*.

Leonard Slatkin and the St Louis Orchestra are not any more musical than the Bernstein set, but this pair of CDs does offer several other Gershwin masterpieces for little extra outlay – the *Piano Concerto in F*, *Catfish Row*, and the *Cuban Overture* are played with fabulous verve and panache.

♫

CARLO GESUALDO
(1561–1613)

The music of Gesualdo is some of the strangest ever written. Even in the context of a period when composers were constantly experimenting with ways of enlivening the words they set, his

music startles through its bizarre and neurotic sensitivity to meaning – his later madrigals especially make for fascinating but at times uncomfortable listening. The eccentricity of the music is mirrored by the details of

Gesualdo's extraordinary life. When, on the death of his elder brother, Gesualdo inherited the title Prince of Venosa, it was felt necessary for him to marry. The choice of bride fell on his twice-widowed cousin Maria d'Avalos and, after special papal permission had been obtained, the two were married in 1586. Four years later Gesualdo found out that his wife was conducting an affair with a nobleman, the Duke of Andria. One night, having left his palace on the pretext of a hunting trip, he returned home suddenly and discovered the lovers in bed together, whereupon he had them both instantly murdered – allegedly they were skewered on a single sword. Gesualdo escaped punishment but unsurprisingly this event seems to have overshadowed the rest of his life. Although he married again, he seems to have become a disturbed and melancholic man, largely cut off from society in the isolation of his palace in southern Italy. In his later years he had himself regularly scourged.

It was not unusual for members of the aristocracy to be musically adept, but it was rare for them to pursue their interest as single-mindedly as Gesualdo did. In 1593 his marriage to Eleonora d'Este (who later tried to divorce him for his violent behaviour towards her) brought him briefly into contact with the ducal court of Ferrara, a lively artistic centre with a particularly strong musical tradition. Here he met Luzzasco Luzzaschi, a skilled madrigalist and one of a succession of Ferrara-based composers who were concerned with finding ever more expressive settings for words. A favoured means of achieving this greater intensity was through chromaticism – in other words, composers began exploiting the interval of the semitone, with the result that the progress of the music became less predictable and regularly threw up peculiar harmonies. This was the catalyst that Gesualdo needed: before Ferrara his work is interesting but relatively conventional; after Ferrara it becomes increasingly original and, at moments, extreme.

MADRIGALS

Gesualdo wrote six books of madrigals, the best of them being books three to six, which were written after his return from Ferrara.

The texts – usually short and almost exclusively about death and the sufferings of love – are set so that the most highly charged words are always dramatically emphasized, either by dissonance or a change of speed or an unexpected note. Unlike Dowland's similarly morbid songs, where consistency of mood invites the listener's identification, Gesualdo's madrigals are distinguished by disruptive and restless changes of mood, so that the end result is rather like eavesdropping on some unresolvable, private agony.

⊙ Madrigals for Five Voices: Les Arts Florissants; Christie (Harmonia Mundi HMC 901268).

This disc provides a selection of seventeen madrigals taken from books three to six, three of which have been arranged instrumentally. Les Arts Florissants are an ideal group for madrigal singing, as each voice is individually recognizable and yet they all blend well. Their responsiveness to the words is also exemplary: they are always keenly aware of shifts in meaning but convey the meaning – as far as is possible with such spasmodic music – in a subtle and unforced manner. The relatively conventional *Sparge la morte* is treated with a subdued and tragic sobriety, for instance, whereas the stark and angular *Merce grido piangendo* veers from a rapturous opening to increasing enervation.

SACRED MUSIC

Gesualdo appears to have been a devoutly religious man – he greatly admired his uncle Carlo Borromeo (later Saint Carlo Borromeo), a leading figure behind the Council of Trent and a patron of Palestrina. Church music accounts for about a quarter of his output, and although it is sombre and restrained in comparison with his madrigals, it carries a far greater sense of the personal and extravagant than that of his contemporaries. Motet settings of gloomy and penitential texts – chosen presumably to reflect his own predicament – comprise the bulk of these works, and stylistically they tend to follows the pattern of Palestrina, but with occasional startling changes of speed that break up the meditative stillness. His greatest religious work, and the closest to his madrigal writing, is the set of responses for Holy Week published in 1611.

⊙ Sabato Sancto Responsoria; Four Motets: Ensemble Vocal Européen de la Chapelle Royale; Herreweghe (Harmonia Mundi HMC 901320; with Gorli, *Requiem*).

This recording provides Gesualdo's nine responses for Holy Saturday plus four motets; Herreweghe's forces are probably larger than Gesualdo would have employed in his private chapel but they never smooth over the music's constant struggle between serenity and anguish. The fill-up piece is a Requiem by a present-day composer.

ORLANDO GIBBONS

(1583–1625)

Gibbons was the outstanding composer of English church music in the generation that succeeded William Byrd. He excelled as a writer of anthems (the English equivalent of Latin motets), building on Byrd's richest and most demonstrative Anglican settings to produce his own vigorous and expressive musical language. He was also a renowned composer of keyboard music, notable for its contrapuntal rigour and inventiveness, and as a keyboard performer he was described as "the best hand in England".

He was born in Oxford into a musical family: his father William was a player in the city band and his brother Edward was master of the choristers at King's College Cambridge, where Orlando served as a chorister and later studied as an undergraduate. In 1603 he joined the Chapel Royal in London and became organist there some two years later – a position he held until his death. His success continued with preferment at court: a gift of £150 in 1615, and four years later an appointment as "one of his Majesty's musicians . . . to attend in his highnes privie chamber". In April l625, as organist of Westminster Abbey, he played at the funeral of King James I and two months later was summoned to Canterbury as part of the royal household to await the arrival from France of King Charles I's new bride, Queen Henrietta Maria. On Whitsunday, a few days before the Queen's arrival, Gibbons died suddenly from an apoplectic fit and was buried in Canterbury Cathedral.

SACRED MUSIC

By Gibbons' time English was the language of the liturgy in Britain, and the anthem had become the main choral display piece. There were two forms: the full anthem, which was closest to the motet, was a polyphonic piece for full choir, while the more dramatic verse anthem contrasted solo sections with choral sections, both accompanied by either organ or strings. Gibbons' most dramatically appealing music is found in his verse anthems, of which the finest, *This is the record of John*, is a gentle yet compelling narrative, sung for the most part by an alto soloist with the chorus echoing the closing chords of each section. It is a peculiarly English mixture of solo and choral interplay, pointing the way towards Purcell's more declamatory style.

⊙ **Orlando Gibbons, Tudor Church Music**: Choir of King's College Cambridge; Ledger (ASV CD GAU 123).

There is currently no recording that really does justice to Gibbons as a composer of sacred music. This 1982 recording is musically very good, with outstanding contributions from alto Michael Chance, who has solos in several of the anthems. The problem is the notorious King's College acoustic: the engineers have tried to retain the resonance without losing the clarity of the voices, and the result creates a curious inbalance between the soloists and the full choir. Its a well-selected programme though, covering the whole range of Gibbon's liturgical music: from the simplicity of the four-part setting of the *Magnificat* and *Nunc Dimittis*, through *This is the record of John* to the lush exuberance of the full anthem *Hosanna to the Son of David*.

SECULAR MUSIC

Gibbons was a versatile and wide-ranging composer. Along with Byrd and John Bull he contributed to *Parthenia* (1613), the first collection of keyboard music to be published in England, and also wrote a set of madrigals on rather sombre texts, the most famous of which is the poignant *O Silver Swan*. His thirty or so pieces for viols are mainly fantasias, which were freely composed works in

several sections that often developed contrapuntally from a particular theme. These were
the most common form of chamber music in
seventeenth-century England.

○ **Fantaisies Royales**: Savall, Coin, Casademunt,
Sonnleitner (Astree E 7747).
◑ **Consort of Musicke by William Byrd and
Orlando Gibbons**: Gould (Sony SMK 52 589).

The three-part and four-part compositions gathered on the
Fantaisies Royales are exceptionally rich and inventive, less
melancholic than Dowland's viol pavans and less cerebral than
Byrd's viol fantasias. Here they are performed by musicians
who are especially responsive to the sensuality of the music,
favouring a full but not a heavy tone, and treating Gibbons' lilting rhythms with a stylish and easy charm.

Though he publically performed just one work by him –
the *Lord of Salisbury Pavan and Galliard* – Glenn Gould claimed
on several occasions that Gibbons was his favourite
composer. He saw the early English keyboard masters as
anticipating the elaborate counterpoint of Bach that was his
major preoccupation as a pianist, a prophetic quality most
apparent in Gibbons' brilliant C major *Fantasy*. Interestingly,
though, he treats several other works more as poetic miniatures than as formal studies, with a hushed rapture that is
particularly evident in the ordered and stately calm of the
pavans on the disc (one by Gibbons and two by Byrd).

═══════════════ ♭♮ ═══════════════

UMBERTO GIORDANO

(1867–1948)

A s with so many *verismo* composers, such
as Leoncavallo and Mascagni, Umberto
Giordano's name has survived on the
strength of a single opera. Typically for
an Italian composer of his time, Giordano was
drawn to opera almost from the start, and his
early life was spent battling with parents who
strongly objected to his pursuing a life in
music. It was not until 1890 that he graduated
from the Naples conservatory, but by then he
had already completed his first opera, the one-
act *Marina*, which he had submitted as an
entry in the 1889 Sonzogno opera competition.
Marina fared no better than sixth place, but it
secured him a commission for a full-length
work, the result of which, *Mala vita*, was one
of the most sensational of all *verismo* operas,
with a plot that contrived to bring together a
prostitute and the Virgin Mary. It was violent,
crude and, for a short time, extremely popular.

His next opera, *Regina Diaz*, was ditched
after only two performances but in 1896,
having moved to the warmer audiences in
Milan, Giordano composed his masterpiece,
Andrea Chénier. Unfortunately its premiere
came less than two months after the first staging, also in Milan, of Puccini's *La Bohème* and
Chénier was inevitably overshadowed to a
large extent. Nonetheless, *Chénier* brought its
composer considerable acclaim, and two years
later he produced another extremely popular
opera, *Fedora* – a work which gave rise to the
witticism "Fedora fè d'oro" (Fedora made
money). Its success was guaranteed when
Caruso, who sang on the first night, gave a
thrilling performance of the opera's only tenor
aria *Amor ti vieta*, which was so well received
that he was obliged to sing it twice.

Of his other operas, only *Madame Sans-
Gêne* achieved anything like the success of
Andrea Chénier or *Fedora*, and he composed
his last, *Il re*, in 1929. For the remaining
nineteen years of his life he composed nothing but songs and a few light salon pieces.

ANDREA CHÉNIER

Like Puccini, Giordano was heavily influenced by the lyricism of Massenet but he is
generally less subtle than both – he was
generally at his best when writing fervent
music for fervent situations. Yet with *Andrea
Chénier*, he created a group of three-
dimensional personalities, a string of memorable tunes, and some of the most dramatic
scenes in all opera.

The eponymous hero is based upon the
real-life Andrea Chénier, an eminent poet in
Revolutionary France, but the events are a
romanticized tale of love across the social

classes, political intrigue, injustice and tragic death. There are some remarkable moments in the course of the four acts – notably Chénier's improvised poem *Un di all'azzuro spazio* in Act One, his beloved's Act Three aria *La mamma morta* (recently used to great effect in the film *Philadelphia*), and Chénier's reflection on his imminent death, *Come un bel di di Maggio* – but the overall orchestration and pacing are just right as well. The eighteenth-century pastiche shows a masterly understanding of the orchestra and Giordano's word-setting must have been the envy of all his contemporaries, excepting Puccini. *Andrea Chénier*'s absence from the opera house stage has more to do with a dearth of genuine heroic tenors than with any intrinsic weaknesses in the music.

◑ del Monaco, Tebaldi, Bastianini, Caruso, Cossotto; Santa Cecilia Academy Orchestra & Chorus; Gavazzeni (Decca 425 407-2DM2; 2 CDs).

◉ del Monaco, Callas, Taddei, Caruso, Protti; Orchestra & Chorus of La Scala; Votto (Verona 28020/21; 2 CDs).

Franco Corelli's studio recording of *Chénier* is due to be released on CD by EMI. When it appears it will be the clear first choice. Until then, the best of a very poor bunch is del Monaco's version with Tebaldi, a thrilling set but one that's consistently vulgarized by del Monaco's penchant for shouting. That said, on January 8, 1955, at La Scala, del Monaco gave a performance opposite Maria Callas that is easily the most exciting performance of the opera ever recorded. He is in astonishing form, producing an unimaginably massive sound, and Callas is similarly passionate – together they set the stage alight. To hear the audience's reaction to del Monaco's *Un di all'azzuro spazio* is a marvellous reminder that opera is not what it used to be. The set is difficult to find, but well worth the effort.

PHILIP GLASS

(1937–)

Philip Glass is the most famous and financially successful serious composer alive, thanks mainly to the instant accessibility of his brand of Minimalism. Whether he's writing for ballet, opera, theatre, film or even for a TV jingle, Glass's style is unmistakeable, with its repetitions of cell-like phrases built usually from brightly coloured keyboard sounds enhanced by soothing vocals and hot horns. Though often criticized as shallow and uneventful, Glass's music is insidiously effective – hear a Glass piece and you won't be able to get it out of your head for the rest of the day.

Of immigrant Jewish parentage, Glass grew up in Baltimore and got a taste for commercial music when he sold Elvis Presley records in his father's music store. He was an accomplished flautist and violinist by the age of fifteen, when he attended Chicago University to major in maths and philosophy. By the late 1950s he was in New York studying with Steve Reich (see p.292) at the Juilliard School, from where he went on to study with Darius Milhaud (see p.235) at Aspen and Nadia Boulanger in Paris. Obviously Glass was en route to a conventional composerly career, but then one day in the mid-1960s he met sitarist Ravi Shankar, who made him aware of his inability to grasp the additive structures of Indian music. Glass promptly set off across India, the Himalayas and North Africa on a new musical quest.

Returning to New York in 1967, Glass threw himself into the bohemian art scene of lower Manhattan, giving loft concerts with Terry Riley and Steve Reich, and forming the Philip Glass Ensemble. From this period came *Music In Similar Motion* (1969) and *Music In Changing Parts* (1970), both written for organs, flute, trumpet and saxes, and combining rock-type grooves with perpetual drones, all played at incredible volume. The real breakthrough came when he met theatre conceptualist Robert Wilson, with whom he produced the hallucinogenic four-hour opera *Einstein on the Beach* (1976) – a sell-out at the Met, this was the work that pushed Minimalism into the mainstream. Assisted by engineer Kurt Munkacsi, Glass built up a

BETTY FREEMAN/LEBRECHT COLLECTION

Philip Glass (left) with Robert Wilson

reputation for technical brilliance in the studio, and his first digital album *Glassworks* (1982) was a smash right across the musical spectrum, from heavy metal fans to Dean Martin lovers. On a larger scale, the operas *Satyagraha* (1980) and *Akhnaten* (1984), drawing on the lives of Gandhi, Tolstoy, Martin Luther King and a sun-worshipping Egyptian pharoah, completed the trilogy begun with *Einstein*, and thrillingly combined his trademark repetitions and overlappings with the ceremonial grandeur of the stage.

Glass maintains a formidable rate of output – he was the first composer to develop a production-line system, using sampling techniques so that every musical sketch could be speedily turned into finished product. He currently lives in the East Village, where he spends each morning composing before taking the short walk to his high-tech Living Room Studios, to oversee record production and the rehearsal of opera and ensemble pieces. The most stimulating project of recent years was his 1990 reunion with Ravi Shankar, *Passages*, a true collaboration in which each gave the other basic material to expand into full compositions.

THE MUSIC

Einstein on the Beach is a landmark in Glass's career and a musical tour de force, with syllabic vocals (doh, ray, mee, fah, etc) and zany texts voiced behind luminous darting keyboard passages to mesmerizing effect. Glass's sense of tension is best heard on "Trial/Prison", where the singer repeats a wacky vocal about an airconditioned supermarket to a seemingly endless chorus of numbers (1, 2, 3, 4) until, at the twelfth minute, the entire instrumental ensemble bursts into life. However, the best way into Glass is to listen to the milder *Glassworks*, a piece mostly made up of tranquil passages of horn, piano, cello and viola spruced up with subtle electronics.

Equally successful in financial terms, the *"Low" Symphony* reveals Glass's sense of tradition, with Romantic and Stravinsky-like orchestrations paying homage to David Bowie and Brian Eno's *Low* – a rock album whose brooding instrumentals were directly inspired by Glass's early works, using techniques of repetition and addition instead of more conventional song structures.

⊙ **Glassworks**: Riesman; Philip Glass Ensemble; Glass, Gibson (Sony MK 73640).

⊙ **Einstein on The Beach**: Riesman; Philip Glass Ensemble; Glass, Gibson, Childs (CBS Masterworks M4K 38875; 4 CDs).

◎ **"Low" Symphony**: Russell Davies; Brooklyn Philharmonic Orchestra (Point Music 438 150-2).

Mixed by Kurt Munkacsi to suit the evolving Walkman market, *Glassworks* was one of the first digital recordings, and remains the essential Glass CD. The original 160-minute CBS (now Sony) version of *Einstein* is still definitive, its crisp almost spiky sound giving you the full rush of a composer at the height of his powers. There's a new version on Elektra (Glass's current label), which is some thirty minutes longer, uses better equipment and has a smoother sound, but the ecstatic ensemble bursts are not as vivid – it's essentially an airbrush job.

For a taste of Glass's more recent work you can't do better than the *"Low" Symphony*, in which he transforms two of the Bowie and Eno album's "songs" and one unreleased track into beautiful symphonic movements.

ALEXANDER GLAZUNOV

(1865–1936)

Glazunov is best known for things other than his own compositions: for helping complete some of Borodin's music, for example, or for teaching Shostakovich, or for conducting the premiere of Rachmaninov's first symphony while drunk, and thereby triggering the young composer's nervous breakdown. With its undisguised assimilations of Tchaikovsky, Rimsky-Korsakov and Scriabin, Glazunov's music might not have the individuality of the music of some of his compatriots, yet it is often attractive and colourful, and it brought him world-wide acclaim in his day.

Glazunov's main problem is his conservatism. This was the charge laid against him long ago by both Prokofiev and Shostakovich, and there is no denying that by the standards of his friend Scriabin, for example, his music showed little advance on that of the nationalist circle surrounding Mily Balakirev, though he did manage to fuse their general techniques with the European-oriented style of Tchaikovsky.

His musical talents were nonetheless prodigious and he soon outgrew Rimsky-Korsakov's tutelage. His first mature works date from the 1880s, when he produced the first two of his eight symphonies (a ninth got no further than a single movement). Three more date from the 1890s, as do the two ballets which brought him more acclaim than anything else he wrote, *Raymonda* (1897) and *The Seasons* (1899). In the year of the latter work he was appointed professor at the St Petersburg conservatory, where he remained until 1930, having become its director in 1905. In the early years of the century he produced the *Violin Concerto* (1904) and the *Eighth Symphony* (1906), and from then on he composed little of any consequence, concentrating instead on his academic responsibilities, thereby managing to stay in favour with the regimes both before and after the Revolution. He settled in Paris in 1932, where he died four years later.

THE MUSIC

Glazunov's symphonies are not consistently good enough to make them all worth investigating, but the youthful *No. 1* is an attractive effort, showing a promise never properly fulfilled. *No. 5* is also appealing, with a headily Romantic slow movement and a lively scherzo, while *No. 8* is the most coherently constructed. The *Violin Concerto* is probably his best known work and, while owing an obvious stylistic debt to Tchaikovsky's concerto, it has its moments of real beauty and harmonic lusciousness. His ballet scores are similarly full of Tchaikovsky, though *The Seasons* emerges as perhaps his most interesting work overall, with its glittering orchestration and apt characterization of the individual seasons.

None of the available versions of the symphonies can be recommended unreservedly, but these Orfeo releases have decent sound quality, even if they are not state of the art. The performances are more than adequate, under Neeme Järvi's typically zealous direction.

Heifetz's stunning recording of the *Violin Concerto* dates from the 1960s, and appears on a generously filled CD alongside typically forceful accounts of the Prokofiev and Sibelius concertos.

Ashkenazy's recording of *The Seasons* outclasses all earlier recordings of the work, and its combination with a first-rate *Nutcracker* makes this an indispensable disc.

MIKHAIL GLINKA

(1804–1857)

Glinka was the father of Russian musical nationalism, the first Russian master of operatic writing, and the first Russian composer to find acceptance in the rest of Europe. He was born into a wealthy land-owning family, and as a thirteen-year-old took piano lessons with John Field, the creator of the nocturne (see p.97). But in 1824 he abandoned his musical studies in favour of a post at the Ministry of Communication, and even

GUUS ONG

though he gave recitals as an amateur singer, he did not fully devote himself to music until 1828, when he began full-time composition lessons.

Two years later he moved to Milan, where his exposure to Italian music forced him to acknowledge the weakness of his native national tradition – every aspect of Russian music at this time, even its folk songs, was contaminated by the overbearing influence of Western European culture. In 1833 he moved on to Vienna, but homesickness and the death of his father forced him to return to St Petersburg where, in 1835, he set about writing his first opera – *A Life for the Tsar*, the first serious attempt at creating classical music with a genuine Russian character, though Italian lyricism is an important element of its style.

The opera's successful production in 1836 proved that Glinka had struck a chord and his subsequent appointment in 1837 as Imperial Kappellmeister cemented his position as Russia's most important composer. Midway through that year, Glinka began to plan an opera based upon Pushkin's poem *Ruslan and Lyudmila*, and even though the poet's death prevented their collaboration, a libretto was patched together. Glinka's second opera was produced in 1842 and its massive success finally secured his fame outside Russia. Numerous aspects of *Ruslan and*

Lyudmila marked it out as essentially Russian: its use of Russian folk polyphony and melodic themes; the recitatives based upon the rhythms of the Russian language; the texture of its sounds, in which instruments such as the balalaika played a significant part. It was a declaration of musical independence, and at Glinka's death in 1857, a generation of composers was ready to continue writing music that was Russian in style, flavour and inspiration – the first such generation in Russia's history.

THE OPERAS

A *Life for the Tsar* – titled *Ivan Susanin* until it was renamed following Tsar Nicholas I's attendence at one of the rehearsals – concerns the troubled period following the death of Boris Godunov, when Poles and Russians were fighting for control of the Tsar's crown. The battling nations are differentiated through unambiguous musical characterization: the Poles are portrayed by "shallow" national dances, while the Russians are portrayed for the most part by slow and elegiac arias and ensembles. This patriotic tale is always being brought out for the openings of operatic seasons in Russia (under Communist rule a few changes to the text turned it into an acceptable piece of socialist realism), but it's not the subtlest opera ever written, and its interest remains chiefly historical.

Ruslan and Lyudmila, on the other hand, stands on its own merits – from the famous, toe-tapping overture to the tuneful, boisterous finale, Glinka's second opera is a thoroughly entertaining piece. Based upon Pushkin's poem, Glinka's magical tale can be seen as anticipating the fantastic and grotesque elements of the operas of Rimsky-Korsakov and Stravinsky. Basically, Lyudmila vanishes from a feast organized for her three suitors. Her father promises her hand to the one who finds her first. Ruslan, the heroic knight, learns that she has been stolen by an evil dwarf, and then battles with a giant decapitated head to win a magic sword with which to defeat the dwarf and rescue Lyudmila. The tale may have its dramatic weaknesses, but the music's overall stylistic cohesion, melodic invention and idiomatic Russian harmonies more than compensate.

Life for the Tsar: Martinovich, Pendachanska, Toczyska, Merritt; Sofia Festival Orchestra; Tchakarov (Sony S3K 46 487).

Ruslan and Lyudmila: Rudenko, Nestorenko, Maslennikov; Bolshoi Theatre; Simonov (Eurodisc GD 69124).

EMI's great recording of *Life for the Tsar* with Nicolai Gedda and Boris Christoff is no longer available, but Sony's version is an extremely worthy replacement. Tchakarov's pacing and control of this very long opera is exemplary, and the soloists are generally very good. There's only one complete recording of *Ruslan* in the catalogue at the moment: Simonov conducts a lively performance although both soprano and sound quality are on the rough side.

CHRISTOPH WILLIBALD GLUCK
(1714–1787)

It was Gluck who put into practice the principle defined by his near-contemporary Pietro Metastasio – "when the music in union with drama takes precedence, then the drama and music itself suffers in consequence". Gluck was the first composer to deny his singers any opportunity to indulge mere display, for in Gluck's operas

the role of the music is to transmit the meaning of the libretto. Technically he may not have been the most accomplished of eighteenth-century composers, but he was the first to write operas in which music and drama achieved a state of complete balance.

German-born, Gluck was educated in Prague then moved to Vienna in 1736 where

MANSELL COLLECTION

Inundated with requests for operas, it was not long before Gluck was working directly with his librettists, rather than accepting completed texts as part of a commission. His collaboration with the poet Raniero de' Calzabigi brought about radical reforms in the composition and production of opera, as typified by *Orfeo ed Euridice* (1762), a work whose dramatic use of orchestration and overall sense of direction were enthrallingly original. *Alceste*, composed in 1767 to a libretto by Calzabigi, furthered the development of Gluck's mission to "restrict music to its true office by serving poetry by means of expression and by following the situation of the story" and "to strive for a beautiful simplicity".

Alceste was not immediately the success it would later become, and in 1770 Gluck left his Vienna position, settling three years later in Paris, in order to fulfill the Opéra's commission for *Iphigenie en Aulide*. Its production was a sensation, as were his revisions of *Orfeo* and *Alceste*. However, his fame resulted in jealousy, and in an episode worthy of a Feydeau farce, a quarrel was engineered between Gluck and his bitter rival Piccini by asking the latter to set *Iphigénie en Tauride*, a libretto on which Gluck was working at the time. Piccini's version was moderately successful, Gluck's was his masterpiece: boasting an astonishingly integrated fusion of dance, drama, chorus and song, it rapidly eclipsed the competition. In 1779, Gluck retired to Vienna where, living in regal splendour, he died after refusing his doctor's orders that he drink no alchohol after dinner.

ORFEO ED EURIDICE

"If my music has had some success, I think it is my duty to recognise that I am beholden for it to him . . . However much talent a composer may have, he will never produce any but mediocre music, if the poet does not awaken in him that enthusiasm without which the productions of all the arts are but feeble and drooping". Gluck was always keen to acknowledge his debt to Calzabigi for it was Calzabigi who had taught him how to write recitative and had persuaded him to banish

he played cello in a nobleman's private orchestra. In 1737 the orchestra travelled to Milan where Gluck took lessons with Sammartini (a pioneer of sonata form), under whose guidance he composed his first opera *Artaserse*. Its success led to the completion of a further seven operas before he left for London in 1745, and although his two London operas failed, his friendship with Handel was to prove of inestimable musical benefit.

Upon leaving London in 1746, Gluck spent the next four years in travel, during which his operas *Semiramide riconosciuta* and *La Clemenza di Tito* were well received, and then settled in Vienna. At the end of 1752 he was appointed Kapellmeister to the Prince of Saxe-Hildburghausen, a position that cemented his dominance of Vienna's musical life. Giacomo Durazzo, the manager of Vienna's state theatres, saw in Gluck's talent an opportunity to capitalize on the popularity of the lively and flexible French opéra-comique, and he engaged Gluck to adapt various existing works in the genre. Gluck responded by producing his own series of "French" comic masterpieces, following the successful premiere of *La fausse esclave* in 1758.

coloratura singing. Their partnership was one of the most productive in operatic history, comparable to Mozart-Da Ponte and Strauss-Hofmannsthal. *Orfeo ed Euridice* was their first joint work and it received its premiere in Vienna on October 5, 1762.

Ironically, Gluck's reformist opera is based upon the myth that had served as the foundation for the first Florentine operas, way back in 1600. Orfeo (Orpheus) is mourning the death of his wife Euridice. Zeus is so taken by his grief that he permits him to attempt to reclaim her from Hades. If, through his playing, he can persuade Pluto to release her, he may guide her back to earth, but he must not look upon her until they have crossed the River Styx. Orfeo succeeds in his task until Euridice, unable to understand his strange behaviour, claims she would rather be dead then be so spurned by him. He turns to look at her, and she is lost – but then touched by his lament, Amor restores Euridice to life, an artificially happy ending typical of the eighteenth-century stage.

Orfeo is today known for little beyond the ballet movement *Dance of the Blessed Spirits*, but it boasts an abundance of fresh, unencumbered melodies that make this Gluck's most engaging work. The eruptions of strong emotion gain added potency from the classical poise with which they are expressed, especially in Orfeo's outpouring of grief, *Che faro senza Euridice* – an aria whose simple profundity is matched only by the closing solo of Purcell's *Dido and Aeneas* (see p.280).

> 🌓 Verrett, Moffo, Raskin; Rome Polyphonic Chorus; Virtuosi di Roma; Fasano (RCA GD87896; 2 CDs).

There are more than ten versions of *Orfeo* in the current catalogue, and several of these are excellent. Most beguiling of the lot is RCA's recording of the original text (ie without the embellishments added to the Paris production), with the delicious Anna Moffo as Euridice. Moffo is peerless in defining the pure shape and style of Gluck's writing for female voice, and while Shirley Verrett has a rather weightier approach, the

writing for the role of Orfeo suits her style. The sense of rapture between the lead roles is beautifully supported by the orchestra, under the supple guidance of the little-known Renato Fasano.

IPHIGÉNIE EN TAURIDE

First performed in Paris on May 18, 1779, *Iphigénie en Tauride* was Gluck's last important work. Its libretto, by Nicholas-François Guillard, is the finest poem set by Gluck, and the opera as a whole comes as close as possible to the composer's ideal of a modern revival of the spirit of Greek tragedy. Listen to this opera and you'll hear the inspiration for the classical scenes composed by Bellini, Berlioz and Strauss.

Ultimately derived from the plays of Euripides (the twists and turns of the plot are too complicated to detail here), *Iphigénie en Tauride* contains some extraordinary moments of great drama, not least the introductory storm (there is no overture) and the chorus of the Furies in Act II, when Orestes' terrible, haunting conscience (he has murdered his mother) is portrayed as if in a dream. The arias throughout are innovatively plain and eloquent, while the finely realized orchestration lifts the ensemble high above the status of mere accompaniment. *Iphigénie en Tauride* is an extraordinarily colourful but plaintive work, which for all its heroic subject matter, set opera squarely on the path to realism.

> 🌑 Montague, Aler, Allen, Argenta, Boulton, Alliot-Lugaz, Massis; Monteverdi Choir; Lyon Opera Orchestra; Gardiner (Philips 416 148-2PH2; 2 CDs).

Gardiner's highly analytical approach often results in attractive if not enthralling music. This recording of *Iphigénie*, however, is a masterly account that buzzes with a sense of purpose and engagement. In the title role, Diana Montague produces an extraordinary, glowing performance; Gardiner rushes some of the ensembles, but his control of the choruses and his attention to clarity are superb.

HENRYK GÓRECKI

(1933–   )

Henryk Górecki's third symphony, the *Symphony of Sorrowful Songs*, is the most remarkable music success story of the past decade. Written in 1976, this cathartic vision of post-Holocaust, post-industrial humanity was recorded several times in Górecki's native Poland without making any great impact elsewhere. Then in 1992 a version was released featuring soprano Dawn Upshaw with the London Sinfonietta, and within a few weeks it had hit the top of the classical charts in Britain and the United States. To date it has sold over a million copies, making a cult figure of its previously obscure creator.

Born near the bleak industrial town of Katowice, Górecki studied at its academy of music in the late 1950s, quickly establishing a reputation for his fierce individualism. He utilized a frenzied form of serialism in his *Symphony No. 1* (1959), which duly outraged the communist officials, as did the subsequent *Scontri* (Collisions) for orchestra, an even more scorching work. After the short-lived post-Stalinist thaw in Poland, the disillusioned composer sought solace in his country's folk songs and in religion, as exemplified by his *Symphony No. 2* (1972), with its setting of texts from the Psalms. Spending much of his time walking in the Tatra mountains, an agricultural area rich in ancient cultural traditions but close to the site of Auschwitz, he then began to conceive of unifying the emotional history of Poland in one great work. The result was the awesome *Symphony No. 3*, for which he took words from the Holy Cross lament and an inscription left by a girl imprisoned by the Nazis at Zakopane, in the Tatras.

Three years later Górecki's frail health forced him to withdraw from teaching, but since then he has written a harpsichord concerto, *O Domina Nostra* for soprano and organ, and *Lerchenmusik* for cello, piano and clarinet, while the Kronos Quartet have recorded his difficult string quartet *Already it is Dusk*. Sales of the *Symphony No. 3* CD have now allowed him to buy a house in his beloved Tatra mountains and enjoy his worldwide celebrity for a work which he views as an "intensely felt revelation of the human condition."

SYMPHONY NO. 3
AND O DOMINA NOSTRA

Elements of the *Symphony No. 3* have been likened to Beethoven and Chopin, and Górecki certainly also drew inspiration for it from Ives and Szymanowski, who experimented with overlapping melodies drawn from folk and church songs. However, the textures of Shostakovich are the main source for the brooding sound of the first movement, where the dense strings rise upward and outward until the aerial vocal takes hold, at which point the strings descend with stubborn slowness back to their place of origin. This "stairway" effect is extremely intense, but the highest pitch comes in the second movement, as the soprano sings the words from the death-camp wall – "No mother, do not weep. Most chaste queen of Heaven" – against a contrastingly light string setting. If you respond to this you'll probably get a lot out of *O Domina Nostra* (1982), a fascinating devotional piece dedicated to the Black Virgin of Jasna Góra, the symbol of Polish independence.

⊙ **Symphony No. 3**: Upshaw; London Sinfonietta; Zinman (Elektra Nonesuch 7559-79282-2).
⊙ **O Domina Nostra**: Eicher; Leonard; Bowers-Broadbent (ECM New Series 437 956-2).

Mastered by rock engineer Bob Ludwig, the London Sinfonietta recording of *Symphony No. 3* has an incredibly panoramic sound with enough depth to please the most uncompromising of hi-fi buffs – and Dawn Upshaw's voice will take your breath away. *O Domina Nostra* is a serenely austere piece that blends medieval plainsong with the strains of Polish folk tunes; Bowers-Broadbent's organ work gives the CD just the right air of solemnity.

CHARLES-FRANÇOIS GOUNOD
(1818–1893)

For most of the first seventy years of the nineteenth century Paris was the great centre of musical Romanticism, but this situation arose more from the city's ability to attract foreign talent – Chopin, Liszt, Meyerbeer et cetera – than from the recognition of its native talent (such as Berlioz). Between 1852 and 1870 only five new French works were added to the Paris Opera's repertory, and it was thanks only to the Théâtre Lyrique that any new French music was heard in the capital at all. Charles-François Gounod was the first home-grown composer to break the trend. Although his debt to German music is undeniable (he had a notorious fondness for Beethoven's late quartets), Gounod is the most thoroughly representative French composer of the mid-nineteenth century, and is the man chiefly responsible for leading French opera away from the elephantine spectaculars of Meyerbeer, France's most popular operatic composer at the time.

His first operatic attempts were far from successful, being pastiche Gluck with thin plots and weak texts, and it was not until 1859 that he hit upon an operatic subject that really stimulated him – Goethe's *Faust*. Deeply religious but with a great weakness for women, Gounod concentrated on that aspect of the poem that spoke to him most directly – he and his librettists duly pulled *Faust* to pieces in order to emphasize the love story of Faust and Marguerite rather than Goethe's wider metaphysical considerations (which is why German writers call the work *Margarethe* rather than honouring it with the same title as their national poet's masterpiece). Reductive though it may be, Gounod's *Faust* is an inspired mixture of melodic invention, religious solemnity and vivid characterization, and gave the country's composers a new sense of direction and identity. It also became the most successful French opera in history. As early as 1863, an English critic was complaining – "Faust, Faust, Faust, nothing but Faust. Faust on Saturday, Wednesday and Thursday; to be repeated tonight, and on every night until further notice." To date, *Faust* has been performed in over fifty countries and translated into twenty-five different languages.

Faust's huge international success did not inhibit Gounod as did the similar triumphs of Mascagni and Leoncavallo (see p.222 and p.195), but despite the quality of what he wrote post-*Faust*, he never again experienced a similar degree of success. Even so, it was Gounod who maintained and promoted characteristic French qualities in serious dramatic music, inspiring the likes of Bizet, Fauré, Massenet (who was known as "the son of Gounod") and Ravel.

FAUST

Gounod's *Faust* is but a distant relative of Goethe's, but the libretto has a directness and lack of pretension that's perfect for the operatic stage, and the score is so stuffed with memorable tunes that it has served as the basis for more instrumental transcriptions, fantasies and variations than almost any other opera. The tenor lead is especially memorable, with the third act's *Salut! demeure chaste et pure* standing out as a sublime example of Gounod's lyric style. Similarly, the duets in Act One for Faust and Mephistopheles, and in Acts Three and Five for Faust and Marguerite, are irresistibly appealing. In short, *Faust*'s seemingly endless stream of hummable melodies make this one of the most completely enjoyable operas ever written.

Corelli, Sutherland, Ghiaurov, Massard, Elkins, Sinclair, Meyers; Ambrosian Opera Chorus; London Symphony Orchestra; Bonynge (Decca 421 240-2DM3; 3 CDs).

There are a number of complete recordings of Faust, but Decca's 1966 recording steals the limelight. Sutherland copes well with the character of Marguerite, while Ghiaurov's powerful and colourful voice brings ominous dimensions to Gounod's potentially spineless Mephistopheles. However, it is the Italian tenor Franco Corelli who dominates in the title role – he might struggle with the French, but he is utterly immersed in the character's emotional turmoil. Bonynge's conducting is thrilling from start to finish, and the recorded sound is exemplary.

ENRIQUE GRANADOS

(1867–1916)

It is not without good reason that Enrique Granados is banded together with his compatriots Isaac Albéniz and Manuel de Falla in most music books. Like them he was taught by the eminent musicologist Felipe Pedrell, who inspired all three to forge an individual style based on indigenous folk music; and, just as Albéniz and Falla did, Granados made the de rigueur student trip to Paris, hotbed of the European avant-garde. All three became masters at taking native folk melodies and overlaying them with a highly spiced chromatic idiom, more often than not French in derivation. When it came to character, however, it was a different matter. The spontaneously warm Granados was closer in temperament to his friend Albéniz than to the drier Falla, and the similarities did not end there. Both Granados and Albéniz were concert pianists of international repute who chose to write primarily for the piano, and their reputations rest primarily on just one concert suite – though the quality of Granados's *Goyescas* and Albéniz's *Iberia* is of the highest order.

Granados started off by composing pretty, salon-type pieces in a post-Lisztian manner. However, with the 1892 premiere of an orchestral version of three of his *Danzas españolas* for piano, it was clear that a new direction in Spanish music was opening up. The *Danzas españolas* were much admired by Massenet, Saint-Saëns and above all Grieg, an endorsement which must have given Granados much satisfaction, as the nationalism of Grieg's music was much appreciated by Spanish audiences and young composers alike. Granados, well aware of prevailing fashions, knew that the best way to get noticed in Spain was to write a zarzuela (a kind of operetta), and a few years later he composed the highly successful *Maria del Carmen* (1898), which gained him a commendation from the king. Although he cashed in on his success with a string of other zarzuelas, over the next decade or so he devoted himself as much to teaching and performing as to composition. From time to time Granados's talents took him

away from music altogether – he once said of himself, "I am not a musician but an artist", and by all accounts he was a fine writer and excellent painter. But despite these creative diversions Granados remained first and foremost a musician, and was in great demand as an accompanist by such virtuosos as the cellist Pablo Casals and the violinist Jacques Thibaud.

During the early 1900s Granados composed a variety of works, most of which are now unknown, but all the while he was contemplating the music of what was to be his most ambitious work to date, *Goyescas*. It was *Goyescas* that made Granados a name to be reckoned with. After its French premiere in 1914, at the Salle Pleyel in Paris, all sorts of honours came his way, including election to the *Legion d'honneur* and a commission from the Opéra to compose a piece of music theatre derived from *Goyescas*. The outbreak of World War I soon scotched the idea of a production, but interest then unexpectedly came from New York's Metropolitan Opera.

The composer travelled over with his wife to be present at the resoundingly successful premiere on 26 January, 1916, then prolonged his stay to play at the White House at the invitation of President Wilson. Consequently they missed a direct boat back to Spain, so decided to travel back to Europe via England. The *Sussex*, the boat they took from Liverpool to Dieppe, was torpedoed by a German submarine with the loss of many lives, including that of Granados and his wife. Just two months before his death, Granados had written to a friend: "I have a whole world of ideas . . . I am only now starting my work."

GOYESCAS

The *Goyescas* were, as you'd guess, inspired by the paintings and etchings of Goya, and rarely has a composer captured the underlying mood of the work of another artist with such clarity as Granados did with this series of piano pieces. Eighteenth-century Spanish music plays an important part in the sound-world of *Goyescas*, but, as the critic Harold Schonberg wrote, it's the general "scent of Spanish rhythms, Spanish melodies, and Spanish life" which makes the suite so memorable. The Andalusian flamenco elements sometimes have a tendency to be a touch over-repetitive, but in the most famous piece, *Quejas, o la maja y el ruiseñor* (known in English as *The Maiden and the Nightingale*), every statement of the plaintive melody and its concluding arabesque is beautifully constructed, with nothing overstated.

◗ **Goyescas; Escenas románticas; 6 Piezas sobre cantos populares españoles**: de Larrocha (Decca 433 920-2; with sonatas by Albéniz and Soler; 2 CDs).

The music of *Goyescas* can sound flat if the pianist can't muster a supercharged rhythmic vitality, but Alicia de Larrocha rises to the occasion – this account of the complete *Goyescas* is beautifully fashioned. She brings an equally evocative flair to the two exhilarating companion sets, the *Escenas románticas* and *6 Piezas sobre cantos populares*.

EDVARD GRIEG
(1843–1907)

Grieg may have been the only internationally successful composer to have come out of Norway, but it would be a mistake to regard him as a peripheral figure. He ranks with names such as Sibelius and Dvořák in the late nineteenth century's upsurge of musical nationalism, inspiring musicians across Europe to follow his example in looking to his country's folk heritage for source material. In Spain, for example, the impact of Grieg's music on the likes of Manuel de Falla (see p.130) was instrumental in the formation of an essentially national school of music. The depth of Grieg's influence is all the more remarkable when you compare his output to that of Sibelius and Dvořák, for whereas they were devoted to mighty large-scale compositions, Grieg was a committed miniaturist. His *Piano Concerto* might be his best-known creation, but it's not at all typical.

His first lessons came from his mother. Then in 1858 the Norwegian violinist and folk enthusiast Ole Bull heard Grieg play the piano and persuaded his reluctant parents to send the boy to the Leipzig Conservatory. Bull was delighted, Grieg was not. He hated his time there, but had the good fortune to attend concerts at which the likes of Clara Schumann and Richard Wagner were regular artists.

In the spring of 1862 his Opus 1 was published, and in May of the following year he settled in Copenhagen, where he was taken under the wing of Niels Gade, Denmark's leading Romantic composer and a close friend of Schumann and Mendelssohn.

ROYAL COLLEGE OF MUSIC

Gade was enthusiastic about the young composer's potential but his optimism was tempered by misgivings about his lack of large-scale work, and so he set Grieg the task of writing his first and only symphony, something for which he was neither technically equipped nor temperamentally suited.

Soon afterwards he met his cousin, the singer Nina Hagerup; a year later, the two were engaged to be married and Grieg was back in Norway, living in the house of Ole Bull. From this point, his artistic personality began to change as he started taking a studious interest in his country's musical heritage, having previously spent a long time away from home or immersed in a middle-class milieu that had been dominated by Danish culture. His commitment to Norwegian nationalism was confirmed by his encounters with Rikard Nordraak, Norway's great hope for the formation of a national school (Rikard died in 1866 aged just 24, having written what is now Norway's national anthem), and by a meeting with Henrik Ibsen in Rome in 1865.

He returned to Norway confident of his mission, and after promoting concerts of his own music he was quickly recognized as one of his country's foremost composers. In 1867 he married Nina and settled in Oslo, where he became a teacher and conductor of international renown. A year later he and his family moved back to Denmark where he composed his *Piano Concerto*; in Italy the following year he presented Liszt with his very badly handwritten draft of the piece, and, to his amazement, Liszt played the whole concerto right through. "Go on, you have the stuff", Liszt is said to have encouraged him.

By 1874 Grieg was so famous and so highly valued that the Norwegian government voted to grant him an annuity, and Ibsen similarly paid his respects by asking him to provide incidental music for his play *Peer Gynt*. His popularity took him to England, where he and his wife gave numerous recitals and, in an extraordinary display of affection, both Oxford and Cambridge granted him honorary degrees. The last twenty years of his life followed a rarely changing pattern of holidays, composition and concert tours and he became one of the elder statesmen of European music.

One year after Grieg's death, Schoenberg composed his first atonal works and within five years Grieg's name had become synonymous with everything outdated in music. There is indeed nothing too challenging in Grieg. His music is on the whole a sweetly harmonic synthesis of folk song and German-based Romanticism the Romanticism of Schumann, not of Wagner, for whose lofty ambitions Grieg felt no affection. Within these limits, however, he is one of the most distinctive and enjoyable composers of his time, a master of small-scale form whose greatest music is, in a sense, his slightest.

> **◗ Historical Recordings – Piano Concerto, Piano Pieces, Chamber Works & Songs**: Rubinstein, Rachmaninov, Kreisler, Bjoerling, Flagstad, Nilsson; Philadelphia Orchestra; Ormandy (RCA 09026 61879 2; 3 CDs).
> **◉ Orchestral Works**: Bonney; Hagegard; Stene; Telefsen; Ziberstein; Gothenburg Symphony Orchestra; Järvi (Deutsche Grammophon DG 437 842-2; 6 CDs).

These two boxes, released to celebrate the 150th anniversary of Grieg's birth, offer very different introductions to the composer's output. RCA's set of historical performances takes in every major field in which he worked, and includes an energetic 1942 performance of the *Piano Concerto* with Rubinstein, a wonderful 1928 performance of the *Violin Sonata No. 3* with Kriesler and Rachmaninov, and a whole disc of Grieg's songs, beginning with performances by Olive Kline in 1913 and ending with Birgit Nilsson in the 1960s.

DG's six-disc box of recent recordings features an excellent disc of songs with Sophie von Otter and a performance of the first version of the *Piano Concerto*, which, like the original of Sibelius's *Violin Concerto*, is substantially different from the better known revision. All in all, it's a fine set, but for beginners it's probably too comprehensive, and the best of Grieg isn't to be found here.

PIANO CONCERTO

Grieg was a fine pianist and hardly a year passed when he did not give concerts either as a soloist or with his wife. He wrote his *Piano Concerto* as a vehicle for his own talents, and its youthful exuberance – reminiscent of Schumann's only concerto, also in A minor – has ensured its place on the CVs of most concert pianists. Composed in 1868 while Grieg was holidaying with his wife and young child in Denmark (although revised to the version played today in 1907), it's replete with a sense of tenderness and well-being, expressed in a proliferation of enchanting thematic ideas. The opening motif – an idea as well-known as the opening of that other virtuoso war-horse, Tchaikovsky's first concerto – is built upon a descending second followed by a descending third, intervals typical in Norwegian folk music.

🔘 Kovacevich; BBC Symphony Orchestra; Davis (Philips 412 923-2; with Schumann *Piano Concerto*).

Stephen Kovacevich's mid-1970s recording holds off fierce competition from the likes of Lipatti, Rubinstein, Richter, Pollini and a host of other stars. Colin Davis occasionally drags the proceedings, but Kovacevich is clear, unaffected and lyrical, showing a great overall awareness of shape and colour.

PEER GYNT

In 1874 Henrik Ibsen decided to adapt his verse play *Peer Gynt* for a performance at the theatre in Christiania (now Oslo). Norway's theatrical tradition at the time was based upon operettas and musical plays, and Ibsen recognized that his sprawling play needed a soothing soundtrack in order to succeed – and accordingly asked Grieg to supply incidental music. The new production was first staged in February 1876 and was hugely successful, playing for several nights until a fire destroyed the sets and costumes.

To give his music an existence apart from Ibsen's drama, Grieg extracted two suites for concert performance, and these two spin-offs – Op. 46 and Op. 54 – contain his most striking orchestral music, showing a directness and freshness that generally eluded him when he came to write for large forces. Its best-known section is the flute's principle theme from *Morning*, but this is one of many examples of a piece of music being identified with a sound-bite from one of its less remarkable moments. Most of the other self-contained episodes make *Morning* sound banal, none more so than *Solvejg's Song*, a piece of wonderfully fragile lyricism.

🔘 **Peer Gynt – complete**: Jorsalfar, Bonney, Eklöf, Sandve, Malmberg; Gothenburg Symphony Orchestra; Järvi (Deutsche Grammophon DG 423 079-2).
🔘 **Peer Gynt – suites**: Hollweg; Royal Philharmonic Orchestra; Beecham (EMI CDM7 64751-2; with orchestral pieces).

Neeme Järvi conducts the whole of the musical score of *Peer Gynt* but includes just the bare bones of Ibsen's text to keep the action clear (the full play can go on for four hours). The Gothenburg Symphony Orchestra respond with delightful enthusiasm to Järvi's sensitive but direct conducting, making this by far the best version of the complete score. For those who prefer the purely musical highlights, go for Beecham's waspish account of the two *Suites*, which is coupled with some other fine Grieg orchestral music.

SONGS

"I loved a young girl who had a wonderful voice and an equally wonderful gift for interpretation. That girl became my wife and my lifelong companion to this very day. For me, she has been – I dare admit it – the only genuine interpreter of my songs." So Grieg wrote to his American biographer Henry Fincke in 1900. Grieg's adoration of his wife was the wellspring of his songs, his greatest body of music, and though she could not be regarded as the the sole inspiration for all 140, there is little doubt that, from Op. 5 onwards, she had a defining influence on their evolution.

Grieg had a rare understanding of the expressive potential of the human voice, allied with a gift for piano writing that gives many of his songs – the later ones in particular – the sort of balance between accompanist and singer that you find in the songs of Schubert. As with Schubert, Grieg's emotional range is vast, and the melodic directness and limpidity of his music allows anyone to grasp immediately the nature of each song – but on the other hand, you'll need a translation to hand in order to appreciate the delicacy with which Grieg augments the content of each text. In contrast to Schubert, most of Grieg's songs are strophic (whereby the same music is repeated with each successive stanza), in honour of their folk inspiration.

🔘 **Songs**: von Otter; Forsberg (Deutsche Grammophon DG 437 521-2).
🔘 **Songs**: Bonney, Hagegard, Steene, Telefsen; Gothenburg Symphony Orchestra; Järvi (Deutsche Grammophon DG 437 519-2).
🔘 **Historic Vocal Recordings**: various artists (RCA 09026 61827-2).

Several outstanding recordings of the songs were issued in 1993, but pride of place goes to two Deutsche Grammophon

POLYGRAM

Anne Sofie von Otter

discs. Anne Sofie von Otter gives marvellously characterful interpretations, beguilingly frank in the folksy pieces, deeply moving in the more intimate songs such as *I Love You* and *Last Spring* – the latter song possessing a melody so perfect that Grieg couldn't resist recycling it for a couple of other compositions. Pianist Bengt Forsberg provides sensitive accompaniment throughout. Grieg's orchestrations of some of his finest songs turn up on the recital from Barbara Bonney and Håkan Hagegård; the orchestra doesn't add anything to the meaning of the songs, but the thicker sonorities certainly give a sense of swoony luxuriance. RCA's historic retrospective is also marvellous; if the prospect of some ancient recorded sound is off-putting, fight it, for some of the finest voices of the century are on this CD. The main problem here is the lack of accompanying text.

LYRIC PIECES

Grieg's talent for uncomplicated, sincere and brief musical ideas is well displayed in his *Lyric Pieces*, ten sets of piano pieces spanning his career from 1867 to 1901. Ranging from forty seconds to four minutes in length, they are extraordinarily crafted compositions, defining a mood in the space of a bar or two, giving it enough time to completely infiltrate the listener's mind, then letting it go. At their best the *Lyric Pieces* are as touching as some of Chopin's miniatures, and even when they amount to little more than whimsical musings, they are never less than tunefully pleasant.

○ **Lyric Pieces (complete)**: Oppitz (RCA 09026 6 1568-2; 3 CDs).
○ **Lyric Pieces (selected)**: Gilels (Deutsche Grammophon DG 419 749-2).

The only complete set of the *Lyric Pieces* comes from Gerard Oppitz, whose generally slow tempi are perfectly suited to the twilight ambience of many of these pieces; his solid Teutonic technique also enables him to hammer his way through the more frenetic outbursts with impressive determination. The best selective recital comes from Emil Gilels, a performance of sublime, fluid romanticism.

SOFIA GUBAIDULINA
(1931–   )

Sofia Gubaidulina has said of herself, "I am the place where East meets West", which is as good a categorization as any. One of the leading innovative composers in the former Soviet Union, she comes from a mixed Tartar and Slavic background, and the influence of Eastern philosophies is clear in many of her attitudes towards spirituality and its expression – whether writing for huge orchestral forces or a few solo instruments, she tends to explore a wide range of sonorities in order to create music that is extraordinarily still and serene, leaving the listener with a sense of timelessness that's rare in Western music.

She started writing her own music at an early age and then studied in Kazan (in the present-day Tatar Republic) before moving to Moscow, where she attended the conservatory until 1963. Until around that time the Soviet regime had been diligent in keeping Russian composers isolated from the corrupting influence of modern Western music, but as the 1960s wore on there was a gradual thawing of official attitudes, marked by visits from avant-garde composers such as Luigi Nono and Pierre Boulez. Having started her career writing in straightforward tonal idioms, Gubaidulina took every possible chance to explore the new languages and techniques, such as serialism, electronics and the use of numerical patterns in composition. Soon she had emerged as one of the country's most interesting contemporary composers, along with the more turbulent Alfred Schnittke (see p.305).

For most of her life Gubaidulina has supported herself by writing music for films and the theatre, disciplines that have enabled her to experiment with a wide variety of sounds and procedures. Another crucial contribution to her work has come from the traditional music of the Soviet Union – in 1975 she founded an improvisation group called Astreya, which made wide use of folk instruments and forms, and had a great influence on her concert-hall pieces. If there is one common denominator to her output, it is her belief in the transforming power of art. Much of her music is rooted in religious imagery, and she believes passionately in the ability of music to establish a sense of connection with the transcendent – a belief that allies her with the likes of Pärt (see p.262) and Tavener (see p.371).

OFFERTORIUM

Gubaidulina's violin concerto, *Offertorium* (1980, revised 1982 & 1986), was one of her first works to become known outside the Soviet Union. It's a moving and virtuosic piece, built entirely around the theme from J. S. Bach's *Musical Offering*. In the first part of the work's single movement the theme is heard several times, but on each hearing it gradually disintegrates; by the end of *Offertorium* the theme has been transfigured and is played in retrograde by the soloist – a moment of calm beauty and resolution.

○ Kremer; Boston Symphony Orchestra; Dutoit (Deutsche Grammophon 427 336-2GH; with *Hommage à T.S. Eliot*).

○ Krysa; Royal Stockholm Philharmonic Orchestra; DePreist (BIS-CD566; with *Rejoice!*).

The best performance comes from Gidon Kremer, for whom the work was written; his passionate account is coupled with *Hommage à T.S. Eliot* (1987) for soprano and octet, a setting of lines from Four Quartets in which Guibaidulina explores Eliot's concept of the transformation of time. The BIS recording of Offertorium is rather less convincing, but it comes with the marvellous *Rejoice!* (1981, revised 1988) for violin and cello, in which the two instruments alternately clash and merge over the course of five movements, each of which is given a subtitle from a Polish parable and from the Mass.

STIMMEN . . . VERSTUMMEN . . .

The twelve-movement *Stimmen . . . Verstummen . . .* (Voices . . . fall dumb . . .), written in 1986, opens with one of Guibaidulina's most original flourishes – an ecstatic D major triad in the wind instruments, over strange scurrying sounds from the strings. The triad is disrupted at the end of the first movement by a menacing D flat from the brass instruments, and throughout this massive and entrancing work movements of static tonal calm are broken by uneasily chromatic episodes. The work reaches an extraordinary climax in the minute-long ninth movement, which is almost completely silent – rhythmic gestures for the conductor are notated in the score at this point, but even without this visual contribution it's a powerfully strange moment.

○ Royal Stockholm Philharmonic Orchestra; Rozhdestvensky (Chandos CHAN 9183; with Stufen).

These excellent performances are conducted by Gennady Rozhdestvensky, the champion of so much new Russian music. The intensity of *Stimmen . . . Verstummen . . .* carries the listener through the almost silent ninth movement, when the pulse of the rhythmic patterns that Gubaidulina has established can still be felt.

CHAMBER WORKS

One of Gubaidulina's most frequently performed chamber works is the radiantly contemplative *Garten von Freuden und Traurigkeiten* (Garden of Joys and Sorrows). Written in 1980, this piece creates an enthrallingly beautiful sound world using all the resources of just three instruments – flute, viola and harp. In *Seven Last Words*, written in 1982, Gubaidulina creates an equally unusual but quite different texture. Here two solo instruments – a cello and a traditional Russian *bayan* or button accordion – play beautiful lamenting melodies and strange, agitated scratching sounds over chant-like passages from the string orchestra. The *String Trio* (1988) is a demanding work for the more conventional line-up of violin, viola and cello, "three characters who reveal their individual wills", to quote the composer's description. The first movement moves from a violently sparse opening through to full rich harmonies and is followed by a second movement of floating pizzicato and ethereal harmonics; the often disturbingly agitated final movement ends with a feeling of uneasy peace.

⊙ **Garten von Freuden und Traurigkeiten; Seven Last Words; String Trio**: Grafenauer, Graf, Mendelssohn (Philips 434 041-2PH).

This CD of live recordings, made at Gidon Kremer's Lockenhaus Chamber Music Festival in 1986 and 1989, offers these important instrumental works in impressive performances but with frustratingly vague sleeve notes.

GEORGE FRIDERIC HANDEL
(1685–1759)

A fter two centuries of achievement English music around 1700 was moribund, and then salvation came in the form of George Frideric Handel. It was Handel who brought to Britain music in which the rationality of the Enlightenment was joined to an acute awareness of the complexities of humanity. Of his contemporaries, only J. S. Bach produced work in which the qualities of robustness, lucidity and passion were so finely balanced.

Handel was born in the north German town of Halle in 1685, son of a surgeon who was convinced that the law was the proper calling for his boy. Yet the musicians at the Court of Saxe Weissenfels, where his father worked, soon introduced Georg Händel (as he was then) to their profession, and recognized his remarkable potential. His teacher, F. W. Zachow, gave him a grounding in counterpoint and instrumentation as well as a bravura keyboard technique, and by 1702 Georg was a major figure in the region – cathedral organist, composer and friend of the mighty Telemann.

In 1705 he presented several operas in Hamburg. Their mixed fortunes convinced him he should learn his operatic trade in Italy: he duly went to Florence, where he came to know both Alessandro and Domenico Scarlatti; and to Venice, where he met Prince August of Hanover, who was looking for a

ROYAL COLLEGE OF MUSIC

Kapellmeister. Perhaps the limitations of what was available in Germany persuaded Handel that he should seek a different market-place for his operatic skills. He settled on England, and marked his arrival in 1711 by the composition of *Rinaldo* in fifteen days flat. The furore it produced – not least when Handel released a flock of sparrows for one aria – made him a household name.

The composition of a magnificent *Te Deum* for Queen Anne secured him a state pension,

and though he was briefly out of favour with the accession of the Hanoverian George I in 1714, the success of *Amadigi* quickly restored his fortunes. In 1716 he was invited to accompany George on a visit to Hanover, where the composer perhaps still retained some ambitions. It was at this point that Handel anglicized his name and took out naturalization papers. It was also the period of the *Chandos Anthems* and the *Water Music* – a period when he was testing himself in all branches of composition.

In 1720 a society of wealthy amateurs founded the Royal Academy of Music, appointing Handel as its director. Its nine seasons drew from him a stream of masterpieces (including *Giulio Cesare*) but the rivalries and fees of a prima donna cast crippled the Academy, as did the success of John Gay's populist *Beggar's Opera*, which was hailed as a bracing respite from the heroics of conventional opera. Handel himself remained solvent, however, and a patriotic potboiler, *Riccardo I, Re d'Inghiltera* (1727), ensured that he stayed in grace with the newly crowned George II. He formed a company called the Opera of the Nobility, which hit trouble when a rival company was set up in 1733 with the backing of the Prince of Wales. Handel retaliated with a new style of opera in which singing was interspersed with ballet, but it was his introduction of the oratorio to London that won him success throughout the 1730s.

Yet by 1741, again a victim of fickle public taste, his finances were ailing once more, and Handel was thrown into despair when his *Messiah* failed to enthrall its first audiences. He was reported "disordered in mind" but the late 1740s saw his reputation revive through oratorios of operatic power and splendour – *Samson*, *Judas Maccabaeus* and then *Solomon*, written in the same year that the *Music for the Royal Fireworks* was produced to celebrate the peace treaty of Aix-la-Chapelle.

In April 1759 Handel fainted during a performance of *Messiah*, and died soon after. He was buried in Westminster Abbey, the only possible resting place for the figure who had become in effect the composer to the nation.

ANTHEMS

Handel's cosmopolitanism is nowhere more pronounced than in his anthems, where a fusion of Italian harmonic intensity, German polyphony and elements of French music and Purcell creates music of strikingly juxtaposed colours. The so-called *Chandos Anthems*, written in 1717–20 for James Brydges, First Duke of Chandos, when Handel was his composer in residence, are typical of Handel's prowess. Alternately ceremonial, penitential and joyful, these early works were significant in laying the foundations of Handel's career as a composer of oratorios. The sixth of the group, *As pants the hart*, is a tour de force of choral writing, though for dramatic impact nothing can match *Zadok the Priest* – one of the anthems written for the coronation of George I in 1727, it has been played at every subsequent coronation.

○ **Chandos Anthems**: Dawson, Partridge; The Sixteen Choir and Orchestra; Christophers (Chandos CHAN 0517).
○ **Coronation Anthems**: Choir of Westminster Abbey; The English Concert; Preston (Deutsche Grammophon Archiv 410 030-2).

The recording quality of the *Chandos Anthems* CD brings body to the Sixteen's singing whilst preserving its clarity and scale. The soloists are at the heart of these performances, lustrous in tone yet capturing the essential intimacy of the music, which was written for James Brydges's small group of resident performers at Cannons House. The *Coronation Anthems* disc presents radiant interpretations of this often jubilant music. *Zadok* is the best-known and the briefest item here, but best of all is *My heart is inditing*, with the Westminster Choir as smoothly assured in the lyrical inner sections as in the cumulative grandeur of the conclusion.

GIULIO CESARE IN EGITTO

Opera took up almost half of Handel's professional career, yet it's an aspect of his output that remains relatively neglected, chiefly because his operas seem undramatic when judged by modern standards. At their best, Handel's operas contain glitteringly inventive music and show an extraordinary capacity to delineate character and express emotion – however grandiose the mythology, his heroes are convincing flesh and blood. Nonetheless, though adventurous companies do occasionally risk a Handel production, it's likely that the operas will remain known mainly for the songs that are lifted out of them for recitals – the most famous being *Ombra mai fu* from *Xerxes*, otherwise known as *Handel's Largo*.

Giulio Cesare in Egitto, written for the Royal Academy of Music in 1724, is perhaps his most fully wrought example of the heroic ideal. Voluptuous and exotic, introducing a new orchestral brilliance and magnificence of spectacle, it was a success from its first appearance – "the house was just as full at the seventh performance as at the first" noted a courtier, Monsieur de Fabrice. It was revived throughout Handel's life, and has retained its standing as his most popular opera.

> ⊙ Lamore, Schlick, Fink, Rorholm, Ragin, Zanasi, Visse; Concerto Köln: Jacobs (Harmonia Mundi HMC 901385/7; 3 CDs).

Where the recording triumphs is in the richness of characterization. Jennifer Lamore has real brio as Caesar, the high-minded conqueror won over by love, but the crucial role is Cleopatra. Handel matches Shakespeare in the infinite variety he reveals in Cleopatra's eight arias, and Barbara Schlick rises marvellously to the occasion: moving from frothy innocence through pathos to seductive insinuation. René Jacobs's genial direction sometimes loses dramatic potency, but he brings out the design of the opera's balanced progression of symphonic movements and gorgeous set-pieces.

MESSIAH

By 1740 Handel realized that his operatic career was finished and, facing an indifferent audience, he contemplated retirement. But in the summer of 1741 came an invitation from William Cavendish, third Duke of Devonshire and Lieutenant of Ireland, to visit Dublin. It was almost certainly to aid charities in Dublin (two hospitals and a debtors' prison) that *Messiah* was written – between August 22 and September 14, including precisely two days for orchestration.

Its plan – divine creation, redemption and the conquest of death – was something quite new for an oratorio, but it's virtually impossible to recapture any sense of the novelty of *Messiah*, so familiar has it become (or at least, so familiar have the *Hallelujah* chorus and other highlights become). As Bernard Shaw observed: "We have all had our Handelian training in church . . . thus we get broken into

the custom of singing Handel as if he meant nothing." Yet this music bears intense meaning in every bar, and has a visionary quality in its evolution from darkness to light. In his deployment of soloists and choruses Handel's sense of timing and proportion is matchless, and the sheer physical pleasure of the sound is remarkable too – never did Handel write more sensitively for each vocal register, or more exquisitely for the airy pastel tones available to the orchestra of his time.

> ⊙ Auger, von Otter, Chance, Crook, Tomlinson; The English Concert & Concert Choir; Pinnock (Deutsche Grammophon Archiv 423 630-2; 2 CDs).
> ⊙ Marshall, Robbin, Rolfe-Johnson, Hale, Brett, Quirck; Monteverdi Choir, English Baroque Soloists; Gardiner Philips 434 297-2; 2 CDs).

In a crowded field, it's the transparency of these two versions, and their sensitivity in capturing the music's development from gravitas to celebration, that makes them outstanding. The immediate dramatics and sense of joy are a little stronger in the Gardiner account, to which the Monteverdi Choir give a fine lightness and rhythmic spring. However, Pinnock's smoother phrasing, his ear for orchestral timbre and his concern for the psychology of each character, added to the generally glossier sound of the recording, makes his account perhaps more remarkable.

JUDAS MACCABAEUS

Ever the consummate opportunist, Handel dashed out *Judas Maccabaeus* after the Battle of Culloden, by way of a compliment to the Duke of Cumberland, the victor of that bloody engagement of April 1746. In his haste Handel lifted sections from his existing oratorios *Joshua* and *Belshazzar*, the rest of the libretto being patched together by the congenial Reverend Thomas Morell, who could match something of the composer's breakneck speed. In the event the premiere had to wait until April 1747.

Perhaps out of fear that his dedicatee might find something offensive in the portrayal of the oratorio's military hero, Handel here avoided the intense personal drama that had characterized *Hercules* and *Belshazzar* – which in any case seemed to have alienated a public used to blander fare. *Judas* deals with the anticipation of events and of reactions to them, rather than with events themselves, yet its contrasts of mood and tempo sustain it well over three acts, and it has endured as one of the finest of all celebratory compositions.

● De Mey, Saffer, Spence, Thomas, Asawa, Kromm; Berkeley Chorus; Philharmonia Baroque Orchestra; McGegan (Harmonia Mundi HMU 9077077.78; 2 CDs).

Nicholas McGegan's small forces add crisp refinement to music which is contemplative rather than theatrical; resiliently phrased, this performance rarely sounds undernourished, as it so easily could.

SOLOMON

Opening on March 17, 1749, Handel's most splendid oratorio was unveiled to a nation in the midst of exuberant mass celebration – the War of the Austrian Succession was over, and in Green Park stood a wooden structure over a hundred feet high, depicting the King amid the Greek gods. "Record him, ye bards, as the pride of our days . . . E'vry object swells with state, All is pious, all is great" – this is the heart of *Solomon*, a piece that idealizes Georgian England through implicit historical comparison. Pantheistic rather than narrowly Christian, *Solomon* is more a pastoral idyll and pageant than a dramatic narrative, with episodes of enraptured lyricism. Handel antic-ipated "above one hundred voices and performers" – huge forces for those days.

● Watkinson, Argenta, Hendricks, Rodgers, Rolfe Johnson, Varcoe; Monteverdi Choir & English Baroque Soloists; Gardiner (Philips 412 612-2; 2 CDs).

John Eliot Gardiner's performance has won many awards for its ebullient pace and lyrical sensitivity. With Barbara Hendricks and Joan Rodgers in especially luscious voice, and with the Monteverdi Choir superlatively clear and precise, this is a landmark not only in authentic performance but in modern Handel interpretation.

THE WATER MUSIC

On July 17, 1717, an event occurred of which the Daily Courant reported: "Many barges with Persons of Quality attended, and so great a Number of Boats, that the whole River in a manner was cover'd; a City Company's Barge was employ'd for the Musick, wherein were 50 Instruments of all sorts, who play'd all the Way from Lambeth . . .the finest Symphonies, compos'd express for this Occasion, by Mr Hendel; which his Majesty liked so well, that

he caus'd it to be plaid three times in going and returning."

The occasion was, simply, that George I had taken a fancy to the idea of a water-party – a reasonably common occurrence, as is indi-cated by the fact that Handel wrote at least three *Water Music* suites (there may have been others). Those with horns or trumpets were most suitable for the outdoors, whereas the softer G major suite (with flutes) was apt for the "choice supper at Lord Ranelagh's villa at Chelsea, where there was another fine Consort of Musick, which lasted until two".

Each of the suites is as sophisticated as it is instantly engaging. Handel had saturated himself in the musical traditions of his adopted country, not least its naval and coun-try dances, but brought to them (in the words of the greatest Handel expert, H. C. Robbins Landon) "far more than the usual international flair: a remarkable fusion of solid German upbringing, Italian training and a thorough acquaintance with French taste." The result is, alongside Vivaldi's *Four Seasons*, the most popular instrumental music before Mozart.

● The English Concert; Pinnock (Deutsche Grammophon Archiv 410 525-2).
3x English Baroque Soloists; Gardiner (Philips 434 122-2).

John Eliot Gardiner, characteristically vital, creates an object-lesson in the articulation of textures and accenting. His sense of the natural growth and fluctuating tension of the music is the key to this recording's spontaneity – the slow movements have a dying fall to them, and rarely have Allegros or Prestos been so effervescent without sounding frenetic. Pinnock, a little less high-spirited, brings out the stateliness of it all, giving his players the space to find the widest range of characterization. If the dynamic range of Pinnock's recording is a little less than Gardiner's, the results are sometimes more poignant.

THE FIREWORKS MUSIC

Within a few weeks of *Solomon*'s first perfor-mance, another spectacular Handel premiere took place. As part of the celebrations for the ending of the war, a pavilion over four hundred feet long was erected in Green Park, and Handel – having composed fire music for his opera *Atalanta* – was asked by George II to create a suite for an immense pyrotechnic display to be held there on April 27, 1749.

There were ructions about orchestration: Handel wanted strings, the King insisted on "martial instruments." The final forces used for the *Music for the Royal Fireworks* are unclear, but included nine trumpets, nine horns, twenty-four oboes, twelve bassoons and three pairs of kettledrums. A rehearsal on April 21 went well, with a hundred musicians playing to a crowd of over twelve thousand, and bringing the centre of London to a standstill. The same could not be said of the big night. "The rockets succeeded mighty well; but the wheels, and all that to compose the principal part, were pitiful and ill-conducted . . . and then, what contributed to the awkwardness of the whole, was the right pavilion catching fire, and being burnt down in the middle of the show." In the end Servandoni – designer of the pavilion – drew his sword on the Comptroller of Fireworks.

The overture is one of Handel's most exhilarating, brilliant creations, and if the remaining numbers are slighter, there is no finer demonstration of Beethoven's comment that Handel knew best how to achieve grand effects with simple means. As Haydn added, "He is the master of us all."

> ◗ The English Concert; Pinnock (Deutsche Grammophon Archiv 431 707-2; with *Alexander's Feast* and *Concerto Grosso Op. 6 No. 6*).

The opening here, all slicing upbeats, has a marvellous bite and sense of pride. The rest is a demonstration of the fine textures and phrasing that authentic Baroque practice can create.

THE CONCERTI GROSSI

The concerto grosso, in which the main body of an orchestra is in dialogue with a small group of instruments, achieved its definitive form in Rome around 1700. Handel's first great contributions to the genre, the Opus 3 of 1734, are concerti grossi with woodwind, featuring a mix of new writing and pieces reworked from existing compositions by Handel and others. Set in the mould established by Vivaldi, Albinoni and Locatelli, they are robust and clearly articulated pieces, making the most of the form's dramatic contrasts of solemn grandeur and vitality.

Handel's instrumental magnum opus appeared five years later – the Opus 6 concerti grossi, published as *Twelve Grand Concertos*. Amongst the most powerful works

of the Baroque era, these concertos form part of a family tree that begins with Corelli, but Handel brings a new vibrancy and motion – his dances are fresh and flexible, his instrumentation lyrically ripe, his polyphony adventurous and tantalizing. "No great music has been more derivative" wrote the musicologist Basil Lam, "yet none bears more firmly the impression of personality."

> ◉ **Concerti Grossi Opus 3**: The English Concert; Pinnock (Deutsche Grammophon Archiv 413 727-2).
> ◉ **Concerti Grossi Opus 6**: Academy of St Martin-in-the-Fields; Brown; (Philips 410 048-2; 3 CDs).
> ◉ **Concerti Grossi Opus 6**: I Musici de Montréal; Turovsky (Chandos 9004-6; 3 CDs).

The Pinnock CD of the Opus 3 concerti is an authentic performance of great charm, fragile where necessary, but very dignified in the slow movements. With Opus 6 you have a choice between two very different but very fine versions. Iona Brown's reading has a winningly uncalculated air – there's real bounce in the Allegros, a great intensity in the slow movements, and the cadences are sculpted beautifully. What Turovsky and I Musici de Montréal offer is playing of dazzling, uningratiating verve and style. If authencity is paramount, opt for the Chandos set; for warmth, go for the Philips.

ORGAN CONCERTOS

Hawkins, Handel's contemporary, leaves a description of him at the organ: "His amazing command of the instrument, the grandeur and dignity of his style, the copiousness of his imagination, and the fertility of his invention were qualities that . . . no one ever pretended to equal." Handel's delight in improvisation is crucial to his finest works for this instrument, his organ concertos – the form of keyboard music to which he devoted himself after 1730. These works were written to be played on the organ or harpsichord, since English organs normally lacked the pedal-boards and multiple manuals fitted to their hefty continental counterparts, and the consequence is that the texture of these pieces is extremely transparent. Many passages were left as skeletons to be fleshed out with improvisation, which is why they demand a performer with thorough knowledge to bring them to life.

> ◉ **Organ Concertos Op. 4 & Op. 7**: Amsterdam Baroque Orchestra; Koopman (Erato 4509 91932-2; 2 CDs).

The Opus 4 set comes from 1738, whereas the Opus 7 was dated January 4, 1757, by which time Handel had lost his sight. Koopman's playing of both sets is elegant and springy and suave, catching the festive sparkle and pastoral homeliness of the music. The interplay between the instrumentalists is lively, and the recorded sound excellent.

JOSEPH HAYDN
(1732–1809)

Until recently, Joseph Haydn was commonly regarded as John the Baptist to Mozart's Jesus Christ, a great man, certainly, but a secondary figure nonetheless. Haydn did the spadework, entrenching the symphony and the string quartet in the cultural landscape, and then dazzling Mozart came along, refining and perfecting what Haydn had doggedly constructed. This misjudgement of Haydn's music was supported by the image of "Papa Joe", a nickname bestowed on him many years before his death. Apart from his occasionally brutish treatment of Frau Haydn, he does seem to have been an agreeable person, well-respected by all, concerned about the wellbeing of others, and – when compared to someone like Beethoven – generous to a fault. But this genial portrait obscures the truth, for Joseph Haydn was one of the great revolutionaries of classical music, making huge advances in structure, harmony and melody, investing every form with inexhaustible potential for expression. He was born into the Baroque age, and went on to write music which prefigures the stormy creations of Beethoven.

Haydn was born in the Austrian town of Rohrau, and in 1761, after a conspicuously ordinary early life, was engaged as vice-Kapellmeister by Prince Paul Esterházy, a Hungarian nobleman. He remained exclusively in that family's employment for the next thirty years, working for Prince Paul and then for his son Nikolaus, at their palaces of Eisenstadt and Esterháza. Unlike Mozart, whose relationships with his patrons was neither easy nor consistent, Haydn lived happily within the confines of his master's world and benefited enormously from the

MANSELL COLLECTION

seclusion and from having a permanent orchestra with which to work. As he later remarked "there was no-one there to confuse me, so I was forced to become original". His duties demanded that he compose almost constantly, but as he travelled rarely and was over-awed at the prospect of having to perform as a pianist, violinist or conductor outside the palaces, his fame as a composer was spread almost solely through publishing.

In 1790 Nikolaus Esterházy died and the court musicians were dismissed by his successor. Haydn was also deemed surplus to requirements but, as a sign of the family's respect for his loyalty, they continued paying his salary and allowed him to keep his Kapellmeister title. He moved to Vienna, but shortly afterwards he received an invitation from the impresario J. P. Salomon to visit England. Fêted by the music world and entertained by royalty, his first stay in England (1791–92) was a remarkable success and his life in London remains the most fascinating episode in what was a fairly uneventful life. He remained in England for some eighteen months, and took enormous satisfaction in receiving an honorary degree from Oxford University.

Having returned from London, he bought a house in Vienna where he taught Beethoven, among others, but in 1794 he was commissioned by Salomon to write six new symphonies and so made the journey back to England. This second visit lasted from February 1794 to August 1795 and brought him even greater fame and success. After his return, he moved back into employment with the Esterházys, but he worked for their household only on special occasions, devoting most of his time to composing. Between 1796 and 1802 Haydn produced some of his greatest music (in particular, the oratorio *Die Schöpfung*), but from 1802 his health began to fail, leading towards an illness from which he died in 1807.

Haydn's life may have been unenthralling, but his music is not. In some ways he was more radical than Mozart: whereas Mozart was obsessed with symmetrical perfection, in which the four- and eight-bar phrase reigned unchallenged, Haydn experimented with phrases lasting three, five, seven, and even nine bars; and while Mozart almost never veered from the sonata convention of first and second subjects, Haydn sometimes built movements on single themes, a procedure that didn't become a convention until the nineteenth century. As with any prolific composer, his output has its pedestrian moments, but his best music is outstandingly fresh and sprightly. Above all, Haydn is the most humane and comforting of composers. In his own words, he wrote music so that "the weary and worn, or the man burdened with affairs, may enjoy a few moments of solace and refreshment."

OPERA

Haydn devoted a lot of time to the opera, and in his day was regarded as one of the most important composers for the stage, greater even than Mozart. Nowadays the judgement has been reversed, and Haydn's fifteen surviving operas (out of twenty) are rarely seen except in productions by small-scale companies. The neglect isn't altogether unjustified, but a handful of the fifteen show a real flair for dramatic orchestration, characterization and use of ensemble – nothing to stand comparison with Mozart's masterpieces, but certainly more sophisticated than contemporaneous Italian opera. Particularly notable is Haydn's penchant for mixing tragic and comic elements, an ability used to the full in his delightful "drama giocoso" *Il mondo della luna*.

IL MONDO DELLA LUNA

A number of Haydn's comic operas were written for the entertainment of guests at Esterházy weddings, birthdays and social gatherings. Supreme among these is *Il mondo della luna* (The World on the Moon). Written in 1777 to celebrate the marriage of Prince Paul's second son, this three-act opera was described by Count Zinzendorf as "une farce pour la populace et pour les enfants" – and it is indeed a work for everyone.

Goldoni's text and the overall premise are endearingly preposterous. Bonafede has two daughters whose proposed marriages to Ecclitico and Ernesto he strongly opposes. Ecclitico tells Bonafede that he has received an invitation to the moon and Bonafede begs that he may travel with him. The two fiancées transform a garden into a lunar landscape and, waking from a sleeping potion, Bonafede believes he is on the moon. Both couples join in the charade and marry "on the moon". When Bonafede discovers the trickery he is unsurprisingly hostile but, eventually, he is reconciled to the marriages.

This farrago clearly engaged Haydn's highly tuned sense of the ridiculous, and his witty music and multi-faceted portrayal of his characters are highly enjoyable throughout.

The ensemble writing in the garden scene is outstanding and Haydn's interweaving of the characters' individuated musical styles must surely have influenced the young Mozart.

● Auger, Mathis, von Stade, Rolfe Johnson, Alva; Orchestre de Chambre de Lausanne; Dorati (Philips 432 420-2; 3 CDs).

Philips recorded eight of Haydn's operas in the 1970s with Antal Dorati – conductor of the first complete Haydn symphonic cycle – and they have all recently been re-released onto CD. Only the most devout Haydn fan would embark on the whole series, but this recording of *Il mondo della luna* is a delight, made with young and brilliantly talented singers (now all major stars) who evidently shared Dorati's enthusiasm for the music. The individuality of each of the voices (especially Auger and von Stade) and the first-rate ensemble work brings wonderful clarity to Haydn's complicated counterpoint. Dorati is at times heavy handed, but his brisk tempi more than compensate for his obsessive attention to detail.

SACRED MUSIC

It has been argued that the essential Haydn is to be found not in the orchestral or chamber compositions but in his sacred and choral music. Certainly there's a lot of it – he composed Masses, cantatas and choruses for most of his life – but Haydn's expressions of faith tend to be almost sentimental, usually lacking the tension and grandeur of Bach or Mozart. The majority of his greatest sacred music was written during the last phase of his career, and the finest of these works is, without question, his penultimate oratorio, *Die Schöpfung* (The Creation).

DIE SCHÖPFUNG

Die Schöpfung was inspired by a performance of Handel's *Israel in Egypt* which Haydn heard in London. Like Handel's oratorio, it is full of fresh and vivid imagery, depicting all the manifold glories of the Creation with a pictorialism that's nothing short of startling. You can hear the worm crawling, the lion leaping, the wind blowing and – in the prelude leading toward the rising of the sun – you can almost feel heat coming off the music.

The overture, depicting Chaos before the first day, is a bleak, formless and dissonant introduction to the arrival of the Archangel Raphael, who shares with the other archangels the narration of subsequent events – the first being the creation of light. With a lapidary simplicity typical of Haydn, the dawning of light is achieved by modulating from the darkness of C minor into a stupendous C major fortissimo chord that foreshadows the similar device in Bartók's *Bluebeard's Castle* (see p.18). The subsequent arias achieve a transcendant simplicity that, perhaps, only Haydn could have brought to such a demanding subject. The choruses are similarly clear in their expression and, notably in *The Heavens are telling the Glory of God*, he shows a genius for multiple voice part-writing.

◗ Janowitz, Ludwig, Wunderlich, Krenn, Fischer-Dieskau, Berry; Vienna Singers; Berlin Philharmonic Orchestra; Karajan (Deutsche Grammophon DG 435 077-2; 2 CDs).

Karajan's recording of *Die Schöpfung* ranks with his account of Beethoven's *Missa Solemnis* (see p.26). Like the *Solemnis* recording, it boasts an incredible cast. – though tragically Fritz Wunderlich died before completing the sessions, and the inadequate Werner Krenn replaced him for those sections left incomplete. Apart from this, Karajan used two singers for the roles of Raphael and Adam, when one singer usually takes both roles, and he brought in Christa Ludwig just for the final movement's *Let every voice sing unto the Lord*. While all this might suggest a fractured performance, it is one of Karajan's most brilliantly realized and cohesive interpretations, and it has a sense of great occasion from beginning to end. With Janowitz, Wunderlich and Berry in glorious form, this romantic, old-fashioned and well-recorded performance is unsurpassed.

SYMPHONIES

Between 1757 and 1795 Haydn composed some 104 symphonies. All the symphonies after *No. 31* are in four movements, each with a second- or third-movement Minuet, and all but one of the last fourteen opens with a slow introduction. However, these are superficial similarities, for each of these symphonies is a markedly original blend of deep feeling and elegance, with the final twelve manifesting a perfect, Mozartian synthesis of form and substance. To discuss them all would require a book in itself, so we've picked out a few exceptional works.

◗ **Complete Symphonies**: Philharmonia Hungarica; Dorati (Decca 430 1002DM32; 32 CDs).

Dorati's complete edition of the 104 symphonies now has challengers from advocates of "authentic" performance, but in many ways it remains the best cycle. This is old-fashioned conducting and the playing has none of the crispness of some more recent versions, but what matters most is that Dorati's approach is human and flexible – communication rather than pedantic exactitude is his priority.

The cycle is available as a box of 32 CDs, and also in smaller packages of three to five discs or, in some cases, as individual CDs. They are all good.

SYMPHONY NO. 45 – THE FAREWELL

Almost a third of Haydn's symphonies have acquired nicknames, most of which – unlike Mozart's symphonic sub-titles – fit the music well. One such case is the *Farewell Symphony*, which was written in 1772, in the course of a particularly prolonged stay at Nikolaus Esterházy's summer residence. Many of the court musicians had had to leave their wives behind at the palace in Eisenstadt, and so Haydn created a piece of music as a hint to the prince that the time had come for a return to their loved ones. In the last movement, one of Haydn's wittiest inventions, the players leave one by one until only two violins and the conductor are left. This is not Haydn's most tuneful symphony but it is one of his most entertaining.

◐ Vienna Concentus Musicus; Harnoncourt (Teldec 2292-44198-2; with *Symphony No. 60*).

Nikolaus Harnoncourt, one of the evangelists of period performance, has conducted surprisingly little Haydn. This recording of the *Farewell Symphony* suggests he should do more – it's an excellent, natural performance, crackling with energy and pacing the music so well that the ending actually comes as a surprise. The playing of his band is crisp, and bounces along with great attention to colour and nuance.

SYMPHONY NO. 94 – THE SURPRISE

Haydn wrote the *Surprise Symphony* in Hertfordshire, in the course of his first triumphant visit to England in 1791. The "surprise" of the nickname comes in the second movement when, halfway through a light and seemingly insignificant Andante, there comes a fortissimo bang from the timpani. It was suggested that Haydn had

placed the explosion there in order to wake up any dozing members of the audience, but he insisted that he had merely wanted to surprise the listener with something new.

◑ London Philharmonic Orchestra; Jochum (Deutsche Grammophon DG 423 883-2GGA ; with *Symphony No. 101*).

Beecham's classic 1958 recording is available on a 2-CD set from EMI, but the best single-disc version is Jochum's – it may not have Beecham's zip, but it bold, earthy and unfailingly charming.

THE LONDON SYMPHONIES

In February 1794, J. P. Salomon began a series of concerts at the Hanover Rooms in London, in the course of which six new Haydn symphonies – the so-called *London Symphonies* – were to receive their premieres. All six are remarkably inventive, but two of them in particular stand out.

Symphony No. 100 – The Military – was performed at the eighth concert on March 31, when it was introduced as a "Grand Military Overture", a reference to the use of a military battery of kettledrums, triangle, cymbals and bass drum in its second movement. The work became especially famous for the final movement, a rondo whose main theme managed to find its way into England's ballrooms. The military flavour returns near the end of the symphony with great grandeur, but the parade-ground pomp is ultimately absorbed into the atmosphere of the salon. This is not a piece of music that should be played with a completely straight face.

The very first bar of *Symphony No. 103* – an unannounced drum-roll – is a marvellous, unprecedented coup, which inevitably led to the symphony's becoming known as the *Drum Roll*. This dramatic flourish announces one of Haydn's most original works, leading into a quiet, sustained phrase for bassoons, cellos and basses which has a mystery comparable to the opening of Schubert's *Unfinished Symphony*. Later in the symphony you get a masterful set of double variations on two themes derived from folk tunes, a Trio that makes intriguing use of the clarinets, and a finale that is ingeniously based upon a single theme.

Symphonies 99–104: Royal Philharmonic Orchestra; Beecham (EMI CMS7 64066-2; 2 CDs).

This set is a marvel of interpretive freshness: Beecham was in astonishing form when he made these recordings, generating a sense of the unexpected and a joyfulness that will make you unaware of the dated sound quality. No conductor has ever shaped Haydn's wondrous thematic lines with such care and understanding or made the climactic moments so shattering.

CONCERTOS

Haydn composed numerous concertos for violin, cello, flute, oboe, trumpet, horn, bassoon, piano and organ, but just three of this tally have entered the concert-hall repertoire – the two cello concertos and the trumpet concerto.

CELLO CONCERTOS

The two cello concertos widely attributed to Haydn (the first is still regarded as spurious in some quarters) were almost certainly written for Joseph Weigl, a cellist in the Esterházy court orchestra – which suggests that their standard of ensemble playing must have been high, as the technical demands of both works are extreme. The first concerto, in C major, was probably written between 1761 and 1765, and opens with a movement that is really nothing more than a virtuoso display; a cheery mood generally prevails throughout the concerto, and the Adagio boasts an extremely affecting and well extended melody. The second concerto, in D major, is notable for the exquisite beauty of its Adagio, but the first movement is far too long for the material upon which it is based; though written in 1784, when Haydn was at the height of his powers, the second concerto is less involving than its predecessor.

Rostropovich; Academy of St Martin-in-the-Fields; Brown (EMI CDC7493052-2).

Rostropovich is temperamentally suited to the vivacity of these concertos, and on these recordings the orchestra is in turn perfectly attuned to his endearing ebullience. He favours quick tempi and a big gruff sound, foregoing the twee delicacy of some other cellists, and the enthusiasm with which he attacks the works' outer movements is highly engaging. His playing of the central Adagios is exquisite – in the C major concerto he produces an ethereal sense of stillness that is breathtaking.

TRUMPET CONCERTO

In the late eighteenth century the trumpet attained great prominence as a solo instrument, its natural limitations gradually being overcome by developments which culminated in a fully chromatic instrument – but with keys, like a keyboard intrument. It was for this keyed trumpet – later superceded by the valved instrument – that Haydn wrote his *Trumpet Concerto* in 1796, for the Viennese trumpet player Anton Weidlinger. It was Haydn's last fully orchestral work, and strangely it found little popularity at first, probably due to the unusual sound of the keyed trumpet. Nowadays it's a favourite vehicle for trumpet virtuosos, who get plenty of opportunity to show off in the first movement's thrilling cadenza. The slow movement is extremely lyrical (making it as demanding for a trumpet player as the fireworks of the cadenza), while the last movement is typical of the restrained exuberance of all Haydn's concerto finales.

Steele-Perkins; English Chamber Orchestra (Pickwick PCD821; with concertos by M. Haydn, Torelli, Telemann, Neruda and Humphries).

Christian Steele-Perkins, one of England's finest trumpet players, is also a renowned expert on the history and playing styles of the natural, keyed and valved instruments. For this recording he prepared all his phrasing, articulation and cadenzas on a keyed trumpet, although his actual performances are on a modern instrument. He makes a clear and vibrato-less sound with a bright and ringing top which, in the extremely high passages, is exceptionally beautiful. His cadenza at the end of the first movement is miraculous, while his playing of the finale is fresh and effortless.

STRING QUARTETS

Like Mozart, Haydn wrote a large amount of chamber music, including over one hundred and twenty trios and more than thirty duos for the baryton, a stringed instrument that most closely resembles the cello. The core of Haydn's legacy as a chamber composer is his work for string quartet: whereas Mozart composed a mere twenty-three string quartets, Haydn completed around ninety – the exact number remains unknown.

Not a single quartet written before Haydn's has survived to modern times, but Haydn wrote within the context of a suffocating Viennese tradition whereby every work ended with a fugal finale. By the time he came to write his *Opus 20* quartets, around the age of forty, Haydn had taken the quartet so far from the formulaic sterility of his predecessors that he could allow himself to end his works with fugues once again – but fugues of such inventiveness as to further widen the gap between himself and the past. Musicologist Hans Keller wrote of Haydn's quartets: "On a conservative count, he composed 45 profound and profoundly different, absolutely flawless, consistently original master quartets, each a violent, multi-dimensional contrast to any of the others." Indeed Haydn seems to have given his quartets more intense attention than his symphonies, for they display a greater thematic, structural and textural richness than any of his orchestral music. No other composer has so completely understood the expressive capabilities of the quartet's four parts, and this body of work represents the apogee of Haydn's genius for outward simplicity and inward complexity.

⊙ Haydn String Quartets: Kodály Quartet (Naxos).

The Kodály Quartet's cycle of Haydn's quartets, a long-term project that's now well under way, features some of the finest playing on disc and, at budget price, the value is superb. As must be the case with Haydn's music, the leader directs the performances with absolute clarity of intention, and the result is at once extremely lyrical, dramatic and spontaneous. For one group to bring such vitality and enthusiasm to so much music is a marvel. Naxos have released the quartets on single CDs, each containing three or four pieces, and have also two five-disc sets. We've picked out the highlights below, but this cycle is so good you shouldn't hesitate about picking up any of them.

STRING QUARTETS OP. 1

It's emblematic of the importance of the string quartet to Haydn that his Opus 1 should be a group of six string quartets. Published 1764 (it's not exactly when they were completed), they follow a standard pattern of five short movements – Presto/Allegro, Minuet, Adagio, Minuet, Presto/Allegro – with the central Adagion nearly always the longest. It is the Adagio of the E flat quartet, the first of the set, that singles it out as the finest of them – the Italianate beauty of the very long principal melodic line is unparalleled in his writing for

quartet. Accompanied by simple harmony, this seamless music melts off the page. Of the other Opus 1 quartets, *No. 6* is also outstanding for its Adagio, less liquid in form than that of *No. 1*, but almost as moving.

⊙ Kodály Quartet (Naxos 8550399 & 8550398; with *Op. 2 No. 1 & Op. 2 No. 2*).

The Kodály Quartet's playing of these very simple works is nothing short of spiritual, especially in the Adagios, where their sonority becomes a single voice. Tempi are always quick and the players avoid anything akin to sentimentality. In short, as an introduction to Haydn's quartets, this cannot be beaten.

STRING QUARTETS OP. 76

The six Op. 76 quartets are, understandably, Haydn's most famous, for they mark the culmination of his quest for expressive perfection. Commissioned by a Viennese nobleman named Count Jospeh Erdödy, who retained their exclusive use for two years, they were completed in 1797, when Haydn had turned sixty-five. He must have felt some satisfaction with the outcome, for they are the strongest and most finely wrought of all his chamber compositions and clearly inspired Beethoven's first attempts at quartet writing – even if he was reluctant to admit the influence.

In the Op. 76 set you can find everything with which Haydn's style is synonymous – ingenious variation, complex fugal writing, folk-influenced melodies, perfect ensemble writing and general transparency. The range of expression is astonishingly wide: the slow movement of *No. 3*, *The Emperor*, is a deeply moving, hymn-like theme composed in response to England's national anthem (it was adopted as the Austrian national anthem and is now the German); the slow movement of *No. 5*, marked *mesto* (sadly) is proto-Romantic in its supple beauty; the forcefulness of Beethoven is prefigured by the first movement of *No. 1*, with its sudden fortissimo outbursts; and the so-called *Witches' Minuet* of *No. 2* is a fine example of Haydn letting his hair down.

⊙ Kodály Quartet (Naxos 8550314 & 8550315).

The Kodály Quartet's performances of Op. 76 possess a steady, reliable elegance that's typical of their entire Haydn cycle. They are expressive without sentimentalizing the often lush writing, and their sense of experimentation makes this sound like music freshly minted.

THE SEVEN LAST WORDS

The *Seven Last Words* occupies a unique place within Haydn's output. It was commissioned in 1785 by the administrators of Cadiz Cathedral, who asked him to provide instrumental music for a special Good Friday service, to be performed between meditations on Christ's seven last words on the Cross. As Haydn wrote: "Each time, at the end of the sermon, the orchestra would begin again and my composition had to be in keeping with the presentation." To compose seven consecutive Adagios, each lasting ten minutes, was a taxing proposition, and Haydn missed his deadline – the first Cadiz performances took place in Holy Week of 1787, though there were performances in Vienna and Bonn the month before.

Haydn's achievement was extraordinary. Not only did he avoid monotony, he produced some of his most innovative and expressive work in the *Seven Last Words*, building music of almost symphonic density around the weighty, declamatory melodic lines that represent the words of Christ. The fact that he reworked the orchestral score into a string quartet (among other formats) shows he was justly proud of this remarkable work.

🔘 Lindsay Quartet (ASV DCA853).

This splendid recording demonstrates that this piece works best in its reduction for string quartet, as the four voices

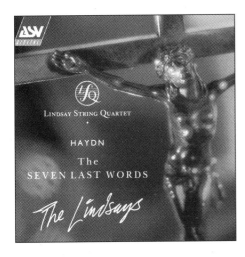

The Lindsays' much praised Seven Last Words

define the harmonic and thematic material more clearly than a full orchestra. The Lindsays give full scope to the pathos and reverence of the music, while losing nothing of its momentum. As usual with this group, the ensemble playing isn't as tight as it might be, but for spontaneity and deep feeling they are without equal.

KEYBOARD MUSIC

Haydn's keyboard music owes most to the instrumental traditions of North Germany and the likes of C.P.E. Bach (see p.7), which means that it possesses a gravity that contrasts with the more elfin spirit of Mozart's work in the same medium. Even concert pianists disagree over the merits of most of Haydn's keyboard sonatas – Glenn Gould played the late ones and was rumoured to have planned to record them all, Sviatoslav Richter plays just a few of them, Stephen Kovacevich steers clear of all of them – but the *Sonata in C minor* is an unqualified masterpiece, as is the astonishingly inventive *Variations in F minor*.

SONATA IN C MINOR

The *Sonata in C minor* dates from 1771 and is something of a watershed, marking a decisive move away from dance-music style and towards the storm and stress of early Romanticism. It is also Haydn's first sonata to carry specific dynamic markings, suggesting that the work was intended for a fortepiano (an early piano) and not a harpsichord, as were all works previous to this. The work's emotional contrasts and overall pacing make it a stylistic companion to the *Farewell Symphony* and the Op. 20 string quartets, and the combination of outright drama and reflective melody – especially in the outer movements – marks the inauguration of the Viennese Classical style, the style which Beethoven was eventually to bring to the point of dissolution.

🌓 Wilde (Collins COLL 30172; with *Sonatas in D major* and *G minor*, and *Variations in F minor*).

Andrew Wilde's marvellous recording is a refreshing antidote to the rather spineless style currently fashionable for playing Hadyn's piano music. He attacks this piece with disciplined muscularity and searching intelligence, finding an inner motivation that propels the music forward unstoppably.

VARIATIONS IN F MINOR

Described by Haydn as "Un piccolo diverti-mento" the *Variations in F minor* stand as one of the pinnacles of the keyboard repertoire. The theme is brilliantly conceived for varia-tion form and the variations themselves are notably innovative, but it is the finale, with its sixty bars of Beethoven-like fury, that is the most striking aspect of this piece. The intensely personal nature of this music has prompted various theories as to the identity of the person to whom Haydn was so openly baring his soul. In all probability there was no such person – in 1773 Haydn had written a piece of music so expressive as to have generations of Romantics looking for an answer to a question that had never been posed.

◉ Staier (Deutsche Harmonia Mundi 05472 77285-2; with other Haydn keyboard works).
◗ Wilde (Collins COLL 30172; with *Sonatas in C minor, D major* and *G minor*) .

The German fortepianist Andreas Staier is working his way through Haydn's keyboard music for Deutsche Harmonia Mundi, and with this CD, Volume Three in the series, he offers one of the most revealing performances ever recorded on a fortepiano. This is heroic playing and in the sixty-bar finale he rips through the music with a force that seems in danger of wrecking the instrument. Andrew Wilde's more poised recording is a perfect foil to Staier's caution-to-the-wind approach.

HANS WERNER HENZE

(1926–   )

Henze is one of the most significant, most approachable and most political of post-war European composers. His social commitment, which grew out of disgust with the Nazi Germany of his youth and his disappointment with the society of post-war Germany, eventually led him into the espousal of communism, an infatuation with the idea of world revolution, and a lengthy sojourn in Cuba. In a whole series of works, concentrated between 1968 and 1980, Henze gave vent to his disaffection with western capi-talism, but he is far from being a straightfor-ward propagandist – on the contrary, Henze is a subtle and complex composer.

His early works show the influence of Stravinsky, Hindemith, Bartók and Schoenberg, yet Henze has always retained a loyalty to classical forms – he has, after all, written seven symphonies. He has always been a profoundly theatrical composer as well: he has stated that all his work ultimately derives from the theatre, and has referred to his hearing *The Marriage of Figaro* as a formative childhood experience. The direct-ness and lucidity of his writing can largely be attributed to his development of a hard-hitting style for the political works he created for small ensembles in the 1960s and 1970s, such as *The Raft of the Medusa*, *La Cubana* and *El Cimarrón*.

One last essential component in Henze's work is its sensuousness, a quality that came to the fore after he left his native country at the age of twenty-seven to live in Italy, which is still his home. Italy has stimulated his work in innumerable ways: through its light and colour; through its freer attitude towards his homosexuality; and, perhaps above all, through its emphasis on community. Of the various popular projects with which Henze has been involved none has been more impor-tant than the festival he created at the Tuscan town of Montepulciano. Here, working with professional musicians and local people, Henze established a forum for the perfor-mance of a range of projects, from new works to little-known Italian operas, most of them staged in the town square. Innovative and highly popular, the festival in Montepulciano epitomizes the best qualities of this prolific composer.

THE MUSIC

Henze's operas have had few productions in the recession-hit recent years, but they comprise a mightily impressive body of stage work. Of those available on CD, *Der junge Lord* makes the best introduction, showing the energizing influence of Italy and its music on Henze's imagination. The story concerns the ridiculous antics surrounding a young English lord who turns out to be an ape in disguise, and Henze plunders the world of Bellini and bel canto opera to produce a beautiful and searingly satirical piece. His greatest opera, however, is *The Bassarids*, a far more sombre creation. Its source is the *Bacchae* of Euripides, worked by Henze into a highly complicated structure which is in effect a single-spanned two-hour symphony with voices. The formal aspects of the opera are demonstrations of a remarkable technical proficiency, but what matters most is Henze's ability to portray the conflicts of sense and sensuality in music that is immediately effective.

The seven symphonies that Henze has so far composed cover an even wider ground than the operas, from the classical forms of the first and the sumptuous late Romantic textures of the second to the agit-prop of the sixth and the dance-inspired music of the seventh. The symphonies are the most accessible part of Henze's output, and the series of seven is now available on three discs.

> ◗ **Der junge Lord**: Mathis, Grobe, Johnson, Driscoll; Deutsche Oper Berlin; Dohnányi (Deutsche Grammophon DG 445 248-2; 2 CDs).
> ◉ **The Bassarids**: Riegel, Schmidt, Tear, Armstrong, Lindsey; Berlin Radio Symphony Orchestra; Albrecht (Schwann 314 006-2; 2 CDs).
> ◗ **Symphonies Nos. 1–6**: Berlin Philharmonic Orchestra; London Symphony Orchestra; Henze (Deutsche Grammophon DG 429 854-2).
> ◉ **Symphony No. 7**; Barcarola: City of Birmingham Symphony Orchestra; Rattle (EMI CDC 7 54762 2).

Dohnányi's performance of *Der junge Lord* is superb, with Edith Mathis outstanding among the generally excellent cast. Gerd Albrecht conducts a similarly fine version of *The Bassarids*: full-bodied singing and good recorded sound make this first-choice recommendation for a work which will repay repeated listening.

Deutsche Grammophon seem to have been slow to release much from their considerable store of Henze recordings, but this mid-price symphony set, conducted by the composer, gives you a fair slice of his best music. The sixth symphony is the problem piece, tending towards a rather stale political attitudinizing, but the set is well worth having for a concise history of Henze's musical development up until the Cuban years.

The finest single Henze recording is Simon Rattle's amazing performance of the *Symphony No. 7* and the *Barcarola*, recorded live in Birmingham. These are perfect interpretations of frequently complex and always rich music – Rattle brings total conviction to the four contrasting dance movements that make up the symphony, and manages the sweep of the *Barcarola* with real panache.

HILDEGARD OF BINGEN
(1098–1179)

The tenth child of a noble family, Hildegard of Bingen spent almost her entire life, from the age of eight until her death at eighty-one, within monastic communities: firstly at the Benedictine monastery of Disibodenberg near Bingen in southern Germany; then, against the wishes of her abbot, at an independent convent which she founded at nearby Rupertsberg between 1147 and 1150, and where she settled with eighteen nuns and her secretary, the monk Volmar.

Hildegard was an ecstatic mystic and from 1141 she had a series of twenty-six visions which were dictated to Volmar and recorded in a book, *Scivias* (Know the Ways). The language of these visions, and of the religious poetry that she set to music, is highly personal and full of startling images, both apocalyptic and sensual – "When I was forty-two years and seven months old, a burning light of tremendous brightness coming from heaven poured into my entire mind. Like a flame that does not burn but enkindles, it inflamed my entire heart and my entire breast . . . ". Hildegard's music has a similar inspired quality. Although it resembles plainsong, being made up of just a single line of melody, it tends to be far more daring and passionate than conventional chant, with an abundance of leaps and florid ornamentation.

The widespread fame Hildegard achieved during her lifetime – she was known as the "Sybil of the Rhine" – was due not so much to her music as to her intellect and influence. As well as two more books of mystical writings she produced important works on natural history (*Physica*) and medicine (*Causae et Curae*) and led four preaching missions throughout Germany. Her many correspondents included two popes, the Holy Roman Emperor Frederick Barbarossa (whom she berated for failing to reply promptly) and the powerful head of the Cistercian order, Saint Bernard of Clairvaux. After her death she was considered for, but never achieved, canonization.

THE MUSIC

In the 1150s Hildegard gathered together her lyrical poems and their musical settings into a collection which she called *Symphonia harmoniae, caelestium revalationum* (Symphony of the harmony of heavenly revelations). The word "Symphonia" signified for her not just the harmonious combination of different musical sounds but also the divine harmony of the cosmos, and she saw the act of making music as a union between the physical and the spiritual that brought the participant closer to the divine. The

collection consists of over seventy works which collectively comprise a cycle of music suitable for the principal feasts of the ecclesiastical calendar. Feast days of saints to whom Hildegard was particularly devoted, namely the Virgin Mary, Ursula, Disibod and Rupert, are the occasions of the greatest amount of music.

◉ A Feather on the Breath of God: Christopher Page; Gothic Voices; Kirkby; Van Evera; Philpot (Hyperion CDA 66039).

Ten years ago few histories of music would have even mentioned Hildegard of Bingen. That there is so much interest in her music today can be largely explained by the success of this outstanding recording. Page is an academic as well as a musician but the great pleasure of this disc is the sense of joy and spontaneity that he manages to get from his singers. The repetition of the same type of melodic patterns in Hildegard's work is mitigated by the skilful variety of vocal combinations and the occasional discreet accompaniment of drone reeds or hurdy-gurdy. He employs both male and female singers (though never together) but it is the female voices, which occur on six of the eight tracks, that best convey the music's special mixture of ecstasy and serenity.

The CD that put Hildegard back on the map

PAUL HINDEMITH

(1895–1963)

Nowadays Paul Hindemith is too often depicted as something of a throwback, the traditionalist antithesis of Arnold Schoenberg. It's true that Hindemith never had much time for Schoenberg and his fellow Viennese iconoclasts, yet he was a more complex character than that. He began his career as the *enfant terrible* of German music, the successor in that role to Richard Strauss, and his earlier style was a sort of Expressionist-Romanticism, reflecting the influences of Wagner and Strauss, even of Stravinsky and Bartók. By the mid-1920s, however, his neo-classical propensities were asserting themselves ever more strongly, and his music was settling into an increasingly contrapuntal and lyrical mode. In a nutshell, Hindemith – like Strauss – began as a radical and ended as a conservative.

Hindemith's earliest studies, between 1913 and 1917, were at the conservatory in Frankfurt, where he took lessons in composition and conducting. In 1915, he became the first violin in that city's Opera Orchestra and, shortly after, he began leader of a major string quartet. Even though he served in the army, he continued composing and playing chamber music throughout the war and in 1918 returned to Frankfurt, where life continued as before. After the scandalous premieres of his sexually provocative one-act operas *Mörder, Hoffnung der Frauen* and *Das Nusch-Nuschi*, Hindemith left the Frankfurt orchestra to concentrate on composition and his role in the Amar Quartet, a group devoted to contemporary music. In 1921, the Amar Quartet gave the first performance of Hindemith's *Quartet No. 2*.

With the production of his opera *Cardillac* in 1926, Hindemith was established as one of Germany's leading young composers, and in the following year he became a teacher of composition at the Berlin School of Music, where he promulgated his theories of *Gebrauchsmusik* (Utility Music), a concept of music as a socially functional activity. (The centrality of music to education was to be a

ROYAL COLLEGE OF MUSIC

constant element in Hindemith's thought, and he wrote many pieces for amateur groups.) In 1929, Hindemith again found himself the subject of scandal, thanks to the premieres of his opera *Neues vom Tage*, which called for a soprano to sing while taking a bath on stage, and of his cantata *Lehrstuck*, with its text by the arch-subversive Bertolt Brecht. Shortly afterwards he visited London for the first time, where his friend William Walton (see p.410) engaged him as soloist at the first performance of Walton's *Viola Concerto*; in 1930 he returned to give the premiere of his own *Viola Concerto*.

In 1933, with Hitler's rise to power, Hindemith began work on *Mathis der Maler*, an opera based upon the life of the artist and social reformer Matthias Grünewald (1475–1528). It had to wait a long time to reach the stage, but in March, 1934 Wilhelm Furtwängler – a champion of Hindemith's music – conducted the first performance of the *Mathis der Maler Symphony*, three interludes extracted from the full score. Its success was immediate but the authorities – in particular Hitler, who had strongly disapproved of the nudity in *Neues vom Tage* – expressed their anger at the choice of Grünewald as subject matter. In November, Furtwängler defended the music and its composer in an open letter, but the controversy resulted in the banning of the symphony and the opera, and, ultimately, to Hindemith's departure for Turkey, where he helped establish a music school. Upon his return, the Nazis were better disposed towards him, but worryingly "demonstrative" applause at the first performance of his new *Violin Sonata* in 1936 led to a ban on all Hindemith's work.

After another brief spell in Turkey, Hindemith returned to Germany to resign from his post, and left for America. In 1938 *Mathis* was staged in Zurich but its production was never reported in the German press. In 1940 he was appointed visiting professor at Yale and head of advanced composition at Tanglewood, where he taught Leonard Bernstein (see p.52). After the war his music again began to circulate in Germany, and his fiftieth birthday was marked by numerous performances. The majority of his remaining years were spent teaching in America and Switzerland, devoting ever less time to composition.

> ◗ **Composers in Person – Hindemith** (EMI CDS 5 55032-2).
>
> This disc includes performances by Hindemith, as violist and conductor, of a good selection of his finest music, including the *Viola Sonata No. 2*, the *Symphonia Serena*, the *String Trio No. 2* and the *Clarinet Concerto*. The sound may be dated, and Hindemith may not be the greatest conductor, but the list of musicians reads like a roll-call of the finest of the time, and performances have real conviction.

CARDILLAC

Hindemith's first three operas, each of them one-act pieces, were outspoken but unpolished productions. His fourth, *Cardillac*, is a very different matter. Dealing with the relationship of the artist to society (a problem that concerned Hindemith all his life), it tells of a master jeweller who is so devoted to his creations that he murders any customers who show an interest in them. An officer witnesses one such attack but blames a third party as he wishes to marry the jeweller's daughter.

Cardillac's shop is threatened with arson and so, rather than have his jewellery harmed, he confesses to the angry mob, who then tear him to pieces. The opera ends with a lush lament for the loss of the artist, a conclusion that's highly distanced from the rest of the opera's music, which is fiercely polyphonic.

The construction of *Cardillac* is traditional, in that it follows the classical principle of furthering the action through distinct numbers, but Hindemith introduces a distancing effect by writing music that progresses in parallel to the text, commenting on the action rather than emphasizing its meaning. Thus the Act One murder takes place to a decorous neo-Baroque piece for two flutes (when Hindemith revised the opera in the 1950s, he incorporated bits of Lully's *Phaëton*). It's a cerebral opera, with no thrilling moments for its singers, but it makes a fascinating comparison with the more aggressive work of Alban Berg, whose *Wozzeck* (see p.43) was premiered one year earlier.

> ◗ Fischer-Dieskau, Grobe, Kirchstein, Söderström, Lorengar; Kölner Rundfunk, Berlin Radio Symphony Orchestra; Keilberth, Ludwig (Deutsche Grammophon 431 741-2; with excerpts from *Mathis der Maler*).
>
> This performance of the original 1926 version of *Cardillac* is brilliantly realized, with an intelligent and responsive cast that includes Dietrich Fischer-Dieskau, who shines in the title role, and the less well-known but no less remarkable Leonora Kirchstein as his daughter. Well recorded, this is a fine introduction to Hindemith.

MATHIS DER MALER SYMPHONY

Though there is a complete recording of *Mathis der Maler* (on the Wergo label), you're best advised to steer clear of the opera until you've heard the *Mathis der Maler Symphony*, the composer's masterpiece. Completed before the opera, in order to give something that Furtwängler could take on a planned tour with the Berlin Philharmonic, the symphony was banned as an example of degenerate music. This might seem odd, in view of the fact that the music represents a distinct move back towards traditional melody rather than away from it, but the symphony was incriminated by the anti-war message of the opera, and its depiction of the corruption of power. Each of the symphony's three movements –

The Angelic Concert, *The Entombment* and *The Temptation of St Anthony* – represents a panel from Grünewald's masterpiece, the *Isenheim Altarpiece*, a work which the opera presented as the distillation of the peasants' hatred of their lords. The final movement, and in particular its brass chorale, is one of Hindemith's most sensational achievements.

⊙ San Francisco Symphony Orchestra; Blomstedt (Decca 421 523-2; with *Symphonic Metamorphosis; Trauermusik*).

This recording is something of a benchmark. Blomstedt has an unmatched empathy for Hindemith's inner torment, and the San Francisco Orchestra respond with uncommon sensitivity, revealing layers of inner voices that are commonly ignored. The accompanying pieces are equally fine. *Symphonic Metamorphosis of Themes by Carl Maria von Weber* is one of Hindemith's most inventive and entertaining orchestral scores. It arose from a commission, in 1940, to compose a ballet based on the music of Weber. When he began to see the shape and form that this ballet was to take – with designs by Dali – Hindemith pulled out from the project, but three years later he returned to the idea, producing a set of transformations that are considerably more rewarding than the originals. The third piece on the disc, *Trauermusik*, for viola and orchestra, is a deeply mournful piece which was written in only six hours to honour the death of George V.

REQUIEM

Hindemith's *Requiem* was composed in 1946 as a lament for President Roosevelt and the dead of World War II – in tribute to his adoptive country during the war years, he took the text not from the Latin Mass but from the Walt Whitman poem *When lilacs last in the door-yard bloom'd*. The *Requiem* is full of technical exercises, such as fugues and marches, but this is not one of Hindemith's didactic displays of classical orthodoxy (there's enough of that in his chamber music) – everything here is subjugated to deeply personal expression. The sonorous opening prelude is occasionally performed separately, but you should hear the work complete – it's one of the rare twentieth-century scores that can invoke the unqualified spiritual devotion of earlier centuries without seeming phoney.

⊙ De Gaetani, Stone; Atlanta Symphony Orchestra; Shaw (Telarc CD 80132).

Hindemith's own recording of the *Requiem* is still available on mid-price CD but this is the sort of music that demands the clarity of digital sound. The conductor of this fine performance was the man who commissioned the *Requiem*.

──────────── ♭♯ ────────────

GUSTAV HOLST

(1874–1934)

Gustav Holst – an Englishman with a Swedish name – was to a large extent hampered by the period into which he was born, a period in which there was no English musical tradition from which to draw and little chance of a favourable reception for new English music. He composed only as and when he felt the urge, was rarely performed in his lifetime, and relied on classroom work for his income. Holst is one of the many composers for whom popularity was posthumous.

As a young man he was prodigiously talented, having his first opera – *Lansdown Castle* – performed in 1893. However, recognizing that the nineteen-year-old needed

further tuition, his father then sent him to the Royal College of Music. It was while at the college that he met and became friends with Ralph Vaughan Williams, who introduced him to English folk music, a passion they shared until Holst's death in 1934 (the same year as Elgar's). Yet Holst did not respond to these folk influences as readily as his mentor, for the presence of Wagner loomed too powerfully, and a large proportion of his early music veered towards the grandeur of Wagner's operas.

Eventually he rid himself of Wagner's influence and produced a steady stream of notably original music, including the *The Planets*, an orchestral suite that gave him his only taste of acclaim. This work, and the late, grim *Egdon Heath*, show what Holst was capable of when he allowed himself to think on a large scale. Much of his music, though, was written in the certainty that professional performances would never come his way, which is one reason why so much of his output was composed for amateur and childrens' groups, such as those at the schools of Dulwich and St Paul's, where he spent most of his life teaching.

THE PLANETS

The Planets, Holst's most brilliantly inventive and famous score, was one of many pieces inspired by the composer's extra-musical interests. In 1913 a friend introduced him to astrology, thus sparking the idea of creating a seven-part tone poem in which the characters of each of the planets would be evoked. This often turbulent and melancholic music was first performed on September 29, 1918, and it was inevitable that *The Planets* would be perceived as an expression of the nation's collective emotions during the war years. Listening to *Mars* they heard the fury of the Somme and Paschendale, yet Holst declared that there was no programme to his orchestral suite, and in the case of this particular episode such a programme was impossible – Holst had finished the movement before August 1914.

Jupiter – source of the patriotic hymn *I vow to thee my country* – is perhaps the best known episode, but listening to *The Planets* for the first time is bound to produce several moments of strange familiarity, as this is one of the most often quoted and plagiarized scores of the twentieth century.

◗ Mitchell Choir; London Philharmonic Orchestra; Boult (EMI CDM7 69045-2).

Sir Adrian Boult gave the first performance of *The Planets* in 1918 and, sixty years later – shortly before his ninetieth year – he entered the studio to record it for the third and last time. His interpretation is coloured by intense passion but also suggests the deep reflectiveness of advancing years. Well recorded, this is a fine and moving introduction to Holst.

EGDON HEATH

The tone poem *Egdon Heath*, composed in 1927 in homage to Thomas Hardy, was Holst's first full-scale orchestral work after *The Planets*. The music is based upon a passage from *The Return of the Native* in which the heath (a fictionalized Salisbury Plain) is described as "a place perfectly accordant with man's nature – neither ghastly, hateful, nor ugly; neither commonplace, unmeaning, nor tame; but like man, slighted and enduring; and withal singularly colossal and mysterious in its swarthy monotony". Witheringly bleak at times, this music is the polar opposite of sunny English bucolicism; Holst believed it to be his finest work.

◗ London Philharmonic Orchestra; Boult (Decca 425 152-2LM; with *Perfect Fool*).

Boult excels himself in *Egdon Heath*, getting as close to the soul of the composer as one is likely to hear on record. As an antidote to this harrowing experience, this CD comes with the magnificently evocative and colourful ballet music from *Perfect Fool* (1918–22), the second of Holst's eight rarely performed operas. Although Boult is here a bit less incisive than in his earlier days, this performance is hugely enjoyable.

ST PAUL'S SUITE

St Paul's Suite, Holst's most famous score for amateurs, was written for the orchestra of St Paul's girls' school in 1912–13. Famous for a final movement that quotes and builds upon the perennial English folk tune *Greensleeves*, it's a good-natured piece of music, with none of the depths of *The Planets* or *Egdon Heath*, but essential listening if you want an idea of Holst's range.

◉ Academy of St Martin-in-the-Field; Sillito (Collins COLL 1234-2; with works by Tippett, Walton and Berkeley).

The *St Paul's Suite* is simple music that demands crisp, attentive playing, and this performance under the leadership of Ken Sillito bristles with enthusiasm. Excellently recorded, this disc features a good selection of twentieth-century English music for strings.

ARTHUR HONEGGER
(1892–1955)

GUUS ONG

Though Honegger spent much of his life in Paris, he retained close links with the German-speaking heritage of his native Switzerland, hence the hybrid Franco-Teutonic character of much of his music. Honegger's earliest significant compositions, such as his violin sonata of 1918, were written around the time that he became one of the chic group of French composers known as Les Six, but his relationship with the other five was always ambiguous, chiefly because of the distinct lack of humour in his outlook – manifested particularly by Honegger's antipathy to the quirky Eric Satie, spiritual guru of Les Six. Honegger wrote at the time: "I have no taste for the fairground, nor for the music-hall, but, on the contrary, a taste for chamber music and symphonic music in its most austere form". When it came to modern French music, Honegger's preference was for Debussy, whom most of Les Six considered decidedly passé, but he was just as likely to draw upon German, Central European and Russian music for inspiration.

Honegger's opera *Antigone*, a collaborative venture with Jean Cocteau, was a disaster on stage, but early success came with the semi-dramatic biblical oratorio *Le Roi David* (1921) and a series of orchestral works including *Pacific 231*, the piece with which he's associated as strongly and unfairly as Ravel is associated with *Boléro*. From the mid-1920s he entered a very productive period, composing several dramatic works, a cello sonata and his first symphony, as well as pursuing the parallel careers of lecturer, writer, music critic and accompanist – he often appeared with his wife, the pianist Andrée Vauraborg, on international and transatlantic tours. Even though Honegger was based in Paris, he maintained firm ties with Switzerland through his close connection with Paul Sacher, the founder and conductor of the Basle Chamber Orchestra. Sacher premiered a significant number of his works and even commissioned two symphonies, the best known being the *Symphony no. 2* for strings and trumpet (1941).

World War II profoundly affected Honegger, whose troubled state found expression in works such as *Cris du Monde*, *Jeanne d'Arc* and the *Symphonie Liturgique*. After the war he could never quite shake off the depression that that conflict had brought him, and although he continued to create, he frequently made it plain that he had become disillusioned with his life – "the profession of a composer is peculiar", he once wrote, "in that it is the principal activity and occupation of a man who exerts himself to produce wares for which no-one has any use". As if continuous depression were not bad enough, Honegger contracted angina on a tour of the USA in 1947, a debilitating condition from which he was never to recover.

THE MUSIC

Honegger held that music required not a change in the rules but "a new player in the same game". This he duly became, producing works that were essentially a natural outgrowth from the tradition of Bach, Beethoven, Wagner and Richard Strauss. However, for one who was so immersed in the

Germanic heritage, Honegger was a surprisingly cosmopolitan composer – his extensive output shows that he was happy to experiment with all sorts of forms, including populist ones such as jazz, which he used to great effect in the 1925 *Piano Concertino*. Characterizing himself as "an honest workman", he even tried his hand composing for the newly emerging film and radio industries, writing the score for Abel Gance's classic movie *Napoléon* (1927). Among the many other sources Honegger drew on were Gregorian chant, the work of Stravinsky and Prokofiev, twelve-tone music (although he was firmly against atonality), Protestant hymns and even – in a little known orchestral piece called *Le chant di Nigamon* (1917) – North American Indian themes.

His best-known creation, the tone poem *Pacific 231*, is more than merely picturesque, which is how it's sometimes dismissively summarized. "What I was looking for in *Pacific*", he declared in 1924, "was not so much to imitate the sounds of a locomotive, but to translate visual impressions and physical enjoyment with a musical construction". As far as Honegger was concerned, the purer the musical structure the better, and with *Pacific 231*, as in so much of his work, he aimed at a Bach-like distillation of means – "I have composed a sort of great, varied chorale", he wrote.

⊙ **Pacific 231; Symphony No. I; Pastorale d'été; Three symphonic movements; Rugby:** Bavarian Radio Symphony Orchestra; Dutoit (Erato 2292 45242-2).

An excellent cross-section of Honegger's oeuvre is featured on this recording from the Bavarian Radio Symphony Orchestra directed by Charles Dutoit. As a counterpoint to the vividly interpreted and rumbustious *Pacific 231* there's the highly accomplished *Symphony No. 1*, whose second movement has rarely sounded so elegantly poised as it does here. *Rugby*, a delightful free-wheeling musical rondo, is an affectionate tribute to one of Honegger's favourite games.

JOHANN NEPOMUCK HUMMEL
(1778–1837)

Hummel was not merely a contemporary of Beethoven – they studied with several of the same teachers (among them Salieri and Haydn) and were both highly gifted pianists. But whereas Beethoven was a daring innovator, both as a composer and as a pianist, Hummel was essentially a conservative – which is why his relationship with Beethoven was rather spiky, and why his music has been largely ignored since his death. This is unfortunate since at his best, particularly when writing for the piano, he is a composer of elegance and charm, with a special facility for producing ornate and lyrical melodies spun out over light and delicate accompaniments.

Hummel began his career as an infant prodigy, impressive enough to be given free lessons by Mozart. Like Mozart he was touted around Europe by an ambitious father, and it was during a trip to England in 1790 that he got to know Haydn, through whom he later obtained the position of Konzertmeister at the court of Prince Nikolaus Esterházy (Haydn was still the prince's Kapellmeister, in title if not in practice). Hummel's time there was not especially successful, but he remained at the court, on and off, until 1811 when he returned to Vienna. Thereafter his career alternates between that of a jobbing composer (Kapellmeister to the Grand-Duchy of Weimar from 1819 until his death) and a concert pianist. His piano playing epitomized the classic Viennese style, and was described by Czerny, Beethoven's most successful piano pupil, as "a modern cleanness, clarity and of the most graceful elegance and tenderness." It was a style that made Hummel, during the 1820s, one of the most celebrated performers in Europe, but the following decade he had been superseded by the more expressive and passionate playing of Romantic pianists such as Chopin and Liszt.

CONCERTOS

The *Trumpet Concerto* is Hummel's most recorded work, largely because trumpet players have so limited a repertoire that they gratefully accept any halfway decent piece that comes their way. That said, it is one of the liveliest concertos for the instrument, with a lyrically wistful slow movement and a virtuosic last movement. Even better are the concertos Hummel wrote for his own instrument, the piano. These are bravura works, written to show off Hummel's pianistic skills especially his ability at playing long highly ornamented melodies. They may not be as poetic as Chopin's two concertos (on which they exerted a very powerful influence) but they are better orchestrated and far more extrovert works, whose neglect over the years is hard to understand.

● **Trumpet Concerto**: Hardenberger; Academy of St Martin-in-the-Fields; Marriner (Philips 420 203-2; with concertos by Haydn, Hertel and Stamitz).
● **Piano Concertos in A minor and B minor**: Hough; English Chamber Orchestra; Thomson (Chandos CHAN 8507).

Håkan Hardenberger plays all four concertos on this CD with astonishing technical expertise and an enormous amount of flair – you would never have believed a trumpet could be made to sound so light. His articulation is always exceptionally clear and bright, and there is wit and warmth in his playing of the Hummel, particularly in the way he rattles through the ebullient last-movement rondo.

The success of Stephen Hough's recording of the two piano concertos has done much to re-establish Hummel's reputation. He tackles the amazingly difficult solo parts not just with ease but with a great deal of artistry, shaping the music's sometimes abrupt transitions from boldness to lyricism with delicacy and style. The A minor concerto is marginally the better work, energetic and exciting, with a breathtaking last-movement coda.

ENGELBERT HUMPERDINCK
(1854–1921)

Humperdinck's masterpiece, *Hänsel und Gretel*, is a fairy-tale opera that's emphatically not for kids. Operas with supernatural themes had dominated German opera since the days of Weber (see p.411), but Humperdinck gave these subjects a new gravity by turning the harmony, orchestration and mythic power of Wagner's operas to the service of the fairy tale. Lightening the ponderousness of his master's music with the use of folk-style music, he perpetuated the Wagner line while taking it to a more populist level.

He was already composing operas at the age of fourteen and by his early twenties had fallen under the spell of Wagner's music, joining a Wagnerite student society in Munich called *The Order of the Grail*. He met the man himself in Naples in 1880 and was invited to Bayreuth to help with preparations for the first performance of *Parsifal* in 1881–82. After Wagner's death in the following year, Humperdinck took up a series of teaching posts in Cologne, Barcelona and Frankfurt, while working on *Hänsel und Gretel*, his most overtly Wagnerian work. Its first performance in Weimar in December 1893 was conducted by none other than Richard Strauss and was instantly popular, receiving some fifty productions in its first year. No other of Humperdinck's works achieved comparable fame, but he continued to write operas, as well as choral, chamber and orchestral pieces – none of which is much heard nowadays. His last conspicuous success was with his opera *Königskinder* (Royal Children), first performed at the New York Met in 1910.

● **Music from Hänsel und Gretel, Königskinder, Dornröschen and The Blue Bird**: Bamberg Symphony Orchestra; Rickenbacher (Virgin VC 7 91494-2).

This CD is the best introduction to Humperdinck if you don't feel ready to jump into one of the full-length operas. It contains the best-known orchestral passages from *Hänsel*, as well as excerpts from *Dornröschen* (Sleeping Beauty), his ballet *The Blue Bird*, and *Königskinder*, the only piece that can be regarded as a worthy successor to *Hänsel*.

HÄNSEL UND GRETEL

Humperdinck's first opera began as a commission from his sister – she asked him to write music for a children's play that she'd adapted from the famous story by the Brothers Grimm. The resulting three-act opera has been a mainstay of the Christmas operatic season since its first performance. Described by Richard Strauss as "a master-piece of the highest quality", it was translated into some twenty languages within a couple of decades of its premiere, and in 1923 became the first opera ever to be broadcast live on radio. Combining the artless charm of German folk-songs with a Wagnerian orchestral magnificence, it brings the natural and supernatural worlds vividly to life, particularly in the interludes of the *Witch's Ride* (shades of the *Ride of the Valkyries*) and *Dream Pantomime*.

◉ Murray, Gruberova, Ludwig, Jones, Grundheber; Dresden Staatskapelle; Davis (Philips 438 013-2; 2 CDs).

Of the several recordings currently available, Colin Davis's is the most enjoyable, mainly because of the beautiful playing of the Dresden Staatskapelle. It boasts a fine cast too, with an ideally characterized pair of children in Ann Murray and Edita Gruberova and a magnificently malevolent portrayal of the witch from veteran mezzo Christa Ludwig.

KÖNIGSKINDER

A rare case of a fairy story that doesn't end with everyone living happily ever after, this tale of a goose-girl and her tragic love for a prince has deeper undertones than the Hänsel and Gretel story. The music, too, has a greater profundity, with a bleakly moving final act which often recalls the spirituality of Wagner's *Parsifal*. The earlier acts are more down-to-earth, but even the bumptious Bavarian inn scene of Act Two ends with a ravishing apotheosis as the goose-girl and prince, rejected by the townspeople for looking too poor to be their rulers, walk off into the sunset.

◗ Dallapozza, Donath, Prey, Schwarz, Ridderbusch; Tölz Boys' Choir, Bavarian Radio Choir; Munich Radio Orchestra; Wallberg (EMI CMS 7 69936 2; 3 CDs).

The opera is well worth investigating in this fine recording by Heinz Wallberg, featuring some of Germany's top singers. The only problems are the absence of an English translation of the German text (there is an English note and synopsis) and the artificial, over-reverberant sound.

CHARLES IVES
(1874–1954)

Charles Ives was one of the most extraordinary innovators Western music has produced, and an equally fascinating man – for years he led a double life, working as a highly successful insurance agent by day, and as a composer by night. His music uses collage, atonality, polytonality, dissonance, quarter tones, asymmetrical rhythms and elements of jazz and ragtime – a panoply of devices that anticipated many of the experiments of Stravinsky, Debussy, Schoenberg, Berg and Webern, before some of them had written their first note. Apart from his wife and a handful of friends and contemporaries, no-one for years understood what he was up to, but Ives could not care less. Composing in virtual seclusion, he went on following his instincts until he stopped writing in his fifties.

Almost every work he wrote contains quotes from the tunes, patriotic songs, hymns and marches he heard while growing up in Danbury, where he received a highly unorthodox musical education from his army bandleader father. He became an intensely patriotic man, whose adoration of his country was often expressed by referring back to his happy Connecticut childhood. Ives had a virtually photographic memory and everything he heard and saw as a child made a

GUUS ONG

lasting impression on him – nothing more so than a baseball rally he once attended, where two marching bands met head on, each playing totally different music. Ives was so entranced by the sound that in adulthood the juxtaposition of different musics became a favourite compositional ploy.

Despite moments of wistfulness and tenderness in works like the *Symphony No. 3*, *The Unanswered Question* and *Three Places in New England*, Ives did not write pretty music, the sort admired by the conventional public. His hardy background gave him an aversion to "cissy sounds", and his opinions on many revered figures were not flattering – Chopin he considered to be "soft . . . with a skirt on", while Mozart was "effeminate". He was a musical Ernest Hemingway – where he came from people "got up and said what they thought regardless of the consequences." Allied to this forthrightness was an earthy idealism, central to which was the belief that art should become part of the fabric of humanity; he looked forward with to the day when "every man, while digging his potatoes, will breathe his own Epics, his own Symphonies (Operas if he likes)". It's no

wonder that he became a hero to America's twentieth-century musicians. Every marginalized composer has at some time or another taken courage from his bold and stoically independent stance, epitomized in his declaration that "the impossibilities of today are the possiblities of tomorrow".

THE ORCHESTRAL MUSIC

If Gustav Mahler had lived a little longer he might well have put Ives on the musical map decades before the old man received his long overdue recognition. Evidently Mahler had come across a score of Ives's *Symphony No. 3* (1901–04) towards the end of his tenure as conductor of the Metropolitan Opera and the New York Philharmonic, and had copied it out ready to perform when he returned to Vienna. It was not to be. The third was indeed to be the first of Ives's symphonies to receive a complete performance, but that was not until April 5, 1946 in New York. To Ives's immense surprise and satisfaction it took the Pulitzer Prize. One of his most popular symphonic works, it is based on music he had played as a young organist at the Central Presbyterian Church in New York, using favourite hymns like *What a friend we have in Jesus* to build the outer movements' melodic and harmonic structures. The end result is a highly ingratiating piece, which is by turns gentle, jaunty and devotional in mood.

In 1906 Ives wrote what has a claim to be his watershed piece, *The Unanswered Question*, the first composition in which he juxtaposed contrasting groups of instruments, each having its own distinctive style. Described as a "Cosmic Landscape", *The Unanswered Question* is a symbolic drama in which the "Perennial Question of Existence" is asked seven times by a solo trumpet against a background of muted offstage strings that represent "the Silences of the Druids – Who Know, See and Hear Nothing". Four woodwinds are unleashed to seek "the Invisible Answer", but to no avail, and they leave the scene before the trumpet reiterates the question for the last time.

The ten years following *The Unanswered Question* were marked by feverish activity. One of the classic works produced in this decade was *Three Places in New England* (1903–14), the second part of which – *Putnam's Camp* – is one of the most celebrated instances of Ives' love of clashing sounds, with a wild march full of duff notes and players missing the beat. This section is preceded by a piece subtitled *Col. Shaw and his Coloured Regiment*, a memorial to America's first black army company, taking the form of a highly effective dreamlike blues, spiced with dissonant harmonies. The final part, *The Housatonic at Stockbridge*, was inspired by Ives' memory of an autumn walk he and his wife took soon after they were married; it's a stunning piece, memorable for the way it sets a simple folk tune against a turbulent orchestral texture and then, at the end, fades into silence.

⊙ **Symphony No. 3; The Unanswered Question; Three Places in New England**: Saint Louis Symphony Orchestra; Slatkin (RCA 09026-61222-2; with other Ives pieces).

When it comes to the interpretation of robust American music there are few American conductors to match what Leonard Slatkin can bring to a performance. He takes hold of Ive's more wildly extravagant moments in the *Three Places in New England* and, rather than taming them, actually heightens the electric charge. By the same token the poetry of *The Unanswered Question* and the folksy imagery of *Symphony No. 3* are brought out with remarkable warmth and finesse.

LEOŠ JANÁČEK

(1854–1928)

Although he was born halfway through the nineteenth century, Janáček's best music belongs decisively to the twentieth. His finest works – the last four operas, the *Sinfonietta*, *Glagolitic Mass*, the *Diary of One Who Disappeared* and the two string quartets – were composed in an astonishing burst of creativity in his last decade, and they are among the most impressive and accessible pieces of the last hundred years, distinguished by terse dramatic power, emotional lyricism, eccentric orchestration and rhythmic bite.

Janáček was the fifth of nine children born into a poor teacher's family in Hukvaldy, northern Moravia. He was educated in Brno, the Moravian capital, and spent most of his life there – the National Theatre in Brno premiered the operas that are the basis of his reputation, and the Czechs' reluctance to place him alongside their beloved Smetana and Dvořák is perhaps due to his being perceived as being too Moravian.

As with so many central European composers, folk music was the liberating ingredient in his career. In 1888 he set off on a tour of northern Moravia with the ethnographer Frantisek Bartos, and this intense encounter with the indigenous culture led to a decisive change in his compositional style. Certain folk tunes made their way into his orchestral and choral compositions, but more generally the short, irregular melodic phrases of Moravian music became integral to Janáček's idiosyncratic constructions, while echoes of folk ensembles influenced his distinctive orchestral sound.

Janáček's work can be seen as a fight against the German domination of his country, and the foundation of the Czechoslovak republic in 1918 was a factor behind the amazing creativity of his last years. But as well as being a Czech patriot, he was also an ardent believer in a pan-Slavic culture – he learnt Russian, visited that country twice, sent his daughter to study in St Petersburg and founded a Russian club in Brno. In 1900 he conducted a concert featuring dances from the various Slav nations for which he wrote a *Serbian Kolo* and *Russian Cossack Dance*. The Russian writers Gogol, Ostrovsky, Tolstoy and Dostoevsky inspired some of his greatest works (the libretto of *From the House of the Dead* was translated by Janáček from

ROYAL COLLEGE OF MUSIC

Dostoevsky), and the monumental *Glagolitic Mass*, with its text in Old Church Slavonic, can be heard as a sort of manifesto for a pan-Slavism.

The other dominating feature of much of Janáček's work is its erotic charge. His marriage, to a pupil ten years his junior, was never very successful – they were formally separated in 1917, when Janáček had an affair with Gabriela Horvátová, singer in the Prague production of *Jenůfa*. Soon afterwards he began the crucial relationship of his last decade, when at the Moravian spa town of Luhačovice he met Kamila Stösslová, a married woman half his age. Janáček conceived an all-consuming but unreciprocated passion for Kamila, to whom he wrote over 700 letters, the most passionate ones being written almost daily in the last sixteen months of his life. (They have recently been published in English, edited and translated by John Tyrrell.) *The Diary of One Who Disappeared* was the first work to be inspired by Kamila, who was then transformed into the heroines of three of his finest operas, *Kát'a Kabanová*, *The Cunning Little Vixen* and *The*

Makropulos Case. However, the most direct expression of their relationship is his *String Quartet No. 2 "Intimate Letters"*, one of the most intimate pieces of music ever written. Less than six months after it was composed, Janáček died of pneumonia from a chill he caught while the aloof Kamila was staying with him in Hukvaldy.

THE EARLY OPERAS AND JENUFA

Janáček composed two operas before his first masterpiece, *Jenůfa*. The first, *Šárka*, is a romantic treatment a Czech legendary subject, very much in the tradition of Smetana and Dvořák. A firm friendship developed between Janáček and Dvořák after they met in Prague in the 1870s, and Janáček revised the score of *Sárka* after Dvorák's criticisms of it – but despite these changes, and further revisions after the success of *Jenůfa* in Prague in 1916, it didn't reach the stage until 1925. Janáček's second opera, *The Beginning of a Romance* (the Czech title, as with most of Janáček's work, is an unmanageable mouthful) was hurriedly composed in 1891 when his passion for folk music was at its height, and is more an ethnic pot-pourri than a drama. Janáček withdrew it after six performances.

The creation of *Jenůfa* lasted nine years (1894–1903), a period in which his whole musical style was undergoing major changes. In addition to finding a way to fully integrate folk music into large-scale pieces, Janáček was abandoning the idea of opera divided into individual set-pieces in favour of through-composed dramatic form. He had also become passionately interested in the melodies of everyday speech, and kept a diary in which he noted down the way people spoke in musical notation – during the composition of *Jenůfa*, he even wrote down the last phrases of his dying daughter, Olga. None of these "speech melodies" were actually incorporated directly into his music, but they honed his dramatic vocal writing so that it approached the ideal that he had defined – "to compose a melodic curve which will, as if by magic, reveal immediately a human being in one definite phase of his existence."

Jenůfa was performed in Brno in 1904 and revived several times, but had Janáček died before 1916, when the opera finally made it to Prague, he would be no more than a footnote in the history of Czech music. When *Jenůfa* was accepted in Prague in 1916 it was on condition that it was revised and re-scored by the artistic director of the National Theatre, Karel Kovarovic. Ironically, it was this watered-down version, with its late-Romantic gloss, that launched Janáček's spectacular international career and his climactic creative surge.

The play on which the opera is based, *Její pastorkyna* (Her Foster-Daughter) by Gabriela Preissová, is a slice-of-life drama set in a Moravian village, a world Janáček had come to know deeply through his folksong collecting. The plot has a brutal simplicity that places it poles apart from the cheery bucolicism of Smetana's *Bartered Bride* (see p.344): two men, Steva and Laca, are rivals for Jenůfa's affection; she gets pregnant by the former, the unreliable one, but is truly loved by the latter; Steva moves on to another girl, whereupon Jenůfa's stepmother drowns the baby; finally Jenůfa and Laca are reconciled, in one of the great moments of opera.

Janáček's absorption of Moravian folk music underpins the entire score, which has a rough-edged veracity that's typical of his mature work, while the use of widely spaced instrumental writing prefigures the more extreme contrasts of his later works. Janáček very often writes for only the high and low strings, leaving out the middle registers for a more unsettling effect – there's a series of incisive chords like this in the prelude to the second act, which were smoothed out in the Kovařovic version. Where a shade more emotional warmth is required, however, he fills out the string texture to cover the full spectrum.

🔘 **Jenůfa**: Söderström; Ochman; Dvorsky; Randová; Popp; Vienna Philharmonic; Mackerras (Decca 414 483-2; 2 CDs).

Mackerras' Decca series of Janáček's operas is unsurpassed, and this premiere recording of Janáček's original score is magnificent in every way. In many ways it's the stepmother that dominates the drama, and Eva Randová brings out every nuance of this tyrannical yet well-meaning character. Elizabeth Söderström and the two male leads are also finely cast, while the orchestral playing is superb.

Jenůfa – one in a series of fine Janáček CDs from Mackerras

KÁT'A KABANOVÁ

Kát'a Kabanová, a story of adultery in a tyranical family setting, was written in 1919–21 and is based on *The Storm* by the Russian playwright Ostrovsky – one of several works Janáček based on Russian literature. His love for Kamila Stösslová is crucial to the psychological portrait of Kát'a, whose love for another man can be read as Janáček's wish-fulfilment. The action is concise and dramatic: Kát'a is reluctantly attracted to Boris, with whom she has an affair while her husband is away, then confesses to her mother-in-law (another strong female character) and is driven to commit suicide in the river. This is probably Janáček's best-constructed work, and it contains some quite extraordinary love music. The opening is especially fine – a brooding orchestral prelude in which the melodic line keeps turning in on itself before reaching the glorious melody that is associated with Kát'a throughout the opera. The timpani then burst in ominously, to return at decisive moments later in the opera.

🔘 Söderström; Dvorsky; Kniplová; Krejcík; Vienna Philharmonic; Mackerras (Decca 421 852-2; with Capriccio and Concertino; 2 CDs).

Made in 1976, this was the first of Mackerras' Janáček opera recordings, and it perfectly evokes the claustrophobic world of this piece. The singing, as ever on these Mackerras projects, is wonderful. The set includes his *Capriccio* and *Concertino* for piano and orchestra as valuable fill-ups.

THE CUNNING LITTLE VIXEN

Kamila Stösslová was again an inspiration for *The Cunning Little Vixen*, this time as self-sacrificing wife and mother – but an equally crucial inspiration was the countryside around his native village of Hukvaldy, where Janáček bought a house in 1921, shortly before starting work on this opera. Derived from a regular cartoon strip that appeared in a Brno newspaper, *The Cunning Little Vixen* is the beguiling anthropomorphic tale of a young vixen called Bystrouška, who is caught and raised by a gamekeeper. She kills his chickens, escapes, finds a mate, and is finally shot by a poultry dealer; at the end of the opera the gamekeeper is found back in the forest, surrounded by a troop of animals including a young vixen, Bystrouška's cub. Conjuring a broad vision of life's richness and transience, and nature's capacity for renewal, *The Cunning Little Vixen* shows Janáček at his most sumptuous and lyrical.

◉ Popp; Jedlička; Randová; Vienna Philharmonic; Mackerras (Decca 417 129-2; 2 CDs).

Full of luscious orchestral interludes, this is probably the most entrancing Janáček opera, and this recording of it is another triumph from Mackerras. Lucia Popp is immensely lively and characterful in the title role, and the Czech supporting cast is very fine indeed.

THE MAKROPULOS CASE

After the erotic passion of *Kát'a* and the fresh vitality of the *Vixen*, Janáček completed his trilogy on different aspects of women with the creation of the captivating, beautiful and cold Emilia Marty, protagonist of *The Makropulos Case* (1925). The opera is based on a dark comedy by Karel Čapek about a woman who has lived three hundred years thanks to an alchemical potion. She makes an uncanny intervention in a long-running court and property dispute, having been the mistress of one of the dispute's protagonists a century back, and the plot gets even more complicated as she begins to exert a powerful fascination on the men now involved. Of course, this portrait of a woman insensitive to the desires of those around her is to an extent a portrait of Kamila.

Lacking much in the way of conventional dramatic excitement, the opera gains its momentum almost purely from its music, which propels the action through the subtle development of a mosaic of motifs and ideas. *The Makropulos Case* is a very powerful piece, but one that reveals itself slowly, by an almost organic process.

◉ Söderström Dvorsky Krejčik, Zítek; Vienna Philharmonic; Mackerras (Decca 430 372-2; with *Lachian Dances*; 2 CDs).

The success of another recording of the *Makropulos Case* depends of course on the casting of Emilia Marty, and Elizabeth Söderström is perfect, managing to convey the vulnerability underneath the chilly exterior. This might not be first-buy Janáček, but it's another masterful set from Mackerras, and has the early orchestral *Lachian Dances* as a fill-up.

FROM THE HOUSE OF THE DEAD

For his last opera, *From the House of the Dead* (1928), Janáček turned to another Russian source, this time Dostoevsky's prison-camp memoirs. This is Janáček's most unorthodox opera and his most spartan score – indeed, the texture is so pared down that it was assumed the work was unfinished. The orchestration was filled out and a more optimistic ending tacked on, and this was how the opera was performed from its posthumous premiere in 1930 until the 1960s, when Janáček's true intentions were realized by Rafael Kubelík and Charles Mackerras.

It's not surprising that Janáček's contemporaries were perplexed, as *From the House of the Dead* has no definable plot and no central character. Consisting of a sequence of events in a Siberian camp, it presents everyday prison life in all its brutality and sickness, leavening the general misery with improvised theatre shows and the release of an eagle at the end – a symbolic embodiment of the line Janáček wrote on the title page of the score: "In every creature there is a spark of God." This might not seem like the place to begin an exploration of Janáček, but it's an amazingly high-spirited and experimental piece for a man of any age, let alone a man of 74.

◉ Zahradníček, Zídek, Zítek; Vienna Philharmonic; Mackerras (Decca 430 375-2; 2 CDs).

The orchestral textures and moods are what make this piece work, and the chamber-like ensemble on this recording of the original Janáček score bring out Janáček's incisive phrasing with exemplary clarity. There are no principal roles, but the Czech cast is strong throughout. The opera is coupled with two of Janáček's most carefree and ebullient works, *Mládí* and *Říkadla*.

THE GLAGOLITIC MASS
AND SINFONIETTA

For several years Janáček conducted a male choir in Brno, and choral music actually comprises the largest element of his output. His masterpiece of the genre is the *Glagolitic Mass*, a piece bursting with brassy fanfares and rhythmic energy, though it has some quieter moments of rapt contemplation. It was written at white heat in a single month in 1926, after an inspirational walk in the woods at Luhačovice, the spa where he had met Kamila. "I felt a cathedral grow out of the giant expanse of the woods," he wrote, "A flock of sheep were ringing their bells. Now I hear the voice of an arch priest in the tenor solo, a maiden angel in the soprano and in the choir – the people. The tall firs, their tips lit up by the stars, are the candles and during the ceremony I see the vision of St Wenceslas and I hear the language of the missionaries Cyril and Methodius."

The text of the *Glagolitic Mass* is written in Old Church Slavonic, and the piece is a patriotic hymn to the greatness of the Czech nation and Slavic culture. Judging by his letters to Kamila, he also imagined the piece as a celebratory wedding mass for the two of them.

Janáček's orchestral tour de force, and justifiably his most popular work, is the *Sinfonietta*, which was written at the same time as the *Glagolitic Mass* and is comparable in its exuberance and overall tone. Encapsulating Janáček's patriotic pride in the newly formed Czechoslovakia, it also – inevitably – has its connection with Kamila. A military band that she and Janáček heard playing in her hometown of Písek gave him the idea of the massive brass fanfares that open and close the piece. The five movements are dramatically scored and highly contrasted, but it's a remarkably coherent piece, thanks mainly to a melodic motif that underpins each part.

● **Glagolitic Mass**: Mackerras; Czech Philharmonic; Söderström, Drobková, Livora, Novák (Supraphon C37-7448).
● **Glagolitic Mass; Sinfonietta**: Palmer, Gunson, Mitchinson, King; City of Birmingham Symphony Orchestra; Rattle (EMI CDC7 47504-2).
◗ **Sinfonietta; Taras Bulba**: Vienna Philharmonic; Mackerras (Decca 430 727-2DM; with *Taras Bulba*).

Janáček's fiendishly high solo writing means that a lot of otherwise excellent recordings of the *Glagolitic Mass* suffer from wobbly and shrieking sopranos. Elisabeth Söderström on the Charles Mackerras recording is very good indeed, and Felicity Palmer is also good with Simon Rattle – a performance that's coupled with a very strong version of the *Sinfonietta*.

Mackerras's recording of the Sinfonietta is rugged and highly charged, and is coupled with a good *Taras Bulba*, a superb score full of glorious melodies.

THE DIARY OF ONE WHO
DISAPPEARED

The first composition to emerge from Janáček's infatuation with Kamila Stösslová was the song cycle *The Diary of One who Disappeared*, a piece which, like *The Cunning Little Vixen*, was spurred by something printed in the Brno paper *Lidové noviny* – in this instance some poems about a young man becoming infatuated with a gypsy girl and forsaking his family. The form of the work is unprecedented: it's a cycle of 22 numbers for tenor and piano, a combination joined in the middle three songs by a female chorus plus a mezzo-soprano to personify the gypsy girl, Zefka. "While writing the *Diary*," Janáček wrote to Kamila, "I thought only of you. You were Zefka!"; unsurprisingly, in view of its heavily autobiographical burden, the story is told principally through the thoughts of the young man, while the gypsy's true feelings remain ambiguous – despite an episode of lovemaking, discreetly masked by a piano solo.

● Keller, Wirz; Venzago (Accord 22031-2).

The *Diary* can sound thin in comparison to the operas, but Peter Keller and the Clara Wirz make a good case for this uncomfortably self-conscious work. The dusky tone of Wirz's voice is especially attractive.

THE STRING QUARTETS

Janáček's two string quartets are amongst the greatest ever written, containing extraordinary textures and sudden juxtapositions of contrasting ideas. The first, written in a week in 1921, is based on Tolstoy's novella *The Kreutzer Sonata*, a portrait of jealousy in a loveless marriage. It's possible to find musical correspondences to the incidents in the story, but it's better to ignore these programmatic elements and simply enjoy the outstanding lyrical and dramatic invention of the score. The same goes for the second quartet, which was written in about three weeks in 1928 and to which Janáček gave the unambiguous subtitle *Intimate Letters*. Judging by Janáček's letters to Kamila, the quartet contains depictions of specific characters and events – the stormy opening theme must represent the composer and the chilling viola reply introduces us to Kamila – but it's futile to speculate on the extra-musical meanings. The passion is what matters, and that's evident in each phrase – in Janáček's own words, "This piece was written in fire." After hearing it played he wrote: "It's a work as if carved out of living flesh. I think that I won't write a more profound and a truer one." Little more than a month later he was dead.

⦿ Talich Quartet (Supraphon 11 1354-2; with *Mládí*).

There are many fine recordings of the quartets and the Talich on Supraphon tops the bunch – the performances are exemplary and the acoustic gives a warm glow to the fantastic musical textures. This CD also contains Janáček's vivacious and exuberant wind sextet *Mládí*, composed shortly after his seventieth birthday.

ARAM KHACHATURIAN
(1903–1978)

K

The conservatism of Khachaturian's music has denied him the critical acclaim awarded to his contemporaries Prokofiev and Shostakovich, but his unashamedly romantic and folk-inflected works, in which he gave international voice to the distinctive melodies and harmonies of his native Armenia and its neighbours, have never lacked an audience.

Khachaturian showed little musical talent until his brother persuaded him to go to Moscow in 1921, where he somehow managed to gain a place at the Gnesin Music Academy to study the cello, an instrument he had never before played. By 1925 he was studying composition too, and he made rapid progress, seeing his first work – a dance for violin and piano – published only a year later. His international reputation was established by his *Piano Concerto*, written in 1936, followed four years later by the *Violin Concerto*, the winner of a coveted Stalin Prize. By the close of the 1940s he had completed three symphonies, but it was two full-length ballet scores – *Gayaneh* and *Spartacus* – that brought him the most widespread attention.

THE MUSIC

Although the *Piano Concerto* was the work that made Khachaturian's name, its swooning romanticism has now gone out of favour. Yet it is well worth exploring, particularly for its folk-like slow movement, which uses the otherworldly sound of a flexatone (a kind of musical saw). The *Violin Concerto*, another instant success, is typical of the composer, with its driving rhythms, hot-house languor and nostalgic colouring.

Khachaturian's first ballet, *Gayaneh*, is best known for the brash *Sabre Dance*. It began life in 1939 as *Happiness*, but went through several revisions before reaching its final state in 1957, by which time *Spartacus*, his 1943 ballet about the Roman slave revolt, had overtaken it in popularity. Like *Gayaneh*, it's famous for one hit tune – the surging *Adagio of Spartacus and Phrygia*, used as the theme music for the BBC series *The Onedin Line*.

Khachaturian's three symphonies lack the immediate impact of his concertos and ballets, but they all have the stamp of individuality. The three-movement *No. 1*, first performed in 1934, introduced a new, personal way of combining his native folk music with symphonic processes. Although having no specific programme, *No. 2* (1943) undoubtedly reflects the wartime circumstances of its composition, with its ominous bells and musical calls-to-arms suggesting the darkness, sacrifice and heroism of the USSR's "Great Patriotic War". Least traditional of the group is *No. 3* (1947), one of many Soviet works to fall foul of the Union of Soviet Composers' proscription of musical formalism in 1948.

> ◉ **Piano Concerto**: Servadei; London Philharmonic Orchestra; Giunta (Hyperion CDA 66293).
> ◉ **Violin Concerto**: Oistrakh; Prague Radio Symphony Orchestra; Kubelík (Praga PR250 017; with *Piano Concerto*).

> ◉ **Violin Concerto**: Mordkovich; Scottish National Orchestra; Järvi (Chandos CHAN8918).
> ◗ **Gayaneh; Spartacus (excerpts)**: Vienna Philharmonic Orchestra; Khachaturian (Decca 417 737-2; with Prokofiev, *Romeo & Juliet*).
> ◉ **Symphonies**: Tjeknavorian, Armenian Philharmonic Orchestra (ASV CDDCS223; with *Battle of Stalingrad suite*; 2 CDs).

Top-rank pianists seem to ignore the *Piano Concerto* and none of the available recordings is particularly distinguished; perhaps the best of a moderate bunch is Annette Servadei's with Joseph Giunti. The *Violin Concerto* has always fared better on disc: the historic 1947 recording by David Oistrakh, for whom it was written, has now been reissued, and there's a fine modern account from Lydia Mordkovich.

No complete recording currently exists of either of the ballet scores, but there are numerous CDs of extracts. The most colourful account, featuring five dances from *Gayaneh* and four from *Spartacus*, comes from Khachaturian himself, conducting the inspired Vienna Philharmonic in a thirty-year-old recording that wears its age well.

Loris Tjeknavorian has successfully recorded all three symphonies with the Armenian Philharmonic, an orchestra which has survived the break-up of the USSR with a less significant loss of national character than some of its Russian counterparts. The symphonies are also available on two separate CDs.

═══════════════ 𝄞 ═══════════════

ZOLTÁN KODÁLY

(1882–1967)

Zoltán Kodály's career was unremarkable after his graduation from Budapest University in 1905. It was then that he encountered Béla Bartók, with whom he was to change the direction of Hungarian music. Shortly after meeting, they embarked upon a pilgrimage to collect folk songs, the first of several expeditions which helped formulate their musical identities and cement their life-long friendship. Kodály later recalled the inspiration behind their studies: "This vision of an educated Hungary, reborn from the people, rose before us. We decided to devote our lives to its realisation." This devotion resulted in a book of Hungarian folk songs with a preface by Kodály, published in 1906, and, later that year, the premiere of his symphonic poem *Summer Evening*.

In 1908 Kodály took over the composition classes at Budapest's Liszt Academy from his own teacher, Franz Koessler, and from then on became closely involved with the formation of the musical curriculum in Hungary's schools. With Bartók, he formed a society for the promotion and performance of contemporary music, a scheme that met with official hostility and public indifference, and their attempts to promote folk song were no more successful, although the pair continued compiling information until the outbreak of war.

In 1923, however, Kodály's fortunes changed with the widespread success of his *Psalmus Hungaricus*, written for the fiftieth anniversary of the unification of Buda and Pest. Soon afterwards a contract with Universal Edition resulted in the publication of a large amount of his music. In 1926 he composed his folk-opera *Háry János*, which was followed by *The Spinning Room* (1932), a work steeped in the folklore of Transylvania. In 1933 Kodály and Bartók were requested by the Hungarian Academy of Sciences to compile a compendium of the country's folk music; with Bartók's departure for America, Kodály assumed editorial control of a project that finally reached the presses in 1951.

Kodály remained in Hungary during World War II, and after Bartók's death in 1945 was hailed as Hungary's greatest living composer, being inundated with invitations to head colleges, universities and artistic institutions, and receiving dozens of governmental decorations. Most of his remaining years were devoted to the composition of choral music and to tours as a conductor, musician and lecturer. He died happy in the knowledge that his two greatest ambitions – the publication of his books of Hungarian folk music and the introduction of daily music lessons into Hungarian schools – had been fulfilled.

Kodály remained a conservative composer throughout his life, in that he had no interest in subverting the established classical forms, and was devoted primarily to melody. Yet his music has a distinctive voice, thanks in large part to the rich mix that went into it – in addition to the folk songs of his native land, he was fascinated with Debussy, and Bach, Palestrina and Gregorian chant all became components of Kodály's sound. Kodály might lack cosmopolitan flair, but his music is an instantly enjoyable and consistently rewarding alternative to the more demanding idiom of his friend and colleague Bartók.

PSALMUS HUNGARICUS

The *Psalmus Hungaricus* represents the climactic fusion of two fundamental elements in Kodály's musical philosophy – his belief in the supremacy of the human voice, and his belief that any musical culture was dependent upon the nurture of amateur performance. He wrote a large amount of choral music for amateur societies, and *Psalmus Hungaricus* is by far the finest. It's a piece that's redolent of the spirit of Hungarian music, yet surprisingly it contains no direct folk quotations: stylisti-

cally, the chief influences are Gregorian melody, Bachian polyphony and Renaissance harmony. For all these decorous influences, *Psalmus Hungaricus* is an urgent and often barbaric composition, showing Kodály at his most thrilling.

🌓 London Symphony Orchestra; Kozma; Brighton Festival Chorus; Kertész (Decca 433 080-2; with *Missa Brevis, Pange Lingua, Psalm 114*).

Kertész's pulsating performance is a marvellous tribute to Kodály, his friend and teacher. This is a controlled but beautifully coloured and passionate account, and the tenor Lajos Kozma gives a finely considered performance, singing with ample weight. It comes coupled with a representative array of other choral pieces.

CONCERTO FOR ORCHESTRA

Kodály's fabulous *Concerto for Orchestra* was composed for the Chicago Symphony Orchestra, who first performed it in 1941 – two years before they gave the premiere of Bartók's *Concerto for Orchestra*. Unlike Bartók's five-movement virtuosic score, Kodály's concerto is a one-movement, twenty-minute piece that rejects what he characterized as "false brilliance" in favour of "melancholy and uncertainty". Again, unlike Bartók's massive score, Kodály's heavily contrapuntal piece is scored for an ordinary orchestra, the only addition to standard forces being the appearance of a triangle. A tension between modernity and more folkloric rhythms and harmonies runs through the concerto, producing music of wonderful emotional intensity.

⚫ London Symphony Orchestra; Frühbeck de Burgos (Collins COLL 10912; with Bartók, *Concerto for Orchestra*).

Frühbeck de Burgos here tackles the two greatest concertos for orchestra, and his performances are scintillating. He evidently feels uncomfortable with fast tempi, but in his sense of balance and colour, and his awareness of Kodály's folk-inspired bite, he is a marvellous interpreter.

HÁRY JÁNOS SUITE

Háry János is a Baron Münchhausen-type tale of a soldier whose fantastic adventures are, to quote the composer "the personification of the Hungarian story-telling imagination." First produced in October 1926, it's a delightful comic opera (or rather, a play with music), but because of the language barrier and its uneven construction it is rarely staged outside Hungary. There is no currently available recording of the complete work, but there are plenty of recordings of the orchestral suite that Kodály created from the opera's main ideas, a translation that secured the opera's fame. You know what you're in for right from the start, when the full orchestra explodes in a huge musical "sneeze", signifying that what follows is not to be taken too seriously. Among the ensuing episodes are a battle scene in which János singlehandedly defeats Napoleon, and the representaion of a Viennese musical clock. Beautifully orchestrated and superbly constructed, the *Háry János Suite* is Kodaly's most entertaining score.

> ◗ Philharmonia Hungarica; Kertész (Decca 443 006-2; with *Dances of Galánta, Dances of Marosszék, Peacock Variations, Symphony*).

Kertész's disc combines lively performances of the suite with some equally brilliant but lesser-known Kodály orchestral pieces – a generous selection, with excellent sound quality.

ERICH WOLFGANG KORNGOLD
(1897–1957)

Erich Korngold was a *Wunderkind* almost on a Mozartian level, having grasped the full panoply of the late-Romantic style by his early teens without obvious influence or tuition. He was labelled a genius by Mahler, his teacher for a time, yet never achieved a comparable depth and humanity in his music and his style changed little through his long career.

As a teenager he established his extremely indulgent Romantic style in his first operas, *Der Ring des Polykrates* (1914) and *Violanta* (1915), the latter a remarkably self-assured tragic drama, full of great sensual power and orchestral finesse. Such was its success that his next opera *Die tote Stadt* (1920), a highly effective expressionist drama, was premiered in both Cologne and Hamburg on the same night. His last and most ambitious major opera, *Das Wunder der Heliane* was completed in 1927, but made no headway once the Nazis came to power, as Korngold was Jewish. In the early 1930s Korngold moved to Hollywood and poured his operatic talents into music for films, and he's best known today for more-or-less creating the typical Hollywood sound in the Thirties and Forties. In his last years he returned to concert music with his *Violin Concerto* (1945), written for the great Jascha Heifetz, and a symphony (1950).

THE MUSIC

Korngold's operas can stand up against those of Richard Strauss in terms of their stagecraft and vocal adroitness. Their continuing neglect is due not to any musical failings, but rather to

Erich Korngold (right) with Jascha Heifetz

the cultural "purism" of the Nazis, which effectively dislodged them from the active repertoire, and to the stigma attached to his film work. Korngold must have had a stormy adolescence if his very adult *Violanta*, composed at seventeen, is anything to go by; an expertly dramatized piece, it tells of a passionate extra-marital affair in Renaissance Venice. His greatest theatrical success, *Die tote Stadt* (The Dead City), is a mysterious tale of a man's inability to come to terms with his wife's death. The characteristically lush and sophisticated score is epitomized by its most famous passage, the opulent *Gluck, das mir verblieb*, which appears on a number of Romantic aria discs. *Das Wunder der Heliane* was Korngold's most ambitious opera. Dealing with grand themes of transcendent love, it's scored for a massive orchestra and is written on a vast scale, with music of late-Romantic complexity taken to extremes of luxuriance and indulgence.

Korngold wrote some of the greatest film scores of his era, including for such classics as Errol Flynn's *The Adventures of Robin Hood*, *The Private Lives of Elizabeth and Essex* and *The Sea Hawk*, gaining two Academy Awards in the process. They are as finely wrought as many of his more "serious" works and are as hot-blooded as his *Violin Concerto* – "More Korn than gold", as the old joke has it, but a mellifluous and well-constructed piece all the same. His *Symphony* is the most uncompromising of all his works, more angular than his earlier compositions, yet no less enjoyable.

○ **Violanta**: Jerusalem, Marton; Bavarian Radio Symphony Orchestra; Janowski (Sony CD79229).
◑ **Die tote Stadt**: Kollo, Neblett, Prey; Munich Radio Symphony Orchestra; Leinsdorf (RCA GD87767; 2 CDs).
○ **Das Wunder der Heliane**: Tomowa-Sintow, Welker, de Haan; Berlin Radio Symphony Orchestra & Choir; Mauceri (Decca 436 636-2; 3 CDs).
◑ **Film music**: National Philharmonic Orchestra; Gerhardt (RCA GD80185).
◑ **Violin Concerto**: Wallenstein; Los Angeles PO, Heifetz. (RCA GD87963; with Rozsa, *Violin Concerto*; Waxman, *Carmen Fantasy*).
○ **Symphony**: Downes; BBC Philharmonic Orchestra (Chandos CHAN9171; with *Abschiedslieder*).

All three of Korngold's best operas now have highly accomplished recordings. Marek Janowski conducts a sumptuous account of *Violanta*, with Siegfried Jerusalem and Eva Marton a dramatic pair of lovers; Erich Leinsdorf's pioneering recording of *Die Tote Stadt* could hardly be bettered; and most recently, *Heliane* has been spectacularly recorded by John Mauceri, with Anna Tomowa-Sintow refulgent in the title role.

Gerhardt's disc is a highly recommendable selection of highlights from the film music, some of which can almost be regarded as miniature tone poems. Heifetz's classic recording of the *Violin Concerto* from 1953 is still the best available. Edward Downes's spaciously recorded performance of the Symphony does it proud, and is accompanied by the first ever recording of the orchestral version of Korngold's fine song cycle, the Mahler-inspired *Songs of Farewell*.

ROLAND DE LASSUS

(1532–1594)

Roland de Lassus (or Orlando di Lasso as he was known in Italy) was a contemporary of Palestrina and, like him, was one of the truly outstanding composers of the sixteenth century. They almost certainly knew each other, since in 1555 Palestrina succeeded Lassus as Maestro di Cappella at the church of St John Lateran in Rome, and their respective careers make an interesting comparison. Lassus travelled throughout Europe, while Palestrina was firmly based in the region of Rome. Both men wrote polyphonic music but whereas Palestrina evolved a style that was notable for its calmness and serenity, Lassus wrote pieces that were altogether more individual and quirky. He was also far more versatile than Palestrina, and his works encompass every major musical genre of the time.

Lassus was born at Mons, in the Franco-Flemish province of Hainaut. He may have been a chorister at the church of St Nicholas, but there is nothing to substantiate the legend that he was kidnapped by talent scouts, on account of the beauty of his voice. However, he was in Italy by the age of twelve, in the service of Ferdinand Gonzaga, the viceroy of Sicily. His prestigious appointment at St John Lateran at the age of twenty-one is a tribute to his remarkable talent, but he was there for only eighteen months before returning north to Antwerp. Shortly after his return, Lassus was summoned to Munich to join the ducal court of Bavaria, firstly as a singer and then in 1562 as Kapellmeister. He was to remain there for the rest of his life, enjoying a unique familiarity with the duke, Albrecht V, and with his son and successor Wilhelm. Lassus's correspondence with Wilhelm has been preserved: written in a mish-mash of languages and full of puns and bad jokes, it shows him as a remarkably lively and affectionate person. He also had his dark side, however, and in his last years suffered from such extreme depression that his music almost dried up.

THE MUSIC

From the middle of the sixteenth century the term *musica reservata* (reserved music) was applied to those composers who were concerned with trying to convey the meaning of the words they set. Of Lassus a contemporary wrote that he could make ". . . the things of the text so vivid that they seem to stand actually before our eyes." Devices such as chromaticism, whereby the melody was made more expressive by employing notes apart from those from the key it was written in, became increasingly common at this time, and in his early work – especially in his songs and madrigals – Lassus employs quite extreme chromaticism, as well as frequent declamatory passages. But as his career progressed his writing became more subtle and economic in its expressiveness. The eight-part *Missa Bell' Amfitrit'altera* has an ineffably radiant but simple opening and its shifts of mood are achieved mostly by varying the musical texture and the rhythm. His final work, *Lagrime di San Pietro* (Tears of St Peter), is an extraordinarily powerful cycle of sacred madrigals in which the music's austerity and intensity of feeling perfectly match the clarity of the poetic imagery.

◉ **Missa Bell' Amfitrit'altera**: Schola Cantorum of Oxford; Summerly (Naxos 8.550836; with Palestrina, *Missa Hodie Christus natus est, Stabat Mater*).
◉ **Lagrime di San Pietro**: Ensemble Vocal Européen; Herreweghe (Harmonia Mundi HMC 901 483).

Schola Cantorum perform the Lassus and Palestrina works in ways that bring out the similarities between them rather than any differences. They are performances very much in the English style, with clear diction, well-blended voices and carefully controlled phrasing. The result is remarkably beautiful if at times a little bloodless. The Ensemble Vocal Européen have a rather more vivid approach, in music where it is certainly more necessary. Their seven voices combine perfectly but are strong and individual, with some wonderfully judged contrasts in dynamics. They are helped by a more sympathetic recording, which brings out the immediacy of the voices yet also suggests the space that surrounds them.

FRANZ LEHÁR
(1870–1948)

In terms of financial success, Franz Lehár was the Andrew Lloyd Webber of his day: within two years of the premiere of *Die lustige Witwe* (The Merry Widow) he was a dollar millionaire, and the show ran for a record 778 performances in London – King Edward VII saw it four times. *The Merry Widow* pioneered the concept of merchandizing, with "Merry Widow" hats, corsets, cigarettes and cocktails going on sale in New York. Several other operettas virtually repeated the success of his best-known work, and *Der Graf von Luxemburg* (The Count of Luxembourg), *Zigeunerliebe* (Gypsy Love) and *Das Land des Lächelns* (The Land of Smiles) were exported to theatres right around the world.

The son of a military bandmaster, Lehár spent his childhood stationed with his father's regiment in various towns across the Austro-Hungarian empire, and for a short while he studied with Dvořák at the Prague conservatoire – "Hang up your fiddle and start composing", he is reputed to have been advised. He had already composed a couple of fairly successful operettas by the time he was given the libretto of *Die lustige Witwe* by Oscar Léon and Leo Stein, the authors of Strauss' hugely popular *Wiener Blut*. In fact Lehár was the second choice as composer – he got the job after being set a trial song, which he composed in a single day and played down the telephone to Léon.

By the time the show was in rehearsal, the Theater an der Wien (Vienna's main operetta theatre) had little faith in the piece, and at one point offered Lehár five thousand crowns to withdraw it. The premiere on December 30, 1905 went well enough, but business was slow and free tickets were handed out to fill the house. But eventually word got round, and *Die lustige Witwe* is still a regular fixture at the Theater an der Wien, even displacing *Cats* from the summer season's programme. After a couple of flops, Lehár hit a winning streak with *Der Graf von Luxemburg* (1909) and *Zigeunerliebe* (1910), both of which had highly successful worldwide runs and are still regularly performed in Central Europe.

Lehár's career then took another downturn until it was revitalized by the tenor Richard Tauber, who became the most celebrated performer of Lehár's music and gave his name to *Tauberlied* – songs that have become far more popular than the operettas that spawned them. The most famous of these *Dein ist mein ganzes Herz* (You are my Heart's Delight) comes from Lehár's last international triumph, *Das Land des Lächelns* (The Land of Smiles), premiered in Berlin in 1929. At Christmas 1930, Lehár's sixtieth birthday year, some two hundred productions of *Das Land des Lächelns* were in progress in Europe, and five hundred different Lehár productions in total. His last major work, *Giuditta*, was premiered at the Vienna State Opera in 1934, the only operetta to have been given that honour, and the show was relayed internationally by 120 radio stations.

Many operetta composers and performers with Jewish blood were forced to emigrate when Hitler came to power, but – although his wife was Jewish – Lehár stayed in Vienna. He is said to have been the favourite composer of Hitler, who as a young man was a regular visitor to the Theater an der Wien's production of *Die lustige Witwe*. After the *Anchluss* Lehár composed a new overture to *Die lustige Witwe*, which he dedicated to Hitler to protect himself and his wife. This didn't help Lehár's Jewish colleagues, however, and Fritz Löhner-Beda, one of the librettists of *Das Land des Lächelns* and *Giuditta*, was murdered in a concentration camp while his work was playing in Vienna. Towards the end of the war, Lehár decided to settle in Switzerland where he died in 1948.

⏻ **Composers in Person – Lehár**: Lehár; Tauber; Schwarz; Novotná (EMI 754838-2).
⏺ **Marilyn Hill Smith sings Kálmán and Lehár**: Marilyn Hill Smith; Chandos Concert Orchestra; Barry (Chandos CHAN8978).

These compilation recordings make fine introductions to Lehár, and the set with Lehár himself conducting is as close as you can get to original-cast recordings. Prominently featuring Richard Tauber – who's essential to any operetta buff's collection – the disc has substantial selections from *Das Land des Lächelns* (recorded in 1929) and Guiditta (in 1934), plus the *Die lustige Witwe* overture dedicated to Hitler in 1940.

The Marilyn Hill Smith CD is by far the best compilation of Lehár (and Kálmán) arias, partly because Hill Smith steers away from the popular favourites and comes up with some little-known but high-quality numbers from *Giuditta*, *Zigeunerliebe* and others. Hill Smith's tone is usually just right, while Stuart Barry brings out the fine orchestration and transparency of the scores.

DIE LUSTIGE WITWE

The story of *Die lustige Witwe* is one of absurd aristocratic intrigue to prevent a wealthy widow, Hanna Glawari, marrying a Frenchman and thereby depriving the fictional Balkan kingdom of Pontevedrino of her fortune. In typical operetta style, Danilo, the man chosen to lure Hanna from the Frenchman, turns out to be her former heart-throb, although there are plenty of diversions on the way. Lehár throws Balkan spice into the score with some folkdances and Hanna's famous *Vilja-Lied* – the *vilja* is a wood spirit from Montenegran folklore. (Furthermore, Danilo's costume for the premiere was closely modelled on that of the Crown Prince of Montenegro). The celebrated Merry Widow waltz and some splashes of French nightclub music further enrich the mix.

◉ Schwartzkopf, Waechter, Gedda, Steffek; Philharmonia Chorus and Orchestra; Matačic (EMI CDS7 47178-8; 2 CDs).

This classic recording, made back in 1962 has never been bettered. Elisabeth Schwarzkopf has all the alluring mystery that Hanna Glawari requires, and her seductive performance of the *Vilja-Lied* has just the right delicacy and poise. Eberhard Waechter and Nikolai Gedda are suitable foils as Danilo and the Frenchman, Camille. The more rumbustious parts of the score are also dashed off with splendid abandon.

Elisabeth Schwarzkopf, the best of all Merry Widows

ZIGEUNERLIEBE

Of Lehár's lesser-known pieces, *Zigeunerliebe* is the most sumptuous, enhancing the exoticism of its eastern European setting with music that has a distinctly Hungarian gypsy flavour. This is also Lehár's most Puccini-like score – the two composers were great admirers of each other's music. Zorika, the heroine, is

torn between two men – the nobleman to whom she is betrothed, and a fiery gypsy fiddler, who, as you can imagine, seems so much more romantic and alluring. The gypsy symbolizes the power of music, but is also an emblem of the unorthodox and risky, so in the end she takes the safe option and marries the fiancé. Those who know Lloyd Webber's *Phantom of the Opera* will realize the basic dilemma's enduring power.

◗ **Zigeunerliebe – highlights**: Schramm; Schoek; Berlin Symphony Orchestra; Stolz (Eurodisc 258 360).

With any operetta it's better to have a highlights disc to avoid the hammy dialogue between numbers – and with *Zigeunerliebe*, unlike *Die lustige Witwe*, there's just such a set available. Margit Schramm is a passionate Zorika and the two men are both sung by Rudolf Schock (suggesting a deeper psychological subtext), but what really sets it off is the splendid solo fiddle playing, the rippling clarinet and the cimbalom effects in numbers like *Ich bin ein Zigeunerkind* and *Hör'ich Cymbalklänge*.

DER LAND DES LÄCHELNS

Apart from *Die lustige Witwe* this is the only Lehár operetta that's staged with any regularity. A reworking of *Die gelbe Jacke* (The Yellow Jacket), which was a flop in 1923, *Der Land des Lächelns* is about the love affair between Lisa, a Viennese countess, and Sou-Chong, the "Minister President of China". It's a much tougher and more profound piece than its glutinous hit song *Dein ist mein ganzes Herz* would suggest, and it has rarity value as an operetta with an unhappy ending – the cultural differences are too great for the lovers, and Lisa is finally taken back to Vienna.

◗ **Das Land des Lächelns – highlights**: Schramm; Schock; Berlin Symphony Orchestra; Stolz (Eurodisc 258 373).

Lehár handed Johann Strauss's conducting baton to Robert Stolz, whose Eurodisc recordings are amongst the best introductions to the operetta repertoire. This highlights disc omits nothing essential, and the pairing of Margit Schramm and Rudolf Schock is excellent – he might be a bit overblown on *Dein ist mein ganzes Herz*, but his mannerisms are nothing compared to Tauber's (see above).

RUGGERO LEONCAVALLO

(1857–1919)

Just as Italians in the eighteenth century would have nothing to do with Gluck, so in the nineteenth century they were extremely uncomfortable with Wagner, an attitude typified by the career of Ruggero Leoncavallo. Enamoured of Wagner's music as a young man, he came to write one of the two great examples of operatic verismo, the low-life counterblast to Wagnerian epic music-drama.

He first experienced Wagner's music in 1878 and was deeply affected by it – or rather, by its literary and dramatic scope. He set about writing *Crespuculum*, a quasi-Wagnerian Renaissance trilogy, but was soon sidetracked into completing a project that had occupied him since his student days, an opera called *Chatterton*, about the young English poet who killed himself by taking strychnine. When the promoter of the premiere disappeared with all the money before the first night, Leoncavallo approached a publisher with a view to issuing *Chatterton* in print. However, the publisher felt Leoncavallo to be a better librettist than composer, and commissioned him to write the text for Puccini's *Manon Lescaut*. Puccini had him removed from the project.

After two years' further dissatisfaction, the ever-ambitious Leoncavallo found his inspiration in the success of Mascagni's *Cavalleria rusticana* (see p.222), the work that launched verismo opera in 1890, and promptly dominated the limelight in Italy. As he later wrote – "I shut myself in my house . . . and in five months I wrote the poem and music of *Pagliacci*". Toscanini gave the first performance of *I Pagliacci* (The Clowns) on May 21, 1892 and overnight Leoncavallo found his fame and made his fortune.

On the back of this success he arranged for the first part of his *Crespuculum* to be performed and, after a blaze of pre-publicity, *I Medici* was duly premiered on November 9, 1893. The evening was a disaster, and from then on he was embroiled in a losing battle with Puccini for the affections of the Italian

people. Leoncavallo's *La Bohème* was performed almost a year after Puccini's and, even though it met with some success, he never came to terms with its inevitable disappearance from the stage. He was one of the first composers to take a serious interest in the gramophone, composing the song *Mattinata* expressly for the G&T record company (Caruso recorded it in April 1904), but life went steadily downhill after *Pagliacci*. The man who had once proposed writing a music drama to rival Wagner's, spent his dying months composing an operetta entitled *A chi la giarettiera?* – or *Whose garter is this?*

I PAGLIACCI

The central idea of *I Pagliacci* – a travelling actor discovers that his younger wife has been having an affair with a friend and colleague, and wreaks a dreadful revenge – was taken from a case that Leoncavallo's magistrate father had judged, and it typified the verismo ideal. From this sordid tale he made one of the finest dramatic operas ever written, showing a command of proportion, timing and characterization that is absent from the rest of his output. The cheated husband (Canio) is one of the greatest dramatic tenor roles in all opera; Nedda, the cheating wife, is a less involved part than that of the adulterer Tonio, but their set pieces and exchanges are riveting in their energy and conviction. The last ten minutes, during which Leoncavallo's play within a play reaches its shocking conclusion, are the ultimate in verismo.

♩ Corelli, Amara, Gobbi, Zanasi, Spina; La Scala Orchestra & Chorus; von Matačic (EMI CMS7 63967-2; with Mascagni, *Cavalleria Rusticana*; 2 CDs).

Matačic's 1960 recording, with Franco Corelli as Canio, Titto Gobbi as Tonio and Lucine Amara as Nedda, is a masterpiece of base emotion and divine inspiration. Corelli's awesome singing is unmatched by any Canio before or since and his massive, ringing sound produces the sort of electric thrill rarely heard from studio recordings. Gobbi's performance is similarly impressive, with all Tonio's contradictory qualities brought to the surface. Amara has a light and unstable voice that produces little of the malice demanded of her role but, ultimately, Matačic's driving direction overcomes these vocal limitations.

GYÖRGY LIGETI

(1923–   )

Ligeti's life has been a series of exiles. He was born in Transylvania just as Hungary was about to lose that region to Romania, and left Hungary permanently in 1956 after the Soviet Union crushed the uprising there. Since then he has lived in Hamburg and Vienna, becoming an Austrian citizen since 1967. His work reflects this rootlessness – it is impossible to classify the music of Ligeti, as he's a composer who changes his style from piece to piece. If one generalization does hold good, it's that Ligeti is the most approachable of all experimental modernists.

Some of his music might sound superficially similar to that of American Minimalists such as Adams and Reich, but Ligeti's Central European background comes through in a variety of ways. A feeling of loss and nostalgia characterizes much of his output, often evoked by use of the strangely haunting five-note scale and half tones of Transylvania's folk music. His penchant for clashing clusters of instruments and the babble of opposed languages links both to the multi-culturalism of his native land and to his wanderings. Equally important is Ligeti's absurdist humour, apparent in works such as his *Poème Symphonique* for one hundred

metronomes, the "music theatre" of *Aventures*, in which three solo singers squeak and gesticulate wildly in ceaseless contradiction, and his operatic tour de force, *Le Grand Macabre*.

THE MUSIC

Ligeti first came to the notice of the general public through Stanley Kubrick's *2001*, in which *Lux Aeterna*, a piece for unaccompanied voices, was used to accompany shots of a descending spaceship in the film. Using a sort of warped polyphony, it shows the contemplative side of Ligeti's nature and his remarkable sensitivity for fine gradations of pitch. The complex textures of the *Chamber Concerto* and the uncertain tonalities of *Ramifications* are further demonstrations of Ligeti's finesse as a constructor of abstract soundscapes, but perhaps his finest work is *Le Grand Macabre*, a savage burlesque written for Stockholm Opera between 1974 and 1977. Set in "Breughelland", a world derived from the visionary paintings of Breughel and Bosch, the opera depicts the end of the world, as experienced by a gang of grotesques – among them the infantile Prince Go-Go, the permanently intoxicated Piet the Pot, the lovestruck Amando and Amanda, and the sluttish Mescalina, who at one point gets ravaged by the opera's master of ceremonies, Nekrotzar. It's a two-hour musical helter-skelter, as raucously enjoyable as anything written since the war.

⚫ **Le Grand Macabre**: Davis, Walmsley-Clark, Smith, Weller, Krekow; Austrian Radio Symphony Orchestra; Howarth (Wergo WER 6170-2; 2 CDs).

◖ **Lux Aeterna**; **Chamber Concerto**; **Ramifications**; **Aventures**: Manning, Thomas, Pearson; Ensemble Intercontemporain, La Salle Quartet; Boulez (Deutsche Grammophon DG 423 244-2).

The Wergo recording of *Le Grand Macabre* reinforces the argument that this is likely to prove one of the most durable of modern operas; the singers vividly characterize Ligeti's nightmarish creations, and the sound is superb. If the prospect of a two-hour opera is daunting, go for the Boulez CD of selected chamber, vocal and choral works – there's no better introduction to the multitudinous styles of this fascinating composer.

FRANZ LISZT

(1811–1886)

In certain circles Franz Liszt is not taken seriously, and the reason for this lies in his brilliance as a performer – Liszt, the argument goes, was all self-promotion and no substance. The accusation is nothing new. In 1874 the critic Eduard Hanslick wrote: "The main objection against Liszt is that he imposes a much bigger – an abusive – mission on the subject of his work: namely either to fill the gap left by the absence of musical content or to justify the atrociousness of such content as there is."

Certainly Liszt was a large-scale character. Born Ferenc Liszt, the son of a minor Hungarian court functionary, he became the greatest pianist of his age – indeed, probably of any age. Like Paganini, he developed his technique to the point at which he had to create his own style of music to do justice to his capabilities, and much of that music did little more than show off his technique. Instead of working from his own ideas, he quarried all available musical sources and reworked the material into show-stoppers that would demonstrate that he could play octaves faster than anyone else, and hit the keys harder (he used to break his wooden-framed pianos). His off-stage character hardly suggested serious devotion to music. Liszt was the ultimate Romantic blend of immorality and piety, an infamous womanizer who yet had the face of Saint Francis carved

on his walking stick – alongside Mephistopheles and Gretchen, heroine of Goethe's *Faust*.

There was indubitably more than a dash of the showman in Liszt, but his contribution to the development of nineteenth-century music was immense. On a practical level, he was an uncommonly generous man who gave freely of his time and money to champion the music of other composers. As for his own compositions, the fireworks represent just the surface, for in his symphonic music he anticipated the tone poems of Strauss and the vast fluid structures of Wagner (his son-in-law), while in his austere late piano music he created perhaps the most prophetic work of his time. As Schoenberg once wrote – "one must not overlook how much there is in his music that is new, musically, and discovered by genuine intuition. Was he not after all one of those that started the battle against tonality?"

Liszt invented the piano recital and the career of travelling virtuoso, but his first major works were created after making a break with his self-established tradition. In 1847, after nearly thirty years as Europe's most revered pianist, Liszt met and fell in love with the Princess Carolyne von Sayn-Wittgenstein, who convinced him that, having sown more oats than most could imagine, he should settle down. Somewhat in awe of the

ROYAL COLLEGE OF MUSIC

princess, Liszt renounced his career as a roaming virtuoso and in 1848 accepted an invitation to become Kapellmeister to the Grand Duke of Weimar. During his ten years at Weimar he wrote or revised most of the pieces for which he is now best known, and made the city a pre-eminent musical centre by conducting a vast number of new works, including music by Schumann, Berlioz, Verdi, Donizetti and Wagner. Weimar became the den of the progressive faction of which Wagner was the figurehead, a group opposed by the Brahms, Hanslick and the traditionalists of Vienna.

In 1860 he moved to Rome, where five years later he took minor orders. His music from this time was soaked in religious sentiment, but his heart was never really in it and in 1869 he began to divide his time between Rome, Weimar and Budapest. The more he travelled, the more he reverted to his old ways, and his amorous adventures once again became the talk of Europe. As his increasing years began to take effect, however, he devoted ever larger amounts of time to teaching and, together with Clara Schumann, he helped produce some of the early twentieth century's greatest pianists. In the 1870s his music entered its final and most radical phase, and he remained active as a composer and performer right to the end of his life – his Jubilee tour, marking his seventy-fifth birthday, was reported across the world. He died soon after. His career had bridged a whole era in the cultural development of Europe: had he been born two years earlier, his lifespan would have overlapped with both Haydn and Stravinsky.

FAUST SYMPHONY

In 1846 Berlioz dedicated his dramatic cantata *La Damnation de Faust* to Liszt. It was to be nearly ten years before Liszt repaid the compliment by dedicating his own interpretation of Goethe's two-part poem to Berlioz. The *Faust Symphony* was one of the major works to emerge from the years in Weimar (along with Liszt's only other symphony, the weaker *Dante Symphony*), but was constantly revised – nineteen years after the first performance in 1861, he was still revising the slow movement.

There are three movements – Faust, Gretchen and Mephistopheles – and each is, essentially, a character study. The grand and sweeping first movement is an extraordinary example of Liszt's technique of transforming his basic themes; lasting nearly half an hour, it is built on just five short phrases. After a second movement of almost chamber-music delicacy, which looks towards the anti-Wagnerian simplicity of his final decade, the finale represents Goethe's "spirit of negation" by grotesque parody of the themes heard in the opening movement. The latter half of *Mephistopheles* depicts "the great struggle" and concludes with his defeat, in which the *Chorus mysticus* (end of Part Two of Goethe's *Faust*) is strikingly set for tenor, male chorus and full orchestra.

◗ Young; Beecham Choral Society; Royal Philharmonic Orchestra; Beecham (EMI CDM7 63371-2).

This is one of Beecham's most famous recordings and rightly so. Taut and disciplined but typically witty, this performance builds to a finale that generates an electric sense of atmosphere. Alexander Young's tenor boasts convincing weight and Beecham's general awareness of balance well serves Liszt's orchestrations.

LES PRELUDES

Liszt can be credited with inventing the genre of the symphonic poem, an extended orchestral piece presented as the interpretation of a non-musical subject. He completed thirteen of them, illustrating subjects taken from classical mythology, Romantic literature, recent history or imaginative fantasy, and while not all of them are successful, *Les Preludes*

(another product of the Weimar years) is a masterpiece. Liszt actually composed the twenty-minute piece before deciding that the music was a paraphrase of a poem by Lamartine, in which life is presented as a series of preludes to the after-life. As with the *Faust Symphony*, the opening theme appears in many guises throughout the work, and more than almost any other of his orchestral compositions, *Les Preludes* is a brilliantly organic, well structured creation.

◗ Berlin Philharmonic Orchestra; Karajan (Deutsche Grammophon 415 967-2GH2; with other Liszt orchestral works; 2 CDs).

Liszt's grand and spectacular music brings out the best in Karajan and his orchestra – this is one of his most exciting recordings, and in the closing measures the music simply tears off the page. This two-disc set is an excellent introduction to Liszt's large-scale work, and features a blazing account of the *Hungarian Fantasia* for piano and orchestra with Shura Cherkassky – it's so highly charged that there is a point near the end of the piece where Karajan appears to have absolutely no idea what is coming next.

PIANO CONCERTO NO. 1

The more famous and certainly more enjoyable of Liszt's two piano concertos is the first, in E flat. It was begun in 1830 then revised for years until, in what must have been one of the concerts of the century, Berlioz conducted the first performance with Liszt himself at the piano in 1855. With its unison opening theme, leading into a series of startling octave leaps, the concerto's opening is one of the most dramatic of any Romantic piano concerto. This introduction is followed by a fiery cadenza which, in turn, leads to a series of calmer, more reflective passages, and the concerto carries on in this exchange of moods, keeping you on the edge of your seat in anticipation of the next burst of pyrotechnics. Moments of incredible banality are dotted through the score, but there plenty of Romantic gestures to distract your attention.

◉ Barere; unknown orchestra; Brockman (Appian CDAPR 7007; various works by Liszt).
◉ Duchâble; London Philharmonic Orchestra; Conlon (Erato 2292 45206-2; with *Piano Concerto No. 2*).

Simon Barere is now almost forgotten but he was quite possibly one of the greatest pianists of the century – as mercurial as Horowitz but equipped with unfailing good taste. This performance was recorded in 1946 at Carnegie Hall and comes with a selection of other Liszt performances from the same venue but on different occasions; featuring an incandescent version of the sonata (see below), there is no more exciting, genuinely Lisztian recital on disc. Of more recent versions, Duchâble's performance for Erato is the best of a surprisingly average bunch.

OPERATIC TRANSCRIPTIONS

Liszt's operatic transcriptions served a double function: on the one hand they enabled Liszt to create a fund of bravura piano music without the sweat of arduous creative thought; and on the other they assisted his colleagues by publicizing contemporary operas – before the age of the gramophone, piano transcriptions were the way most people got to hear the operas of Wagner, Berlioz, Verdi, Tchaikovsky, Bellini, Donizetti, Gounod and Meyerbeer. Sometimes Liszt made a straightforward bar-for-bar transcription, as in the works of Rossini and Wagner (whose music he felt was perfect to begin with), but of his sixty works in this genre, a number are a good deal better than the originals upon which they were based. He composed an opera as a child of thirteen, and you can only regret that his interest in opera was stifled by his enthusiasm for the work of others.

⦿ Howard (Hyperion CDA 66371-2; 2 CDs).

As an introduction to Liszt's operatic transcriptions, there is nothing finer than Leslie Howard's two-disc survey, which encompasses *Faust*, *Norma*, *Don Giovanni*, *Aida*, *Eugene Onegin*, *Tristan und Isolde* and *Lucia di Lammermoor*, to name just a few. His playing is at times splashy and thumping, but he's an excellent, dramatic pianist and his continuing project to record all Liszt's solo piano music for Hyperion is a great recording event.

ÉTUDES D'EXÉCUTION TRANSCENDANTE

Liszt's eight *Études d'exécution transcendante* (or *Transcendental Studies*) comprise one of the great documents of musical Romanticism and a landmark in the history of the piano, amounting to nothing less than the creation of modern piano technique. These studies teem with such outrageous difficulties that, in their day (1831), they were the most

difficult works ever written for the piano; even now, there's but a handful of pianists able to play them authoritatively. The versions most commonly performed today are Liszt's revisions of 1851, which cut back on the pyrotechnics but, even so, are as fiendish as anything written since. If played well, this music rises above mere display to reach a plateau of intense emotional conviction – especially the first four.

⦿ Ovchinikov (EMI CDC 749821-2).

Both in terms of the performances and the sound quality, Vladimir Ovchinikov's version of the studies is one of the finest Liszt recordings ever made. He adopts such quick tempi that in places (eg *Mazeppa*) he seems to have three hands, yet he never fails to maintain his imperious sense of structure. Where others cheat by overpedaling to create a fog of sound, Ovchinikov plays everything cleanly, as it was written. This sort of technique is extremely rare.

HUNGARIAN RHAPSODIES

A lot of Liszt's music bears the stamp of his Hungarian heritage, and of all his quasi-gypsy compositions the most inventive and popular are the nineteen *Hungarian Rhapsodies*. Growing out of Liszt's renewed interest in the folk music of his native country, the first fifteen were written between 1840 and 1847, whereas the last three were not added until the 1870s. This is not his greatest work, often being contrived and superficial, but his rhythms and melodies are immediately infectious, and his transcriptions of the sounds of a gypsy orchestra (solo violin, clarinet, cimbalom and strings) are breathtaking. You'll recognize the second rhapsody – Tom and Jerry and Daffy and Donald all skittered around to it.

◗ Cziffra (EMI CMS 764882-2; with *Années de pèlerinage* Books 1 & 2; 4 CDs).

Remembered as one of the greatest Lisztians in history, the Hungarian pianist Georges Cziffra died at the end of 1993, aged 72. In his memory, EMI have released this mid-price box set of what are probably his finest recordings, the complete Hungarian Rhapsodies and the first two books of Années de pèlerinage. Unpredictable and risk-taking, Cziffra produces just about the most hair-raising playing on record – hearing this, you'll understand why people thought his sound must have been produced by overdubbing. Marvellous entertainment, this four disc set is a worthy tribute and a superb introduction to the very best and the very worst of Liszt's piano music.

SONATA IN B MINOR

As you'd expect, works for solo piano make up the largest part of Liszt's output, and the greatest of these is the *Sonata in B minor*, a monumental construction that stands apart from almost everything else he wrote. Liszt purged his language of all unnecessary virtuosity, creating a piece in which the dramatic changes of mood are subsumed into the overall construction – and here the construction is purely musical, as Liszt attached no programme to the sonata.

Composed between 1851 and 1853, and dedicated to Schumann (who died the year before its 1857 premiere), it is cast as three movements to be played without a pause, the whole musical span being underlaid by a series of themes and motifs that grow, fuse and eventually expire. It's a piece that traverses enormous distances: the music at the start and at the close of the sonata gives a foretaste of the sparse angularity of Liszt's late style; in between lie passages of fulminating emotion, as thrilling as anything Liszt ever wrote.

Nikolai Demidenko – brilliant in the fearsome B minor sonata

HYPERION

> ◗ Argerich (DG Galleria 437 252-2 with Schumann, *Piano Sonata No. 2*; Brahms, *Rhapsodies*).
> ◉ Demidenko (Hyperion CDA 66616; with *Two Legends*, *Scherzo* and *March*).

Marta Argerich's recording of the sonata is a magnificent high-voltage account, in the opinion of many the finest thing she has ever recorded. Whereas Argerich is all about passion, Demidenko gives a brilliant performance that is marked by structural cohesion and an affinity with the sober, unworldly side to Liszt's genius. Both are wonderful.

MEPHISTO WALTZ NO. 1

The first of Liszt's three *Mephisto* waltzes – an orchestral piece transcribed for piano in 1881 – is a virtuoso's delight and one of his most popular works for piano. Lasting only ten minutes, it is full to bursting with Romantic imagery, including evocations of violins, nightingales, the play of starlight and village dances. When it first emerged, *Mephisto No. 1* caused a sensation, provoking the *Boston Gazette* into suggesting that "it has about as much propriety on a programme after Schumann and Handel as a wild boar in a drawing room".

> ◉ Ashkenazy (Saga SCD 9014; with performances by Richter of Chopin, Liszt and Haydn).

Vladimir Ashkenazy was a tender eighteen years old when this live recording was made in 1955. Although he has never been particularly associated with Liszt's music, this is a blistering performance, adopting dangerous tempi which, on record, no other pianist has been able to pull off.

ANNÉES DE PÈLERINAGE

The first two volumes of Liszt's *Années de pèlerinage* (composed and revised from the 1830s to the 1870s) are perhaps the most complete overview of his talents as a composer. (The third volume, compiled against Liszt's will and published posthumously, is inferior to the other two.) Standing in complete contrast to the glitter and dazzle of the studies, these pieces are principally lyrical miniatures, and are more concerned with the creation of atmosphere than the construction of a literal narrative. The first book, dealing with his travels through Switzerland, includes the exquisite *Au bord d'une source* and *Vallée d'Obermann*, both of which are as fresh as the landscapes they portray. In the second volume, the so-called "Italian book", art and literature are the subjects, and here the music is, if anything, even more beautiful. *Sposalizio* and *Petrach Sonnet 104* are two of the most translucent, unaffected piano pieces he ever wrote, and if *Après une lecture du Dante – Fantasia quasi Sonata* looks back to the virtuosic indulgence of his youth, it does so in the spirit of re-evaluation.

⚫ Cziffra (EMI CMS 764882-2; with *Hungarian Rhapsodies*; 4 CDs).

Part of EMI's Cziffra retrospective, these performances perfectly capture the essence of Liszt's deeply considered poetry – a stark contrast to the circus-act of the *Hungarian Rhapsodies*.

THE LATE PIANO PIECES

While his contemporaries were piling more and more notes into their scores and trying desperately to out-Wagner Wagner, Liszt pushed music to the opposite edge in his late piano works. With their raw dissonances and attentuated textures, their use of silence as a dramatic means, their denial of absolute tonality and their lack of any audible themes, these terse utterances are prophetic of the world of Schoenberg and Webern. Many of them speak of an obsession with death and repentance, as typified by the two pieces entitled *La lugubre gondola*, which were inspired by Liszt's premonition of Wagner's death two months before it occurred, in Venice in 1883. Clashing chords and ideas that offer no centre or direction suggest an emptiness and despondency that is nothing short of desolate.

⚫ Howard (Hyperion CDA66445).

Leslie Howard gives superb accounts of thirty of Liszt's final works for piano, five of which have never been recorded before. His playing is always deeply infused with emotion, and in the four pieces associated with Wagner's death the sense of loss and desperation is movingly portrayed without any recourse to sentimentality. A brilliantly programmed recording boasting equally memorable performances.

═══════════════════ ♭♮ ═══════════════════

JEAN-BAPTISTE LULLY
(1632–1687)

Rarely has a composer so dominated a cultural environment as Lully dominated the French court in the reign of Louis XIV. Through his friendship with the king, and some unscrupulous wheeler-dealing, he managed to achieve almost complete control of the musical life of Paris and Versailles. He was also extremely talented: he wrote sprightly and energetic dance music which, collected together as suites, exerted a strong influence on European orchestral music until the middle of the eighteenth century; and much of his more serious music, including his operas, possesses a powerful stateliness, though it can, on occasions, subside into pomposity.

Lully was born an Italian but went to France at the age of fourteen as a servant to a cousin of Louis XIV. Though an outstanding violinist, he first attracted attention as a dancer and a mime, performing alongside the young king in a court ballet in 1653. In the same year he joined the royal household as Composer of the King's Instrumental Music, and composed a number of ballets that were performed by his own orchestra, La Petite Bande – an ensemble that he moulded into one of the finest of the age. During the 1660s he produced a series of *comédies-ballets* in collaboration with the playwright Molière, the most famous of which was *Le Bourgeois Gentilhomme* (1670).

Lully's increasing control of French theatre music was consolidated in 1672 by his purchase of the exclusive right to produce opera. His first theatre was a converted tennis court, but with Molière's death he moved,

GUUS ONG

rent-free, into the theatre of the Palais Royal. For the next fifteen years he produced an opera per year, mostly to librettos by the tragedian Phillipe Quinault. His unrivalled power – he even forbade music in the marionette theatre – made him many enemies. One resentful entrepreneur, Henri Guichard, allegedly tried to have him poisoned by putting arsenic into his snuff. More damaging were reports of Lully's homosexuality which reached the ears of the king, who threatened to make an example of him. His death was a strange mixture of grandeur and farce: while conducting his *Te Deum*, in celebration of the king's recovery from illness, he jabbed one of his toes with the stick he was using to beat time. A gangrenous abcess developed but he refused amputation and died – an immensely wealthy man – some two months later.

ARMIDE

Lully virtually created French opera, or *tragédie lyrique* as it was known, by fusing the courtly ballet with the conventions of classical French tragedy into one enormous and lavish spectacle in which the setting, the scenic effects and the choreography were all as important as the music. The elaborate, often fantastical, plots – usually taken from Greek myths or from the epics of chivalry – were combined with the examination of moral issues in such a way as to pay flattering tribute to the sagacity of the king for whom they were written. One highly influential innovation was the introduction of an overture in two sections: the first slow and stately, the second more animated and usually fugal. Lully also developed a type of recitative which was less florid than the Italian model and supposedly based on the declamatory style of the French tragedians like Racine and Corneille. To a modern audience much of the proceedings, if not the music, can seem cumbersome and laboured, and today Lully's operas are rarely staged outside France.

Armide, a late work, is his masterpiece. The libretto, by Quinault, is based on a story from Torquato Tasso's *Gerusalemme Liberata*, the great chivalric poem of Renaissance Italy. Armide (Armida in the original) is a sorceress obsessed by the Christian knight Renaud (Rinaldo), who seems impervious to her beauty. She captures and plans to kill him, but instead falls in love with him. Renaud is bewitched into loving Armide but he is rescued by two of his fellow knights and she flies away as her palace is destroyed by demons. It is a plot with a similar outline to Purcell's *Dido and Aeneas*: a noble warrior is unmanned by love until duty prevails and the joys of the flesh are abandoned. That Lully turns this into such a compelling drama is a tribute to his flexible vocal writing, which generates a powerful dramatic momentum. His recitatives are never far away from the rhythms of normal speech and even the more elaborate airs do not stop the action in the manner of an Italian operatic aria.

⊙ Laurens, Crook, Gens, Rime, Deletre, Ragon; Collegium Vocale, La Chapelle Royale; Herreweghe (Harmonia Mundi HMC 901 456.57; 2CDs).

No recording of a Lully opera can represent anything like the totality of the proceedings, but this forceful and persuasive performance goes a long way to making Lully's music seem dramatically feasible on its own. There is a great deal of contrast and variety here, ranging from the sprightly rhythms of the ever-present dance music to the meltingly beautiful prelude at the beginning of the third scene of Act Two. Herreweghe is well served by his soloists, with Guillemette Laurens brilliant at conveying the ambivalent emotions of Armide, nowhere more powerfully than in her final air, which wavers between rage and despair. Howard Crook's Renaud is necessarily a rather bloodless characterization, but he has an unerringly elegant sense of the music's line.

WITOLD LUTOSŁAWSKI

(1913–1994)

The resurgence of interest in Polish music – exemplified by the vogue for Gorécki (see p.150) and the reassessment of Szymanowski (see p.367) – has much to do with the achievements of Penderecki (see p.264) and Witold Lutosławski. Sometimes sounding like nineteenth-century Romanticism laced with wrong-note harmonies, and only rarely (unlike Penderecki) expressing Poland's trauma during the war years, Lutosławski's music is among the most accessible of the twentieth century.

Born into a privileged family who saw to it that he received a well-rounded education, he studied mathematics and music before eventually electing for the latter discipline. The influence of his mathematical training is evident in the organization of some of his compositions and in the titles of works such as *Chain 1*, *Chain 2* and *Chain 3*. His composing career was brought to a sudden halt by the occupation of Warsaw by the Nazis, and after the war he found the new Communist government antagonistic to his work – his first symphony was promptly banned for being "formalist", a catch-all term applied to anything tainted by the capitalist avant-garde.

During the ensuing difficult years, Lutosławski earned his living by writing film and radio scores, and music for educational purposes. In the late 1950s, however, there came a relaxation within the arts and Lutosławski was able to take up serious composition again; a turning point came with his *Funeral Music* of 1958, widely performed and accepted on both sides of the Iron Curtain. Thereafter, Lutosławski's music openly displayed the influences of Debussy and Ravel, as well as of Schoenberg, Berg and Webern, although he never fully embraced the techniques of the Second Viennese School. Lutosławski's rehabilitation was completed with the fall of the Communist regime, when he became something of a musical ambassador for his country, touring all over the world in the double capacity of composer and conductor.

THE MUSIC

Lutosławski was never an over-prolific composer: the first symphony took years to complete, the third was begun in 1972 but not finished until 1983, and his fourth and final symphony was given its premiere only a year before his death. The symphonies are central to his development, and the best way to get to grips with him is to listen to the first – a fairly conventional piece, full of easily recognizable tunes – and then the third, a much more intensely personal work, and the latest one to be recorded.

The *Concerto for Orchestra*, one of Lutosławski's most enjoyable compositions, dates from the early 1950s, when he was under pressure to produce easily digestible music. Obviously based on Bartók's similarly virtuosic piece of the same title, the *Concerto* is filled with quotations from folk tunes, all integrated into the work's symphonic fabric.

The three orchestral pieces known as *Chains* were composed in the mid-1980s in the wake of the third symphony and share that work's intense musical language. Constructed so that each forms a self-contined unit that nonetheless connects with the other two, like links in a chain, they incorporate fully written sections and episodes in which the instrumentalists are given some leeway to improvise. Of the three, the best is the second, which was written specifically for the violinist Anne-Sophie Mutter.

◗ **Symphonies Nos. 1 & 2**: Polish Radio Symphony Orchestra; Lutosławski (EMI CDM 5 65076-2; with *Variations, Funeral Music*).
◗ **Symphony No. 3**; Concerto for Orchestra: Chicago Symphony Orchestra; Barenboim (Erato 4509-91711-2).
◗ **Chain 2**: Mutter; BBC Symphony Orchestra; Lutosławski (Deutsche Grammophon DG 423 696-2; with *Partita*; Stravinsky, *Violin Concerto*).
◗ **Chain 1, 2 & 3**: Jakowicz; various conductors & orchestras (Polskie Nagrania PNCD 044; with *Symphony No. 3*).

The Polskie Nagrania label has issued an invaluable survey of Lutosławski's music, but many of their recordings are often quite aged. When it comes to the symphonies you're best advised to choose the EMI version of the first two, with the composer conducting, and Barenboim for the third. The latter is especially good, with Barenboim bringing out all the drama and the passion of the music's single sweep; it comes with a dazzling performance of the *Concerto for Orchestra*. The Polskie Nagrania disc of *Chain* has the merit of presenting the composer's conception in its entirety, but there is something really special about Mutter's performance of *Chain 2*; boasting committed accompaniment and fine recorded sound, as well as a splendid performance of the Stravinsky concerto, this DG disc is the obvious place to begin exploring Lutosławski.

ELISABETH LUTYENS
(1906–1983)

Nicknamed "twelve-tone Lizzie", Elisabeth Lutyens was one of the most radical British composers of her generation. Although music by the Viennese serialists Schoenberg and Webern was being played in London while she was a young woman, Lutyens always claimed that she had developed her twelve-note technique independently of them, and certainly she was to display a staunch self-reliance throughout her career. Her style was constantly changing and developing, and her complex but ultimately rewarding music has gone in and out of fashion, although the best of it has never received the attention it deserves.

She was born into a well-to-do artistic family: her father was the architect Edwin Lutyens and her mother, Lady Emily Lytton, became a devoted follower of Krishnamurti and theosophy. Determined from an early age to become a composer, Lutyens studied briefly at the École Normale in Paris in her late teens and then at the Royal College of Music. It took her some years to find a musical language with which she was satisfied and she later withdrew most of her works before the ground-breaking *Chamber Concerto No. 1* (1939–40).

The early 1940s were a period of experimentation, culminating in her glorious cantata *O Saisons! O Châteaux!* (1946), to words by Rimbaud. By this time she had left her husband for Edward Clarke, a former pupil of Schoenberg and a leading figure in contemporary music circles. He was also frequently unemployed, leaving Lutyens with the responsibility of providing for Clarke and her four children, which she did by writing countless scores for film and radio. She became a well-known figure amongst the writers and artists who frequented the pubs of London's Fitzrovia, hanging out with such luminaries as Dylan Thomas, Louis MacNeice and Francis Bacon.

After overcoming a nervous breakdown and alcoholism at the beginning of the 1950s, Lutyens started to produce some of her most striking works. Yet compositions such as the *String Quartet No. 6* (1952), and her Wittgenstein-inspired *Excerpta tractatus-logico philosophici* (1952) were simply too advanced for the British musical establishment, and she was rarely performed. The successful first performance in 1962 of the powerful *Quincunx* for baritone, soprano and orchestra saw the beginning of a change in the reception of her music. The more adventurous musical climate of the 1960s and 1970s was more open to her uncompromising ways, and she produced a stream of important works, such as *And Suddenly It's Evening* (1966), a setting of four poems by Salvatore Quasimodo for tenor and instrumental ensemble, and *Essence of our Happiness* (1968), which used Islamic texts and words by John Donne.

During this late period her music became less dry and more immediately lyrical, but by the time of her death Lutyens had become as well-known for her caustic wit and outspoken opinions on the British musical establishment as for her music.

CHAMBER MUSIC

Luytens' large-scale works are absent from the CD catalogue, but there is a wealth of dramatic and expressive music to be found among the chamber works that have been recorded. One of the earliest pieces she was later prepared to acknowledge was her *Chamber Concerto No. 1*, the first of six chamber concertos composed during the 1940s. Its bare textures and serial language piece must have seemed unrelentingly austere to its first audience in 1943. By 1957, when she wrote *6 Tempi For 10 Instruments*, Lutyens was experimenting with different ways of using rhythm: this work, which was admired by Igor Stravinsky, comprises six short movements which are all of the same duration but use that time in very different ways.

Much of Lutyens' work in the 1960s was vocal, and her chamber music from this decade includes *The Valley of Hatsu-Se* Op. 62 (1965), settings of eight ancient Japanese poems for soprano, flute, clarinet, cello and piano, and *Lament of Isis on the Death of Osiris* (1969), which was extracted from Lutyens' unsuccessful opera *Isis and Osiris*. Using writings by Plutarch and from the Egyptian Book of the Dead, the *Lament* makes strenuous use of the soprano soloist's full emotional and technical range.

Lutyens' later, more lyrical writing can be heard in two works dating from 1971, *Requiescat* for soprano and string trio, and *Driving out the Death* for oboe, violin, viola and cello. Brief yet deeply moving, *Requiescat* was commissioned by the music magazine *Tempo* in memory of Stravinsky and uses as its text a passage from *The Couch of Death* by William Blake. *Driving out the Death*, probably the most frequently performed of all Lutyens' work, was inspired by ancient rituals marking the changing seasons; in six sections, it opens with an oboe call, and it is the expressive voice of the oboe that dominates the whole work.

> ◉ **Chamber Concerto No. 1; 6 Tempi for 10 instruments; The Valley of Hatsu-Se; Lament of Isis on the Death of Osiris; Requiescat; Triolet I and Triolet II**: Jane's Minstrels; Manning (NMC DO11).
> ◉ **Driving out the Death**: Redcliffe Ensemble (Redcliffe Recordings RR 006; with works by Rawsthorne and Routh).

All credit to NMC for issuing the only currently available CD to consist entirely of Lutyens' music. It presents a wide-ranging selection of her chamber music in excellent performances, with the vocal works performed by Jane Manning, for whom both *The Valley of Hatsu-Se* and *Lament of Isis on the Death of Osiris* were written. The Redcliffe Ensemble, a chamber group specialising in the music of British composers, gives a passionate performance of the Lutyens quartet on their recording of music for oboe and strings.

GUILLAUME DE MACHAUT
(c.1300–1377)

Round about the year 1320 the French composer and theoretician Philippe de Vitry wrote a treatise entitled *Ars Nova* (New Art) in which he claimed that the recent technical innovations in music amounted to a major break with the music of the immediate past. Musicologists later employed the term Ars Nova for the developments that took place in French and Italian music in the fourteenth century, designating the previous period – the period of early polyphony (c.900–1250) – Ars Antiqua.

Guillaume de Machaut was the outstanding Ars Nova composer, exploiting new musical techniques that make much of his work sound startlingly modern. One of the most significant innovations was that of isorhythm, whereby a fixed rhythm was applied to the cantus firmus, the borrowed melody that often underpinned a new composition. This fixed rhythm might have a different number of notes from the main melody, so that each time it was repeated it would begin at a different point along that melody – a numerical system of composing that has led to Machaut being bracketed with Schoenberg as an essentially intellectual composer. In addition, Machaut also employed musical forms that were in decline, and many of his most moving songs are monophonic.

Machaut was almost certainly born in Rheims, a city where he spent most of his later years. Around 1323 he joined the household of John of Luxembourg, the King of Bohemia, serving as his secretary on many military and diplomatic expeditions. When King John died at the battle of Crecy in 1346 Machaut went on to serve a succession of aristocratic patrons including the king's daughter Bonne, King Charles the Bad of Navarre, the King of Cyprus and the dukes John of Berry and Amadeus of Savoy. As a priest much of his income came from a number of largely honorary positions awarded him by various churches throughout France.

Machaut's fame during his lifetime was gained as much by his skills as a poet as by his musicianship, and he was admired as such by his great English contemporary Geoffrey Chaucer. In his later years, he fell in love with a woman much younger than himself and he tells their story – the source of much biographical detail – in a long poem, *Voir Dit* (The Tale of Truth). "All my works", wrote Machaut to his beloved, "were made from your feelings, and are for you especially."

THE MUSIC

Machaut exemplifies the poetic and courtly conventions of his day. Despite his income from the church, nearly all of his compositions are secular songs about love, the courtly, spiritual love of the Middle Ages which requires the love object to be an unattainable woman of unrivalled beauty. Her devoted admirer pays extravagant tribute to her, and swears undying devotion, even though she is the cause of as much pain as pleasure. Machaut's language is in the

tradition of the troubadours of northern France, poet-musicians who performed their work at the chateaux of the nobility. One of his favoured song forms is the *virelais*, in which a refrain alternates with three stanzas, and these compositions have all the simple directness of folk song. His polyphonic songs, on the other hand, are more adventurous and possess greater rhythmic variety, often using a form of syncopation called the hocket (from the Latin for hiccup), which breaks up the line of a melody in one voice by inserting sudden gaps which are then filled by the other voices, thus creating a gentle undulating quality.

Machaut's most important work for the church was the four-part *Messe de Notre Dame*, the first polyphonic setting of the Ordinary of the Mass which shows some kind of stylistic unity between the sections. (The Ordinary of the Mass is those parts of it which are constant – ie the Kyrie, Gloria, Credo, Sanctus and Agnus Dei – as opposed to those sections whose texts vary according to the occasion, and which are called the Proper of the Mass.)

⊙ The Mirror of Narcissus – Songs of Guillaume de Machaut: Kirkby; Philpot; Covey-Crump; Gothic Voices; Page (Hyperion CDA 66087).
⊙ Messe de Notre Dame; Le Lai de la Fonteinne; Ma fin est mon commencement: The Hilliard Ensemble; Hillier (Hyperion CDA 66358) .

The Gothic Voices' decision to perform the songs with voices only – a valid alternative would have been to have instruments in the lower parts – is fully justified by the wonderful textual clarity that results. Unaccompanied performances of these three- and four-part songs show off their complexity and energy in a much more immediate way. This is especially true of the one sacred work on the disc, the motet Inviolata genitrix, where it really does sound, at moments, as if three people were singing completely different songs simultaneously. The way it all fits together, and the haunting harmonies that are thrown up, are what makes this such a powerful and pleasurable work.

Austerity is the chief characteristic of the *Messe de Notre Dame*, in which the general simplicity of the word-setting places the few dramatic moments in sharp relief. The Hilliard Ensemble's approach to this music is to avoid the obviously expressive and to concentrate on making the music's constant rhythmic ebb and flow sound coherent. The result creates an atmosphere of extraordinary devotional intensity.

JAMES MACMILLAN
(1959–   )

James MacMillan, one of Britain's leading young composers (a recent Edinburgh Festival featured no fewer than seventeen works by him) is a man proud to wear his "Catholic left-wing traditionalist" principles on his sleeve. His work tends to be placed alongside the compositions of other deeply religious composers, such as John Tavener and Arvo Pärt, but his music is more raw and turbulent than theirs, befitting a world-view that is markedly different. As MacMillan himself has remarked of his kinship with Tavener: "Tavener has always said that for him the most important image is that of the Risen Christ. For me, it's Christ Crucified. It shows in our music: in Tavener's, it's as if Heaven is already attained. In mine, it's still to be fought for". Since discovering liberation theology in the 1980s, MacMillan has written several works embodying the plight of oppressed peoples, particularly those of South America. One of his most moving and harrowing pieces, the theatre piece *Busqueda*, draws on poems by Argentina's Mothers of the Disappeared and brilliantly weaves sections of the Latin Mass around them. It's a perfect illustration of his belief that "you cannot divorce the religious and political".

In interviews and in articles MacMillan has addressed the need to fight against "the old guard of the avant-garde" who "are deeply suspicious of any significant move towards tonality, any hint of pulse that is actually discernible, and any music which communicates successfully with a non-specialist audience". Despite his own orthodox musical education, everything that he is trying to achieve as a composer has to do with direct emotional and dramatic communication, an enterprise in which Scottish traditional music

is an important source of inspiration. Ayrshire born and bred, MacMillan is often presented as the musical voice of Scottish nationalism. However, MacMillan is too much of a universal humanist to get caught up in any extreme manifestations of nationalist sentiment. Extremism, in whatever guise, is something that repels him, as is evident from his main work to date, *The Confession of Isabel Gowdie*.

THE CONFESSION OF ISOBEL GOWDIE

If one occasion in particular could be said to have marked the turning point in MacMillan's professional life, it was the 1990 Proms debut of *The Confession of Isobel Gowdie*. It's not difficult to see why this large orchestral work has become such a firm favourite. With its references to the Scottish ballad tradition and Gregorian chant, not to mention suggestions of Stravinsky, Messiaen, Berg, Vaughan Williams and Purcell, this is a composition of resonant textures and violent dynamics. The title refers to the trial of Isobel Gowdie, who in 1662 was tortured into confessing herself guilty of witchcraft, an incident that serves as a metaphor for MacMillan's "fears about the new rise of fascism" in Europe.

⊙ **The Confession of Isobel Gowdie; Tryst**: BBC Scottish Symphony Orchestra; Maksymiuk (Koch/ Schwann 3-1050-2).

Jerzy Maksymiuk and the BBC Scottish Orchestra – the combination that gave *The Confession*'s premiere – sensitively mould every phrase of MacMillan's slow-moving musical ritual, handling the abrupt and shocking change of gear in the work's *Rite of Spring*-ish middle section with great virtuosity. It's coupled with a half-hour instrumental piece, *Tryst*, another single-movement work with elements of medieval chant in its musical fabric.

ELIZABETH MACONCHY

(1907–   )

Elizabeth Maconchy has described her work as "an impassioned argument", and indeed her compositions are characterized by the combination of heartfelt lyricism and clear logical structures. Her vigorous music, which has remained rooted in tonality except for an experiment with twelve-note techniques during the 1940s, is among the most dynamic to have been produced in twentieth-century Britain, and deserves to be far more widely heard than it is at present.

Maconchy spent most of her childhood in the countryside of England and Ireland with little exposure to any music other than what she played on the piano or made up for herself. At sixteen she went to the Royal College of Music in London, where she studied with Ralph Vaughan Williams and explored new music by composers such as Béla Bartók, while developing her own highly personal musical language. She first sprang to public attention at the age of 23 when her powerful orchestral work *The Land*, based on a poem by Vita Sackville-West, was premiered at the Proms in August, 1930, to enthusiastic reviews.

In 1932 Maconchy developed tuberculosis, the disease which had killed her father ten years previously. She cured herself by moving out of London and living in a shed at the bottom of the garden of her house in Kent. In spite of this enforced isolation, her music continued to be performed all over Europe throughout the 1930s, although some British critics found the modernity and intellectual power of her music hard to accept in a woman. Having married in 1930, Maconchy had two children in 1939 and 1947, and had to spend much of her time looking after her family. Nonetheless, in the face of resistance from the male-dominated establishment, she continued to compose and to develop, enhancing her reputation with music such as the prize-winning overture *Proud Thames* and her *Symphony for Double String Orchestra*, both from 1953, and adding to the body of chamber music that is central to her output. In the later years of the decade Maconchy turned to writing opera and produced a series of three one-act works – *The Sofa*, *The Departure* and *The Three Strangers* – as well as several works for children and amateurs.

An increasing volume of commissions from performers, institutions and festivals came her way in the 1970s and 1980s, but her innovative edge was not blunted by her increasing success. Works from this period include her large choral work *Héloise and Abélard* (1979) and the exuberant *Music for Strings*, first performed at the Proms in 1983.

THE MUSIC

Throughout her life Maconchy has written string quartets, a genre that's central to her output and perfect for her closely argued musical language. All fourteen of her quartets demonstrate her fascination with counterpoint, both of melodic line and of rhythm, and all of them are well worth investigating, though a few are particularly rewarding.

Maconchy has described her *Quartet No. 1*, written when she was 25, as "extrovert, direct and rhythmical"; its high-spirited energy is apparent from the characteristic driving rhythms of the opening bars. The dramatic and darkly brooding *Quartet No. 4*, written during World War II, demonstrates Maconchy's technique of building the material of a work from one cell, in this instance an idea first heard in the opening cello pizzicato. Her *Quartet No. 5*, written in Ireland in 1948, was her own favourite and contains an achingly beautiful slow movement. Another key work is her *Quartet No. 9*, with its deeply moving, elegiac slow movement written in August 1968, at the time of the Soviet occupation of Prague. The viola was Maconchy's favourite instrument and this can be clearly seen by its central role in the two single-movement quartets of the 1970s, *Quartet No. 10* and *Quartet No. 11*, both characteristic of Maconchy's later, more condensed style. She herself has described her eleventh quartet as like "a piece of woven material, with contrasting colours and patterns running through it".

Perhaps Maconchy's most haunting work is *My Dark Heart* (1981), a setting of three of the Irish writer J. M. Synge's prose translations of Petrarch's sonnets, in which the singer laments lost love while recalling moments of past happiness. Synge's words have a particularly Irish cadence which is echoed in Maconchy's finely judged lyrical writing.

Maconchy's two works for clarinet and orchestra show clearly the changes in her style over the years. The first, *Concertino No. 1* (1945), is a richly ominous work in three movements with exciting, driving rhythms and dramatic brooding passages. *Concertino No. 2* was written in 1984 and is a shorter, more exposed work, although still in three movements. The clarinet is here accompanied by an orchestra that includes wind, brass and timpani (the first used just strings), creating an enthralling sound world in which stark harmonies and textures are reconciled with lyrical warmth.

⊙ **String Quartets Nos. 1–4**; Hanson Quartet (Unicorn Kanchana DKPCD9080).

⊙ **String Quartets Nos. 5–8**: Bingham Quartet (Unicorn Kanchana DKPCD9081).
⊙ **String Quartets Nos. 9–13**: Mistry Quartet (Unicorn Kanchana DKPCD9082).
⊙ **My Dark Heart**: Manning; Lontano; de la Martinez (Lorelt LNT 101; with LeFanu, *The Old Woman of Beare*).
⊙ **Clarinet Concertinos**: King; English Chamber Orchestra; Wordsworth (Hyperion CDA66634 (with works for clarinet and orchestra by Arnold and Britten).

The Unicorn series of three CDs presents all but one of Maconchy's quartets in exciting performances by young British ensembles, forming an essential introduction to a composer whose work is an important part of the quartet repertoire. Each volume contains invaluable notes on the individual works as well as an interesting essay on writing string quartets, all written by the composer.

The marvellous performance of *My Dark Heart*, by the versatile Jane Manning and the contemporary music group Lontano, comes with an good account of *The Old Woman of Beare* by Maconchy's daughter Nicola LeFanu. This expressive work for soprano and instrumental ensemble was written in the same year as *My Dark Heart* and sets the memories of a ninth-century courtesan living out the end of her life on the wild Irish coast.

The Hyperion recording of the *Clarinet Concertinos* is the only available CD to contain any of Maconchy's orchestral writing. Clarinettist Thea King, who has recorded many little-known works by British composers, gives a glorious performance, with sensitive accompaniment from the English Chamber Orchestra.

GUSTAV MAHLER
(1860–1911)

Until little more than thirty years ago, Mahler's heady, epic compositions were regarded with a degree of suspicion similar to that which still dogs many of his contemporaries, such as Zemlinsky and Schreker. In his own time he was known far more for his conducting than for his music and it took many decades of proselytizing by conductors such as Bruno Walter, Wilhelm Mengelberg and, later, Leonard Bernstein, before the symphonies became the audience-pullers they are today – though there were always pockets of support, notably in the Netherlands and New York, both places where Mahler frequently conducted. That the symphonies finally caught on in a big way after World War II is doubtless due to an affinity between their unstable, angst-ridden content and the complex world of the late twentieth century.

Sigmund Freud, to whom Mahler turned for analysis in later life, found the roots of the composer's neuroticism in his childhood, which was spent in a somewhat tense family atmosphere. One memorable event occurred when the young Gustav rushed out into the street to escape a particularly heated parental argument, to be confronted with the playing of a military band (they lived next to a barracks) – an incident often seen as prophetic of

Mahler's later juxtaposition of widely contrasting moods in his music. In a Mahler symphony one passes from the tragic to the commonplace, from the ingenuous to the ironic, from rustic folk song to spiritual ecstasy, in the space of a moment.

Mahler was born into a Jewish-Bohemian family at a time when official attitudes to Jews in the Austro-Hungarian Empire were relaxing after years of residence restrictions. Thus he was able to benefit from a decent education in Prague and later at the Vienna conservatory, where his fellow pupils included Hugo Wolf (see p.418) and Hans Rott. A recently rediscovered symphony by Rott (available on Hyperion CDA 66366) gives an intriguing insight into Mahler's early work: it predates Mahler's own symphonies yet prefigures many of their musical themes, suggesting that Rott, who died insane at the age of 26, was a significant influence. Among the many other influences on Mahler in Vienna was the music of Bruckner who, though only beginning to receive the recognition he deserved, was idolized by Mahler and his fellow students.

Just as he was beginning to find his voice as a composer in the dramatic cantata *Das klagende Lied* (1880) and other early songs, Mahler discovered his talents as a conductor and soon won renown for his performances of the operas of Mozart, Beethoven and Wagner. By 1888 he was chief conductor at the Budapest Opera and within a few years was in charge at the more prestigious house in Hamburg, where his thoroughly prepared performances – at a time when rehearsal was often seen as an encumbrance – gained him more plaudits. It was also during this period that he established the pattern of composing that would last until his death: with concert and opera seasons taking up most of the year from autumn to spring, he had to confine his writing to the summer months, usually retiring to the idyllic surroundings of the Carinthian lakes in southern Austrian. To Mahler, it was a life of great continuity, for he saw little distinction between bringing masterpieces to life in the concert hall and opera house, and expressing his innermost thoughts in his own music. Refusing to separate life from art, Mahler embodied the apotheosis of Romanticism.

MARY EVANS PICTURE LIBRARY

As Mahler became disenchanted with musical life in Hamburg he set his sights on Vienna and went to the lengths of converting to Roman Catholicism to make himself acceptable to the anti-Semitic Viennese court that ran the opera house. He was duly appointed principal conductor in 1897 and survived ten acrimonious years at the head of one of Europe's top musical establishments, where he raised musical and dramatic standards to unforeseen heights, but at the expense of never-ending battles with orchestral players, singers and critics. (The top job at Vienna is still one of the most antagonistic posts in the music world.) Mahler rarely conducted his own music in Vienna, not wanting to be seen taking advantage of his position, but toured widely through northern Europe with his symphonies and song cycles.

In 1907 he resigned from his Viennese post and accepted the offer of a contract at the Metropolitan Opera in New York, but ended up becoming more involved in the regeneration of the New York Philharmonic. At the same time a serious heart disease began to manifest itself, a bacterial infestation brought on by the throat infections that had plagued him throughout his life. His last compositions, the ninth and tenth symphonies and the song cycle *Das Lied von der Erde*, are overwhelmingly imbued with premonitions of his death, which finally occurred on May 18, 1911, after a fruitless visit to a bacteriologist in Paris on the way back from his final American trip.

SYMPHONIES

"The symphony is a world", proclaimed Mahler to Sibelius, and indeed few if any composers have crammed so much into their symphonies, from funeral marches to vast images of nature, from ironically quoted popular tunes and dances to great apostrophes to love. These are not purely abstract works in the tradition of Brahms and Bruckner: all have strong extra-musical elements, incorporating poems or religious texts, or possessing an ambitious philosophical "programme". On the other hand, these programmes are not the detailed paraphrases that you'll find in symphonic poems of Berlioz or Strauss, and it's not necessary to know the "meaning" of the piece before listening to it – Mahler himself regarded his explanatory subtitles as mere crutches, and often deleted them from his revisions. Most of the symphonies describe a dramatic progression of some sort, and accordingly demonstrate "progressive tonality", where the symphony ends in a different key from that in which it began.

The first four were influenced by the folk-like verses of *Des Knaben Wunderhorn* and his own settings of them (see below), and three of them incorporate solo singers and/or choirs. There followed three purely instrumental works of enormous power and range, but he returned to the vocal symphony with *Symphony No. 8* – in terms of number of performers required, his most massive work. After came the incomparable, valedictory *No. 9* and an attempt at completing a tenth (since reworked into a performable version). Of the ten, the first and fifth are probably the best places to start.

>) **Symphonies Nos. 1–9; Adagio of No. 10:**
> **Adagio**: Kubelík; Bavarian Radio Symphony Orchestra
> (Deutsche Grammophon DG 429 042-2; 10 CDs).
>
> When Simon Rattle gets around to recording the whole set (he has spoken of having reservations about *No. 8*), his could well prove to be the first choice for a complete symphonic

cycle. In the meantime the choice lies between the cycles from Bernstein, Haitink, Inbal, Kubelík, Maazel, Solti and Tennstedt, all of which are available at mid- or bargain price. Inevitably in a body of work with such a range of challenges it would be a miracle if a single conductor were to produce the ideal performance of each and every symphony, but the most consistently satisfying attempt is Rafael Kubelík's. Even if the symphonies do not merit a first choice individually, this is a low-cost way of getting hold of the lot in more than merely adequate performances.

SYMPHONY NO. 1

Mahler's *Symphony No. 1* (1885–88) began life as a symphonic poem, and a vestige of this early draft survives in the subtitle that is occasionally attached to it, *Titan*, and in the appearance on some recordings of a subsequently discarded movement entitled *Blumine*. The flower imagery of this movement provided an interlude in the rather confused narrative of the original, which was based on a novel by Jean-Paul, in which the hero figure's contemplation of nature leads to a fatal self-absorption. Suggestions of this extra-musical programme remain in the work's evocative, primordial opening, the slow movement's funeral march (based upon *Frère Jacques*) and the presence of song tunes from Mahler's own *Lieder eines fahrenden Gesellen* (see below). It is remarkably original for a first symphony and its direct influences are hard to define, beyond a melodiousness recalling Schubert and a sense of scale derived from Bruckner.

> ● City of Birmingham Symphony Orchestra; Rattle (EMI
> CDC 7 54647 2; with *Blumine*).
>
> Simon Rattle's live recording with CBSO best captures the music's scale, with the twilight opening played at an extreme pianissimo and evolving into a most magical evocation of awakening nature. The rustic Scherzo has a real Austrian rumbustiousness, with the horns playing at full tilt, while the sense of irony in the funeral march is never far from the surface, and the climax of the finale is truly breathtaking.

SYMPHONY NO. 2 –
THE RESURRECTION

The first movement of the *Symphony No. 2* (1888–94) also began life as a symphonic poem, *Totenfeier*, or "Funeral Rites", in which Mahler claimed to show the "hero" of his first symphony being "borne to his grave".

He later reworked this as the first movement of a symphony broadly expressing the concept of the life force's ability to rise again from the ashes of fate through faith in God – hence the symphony's subtitle.

The first three movements are purely instrumental, the self-explanatory funeral march being followed by two interludes looking back on the happy and bitter times of life; in the fourth movement, the "hero" hears the call of God in an evocative alto solo, *Urlicht* (Primeval Light); and in the finale he has to face the Day of Judgement before being granted immortality. Such a grand theme called for grand treatment and Mahler uses a vast orchestra (including ten horns and eight trumpets), together with two solo singers and a choir, in a work that lasts some ninety minutes.

◉ Augér, Baker; City of Birmingham Symphony Orchestra & Chorus; Rattle (EMI CDS 7 47962 8; 2 CDs).

Simon Rattle is again the recommendation here. He shapes phrases with attention paid to every nuance of the score, while the grand sweep remains paramount; his performers play and sing magnificently and the recording is often overwhelming.

SYMPHONY NO. 3

Whereas *Symphony No. 2* is a hymn to humanity's salvation through spirituality, *Symphony No. 3* (1895–96) is a hymn to the natural world. Conceived as a seven-movement paean entitled *The Joyful Knowledge* or *A Summer Morning's Dream*, it originally bore movement headings such as *Summer marches in*, *What the meadow flowers tell me* and *What love tells me*, and ended in a child's view of heaven. In the event, Mahler turned this last movement into the finale of *Symphony No. 4*, and as with *No. 1*, he suppressed the somewhat twee details of the programme.

Although written for a slightly smaller orchestra than *No. 2*, it uses extravagant vocal forces (soprano, boys' chorus, women's chorus) for two brief movements. This was to be Mahler's broadest work in terms of scale, with a vast first movement suggesting the awakening of primeval life from the depths of winter, four contrasting middle movements (one a setting of Nietzsche's *Midnight Song*,

another of a naive *Wunderhorn* poem), and an extended Adagio finale culminating in an apotheosis in which, in Mahler's words, "Nature in its totality may ring and resound".

◗ Procter; London Symphony Orchestra, Wandsworth School Boys' Choir, Ambrosian Singers; Horenstein (Unicorn-Kanchana UKCD2006/7; 2 CDs).

For the best recording of this symphony you have to go back to Jascha Horenstein's classic recording with the LSO in the 1960s: no-one has delved deeper into this majestic work. The sound quality might leave something to be desired by modern standards, but this is one of those cases where the music has to come before technology.

SYMPHONY NO. 4

The projected finale of *Symphony No. 3*, a soprano setting of the *Wunderhorn* song *Das himmlisches Leben* (The Heavenly Life), became the climax of *Symphony No. 4* (1899–1901), a much more restrained work than its predecessors. The orchestra is of a normal size, there are only four movements and the childlike sentiments of the finale's text affect the whole work; it is not devoid of weightier moments, however – its Scherzo requires the lead violinist to tune the violin up a tone to add a sinister touch to proceedings.

◗ Lott; London Philharmonic Orchestra; Welser-Möst (EMI CD-EMX2139).

Although Franz Welser-Möst had a rough critical ride as music director of the LPO, his performance of this symphony is completely successful, with a perfect balance between the music's naivety and irony, and Felicity Lott singing radiantly in the last movement.

SYMPHONY NO. 5

With his *Symphony No. 5* (1901–02), Mahler abandoned the use of vocal forces for a five-movement symphony that for once has no preconceived programme, though it follows the dark-to-light pattern of the earlier symphonies, beginning with a funeral march and ending with a triumphant, exuberant finale. The intervening episodes are a ferocious Allegro, whose mood is then completely banished by the ensuing, uninhibitedly jolly Scherzo and the ineffably tender Adagietto for harp and strings, a piece of music made famous by Visconti's film of *Death in Venice*.

● Vienna Philharmonic Orchestra; Bernstein (Deutsche Grammophon DG 423 608-2).

Only the first symphony is more often recorded than the *Symphony No. 2*. The most invigorating account is undoubtedly Leonard Bernstein's live recording with the Vienna Philharmonic: his self-indulgent way with Mahler has always had its detractors, but here his empathy with the composer's intentions is unsurpassed. The playing conveys the excitement of a live event and the recording is unusually spacious.

SYMPHONY NO. 6

The *Symphony No. 6* (1903–04) was Mahler's only symphony to follow the conventional four-movement pattern and to be centred on a single key, A minor. He at first toyed with the idea of naming it the *Tragic* and, while there may be no specific text attached to the work, it's a powerful, pessimistic composition. In its first version, the last movement contained three crashing blows, marked to be played with a sledge-hammer on a resonant surface; intended to represent the hammer-blows of fate, they were to prove prophetic when a year after the first performance in 1906 he lost his position at the Vienna Opera, his daughter died and his heart condition was diagnosed. Mahler was highly superstitious and later excised the third of the blows from the score as if to ward off his death, yet the bleakness of the work's ending is matched only by Tchaikovsky's sixth symphony and Mahler's own ninth.

● Berlin Philharmonic Orchestra; Karajan (Deutsche Grammophon DG 415 099-2; with *Rückert-Lieder*; 2 CDs).
● City of Birmingham Symphony Orchestra; Rattle (EMI CDS 7 54047 2; 2 CDs).

Only Herbert von Karajan's Berlin Philharmonic had the power to make the most of this titanic work, from the savage intensity of the first movement and Scherzo to the soaring violin lines of the last movement. Simon Rattle's CBSO might not reach the refined heights of their Berlin counterparts, but Rattle's interpretation is arguably more searching and the finale gets to grips with the tragedy in a truly convincing way.

SYMPHONY NO. 7

As if trying to exorcise the gloom of *No. 6*, Mahler's *Symphony No. 7* (1904–5) ends with his most uninhibited attempt at being cheerful, in a finale that combines allusions to Offenbach's *Can-Can* and Wagner's *Die Meistersinger* in a general mélange of C major joyfulness that can seem merely gaudy in the wrong hands. It is probably this movement that has led to the work's relative neglect until recent years, when the glories of its other movements have at last been recognized. The funereal first movement may not be one of his most profound symphonic essays, but is made up for by the three movements that follow. The outer pair are entitled *Nachtmusik* (Night Music) and combine the moods of the nocturne with those of a serenade (the song-like second includes important parts for mandolin and guitar), while the central movement is one of Mahler's most miraculous creations – a ghostly Scherzo revealing his mastery of orchestral colour.

● City of Birmingham Symphony Orchestra; Rattle (EMI CDC 7 54344 2).

No-one has brought this music quite as vividly to life as has Simon Rattle. The symphony has been in the CBSO's repertoire for many seasons and this live recording combines the advantages of familiarity with the risks inherent in live performance. The acoustic is perhaps a little dense for the large forces used, but the whole enterprise is thrillingly executed, with every detail in the score given its proper weight.

SYMPHONY NO. 8 –
THE SYMPHONY OF A THOUSAND

If *Symphony No. 6* descends to Hell, *Symphony No. 8* (1906) rises heavenward. It is in two parts, the first a setting of the Pentecostal Latin hymn *Veni Creator Spiritus*, the second a setting of the closing scene from Goethe's *Faust*. Thus Mahler returned to the use of vocal forces, and not simply for the odd movement, as in the second, third and fourth symphonies: here he calls for eight soloists, a boys' chorus and large mixed chorus, hence the nickname of the *Symphony of a Thousand*. The result is a wide-ranging work, the rigorous counterpoint and earnestness of the opening hymn contrasting with the lush treatment of the Goethe; but the two parts are linked by certain musical themes and by their conceptual similarity – the first is a humanist interpretation of a Christian text concerning the search for enlightenment, the second a portrayal of Faust's redemption through wisdom and love.

Klaus Tennstedt

⊙ Harper, Auger, Popp, Minton, Watts, Kollo, Shirley-Quirk, Talvela; Chicago Symphony Orchestra; Solti (Decca 414 493-2; 2 CDs).
⊙ Connell, Wiens, Lott, Schmidt, Denize, Versalle, Hynninen, Sotin; London Philharmonic Orchestra & Choir, Tiffin School Boys' Choir; Tennstedt (EMI CDS 7 47625 8; 2 CDs).

The choice of recordings rests between Solti and Tennstedt, both superb but quite different in approach. Solti's is an operatic reading, stunningly recorded and with a first-class roster of singers; the engineers capture the scale of the work like no others, from the pungent organ at the opening and close to the tintinnabulating pianos and harps in the second movement. Tennstedt's recording, on the other hand, while no less massive in overall concept, is a more personable account, with greater care taken over orchestral detail and more air around the notes. A difficult choice, then: Solti for greater physical impact, Tennstedt for greater musical qualities.

SYMPHONY NO. 9

Mahler was a very ill man by the time he wrote his *Symphony No. 9* (1908–11). Ever superstitious, he attempted to trick fate out of its habit of terminating composer's lives after their ninth symphonies (as in the cases of Beethoven, Bruckner and Dvořák), by pretending that this was really his tenth, with his intervening symphonic song cycle *Das Lied von der Erde* (see below) as the true *No. 9*. This sleight of hand did nothing to lighten the tone of the music, for this symphony is the most desperately death-ridden piece Mahler ever wrote. The opening movement, in which you can hear ominously tolling bells, the tread of a funeral march and a faltering heartbeat, gives way to a deliberately charmless rustic Ländler with a vulgar, distorted waltz at its centre. The Rondo-Burlesque third movement is, in the words of Mahler scholar Deryck Cooke, a "contrived chaos . . . a ferocious outburst of fiendish laughter at the futility of everything". From this emerges the Adagio finale, in which death is stoically accepted and the music fades into tranquillity.

⊙ Berlin Philharmonic Orchestra; Karajan (Deutsche Grammophon DG 410 726-2; 2 CDs).

The ninth is the most difficult of Mahler's symphonies to bring off in performance – its colossal structures, drastic changes of tone and profound solemnity require the greatest conductors and orchestras to do it justice. Herbert von Karajan and the Berlin Philharmonic are such a partnership. Their live concert performance, recorded in 1982, is immaculate, displaying an intensity rarely found in other performances of the work, with the orchestra playing as if their lives depended on it.

SYMPHONY NO. 10

In the summer of 1910 Mahler made a sketch of a new symphony, but left it in an unfinished state when he died the following spring. All five movements of the *Symphony No. 10* had a continuous line of music and three of them were filled out in more detail and partially scored for orchestra. Two movements were edited for performance in 1924, but it wasn't until the early 1960s that Deryck Cooke produced a performing version of the whole work, judiciously filling out passages that Mahler had not had time to expand beyond a single melodic line. This version took a while to be accepted by the musical establishment and there are still many eminent conductors who refuse to touch it on the grounds that it never can be a true representation of Mahler's intended completion. Yet those who do ignore it ignore a valuable insight into Mahler's state of mind a year after completing the doom-laden ninth. Here, death is again very much a subject of the work, but the overall impression is one of achieved peace, as if Mahler had at last exorcized his terrors.

MAHLER **215**

◉ Bournemouth Symphony Orchestra; Rattle (EMI CDC 7 54406-2).

One conductor who has never had any doubts about the completion of the work, and indeed has included his own editorial additions in performance, is Simon Rattle. His recording with the Bournemouth Symphony Orchestra precedes his partnership with the CBSO, but is as assured a performance as his later ones in Birmingham.

VOCAL MUSIC

A smaller but no less important part of Mahler's heritage is his contribution to German song, as significant in its own way as that of Schubert, Wolf and Strauss. Like Schubert, he had a supreme melodic gift, with a vocal style that was honed by setting various folk texts in his early songs – and indeed, the folkloric element remained central to all his vocal work, including the solo and choral sections of his symphonies. Virtually all his songs exist in versions accompanied by piano or orchestra (even the symphonic *Das Lied von der Erde* has an authentic piano version), but, given Mahler's skills in orchestration, the fuller alternatives are invariably more effective.

DAS KLAGENDE LIED

Das klagende Lied, a cantata for four soloists, chorus and orchestra, setting Mahler's own poem relating a folk tale about a fratricide, sounds too accomplished to be the work of a twenty-year-old. This immensely accomplished piece is the composition in which he "found himself as Mahler", as he once said, and apart from a few songs and a movement for piano quartet he destroyed everything that had preceded it. In the 1890s he revised the cycle and discarded its first movement, which he felt to be superfluous to the story telling, but fortunately this inspired if sprawling movement has now returned to circulation – though beware that some older recordings still omit it.

◉ Dunn, Baur, Fassbaender, Hollweg, Schmidt; Berlin Radio Symphony Orchestra, Düsseldorf City Music Society; Chailly (Decca 425 719-2).

Riccardo Chailly's recording of the complete work is magnificent in every way. He has a superb orchestra and a fine quintet of soloists – a quintet, since the imaginative decision has been taken to have a boy treble sing the murdered brother's lament, rather than the marked mezzo-soprano, an evocative and eerie touch. The recording is up to Decca's best standards, with the off-stage band in the finale (representing the behind-the-scenes revelry of the wedding feast) at just the right distance, and the main orchestra and chorus caught to thrilling effect.

THE SONGS

The text of Mahler's first song cycle, *Lieder eines fahrenden Gesellen* (Songs of a Wayfarer; 1883–85) is again his own, and is again in the style of the poetry from the immensely popular collection of folk texts titled *Des Knaben Wunderhorn* (The Boy's Magic Horn). There are four songs, all dealing with a rejected lover's attempts to find solace in nature and, ultimately, in death – the second song became the main theme in the first movement of *Symphony No. 1*, the composition of which followed immediately on from these songs.

Mahler's settings from *Des Knaben Wunderhorn* itself do not form a cycle as such, but are a collection of individual songs composed between 1892 and 1901. The range of these songs – some of which percolated into the symphonies written during this period – is impressively wide, from the mournful *Das irdische Leben* (Earthly Life) to the witty *Lob des hohen Verstandes* (Praise of Lofty Intellect), and they are usually shared between a female and a male singer.

After such folksiness, the *Kindertotenlieder* (Songs on the Deaths of Children; 1901–04) are made of sterner stuff. Although these settings of five poems by Friedrich Rückert pre-date the tragic death of one of Mahler's children, they seem an expression of an overwhelming fear for their well-being. While working on these songs, Mahler composed five more settings of poems by Rückert; these *Rückert-Lieder* are no more a cycle than is the *Wunderhorn* series, instead dwelling on a variety of Mahlerian themes, from love and life to loneliness and death.

◉ **Lieder eines fahrenden Gesellen; Kindertotenlieder; Rückert-Lieder; Des Knaben Wunderhorn** (3 songs): Fassbaender; German Radio Symphony Orchestra; Chailly (Decca 425 790-2).

⦿ **Des Knaben Wunderhorn**: Schwarzkopf, Fischer-Dieskau; London Symphony Orchestra; Szell (EMI CDC 7 47277 2).
⦿ **Des Knaben Wunderhorn**: Hampson, Parsons (Teldec 9031-74726-2).

The mezzo-soprano Brigitte Fassbaender has no equal in the early cycles, and her disc with Chailly is nothing short of stunning, giving each song a character and personality of its own. In terms of tone quality, her voice is perhaps coarser than many of her rivals (both male and female), but its innate expressiveness is totally involving. For the *Wunderhorn* songs, Elisabeth Schwarzkopf and Dietrich Fischer-Dieskau are the most effective pairing in their classic 1968 recording with Georg Szell conducting the London Symphony Orchestra. Both singers are renowned for the way they stress the meaning of the words, and the result here is particularly characterful and communicative. Thomas Hampson and Geoffrey Parsons have resurrected Mahler's original piano versions of the *Wunderhorn* songs on a splendidly sung and played recording; most other piano-accompanied recordings use an edition made from piano reductions of the orchestral score, whereas this version uses a piano score which preceded the orchestration.

DAS LIED VON DER ERDE

The valedictory song-cycle *Das Lied von der Erde* is one of Mahler's most personal works and is perhaps his most beautiful, combining symphonic scale and structure with the narrative clarity of a song-cycle. The six songs are settings of translated Chinese poems conveying the relationships between death and nature, with human life presented as a transient stage in the ever-renewing processes of the earth. Mahler emphasized the message with some words of his own at the end of the last song, as the music fades away: "The dear earth everywhere/Blossoms in spring and grows green again!/Everywhere and eternally the distance shines with a blue light!/Eternally . . . eternally . . .". The cycle calls for a tenor and mezzo-soprano, who alternate between songs of defiance and resignation, but the dominant performer is the mezzo, who has the final thirty-minute movement to herself.

⦿ Fassbaender, Araiza; Berlin Philharmonic Orchestra; Giulini (Deutsche Grammophon DG 413 459-2).

Few mezzos have penetrated more deeply into this profound music than Brigitte Fassbaender, whose voice takes on a truly gut-wrenching quality at the moment of death towards the end of the last poem. Her tenor is Francisco Araiza, forthright and assured, but also more lyrical than some of his rivals. Giulini conducts the Berlin Philharmonic in a slow but passionate, heart-rending account of the score.

POLYGRAM

Brigitte Fassbaender – a superlative interpreter of Mahler's songs

FRANK MARTIN
(1890–1974)

Swiss culture has always been a bridge between the Germanic and Latin worlds, a situation embodied in the person and music of Frank Martin, who was born into a Geneva-based family of French Protestant descent but was more inclined towards the German approach to art. Martin was taught harmony and counterpoint but never underwent any formal conservatory-level training – he actually began, but never completed, a course in mathematics and physics. Initially he was more interested in music theory and education than in composition (he became a renowned teacher and lecturer), and the now more-or-less forgotten works from the 1920s were let down by their excessively theoretical basis. Then in the 1930s his work gained more focus with the development of a personal language which, rather like Berg's, was founded upon a supple adaptation of Schoenberg's twelve-tone principles.

His best-known works date from the 1940s, in particular the oratorio *Le vin herbé* (1941) and the ingenious *Petite symphonie concertante* (1945). He later wrote a pair of operas, *Der Sturm* (1955), based on Shakespeare's *The Tempest*, and *Monsieur de Pourceaugnac* (1962), based on Molière, and there are numerous chamber and vocal works sprinkled throughout his career, as well as a series of concertos. Only a small portion of his output is performed with any regularity, but a moderate proportion is now available on CD, if largely in unsatisfactory broadcast transfers, some conducted by the composer himself.

THE MUSIC

The *Petite Symphonie Concertante*, arguably Martin's masterpiece, was written as a commission from the Basle-based conductor and impresario Paul Sacher, who asked Martin to compose something that gathered together all the common stringed instruments – harp, harpsichord, piano and string orchestra. Martin came up with a piece that used the eighteenth-century concerto grosso as its model, but reversed the priorities of that form by giving prominence to the harp and harpsichord, the parts conventionally associated with the accompanying role. Martin's deployment of this unique combination of instruments is highly resourceful, and like many of his works it is constructed from themes using

all twelve tones of the chromatic scale, but clothed in a harmonic style that makes the music sound almost tonal.

One of the most intriguing of Martin's other works is the *Concerto for Seven Wind Instruments* (1949), an instantly appealing and occasionally astringent piece, spiced with musical allusions – a jibe at a Ravel-like waltz in the first movement, and allusions to Haydn's *Clock* symphony in the steady tread of the slow movement. Of his vocal works, the only one that's often recorded is the *Sechs Monologe aus "Jedermann"*, a setting of six monologues from Hofmannsthal's modern German version of the Everyman medieval mystery play. A gift to a characterful baritone, it's a profound work that makes you regret that Martin's operas have been so neglected.

⦿ **Concerto for Seven Wind Instruments**: Chamber Orchestra of Europe; Fischer (Deutsche Grammophon DG 435 383-2; with *Polyptique* & *Études*).
⦿ **Petite Symphonie Concertante**: Jordan; Suisse Romande Orchestra (Erato 2292-45694-2; with *Wind Concerto* & *Sechs Monologe*).
⦿ **Sechs Monologe aus "Jedermann"**: van Dam; Lyons Opera Orchestra, Nagano (Virgin VC7 59236-2; with pieces by Ibert, Ravel and Poulenc).

The recording from the Chamber Orchestra of Europe under Thierry Fischer is the most successful version of *Concerto for Seven Wind Instruments*; featuring some of Europe's best instrumentalists, the performance sounds effortless but by no means staid. With Ernest Ansermet's classic 1951 account of the *Petite Symphonie Concertante* currently out of the catalogue, the best paced and most atmospheric version comes from Armin Jordan and the Suisse Romande Orchestra. It's coupled with a decent performance of the *Sechs Monologe* – but far better is the version sung by José van Dam, whose account with Kent Nagano and his fine Lyons Opera Orchestra is included in an adventurous collection of French song.

═══════════════ ♫ ═══════════════

BOHUSLAV MARTINŮ
(1890–1959)

After Janáček, Martinů is the leading Czech composer this century, but – like Milhaud and Villa-Lobos – his reputation has suffered because he was so prolific and inconsistent. He often wrote at high speed, almost never revised his scores and was curiously indifferent to performance or acclaim. There's always a lyrical ingredient in his work, a strong rhythmic drive and, often, a sense of ebullience and fun.

Martinů was born in the little town of Polička in the Bohemian-Moravian highlands, an area remarkable for the richness of its musical traditions (Smetana and Mahler came from this region too). His family lived in a tiny room at the top of a church tower, where his father – a cobbler by trade – earned money by keeping an eye open for fires in the town below. For the rest of his life Martinů carried a postcard of the view from the tower, and his home town was to remain an inspiration for him even after World War II had forced him permanently into exile. A sickly child, he spent most of his time closeted in the tower until the age of six, when school brought his first real confrontation with the outside world – a disorienting experience later echoed when he uprooted himself to live in Prague, Paris and the USA.

Martinů learned the violin, started composing aged ten, and in 1907, thanks to local donations, was sent to the conservatory in Prague, where he was not a very successful student. Though his *Czech Rhapsody*, written to celebrate the founding of the new republic in 1918, was played in the presence of President Masaryk, Martinů was a late developer as a composer – it wasn't until he was regularly playing the violin in the Czech Philharmonic in the early 1920s that his musical education really began. In 1923 he took advantage of a small grant from the ministry of education and went to Paris, intending to stay just a few months. He remained there for over seventeen years.

Paris was then the artistic capital of Europe, and Martinů – despite his shyness and inability to speak French – threw himself into the maelstrom. He went to the composer Albert Roussel for lessons and, fascinated by Stravinsky, popular music and jazz, dashed off a couple of noisy orchestral pieces and some experimental ballet scores, culminating in *La revue de cuisine*, in which various kitchen utensils dance the charleston, tango and foxtrot. Later Parisian works included his most interesting opera, *Julietta*, a number of works on Czech folk themes – notably the ballet *Špalíček* (a huge success in Prague in 1933) and the beautiful cantata *Kytice* – and several concertos and *concertante* pieces in a sort of neo-Baroque style. In 1940, soon after the premiere of the magnificent *Double Concerto* (his best work), Martinů was blacklisted by the Nazis and his music was banned in Czechoslovakia. He and his wife fled Paris with no more than a suitcase and went to start a new life in America.

Like Bartók, Martinů didn't feel at home in the USA, although he was highly regarded by influentiual conductors such as Serge Koussevitsky and Eugene Ormandy, and received plenty of commissions. After the war ill-health prevented Martinů returning to Czechoslovakia and with the arrival of the communist regime in 1948 he decided reluctantly to stay in America.

The most important works from this period of exile were the six symphonies composed between 1942 and and 1951, but some of Martinů's best and most deeply Czech music was written after his return to France in 1953. There he composed a series of four cantatas inspired by the poems of Miloslav Bures, a poet from his home town and an opera, *The Greek Passion*, based on a story by Nikos Kazantzakis of *Zorba the Greek* fame. Martinů died in a Swiss hospital before the first

LEBRECHT COLLECTION/MARTINŮ COLLECTION

performance; twenty years later his body was transferred to the family grave in Poliaka, in sight of his beloved tower.

THE OPERAS

Martinů wrote fourteen operas and even more ballets in a wide variety of styles, but his greatest stage work, and his personal favourite, was the opera *Julietta* (1936–37). Based on a surreal play by the French writer Georges Neveux, it doesn't have a plot as such, being more an exploration of dreams and reality in a world where everyone has lost his or her memory. A young man named Michel comes into this strange world in search of Julietta, a young girl with whom he's been obsessed since his previous visit to the harbour town in which the opera is set, but he never manages to find anything tangible to grasp. Martinů kept the score of *Julietta* beside him on his deathbed, and it's easy to see why the work held a particular personal significance for a man who was a traveller and exile for much of his life. He associated the figure of Julietta not only with his wife, Charlotte, but also with a young piano student named Vítězslava Kaprálová – when she died, aged only 25, her last words were "Julietta, Julietta", and the musical motif associated with her crops up in subsequent works.

Martinů's last opera, *The Greek Passion* is the only other one to have been widely performed outside Czechoslovakia. Telling of a passion play that becomes tragically real, it contains some of Martinů's most lyrical passages and some fine choral writing.

> ◉ **Julietta**: Tauberová; Zídek; Orchestra of the Prague National Theatre; Krombholc (Supraphon 10 8176-2; 3 CDs).
> ◉ **The Greek Passion**: Mitchinson; Field; Tomlinson; Brno Philharmonic; Mackerras (Supraphon 10 3611-2; 2 CDs).

On stage Julietta is a fascinating work, but is inevitably less captivating on disc – that said, the splendid recording from the Prague National Theatre captures as much of its haunting beauty as any CD could. The Welsh National Opera version of the Greek Passion – using an English text based on a version prepared by the composer for Covent Garden – is very good indeed. The cast is uniformly strong, and Mackerras once again shows himself to be a master of twentieth-century Czech repertoire.

CHORAL MUSIC

All of Martinů's finest choral music was written to folk texts, and perhaps the most beguiling examples of the genre are the four chamber cantatas composed as an act of homage to his home town at the end of his life. Setting texts by local writer Miroslav Bureš, the cycle follows a seasonal sequence beginning with *Otvírání studánek* (The Opening of the Wells), celebrating a Maytime custom in the Moravian countryside when processions go into the hills to cleanse the wells and springs. Written for soloists, female chorus and a chamber group of two violins, viola and piano, this piece is fresh and naive, whereas there's a greater intimacy and softness to *Romance z pampelišek* (Romance of the Dandelions), for unaccompanied mixed chorus and soprano solo. *Legenda z dymu bramborové nati* (The Legend of the Smoke from Potato Fires), recounts the harvest-time legend of how the Virgin Mary steps down from a stained glass window to work in the fields as a peasant; the soloists and chorus are accompanied by an ensemble of piano, recorder, clarinet, horn and accordion, which creates a sound rather like a band of village folk musicians. *Mikeš z hor* (Mikeš of the Mountains), for the same ensemble as the first cantata, tells how a shepherd boy settles his flock on a mountain so that the frost mistakes their white coats for snow and moves elsewhere, leaving them to enjoy a mild winter.

> ◉ **Chamber Cantatas**: Kühn Mixed Chorus and soloists; Kühn (Supraphon 11 0767-2).

The cantatas are amongst Martinů's most profound celebrations of his homeland, and three of them are on this disc (*The Romance of the Dandelions* is coupled with the Špalíček CD listed below). *The Opening of the Wells* is sung with unsentimental freshness and is given a spirited instrumental accompaniment, though it's a little spoiled by an over-intrusive narrator – thankfully, he's absent from the other two cantatas. The recording of all three is crystal clear.

BALLETS

Martinů wrote a series of ballets in Paris, several of which were experiments involving film, puppets, projections and impossible sets. Typical of this period is *Vzpoura* (Revolt), a ballet-fantasy in which bedlam breaks out among the musicians and sounds: black notes fight against white notes, high notes against low ones; the gramophone mutinies against ragtime and jazz; critics commit collective suicide and Stravinsky emigrates to a desert island. From the chaos a Moravian girl in national costume emerges singing a folksong, and a lyrical order is restored. *Špalíček*, written in the early 1930s, was Martinů's first large-scale work drawing primarily on Czech folk material – he called it a ballet of "popular plays, customs and fairy-tales". It's a piece that also bears the influence of Stravinsky's *Les Noces*, in that the texts sung by the soloists and chorus are integral to the score.

⦿ **Vzpoura; Échec au roi**: Prague Symphony Orchestra; Bělohlávek (Supraphon 11 1415-2).
⦿ **Špalíček; Romance z pampelišek**: Brno Philharmonic Orchestra; Jílek (Supraphon 110752-2; 2 CDs).
⦿ **La Revue de Cuisine; Nonet; Trio in F**: Dartington Ensemble (Hyperion CDA66084).

The Bělohlávek CD is the premiere recording of *Vzpoura* and the chess ballet *Échec au Roi*, and is the disc that best conjures up the cartoon-like exuberance of Martinů's music in the 1920s. The colourful and fresh recording of *Špalíček* also includes *Romance z pampelišek*, one of the four cantatas to verses by Miroslav Bureš composed in the 1950s (see above).

The last of these CDs is another splendid introduction to Martinů's music. *La Revue de Cuisine*, written in 1927, is a witty and irreverent piece for a sextet of instruments, and includes a tango and a couple of charlestons. It's coupled with two fine specimens of Martinů's wealth of chamber music, the best of which has a fluency and sparkle unmatched in his larger-scale pieces. If the *Nonet* and *Trio in F* whet your appetite for the more carefree side of Martinů, pick up the Dartington Ensemble's second collection (Hyperion CDA66133), on which they play four instrumental works described by Martinů as madrigals – including one written for physicist and amateur violinist Albert Einstein.

SYMPHONIES AND CONCERTOS

Martinů's orchestral sound is very recognizeable, with its driving momentum tempered by Czech lyricism, and the texture of the orchestra almost always given extra bite by a piano part. The remarkably varied six symphonies, all of which were written in America, are the most impressive of his orchestral pieces. *Symphony No. 1*, written in only fifteen weeks, is very lyrical and epic in

scale; *No. 2* is pastoral and distinctly Czech sounding; *No. 3* has an undertow of tragedy, reflecting its creation in wartime; *No. 4* is closer in spirit to the first symphony, and is reminiscent of Dvořak; *No. 5*, written at the end of the war, is more gentle and understated; and *No. 6*, subtitled "Fantaisies Symphoniques", is full of changing moods and intriguing textures, and includes a quotation from his fantasy opera *Julietta*.

Many of Martinů's huge number of concertos and *concertante* works settle into a note-spinning neo-Baroque groove which can be long-winded and tedious, but his *Double Concerto* – for two string orchestras, piano and timpani – is one of the masterpieces of twentieth-century music. Written in 1938 for Paul Sacher and his Basle Chamber Orchestra (who commissioned many other works by such greats as Bartók and Stravinsky), this taut and powerful work was composed as a direct response to the imminent Nazi invasion of Czechoslovakia, and marks a turning point in his life. After 1938 Martinů was never to see his family or homeland again.

⦿ **Symphonies 1–6**: Bamberg Symphony Orchestra; Järvi (BIS CD 362, 363 & 402).
⦿ **Symphony no. 4; Polní Mše; Památník Lidicím**: Czech Philharmonic Orchestra; Bělohlávek (Chandos CHAN 9138).
⦿ **Double Concerto; Sinfonietta giocosa; Rhapsody-Concerto for viola and orchestra**: Brno Philharmonic Orchestra; Mackerras (Conifer CDCF 210).
⦿ **Double Concerto; Concerto for string quartet and orchestra; Sinfonia concertante**: City of London Sinfonia; Hickox (Virgin VC 791099-2).

Several versions of Martinů's symphonies are now available, but Neeme Järvi's have the edge: the playing is both lyrical and dynamic, with a splendid sinewy quality in the syncopated rhythmic passages, and the recordings are very clear with a great dynamic range. If you want to sample just one disc from the series of three, begin with the CD of symphonies 3 and 4, as the two works are very contrasted and the fourth is one of Martinů's most immediately appealing works. Alternatively you could go for the Chandos CD of the fourth symphony, a fine performance coupled with two important wartime works: *Polní Mše* (Field Mass) sets poetic texts alongside liturgical verses for men's voices and a military band, while *Památník Lidicím* (Memorial to Lidice) is an impassioned response to the Nazi massacre and destruction of the village of Lidice in 1942.

The *Double Concerto* is Martinů's most widely recorded work, but Conifer's disc heads the field, not least because of the other delightful works on the CD – the neo-Baroque

Sinfonietta giocosa and the unashamedly romantic *Rhapsody-Concerto*. This is the place to start your Martinů collection. The rival Virgin CD of the *Double Concerto* is also very fine, and has the advantage of being slightly easier to find; it's coupled with the rather dry *Concerto for string quartet and orchestra* and the more appealing *Sinfonia concertante*, in which the array of oboe, bassoon, violin, cello and orchestra create some interesting textures.

PIETRO MASCAGNI
(1863–1945)

Verismo opera, which flared onto the musical landscape of Italy during the last ten years of the nineteenth century, foreshadowed the world of soap opera. In verismo operas emotions are extreme, characters are one-dimensional, the tension is high, the pace is fast, and the attention-span is short – the two most successful verismo operas, Mascagni's *Cavalleria rusticana* and Leoncavallo's *I Pagliacci* (see p.195), last only an hour.

Pietro Mascagni, the father of "realistic" opera, shot to prominence on May 17, 1890, with the Rome premiere of *Cavalleria rusticana*, or "Rustic Chivalry". Things might have turned out very differently. Reading, by chance, of a competition for one-act operas, he prepared to send in the fourth act of his full-length opera *Ratcliff* but, unknown to him, his wife had already submitted the recently completed *Cavalleria* on his behalf. It was one of three winners, and received its first performance in front of a half-empy but wildly enthusiastic house.

The rapid international vogue for *Cavalleria* was unprecedented and its popularity remains undimmed – every opera house plays it once every few years, invariably on a double bill with *I Pagliacci* (*Cav & Pag*, as it's known in the trade). However, unlike Leoncavallo, Mascagni found success beyond his name-maker, and went on to produce some extremely fine music, most notably the three act opera *L'amico Fritz*. He was also a highly respected conductor and assumed some of Toscanini's duties at La Scala when the maestro resigned in protest over the fascist regime. Mascagni's acceptance of the post led to his becoming the official composer of the government, which in turn led to a sharp decline in his reputation. Nowadays he's back in the ranks of the one-hit wonders.

CAVALLERIA RUSTICANA

Set in Sicily, the plot of *Cavalleria rusticana* revolves around the relationship between Santuzza and Turiddu. Before the action starts, the latter has seduced the former, then deserted her for Lola, a former lover, now the wife of Alfio. In revenge, Santuzza reveals all to Alfio, who takes it rather badly and ends up killing Turiddu in a duel behind the church (to heighten the pathos, this all takes place on Easter Sunday). It's a cheap and cynical tale, similar to that of *I Pagliacci*, but *Cavalleria rusticana* is musically the superior – melodically, it stands up to comparison with the bulk of Puccini. The Intermezzo has been used time and time again in advertising campaigns, but the best part of the opera is the final fifteen minutes, during which Turridu, the tenor lead, sings his marvellous testament to the wonders of wine *Viva il vino* and his concluding lament *Mama, quel vino e generoso* – the latter is an extraordinary, highly moving bit of music. Alfio's involvement is one part bluster and one part ballast, but Santuzza gets some excellent writing, not least *Voi lo sapete*, in which she sings of her betrayal.

⊙ Arragal, Evstatieva; Bratislava Radio Symphony Orchestra; Slovak Philharmonic Chorus; Rahbari (Naxos 8 660022).

Though you can buy versions with flashier singing and finer sound quality, Naxos's account with the splendid Giacomo Arragal as Turridu and Stefka Evstatieva as Santuzza wins hands down on purely musical terms. Rahbari's conducting has a few moments of indiscipline, but for the most part he's worthily solid and he avoids the self-consciousness and senti-mentality so common amongst his better-known colleagues. The Slovak Philharmonic's playing does not stand comparison with that of Karajan's Berlin Philharmonic on DG, but the performance is blessed with an integrity and a sense of occasion sorely missing from that full-price "bench-mark".

JULES MASSENET
(1842–1912)

With the advent of Wagner, French composers such as d'Indy, Chausson and Chabrier reacted by creating their own vast Gothic operas, which usually amounted to little more than Teutonic heroics in French fancy dress. Jules Massenet, nineteenth-century France's finest prolific composer of opera, offered an alternative by re-defining the lyrical French tradition – the tradition of Gounod (see p.151) – in the light of Wagner's advances in dramatic structure. Massenet was uninterested in profundity of any sort, but few composers have ever created such attractive surfaces.

After studies with Ambroise Thomas, Massenet won the Prix de Rome in 1863, then spent three years in Italy, where he visited Liszt, and got married. He had his first opera performed in 1867 and, after interruptions from the Franco-Prussian war, achieved his first major success in 1872 with *César de Bazan*. This was followed a few months later by the yet more popular *Marie-Magdeleine*, a work of "discreet and pseudo-religious eroticism", to use d'Indy's words. This eroticism, together with an affection for orientalism, coloured most of Massenet's subsequent work, and he was openly cynical about pandering to the French taste for religiose themes, declaring "I don't believe in all that creeping Jesus stuff, but the public likes it and we must always agree with the public".

In 1881, after a string of finely constructed oratorios, he produced *Herodiade*, a work whose free and semi-declamatory melodies can be seen as anticipating Debussy's *Pelléas* (see p.105). His next success, *Manon* (1884), used leitmotifs and weightier brass, a development that led to the composer's being labelled "Mademoiselle Wagner", a jibe produced partly by envy, for by now Massenet was the country's most popular opera composer. After *Manon*, Massenet produced three notable failures – *Le Cid*, *Le Mage* and *Esclarmonde* – but in 1892 he came up with his masterpiece, *Werther*. Taking his inspiration from Wagner's *Parsifal* and Goethe's *Sorrows of Young Werther*, Massenet here achieved a genuinely moving work which contrasts the Germanic sobriety of Charlotte, Werther's love, with the Gallic charm of Sophie – and in the characater of Werther himself he created his finest tenor role.

For a while Massenet produced verismo operas (after all, the French opera *Carmen* was the progenitor of verismo), but he finally settled back into his natural style of light, lyrical and saccharine music. His younger contemporaries were, however, unimpressed by his crowd-pleasing rhetoric. Indeed, it was Debussy's hatred of Massenet and his easily won success that drove him to complete *Pelléas et Melisande*, a work which set the seal on Massenet's fall from grace. After *Sapho* (1897) only *Don Quichotte*, produced in 1910, brought Massenet any reminder of past glories, and he died bitter at the direction in which, in Debussy's hands, French music was now heading.

WERTHER

Like Puccini, Massenet was obsessed with melody. Tender, sweetly sensuous, never violent or uncomfortably dramatic, his melodies determine the texture of the music as a whole, and there instances in which Massenet produced strings of tunes that have little or nothing to do with what's happening on stage. With *Werther*, though, he achieved a perfect balance between drama, characterization and beauty of sound.

Based upon Goethe's novel, the tragedy principally concerns the affections of Werther, Charlotte and Albert. The poet Werther loves Charlotte, who loves Werther but is engaged to marry Albert. Werther leaves, returning to find Charlotte married. She begs him to leave her alone but upon finding that her husband has loaned him his pistols, she rushes through a blizzard to find him dead. As you might imagine, the opera is remarkable for the pathos of much of the music, and it boasts moments of thrilling atmosphere. It also shows Massenet's fascination with the psychology of women, again like Puccini, and if Charlotte lacks the insight of some of Puccini's heroines, Massenet nonetheless gives her a highly convincing and sympathetic gravity. The first act which contains the majority of *Werther*'s finest writing, but the Act Three reconciliation scene is perhaps the most impressive demonstration of Massenet's understanding of the human voice, while the finely constructed development towards the tragedy of Werther's death is unforgettable.

🔘 Bergonzi, Casoni, Trimarchi, Ravaglia, Pezzetti; San Carlo Opera Orchestra & Chorus; De Fabritiis (Nuova Era 2340/1; 2 CDs).
🌓 Gedda, de los Angeles, Soyer, Mesple; French Radio Maitraise; Paris Orchestra; Prêtre (EMI CMS7 63973-2; 2 CDs).

Carlo Bergonzi's live 1969 performance of the title role (in Italian) is a masterpiece of vocal characterization – indeed, it's one of the greatest of all his interpretations. The sound is fine for its time and he is ably supported by Biancamaria Casoni as Charlotte; De Fabritiis is a master of Massenet's orchestration. Prêtre is less engaging on EMI's recording with Gedda and de los Angeles, but the two principal singers are magnificent – and it's in the original French.

MANON

The source for Massenet's *Manon* is the same as that to which Puccini turned for his third opera – *Manon Lescaut*, by Abbé Prevost. As with *Werther*, the tale offers plenty of opportunities for lavish emotionalism – humble

Manon elopes with the young nobleman Des Grieux, abandons him, returns to him after he has joined the priesthood in despair, is accused of prostitution and finally dies in a prison cell, in the arms of her lover. Though Massenet doesn't go for the extreme passions that Puccini wrung out of his source, his most affecting music is to be found in the five acts of this melodious tragedy – not least in the seminary scene, where Manon begs Des Grieux to leave the priesthood, and in Manon's death scene. Less dramatic but more emotional than *Werther*, this is a beautifully written opera, and of all his heroines, Manon is the most alive.

🌓 de los Angeles, Legay, Dens, Borthayre; Paris Opéra Comique Chorus & Orchestra; Monteux, EMI [2] CMS 7 63549-2).

There is only one recording of Manon currently available, and it's the finest ever made, with Victoria de los Angeles in glowing voice. It is a role for which she is understandably famous and her underlining of the character's weaknesses is a joy. The supporting cast is also highly efficient but Pierre Monteux is the real co-star. He was already thirty-seven when Massenet died and his conducting gives a good idea as to how Massenet's music was performed in its day. Excellent sound for its time.

Victoria de los Angeles – the finest Manon on record

NICHOLAS MAW

(1935–)

Like his contemporaries Peter Maxwell Davies (see p.226) and Harrison Birtwistle (see p.54), Nicholas Maw has absorbed the legacy of serialism, yet his strongest affinities are with the luxuriant opulence of the late Romantic movement. The reconciliation of these influences has taken years to achieve, but has produced at least one work of major status.

Maw studied at the Royal Academy of Music in the mid-1950s, and in 1958 produced his first signicant piece, *Nocturne*. Written under the tutelage of the neo-classicist Lennox Berkeley, and owing much to Bartók, *Nocturne* won him a French government scholarship which allowed him to study in Paris with two of the most eminent teachers of his day, Max Deutsch (a pupil of Schoenberg) and Nadia Boulanger. A period of creative sterility followed, in which Maw eked out a living as a writer and teacher. His breakthrough came with the *Scenes and Arias* of 1962, a setting of twelfth-century texts for three sopranos and orchestra, in which the hedonism of Richard Strauss – and something of the attack of the Second Viennese School – found fresh chromatic richness. Developing this new idiom took the next eight years, an evolutionary process which Maw referred to as "my second apprenticeship". His series of operas from the mid- and late-1960s – *One Man Show*, *The Voice of Love* and *The Rising of the Moon* – are full of lyrical music, as deeply argued as before, yet more clear-cut in its effects and now revealing the influence of the young Alban Berg alongside Strauss, Britten, Wolf and Brahms. Yet Maw's operas enjoyed limited success, which some have attributed to the crassness of some of the librettos – they include, for example, the sexual initiation rites of British soldiers in nineteenth-century Ireland.

In the 1970s Maw further developed his finesse in orchestration, blending colours and timbres in a way that gave clarity to music in which melodic motifs were elaborated with increasing drama, and at ever greater length. This is the period to which *Odyssey* belongs.

ODYSSEY

Written between 1973 and 1979, then revised until 1985, *Odyssey* is the summation of Maw's expressive progress over the years, and is a journey in itself. It was composed in its playing order, and during its development Maw's style became less ambiguous, his debt to tonal music more blatant. Lasting ninety minutes, the whole gigantic structure is spun out of a 44-bar melody and owes something to Bruckner's sense of epic symphonic form. It begins with an Introduction which the composer has summarized as "a gigantic upbeat groping towards articulation", and moves through four contrasting movements before reaching an Epilogue which closes the music serenely.

⊙ City of Birmingham Symphony Orchestra; Rattle (EMI CDS 7 54277 2; 2 CDs).

Simon Rattle, the conductor in this premiere recording, rates Maw as the spiritual heir to William Walton and comments, "I am convinced that *Odyssey* is a masterpiece, a whole world of ideas miraculously welded together: new, alert and alive." Rattle's interpretation, transparent and unforced, makes a case for *Odyssey* as a solid contribution to the English lyric tradition.

PETER MAXWELL DAVIES
(1934–)

With the English pastoral tradition flogged almost to death, and with serialism a battle won long ago, Peter Maxwell Davies has found a fresh source of inspiration in quotation from past ages and styles – but quotation lifted beyond pastiche onto an entirely individual level. His preoccupations are not merely stylistic. He presents himself as a composer "torn by the fundamental question of good and evil", writing in the face of a modern world which seems to look upon past atrocities and pronounce "They couldn't happen now."

Born in Manchester, he studied at the Royal Northern College of Music with Harrison Birtwistle, John Ogdon and Alexander Goehr, and soon became identified with the "Manchester Group" and its commitment to the serialist avant-garde. At the same time he developed an affection for medieval music – not just for its rhythmic devices but also for its notions of damnation. The stamp of medievalism would be audible in Maxwell Davies's work for years to come.

In 1957 Maxwell Davies won a scholarship to study composition in Rome, and two years later his orchestral piece *Prolations* won the Olivetti Prize. He returned to England and took up the post of music director at Cirencester grammar school, at first just to make ends meet. The experience proved invigorating, and made his music clearer and simpler. His pleasure in writing for young people, evident in the 1960 carol sonatas *O Magnum Mysterium*, has remained with him.

Maxwell Davies's fascination with the life and music of John Taverner (see p.372) gave rise to two orchestral fantasias, the opera *Taverner* (1962–70) and other works developed from plainsong fragments. His methods were similar to those used in "parody" Masses in the fifteenth and sixteenth centuries, where the material of one composition is used to create another, but they also allowed parody in our modern sense – parody as critique. Thus *St Thomas Wake* is a "foxtrot for orchestra" based on a pavan by John Bull.

In 1968 – after periods at Princeton and at Adelaide University – Maxwell Davies returned to Britain and founded, with Harrison Birtwistle, the Pierrot Players, later renamed the Fires of London. Before long Maxwell Davies was writing most of his music for them: for instance, *Eight Songs for a Mad King* (1969), one of several music-theatre spectacles exploring extremes of delusion and hysteria. In chamber pieces composed for the group Maxwell Davies refined his elaborations of the rhythmic involutions of medieval scores, while the sonorities of certain instruments began to spark a new sharpness and clarity of ideas. The astringent tones of out-of-tune instruments connected with Maxwell Davies's fascination for "music of the absurd".

In 1971 he moved to Orkney. The sounds, landscapes, literature and history of the place have inspired many works since, including the first and second symphonies (1976 & 1980). His religious thought has become more mystical than it used to be, as exemplified by his *Hymn to St Magnus*, based on a twelfth-century psalm to the Orcadian saint. Crucial too has been the work of local writer George Mackay Brown, whose texts Maxwell Davies used for *St Magnus* (who now finds himself transposed to a concentration camp), and *Black Pentecost*.

These more recent works are the most immediately appealing, demonstrating his success in creating a harmonic language within a non-tonal idiom. Craggy and uncompromised, sometimes with a gruelling obsession for working through the formal implications of the music (first hearing can be exhausting work), Maxwell Davies is one of Europe's most challenging and theatrical composers.

WORLDES BLIS

Worldes Blis (1969) took three years to create, and painstaking craft is evident in every section of this granitic work. In the composer's own words, *Worldes Blis* develops "slowly in extremely articulated time-spans . . with a minimal presentation of the material in such a way as to make the structural bones as clear as possible." The title is taken from a thirteenth-century monody ("worldes blis lasts no time at all"), and the piece flows from isolated musical cells towards the theme of this source material through ever-changing melodic, rhythmic and harmonic contours, moving from serenity though tension to an explosive climax. It's as if traditional symphonic development, which sets out with the exposition of the subject, has here been thrown into reverse.

⊙ Manchester Cathedral Choir; Royal Philharmonic Orchestra, BBC Philharmonic Orchestra; Maxwell Davies (Collins 13902; with *The Turn of the Tide*).

Maxwell Davies paces this performance immaculately, maintaining the flow through each successive part. Its coupling, *The Turn of the Tide* (1992), depicts the creation of life on earth and the threat humanity poses to the rest of nature; intended to be played by professionals, with interludes in which schoolchildren can improvise, it shows Maxwell Davies at his most accessible.

BLACK PENTECOST

Written in 1979, *Black Pentecost* is a four-movement, polemical symphony with voices. Its title is taken from George Mackay Brown's poem *Dark Angels* ("Now, cold angels, keep the valley from the bedlam and cinders of a Black Pentecost") and the text is from his novel *Greenvoe*, set on the imaginary island of Hellya as it is ripped to bits by commercial exploitation. What set Maxwell Davies work-ing was the threat of uranium mining in Orkney. "But it could be anything," he has said. "The pollution is there, and the kicking of people out of their houses is there, and the destruction of a way of life is there. The LSO commissioned it," he added, "but when they found out what it was, they didn't want to touch it."

The piece plays out a dramatic encounter between a baritone, in the role of Operation Black Star, and a mezzo-soprano who takes on the personae of both narrator and of Bella Budge, one of Black Star's innocent victims. An orchestral introduction, which hovers between menace and meditative stasis, sets the scene before the singers explore the moral consequences of "the catastrophe of nations" as "piecemeal a village died, shrivelled slowly with the radiance of Black Star." Relentlessly slow-paced, with episodes of savage parody and near-chaos, vocal interludes that vacillate between lament and hysteria, cavernous resonances and abrasive outbursts, *Black Pentecost* is an arduous masterpiece, comparable in its fatalism and ambition to Mahler's *Das Lied von der Erde*.

⊙ Jones, Wilson-Johnson; BBC Philharmonic Orchestra; Maxwell Davies (Collins 13662); with *Stone Litany*).

The composer's insight is invaluable in teasing out the densely unfolding musical rhetoric of *Black Pentecost*, and the performance is excellently recorded. The coupling, *Stone Litany* (1973) again features a haunted orchestral landscape which is shattered by vocal interpolation, here symbolizing the birth of speech. Della Jones handles with aplomb the pyrotechnics which Maxwell Davies imposes on the sparse Old Norse text.

━━━━━━━━━━━━ ♭♪ ━━━━━━━━━━━━

FELIX MENDELSSOHN

(1809–1847)

The conductor Hans von Bülow said of Mendelssohn that he began as a genius and ended as a talent, and Mendelssohn was indeed a terrifyingly gifted child. He painted with skill, wrote fine poetry, was an excellent athlete, spoke several languages, played many instruments and in 1825, aged only sixteen, he composed one of the greatest pieces of chamber music – his *Octet for strings*. With this work he set himself impossible standards, and though he went on to produce much excellent music, he never again came so close to perfection.

He was born into a wealthy Jewish-German family, and his talents were encouraged by his mother and elder sister, Fanny, who was

MARY EVANS PICTURE LIBRARY

almost as gifted a pianist as her brother. He made his concert debut in 1818 and had some of his music performed the following year. In 1821, aged twelve, he was taken to meet the seventy-two-year-old Goethe in Weimar, and the two became strong friends. In 1826, a year after the composition of the *Octet*, he wrote his overture to *A Midsummer Night's Dream*, a work that established his name internationally, yet remarkably it was not until he had completed three years' study at Berlin University that he finally decided upon a career in music. In March 1829 he gave the first performance of Bach's *St Matthew Passion* since the composer's death in 1750, and he was to be one of the principle influences behind the European revival of Bach's music. Near the end of that year he made his first visit to England where, apart from conducting concerts of his own work, he played the piano in the first English performance of Beethoven's *Emperor Concerto*. The English loved him and for many years he was the country's most popular foreigner.

After touring Scotland (where he met Sir Walter Scott) he returned to mainland Europe, to spend two years touring Germany, Austria and Italy. Further visits to England in

1832 and 1833 cemented his position within that country's musical life and he became a frequent guest artist with the Philharmonic Society Orchestra. In 1835 he became conductor of the Leipzig Gewandhaus Orchestra, and in 1837 he married. The next few years saw him produce a wide range of superb music, including his *Violin Concerto*. In 1843 he established a new conservatory of music in Leipzig, where he was assisted by Robert Schumann, and in 1847 he made his tenth and last visit to England, when he became friends with Queen Victoria and Prince Albert, teaching the latter at the piano. In May of that year his beloved sister Fanny died and the shock of this loss, together with the pressure of severe overwork, led to his own death six months later.

It had been a brilliant career and yet also something of an anticlimax. Mendelssohn was described by von Bülow as the most complete master of musical form after Mozart, and this very mastery is perhaps the chief reason for his relapse into self-conscious *politesse* – the creation of pleasing, impeccably structured music came easily to him. His music is as bereft of struggle as was his life. Never did he lack money, praise or support, and not until the death of his sister did he experience genuine misery – and by then it was too late. No other great composer experienced such complete insulation from hardship, and there is little question that his cushioned existence impaired his creative development. His emotional range never really broadened, so is it surprising that his music remained consistent? One example tells the whole story – his *A Midsummer's Night Dream*. He wrote the overture in 1826 and, seventeen years later, added the incidental music. As if but seventeen days divided its composition from that of the overture, the additional music is identical in style, showing not the slightest evidence of creative evolution in its hugely enjoyable, supremely elegant and completely untroubling pages.

A MIDSUMMER NIGHT'S DREAM

Mendelssohn's most popular work is now the *Violin Concerto* but it hasn't always held that place in the public's affection – previously his best-loved piece was the overture to his *A Midsummer Night's Dream*, source of the famous *Wedding March*. Deeply impressed by Schlegel's translations of Shakespeare, Mendelssohn composed the overture when he was only seventeen, and it beautifully captures the elfin atmosphere of the original. The incidental music, composed in 1843, is rarely performed complete, which is a pity, for as Schuman rightly commented, it glows with "the bloom of youth". Innovatively constructed from motifs heard in the overture – thus, for example, the opening chords are used as the basis for the entry of Oberon and Titania in the finale – it's a wonderfully evocative series of musical tableaux.

> Mathis, Boese; Bavarian Radio Chorus & Orchestra; Kubelik (Deutsche Grammophon 415 840-2GGA).

Kubelik's performance is true to Mendelssohn's lightness of touch and deft use of colour, and he directs the music with unfailing charm. In this he is aided by the beautiful voices of soprano Edith Mathis and mezzo Ursula Boese, whose vocal combination has a real glow.

ELIJAH

Mendelssohn's extraordinary popularity in England was due mostly to his oratorios and other religious works, in which he satisfied the Victorians' craving for pious tunes and grand choruses. Of the pious tunes the finest is his beautiful hymn *Hear my Prayer*, which contains *O for the wings of a dove*. Of the more grandiose sacred compositions, the most rewarding is his oratorio *Elijah*, written in the summer of 1844, some eight years after Mendelssohn had first approached his librettist about a possible collaboration on a work celebrating the prophet. Dominated by the bass role of Elijah and the chorus, the oratorio is very dramatic in a civilized sort of way, combining vivid sound-pictures of oceans, earthquakes and fires with more urbane passages of orchestral music. As you'd expect from someone who spent so much time in England, Mendelssohn pays homage to Handel in his choral writing, and he also shows his proficiency in Bach-like counterpoint. *Elijah* is an engaging piece, but it is long and potentially demanding, so don't start here.

> Donath, Klein, van Nes, George, Miles; Leipzig Radio Choir; Israel Philharmonic Orchestra; Masur (Teldec 9031 73131; 2 CDs).

Kurt Masur is often a leaden conductor, which makes it strange that he should be tackling so much Mendelssohn as part of his Teldec contract. His direction here is a touch stolid in places, and he plays down the excitement wherever possible, but this set is lifted to another plane by the singing: Alastair Miles is particularly forceful voice in the title role, and Helen Donath gives a finely considered performance. The chorus is fine, as is the sound quality.

SYMPHONY NO. 4 – THE ITALIAN

Of Mendelssohn's five mature symphonies (he wrote a group of string symphonies as a child), the fourth, the *Italian*, is the one that shows the composer at his most winning. Written in Berlin in the winter of 1832, a few weeks after his return from Italy, the symphony's ebullient mood reflects the wealth of pleasures he found there, in the country's landscapes, art and people. Apart from the brilliant and lively Neapolitan tune that forms the basis to the last movement, there's nothing that's specifically Italian about the music – indeed, one of Mendelssohn's contemporaries insisted that the Andante was based upon a Czech pilgrim folk song, while the boisterous Scherzo that follows it was inspired by Goethe's poem, *Lilis Park*. The overall ambience, however, is one of Mediterranean spontaneity and expansiveness, and its life-affirming attitude is established right at the outset with the opening movement's skipping main theme, prelude to one of the composer's most delightful movements.

> Leipzig Gewandhaus; Masur (Teldec 2292-4346-2; with *Symphony No. 3*).

This is the best of Masur's Mendelssohn cycle to date, with an intoxicating sense of momentum which is much more effective than mere speed. What was once Mendelssohn's orchestra now produces a fairly ordinary sound but they play enthusiastically and are excellently recorded. It's coupled with a similarly good version of Mendelssohn's *Scottish Symphony*, which was partly inspired by the story of Mary, Queen of Scots, but is no more programmatic than is the Italian – indeed Schumann famously reviewed a performance of the *Scottish* and he was hearing the piece that Mendelssohn had labelled the Italian. He found it redolent of the "old melodies of beautiful Italy".

VIOLIN CONCERTO IN E MINOR

As a young boy Mendelssohn wrote two concertos for violin, both of them immensely accomplished works, but scarcely anticipating the breathtaking originality of his *Violin Concerto in E minor*, which he composed in 1844. One of the summits of his output, it is stuffed full of tunes, all of them instantly memorable. The passionate and forceful first movement is linked by a solo bassoon note to an Andante whose mood can perhaps best be described as rapturous melancholy (you may recognize the source of a Lloyd-Webber tune here); in the final movement, Mendelssohn's complete understanding of the instrument is realized in a superb display of virtuoso writing that demands as much of the orchestra as of the soloist. No concerto ends with such brilliant éclat.

> ◗ Heifetz; Boston Symphony Orchestra; Munch (RCA RD85933; with Tchaikovsky, *Violin Concerto*).

Heifetz's performance with Munch is a classic account that has never really been surpassed. It's a recording that shows signs of its age, but no-one can match Heifetz's sweet tone, which is what this music requires more than anything else. Most other versions make a meal of music's virtuosity; Heifetz is almost alone in making it sing effortlessly.

OCTET

No-one, not even Mozart, created anything as profound as the Mendelssohn *Octet* at so young an age. In its structure the *Octet* is purely conventional, but it possesses an intensity and dynamic thrust that none of the composer's later works recaptured. The wisp-like Scherzo is best known for its use as an orchestral showpiece but it is the final movement that marks the work out for greatness – its jubilant energy and tight fugal construction give it a power that is equalled by few other finales in chamber music, and the final three minutes are the most exciting thing Mendelssohn composed. A towering achievement, the *Octet* makes the best introduction to its composer.

> ◗ Academy of St Martin's Chamber Ensemble (Chandos 8790; with Raff, *Octet*).

The Academy Ensemble have recorded this extraordinary work more than once but their performance for Chandos, led

superbly by Ken Sillito, is the finest in every respect. The eight players employ tempi quick enough to maintain the tension but they do not rush the outer movements; conversely, they do not indulge the sentimentality of the central Adagio. The Scherzo is almost brushed off the strings, so delicate is the delivery, but the final movement is the performance's glory, leading towards a conclusion that is at once inevitable and revelatory.

STRING QUINTET NO. 2

Mendelssohn completed his second quintet in 1845, more than twenty years after his first essay in the genre and nearly twenty after the *Octet*, a work with which it has some similarities. As with the *Octet*, each of the instrumental parts is given almost equal weight, and any good performance will clearly reveal Mendelssohn's genius for counterpoint. The first movement Allegro is a perfect example of multi-thematic writing, showing his consummate ability to juggle more than four voices at once. Full of elegaic tunes, especially in the haunting Adagio, the *String Quintet No. 2* looks forward to the world of Brahms's mature chamber music, and is Mendelssohn's most rewarding chamber piece after the *Octet*.

> ◗ Laredo, Kavafian, Ohyama, Kashkashian, Robinson (CBS CD45883; with *String Quintet No.1*).

Recorded at the Malboro Festival, this group of young musicians gives a refreshing performance of Mendelssohn's late quintet. The recording is less than perfect and the aggressive tone occasionally frustrates the music's lyricism, but this hardly matters in the face of such joyful commitment. Especially fine is the cello playing in the Adagio, an extremely difficult part which is carried off with seemingly no effort at all.

SONGS WITHOUT WORDS

Mendelssohn wrote three large-scale piano sonatas, a fantasia and a major set of variations, but his reputation as a composer for the piano is dominated by the *Lieder ohne Worte – Songs without Words*. Composed from 1830 onwards, these forty-eight miniatures were published in six cycles of six during his lifetime, with two other sets issued posthumously. Combining surface virtuosity with a lyrical sense of line, they are exquisitely constructed and intimate little pieces, but some of them have proved too tuneful for their own good: numbers such as the *Bee's Wedding, Andante and Rondo Capriccioso, Funeral March* and *Spring Song* have been repeatedly quarried by jingle-writers and other hacks.

◗ Barenboim (Deutsche Grammophon 423 931-2GGA2; 2 CDs).

Barenboim's account of the complete set is suitably light and unfussed, with none of the didactic ponderousness that some-times creeps into his playing. He gives relaxed and engaging performances, which are ideally captured on a well engineered recording. Bear in mind that the *Songs without Words* were not intended to be heard in a continuous stream – make judicious use of the scanning button, otherwise this will just become background music.

OLIVIER MESSIAEN

(1908–1992)

The greatest twentieth-century French composer after Debussy, Olivier Messiaen was an intriguing mixture of the ascetic and hedonistic. On the one hand he was a devout Catholic who found inspiration in medieval chant, wrote a vast opera on the life of Saint Francis of Assisi, and had the Trinité church in Paris as his postal address. Yet his music is also an ecstatic cele-bration of earthly life, deriving much of its material from the natural world – when Messiaen went on a pilgrimage to the Holy Land in the last decade of his life, he spent the time between prayer transposing the songs of the local birds. The inventor of a thrillingly sensuous music of bright acoustic colours and resonant fades, he single-handedly created a vocabulary that was eagerly seized on by Xenakis, Boulez and most importantly Stockhausen, who applied Messiaen's detailed work on note durations, attack and intensities to electronic music. Furthermore, Minimalists such as Steve Reich and Philip Glass owe their interest in non-Western musics to Messiaen's wide-ranging precedent.

Born in Avignon, Messiaen was a self-taught musician, and he was composing by the age of seven. After World War I he attended the Paris Conservatoire, where his brilliant piano playing won all available prizes, while he began privately studying Eastern musical scales and rhythms. His first major composition, *Preludes* (1929), owed much to Debussy but shimmered with the exotic sound of what he termed his "modes of limited transposition", special scales which

HULTON DEUTSCH

lent his music a strange harmonic richness. It was during this period that he was appointed organist at the church of La Trinité, where he was to play for over five decades.

From 1936 to 1940 he was professor of music at the École Normale in Paris, where he demonstrated his fierce nationalism by found-ing La Jeune France, a group devoted to the propagation of a French music aesthetic to counter the influence of the Germanic tradi-tion. The outbreak of war saw Messiaen conscripted as a medical auxilliary but he was then interned by the Germans in Stalag VIIIA at Görlitz. Finding himself in the company of three other French musicians, a clarinettist, a violinist and cellist, Messiaen strove to overcome the hunger, squalor and bitter cold by writing an eight-part quartet to "bring the listener closer to eternity in space, to infinity." Based on the Book of Revelation, it was titled *Quatuor pour la fin du temps* (Quartet for the end of time), was premiered with a banged-up piano and a broken cello in front of 5000 prisoners on January 15, 1941, and was to prove one of the seminal works of the twentieth century.

At the war's close he was made professor at the Paris Conservatoire, a post he held until 1978 and which was to provide a platform for the dissemination of his immensely influential ideas. Also in 1945, entranced by the pianist Yvonne Loriod, Messiaen wrote *Harawi*, a song cycle full of bird song, Peruvian lore and echoes of the Tristan myth. He subsequently visited the USA, where he conceived the monumental *Turangalîla-symphonie* (1948), an epic celebration of America's vistas and of his passion for Loriod. Featuring the unique tones of the ondes martenot (an early electro-acoustic instrument with a distinctive quivering sound), and shot through with the bell-like sounds of the Javanese gamelan, it was an instant classic.

From 1953 he committed himself wholly to notating the sounds of birds, roaming rural France with pen and paper in hand to transpose every song. The project bore fruit with the massive piano piece *Catalogue d'oiseaux* (1956–58), in which Messiaen utilized Greek and Indian rhythms to convey the cries of the alpine chough, tawny owl and numerous other species. His love of nature reached overflow with *Chronochromie* (1960) – meaning "the colour of time", it was a ten-part homage to the Alps, full of luminous percussion and shifting dense string parts. In 1962 Messiaen finally married Loriod, his first wife – the violinist Claire Delbos – having died in 1959 after a long illness.

A visit to Japan left an Eastern imprint on *Et Expecto Resurrectionem Mortuorum* (1964), written for woodwind and percussion, and intended for "vast spaces, churches, cathedrals and the open air of the mountainside." Returning to America in the early 1970s, he was amazed by the landscapes of Utah, which resulted in the intoxicating *Des canyons aux étoiles* (1971–74) for piano and orchestra, a ninety-minute merging of natural sounds, Christian contemplation and the grander themes of American symphonic music. In a search for a "music that touches everything and at the same time touches God", Messiaen then spent nearly a decade on the most ambitious of all his works, *Saint François d'Assise* (1975–83), a four-hour opera which assailed audiences with blocks of almost static sound. The culminating statement of his religious dedication was the *Livre du Saint-Sacrement* (1984), a brilliantly innovative organ cycle in eighteen movements, incorporating scenes from the Gospels and the liturgy of the Eucharist.

If you just want to sample Messiaen's music before committing yourself to an entire piece, get hold of *To The Edge of Dream* (Sony SMK 53473), which features two movements from *Turangalîla* as well as the vaporous "Song of the Star" section of *Des canyons aux étoiles*. It's an excellent sampler, brilliantly marshalled by Esa-Pekka Salonen, and should whet your appetite for more ambitious listening.

QUATUOR POUR LA FIN DU TEMPS

The symmetry and quiet beauty of Messiaen's great quartet belies the terrible circumstances under which it was created – this 45-minute free-flowing masterpiece is one of the century's supreme examples of transcendant art. The score is prefaced by a quotation from the Revelation of Saint John, in which the angel of the apocalypse shouts "There shall be time no longer", yet the music is hauntingly beautiful, its labyrinthine sounds replete with the shimmering harmonies and archaic tones that Messiaen codified in his *Techniques of My Musical Language*, published in 1944. The piano, "enveloped in pedal", insistently keeps time through most of the piece, while the clarinet – especially in the solo *L'abîme des oiseaux* (Abyss of the Birds) – follows a path like a bird's song. It's a work of delightful contrasts too, as when a surprisingly light, dancy interlude gives way to the seductive slow cello phrases of *Louange à l'éternité de Jésus* (Praise to the Eternity of Jesus). This fervently devotional work reaches its climax with the last movement's *Louange à l'immortalité de Jésus*, an extensive violin meditation in which the instrument is slowly extended to its highest register, expressing Messiaen's spirituality at its most direct.

⊙ Chamber Music Northwest (Delos CD 3043; with Bartók, *Contrasts*).

This is a superlative recording of a joyful performance, with especially fine interplay between piano and violin. Interesting sleevenotes by pianist Williams Doppmann further enhances its attraction.

TURANGALÎLA-SYMPHONIE

The title of the *Turangalîla-symphonie*, derived from Sanskrit, can be translated as the "speed of life", and the sound explosions of this colossal work certainly live up to the name. Messiaen imparts a certain amount of subtlety to the loud sonorities by use of glockenspiel, vibraphone and above all the ondes martenot, an instrument whose ethereal tones are perhaps the most distinctive feature of *Turangalîla*. It creates a kind of Hollywood horror effect in the third movement, but it's in the pivotal sixth movement – the exquisite slow *Jardin de sommeil d'amour* (Garden of Sleeping Love) – that the metallic timbre and delicate harmonies of the instrument come into their own. Set against rhythmic piano and floating strings, the ondes martenot make

parts of *Turangalîla* sound Ambient and Minimalist, years before the forms had been invented.

⊙ Salonen; Philharmonia Orchestra; Crossley; Murail (Sony M2K 42271; 2 CDs; with Lutosławski, *Symphony No. 3 & Éspaces du Sommeil*).

Finnish conductor Esa-Pekka Salonen and the Philharmonia are in sprightly form on this recording, giving Messiaen's sprawling magnum opus the whirlwind treatment. This is a performance that stresses the angular, jazzy aspects of the symphony, where others have lingered over its more ingratiatingly sensual side.

LIVRE DU SAINT-SACREMENT

The sprawling *Livre du Saint-Sacrement* is the most extensive of Messiaen's explorations of the capabilities of the solo organ. Throughout its eighteen sections, which celebrate the transubstantiation of Christ during Holy Communion, Messiaen demonstrates a total control over the dynamics and harmonic possibilities of his favourite instrument. Though initially austere, *Livre du Saint-Sacrement* gradually transforms itself through the incorporation of birdsong, Indian melody and a host of other musical devices into a stunningly inventive display, where silences and lengthily sustained notes create a sound-world never previously envisaged for the organ.

⊙ Ericsson (Bis CD-491/492; 2 CDs).

This definitive recording is the sixth instalment in Hans Ericsson's cycle of Messiaen's complete organ works, and comes with exemplary notes by Anders Ekenberg on Messiaen's birdsong transcriptions, explaining how their elements are transformed in the organ music.

GIACOMO MEYERBEER
(1791–1864)

During the first half of the nineteenth century French opera was dominated by outstanding but decidedly non-French talent. Berlioz, in particular, was forthright in his condemnation of his country's "occupation", directing his frustrations at the composer who, he believed, was most respon-

sible for the neglect that Berlioz suffered. For him, Giacomo Meyerbeer's influence upon managers, artists, critics and public had put a stranglehold on the Paris Opéra, an institution he accused of being "madly in love with mediocrity". Posterity has tended to side with Berlioz, and the very qualities that ensured

Meyerbeer's success in his lifetime are those for which he is now condemned. The public demanded grand Romanticism and Meyerbeer gave it to them, in huge melodramas that required armies of musicians and extraordinary stagings – so extraordinary that eventually what the audience saw was more important than what they heard.

Born in Germany, of Jewish descent, Meyerbeer began as a piano virtuoso but, nursing an ambition to write opera, attempted a number of oratorio-like dramas, each of which proved as disastrous as the last. Salieri advised him to study in Italy, and within a few months of arriving he had composed six "Italian" operas and was being compared to Rossini. However, this change of direction did him no favours in Germany, and though Weber produced Meyerbeer's operas, he did so while complaining of his Italian "aberration".

The massive success of *Il crociato in Egitto* in Venice 1824 encouraged Meyerbeer to take the work to Paris, which he did the following year. The first night inspired the sort of lunatic fuss that would not be seen again until the appearance of Paganini six years later. With this single piece Meyerbeer was established as the dominating influence in French grand opera, a position strengthened by the success of *Robert le Diable*, *Les Hugenots* and a whole series of unfailingly popular operas.

His influence was not maintained entirely by his music. Meyerbeer possessed enormous inherited wealth, and many of France's critics, managers and musicians came to him for loans, a situation that assured him of praise. In one instance, however, Meyerbeer's largesse produced the opposite result. He helped Wagner produce his first two operas by lending him a regular monthly retainer, but after Meyerbeer heard of Wagner's resentment of this patronage he removed his support, provoking Wagner to turn upon Meyerbeer as the principle target of his outrageous anti-Semitism. And yet Wagner's early music attests to the influence of Meyerbeer, for Wagner's *Rienzi* is but a grand imitation of Meyerbeer's style, trumping his massive choruses, set pieces and Gothic settings. Meyerbeer's ideal of Grand Opera is equally evident as an influence on Verdi's *Don Carlos* and *Aida* as well as on countless other nine-teenth-century works. His operas might contain lots of empty eclecticism and bombast, but there remains much of real quality – most notably in *Les Hugenots*, in which his effulgent orchestration, incisive dramatic pacing and glorious vocal melody combine to produce one of the most entertaining operatic spectacles of its time.

LES HUGENOTS

Meyerbeer's extravagance keeps his work off the stage, and only three of his sixteen operas are presently available on CD – fortunately, *Les Hugenots* is one of them.

Les Hugenots is set during France's Wars of Religion, a subject that had never been set to music before. It's doubly unique in that Meyerbeer, when approaching this work, became the first major opera composer to carry out research into musical history as part of the composition process: to establish the appropriate historical tone, he spent a long time studying sixteenth-century manuscripts in the national library, and also incorporated traditional Jewish music into the score. The opera is probably his finest for voices and the roles of Raoul and Marguerite, in particular, are marvellous examples of Meyerbeer's melodic talents – Raoul's *Romance*, in Act One, is an extraordinary piece of tenor writing, as is the seventeen-minute tenor and soprano duet that ends the second act. Marguerite's role might be less exciting, but her Act Two aria *O beau pays de la Touraine* perfectly complies with Richard Strauss's dictum, "Give the aria its due by keeping the orchestra quiet".

⬤ Sutherland, Arroyo, Tourangeau, Vrenios; Ambrosian Opera Chorus; New Philharmonia; Bonynge (Decca 430 549-2DM4; 4 CDs).

Franco Corelli's astounding live performance from La Scala in 1962 is at the moment unavailable, which leaves Decca's recording, made seven years later, as the best option. It features a fine cast, including Arleen Auger, Martina Arroyo, a very young Kiri Te Kanawa and Joan Sutherland as Marguerite – the only vocal weakness is the tenor of Anastasios Vrenios, who is lacking in both weight and colour. Richard Bonynge offers fine and sensitive support, and if he does sometimes allow Sutherland too much room to manoeuvre, then the beauty of her singing more than compensates for the loss of direction. A well recorded and exciting performance, and a perfect introduction to Meyerbeer.

DARIUS MILHAUD

(1892–1974)

The key to Milhaud's musical personality lies in the very first words of his autobiography: "I am a Frenchman from Provence". He was born into a wealthy Jewish family in Aix-en-Provence, and his musical style is underpinned by his enduring affection for his native region. His unselfconscious ability to soak up folk materials can be traced to the earthy culture of Provence, while his characteristic polytonality (the simultaneous use of more than one key), was not a mere trendy musical excursion on Milhaud's part, but – at least in part – a further legacy of the Provençal landscape, as refracted by the painter Cézanne.

Showing prodigious musical talent, Milhaud started to learn the violin at the age of seven and made brilliant progress. Although he entered the Paris Conservatoire as a violin student he soon became convinced that composing was his true vocation, and he began to take lessons from such illustrious teachers as Paul Dukas and Charles-Marie Widor. In the late 1910s Milhaud became a central figure in Les Six and came under the influence of Jean Cocteau, which was something of a mixed blessing. While he was undoubtedly a dynamic character with an uncanny knack of turning modish ideas into genuine art, Cocteau was also a charmingly unscrupulous man who used people very much to his own ends. At the instigation of Cocteau, Milhaud found himself composing a self-conscious ballet called *Le Boeuf sur le toit* (1919), and overnight he became the talk of Paris – not as a serious musician but rather as a joker who had jumped on the bandwagon of high fashion. It was to take him a good few years to shake off the tag.

Milhaud was already highly receptive to the folk music of the Americas, having accompanied the poet and diplomat Paul Claudel to Brazil, an episode that was the inspiration for the nostalgic piano pieces titled *Saudades do Brazil*. Then in 1920 he visited London and got his first taste of jazz, which prompted him to set off to New York in order to explore this new musical language at first hand. After that he developed strong sympathies with Viennese expressionism, doing much to help the success in Paris of Schoenberg's *Pierrot Lunaire*. Throughout this decade and the 1930s Milhaud broadened his composing activities to include writing for the cinema (including the score for Renoir's *Madame Bovary*, 1933), for children's and amateur groups, and for the stage (most notably *L'annonce faite à Marie*, 1932, and *Le trompeur de Seville*, 1937).

Fleeing France in 1940, he took refuge in the USA, where he started teaching at Mills College in Oakland, California, a post he was to hold in tandem with the professorship of composition at the Paris Conservatoire after 1947. Much of the vitality went out of Milhaud's work now that he was distanced from his rural roots, but he found some compensation for his dislocation through his growing awareness of his Jewish heritage – the stimulus for fine pieces such as the ballet *Moisé* (1940) and the *Service sacré* (1947). Crippling rheumatoid arthritis finally forced him to quit Mills College, and he retired with his wife to Geneva in 1971. Tenacious and

GUUS ONG

optimistic as ever he went on composing into his eighty-first year – his last work was a cantata written for the 1973 Festival of Israel.

THE MUSIC

As a boy, Milhaud experienced the Provençal sky and landscape in a manner he later described in quasi-mystical terms – it was like "a thousand different simultaneous musics rushing towards me from all directions". These vivid sensuous experiences were clearly an important source of Milhaud's polytonality, a technique heard to stunning effect in pieces like the *Ouverture mediterranéenne*, the *Suite provençale* and the *Symphonie rurale*, in which he tried to capture the dazzle of his native land in the same way as Cézanne had depicted the harsh colours and the jagged contours of Provence.

Milhaud was almost as entranced by the melodic lines, rhythms and percussion play-

ing he heard in the jazz clubs of Harlem, and on his return to Paris he composed *La création du monde*, widely regarded as the best jazz-based piece by a European classical composer. This seminal ballet portrays the creation of the world as told in African legend, and is scored for a small ensemble including saxophone and piano, a line-up modelled on those Milhaud had seen in New York; it's a near-perfect synthesis of jazz elements with classic Western procedures.

◗ **La création du monde; Suite provençale**: Boston Symphony Orchestra; Munch (RCA GD 60685; with Honegger, *Symphonies Nos. 2 & 5*).

These performances of seminal Milhaud works by Charles Munch and the Boston SO were recorded in the 1960s and have come out of their transfer to CD sounding better than ever. Showcasing two contrasting sides of the composer's oeuvre, this is perfect for newcomers to Milhaud's music: the jazzy *La création* is played with verve and melancholic elegance, while the sun-soaked *Suite provençale* gets a performance that is as fresh as paint.

CLAUDIO MONTEVERDI
(1567–1643)

Monteverdi's career coincides with a period of profound change in European music. From the time of Josquin (see p.113), composers had become increasingly concerned with how best to communicate the meaning of the words that they set to music. By the end of the sixteenth century progressive composers were beginning to reject polyphony for a new form of music, called monody, in which the melody was confined to just one part – any additional parts provided a supportive role, filling in the harmony underneath the melody, usually in the form of chords. The increased verbal clarity of this new method gave composers greater scope for expressing ideas and emotions, and no composer was more concerned with affecting the emotions than Monteverdi. However, he did so not by concentrating on one style alone but by using choosing a particular style whenever it seemed most appropriate. His greatest works, the operas and the *Vespers*,

combine a range of musical methods – from monody to madrigalian choruses – which succeed in creating an exuberantly varied and, above all, dramatic whole.

Monteverdi was born in Cremona in northern Italy, the son of a pharmacist-cum-barber-surgeon. After studying with Marc'Antonio Ingegneri, the maestro di cappella at Cremona Cathedral, he joined the ducal court of the Gonzaga family at Mantua, where he was employed for over twenty years. This was a highly cultivated if somewhat claustrophobic working environment: Duke Vincenzo I was tyrannical and demanding, and Monteverdi frequently felt under-appreciated. The Gonzagas were not one of Italy's most politically powerful families but they lived in great style, employing several important artists including the painter Rubens and, as their maestro di cappella, Giaches de Wert – an important influence on his younger colleague.

HULTON DEUTSCH

In 1599 Monteverdi married one of the court singers Claudia de Cattaneis, and by 1602 had become maestro di cappella at the ducal chapel of Santa Barbara. His first opera, *Orfeo*, was performed in 1607, at the instigation of the Duke's eldest son Francesco. In the same year, the death of his wife sent Monteverdi into a deep depression. He returned to his father in Cremona but was summoned back to court in 1608 to write a new opera, *Arianna*, for the wedding of Francesco Gonzaga. The work was an enormous success but, unlike *Orfeo*, it was never published and only a fragment of it, the lament of Arianna, has survived.

Monteverdi's final years in Mantua seemed to have been frustrating, and his famous *Vespers* of 1610 was published with a dedication to the pope in an attempt to find employment in Rome. Nothing came of it, and when Francesco Gonzaga succeeded to the dukedom in 1612, Monteverdi found himself out of a job. Once again he returned to Cremona before unexpectedly being offered the post of maestro di cappella at St Mark's in Venice. He greatly improved musical standards at St Mark's, and in turn he was better appreciated, enjoying a substantial and regular salary.

Following the terrible plague that hit Venice in 1630 he became a priest and his final years might have passed quietly but for the opening of the first public opera house in Venice, the *San Cassiano*, in 1637. For the remaining years of his life he wrote regularly for the opera but unfortunately only two works have survived: *Il ritorno d'Ulisse* (1641) and, one of his greatest works, *L'Incoronazione di Poppea* (1642).

ORFEO

Monteverdi did not invent opera but he produced its first masterpieces, works that – though neglected between his death and the twentieth century – are now firmly established in the operatic canon. Opera had emerged in the last decade of the sixteenth century partly from theoretical discussions about the nature of Greek theatre. A scholar named Girolamo Mei proclaimed that all the words in Greek tragedy had been sung, not polyphonically but to a single line of music, an idea taken up by a group of Florentine intellectuals known as the Camerata. One of their number, Vincenzo Galilei (father of the astronomer), agreed that polyphony was hopelessly complex for conveying the meaning of poetry, and he advocated the single-line approach, monody, to contemporary composers.

The earliest composers to adopt monody were Caccini, Cavilieri – who wrote the first oratorio – and Jacopo Peri, who wrote the first opera, *Dafne* (now lost). It was Peri who developed a form of rhythmically free, declamatory singing called *recitativo*, which was used for dialogue and narration. It was Monteverdi who showed how this new genre could be used for the creation of a dramatic narrative, by combining a wonderfully varied and flexible *recitativo* with a wide range of musical styles to provide contrast and depth.

Orfeo, Monteverdi's first opera, took as its subject the classical myth of Orpheus, a theme treated by Peri in his second opera, *Euridice*. Both operas tell of the death of Euridice, and how her betrothed, the poet and singer Orpheus, journeys to the underworld in an attempt to bring her back from the dead. The power of his music persuades Pluto into letting her return, on condition that Orpheus should not look back as he leads her to the upper world. At the last moment he does so and loses her once more. In the original versions of the story Orpheus despises all women after his loss, and is torn to pieces by the frenzied female followers of Bacchus. This ending was changed after the first performance of the opera, to one in which the god Apollo, Orpheus's father, conveys Orpheus to the heavens, where he is able to view the likeness of Euridice in the stars.

⦿ Ainsley, Gooding, Bott; New London Consort; Pickett (L'Oiseau Lyre 433 545-2; 2 CDs).

From the sparkling attack of the opening toccata it is clear that this is going to be a spirited account. Pickett's sleevenotes give detailed reasoning about his choice of instrumental combinations, and the result brilliantly communicates the freshness and the intimacy of the drama. The dilemmas and emotions of the protagonists seem real and immediate, not simply because of the consistently convincing characterization but also because the instrumental colouring does so much to create a context for the action. Orfeo himself is a complex and self-centred character, qualities strongly conveyed by John Mark Ainsley's well-judged performance. Also excellent are Julia Gooding's poignant Euridice and Catherine Bott in the multiple roles of Prosperina, the messenger who brings news of Euridice's death (a particularly moving moment), and as Music, who presents the prologue to the main action.

IL RITORNO D'ULISSE IN PATRIA

A gap of over thirty years separates *Orfeo* from Monteverdi's second surviving opera, *Il ritorno d'Ulisse*, which was first staged at the San Cassiano theatre in 1640. Its libretto, by Giacomo Badoaro, is based on Homer's *Odyssey*. While Ulysses has been away for twenty years (fighting at Troy and then attempting to return home to Ithaca), his wife Penelope has remained faithful to him, despite the attentions of several suitors. At the opera's conclusion Penelope holds a contest: whoever can draw the bow of Ulysses will win her hand. They all fail with the exception of Ulysses who, disguised as a beggar, not only draws the bow but kills all of the suitors. Penelope, fearing a trick, refuses to acknowledge that it is indeed her husband until he describes the embroidered cover of their wedding bed.

Il ritorno d'Ulisse is the most neglected of Monteverdi's surviving operas, perhaps because it is the most courtly, yet its fabric is more varied than that of *Orfeo*. *Recitativo* is still the major vehicle for expression here, but

arias occur regularly to intensify the drama – most notable being Penelope's moving *Illustratevi, o cieli* in Act Three.

⦿ Pregardien, Fink, Hogman, Hunt; Concerto Vocale; Jacobs (Harmonia Mundi HMC 901427.29; 3 CDs).

This is a rather more epic work than *Orfeo* and here receives a correspondingly larger and more obviously operatic performance. The instrumental combinations are darker than in *Orfeo*, and Jacobs' choice of singers also tends towards the overtly expressive, particularly in the near-neurotic Penelope of Bernarda Fink. The recording's one drawback is that it occasionally lacks the energy and spontaneity of Pickett's *Orfeo*.

L'INCORONAZIONE DI POPPEA

Monteverdi selected another classical theme for his last and greatest opera, but this time from history rather than mythology – the first known example of an opera based on fact. The choice of subject for *L'Incoronazione di Poppea* might seem strange, since it concludes with the complete triumph of immorality. The Roman Emperor Nero decides to cast aside his wife Ottavia and to marry his new mistress, Poppea. When his tutor, the philosopher Seneca, is critical of his decision, Nero – goaded on by Poppea – orders his execution. Ottone, Poppea's former lover, is blackmailed by Ottavia into making an attempt on Poppea's life. He does so disguised as Ottavia's maid Drusilla who is in love with him. His failure duly brings him capture and exile. Nero then divorces and exiles his wife, and the opera ends with Nero and Poppea luxuriating in their success and their love for each other in a highly sensual and disturbingly moving duet.

There are several features that distinguish *L'Incoronazione* from its predecessors, apart from the likelihood that it contains music by more than one composer. Its orchestration is pared down from that used in *Il ritorno*, and the music is characterized by more marked contrasts between juxtaposed sections, as when Seneca's preparations for suicide are followed by the badinage of Nero's decadent flunkeys. The arias here are longer and more prominent as well, and the characterization is more complex than anything Monteverdi had attempted before – Nero is the most rounded of his creations.

🔵 Donath, Söderström, Esswood; Concentus Musicus Wien; Harnoncourt (Teldec 2292 42547-2; 4 CDs).

Since Virgin Classics inexplicably deleted their marvellous recording, the best alternative is this 1974 set from Teldec. It does rather sound its age, with large and at times strident instrumental forces, but its great strength is its soloists: Elizabeth Söderström and Helen Donath make a well-matched Nero and Poppea, brilliantly conveying the obsessive nature of their love – the mixture of depravity and beauty in their final duet creates a real frisson. Also outstanding is the Ottavia of Cathy Berberian, a psychological portrait of great subtlety and depth which brings out the conflicting impulses of duty and the desire to be revenged.

THE VESPERS

The Gonzagas employed Monteverdi primarily as a composer of secular music and, despite becoming maestro di cappella in 1601, his religious output was fairly small before his appointment to St Mark's in Venice. Undoubtedly his greatest achievement in the field of religious music was the *Vespro della Beata Vergine*, a collection of music for the service of Vespers, published in 1610. For what occasion this music was written has proved difficult to establish, but it is fairly certain that Monteverdi intended its publication as a showcase for his skills, above all for his ability to write effectively in a variety of styles both old and new. The Vespers provides an extraordinarily theatrical approach to church music, with a range of startling effects throughout the service, from the opening fanfare to the use of an echo in the motet *Audi coelum*, or the dramatic ornamentation of the part for three tenors at the end of *Duo Seraphim* – not to mention the consistently sumptuous instrumental writing.

⚫ Kirkby, Rogers; Taverner Consort and Choir; Parrott (EMI CDS 747078-2; 2 CDs).
⚫ Figueras, Kiehr; La Capella Reial; Coro del Centro Musica Antica di Padova; Savall (Astree E 8719; 2 CDs).

Parrott's was a trail-blazing recording when it appeared in 1984, being the first to place Monteverdi's music in a complete liturgical context through the addition of chants and material by Monteverdi's contemporaries. The approach is largely soloistic rather than choral and Nigel Rogers, an expert in Monteverdian ornamentation, gives an outstanding performance of the *Audi coelum*.

Savall's performance, though not in a liturgical context, has the advantage of being generally more atmospheric: the recording was made in the ducal chapel of Santa Barbara in Mantua – possibly the site of its original performance – and the warm and resonant acoustic has been beautifully captured. Its other main attraction is the use of continental singers with consistently rich vocal timbres. This is at its most marked in the darkly expressive tones of soprano Montserrat Figueras, a penetrating voice but one that combines well with others, most beguilingly with the more reticent Maria Kiehr in an intense performance of *Pulchra* es. There is also some thrillingly lively instrumental playing especially in the *Sonata sopra Sancta Maria*, essentially an instrumental piece over which the words "Holy Mary pray for us" are repeatedly intoned by the chorus.

MADRIGALS – AND IL COMBATTIMENTO

Monteverdi had already published two collections of madrigals by the time he reached Mantua in 1592. These were in the standard five-part polyphonic fashion and show great charm and imaginative word-setting. At Mantua, under the influence of de Wert, his madrigals became much bolder especially in their use of dissonance and in a tendency towards a more declamatory mode of expression. This prompted a conservative theorist named Artusi to launch a biting attack on Monteverdi, particularly his use of dissonance. Monteverdi's defence, later amplified by his brother Guilio Cesare, appeared in the preface to the fifth book of madrigals (1605), where he makes a distinction between the old style of composing (the *prima prattica*), where the music governed the words, and his new style (the *seconda prattica*), where the words governed the music.

Monteverdi's eighth book of madrigals, subtitled "Madrigals of war and love", had an aesthetic agenda which he outlined in a foreword. Harking back to classical ideas, he argued that music should be able to evoke in the listener the contrasting states of calmness, love and war. This move towards an even more graphic form of musical realism can be seen most clearly in the dramatic piece included in the eighth book, *Il Combattimento di Tancredi e Clorinda* (The Combat of Tancred and Clorinda), an oddly unclassifiable work that's not quite an opera but more than a madrigal. First performed in 1624 at the home of the Venetian nobleman Girolamo Mocenigo, it takes its story from Tasso's chivalric epic *Gerusalemme liberata* and tells, mainly through a narrator, of a duel between a disguised Saracen woman, Clorinda, and a Crusader knight, Tancredi. Monteverdi employs several startling imitative effects, including the trotting of the horse and the clashing of swords, but the essence of *Il Combattimento* is its expressive vocabulary. He selected Tasso because of the wide range of emotions in his work, and the success of Monteverdi's setting rests in the extent to which he convincingly conveys these emotions through music. The original performance is said to have reduced its audience to tears.

MONTEVERDI
Altri Canti
Les Arts Florissants
WILLIAM CHRISTIE

harmonia
mundi
FRANCE
1901068

musique d'abord

One of the best anthologies of Monteverdi's songs

◉ **Il Quarto Libro dei Madrigali**: Concerto Italiano; Alessandrini (Opus III OPS 30-81).
◉ **Altri Canti**: Les Arts Florissants; Christie (Harmonia Mundi HMA 1901068).
◉ **Il combattimento di Tancredi e Clorinda**: Les Arts Florissants; Christie (Harmonia Mundi HMC 901426).

The fourth book of madrigals was published in 1603 but contains several works written considerably earlier. The music is still unaccompanied five-part polyphony, but the harmonies are more adventurous than in earlier books and there is an increased emphasis on declamation (making the words follow the pattern of speech), notably at the beginning of *Sfogava con le stelle*, where the dominance of a single chord gives the impression of chanting. Concerto Italiano, a group of young Italian singers, are the best performers of this type of repertoire: sensitive, passionate, theatrical when necessary, but always making the often extreme harmonies seem natural and unforced.

Both the seventh and eighth book of madrigals employ accompanying instruments, and Monteverdi continuously varies the combination of voices – there are songs for solo and duet as well as three-, four- and five-part settings. The selection from Les Arts Florissants contains three pieces from book seven and six from book eight, ranging in style and mood from the frisky to the lyrical. Best of all is *Hor ch'el ciel a la terra* an astonishing example of word setting that culminates in one of the most serene and poignant closing lines in all Monteverdi's output. Les Arts Florissants are a lively and highly expressive group: there are occasional moments of poor tuning and an unfortunate edit in *Hor ch'el ciel* but this disc makes a fine introduction to the later madrigals. Regrettably, however, none of the words are printed with the sleeve notes.

The performance of *Il Combattimento* from Les Arts Florissants works almost perfectly because the details and the spirit of the piece are so closely adhered to. Nicolas Rivenq makes an outstanding narrator and the instrumentalists bring the work to life through the variety and refinement of their tone colour.

═══════════ ♫ ═══════════

WOLFGANG AMADEUS MOZART
(1756–1791)

❝ **I**t is a mistake to think that the practice of my art has become easy to me – no one has given so much care to the study of composition as I have. There is scarcely a famous master in music whose works I have not frequently and diligently studied.❞ Thus wrote Wolfgang Amadeus Mozart to his father, Leopold. The idea that Mozart had to work at anything doesn't quite match the received image. We know Mozart as the artless child of nature, producing music in unconscious, effortless profusion, untrammelled by knowledge of the heights and depths of human experience. It's an immensely alluring image, as attested by the success of the film *Amadeus*, which marketed a caricature of the composer as prodigious superbrat. Like any caricature, it necessarily bears a recognizeable relationship to reality – there are numerous stories of Mozart completing an entire symphony in the course of a coach journey, and many of his manuscripts are entirely free of second thoughts, as if he had been taking dictation from the Almighty. But to categorize Mozart as a brilliant freak who exhaled music as others exhale air is to diminish him. Mozart possessed a profound and profoundly self-aware mind, and his unequalled facility was founded upon a comprehensive knowledge of the traditions within which he was working. And he crammed more work into a couple of decades than many composers managed in a lifetime – Mozart's complete output would fill almost two hundred CDs.

He started working earlier than most, of course. Mozart learned how to play the keyboard at the age of three and was composing from five. From 1762, his father toured Wolfgang and his sister throughout Europe, during which the six-year-old learned to play the violin without any formal teaching. During these tours, he met and played for some of the world's most powerful figures, including Louis XV at Versailles and George III in London. Not until 1766, when he was ten, did he return home to Salzburg. Two years later he completed two operas and journeyed to Italy, where he was acclaimed as the "greatest genius in all music". While he was in Rome, he heard a performance of Allegri's *Miserere* and wrote it down from memory to spite the authorities who had refused him access to a copy of the score. After returning to Austria then making further trips to Italy, he came home to work for the Archbishop of Salzburg. Neither liked the other, however, and in 1777 Mozart once again left on tour, this time with his mother.

In 1778, while they were in Paris, she died, leaving the twenty-two-year-old in a state of deep distress. Unable to find a court position such as Haydn had procured, Mozart again returned to Salzburg, where he spent the next two years as court and cathedral organist to the Archbishop, but their relationship steadily disintegrated to the point where in 1781 a climactic confrontation led to the composer's resignation. In 1782 he moved to Vienna, where he married Constanze. There

POPPERFOTO

he gave many concerts as conductor and pianist, and spent a great deal of energy on composing opera, an area in which he excelled even his own standards by writing *Don Giovanni* in only a few months in 1787. After his father's death in the following year, he wrote his last three symphonies in a matter of weeks and from then on pretty much devoted himself to his last three operas, *Così fan tutte*, *Die Zauberflöte* and *La Clemenza di Tito*. In July 1791 he was commissioned by an anonymous patron to write a *Requiem*; he died on December 5 of that year, leaving the *Requiem* incomplete. He was buried with a number of other bodies in a communal grave, the location of which has never been identified.

These brief facts give no idea of the complexity of his short life, but his music is easier to break down. As with most composers, his early music is very much of its time and there is little that's remarkable about his first attempts except that they were composed by a boy. His "middle period" begins in his sixteenth year, a curious passage of nine years during which much of Mozart's composition reflected his general unhappiness with life, ruled as it was by his strict patron, the Archbishop of Salzburg. As he wrote to his father in 1778: "Frequently I fall into a mood of complete listlessness and indifference; nothing gives me any pleasure".

In his twenty-fifth year he broke free of the claustrophobic patronage of the Archbishop, and what followed was one of the most remarkable decades in musical history. The list of pieces composed between 1781 and 1791 takes in almost everything for which Mozart is best known, music which has no parallel in its achievement of depth without pomposity, clarity without banality and simplicity without shallowness. This music is a synthesis of many different elements, each adopted, modified and then outgrown. As a travelling virtuoso he absorbed an enormous variety of European music – England, Germany, France and, most importantly, Italy (especially Italian opera) all left indelible marks on his musical character. Except in the world of opera, Mozart was thus no innovator, but – unlike Haydn and Beethoven, who were – he excelled in every genre current in his time. This universality, this limitless proficiency, is unique, as is the prevalent tone of Mozart's music, an atmosphere of serenity achieved through hardship, of complex experience sublimated into outward simplicity. No other composer has been so revered by other great figures. Perhaps the most powerful testimony came from Richard Strauss; shortly before his death, he placed his hand upon a score of Mozart's clarinet quintet and said "I would give everything just to have written this."

OPERA

The most obvious distinction between Mozart and the majority of opera composers is that he was the master of all other branches of composition. Almost every great composer of opera after Handel specialized in writing operas and left it at that. Mozart's operas are the product of a mind that thought symphonically – so even if you haven't got a clue what's going on, you can tell that you're listening to an extended piece of music in which the dramatic incidents form part of a perfectly coherent whole. Mozart set some excellent libretti (those of Lorenzo da Ponte are just about the best texts a composer ever had to work with), yet the music is always the dominant element, giving the action inflections of meaning that the words alone wouldn't bear. Furthermore, until Mozart's emergence operatic characters were generalized and typical, often superhuman or supernatural. As they were at the beginning of an opera, so they were at the end. Mozart was the first to put real people on the stage, individuals whose emotions were inconsistent and whose personalities were evolutionary. In short, Mozart's combines the playwright's psychology with the musician's sense of form.

In all, Mozart wrote twenty-two operas, half a dozen of which are performed regularly in all the world's major opera houses, with another half-dozen receiving attention from smaller companies. To discuss all of them in any detail would obviously take up an entire book – we've singled out what we think are the four finest.

LE NOZZE DI FIGARO

Le Nozze di Figaro (The Marriage of Figaro) was first performed in Vienna on May 1, 1786. In keeping with that decade's vogue for Italian rather than German opera, Mozart chose to set a text by Vienna's most gifted librettist, Lorenzo Da Ponte. Da Ponte's text was based upon Beaumarchais' recently banned comedy *La Folle Journée, ou le Mariage de Figaro*, in which a libidinous Count attempts to seduce the fiancée of his servant, but is outwitted by an alliance between the serving classes and his own long-suffering wife. The plot is bursting with intrigue and misunderstanding, and Mozart responded to it by creating an extraordinarily witty piece of music, in which even the most minor characters are precisely characterized. But the magic of *Figaro* lies not in the panache with which Mozart handles the logistics of farce, but rather in the profundity of emotion that he reveals, through some of his most moving arias and perhaps the greatest ensembles ever written. There is no more potent demonstration of Mozart's economy of means than the opening of the second act:

virtually everything up to that point has been knockabout humour; within the space of a single two-minute aria from the heartbroken Countess, Mozart changes the mood of the opera completely.

> 🌓 Siepi, Gueden, Poell, della Casa, Danco, Rossl-Majdan, Corena; Vienna State Opera Chorus; Vienna Philharmonic Orchestra; Kleiber (Decca 417 315-2DM3; 3 CDs).

There are over twenty studio recordings of *Figaro* and around twice that number of live recordings in the catalogue, and many of these (such as Böhm's DG studio version) are superb. None, however, is better than Eric Kleiber's 1954 recording, made with what must be one of the greatest Mozart casts ever assembled. The characterization and dramatic direction are impeccable from first to last, and the singing is a testament to one of opera's golden ages – this set would be worth the money just for the vitality and freshness of Hilda Gueden's Susanna and Lisa della Casa's Countess Almaviva.

DON GIOVANNI

Mozart's next opera was commissioned from the Prague opera house as a result of Figaro's success there, and again he turned to Da Ponte for his libretto. The plot of *Don Giovanni* is the familiar morality play concerning the philandering Don Juan and his eventual damnation, but Mozart transforms this cautionary tale into an enthralling assembly of character studies. The Don himself is a monster, but he is an irresistible monster: the seductive beauty of his famous serenade (sung to the servant of one of his thousands of deceived lovers), the superhuman energy of the "champagne aria", and the ambiguous passions he inspires in the women he encounters, all prompt the suspicion that Mozart was, as Blake said of Milton, a covert member of the devil's party. The action of *Don Giovanni* oscillates between high farce and deep tragedy, culminating in an extraordinary banquet scene, during which Giovanni refuses to repent and is dragged to hell by the ghost of the man whom he had murdered in the first scene. Two hundred years later, it is still one of the most terrifying scenes in opera.

> 🌓 Siepi, Danco, della Casa, Gueden, Dermota, Corena, Berry; Vienna State Opera Chorus; Vienna Philharmonic Orchestra; Krips (Decca 411 626-2DM3; 3 CDs).

This is the most recorded of all Mozart's operas, and is also the most demanding for the conductor, as *Don Giovanni* falls apart if the conductor lacks a tight grip. The sadly underrated Josef Krips is indubitably in charge in this recording, featuring a stupendous cast that's almost identical to the one assembled for Kleiber's *Figaro* – his disciplined approach and brisk tempi produce an almost uninterrupted excitement. No other recording makes the final act sound so disturbing.

COSÌ FAN TUTTE

After *Don Giovanni*, Mozart and Da Ponte produced their last opera together, *Così fan tutte* – or in full, *Così fan tutte, ossia la scuola degli amanti* (Thus do they all, or The School for Lovers). Though repeated ten times in 1790, the year of its premiere, *Così* did not achieve the popularity of the other Mozart-Da Ponte operas, and by the 1830s it had disappeared from repertoire, resurfacing only when the likes of Mahler and Strauss began to promote its cause. Beethoven attacked the "immorality" of *Così*, and squeamishness about its apparent cynicism probably goes a long way to explaining its neglect. The plot has the dovetailed perfection of farce: two young men, riled by a friend's insinuations about the trustworthiness of their girlfriends, disguise themselves in order to attempt to seduce them. They expect to fail but in fact succeed; a reconciliation is finally achieved. Mozart takes this formulaic plot and makes it the vehicle for some uncomfortable irony, writing superlatively melodious music whose cheerfulness often has an undertow of melancholy and disillusionment. It's an opera with no hero, not even in the sense of a main character – the six lead roles are all equally important, and more than any other opera this one is carried by its ensembles.

> ⏺ Janowitz, Fassbaender, Grist, Schreier, Prey, Panerai; Vienna State Opera Chorus, Vienna Philharmonic Orchestra; Böhm (Deutsche Grammophon 429 874-2GX2; 2 CDs).

Karl Böhm's third recording of *Così* was recorded when the conductor had reached his eightieth year, and in many respects it's superior to the earlier versions. Böhm cuts the score slightly (not uncommon practice), and takes the music at a quick pace, producing a performance that's bright and quixotic, with Fassbaender and Prey shining as Dorabella and Guglielmo. The CDs are well engineered and excellently annotated.

DIE ZAUBERFLÖTE

After the comparative failure of *Così*, Mozart made an unexpected return to the fantasy and magic of Gluckian opera. Mozart was a freemason for most of his adult life and the masonic sub-plot of *Die Zauberflöte* (The Magic Flute) has provoked reams of academic commentary since the opera's first performance in 1791. The ritualistic element of *Die Zauberflöte* is undeniable, but you do not need to know anything of masonic esoteric teaching to enjoy this opera, for it can heard simply as an incident-packed tale of love tested and found true. *Die Zauberflöte* ranges from buffoonery to hieratic solemnity, and features some of the most unusual and vivid characters in all opera – such as Papageno the guileless bird-catcher, the flamboyantly evil Queen of the Night (who gets two of the most startling arias you'll ever hear), and the comically thuggish Monostatos. In short, The Magic Flute is a pantomime for grown-ups.

> ◗ Gueden, Lipp, Simoneau, Berry, Schoeffler, Ludwig; Vienna State Opera Chorus, Vienna Philharmonic Orchestra, Böhm (Decca 414 362-2DM2; 2 CDs).
> ◉ Lear, Peters, Wunderlich, Fischer-Dieskau, Crass, Hotter, Otto, King, Talvela; Berlin RIAS Chamber Choir, Berlin Philharmonic Orchestra; Böhm (Deutsche Grammophon 3371 002; 3 CDs).

These are both superb performances. The later Berlin recording is much slower than the Vienna performance, but the tempi are cohesive and they reflect the considered judgement of a man whose affinity with Mozart's music had lasted over a half a century. Beyond this aspect to the performance, Deutsche Grammophon's recording also boasts the one-in-a-million talents of Wunderlich, Hotter and Otto. The Decca version has its individual strengths – the performances by Gueden, Lipp and Berry are astonishingly fresh and alive – but it's the overall unity of purpose that distinguishes this account. It may not be as well engineered as the Deutsche Grammophon recording, but this Decca set is conspicuously immersed in the Viennese repertoire traditions.

SACRED MUSIC

Ever since Mozart's day it has been suggested that the bulk of his sacred music was written as a means of remaining in favour with his patrons. This is unlikely, but even if it is true it makes no difference to the meaning of the music, for even the earliest of his Masses (he

wrote nearly twenty) express a deep, childlike and unquestioning faith. Two works in particular warrant comparison with the finest devotional music of Bach – the *Mass in C minor* and his last work, the *Requiem*.

MASS IN C MINOR

Mozart's *Mass in C minor* was his first noncommissioned Mass, which may well explain the music's breathtaking sense of personal utterance, but what remains unexplained is why he chose to leave the score incomplete. A number of suggestions have been made – the most watery-eyed being that he did not know how to finish a score already beyond perfection – but nothing convincing has yet emerged. Whatever the truth, movements such as the Qui tollis, with its soulshuddering *subito piani* (sudden quiet), eclipse anything in the *Requiem* and only the latter half of Beethoven's *Missa Solemnis* stands comparison with this extraordinary, solemn, God-fearing work.

> ◉ McNair, Montague, Rolfe Johnson, Hauptman; Monteverdi Choir, English Baroque Soloists; Gardiner (Philips 420 21-2PH).

John Eliot Gardiner's semi-academic methods often result in performances that inspire admiration rather than affection. However, for his recordings of the *Mass in C minor* and *Requiem* he struck gold. The depth and range of expression is overwhelming, and in Silvia McNair (then an unknown), he found the perfect soprano – in particular, her performance of *Et incarnatus est* has a wondrous, unaffected purity.

THE REQUIEM (MASS IN D MINOR)

The anonymous commission for the *Requiem* is now known to have come from Count von Walsegg, who wished to pass the composition off as his own. Walsegg did not kill Mozart but he might as well have placed a pistol in the sick man's hand, so disastrous was the commission's effect on his health. Other than a small funeral motet *Ave verum corpus*, it was his first sacred composition since the abandoned *Mass in C minor* and it too was to remain incomplete – Mozart died while working on it, and it was left to one of his pupils, Sussmayr, to finish it. If Sussmayr was telling the truth (and many people think he aggrandized his contribution), then he composed a substantial amount of the *Requiem*, using Mozart's sketched bass parts as a guide to harmonic and melodic direction. Whatever Sussmayr's role, much of the *Requiem* bears Mozart's unmistakeable stamp, and its strong contrapuntal element reflects Mozart's immersion in the music of Bach and Handel towards the end of his life. It's impossible to hear the *Requiem* as anything other than Mozart's acceptance of fragile mortality, the last testimony of the man who wrote – "I never lie down in my bed without reflecting that perhaps I, young as I am, may not live to see another day."

◉ Bonney, von Otter, Blochwitz, White; Monteverdi Choir, English Baroque Soloists; Gardiner (Philips 420 21-2PH).

Gardiner's performance boasts some superb talent, and as with the *Mass in C minor* he achieves a sense of occasion that is palpable from start to finish. The rock-steady voices of Barbara Bonney and Anne Sofie von Otter are perfectly suited to the plainer and more linear style of the *Requiem*, and the small orchestra and choir contribute greatly towards the intimacy of expression.

SYMPHONIES

Mozart's forty-one symphonies represent but a fraction of his enormous output of orchestral music. It's an amazing volume of work, especially when you consider that, unlike Haydn, Mozart was not working in circumstances that guaranteed performance of whatever he wrote. But also unlike Haydn, Mozart's symphonies do not constitute a great body of work – the first dozen or so are the weightless creations of a prodgiously adept boy, and even in the "middle period" symphonies there are tracts of hack-work. There is thus no point, unless you have a mania for completeness, in buying a colossal set of the Mozart symphonies. With the last three symphonies, however, it's a different story, for they represent one of the most remarkable feats of composition ever accomplished. All three – nearly an hour and a half's music – were uncommissioned and were completed in less than six weeks, a period in which Mozart was busy writing other, money-earning, music. These three masterpieces are the expression of an inner compulsion that demanded satisfaction.

SYMPHONIES NOS. 39–41

Although they were composed close togther, the last three symphonies are widely contrasted. *Symphony No. 39* is a smiling work, full of sunlight and mellow, flowing lines – once, that is, the discordant and angry introduction has passed by. The *Symphony No. 40* is a tragic utterance quite unlike anything previously written by Mozart. The bleakness is crystallized in the second movement, a piece of music as profoundly spiritual as anything in the symphonic repertoire, but just as remarkable is the first movement, a splendid conception which, like the opening of Beethoven's fifth symphony, is built upon a single idea whose interest is primarily rhythmical.

It was the haughty and imperial nature of the first movement of the *Symphony No. 41* that earned it the title "Jupiter" early in the nineteenth century – when you hear the opening's march-like progress and forceful trumpets and drums, you'll know why the association caught on. Haydn echoed the wonderful middle movement in the slow movement of his *Symphony No. 98*, as a tribute to his friend and one-time pupil upon Mozart's death three years later. For complexity and sheer excitement, there is nothing comparable to the finale: there are no fewer than six distinct themes here, and Mozart juggles each throughout the movement until, in the coda, he unites them all in a dazzling display of invention.

◗ **Symphonies Nos. 39–41**: Columbia Symphony Orchestra, Walter (Sony SM3K 46511; with *Symphonies Nos. 35, 36 & 38*; 3 CDs).

SONY

Bruno Walter – famous for Mahler, just as good in Mozart

Bruno Walter is renowned for his Mahler, but critics have tended to ignore his refreshingly imaginative approach to Mozart and, in particular, the symphonies. His recordings of the last three is a fine set indeed. Completely devoid of pomposity (a common fault in other conductors), he leads the purposeful Columbia Symphony Orchestra through performances that give the music a bracing sense of freedom (where many have imposed metronomic regularity).

Complete Piano Concertos: Anda, Salzburg Mozarteum Camerata Academica (Deutsche Grammophon 429 001-2GX10; 10 CDs).

Geza Anda's concerto cycle established a benchmark back in the 1960s, and though it now has several excellent rivals (eg from Murray Perahia and Andras Schiff), none has surpassed it. Anda's style is intimate, romantic and unfussy, the sound is good for the time, and the set is excellent value for money.

CONCERTOS

Mozart's twenty-seven piano concertos dominate his concerto output, and they are remarkably consistent in form. Eighteenth-century pianos were incapable of offering any dynamic challenge to the orchestra – small though it was – and so much of the writing follows the simple system of exchange, whereby the orchestra plays a theme which is then repeated or developed by the pianist and vice-versa. All but one of the concertos opens with a straightforward orchestral statement, presenting the main movement subject as well as any other relevant themes, and then the piano takes over. But if the structure remains essentially the same, the inventiveness within that structure is astonishing. The music can seem brittle at first, with decoration after decoration poured onto simple melodic lines, but beneath the elegant façade is a spirit of immense strength and imagination. Mozart didn't write a proper piano concerto until he was seventeen (the first four concertos are arrangements of other people's music), and so – unlike the symphonies – they comprise a body of work that's of consistently high quality. If you don't want to commit yourself to the lot straight away, sample the three we've selected below – the first will give you a taste of middle-period Mozart, the other two reveal him at his peak.

At the age of nineteen Mozart wrote five violin concertos at the instigation of his father (a noted violin teacher), who believed that they would make his name abroad. Composed within a matter of months, for performance by the Italian violinist Brunetti and his court orchestra in Salzburg, they are all extremely pretty, but the fifth is superior to the rest. Of his other concertos, the *Clarinet Concerto* is the finest of his numerous works for wind instruments (he also wrote two for flute, one for flute and harp, and four for horn).

PIANO CONCERTO NO. 12

The delightful *Piano Concerto No. 12* was produced soon after Mozart had resigned from the service of the Archbishop of Salzburg, and the music's cheerfulness might betray his relief. It was one of a set of three concertos, of which he wrote to his father: "These concertos are a happy medium between what is too easy and too difficult; they are very brilliant, pleasing to the ear, and natural without being vapid. There are passages here and there from which connoisseurs alone can derive satisfaction; but these passages are written in such a way that the less learned cannot fail to be pleased, though without knowing why."

Schiff; Salzburg Mozarteum Camerata Academica; Vegh (Decca 417 886-2DH; with *Concerto No. 14*).

Although he plays on a massive nine-foot Bösendorfer, Andras Schiff is able to produce a delicate and highly varied tone which is perfectly suited to this uncomplicated, light and colourful concerto.

PIANO CONCERTO NO. 21

Everybody knows the slow movement of the *Piano Concerto No. 21* since Bo Widerberg used it for the soundtrack of his soppy film *Elvira Madigan* – indeed, it now appears as "The Elvira Madigan" on concert programmes, as if Mozart dreamed up the title. The association does the concerto a disservice, for this is a serene rather than a sentimental work, eschewing the virtuosity so popular with Viennese audiences in favour of exquisite melodies and limpid textures.

Anda, Salzburg Mozarteum Camerata Academica (Deutsche Grammophon 429 522-2GR (with *Concerto No. 17*).

Geza Anda's lyrical performance on Deutsche Grammophon is beautifully constructed, and the recording is bright and well focused.

PIANO CONCERTO NO. 27

The *Piano Concerto No. 27* was Mozart's last: he completed it on January 5, 1791, eleven months before his death. It followed two years of extreme hardship, in which his relationship with Constanza had disintegrated and his financial situation had become critical. The least virtuosic of all his concertos, it is characterized by a mood of introspection and resignation that is typical of his late work.

⊙ Gulda; Vienna Philharmonic Orchestra; Abbado (Deutsche Grammophon 437 014-2GCA; with *Concerto No. 20*).

Frederic Gulda now spends most of his time performing and writing jazz music, and an improvisatory approach infuses this immensely flexible performance. An illuminating sense of the unexpected is also to be found in the coupled performance of *Piano Concerto No. 20*, which boasts another of Mozart's sublime slow movements.

CLARINET CONCERTO

Mozart's *Clarinet Concerto* has for many years been the subject of controversy. While it is quite clearly the finest ever written for the instrument (and therefore almost certainly by Mozart), no-one really knows how much of it is actually Mozart's – but for 199 bars of the first movement, there is no complete manuscript in the composer's hand. However, the music is seductive throughout, and the slow movement takes pride of place next to the central movement of the *Piano Concerto No. 21*.

◗ Goodman; Boston Symphony Orchestra; Munch (RCA RD85275; with *Clarinet Quintet*).

Benny Goodman was the dedicatee of works by Bartók, Hindemith and Copland, but the bulk of his recordings were made as a jazz clarinettist and swing band leader. His recording of Mozart's concerto, however, is probably the most famous ever made; the recording is old but its age is more than compensated for by Goodman's shimmering beauty of tone.

VIOLIN CONCERTO NO. 5

What distinguishes the fifth violin concerto from the rest of the set is the greater responsibility given to the orchestra – in the other four, the orchestra does little more than merely accompany the soloist. The melodies are engaging and instantly memorable, especially in the "Turkish" episode within the finale, a piece of music reflecting the current vogue for all things Ottoman.

⊙ Zukerman; St. Paul Chamber Orchestra (Sony CD46540; with *Concerto No. 4, Rondo and Adagio*).

Zukerman gives a witty performance and milks the music for every drop of emotion, especially in the slow movement. The small size of his chamber orchestra ensures that the contrapuntal writing is not lost beneath washes of thickly vibrating strings, as happens on many recordings.

CHAMBER MUSIC & PIANO SONATAS

Mozart's twenty-three string quartets, six string quintets and eighteen piano sonatas represent but the tip of an iceberg, for Mozart wrote a bewildering amount of music for chamber groups and solo keyboard. Much of the chamber music is of variable quality, but most of these quartets, quintets and sonatas are interesting, at the very least. The best way to begin tackling this area of Mozart's output is to listen to the works we've ruthlessly picked out from the rest.

THE "HAYDN" QUARTETS

The *"Haydn" Quartets* (Nos. 14–19) were written between 1782 and 1785, and were commenced soon after Mozart first made the elder composer's acquaintance. Where or how they came to meet is unknown, but their friendship was probably cemented at "quartet" parties, during which Haydn played first violin to Mozart's viola – as they did for the first performances of these six quartets. At one such gathering, Mozart's father was confronted by Haydn who announced that "Before God, and as an honest man, I tell you that your son is the greatest composer known to me in person or by name. He has taste and, what is more, the greatest knowledge of composition." Mozart returned the compliment by dedicating these works to the universally acknowledged master of the string quartet, thereby sacrificing an excellent opportunity at pleasing a potential patron.

The second of the six is a particularly strong and determined work – according to Constanza, the Trio of the second movement was her husband's response to her difficult labour prior to the birth of their first son, which took place in the bedroom next to Mozart's workroom. Its use of fugues, canons and variation form can be seen as a homage to Haydn's compositional processes, and Haydn is again a strong presence in the fourth of these quartets, the *Hunt* (so named after the galloping opening). This quartet was a clear attempt at mastering not just four part harmony but four part "discourse" – the Adagio boasts some richly organized textures that could easily have been composed early in the nineteenth century, while the Minuet is a brilliant and suitably brief study of sophisticated invention.

The shocking discords that open the last of the *"Haydn" Quartets* earned it the subtitle the *Dissonance* after Mozart's death. As with all these quartets, it is an astonishingly complex piece of music and plunges to depths that always remained beyond Haydn's grasp. The dissonant turns out to be a ruse, misleading the listener into believing that the remainder of the work will be of a similarly haunting sobriety. Nothing of the sort happens, although the second movement does hark back to the weight of the first movement. Mozart has never been particularly associated with innovation, but the chromaticism of this quartet is one instance of Mozart employing musical language that would not become acceptable until the following century.

◉ Emerson Quartet (Deutsche Grammophon 431 797-2GH3; 3 CDs).

These performances are intelligent and spontaneous, exploring avenues of expression closed to less accomplished or less inquisitive musicians. There are times when their tone does become over-harsh but, otherwise, you can but marvel at their unity of vision. This standard of playing is very, very rare.

STRING QUARTET IN G MINOR

In the spring of 1787, shortly after the enormous success of the *Le Nozze di Figaro* in Prague, Mozart composed two string quintets, of which the one in G minor is superior in almost every respect. Written at a time when Mozart had become resigned to the hostility of the audiences in his home city of Vienna, it's evidently a work composed solely to satisfy his own requirements. This deeply felt quintet speaks of resolution and self-reliance, and its third movement is very probably the most wonderful thing he ever wrote for a chamber ensemble.

◉ Heifetz, Baker, Primrose, Majewski, Piatigorsky (RCA GD87869; with *Violin Concerto No. 5, Violin Sonata No. 26*).

There is only one recording of this piece worth discussing. Recorded in 1954, with Heifetz joined by Gregor Piatigorsky, William Primrose and two of the finest session musicians of the day, this is the ultimate interpretation. Heifetz is the dominant voice, but this performance radiates a sense of complete accord.

CLARINET QUINTET

Mozart first met Anton Stadler, a famed member of the Viennese Imperial Court Orchestra, in 1782, and the two men – both freemasons – quickly became close friends. Stadler frequently took financial advantage of the far from wealthy composer, borrowing large sums that were never paid back, but this did not dent Mozart's admiration for the way Stadler played the clarinet, an admiration that resulted in a concerto, a quintet and a trio. The first two are masterpieces, showing a complete mastery of the instrument's particular tone and blending capabilities – and the quintet, unlike the concerto (see above), is known to be wholly by Mozart.

The king of swing plays Mozart

It was composed in 1789 and received its first performance on December 22 of that year, with both Stadler and Mozart taking part. Mozart included plenty of opportunities for Stadler to show off his and the instrument's dexterity, but this is not merely an exercise in great technique – the second movement is intensely romantic, for example, and the final movement has moments of almost unbearable yearning. With its wide palette of colour, extreme emotional contrasts, wonderful melodies and innovative exploration of the clarinet's range, "Stadler's Quintet" (as Mozart titled it) is one of the composer's most brilliant and characterful creations.

🌓 Goodman, Boston Quartet (RCA RD85275; with *Clarinet Concerto*).

Goodman first recorded the *Clarinet Quintet* in 1938 with the great Budapest Quartet; this second version, with the Boston Quartet, was made at the same time as his recording of the concerto (see above) and while the American quartet do not compare with the Hungarians, Goodman is in fine form, and the sound quality is vastly better.

PIANO SONATA NO. 14

Mozart did not begin writing piano sonatas until 1774, by which time he was already famous as the composer of an enormous catalogue of music. Before then, he had written only variations and some sonatas for four hands – composed for him to perform with his sister. However, within six months he had composed six sonatas, only the last of which was published, and all of which betray Haydn's deep influence. The later sonatas display a far greater harmonic ingenuity and melodic richness, and of these the most enjoyable is the *Sonata No. 14*, in C minor, written in 1784. Mozart's grandest solo work, it is terse, pithy and inward-looking, in marked contrast to the effervescence of most of his piano works.

⦿ Eschenbach (Deutsche Grammophon 429 808-2GMM; with *Sonatas Nos. 11 & 16, Variations and Fantasia in C minor*).

Christoph Eschenbach is a perceptive and intelligent musician whose name should be far more widely known than it is. This recording boasts some liquid but powerful playing that flies in the face of modern Mozartian performance practice, which tends to favour fragility above all else. It comes with two other sonatas and the bubbling *Fantasia in C minor*. Published together with the *C minor Sonata* but written over a year later, the *Fantasia* is a perfect counterweight to the sonata, with a tremendously exciting finale that might remind you of the Keystone Cops.

MODEST MUSSORGSKY

(1839–1881)

Of all the composers in the Russian nationalist school known as "The Five" or "The Mighty Handful", Mussorgsky is arguably the greatest. True, Rimsky-Korsakov's highly colourful style left its mark on the likes of Glazunov and Stravinsky, but Mussorgsky's works were invariably ground-breaking, though few in number. Indeed, Mussorgsky's music was too innovative. Rimsky-Korsakov, while recognizing that Mussorgsky was "talented, original, full of so much that was new and vital", asserted that his manuscripts also revealed "absurd, disconnected harmony, ugly part-writing, sometimes strikingly illogical modulation . . . unsuccessful orchestration . . " and began a dedicated project to make his music more performable, either by completing works Mussorgsky had failed to finish or by the wholesale rewriting of complete compositions. Yet these are the very elements – power, earthiness and sheer invention – that gave Mussorgsky his unique musical personality.

Mussorgsky was born into a land-owning family and led a rather dilettantish early life. He found his way into Balakirev's circle in the late 1850s and began composing in earnest, under Balakirev's guidance. After

GUUS ONG

BORIS GODUNOV

Boris Godunov is roughly based on the life of the man who became tsar in 1598, having murdered his rival, and the plot depicts the attempt of a pretender to the throne, who knows of the murder, to usurp him. Mussorgsky exploits the dramatic potential of this scenario to the full, creating a powerful contrast between the spectacle of the Coronation Scene and Boris's inner torment as he tries and fails to come to terms with his guilt. His greatest achievement, however, in his musical characterization, in which the words, thoughts and moods of the protagonists are mirrored in the orchestral accompaniment. Composers as diverse as Debussy and Janáček were undoubtedly influenced by Mussorgsky's skill in word-setting, in particular his way of setting dramatic prose so that the music reflects the inflections of the spoken text.

The work exists in three versions: Mussorgsky wrote two (in 1873 he added two scenes set in Poland, but cut a scene in the last act), and Rimsky-Korsakov produced one soon after the composer's death with the intention that it should help the reception of the opera, while admitting that a time might come when it was superseded by a reappraisal of Mussorgsky's original. This has now happened and, while Rimsky's version is undoubtedly colourful, it misses the profundity and dark hues of the original orchestration.

the emancipation of the serfs in 1861, his family lost much of its wealth and he had to find work with the engineering department of the Ministry of Communications, and later with the forestry department of the Ministry for State Property. (As with many of his contemporaries, composition was always a spare-time activity, though his dipsomania probably had a more deleterious effect on his writing than did his lack of time.)

In the meantime, he had been gaining a growing reputation for his song-writing abilities, bringing a new sense of realism and integration to the form. He also worked on a couple of operas that he never got round to completing, *Salammbô* (1863–66) and *The Marriage* (1868) – from the former emerged one of his best-known works, *St John's Night on the Bare Mountain* (1867). He then embarked on an operatic adaptation of Pushkin's play *Boris Godunov*, which went through two versions in his own lifetime (1869 and 1873), and found lasting success in the second. In 1874 he wrote his best known work, *Pictures at an Exhibition*, a piano suite more often heard today in orchestral guise. His last great projects, which vied for his attention and thus were never finished, were another historical opera, *Khovanshchina* (1872–80, completed by Rimsky-Korsakov) and the Gogol-based comedy *Sorochintsy Fair* (1874–80, completed by Liadov).

◉ Kotcherga, Ramey, Lipovšek, Leiferkus, Langridge; Berlin Philharmonic Orchestra; Abbado (Sony S3K 58977; 3 CDs).

◉ Ghiaurov, Spiess, Vishnevskaya, Talvela; Vienna Philharmonic Orchestra; Karajan (Decca 411 862-2; 3 CDs).

Claudio Abbado's recording is the most successful, concentrating on character perhaps at the expense of spectacle (the bells at the coronation could be more atmospheric), but boasting a finely integrated cast and beautifully detailed orchestral playing. Like many recent accounts of the work, Abbado's amalgamates Mussorgsky's two versions; Karajan's sumptuous recording uses the Rimsky version – it's worth a listen after getting to know the original.

KHOVANSHCHINA

Khovanshchina (The Khovansky Affair) is set some eighty years later than *Boris Godunov* and depicts the religious and political upheavals leading up to the accession of Peter the Great in the 1680s. Mussorgsky failed to complete it before his death and Rimsky came to the rescue once more, though again his version has been superseded by a more faithful completion and orchestration – this time by Shostakovich, with a little help in the final scene from Stravinsky. The characterization is less coherent in this later opera, due to Mussorgsky's less than whole-hearted involvement in the project, but the music itself is just as fine and memorable.

⊙ Haugland, Atlantov; Vienna Philharmonic Orchestra; Abbado (Deutsche Grammophon 429 758-2; 3 CDs).

Abbado is perhaps the greatest living conductor of Mussorgsky's music, and he gives an impressively coherent and dramatic account of this score. This live recording reeks of the theatre, with vivid performances from all the main soloists.

PICTURES AT AN EXHIBITION

When Mussorgsky's close friend the architect-painter Victor Hartmann died in 1873, a mutual friend named Vladimir Stasov arranged a memorial exhibition of the artist's work in St Petersburg. Visiting the exhibition, Mussorgsky conceived his own tribute in the form of a suite of piano pieces depicting a selection of the works on show, with a recurring theme (the *Promenade*) representing the viewer walking between the pictures. Although completed in 1874, the suite wasn't published until after Mussorgsky's death, and the pictorial quality of these pieces inevitably drew the attention of other composers and arrangers – it's only surprising that Rimsky didn't attempt an orchestral arrangement himself. Of the many subsequent orchestrations, the most successful, if hardly the most Russian, is that made by Ravel in 1922.

⊙ **Piano version**: Pletnev (Virgin VC 7 59611-2; with Tchaikovsky, *Sleeping Beauty* – excerpts).
⊙ **Ravel orchestration**: London Symphony Orchestra; Abbado (Deutsche Grammophon 423 901-2; with Stravinsky, *Petrushka*).

Mikhail Pletnev gives a strong reading of the original piano suite, with playing that sometimes makes one think that orchestration didn't really add anything substantial. Abbado's excellent LSO performance of Ravel's version can't prevent the piece sounding less like Mussorgsky than like Ravel, but there is plenty of character here.

ST JOHN'S NIGHT ON THE BARE MOUNTAIN

Mussorgsky's only major orchestral work – *St John's Night on the Bare Mountain* – is another work that Rimsky wouldn't leave to fend for itself. It exists in two versions, Mussorgsky's original (intended as an episode in his opera *Sorochintsy Fair*) and Rimsky's beefed-up recomposition, incorporating other Mussorgsky fragments. The work is a portrait of midsummer night when, according to Russian folklore, a witches' sabbath is held on the Bare Mountain near Kiev; the musical whirlwind at the heart of the piece is one of those bits of music that hi-fi shops use to impress customers.

☽ **Original version**: London Symphony Orchestra; Abbado (RCA 09026 61354 2; with other orchestral works).
◉ **Rimsky-Korsakov version**: Royal Liverpool Philharmonic Orchestra; Mackerras (Virgin 7243 5 61135 27; with *Pictures at an Exhibition*; Borodin, *Prince Igor* – excerpts).

Although not nearly as well known as Rimsky's reworking, the original is arguably a more effective portrait of the midsummer mayhem, and Abbado's fine recording of it comes coupled with an invaluable collection of rarely heard choral and orchestral pieces. The most recommend`able account of the bastardized version is Mackerras's spirited performance with the Royal Liverpool Philharmonic – it's a potent piece, but make sure you hear the Mussorgsky version as well.

CARL NIELSEN

(1865–1931)

Of all Scandinavian composers, one of the most accomplished and original is Carl Nielsen, who was born into a peasant island community in eastern Denmark, and went on to become his country's musical figurehead. The first step in his career came at the age of fourteen, when he joined a military band in Odense; ten years later he joined the violins of the Royal Theatre Orchestra in Copenhagen. He had already begun composing by this stage and his first symphony was premiered by the orchestra in 1894. From then on his rise was rapid. His two operas, *Saul and David* (1902) and *Maskarade* (1905) were both performed under his direction, then he left the orchestra to concentrate on composing, though he returned three years later to be its principal conductor.

The rest of his life was taken up with composition – he once wrote that his life was lived through music rather than out in the everyday world. He wrote concertos for flute, clarinet and violin, and some fine tone poems, including *Helios* (1903), a short evocation of sunrise, and *Pan and Syrinx* (1918), an impressionistic depiction of characters from Ovid. But his fame rests solidly on his symphonies, works which are characterized by an emotional directness devoid of sentimentality, and by a constant search for clarity in line and orchestral texture, spinning out long lines of melody that build into complex yet clearly defined contrapuntal melées. His orchestration can often be stark in its sustained concentration on just a few instruments, yet come the climax of a movement or work Nielsen can unleash the orchestra's full force in a blaze of energy.

THE SYMPHONIES

Nielsen's six symphonies are almost contemporary with the seven of Sibelius, yet they could hardly be more different in style, form and intent: where Sibelius seemed to be aiming for ever greater concision, Nielsen's symphonies get more adventurous and wide-ranging as the cycle progresses. The ones to explore first are Nos. 3, 4 and 5, the first of these being the most immediately appealing.

The last few years have seen a real boom of Nielsen symphony recordings, with the result that there are now complete sets from the likes of Herbert Blomstedt, Bryden Thomson and Neeme Järvi, plus other single discs from Simon Rattle, Leonard Bernstein and others. At the moment, however, there is no good mid-price cycle, so the best thing to do is put together a cycle from the CDs recommended below.

SYMPHONY NO. 1

Even in his first symphony (1890–94) Nielsen was striking out in new directions. While his model was undoubtedly the Romantic classicism of Brahms (whom he met in the year of its composition), there is plenty to mark it out as the work of a fresh talent, including the concept of "progressive tonality", a Nielsen hallmark whereby the work ends in a different key from the one in which it began.

◉ San Francisco Symphony Orchestra; Blomstedt (Decca 425 607-2; with *Symphony No. 6*).

This disc couples Nielsen's first and last symphonies, showing how far he travelled in the thirty years that separate them. Blomstedt brings a sense of spontaneity to the exuberant early work and the recording quality is among the best ever heard on CD.

SYMPHONY NO. 2 – THE FOUR TEMPERAMENTS

Nielsen's second symphony emerged nearly a decade later, in 1902. It was inspired by a chance sighting in a village pub of a painting representing the four temperaments that were thought in medieval times to make up the human personality: choleric, phlegmatic, melancholic and sanguine. Here he found the "characters" for the four movements of his symphony, where the temperaments are suggested both by the tone of the music and the degree of sloth or energy with which it progresses.

● San Francisco Symphony Orchestra; Blomstedt (Decca 430 280-2; with *Symphony No. 3*).

Blomstedt's superb Decca recording is again the top choice, his San Francisco orchestra characterfully portraying the great mood swings from movement to movement.

SYMPHONY NO. 3 – SINFONIA ESPANSIVA

Another "theme" dominates Nielsen's third symphony (1910–11) – expansiveness – and again it works at every level, with the musical material seeming to be pushing inexorably further beyond its righful bounds through its repetitive rhythms, onward-forcing harmonic progressions and endless melodies. Another dimension of spaciousness is achieved in the marvellous slow movement, in which distant wordless voices join the melodic mélange.

● Isokoski, Hynninen; Gothenburg Symphony Orchestra; Järvi (Deutsche Grammophon 439 776-2; with *Symphony No. 4*).

Neeme Järvi has come late to Nielsen in his exploration of Scandinavian music, but he brings to this music all the personality and attention to detail that's evident elsewhere in his vast discography. Here he conducts an account of the *Espansiva* that seems ready to burst its seams.

SYMPHONY NO. 4 – THE INEXTINGUISHABLE

The life spirit is at the heart of the third symphony, and the same goes for *Symphony No. 4, The Inextinguishable* (1914–16). As Nielsen wrote in the foreword to the published score: "The composer has sought to indicate in one word what only music has the power to express in full: the elemental Will of Life. Music is Life and, like it, inextinguishable." It was written at a difficult time: World War I was raging (though Denmark remained neutral); his marriage was on the rocks; and he had resigned from his conducting post at the Copenhagen Opera. This symphony is patently a kind of emotional exorcism, culminating in a musical battle between two sets of timpani, a conflict resolved in the recall of a lyrical melody from the first movement.

● San Francisco Symphony Orchestra; Blomstedt (Decca 421 524-2; *Symphony No. 5*).

In the absence from the catalogue of Karajan's dramatic account, Blomstedt's is the most exciting performance currently available, recorded with splendid presence and bite.

SYMPHONY NO. 5

This sense of conflict resurfaced in Nielsen's *Symphony No. 5* (1921–22). Here a tense, sparely scored opening gradually breaks out into a battle for supremacy between a solo sidedrum and the rest of the orchestra – depicting, according to the composer, a fight between good and evil. The orchestra triumphantly subsumes the side-drum's martial improvisations and, after a warmly scored Adagio, the first movement ends quietly with the sidedrum heard again in the distance over a plangent clarinet solo. As this movement had contained both the traditional opening and slow movements, so the second exuberantly combines Scherzo and finale.

● San Francisco Symphony Orchestra; Blomstedt (Decca 421 524-2; *Symphony No. 4*).

Performances and recordings of this symphony often disappoint in the most vital place – the sidedrum battle, which can often sound too easily won. Not so in Blomstedt's account, which is a worthy partner to his recording of *No. 4*.

SYMPHONY NO. 6 – SINFONIA SEMPLICE

Nielsen's last symphony (1924–25) seems to convey his uncertainties about the way music was going in the 1920s. At once good-humoured, ironic (as is the title, "Simple Symphony") and intensely moving, it alternates passages that seem to be poking fun at atonal modernity with others that suggest deeper soul-searching. The whole enigmatic work ends with an unmistakeable bassoon "fart". It is often unclear whether Nielsen meant his audience to laugh or scream at this music, but this is one of his most fascinating and phantasmagorical works, looking forward to the irony of Shostakovich and nostalgically back at his own achievements.

● Gothenburg Symphony Orchestra; Järvi (Deutsche Grammophon 439 777-2; *Symphony No. 5*).

Blomstedt's recording of this symphony may be more stunningly executed, but Järvi provides a truer, more nightmarish experience.

MICHAEL NYMAN

(1944–   )

To date, the career of Michael Nyman is like the career of Erich Korngold (see p.190) played backwards. Korngold began by composing concert music but later devoted himself to highly successful film scores; Nyman began by writing highly successful film scores and has, ever since, been straining for recognition as a composer of concert music. It looks like being an uphill struggle. The recent album *Time will Pronounce* (see below) went some way to proving that his eighteen soundtracks for Peter Greenaway represented but one aspect of the composer, but then along came Jane Campion's *The Piano*, with its soundtrack by Michael Nyman. His prompt conversion of that score into a *"Piano" Concerto* is unlikely to win much respect from the opinion-formers, but even had *The Piano* never happened, Nyman's financial success would have been enough to antagonize the contemporary music scene in Britain.

If he doesn't manage to exorcise his cinematographical curse, it won't be for lack of trying. Nyman is an immensely prolific composer, and he celebrated his fiftieth birthday by embarking upon a series of major commissions: a *Trombone Concerto* for Christian Lindberg, a *Concerto for Cello and Saxophone* for Julian Lloyd-Webber and John Harle, and a *Double Piano Concerto* for the Labèque sisters. He has also been commissioned by the BBC Symphony Orchestra to write a piece to celebrate Purcell's tercentenary in 1995.

THE MUSIC

Nyman's music is immediately recognizeable as the work of a composer who knows his stuff. (He worked as a music critic from 1968 to 1978, and his book *Experimental Music – Cage and Beyond* is a classic text.) The film scores – in particular, the music for *The Draughtsman's Contract*, *The Cook, The Thief, His Wife and Her Lover* and *Prospero's Books* – are extremely well constructed, making very effective use of neo-Baroque instrumentation, greatly drawn-out melodies and an inflexible, unremitting pulse. These film scores do their job extremely well; the problem is that many of Nyman's concert compositions sound too similar to the film music. The pieces that convey the greatest sense of personal expression are the ones commissioned by or written for specific musicians – his songs for Ute Lemper, for example, or his music for the Balanescu Quartet. Four such pieces, all commissioned in 1993, are featured on the CD below.

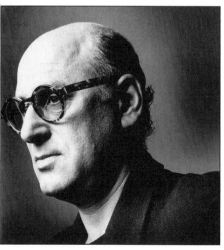

MATT ANKER

○ **Time will Pronounce**: Bowman; Fretwork; Trio of London; Black; London Brass (Argo 440 282-2).

This collection represents the most varied and revealing cross-section of Nyman's output. Each of the works is performed by the musicians for whom it was written, ranging from the counter-tenor James Bowman to the London Brass ensemble. Therefore the degree of commitment is high and the musical textures are radically different throughout, even if some of the pieces can become tiring in their insistence. All are immediately accessible and excellently crafted, especially the *Self laudatory hymn of inanna and her omnipotence*, consummately written for the pure voice of James Bowman.

JOHANNES OCKEGHEM

(c.1420–1497)

When Ockeghem died, Josquin Desprez – who may have studied with him – wrote a lament describing him as "Music's very treasure and true master," a fair reflection of the esteem in which he was held during his lifetime. This esteem virtually vanished with his death, and when musical scholarship finally caught up with him in the nineteenth century, he suffered the indignity of being dismissed as too clever by half, a purveyor of over-elaborate formal tricks. This is a difficult conclusion to reach once you have heard his music, for in works like the motet *Intemerata Dei Mater*, Ockeghem possesses a pellucid and ethereal beauty.

Unlike his two great Franco-Flemish contemporaries, Dufay (see p.117 and Josquin (see p.113), very little documentary information about Ockeghem's life has survived. He may have been born at the village of Ockeghem in eastern Flanders and may have studied with Binchois (he wrote a lament on Binchois' death), but there is no real evidence to support either theory. It is known that in the mid-1440s he served at the court of the Duke of Bourbon at Moulins, and that by 1453 he was in the service of the King of France, Charles VII. He remained a favoured member of the royal chapel until his death, serving Charles VII, Louis XI and Charles VIII as their premier chaplain, and was awarded the honorific and highly lucrative position of treasurer at the abbey of St Martin-de-Tours. His contemporaries admired him not just for his music but also for the remarkable sweetness of his singing voice. Several accounts suggest an exceptionally attractive character; one, by Francesco Florio, states – "you could not dislike this man, so pleasing is the beauty of his person, so noteworthy the sobriety of his speech and of his morals and his grace."

SACRED MUSIC

Considering that he lived so long and was so revered, Ockeghem was a curiously unprolific composer. About twenty secular songs have survived, plus nine motets, and some fifteen Masses, including the earliest surviving polyphonic setting of the Requiem.

Ockeghem's reputation for complexity derives from his four-part *Missa Prolationum*, in which two separate canons are sung simultaneously. In contrast, the three-part *Missa Ecce Ancilla Domine*, the only Mass by Ockeghem based on a plainsong cantus firmus, is on the whole a model of simplicity, though its later sections contain some florid writing. Probably composed for the funeral of Charles VII in 1461, it incorporates the plainsong chants traditionally used for the Requiem into the texture of the polyphony, usually placing it with some ornamentation in the highest voice.

⦾ **Requiem**: Ensemble Organum, Pérès (Harmonia Mundi HMC 901 4413.

⦾ **Missa Ecce Ancilla; Ave Maria; Intemerata Dei Mater**: The Clerks' Group, Wickham (Proudsound PROU CD 133; with motets by Obrecht and Josquin).

The Ensemble Organum set their performance of the *Requiem* firmly in a liturgical context (including plainsong settings as well as settings by another composer), and they succeed triumphantly in their attempt to evoke a definite sense of occasion. The individual voices of the all-male choir have rather more warmth and character than is favoured by English early music groups, and they manage to create the impression of having completely inhabited the spiritual world of the music in the same way that the greatest monastic choirs do.

The Clerks' Group is a young choir with a fresh and clear sound that effectively brings out the elasticity of Ockeghem's vocal lines, notably in the bright performance of the motet *Intemerata Dei* (Inviolate Mother of God) in which they employ women's voices on the top line. All the other Ockeghem works on the disc are sung by the men alone, but still with a strong sense of the music's rhythmic flow and an emphasis on clarity.

O

JACQUES OFFENBACH
(1819–1880)

GUUS ONG

Jacques Offenbach, "the Mozart of the Champs-Elysées", was the composer who made operetta an international art form, and so paved the way for Lehár (see p.192), Sullivan (see p.366) and the musicals of this century. Fusing dialogue and show-stopping set-pieces in productions of unrivalled musical verve and satirical bite, he deflated the morals and manners of the Second Empire in its prime – and they paid him for it.

Jacob, as he was named, was born in Cologne in 1819, seventh of ten children. He was taught music in his native city, then in 1833 the family resettled in Paris, allowing him to study at the Conservatoire. Joining the orchestra of the Opéra-Comique, he published waltzes and concert pieces for his own instrument, the cello. Throughout the 1840s he survived as a virtuoso performer, failing to get his stage works performed except when he paid for the privilege, but his luck changed in the following decade. In 1850 he was made conductor of the Théâtre Français, which in 1855 accepted his *Oyayaie, ou La reine des iles*. Its success gave him the cash and the credibility to set up as composer and stager of his own music, despite the disdain of Paris's "respectable" cognoscenti.

His two-act *Orphée aux enfers* (Orpheus in the Underworld), unleashed the can-can on the world in 1858, and typified Offenbach's irreverence – the opera's starting point is that Orpheus is bored with Eurydice and she is being driven to distraction by his violin-playing. His big hit of 1864, *La belle Hélène*, was concerned with the infidelities of Helen of Troy, lampooning Donizetti and Wagner in the process. Two years later came *Barbe-Bleu*, in which Bluebeard searches for his sixth wife (see p.18), and *La vie parisienne*, a glittering portrait of contemporary Paris society. In 1867 his mordantly satirical *La Grande-Duchesse de Gérolstein* (1867) was described by George Bernard Shaw as "an original and complete work of art which places its composer heavens-high", and was a colossal

box-office success. The risqué *La Périchole* (1868), which concerns the adventures in Lima of a pair of down-at-heel street singers, marked the end of Offenbach's heyday, a period during which he had composed some ninety operettas.

He had made his name amid the frivolous decadence of the Second Empire. Public taste changed after the Franco-Prussian War of 1870–1871, and Offenbach, once made a Chevalier of the Legion of Honour, was now branded "the great corrupter" of decorous taste. He fled to the admiring audiences of England and the USA, and from 1877 was occupied with the work that would become his masterpiece, *Les contes d'Hoffmann*. He died leaving much of it still in piano-score.

LES CONTES D'HOFFMANN

Produced in 1881, *Les contes d'Hoffmann* (Tales of Hoffmann) is Offenbach's most sober piece, his attempt to show himself worthy of the great German tradition. If it doesn't merit inclusion in the exalted ranks of Gluck and Mozart, it's nonetheless a highly accomplished and melodic fantasy. It takes its text from three tales by the German Romantic writer E. T. A. Hoffmann, presenting them as the disillusioned reminiscences of the writer himself. Hoffmann entertains the customers of a Nuremberg beer cellar with a recital of his three great loves, then is told by his Muse that all three were personifications of his latest love, Stella. Miserably self-absorbed, Hoffmann allows Stella to be drawn away by his rival, whereupon his Muse consoles him with the thought that his writing will be enriched by his woe. The great strength of *Les contes d'Hoffmann* is its vocal writing: some wonderful ensembles punctuate the action, the multi-faceted female lead is a consistent delight, and there is at least one fabulous duet – the Act Four barcarolle, *Belle nuit, o nuit d'amour.*

● Domingo, Sutherland, Tourangeau, Bacquier, Cuénod; L'Orchestre de la Suisse Romande, Radio Suisse Romande Chorus; Bonynge (Decca 417 363-2; 2 CDs).

The sweep and wit of Offenbach's score is supremely caught by Bonynge in a reading which tingles with frenetic urgency while bringing out the lushness of Guiraud's orchestration. Domingo is in his richest voice, summoning the impetuous ardour of Hoffmann, and Sutherland excels in one bravura aria after another.

CARL ORFF
(1895–1982)

Carl Orff is generally known as the creator of the hedonistic *Carmina Burana*, one of the most popular of all twentieth-century pieces, but he was both more prolific and more versatile than his reputation suggests. As well as composing nearly twenty music-theatre works, he was a highly influential educationalist, whose teaching methods are still in use all over the world.

Scion of an old Bavarian military family, Orff showed precocious musical gifts and quickly learnt to play the piano, cello and organ. He graduated from the Munich Academy of music in 1914, and the outbreak of World War I did not particularly hinder his advancement: he held the position of Kapellmeister at the Munich Kammerspiele from 1915 to 1917, going on to work at Mannheim's Nationaltheater and the Landstheater in Darmstadt. By this time Orff had several works behind him, the earliest of them bearing the mark of Debussy, whose influence soon gave way to that of Austro-German masters such as Schoenberg and Strauss.

However, he was later to disown all the compositions written before 1924, the year he and Dorothy Günther founded the Güntherschule in Munich. Working from the belief that everyone has inherent musical understanding and that movement and music cannot be separated, this innovative institution took its young adult students through a coordinated course of music, gymnastics and dance. In the early 1930s the Ministry of Culture recommended that a simplified version of the Güntherschule curriculum be adopted in elementary schools, but the project was thwarted by the rise of the Nazis, who were inimical to the radicalism of the school, with its emphasis on improvisation and percussion-based music.

In 1930 Orff found time to take up the post of conductor of the Munich Bach Society, and during his three-year tenure he became steeped in the compositions of the seventeenth and eighteenth centuries, especially Bach and Monteverdi. Augmented by his fascination with classical tragedy, Bavarian peasant life, primitive musical forms and Christian mysticism, this immersion in early music led to the creation of *Carmina Burana*, which was premiered at Frankfurt am Main in 1937.

After World War II Orff continued to refine his ideas about a "total theatre" in which music, speech and movement would combine to produce a spectacle both mentally stimulating and visually exciting. This conception of music as an essentially dramatic art form bears similarities with Wagner and his notion of the Gesamtkunstwerk, but Orff's methods were fundamentally simpler than those of his predecessor, employing punchy harmonic effects to create music of immediate sensuality. The compositions with which he consolidated his reputation as a dramatic composer drew on the classic stage repertoire for their raw material: *Antigonae* (1949) and *Oedipus der Tyrann* (1959) were derived from Sophocles, *Ein Sommernachtstraum* (1966) from Shakespeare.

Although Orff continued composing into old age (for example, writing a piece for the opening of the Munich Olympics in 1972), it was as a teacher that he was most influential. His educational activities were given fresh impetus when, in 1948, the German radio authorities commissioned him to adapt the Güntherschule's exercises as a series broadcasts for children. Running for five years, these programmes were so successful that the transcripts were translated into languages as diverse as English, Welsh, Japanese and Greek, and in 1961 Orff was invited to set up the Orff Institute in Salzburg, in order that his methods could be taught at first hand. In the final analysis, those methods, and the *Carmina Burana*, are his chief legacy.

CARMINA BURANA

Though nowadays performed as a choral concert item, *Carmina Burana* was conceived as a "scenic cantata" for the stage. Orff took the libretto from a sequence of medieval Latin lyrics that mix Christian piety with a celebration of the world's delights, but the latter element sets the dominant tone here, as you can tell from the titles of the work's three parts: *Spring, In The Tavern* and *Love*. The musical style of *Carmina Burana* owes a considerable debt to Stravinsky's *Les Noces* and *Oedipus Rex*, a connection most evident in Orff's use of the chorus and his use of rich percussive orchestration. Unlike Stravinsky, however, Orff makes little use of extended melodic writing, thematic development or polyphony – with him the rhythm is paramount. Allied to explicit harmonies, this rhythmic drive gives *Carmina Burana* a sense of wild abandonment.

Haranyi, Petrak, Presnall; Rutgers University Choir; Philadelphia Orchestra; Ormandy (Sony SBK 47668). Walmsley-Clark, Graham-Hall, Maxwell; Southend Boy's Choir; London Symphony Orchestra & Chorus; Hickox (Pickwick; PCD 855).

Of the many excellent versions on CD, the cream of the crop is the 1960 version from Eugene Ormandy and Philadelphia Orchestra, a performance in which it's abundantly clear that everyone had a roisteringly good time. The soloists hit a perfect balance between vivid characterization and vocal accuracy, the Rutgers University choristers bring an appealing roughness, swagger and wit to their singing, and Ormandy's orchestra projects an ideal combination of rugged power and warmth. Richard Hickox's budget-price recording also offers a thrilling ride, with the orchestra and chorus giving it all they have got, while the soloists are full of sexual knowingness. The only real reservation is that there is no line-by-line translation of the Latin, though a synopsis is provided.

NICOLÒ PAGANINI

(1782–1840)

Nobody had ever played the violin like Nicolò Paganini. The first musician to employ an agent, he was part Jascha Heifetz, part P. J. Barnum. People flocked to hear him play, not just for the promise of astonishing technical virtuosity but also because of the whiff of scandal that surrounded him. One persistent rumour suggested that his extraordinary talent was a result of a pact with the devil. Certainly their was something demonic about him: as a boy he mutilated his left hand in order to increase the spread of his fingers, and most contemporary portraits of the adult Paganini present an almost demented figure: gaunt, long-haired and with an intense, piercing gaze. Like all

ROYAL COLLEGE OF MUSIC

virtuosos of the time he mostly performed his own compositions, works which were designed to show off the whole range of his skills, from the lyrical to the acrobatic – his party piece was to break three strings on his violin and still keep playing. His music is rarely if ever profound, but its combination of easy-going charm and flagrant exhibitionism exerts a fascination above that of mere curiosity.

Paganini's world-wide reputation as the greatest violinist of the age followed a series of recitals that he gave in Vienna in 1828, and his triumphant progress throughout Europe continued for the next six years. Some musicians, like Spohr, denigrated him for the superficiality and trickery of his playing but his many admirers included Chopin and Schumann – both of whom wrote musical tributes to him – and above all Liszt, who successfully transformed himself into the Paganini of the piano. By 1834 Paganini was pretty well burnt out, worn down by exhaustion, illness, and persistent press rumours of

his miserliness and immorality. He retired to Parma and performances became increasingly infrequent. A venture in 1837 to start a casino in Paris bearing his name lost him large sums of money, and three years later he died in Nice from a disease of the larynx, resolutely refusing to see a priest.

VIOLIN CONCERTO NO. 1

Of Paganini's six violin concertos only the first two are now performed with any regularity. The first, the most uninhibited and most enjoyable, was written in 1817–18 when Paganini's fame was still confined to Italy. Like many virtuoso concertos of the period, including the piano concertos of Hummel (see p.179), the influence of Italian opera, particularly of Rossini, looms large. The work begins with a long and extremely bouncy orchestral introduction (with a lot of cymbal crashing) before the soloist enters with a theme full of leaps and runs which eventually leads into a sweet if rather simpering melody. The short slow movement is darker and more thoughtful, and it's not until the last movement that the technical stops are pulled out, with high chords, brilliant runs and "ricochet" bowing, a Paganini speciality in which several bouncing notes are played on one stroke of the bow.

⦿ Perlman; Royal Philharmonic Orchestra; Foster (EMI CDC 7 47101 2; with Sarasate, *Carmen Fantasy*).

Many violinists are now technically capable of playing Paganini's music, but few bring to it the finesse and the panache of which Perlman is capable. As usual with Perlman, the warmth and sweetness of tone is beguiling, but on top of this is the fact that he enters so fully into the spirit of the music, treating the insinuating first movement melody completely seriously, but injecting a witty playfulness into the music when it demands it. The concerto is coupled with another show-stopper, the *Fantasy on themes from Bizet's Carmen* by Sarasate, a great violin virtuoso of the second half of the nineteenth century.

THE CAPRICES

Paganini's *24 Caprices*, published in 1820, are the most famous of all his compositions. Like Chopin's *Études* (which they directly inspired), the *Caprices* are technical exercises that transcend the pedagogic limitations of the genre to become virtuosic miniatures –

not as wide-ranging in mood as Chopin's pieces but no less brilliant. Paganini dedicated them "Agli Artisti" (to the artists), but there could have been few artists capable of performing them, apart from himself. Each one explores a different aspect of violin technique: fast passages of double stopping, trills, harmonics, the combination of pizzicato and bowing, are just some of the more spectacular examples. *Caprice No. 24* is the best known, having been used by a wide number of composers (Brahms, Rachmaninov, Lutosławski, Andrew Lloyd-Webber) as the theme for sets of variations.

● **24 Caprices**: Perlman (EMI CDC 7 47171 2).

As with the concertos, many violinists can now play the *Caprices* (selections are often employed as encore pieces), but few can make their pyrotechnical bravura and quirkiness seem really musical. Perlman manages it with ease: whether in the Bach-like opening of *No. 2*, the mysterious trilling of *No. 6*, or the sheer chutzpah of *No. 24*, his response always suggests something more than mere showmanship.

═══════════════ 𝄢 ═══════════════

GIOVANNI DA PALESTRINA
(c.1525–1594)

Giovanni Pierluigi da Palestrina wrote music for the Catholic Church during one of the most traumatic periods of its history, a period during which its leaders were looking for ways to reverse the damage caused by the Reformation and the popularity of Protestantism. The function of church music was one of the many subjects under discussion. To its critics polyphony had become an over-elaborate web of sound that obscured rather than enhanced the meaning of the sacred words. Some, like the Bishop of Modena, even advocated a return to plainsong.

Palestrina is often credited as the composer who single-handedly saved polyphony: with the Church on the brink of abolishing it, he was requested to compose a Mass which would show decisively that the polyphonic style was not irreconcilable with clarity of meaning or a truly devotional spirit. The result, the *Missa Papae Marcelli* (the Mass of Pope Marcellus), swayed the critics and saved the day, at least till the end of the century. This story forms the basis of Pfitzner's opera *Palestrina* (see p.267), and although it is now regarded as more legend than fact there is an important element of truth in it. Palestrina had indeed begun his career by learning and assimilating the techniques of the great Franco-Flemish composers, such as Josquin Desprez, but had gone on to forge his own more simple and direct style,

one which combined polyphony with sections of more simple homophony – music in which the individual parts are melodically different, but are rhythmically in step with each other.

Palestrina took his name from the hill-town near Rome where he was born. After serving as a chorister at the church of Santa Maria Maggiore in Rome he returned to Palestrina in 1544 to be the organist at the cathedral of Sant'Agapito. He might well have remained in provincial obscurity had not the Bishop of Palestrina been elected Pope Julius III and in 1551 appointed him maestro da cappella at the Cappella Giulia, one of the choirs at St Peter's. Palestrina also sang in the Sistine Chapel choir, and almost certainly composed the *Missa Papae Marcelli* on the accession of Pope Marcellus II, possibly in response to the new pope's directive to his singers that the music for his enthronement "must be sung in a proper manner".

Dismissed in the same year from the Sistine Chapel for being married (it was meant to be a choir of celibates), Palestrina spent five fruitless years at the underfunded church of St John Lateran before being appointed to the rather more affluent Santa Maria Maggiore. By the 1560s his fame was such that several aristocratic patrons sought him out. In 1571 he was re-appointed maestro to the Cappella Giulia, a post he kept until his death. The deaths of both his sons in the

1570s and of his wife in 1580 led him to consider joining the priesthood but instead he got married again, to a wealthy widow with a thriving business in the fur trade, thus enabling him to spend his final years in relative financial security.

SACRED MUSIC

Although Palestrina wrote many madrigals (a source of pious embarrassment to him in later years), the main body of his work is made up of sacred music. As well as the one hundred and four Masses, there are at least two hundred and fifty motets and seven settings of the Magnificat. Obviously such a long and prolific career is bound to contain a great deal of variety, nevertheless Palestrina's name, especially after his death, came to be synonymous with the classic style of Catholic church music, a style characterized by clarity, sweetness of sound and a serenely optimistic mood. He avoids the startling dissonances then in vogue with avant-garde composers like Gesualdo (see p.139), and makes the music unfold in slow, steady steps – there are rarely any great interval leaps in his work. Comparisons are frequently made with the Renaissance painter Raphael, another artist striving to create an ideal world of balance and harmony. Some have found this ordered and reverential approach unrewarding and even boring, but at its best Palestrina's music creates a powerful impression of spiritual joy, unencumbered by doubt.

⦿ **Missa Papae Marcelli; Missa Brevis**: Westminster Cathedral Choir; Hill (Hyperion CDA 66266).
⦿ **Missa Hodie Christus Natus Est; Stabat Mater**: Schola Cantorum of Oxford; Summerly (Naxos 8.550836; with Lassus, *Missa Bell' Amfitrit' altera*).

The ethereal purity of the *Missa Papae Marcelli* is well served here by a great choir. The trebles have a bright, strong sound that is especially appropriate for the sense of line and momentum in Palestrina's melodies. Particular moments are given a restrained emphasis, for instance in the traditional slowing down of the words *et incarnatus est* (and was incarnate) in the Creed, or when the solemn treatment of the *Benedictus* is followed by the exuberant joyousness of the *Hosanna*. Such moments are brought into relief by a flexible but subtle attitude to dynamics and tempi. The performance of the *Missa Brevis*, one of Palestrina's best-loved and most often performed works, is equally effective; this is a rather more lively and less rarified *Mass* than the other but no less radiant.

Written for Christmas Day, the *Missa Hodie Christus Natus Est* (Today Christ is born) is one of Palestrina's most buoyant and energetic Masses. A Mass for double choir, it is based on the motet of the same name, which is also included on the disc and is given an equally exuberant performance by the Schola Cantorum. Palestrina's *Stabat Mater* is one of his most celebrated and glorious works. Its static and supremely tranquil music makes a startling contrast to the *Mass*, and the separation of the two choirs at its opening creates a wonderfully mysterious effect. The Naxos disc has a rather dry and ungiving acoustic, but that is its only failing.

HUBERT PARRY

(1848–1918)

Hubert Parry seems doomed to be known solely as the composer of *Jerusalem*, a piece of music that has become a sort of deputy national anthem. However, Vaughan Williams was acutely aware of the magnitude of Parry's contribution: "We pupils of Parry have . . . inherited from him the great English choral tradition which Tallis passed on to Byrd, Byrd to Gibbons, Gibbons to Purcell, Purcell to Battishall and Greene and they in turn through the Wesleys to Parry. He has passed the torch to us, and it is our duty to keep it alight." As composer, scholar and teacher (he became director of the Royal College of Music), Parry exercised a revitalizing influence upon British musical life at a time when it desperately needed it.

At Oxford, he studied with Schumann's friend Sterndale-Bennett but in 1871 he gave up music to pursue business interests. Within three years, he returned to his musical studies, and after piano lessons with Dannreuther (a friend to both Tchaikovsky and Wagner), he had his first piano concerto performed in 1880. However, it was the premiere, seven years later, of his cantata *Blest Pair of Sirens* that established him as one of England's leading composers. His deep affection for Wagner's music and his immersion in the British sacred traditions nurtured a distinctively Romantic voice that found clearest expression in his work for the voice – and, in particular, choral music, much of it written for English choral music festivals. Hymns and anthems comprise but part of an output that was perhaps too vast for the good of Parry's reputation. At its best, however, Parry's music is a tuneful and enjoyable alliance of Edwardian grandiosity and highly original polyphony.

THE MUSIC

Parry was an avowed agnostic yet he produced some of Britain's finest sacred choral music. His three best known choral pieces are the anthem *I was Glad*, the cantata *Blest Pair of Sirens* and the hymn *Jerusalem*. Of these, the masterpiece is the first – written for the coronation of Edward VII in 1902, it contains some of the most ecstatic, jubilant music ever written for a choir. Most famous is of course *Jerusalem*, which was first heard in 1916, in the depths of World War I, and still makes many a British heart beat faster; there are indeed few hymns more stirring, even if it is debatable whether the music obscures or enhances the meaning of Blake's militant poem.

When Elgar's *Symphony No. 1* was premiered in 1908, it was hailed as a "first" by an English composer; the distinction really belongs to Parry's *Symphony No. 1* of 1882. An extraordinary achievement, it's a work bursting with youthful enthusiasm, and is full of beguilingly simple tunes that at times recalls Mendelssohn. The best of the subsequent symphonies are the third and the fifth, both of which display the controlled expansiveness of the true symphonist – *Symphony No. 5* is an especially fine example of ardent Romanticism. As a group, Parry's symphonies may not reach the exultant heights of Elgar's two, and they lack the humanist gravity of Vaughan Williams's symphonies, but there is much to enjoy here.

◉ **I was Glad**: Westminster Abbey Chorus; London Brass; Neary (Pickwick PCD 919; with other English anthems).

◉ **Jerusalem; Blest Pair of Sirens**: Winchester Cathedral Choir, Waynflete Singers; Bournemouth Symphony Orchestra; Hill (Argo 430 836-2ZH; with other English anthems).

◉ **Symphonies 1–5**: London Philharmonic Orchestra; Bamert (Chandos 9120-22; with *Symphonic Variations*; 3 CDs).

The Westminster Abbey Chorus is now one of the greatest treble-led choirs in the world, and their finely engineered recording of English anthems boasts a jubilantly sung account of Parry's masterpiece. Neary's well paced direction keeps the music from descending into sentimentality. David Hill's account of *Jerusalem* makes the most of the composer's thick orchestration, and the singing of the Winchester Cathedral Choir is angelic; also on this recording is a fine performance of *Blest Pair of Sirens* and various other English favourites.

Chandos have carried the flag for Parry by recording a large amount of his orchestral music. Best of all their efforts is this cycle of the complete symphonies, the first undertaken since the composer's lifetime. Occasionally you get the feeling that Bamert is more enthusiastic than the orchestra, but on the whole the symphonies are played with wonderful lucidity, colour and conviction.

ARVO PÄRT

(1935–)

If any one composer can be said to be responsible for creating a public receptive to the "sacred minimalism" of John Tavener and Górecki's third symphony, it's the monkish Estonian composer Arvo Pärt. Trained at Tallinn's conservatory, he began – like Górecki – as a recalcitrant serialist, using the dissonances of atonal music to kick against the Soviet system. In addition to these exercises in difficult, noncomformist music, he wrote over fifty film scores while working as a technician for Estonian Radio from 1958 to 1967. Towards the end of this period, having composed a depressing *Second Symphony* (1966), he embarked on a study of medieval Franco-Flemish choral music that resulted in his first religious piece – a *Credo*, which was duly banned by the secularist state. The more serene *Third Symphony* (1971), mixing seventeenth-century elements with Orthodox chant, indicated the way Pärt's music was to move forward by looking back.

Years of meditation and religious consultation yielded three stunning compositions in 1977 – *Tabula Rasa*, *Fratres* and *Cantus in Memory of Benjamin Britten*, the first examples of Pärt's unique species of highly charged minimalism. A year later, Pärt and his Jewish wife and two children were granted permission to go to Israel; instead he fled to Vienna, where he lived for twelve years until finally settling in Berlin. Since the late 1970s he has unwaveringly followed a spiritual path, and has been steadily productive: *Passio* (1982), an eighty-minute rendition of the Passion according to Saint John, was followed by a succession of smaller works such as *Arbos* (1987), which was dedicated to the great Russian film-maker Andrei Tarkovsky, and then by a wonderful *Te Deum*, released on CD in 1993.

THE MUSIC

The serialist music of Pärt's early career hasn't been widely recorded and is unlikely to make converts to his cause anyway. The pieces composed since the mid-1970s are a different matter. When Manfred Eicher founded ECM in 1969 he announced his intention of recording "the most beautiful sound next to silence", and when he first heard Pärt's passionately quiet music he knew he'd found what he wanted – he described it as being like "slowly beating

wings". The subsequent series of superlative ECM releases have generated a cult following for the composer, and though other labels are now recording Pärt's music, the best introductions are the CDs reviewed below. Some might balk at the limitations of these pared-down compositions – not a lot happens in twenty minutes of Pärt – but if you can get on the same wavelength, you'll find this some of the most nourishing music of the post-war years.

⦿ **Tabula Rasa; Fratres; Cantus**: Sondeckis, Russell Davis; Lithuanian Chamber Orchestra, Berlin Philharmonic, Stuttgart State Orchestra; Kremer, Jarrett, Schnittke (ECM New Series 817 764-2).

⦿ **Arbos; Pari Intervallo; An den Wassern zu Babel; De Profundis; Es sang vor langen Jahren; Summa; Stabat Mater**: Russell Davies; Stuttgart State Orchestra; Hilliard Ensemble; Kremer, Dawson, Bowers-Broadbent (ECM New Series 831 959-2).

⦿ **Te Deum**: Estonia Philharmonic Chamber Choir; Tallinn Chamber Orchestra (ECM New Series 439 162-2).

The ECM issue of *Tabula Rasa*, Pärt's breakthrough in the West, is one of the late twentieth century's finest recordings. Beginning with effusive strings which give way to a music of deep silence and simple triads, *Tabula Rasa* is given a fittingly intense performance by Alfred Schnittke (on prepared piano) and the violinist Gidon Kremer, a frequent collaborator with the composer. The briefest piece on this CD, *Cantus*, recalls the adagio of Mahler's fifth symphony with its lush, yearning strings, but its tolling bells and hieratic grandeur are wholly Pärt. *Fratres* is performed here in two versions, a dramatic one for violin and piano and a more solemn one for twelve cellists.

The selection of smaller-scale pieces on the *Arbos* CD is equally fascinating, with the plaintive voices and almost static organ sound of Arbos itself – intended to suggest the slow organic growth of a tree – preparing the way for the uncompromising *Stabat Mater*, an extreme case of Pärt's hypnotic simplicity. After that, you could totally immerse yourself in Pärt's world by tackling the *Te Deum*, a mighty work that demonstrates Part's absolute mastery of his chosen form. Recorded in a Finnish church, this celebration of God uses acoustic resonance, bursts of strings and choral voices to devastating effect, alternating silence with soaring chant. The precise orchestral embellishments which colour the voices are exquisite, particularly the high/low string decoration of the Sanctus.

KRZYSZTOF PENDERECKI

(1933–   )

Of the Polish composers who burst onto the Western musical scene with the relaxation of socialist-realist dogma in the 1960s, the one who made the greatest impact was the versatile Krzysztof Penderecki. Having completed his studies at the Kraków Academy in 1958, he won the Polish Composer's Union competition in the following year, and in 1960 unveiled his *Threnody for the Victims of Hiroshima*, a piece singularly well attuned to the mood of the coming decade. Much of the 1960s was spent travelling throughout Europe and the United States, teaching at various institutions and absorbing the latest artistic movements. The *St Luke's Passion* of 1966 marked his arrival as a composer of international status, and epitomized his talent for creating a feeling of space and epic duration.

Penderecki had all the techniques of modernism at his finger tips – note clusters, indeterminate pitch, extremes of volume and register, shouting and hissing, sudden bursts of energy and moments of calm. Since the late 1970s, however, he has become an increasingly conservative musician, with works such as his second symphony showing a predilection for post-Romantic luxury.

THE MUSIC

Penderecki's orchestral works range in length from concise utterances such as the six-minute *Anaklasis* to his two full-scale symphonies and concertos for viola, violin and cello. More important is their stylistic range – it's a long way from the terseness and raw emotion of the earlier avant-garde pieces to the more accessible but sometimes unspontaneous world of the music written after Penderecki's "return to melody". With its quotation from the carol *Silent Night*, the *Symphony No. 2* (1980), subtitled the *Christmas Symphony*, sounds as if it could not have been written by a man who was once the arch-experimenter of the 1960s, and the same goes for the *Violin Concerto* (1976), a conventional, richly melodic, two-movement work based on Berg's violin concerto.

Penderecki's terrifying opera *Devils of Loudon* has not yet been recorded, which means that his vocal and choral music is best represented on disc by the *St Luke's Passion* and the more recent *Polish Requiem*. The *Passion* was commissioned in 1963 by West German Radio for the seven hundredth anniversary of Münster Cathedral, which also coincided with the thousandth anniversary of Christianity in Poland. Loosely based on the structure of Bach's Passions, it uses some dramatic untraditional effects (such as crowd noises) to convey a genuinely devotional feeling. Penderecki's Catholicism and liberal politics come together in the *Requiem* (1980–84), a piece that is inextricably bound up with the events of the time in Poland – the Lacrimosa was written for the unveiling of a Solidarity monument, the Agnus Dei for the funeral of Cardinal Wyszynski, the leader of the Polish Church. Reminiscent of the Requiems of Verdi and Britten, it concludes with a Polish hymn sung against the Latin text. Not surprisingly, it became something of a rallying call for Poles in a time of trouble.

❍ **Anaklasis; Threnody; Canticum Canticorum and other works**: Polish Radio Symphony Orchestra, London Symphony Orchestra; Penderecki (EMI CDM 5 65077 2).

❍ **Violin Concerto; Symphony No. 2**: Kulka; Polish Radio Symphony Orchestra; Penderecki, Kasprzyk (Polskie Nagrania PNCD 019).

❍ **St Luke's Passion**: von Osten, Roberts, Rydl, Lubaszenko; Polish Radio Symphony Orchestra; Penderecki (Argo 430 328-2).

❍ **Polish Requiem**: Haubold, Winogradska, Terzakis, Smith; Polish Radio Symphony Orchestra; Penderecki (Deutsche Grammophon DG 429 720-2; 2 CDs).

EMI's anthology of short works, spanning the years 1959 to 1974, is the ideal introduction to Penderecki, charting his progress from the unyielding early pieces through the archaic and religious sound worlds that he began to explore in the 1960s. Threnody and Anaklasis are particularly well played and the short choral *Canticum Canticorum* is a marvellous wallow in sound for sound's sake. To complete the chronological survey of the orchestral music, the Polskie Nagrania disc of the *Violin Concerto* and *Symphony No. 2* provides fine performances and acceptable sound. Penderecki has recorded the *Passion* twice, the better version being this second record-ing from Argo, which has the extra clarity of digital sound. The composer's own reading of the *Requiem*, recorded live in 1989 with excellent soloists and chorus, is the best available.

=== 🎵 ===

GIOVANNI BATTISTA PERGOLESI
(1710–1736)

Though only a moderately successful composer during his short life, Pergolesi managed to write two works that not only brought him posthumous fame but significantly influenced the direction of vocal music in the eighteenth century.

The first, *La Serva Padrona* (The Maid as Mistress), was an early example of comic opera, or opera buffa, in which the characters were drawn from everyday life. Pergolesi worked mainly in Naples, where an operatic style had developed which emphasized the beauty and virtuosity of the solo voice, often at the expense of dramatic unity. *La Serva Padrona* introduced a more naturalistic tone, but its notoriety came about after the composer's death, when a performance in Paris in 1752 instigated a furious theoretical debate about the respective merits of Pergolesi's opera buffa as opposed to the more formal and serious French opera.

The second, a setting of the Stabat Mater for two solo voices and strings, pioneered a style of church music which combined emotional directness with an elegant and graceful expressiveness. Here, as in his operatic work, Pergolesi epitomized a progressive tendency which was championed by the philosopher Jean-Jacques Rousseau, who described the opening of the *Stabat Mater* as "the most perfect and most touching to have come from the pen of any musician".

THE MUSIC

The *Stabat Mater* is Pergolesi's masterpiece: the great medieval text, detailing the Virgin's suffering at the foot of the Cross, drew an enormously intense response from him, in which the expressive use of pauses and of dissonances is much in evidence. If it sounds rather operatic for a religious work, it is largely because Pergolesi dispenses with a chorus in order to present the text through the immediacy of the solo voice – each of the twelve sections is allocated either to the soprano or the alto or to both in duet. The music is astonishingly varied given that the prevailing mood is one of pain and supplication, though there are a couple of sections of relative liveliness. According to legend it was the last work Pergolesi wrote before his death, probably from consumption, at the Franciscan monastery in Pozzuoli near Naples. What is certainly true is that it became one of the most popular and enduring works of the entire eighteenth century.

La Serva Padrona should be approached with a certain amount of caution. Several of the arias are charming and inventive (and sound surprisingly Mozartian) but over a third of the opera takes the form of long recitatives which, though possibly tolerable with accompanying stage business, can be wearisome on record. The plot tells of how a tyrannical maid-servant (Serpina) tricks her elderly master (Umberto) into marrying her by disguising a fellow servant (Vespone) as a prospective suitor. Much of the comedy derives from the fact that the role of Vespone is mute, thus providing scope for several comic misunderstandings.

🔵 **Stabat Mater; Salve Regina in C minor**: Kirkby, Bowman; The Academy of Ancient Music; Hogwood (L'Oiseau Lyre 425 692-2).

🔵 **La Serva Padrona**: Bonifaccio, Nimsgern; Collegium Aureum; Maier (Deutsche Harmonia Mundi RD 77184).

Past recordings of the *Stabat Mater* have tended to sentimentalize the work by using a lush orchestral sound and two female operatic voices. More recently, in the name of authenticity, there has been a tendency to pare down the accompaniment and use a male alto with a female soprano. This is such a recording, and the advantages are immediately apparent: there is a clarity and a directness to the sound, and both of the well-matched soloists seem to have found just the right balance between passion and restraint. Pergolesi wrote several settings of the *Salve Regina*, of which the C minor version for soprano and strings is the most well known. Emma Kirkby's performance touches through its simplicity and directness.

The Deutsche Harmonia Mundi CD of *La Serva Padrona* is the best available; unfortunately, however, its provides no translation of the libretto.

PÉROTIN
(c.1170–c.1236)

T he earliest composers of polyphonic music whose names have come down to us are Leonin (c.1159–1201) and Pérotin, both of whom were part of an extraordinary flowering of culture that took place in Paris in the late twelfth century. Almost nothing is known of their lives. They probably had some connection with the new cathedral of Notre Dame, but the theory that Pérotin was taught by Leonin and succeeded him as choir-master of Notre Dame is now generally discredited. Leonin's music is relatively simple two-part writing, whereas Pérotin wrote in three and sometimes four parts – strange but utterly compulsive music, in which harmonic plainness is carried joyously along by rhythmic suppleness.

Up to the time of Pérotin, the dominant musical form of the Christian church had been monophonic chanting – that is the singing of a single line of music, either by one voice or by several voices. This became known as plainsong (or plainchant), and several different versions of it existed, the best known of which, Gregorian Chant, seems to have developed in France between the eighth and tenth centuries. Sometime in the ninth century the addition of another voice with its own independent line of music marks the beginnings of polyphony. At first it was very simple: the added line moved in parallel to the plainsong melody, usually beneath it, at a fixed interval. The plainsong melody was known as the cantus firmus (fixed song), the voice that sang it was the vox principalis and the added voice the vox organalis. This simple form of polyphony was called organum

and it was employed as an occasional, ornate addition to liturgical plainsong rather than as a replacement for it.

This parallel duplication of the melody had obvious musical limitations, and freer developments soon began to appear, such as the use of more than two voices. One especially important progression was that vox organalis, instead of moving note-on-note with the cantus firmus, was placed on top of the cantus firmus and was made rhythmically independent and melodically dominant, employing as many as twenty notes to one in the lower part. The voice singing the cantus firmus became known as the tenor (from the Latin "to hold") since the plainsong was drawn out to accommodate the ornate phrases above it. This style was called florid or melismatic organum and it existed alongside the older note-on-note style, which became known as discant.

In Pérotin's hands organum became increasingly lively and exciting – two of his most moving contributions to the genre, the extraordinary *Viderunt omnes* and *Sederunt principes*, are the earliest examples of Western music written in four parts. Both contain startlingly dance-like rhythms in the higher voices, which lilt and weave their way around the drawn-out line of the cantus firmus, echoing each other's material in a way that dissolves the dominant melodic line to create, in Paul Hillier's words, "a kaleidoscope of constantly shifting textures".

● Pérotin: The Hilliard Ensemble; Hillier (ECM 837 751-2).

This CD of music attributed to Pérotin and his contemporaries is no archaeological curiosity – on the contrary, the Hilliard

Ensemble's performances are direct and deeply moving, their wonderfully flexible approach creating an image of the Gothic as something delicate and light-filled. Of the nine pieces on this disc, four (all by Pérotin) are organum while the other five (two by Pérotin) are conductus, a simple form of music which was employed for ceremonial or processional occasions within the church. The one minor irritation is that the sleeve-notes include the Latin texts but no translation of them.

HANS PFITZNER
(1869–1949)

The Third Reich effectively wrecked the reputation of Hans Pfitzner. Though he may have liked to regard himself as apolitical, he held strongly anti-Semitic nationalist views and complied with what the Reich demanded of him, allowing them to use his good name as and when they chose. Pfitzner's self-consciously Wagnerian music was lauded for upholding the best in the German tradition, and he was used by the Nazis as a stick with which to beat the "degenerate" Richard Strauss, a composer whose success Pfitzner deeply envied. Works such as *Von deutscher Seele* and *Das dunkle Reich* (fine pieces in themselves) became musical propaganda, paraded as evidence that there was an abundance of great non-Jewish Teutonic music. It is scarcely surprising that his music is unfairly seen as nothing more than a reflection of Germanic insanity.

It's ironic that, he was born in Moscow, where his father was working as a violinist. Moving to Frankfurt as a child, he studied at the conservatory until 1890 then he began teaching in Coblenz from 1892. Teaching and conducting dominated the next twenty years of his life, although Mahler conducted two of his operas in Vienna and his songs, chamber music and early symphonies all found champions. His status as a composer was sealed in 1917, with the premiere of his music-drama *Palestrina*, a composition that defined his Romantic-conservative stance against the radicalism of Schoenberg and Busoni. His career prospered under the Nazis but ended pathetically. At the end of the war his house in Munich was destroyed by Allied bombing, and in 1946 the president of the Vienna Philharmonic Orchestra found him living in a home for the aged in Salzburg. Supported by the orchestra, he lived out the rest of his days in Vienna.

PALESTRINA

Composed between 1912 and 1915, while Pfitzner was director of Strasbourg opera, *Palestrina* was his most successful and finest work. Set in 1563, it concerns the legendary incident in the life of the eponymous composer, when, at the instigation of Cardinal Borromeo, he saved the polyphonic tradition by composing the brilliant *Missa Papae Marcelli*, a piece that demonstrated to the Council of Trent that the Catholic Church could repel the Protestant onslaught through beautiful polyphonic music (see p.261 for more). It's a long, doggedly serious work, but Pfitzner sustains concentration throughout the three acts by a skilled deployment of devices learned from Wagner. The orchestration of *Palestrina* is decidedly Wagnerian, as are Pfitzner's extended mystical moods, dissonant contrapuntal textures and long-breathed melodic lines – and as a true Wagnerian he also wrote his own libretto, after spending two years researching the history of the Council of Trent. Musical motifs from the *Missa Papae Marcelli* are incorporated into the score, underlining the point that this is, in essence, Pfitzner's aesthetic manifesto as defender of the faith against the philistines and modernists.

Ridderbusch, Wiekl, Steinbach, Fischer-Dieskau, Prey, Gedda, Donath, Fassbaender; Tolz Boys Choir, Bavarian Radio Chorus, Bavarian Radio Orchestra; Kubelik (Deutsche Grammophon 427 417-2GC3; 3 CDs).

Kubelik's monumental and widely acclaimed account has an incredible cast, including Fischer-Dieskau as Borromeo, the superb Karl Ridderbusch as Pope Pius IV, and Nicolai Gedda as Palestrina – a wonderful performance, creating a sense of fragility well suited to this semi-autobiographical role. As with most of Kubelik's work, he maintains brisk tempi throughout, and he achieves a clear orchestral sonority that serves Pfitzner's orchestrations well.

— ♫ —

FRANCIS POULENC

(1899–1963)

For years Francis Poulenc was pigeonholed as the playboy of French music. Superficially there's some justice to the charge. He was born into money and had a privileged social position. He was a member of the Les Six, a group who – egged on by Cocteau – made it their business to jeer at the old masters and to embrace all manner of low-brow musical forms. And of all that gang, Poulenc seemed the most facile and clownish, the man with the permanent grin on his face. But be that as it may, he was from the outset a serious craftsman, and was the only one of the sextet who continued to develop in new directions. By no stretch of the imagination could Poulenc be described as a modernist, yet he always had a keen interest in the international scene – for example, he accompanied Milhaud to Vienna in 1921 to meet Schoenberg and his pupils. Even towards the end of his life he considered it his duty to keep abreast of what was happening, even if it involved young turks who were so scathing of his generation. In 1961 he wrote of the premiere of a Boulez piece – "I'm truly sorry to miss *Pli selon pli*, because I'm sure it's well worth hearing".

Like many young French composers of the inter-war years, he was immensely taken by the irony of Stravinsky's early neo-classical works. His masterstroke was to be able to take this irony and turn it into something beguilingly French. In this project, the influence of his friend Jean Cocteau was never far away, and the rather brittle, jewel-like works of these years show Poulenc taking to heart Cocteau's principle that artists must aim for a coolly elegant modernity, braced with a quasi-classical sense of proportion. There is artifice aplenty in the *Aubade* for small orchestra, the ballet *Les Biches* and the *Mouvements perpetuels* for piano, but there is also much ingenuity in the way he achieves fresh sounds with conventional materials.

In 1935 Poulenc rediscovered Catholicism, but although henceforth he concentrated on liturgical music, he never lost his lightness of touch nor his dash of Parisian worldliness. The war years were spent in France where his form of resistance was to compose lightly veiled barbs against the occupying forces. Once peacetime came he spent much of his time accompanying his friend the brilliant singer Pierre Bernac, with whom he gave numerous recitals of French song, as well as recording songs by himself, Satie and Chabrier. In the second half of his life he achieved growing respect as a composer – perhaps his greatest success being the performance of his first opera, *Les mamelles de Tiresias*, in 1947.

The best summary of Poulenc's place in the history of modern music is contained in a letter he wrote in 1942. "I know perfectly well that I'm not one of those composers who have made harmonic innovations like Igor [Stravinsky], Ravel or Debussy, but I think there's room for new music which doesn't mind using other people's chords. Wasn't that the case with Mozart-Schubert?" For all his chic use of spicy dissonances and his flirtation with advanced techniques such as polytonality, Poulenc was quite happy to be seen as part of a French tradition stretching back through Chabrier and Fauré deep into the nineteenth century.

SONGS AND CHORAL WORKS

Poulenc had no doubts as to which part of his output gave him most satisfaction: "I think I put the best and most authentic side of myself into my choral music. Excuse my lack of modesty, but I have the feeling that it is truly in this domain that I have contributed something new." Poulenc's great strength was as a lyrical melodist and a writer for the voice – few could match the exquisite delicacy of Poulenc's word-setting, which displayed a feeling for every nuance of his native tongue. What makes his work in this form so pleasurable was his return to an early seventeenth-century aesthetic that saw no division between what was musically appropriate for sacred texts and what was fitting for more earthly subjects. Poulenc's religious choral music is as warm and humane as his secular songs, for Poulenc saw everything as a product of the heavenly father. His subjects range from the Catholic mass, through the surreal texts of Apollinaire and Eluard (inspiration

for the *Sept chansons* of 1936), to simple French folk-tunes like those that form the basis of his *Chansons françaises*, written to celebrate the return of peace in 1946.

> ◉ **Salve Regina; Messe en sol majeur; Un soir de neige; Chansons françaises; Chanson a boire; Sept chansons**: The Sixteen; Christophers (Virgin VC7 59311-2).
> ◉ **Figure humaine; Laudes de Saint Antoine de Padoue; Quatre Motets pour le temps de Noel; Quatre Motets pour un temps de penitence; Quatre Petites prières de Saint Francois d'Assise**: The Sixteen; Christophers (Virgin VC7 91075-2).

Harry Christophers and The Sixteen have a great reputation for unaccompanied vocal music, and they bring a suitably wide interpretive range to these two recordings of Poulenc's religious and secular choral compositions. On the first of these CDs the sensitivity of *Un soir de neige* is particularly special, as is the vigour and freshness of *Chanson à boire*, a delightfully off-the-wall collection of drinking songs written for the Harvard Glee Club in 1922, but not publicly performed until Prohibition had ended. The companion CD of exclusively religious pieces cannot be recommended highly enough; it includes some of Poulenc's best-loved a cappella motets, as well as the cantata for double choir, *Figure Humaine*.

SERGEY PROKOFIEV
(1891–1953)

Though he was regarded as impossibly avant-garde in his youth, Sergey Prokofiev in fact belongs squarely to the same great tradition of Russian music as Tchaikovsky and Mussorgsky, a tradition resonant with a sense of the country's history. Writing in an immediately recognizeable style which reconciles progressive technique with melodic traditionalism, he produced some of the most enjoyable of all twentieth-century compositions, and contributed to almost every musical genre. It's an achievement all the more remarkable in view of the fact that much of it was achieved in the face of the dogmatic repression of Stalinism, and in the midst of Russia's suffering in World War II.

Born in the Ukraine, he soon displayed prodigious talent as a composer and as a

LEBRECHT COLLECTION

pianist, as well as a somewhat over-developed sense of his own importance. At the St Petersburg academy he proved rebellious, disruptive and totally unsuited to the disciplines of academic study, earning the hostility of, among many others, Glazunov (see p.145). Stifled by conservative Russia, he packed his bags after graduation in 1914, and left for a spell in London, where he met Diaghilev and Stravinsky.

Stravinsky's music had a deep and lasting impact on the young man – although it was one that Prokofiev, curiously, always failed to acknowledge – and his relationship with Diaghilev was equally productive. The great impresario of the Ballets Russes set Prokofiev to work on three different ballets and also encouraged him to remain away from Russia. This resolve, though weakened by intermittent concert tours and visits to his homeland, held out until 1926, when he began a correspondence with the concert authorities in the USSR. Cautiously, he accepted their invitation to make an extensive tour of western Russia, his first visit for nine years. To his surprise, Prokofiev was treated as a celebrity and a hero of Russian music, and the great success of the series of twenty-one concerts, coupled with his joy in renewing old friendships, must have made the prospect of a permanent return seem very attractive. He managed to avoid the inevitable for another seven years until 1933, when Prokofiev and his wife left Paris and went home to Russia for good. It was the worst decision of his life.

He could have stayed in the West – as had Rachmaninov and Stravinsky – but he saw himself as an apolitical artist and disregarded the political implications of his return, believing that the Soviet authorities would grant him immunity as a famous composer. Prokofiev genuinely felt that the pressures being brought to bear on other composers, such as Shostakovich, would somehow not apply to him. His timing could not have been worse. By 1936 the musical establishment was run by politicians, and when he arrived in Moscow, Prokofiev effectively threw himself upon the mercy of a system that now expected composers – without exception – to write music for "the people", extolling the brave new world of Soviet socialism. The ensuing

years were hard. His relationship with the authorities, though stable to begin with, rapidly disintegrated and he suffered frequent humiliation, often having to thank the authorities for belittling him and his music in the press. When war broke out, ill-health and deep-seated resentment towards his country prevented him from taking any involvement and in 1941 his relationship with a 25-year-old student, Mira Mendelson, ended his marriage.

For all that he suffered, Prokofiev wrote some superb music during the war years, including the opera *War and Peace*, the violin sonatas, the film score to *Ivan the Terrible* and the ballet *Cinderella*. Through works such as these he attained a dominant position within the Russian musical world, and for the first few years after the war, it seemed that he was above persecution. In 1948, however, it became clear that Prokofiev's position was not as secure as he had imagined. The Central Committee of the Communist Party held a meeting at which Prokofiev, Shostakovich and many others were accused of "formalism", a catch-all term applied to any music that had no immediately utilitarian function. The errant composers were charged with "anti-democratic tendencies that are alien to the Soviet people and its artistic tastes" and condemned for writing music "strongly reminiscent of the spirit of contemporary modernistic bourgeois music of Europe and America." Unequivocal apologies were wrung out of all the "defendants".

After this idiotic and brutal farce, all sense of purpose was knocked from Russia's composers and Prokofiev was reduced to turning out pallid and predictable scores, almost entirely derived from Russian folk music. The opera *War and Peace* is the only work that stands out from the morass – the rest is the musical equivalent of the paintings of agricultural labour that the country's artists were obliged to churn out. Prokofiev died on March 3, 1953 – only a few hours before Stalin. The irony would have appealed to him.

THE LOVE FOR THREE ORANGES

Prokofiev's relationship with the theatre was lifelong but never particularly happy. Before

the end of his student days he had already
written over half a dozen complete operas. His
first work after graduation remained
incomplete while his second, based upon
Dostoyevsky's *The Gambler*, was beset by so
many problems – orchestra and singers who
hated the violent music, a director who
resigned – that it wasn't performed until 1929,
and even then the music was substantially
revised from the original of 1917.

The Love for Three Oranges, Prokofiev's
first successful opera, was written between
1919 and 1921 while he was living in
America. Re-working the *commedia dell'arte*
traditions of Gozzi's eighteenth-century play
Fiaba dell'amore delle tre melarancie, *Three
Oranges* is whimsical, melancholy and very
strange, as you can tell from a glance at the
cast list which features ten "ridiculous
people", a chorus of "little devils", a
"Gigantic Cook" and a smattering of prin-
cesses. Prokofiev was deeply impressed by
Meyerhold's theories on drama, which
included "the diminution of the role of the
actor and a challenge to conventional audience relationships", and in Gozzi's lunatic
plot he found the perfect vehicle for such a
challenge. Displaying Prokofiev's talent for
musical grotesquerie, *Three Oranges* places
mock neo-classicism against barbarically
rhythmic modernism, and interweaves bizarre
choruses with tortuous solo parts. The orchestration is sparse yet colourful, but the only
real tunes materialize in the well-known
March and Scherzo.

Kent Nagano's award-winning Oranges

⬤ **Love for Three Oranges – complete**: Bacquier;
Viala; Perraguin; Le Texier; Gautier; Henry; Reinhart;
Lyon Opera Chorus & Orchestra; Nagano (Virgin VCD7
91084-2; 2 CDs).
⬤ **Love for Three Oranges – excerpts**: Scottish
National Orchestra; Järvi (Chandos 8729).

The Virgin recording won the 1989 Gramophone Award for
best opera and it is easy to see why. Nagano's handling of the
dramatically anti-Romantic score is intelligent and exciting (if
sometimes over-aggressive), and the cast revel in the surrealism of the characters. It should be said that, as with *War and
Peace*, the opera relies so much on the visual element that
much of its dramatic motion is lost on disc. With that in mind,
you might prefer to go for the March and Scherzo, as
arranged by Prokofiev for concert performance – it's entertainingly thrashed out by Järvi on a Chandos recording that
includes various other scenes.

WAR AND PEACE

After returning to Russia in 1933, Prokofiev
struggled to tailor his pungent, often dissonant earlier style to the demands of the country's leaders. The difficulties of this
adaptation are highlighted by his last opera,
War and Peace, which was composed during
the war to a libretto co-written with his
mistress, Mira Mendelson. He submitted a
piano score for official scrutiny in 1942, and
was duly asked to increase the patriotic
element, a request that set in motion a
sequence of revisions that continued right up
to Prokofiev's death. It was violently attacked
in the 1948 tribunal, and Prokofiev never saw
a staging of the complete work.

In its final form, as premiered in 1955, *War
and Peace* is an epic thirteen-scene construction, with an extraordinary range of characters matched by music of corresponding
variety. As in previous works, he makes
exacting use of recurring themes, but here the
vocal writing is more lyrical than before, and
the music is tonal and expressive throughout.
This does not mean that *War and Peace* is
easy to digest – like the novel, it is very, very
long and complicated. Nonetheless, it places
Prokofiev firmly in the great tradition of
Russian opera: profoundly nationalist in
spirit, and yet profoundly humanistic.

🌓 Miller, Vishnevskaya, Ciesinski, Paunova, Petkov,
Ochman, Gedda, Smith, Ghiuselev, Tumagian;

French Radio Orchestra & Chorus, Rostropovich. (Erato 229-45331-2; 4 CDs).

⦿ Okhotnikov, Gergalov, Prokina, Gregorian, Borodina, Bogacheva, Ognovenko, Gerelo; Kirov Opera and Orchestra, Marinsky Theatre; Gergiev (Philips 434 097-2; 3 CDs).

Rostropovich was asked by the composer – with whom the cellist was friendly in the late 1940s – to see that his grandest opera was performed and recorded. In the 1970s he managed to keep his word with this, the first ever recording. However, Rostropovich is a cellist and has rarely, if ever, lived up to his potential on the podium: he has a fine cast (the cast is massive) but his affection for the composer leads him into a sentimentality that does not do justice to this fearsome and unwieldy score. Gergiev, on the other hand, drives the score with urgency and his cast, while less polished, offer more characterful performances, with a greater sensitivity to colour. The Philips set on balance is the more convincing attempt to scale the unscaleable.

THE SYMPHONIES

Prokofiev's seven symphonies span the years 1917 to 1952. They are, in general, tremendously exciting works but all except two of them are marked by sharply antagonistic harmonies, rhythmic percussiveness and a paucity of melodies, so they may take some getting used to. Prokofiev's most accessible orchestral work is the twenty-minute *Symphony No. 1*, a tuneful piece that clearly reflects the neo-classicist influences of Stravinsky and his circle, with whom Prokofiev was in contact when he composed the work. If you don't have the stamina to tackle all the rest, concentrate on *Symphony No. 5*, which was completed in 1944 and received with great enthusiasm throughout Russia and the USA. Prokofiev's intention here was to "sing of man, free and happy, of his strength, generosity, and the purity of his soul" – a goal realized in the Adagio, one of his most eloquent creations.

⦿ **Symphonies 1–7**; Scottish National Orchestra; Järvi (Chandos CHAN8931–4; 4 CDs).
⦿ **Symphony No. 5**: Philadelphia Orchestra; Szell (Orfeo 87689-2; with Haydn, *Symphony No. 93*).

The most reliable of the three complete cycles currently available is Chandos's with Järvi, available as four separate CDs. He has a solid grasp of Prokofiev's irregular architecture and is keen to move the music on, without resorting to the histrionic savagery that some conductors indulge in. The recorded sound is excellent on each of the CDs.

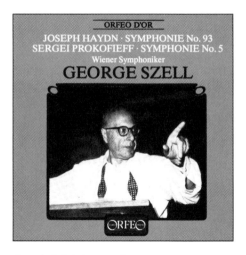

George Szell's Prokofiev – one of the best things he ever did

The best account of Prokofiev's greatest symphony is the thrilling, uninhibited perfomance from George Szell on Orfeo – a live recording in every sense of the word. Szell's conducting was at its most athletic in the heavy Slavic music, where rhythmic considerations predominate over melodic, and his performances of Prokofiev's symphonies were renowned. This recording of the fifth shows him at his zenith.

ROMEO AND JULIET

The ballet music for *Romeo and Juliet* (1936) is one of Prokofiev's greatest achievements. The emotional scope and scale of this piece has no rival in ballet music and no other composer has so perfectly interpreted this play – indeed, only Verdi's late Shakespearean operas, *Falstaff* and *Otello* (see p.395), can compare with it. Prokofiev was long troubled by the ending of the ballet for, as he said, "living people can dance, the dying cannot". As did Rossini with his *Otello*, Prokofiev rewrote the ending so that Romeo arrives just in time to prevent disaster, thus ending the ballet happily. However, he had his mind changed for him by the choreographers who assisted the composer in following the play almost to the letter – Juliet gets rather longer to expire than Shakespeare allowed her.

⦿ **Romeo and Juliet – complete ballet**: Cleveland Orchestra; Maazel (Decca 417 510-2; 2CDs).
⦿ **Romeo and Juliet – Three Suites**: Scottish National Orchestra; Järvi (Chandos CHAN8940).

Maazel's performance of the complete work is the best of an ordinary bunch, but the recording is rather dry and necessarily lacks the warmth that comes from a live ballet performance. On balance, the best alternative to seeing Romeo and Juliet in the theatre is to buy Järvi's recording of the three suites (1936, 1937 & 1944) into which Prokofiev divided the work's main numbers. Järvi's is a wonderful account, principally because he adopts some undanceably slow tempi – they would incite backstage revolt, but on CD his approach is inventive, original and entirely successful. A marvellous, well-engineered recording.

PIANO CONCERTOS

It's baffling that Prokofiev's piano concertos are so infrequently performed, as they are among the most inventive ever written. The first was written in 1912; two years later Prokofiev used it to get back at his piano teachers when he graduated not with the standard performance of a classical composition, but with a piece of his own. He won first prize and widespread resentment. The second is notable for the terrifying difficulty of the piano part and, especially, for the maniacal demands of the opening movement's cadenza. The third, the most popular, was composed as a virtuoso vehicle for himself, and though its stylistic diversity lends a sense of detatchment to the music, much of it is demonically exciting.

The fourth, composed ten years later, was commissioned by Ludwig Wittgenstein's brother Paul, a brilliant pianist who lost his right arm in World War I (he also commissioned a one-handed concerto from Ravel). It dominated Prokofiev's attention over the summer of 1931, and emerged modest in scale but awesomely demanding; Wittgenstein didn't understand it and never played it, but held onto the score until 1956 when it finally had its premiere. Prokofiev's last concerto began as a slight almost backward-looking composition, but the performer in him took over and the concerto evolved as yet another barnstorming test of digital prowess. Its five movements are more like a suite than a concerto, and its consequent lack of cohesion has contributed to its lack of popularity.

◉ **Piano Concertos Nos. 1–5**: Gutierrez; Concertgebouw Orchestra; Järvi (Chandos CHAN8938; 2 CDs).

◉ **Piano Concertos Nos. 1–5**: Krainev; Frankfurt Radio Symphony Orchestra; Kitaenko (Teldec 9301-73257-2; 2 CDs).
◖ **Piano Concerto No. 3**: Argerich; Berlin Philharmonic Orchestra; Abbado (Deutsche Grammophon 415 062-2GH; with Tchaikovsky, *Piano Concerto No. 1*).

The thumping, thrashing performances recorded by Gutierrez take some of the risks that Prokofiev obviously wanted the soloist to take, and Järvi's conducting is suitably characterful, though the recorded sound is not up to the Chandos label's normal standards. Krainev and Kitaenko are better recorded and they are working with a more responsive, flexible orchestra. There are places where the pianistic demands seem to get the better of the soloist, resulting in a loss of line and direction, but Krainev gives an interestingly less tense view of the music than Gutierrez. It all comes down to taste.

Argerich is rightly famous for her playing of the third concerto. Its explosive energy and sharply contrasted character suit her mercurial temperament perfectly, and though the studio removes some of the fire from her playing, this recording is required listening.

VIOLIN CONCERTOS

Together with those by Bartók and Shostakovich, Prokofiev's two violin concertos are the finest written this century. The first was composed in 1917, shortly before he left Russia for his long sojourn in Europe, and was premiered by the leader of a Paris orchestra, Marcel Darrieux, after a string of much grander names had declined to learn the very difficult score. Though it ends in a dreamy, lyrical mood, this concerto is far more prickly than the later one, being pivoted on a fierce and angular central Scherzo. It was Prokofiev's intention that the second concerto be "altogether different", and so it is. Composed after his return to Russia in 1935, it has a quality of emotional transparency similar to *Romeo and Juliet*, on which he was working at the same time. The soloist dominates far more than in its predecessor, and the only real harmonic irregularities occur in the first movement. The second movement is one of Prokofiev's most inspired creations, a huge and plaintive melody coloured by rapturous modulations and a jaunty accompaniment. A sprightly dance-like finale rounds off the concerto.

◉ **Violin Concertos Nos. 1 & 2**: Mordkovich; Scottish National Orchestra; Järvi (Chandos CHAN 8709).
◖ **Violin Concerto No. 2**: Heifetz; Boston Symphony Orchestra; Koussevitsky (Biddulph LAB018).

Lydia Mordkovich, studied with Prokofiev's friend David Oistrakh, and her limpid tone suggests that he taught her well. She is more than equal to the barbarism of the aggressive first concerto, while in the second she produces a sweeping, energetic perfromance that is as fine as any to be heard on digital CD.

Although the second concerto was commissioned by the French violinist Robert Soetans, it was first recorded by Jascha Heifetz in 1937, two years after its completion, with Koussevitsky conducting his Boston Symphony Orchestra. Biddulph Records have brilliantly transferred the 78s onto CD and the perfomance is nothing short of miraculous – Heifetz's sound has never had an equal and the singing, unaffected legato of the slow movement is exquisite. As legendary as recordings get.

STRING QUARTETS

Prokofiev's two string quartets epitomize his stylistic schizophrenia. The first quartet was commissioned during a visit to America in 1929–30 and received its first performance in 1931 at the Library of Congress in Washington. At that time, Prokofiev had recently immersed himself in the quartets of Beethoven, so it is no surprise that the opening movement is classical in feel, though this classicism is tempered by pungent dance-like rhythms that colour a string of memorable tunes. This energetic movement leads to an Andante of deceptive tranquillity – almost immediately the quartet breaks into a forceful Scherzo, which leads into a disturbing section where the players are directed to use the heel of their bows, a technique that puts violent pressure on the strings. The finale is the work's slow movement, which by classical rules should have preceded the Scherzo; profoundly expressive, and detailed with moments of sweet lyricism, it closes with a mournful recapitulation of the movement's opening theme.

The second quartet was completed a decade later, "for the people", and is too much a product of its environment; evidently the work of a composer working under constraint, it contains none of the idiosyncratic wit of the first.

⊙ **Emerson Quartet** (DG 431 772-2GH).

This CD has no rival. The Emersons are one of the best quartets in the world and have matured in recent years to produce performances of unfailing clarity and freshness. On occasion their staggering technique might create a slightly sterile atmosphere, but with these two quartets they are at their finest, giving performances full of wit and genuine emotion.

VIOLIN SONATAS

The first violin sonata, begun in 1938 and completed eight years later, is a bleak and sombre work. The second sonata, on the other hand, though completed in 1944, is a positive composition that conveys no sense of the strain the composer was under. It was written as a flute sonata (and has been recorded in this original state many times) and was only later transcribed for the violin, at the insistence of David Oistrakh. Although flautists would argue, it works better in the hands of a good violinist, taking on a life that the colourless flute can't give it.

⊙ **Violin Sonatas Nos. 1 & 2**: Mintz; Bronfman (Deutsche Grammophon 423 575-2GH).
⊙ **Violin Sonata No. 1**: Oistrakh; Oborin (Chant du Monde LDC278 91; with *Violin Concerto No. 1*).
⊙ **Violin Sonata No. 2**: Kogan; Walter (Vogue 672009; with works by Strauss, Falla and Shostakovich).

Schlomo Mintz's recording sometimes plays it safe, but his account is the most revealing single CD of the two sonatas. If, however, you can afford to invest in the sonatas separately, seek out the pair of amazing live performances from Oistrakh and Kogan.

PIANO SONATAS

As can be heard on his own recordings (on the Pearl label) Prokofiev possessed an awesome piano technique, and as a young man his muscular approach confused and shocked his contemporaries, who were then revelling in the meanderings of the Scriabin and post-Debussy schools of performance. The tempestuous music of his nine piano sonatas demand a flawless technical command, but many pianists allow them to sink into empty ostentation – this is sharply characterized music that demands a sense of structure and momentum, as well as fingers of flexible steel. Prokofiev's greatest work for solo piano is the seventh sonata (1947), a titanic construction with a piston-driven last movement that distills the fury and violence of World War II – it's a fierce, draining experience, making terrible demands on the pianist.

○ **Piano Sonatas Nos. 1–9**: Nissman (Newport
NCD60092, NCD60093 & NCD60094).
○ **Sonata No. 7**: Pollini (Deutsche Grammophon DG
419 202-2GH; with pieces by Stravinsky, Boulez &
Webern).

The under-recorded American pianist Barbara Nissman plays
all nine sonatas (plus the incomplete fragment of the tenth)
with a wide tonal range and sharply drawn contrasts that
single her out as someone fully in command of the music's
intricate detail. The energy and sense of occasion make this
the best complete sonata cycle, even if she can't quite hit the
heights of Maurizio Pollini's recording of the seventh sonata, a
performance that has acquired legendary status since its
release in 1977. Pollini commands unrivalled power, concentration and dynamic range, assaulting the listener in a scorching performance that becomes almost diabolical in the last
movement. The performances of the other pieces on this CD
are of comparable brilliance, making this possibly the most
exciting of all recitals of twentieth-century piano music.

GIACOMO PUCCINI
(1858–1924)

I
t has been said that Wagner's music is
better than it sounds. Conversely,
Puccini's often sounds better than it is.
Puccini had a taste for melodrama, and
possessed in abundance the talents necessary
to achieve his ends, principally a highly developed sense of theatre and an uncanny facility
for memorable melodies. His genius for
emotional blackmail soon settled upon the
most effective techniques and then stuck to
them – from his third opera, *Manon Lescaut*, to
his twelfth and last, *Turandot*, his style
evolved only slightly. He was frequently
accused of decadence, as he still is, but judged
by box-office receipts Puccini is the most
successful of twentieth-century composers.

He was born into a long line of Italian
church musicians and, as was expected, first
became a church organist. Then in 1880 he
entered the Milan conservatory, where he
took lessons with Amilcare Ponchielli, who
steered Puccini towards opera. With
Ponchielli's encouragement he entered the
Sonzogno opera competition in 1883, submit-
ting the one-act *Le Villi*; it was not a success,
but it did indirectly lead to a commission,
five years later, for a second opera, *Edgar*.
Premiered the following year, it too was a failure, but in 1893 Puccini produced his first
masterpiece, *Manon Lescaut*, a verismo opera
to rank with those of Mascagni and
Leoncavallo. In part inspired by Massenet's
similarly ardent interpretation of Prevost's
play, *Manon Lescaut* made use of five libret-

MANSELL COLLECTION

tists (including Leoncavallo) and inspired
George Bernard Shaw to proclaim Puccini the
rightful heir to Verdi.

Remarkably, his next opera didn't get the
same acclaim as *Manon* when it was first
produced in 1896, but within a year *La
Bohème* had become what it remains today –
the most popular opera ever written. It established Puccini as Italy's supreme master of
the human voice, a reputation further

enhanced by the similarly effulgent *Tosca*, premiered in 1900. His career suffered a slight hiccup with the disastrous opening of *Madama Butterfly* at La Scala in 1904; he withdrew the work, re-scored it in three acts, and gave it a second premiere three months later, when it was duly acclaimed as a triumph. Puccini turned to the author of *Butterfly*, Belasco, for his next opera, *La fanciulla del West*, but even though Caruso sang at its first performance, it never attained the popularity of its predecessors, chiefly because it contains no show-stopping arias.

La Rondine didn't set the world alight, but the composer's ailing fortunes were restored by his penultimate work, *Il Trittico*, which comprised three brief operas – a thriller, *Il Tabarro*, a sentimental religiose drama, *Suor Angelica*, and a comedy, *Gianni Schicchi*. Puccini's last opera, *Turandot*, remained incomplete at his death in 1924; however, Toscanini engaged Franco Alfano to complete the work and the opera received its first performance in front of an ecstatic Milanese audience on April 25, 1926.

Puccini was prone to glutinous sentimentality, and a sadistically misogynistic streak is evident in the casting of most of his heroines, who are generally helpless and weak creatures at the mercy of callous, domineering men. While he was unquestionably a verismo composer, his plots are often absurd or trivial, and many of his realistic details – such as the bells in *Tosca*, the Americanisms in *Fanciulla* – amount to little more than cheap motivic imitation. For most audiences, however, these objections ultimately don't matter. The important thing is that Puccini's twelve operas contain some of the most beautiful vocal music ever written, carrying into the twentieth century the bel canto tradition of Bellini, Donizetti and Verdi.

MANON LESCAUT

The plot of Puccini's *Manon* is more or less identical to that of Massenet's (see p.224), but Puccini's treatment of the story is unremittingly intense. *Manon Lescaut* establishes Puccini's ultimate goal, which was the creation of a flexible, through-composed structure in which all the elements are subordinated to

dramatic melody – where other verismo composers went for a continuous sequence of melodramatic shocks, Puccini tried writing an opera carried entirely by melodic high-points. Rejecting Verdian structures of interspersed arias, recitatives and choruses, the gushing, momentous score of *Manon* takes a grand step towards Straussian opera. The problem with *Manon* is that Puccini keeps the tension consistently high, with no points at which the senses can recover before the next emotional crisis – the effect is rather like a banquet of desserts. To an extent all Puccini's music is prone to this weakness of excessive strength, but *Manon* is particularly concentrated. Nonetheless, it has a glut of good arias and the duets with Des Grieux and Manon are very effective.

● Bergonzi, Kirsten, Sereni, Baccaloni; Orchestra and Chorus of the Metropolitan, New York; Cleva (Golden Age of Opera GAO113/14; 2 CDs).
◗ Tebaldi, del Monaco, Boriello, Corena; Santa Cecilia Academy Chorus and Orchestra; Molinari-Pradelli (Decca 430 253-2DM2; 2 CDs).

Bergonzi's live performance from the Met in 1960 is the most perfect realisation of this score ever recorded. Bergonzi is in extraordinary voice, resonant, lyrical and declamatory, while Cleva's dramatic conducting maintains so fraught a momentum that you can't imagine why the whole show doesn't collapse, as was surely Puccini's intention. Well-recorded and outstandingly performed, this is a one-in-a-million document. The Decca recording, on the other hand, will be easier to find, and it's a fine performance. Molinari-Pradelli's tempi are appropriately quick, and though del Monaco's penchant for yelling does wear you down a bit, the atmosphere is tight enough for the performance to succeed despite this limitation.

LA BOHÈME

La Bohème is the finest lyric opera ever written. Set in Paris around 1830, the drama unfolds amongst a group of impoverished students, one of whom – Rodolfo – is a struggling poet. He meets and falls in love with the seamstress, Mimi, but by the third act they have agreed to separate, largely because Rodolfo can't cope with the fact that Mimi is dying from consumption. At the opera's close, Mimi duly expires leaving Rodolfo and his colleagues distraught, and not a dry eye in the house. Puccini's score is superbly constructed and littered with classic arias – including *Che gelida manina*, otherwise known as *Your tiny hand is frozen*. Lush orchestration and a cast of vividly defined sub-characters add to the pleasures of the ultimate operatic tear-jerker.

◗ Tebaldi, Bergonzi, d'Angelo, Bastianini; Santa Cecilia Academy Chorus and Orchestra; Serafin (Decca 421 049-2; 2 CDs).

The most famous *Bohème* is the Pavarotti and Freni account with Karajan on Decca, but the finest is sung by Bergonzi and Tebaldi, conducted in 1958 by Puccini's friend and Bergonzi's mentor, Tullio Serafin. The wondrous, meltingly lyrical voice of Bergonzi is perfectly suited to the part of Rodolfo. He may not have the ringing tone that Pavarotti boasted in 1976 but his sound is powerful and his characterization unmatched. He is ably matched by the equally fresh-sounding Renata Tebaldi, and they are well supported by Serafin's sense of pace and style.

Carlo Bergonzi at around the time of his recording of Bohème

TOSCA

Based on a play that had been a great success for Sarah Bernhardt, *Tosca* was soon labelled "A shabby little shocker". It is indeed a heady mixture of sex and violence. The beautiful singer Tosca loves the painter Mario Cavaradossi, but she suspects him of having an affair with a local noblewoman. Meanwhile, Tosca is being lecherously pursued by the chief of police, Baron Scarpia

(perhaps the most disgusting character in opera), who is consumed by hatred for the revolutionaries – one of whom, Angelotti, is being protected by Cavaradossi. For this Cavaradossi is arrested by Scarpia and horribly tortured (off-stage). After murdering Scarpia with a table knife and seeing her lover executed by firing squad, Tosca hurls herself off the walls of Castel Sant'Angelo, one of Rome's most famous landmarks.

Puccini spent a long time working on *Tosca* and the effort paid off. The harmonies are even richer than *La Bohème*, and Puccini's leitmotifs – a feature of *Bohème* – are refined to the point that anyone can recognise, for example, the Baron's signature tune. The opera has a dozen classic moments, including the two arias for Cavaradossi, the Act One duet between him and Tosca, the Scarpia's *Credo*, the final duet *O dolci mani* – and, most famous of all, Tosca's Act Two aria *Visi d'arte*, in which she laments the misery of her fate. This "prolonged orgy of lust and crime", as it was called, is the perfect foil to the saccharine sadness of *La Bohème*.

◉ Callas, Gobbi, di Stefano; La Scala Chorus and Orchestra; de Sabata (EMI CDS 7 47175-8; 2 CDs).

Maria Callas recorded the work twice, once in the early 1950s, conducted by Victor de Sabata, and again in the early 1960s, conducted by Georges Prêtre. Do not confuse the two. De Sabata's Callas is at her thrilling, un-selfconscious peak, Tito Gobbi's portrayal of the vile Scarpia is similarly convincing, and though di Stefano is miscast he manages a committed portrayal of Cavaradossi, relishing de Sabata's inspired conducting. Although the mono recording has its limitations, this blistering *Tosca* is a clear first choice.

MADAMA BUTTERFLY

Butterfly is the archetypal Puccini woman, crushed by the selfishness and cruelty of man. Based upon a David Belasco play which in turn was based on real events, *Madama Butterfly* is set in Nagasaki during the early part of the twentieth century. A geisha called Cio-Cio-San (Madama Butterfly) marries Pinkerton, an American naval officer, who duly deserts her shortly after the service. Butterfly, bearing their child, faithfully awaits his return. When Pinkerton does come back, it's in the company of Kate, his American wife; Butterfly kills herself with her father's ceremonial sword, leaving the child to the care of Pinkerton and Kate.

In one respect at least, *Madama Butterfly* is even more gruesome than *Tosca*, for the cruel drama is accompanied by some of the most seductive music Puccini ever composed – even when Pinkerton is finally revealed as a monster, the music is pleasingly light, reflecting nothing of his crimes. The growing sophistication of Puccini's technique is demonstrated by the first act's closing twenty-minute duet between Butterfly and Pinkerton, a gorgeous piece of writing in which the Japanese harmonic traits associated with Butterfly are blended with Pinkerton's more robust New World style. Although he dominates the opening act, Pinkerton hardly makes another appearance, leaving the opera almost entirely to Butterfly; when performed by a singing actress capable of impersonating the fifteen-year-old bride of Act One as well as the mature woman of Act Three, *Madama Butterfly* becomes one of Puccini's most moving operas.

🔊 Tebaldi, Bergonzi, Sordello, Cossotto; Santa Cecilia Academy Chorus and Orchestra; Serafin (Decca 425 531-2DM2; 2 CDs).

Both Tebaldi and Bergonzi recorded this opera twice but neither managed to recapture the glorious performances they produced in their first studio recording, in 1958. This is one of the great lyric partnerships of the post-war years, rising to rapturous heights of emotion – the duet is sung magnificently, even if Serafin's tempi do not quite generate a sense of sexual ecstacy. The Decca recording brings the orchestra too close to the ear but otherwise this is an astonishing set.

LA FANCIULLA DEL WEST

Puccini considered numerous plots for his next opera before settling on another play by David Belasco, *The Girl of the Golden West*, which he saw in New York in 1907, on a visit for the US premieres of *Manon* and *Butterfly*. Puccini's cowboy opera centres on gun-toting, whisky-swigging, thigh-slapping Minnie, who runs a saloon in a gold-prospecting camp in the American West. Recipient of the unwelcome attentions of the sheriff, Jack Rance, she falls in love with a dangerous bandit, Dick Johnson (alias Ramerrez). After Rance finds Dick lying wounded in Minnie's loft, he and Minnie play poker for the bandit's life.

Cheating, she wins, but the lynch mob drag Dick to the scaffold and place a noose around his neck. Minnie arrives just in time, eventually persuades them to set Dick free, and together they ride off into the sunset.

The plot can seem risible, but the score is one of the composer's strongest, even if it does lack the big arias that so efficiently promoted his earlier works. The tenor role of Dick Johnson, first sung by Caruso, has only one hit tune, and it's so difficult that most tenors keep away from it. Nonetheless, *Fanciulla* comes close to achieving the artistic goals first set out in *Manon Lescaut*, absorbing its melodies into a fluent, uninterrupted dramatic whole. And at least Minnie can look after herself.

🔊 Tebaldi, del Monaco, MacNeill; Santa Cecilia Academy Chorus and Orchestra; Capuana (Decca 421 595-2DM2; 2 CDs).

Tebaldi is supreme as Minnie, delivering an involved and suitably pugnacious account of Puccini's rough and ready heroine. McNeill is slightly dry as Jack Rance, but del Monaco is thrilling as Dick Johnson (his aria is given a showstopping performance), even if he does insist on shouting through all his ensemble work. Overall, this is a fine production, with tight direction from Capuana. Well recorded for 1958 and excellent value at mid-price.

TURANDOT

Pavarotti's rendition of *Nessun Dorma* was a great choice of signature tune for the 1990 World Cup, but it gave people the wrong idea about the opera from which it's taken. *Turandot* is a grand but profoundly unpleasant work, being the most disturbing example of Puccini's affection for violence against women. The action is set in Peking during "legendary" times. The evil Princess Turandot anounces that she will marry the first man to answer her three riddles – unsuccessful candidates will be decapitated. The deposed King of Tartary, Timur, recognises his son, Calaf, in a crowd assembled to witness one of these executions. Timur is with the slave girl Liù, who loves Calaf. Calaf, however, loves Turandot and he resolves to solve her riddles. Turandot ridicules Calaf's quest for her hand, and is less than happy when he answers her questions correctly. In an uncommonly generous move Calaf tells

Turandot that if she can guess his name before the following dawn, she may, after all, have him killed. Turandot promptly orders mass executions if his name is not brought to her, so the people turn against him. They capture Liù and Timur, and Liù kills herself rather than give up the name of the man she loves. Calaf then professes his love for Turandot and melts her icy heart.

The score shows Puccini's absorption of contemporary trends (Debussy and Schoenberg are recognisable in the orchestral textures), but *Turandot* is still essentially a work of committed romanticism. It contains some marvellous vocal writing apart from Calaf's *Nessun Dorma* – Calaf's *Non piangere*, *Liù* and *Principessa di morte*, for example, and Turandot's *In questa reggia*, one of the most powerful and chilling arias ever composed for a dramatic soprano. The use of exotic harmonies and melodies is more subtle here than in *Butterfly*, and the roster of leit-motifs is considerably larger. On the other hand, the dramatic cohesion is less pronounced than in *Fanciulla*, and the sadism of the opera might leave you with a bitter aftertaste.

○ Nilsson, Corelli, Scotto, Mazzini, Ricciardi; Rome Opera Chorus and Orchestra; Molinari-Pradelli (EMI CMS7 69327-2; 2 CDs).

Franco Corelli's bari-tenor was ideally suited to the declamatory role of Calaf, and his partnership with Birgit Nilsson, recorded for EMI in 1965, sets unmeetable standards. Even if Molinari-Pradelli's conducting is often too slapdash for the drama to unfold naturally, there is no better introduction to the opera.

HENRY PURCELL

(1659–1695)

Before Elgar came to international prominence in the 1930s, English music was famed exclusively for a single composer, Henry Purcell. He's a pivotal figure, through whom the art of Palestrina (see p.260) and Byrd (p.87) flows into the Baroque era of J. S. Bach, and his importance was fully recognized during his lifetime. As Byrd was without equal in the sixteenth century, so Purcell remained peerless in the seventeenth.

He was probably the son of Thomas Purcell, one of the court musicians to King James II, and became a chorister at the Chapel Royal. Music attributed to him was published in 1667, although it is not clear whether he was indeed its author. His voice broke in 1673 and the following year he was appointed tuner of the organ at Westminster Abbey. Three years later, he succeeded Matthew Locke as "composer to the King's Violins" and in 1679 he took over as organist of Westminster Abbey. By any standards, it was a remarkable start in life.

From 1682 he was one of three organists at the Chapel Royal and in 1685 he produced his first major work – the anthem *My heart is Inditing*, composed for the coronation of

James II. Four years later he provided music for the coronation of James's daughter Mary and her husband William III; in the same year his only opera, *Dido and Aeneas*, was performed at a girl's school in Chelsea. His last years were extremely prolific, producing a large amount of extraordinary church music, including his music for the funeral of Queen Mary, a work that was performed at his own funeral only months later.

During his thirty-six years Purcell wrote a bewildering volume and range of music, some of it weak, most of it strikingly expressive. With its heavy chromaticism and emotional directness, Purcell's style has no true precedent in English music, and in his writing for voice – in particular, in *Dido and Aeneas* and the funeral music for Queen Mary – Purcell was to have no worthy heir until the time of Benjamin Britten.

DIDO AND AENEAS

In 1698, Henry Playford wrote of Purcell: "The author's extraordinary Talent in all sorts of Musick is sufficiently known, but he was especially admired for the Vocal, having a peculiar Genius to express the Energy of English Words, whereby he mov'd the Passions of all his Auditors." Nowhere is Purcell's use of language in music better demonstrated than in *Dido and Aeneas*.

Purcell composed prolifically for the stage, contributing music to more than forty plays and writing four "semi-operas" – *The Prophetess*, *King Arthur*, *The Indian Queen* and *The Fairy Queen*. He wrote only one proper opera, however, and *Dido* was a work with no English precursors and no immediate successors. Even though *Dido*'s premiere in 1689 was said to have been successful (documentation is scant), it would seem that the response was not enthusiastic enough to encourage further attempts.

Composed in three brief acts, to a feeble text by the comprehensively untalented Poet Laureate, Nahum Tate, *Dido* was first performed at a girl's school in Chelsea, London. A number of its performers would almost certainly have been pupils at the school, and accordingly the music makes comparatively light demands of its singers and instrumentalists. The simplicity and clarity of its melodic writing is what makes *Dido* so powerful a drama, transcending the limitations of Tate's doggerel. In the first act, the air *Pursue thy conquest*, with its antiphonal responses, is brilliantly effective and original, while the duet *Fear no danger* is an innovative re-working of a style thought perfected by the school of Lully (see p.202). There are many other memorable moments, but the finest comes last – Dido's final lament, *When I am laid in earth*, is as heart-rending an expression of grief as anything in all opera.

 von Otter, Varcoe, Dawson, Rogers, Leonard, Priday; English Concert Chorus; English Consort; Pinnock (Archiv 427 624-2AH).

Pinnock's is a wonderfully lyrical rendition of Purcell's opera. An Olympian array of talent – with Anne Sofie von Otter as Dido and Stephen Varcoe as Aeneas outstanding – produces a cohesive vision in which the characters are given depths that most singers obscure through vocal affectation. The English Consort, as ever, create a tightly controlled and earthy instrumental sound. With good sound quality and excellent notes, this is an essential buy.

FUNERAL MUSIC FOR QUEEN MARY II

Purcell wrote a fair amount of music for Queen Mary, including a set of six enormous odes for her birthdays between 1689 and 1694. There is little to suggest that Purcell and his patron were personally acquainted, for musicians were servants like any others, and, unlike Elizabeth I, Mary was not known for her artistic enthusiasms. Yet it seems that Purcell felt strongly about her character and strength of purpose, and her death from smallpox in 1694 clearly caused him much anguish. The composition he wrote for her funeral is an extraordinarily oppressive and despairing creation, enshrining in a mere seventeen minutes of music the mourning of a nation and one man's intense affection for his dead monarch. It's in seven sections, alternating music for choir and drums with passages for solo brass and drums; the opening of the second section, *Man that is born of a woman hath but a short time to live, and is full of misery*, is the work's crowning achievement, with a chromatic foundation that is astonishingly advanced for its time.

⊙ Lott, Brett, Williams, Allen; Monteverdi Choir & Orchestra; Equale Brass; Gardiner (Erato 2292-45123-2; with *Come ye sons of art, away*).

This is perhaps the finest of all John Eliot Gardiner's period performances. Absolute restraint and discipline are maintained throughout, accentuating the air of doom established by the opening march, and purging all sentimentality for the settings of *In the midst of life* and *Thou knowest, Lord*. The gravity and weight of this finely researched performance will leave you with a heavy heart. The similarly fine performance of Purcell's last birthday ode for Queen Mary – composed eight months before the funeral music – make this recording by far the best introduction to the music of England's greatest composer.

SERGEY RACHMANINOV

(1873–1943)

HULTON DEUTSCH

Sergey Rachmaninov was a displaced person in more than one sense – a Russian who spent much of his life outside the mother country, and a Romantic who embodied a brooding stereotype that belonged to a previous era. A virtuoso of Liszt-like abilities, and a composer of music as expansive as any nineteenth-century symphony, he upheld the Romantic tradition – in particular the tradition of his idol, Tchaikovsky – with a granitic integrity, unmoved by the onslaughts of modernism or the disdain of progressive critics. Stravinsky summarized him thus: "Rachmaninov's immortalizing totality was his scowl. He was a six-and-a-half-foot-tall scowl . . . he was an awesome man."

Rachmaninov's doom-laden appearance and taciturn manner were acquired quite young: he was born into wealth but his father was profligate, so by the time Rachmaninov was nine the family was left with nothing. In 1885 he moved to Moscow where he began piano lessons, which in turn led to his first attempts at composing. In 1891, after further studies with various teachers, he completed his *Piano Concerto No. 1*, following it a year later with his most celebrated work for solo piano, the *Prelude in C sharp minor*. His opera *Aleko* met with similar acclaim in 1893, but his first symphony was a complete disaster (see below). Rachmaninov's reputation as a pianist continued to blossom, yet from 1897 he put almost all his energies into his conducting position with the Moscow Private Russian Opera Company. It was in this capacity that he made his first professional trip abroad, when he journeyed to London in 1899.

Around this time Rachmaninov began to suffer bouts of self-doubt so severe that he lost all faith in his abilities as a composer. A doctor named Nikolai Dahl came to the rescue with a course of hypnosis, through which Rachmaninov overcame his insecurities and began work on his second piano concerto. The first performance in 1901 was an enormous success, and the work has remained his most popular. From then on, he composed fluently but for the next three years he was possessed by an enthusiasm for opera, an area of his output that's now all but forgotten. By 1906 he was becoming worried by Russia's social instability, and he spent extended periods of time outside the country – in 1909, for example, he toured all over America, playing nothing but his own music, including the recently completed *Piano Concerto No. 3*. Shortly after the 1917 Revolution, an invitation to conduct in Stockholm was the catalyst for the inevitable decision, and Rachmaninov and his family left Russia for the last time.

Shrewdly, if reluctantly, he recognised America as the answer to his financial worries and it was in New York that he finally settled in November 1918. His remaining years were dominated by performing engagements, with little time to spare for composing – part from the fourth piano concerto, the *Paganini Rhapsody*, the third symphony and the *Symphonic Dances*, he produced little of note in the last third of his life. His last American home was a metaphor for his career and his music – it was a complete replica, down to the food and drink, of his home in Moscow.

) The Complete Rachmaninov Recordings (RCA 09026 612652; 10 CDs).

Rachmaninov had enormous hands (it's been suggested that he suffered from a rare bone disease), which enabled him play with ease what other pianists would find impossible. Thus much of his own music makes terrible demands upon the soloist, and very few recordings of Rachmaninov's works even begin to approach the composer's own. This dazzling set includes all four piano concertos, the *Paganini Rhapsody*, the third symphony (conducted by Rachmaninov) and a large selection of his solo piano music – but, sadly, there is no recording of the second sonata. In addition to Rachmaninov's incredible performances of his own music, this invaluable document also includes pieces by Beethoven, Grieg, Schumann, Mendelssohn, Schubert, Tchaikovsky, Scriabin, Liszt, Debussy and others.

SYMPHONY NO. 2

The premiere of Rachmaninov's first symphony was a spectacular failure, thanks to its conductor, Glazunov (see p.145), who arrived at the podium tanked up on vodka and turned the performance into a humiliation for the young composer. In the wake of this debâcle, Rachmaninov pronounced the symphony "weak, childish, strained and bombastic", withdrew it from public use, and never heard it again. The *Symphony No. 2*,

however, is a work of immense power and maturity – coming, as it did, twelve years later. It may be over-long, but it's more disciplined than its predecessor, and the richness of its themes makes it the most absorbing of Rachmaninov's three symphonies. In particular, the Adagio is one of the greatest symphonic movements in all Russian music. A song for orchestra, the Adagio becomes perilously sentimental in places, but its lush harmony and exquisite orchestration are so genuinely felt that you'll forgive any excesses.

○ St Petersburg Philharmonic Orchestra; Jansons (EMI 55514028; with *Vocalise and Scherzo*).

Perhaps the finest recording of recent years is Mariss Jansons' second account of the score, with the St Petersburg Philharmonic. It might be at times too slick and precise, but overall the passion of the interpretation is thrilling, and Jansons maintains a tight balance and responsive tempi throughout.

PIANO CONCERTOS

In view of Rachmaninov complete technical command of the piano, it's amazing that he should so rarely have succumbed to the temptation to write bravura music. His piano concertos are all very difficult to play but, with the exception of the blatantly taxing third concerto, there are few moments where it sounds like it. Of the four, the *Piano Concerto No. 2* is understandably the most popular. Dedicated to Doctor Dahl, the hypnotherapist who restored Rachmaninov to composition, it is a wonderfully optimistic work, opening with a famous eight-chord progression and crammed with soaringly beautiful music. Remarkably, at no point in the first movement does the soloist take up the main opening theme, and there is a notable sense of self-denial throughout the solo part – which is not to say that the orchestral music doesn't have its moments of wallowing.

Rachmaninov's *Piano Concerto No. 3* is a production of the fruitful years following his aberrant "operatic" period. Commenced at the same time as the second symphony and completed in 1909, it is his grandest concerto, reflecting a confident mastery of melodic writing and the resources of the orchestra. Here he finally overcomes his habit of signposting the introduction of new material by bringing the

Vladimir Horowitz, who made amazing recordings of Rachmaninov's third concerto and second sonata

music to a screeching halt, and his subtle metamorphosis of the first movement's thematic core into a leitmotif for the whole work gives the concerto a continuity unprecedented in Rachmaninov's work. However, the most important aspect of the *Piano Concerto No. 3* is its scale and violently Romantic vision: it was dedicated to the great Josef Hofmann (see p.95), and although Hofmann never played the piece, it was clearly written with his thunderous abilities in mind.

> ⦿ **Piano Concertos Nos. 2 & 3**: Gieseking; Concertgebouw; Mengelberg (Music & Arts MACD-250).
> ⦿ **Piano Concerto No. 2**: Richter; Warsaw National Philharmonic Orchestra; Wislocki (Deutsche Grammophon 415 119-2GH; with Prokofiev, *Piano Concerto No. 5*).
> ⦿ **Piano Concerto No. 3**: Horowitz; RCA Victor Symphony Orchestra; Reiner (RCA GD87754; with *Piano Sonata No. 2* and other works).

These two recordings of the second concerto stand out from nearly seventy in the current catalogue. The first dates from 1940, when the conductor, Wilhelm Mengelberg, was a revered musician – his Nazi sympathies soon put paid to that. He and Walter Gieseking, one of Germany's greatest pianists, give a monumental performance; the sound is poor, as one might expect from a live recording of this date, but the intense, dramatic atmosphere makes for rewarding listening. The coupled recording of the third concerto is almost as good, with only Mengelberg's direction of the finale letting the voltage slip. Less idiosyncratic, but a more obvious choice for a first-time buy, is Sviatoslav Richter's 1966 recording of the second concerto for DG, an interpretation that resolutely avoids all gushing indulgence.

Horowitz made three versions of the third concerto, and the best of them is the RCA recording from 1951. Horowitz is in staggering form, producing one of the most thrilling, percussive performances of his life. Do not confuse this with the better-known 1976 recording with Ormandy, which is pretty horrendous.

RHAPSODY ON A THEME OF PAGANINI

The last of Paganini's twenty-four *Caprices* (see p.259) has spawned more sets of variations than almost any other piece of music. Rachmaninov's response to it, the immensely popular *Rhapsody on a Theme of Paganini* (1934), is a set of variations for piano and orchestra, a sequence that's strictly constructed (the main theme is never far away) but has as strong a Romantic sweep as any of the symphonies or concertos – indeed, it's perhaps best described as a quasi-concerto. Particularly effective episodes are variation number seven, which invokes the Dies Irae chant so popular with Romantic composers (cf Berlioz), and the swoony variation eighteen, perhaps Rachmaninov's greatest hit. The last six variations form a highly charged coda, but the work ends with a barely audible flutter of notes that is almost as capricious as Paganini's original.

⊙ Pletnev; Philharmonia; Pešek (Virgin VC7 59506-2; with *Piano Concerto No. 1*).

Pletnev's performance is a thrilling modern alternative to the composer's own recording (see above). Tightly constructed and aggressive, it refuses all the music's invitations to self-indulgence.

PIANO SONATA NO.2

Neither of Rachmaninov's piano sonatas has entered the standard repertoire, a neglect attributable to their extreme technical demands and to a fin-de-siècle opulence that many find offputting. In the case of the first sonata this is fair enough, but the *Sonata No. 2* is a different proposition. It was written between January and September 1913, and it soon became a mainstay of Rachmaninov's own concert programmes. In the 1930s, having doubts about the volume of "surplus material" in his early music, he cut the sonata down, but the revision did nothing to improve a work that succeeds by its very expansiveness. The opening is a declamatory and rugged movement that moves into a central Adagio in which the harmonies recall Scriabin. None of this prepares you for the breathtaking finale, a polyphonic Romantic drama of immense grandeur and virtuosity. The wild and jubilant final section is almost crazed with energy.

◗ Horowitz (RCA GD87754; with *Piano Concerto No. 3* and other works).

Vladimir Horowitz championed this sonata to such an extent that the composer reputedly felt embarrassed at performing the work himself. This is possibly a publicist's myth, but Horowitz's playing of the sonata was monumental, as many recordings attest, and Rachmaninov certainly took the pianist's advice on how the score could be improved – he approved Horowitz's preparation of a version that restored most of the passages trimmed by the revision. The version for RCA, made live in 1980, is one of the most stupendous, full of the clanging freneticism for which his playing of this work was famous – the finale is one of the greatest displays of piano-playing ever

captured on record. Coupled with a magnificent performance of the third concerto (see above), this CD is probably the most complete introduction to the composer, except for the bumper RCA Rachmaninov set.

PRELUDES

Like Chopin's, Rachmaninov's *Preludes* comprise a sequence of miniatures in every major and minor key and, as with Chopin, the self-imposed constraints inspired some of the composer's most original ideas. Comprising the famous C sharp minor *Prelude* (Op. 3 No. 2) plus two later sets (Op. 23 and Op. 32), the *Preludes* are on the whole more economical than the ripe piano music of Rachmaninov's early career. Melody is a less dominant element than you might expect, for many of these pieces are built upon rhythmic patterns that lead towards the establishment of a melodic pattern that reflects the rhythmic pulse. This is not especially warm music – and you certainly shouldn't tackle the whole series in one sitting – but the *Preludes* are essential listening if you want to get a rounded picture of Rachmaninov.

⊙ Weissenberg (RCA GD60568).

Alexis Weissenberg's punchy sound is well suited to this frequently percussive music, and his searching approach highlights Rachmaninov's inner, contrapuntal voicing to great effect. This recording is presently without equal.

CELLO SONATA

As with the majority of nineteenth-century Russian composers, Rachmaninov wrote a small amount of chamber music, and the only work in this field that shows him at his best is the *Cello Sonata* of 1901. It displays an exceptionally detailed knowledge of the expressive qualities of the instrument, a knowledge doubtless acquired with the help of his cellist friend Brandukov, to whom the work is dedicated and by whom it was first performed. After a brief introduction, the cello plays the opening movement's yearning first subject but the piano is given the responsibility of carrying the second. Thereafter, the piano is the dominant partner, and only in the elegiac Andante – one of Rachmaninov's greatest achievements – does the cello come back into its own.

● Starker; Neriki (RCA RD60598; with cello transcriptions of pieces by Brahms and Schumann).

Janos Starker is highly suited to music that thrives off the projection of a sweet tone. This is a surging, urgent vision of the score: the outer movements are dashed off with considerable passion, while the Andante's emotional assault course is traversed with great dignity, although Starker and Neriki sometimes indulge in a little too much structural flexibility.

JEAN-PHILIPPE RAMEAU
(1683–1764)

Rameau achieved fame as a composer relatively late in his career. In 1733, when he was fifty years old, his first opera, *Hippolyte et Aricie*, created a storm of controversy because it dared to challenge the model for French opera established by Lully some fifty years earlier. In fact Rameau claimed to be a follower of Lully, but his music is much more dynamic and harmonically adventurous – qualities that his critics decried as being forced and unnatural. Success had been long in coming partly because he had spent the first forty years of his life in provincial obscurity, and partly because what reputation he had made was as a music theorist, an occupation thought to be incompatible with the actual business of composing, though Rameau himself rated it more highly. Despite his academic background, his music does not sound especially intellectual – rather it has the charm and elegance of Couperin (see p.103), but with rather more bite and vigour.

Rameau was born in Dijon, the seventh of eleven children. His father – who taught him music – was the organist of the cathedral of Notre Dame in Dijon, a post to which Jean-Philippe succeeded in 1709. His early career was spent largely as an organist at a series of other French cathedrals, including Clermont-Ferrand, where in 1722 he published his *Traité de l'harmonie* (Treatise on Harmony), in which he examined the origins of harmony and the relationships of chords.

The following year he left for Paris but achieved only modest success writing light theatrical works and teaching the harpsichord, before being taken up by one of the city's greatest artistic patrons, the financier La Riche de la Pouplinière. One of the wealthiest men in France, La Pouplinière was prodigal in his expenditure on art. Among his several homes was a château at Passy near Paris, where he had a private chapel, kept an orchestra of fourteen players, and gave regular concerts and musical festivities. Rameau was his music director from 1731 to 1753, and it was La Pouplinière who provided the contacts and the money that launched his late-flourishing operatic career. Within just a couple of decades Rameau's status as a radical innovator had been reversed, and he was held up as exemplifying all that was best about the French operatic tradition in the quarrel that followed the performance of Pergolesi's *La Serva Padrona* in 1752 (see p.265).

CASTOR ET POLLUX

Rameau's operas conform to the general pattern of Lully's *tragédies lyriques*: they are in five acts, preceded by an overture and a didactic prologue, and in each act there is a lavish *divertissement* for dancing or spectacular scenic effects. The musical differences, however, are so great that audiences at the time were forced to take sides either as Lullistes or Rameauistes. For one thing Rameau's orchestration is much more imaginative, using novel combinations of instruments to create specific descriptive effects (like the storm scene and its sunny aftermath in Act Five of *Castor et Pollux*) – indeed it was for this pictorial skill that he was most admired during his lifetime. As well as this, his harmonies were much richer and bolder than Lully's, and one moment in *Hippolyte et*

Aricie was regarded as so bizarre and cacophonous that Rameau was forced to withdraw it after the first performance.

Castor et Pollux is Rameau's operatic masterpiece. The libretto is based on the classical tale of two half-brothers, one mortal (Castor) the other the son of Jupiter (Pollux). When Castor dies, Pollux intercedes with his father who allows Castor to return to life only if Pollux takes his place in Hades. The story is a simple one of fraternal love and loyalty, made complicated by the fact that Pollux is in love with his brother's lover, Telaira, but not in love with the woman who loves him, Phoebe. Rameau clothes the story in extraordinarily rich and varied music, often juxtaposing profoundly contrasting moments, as when Telaira's meltingly tender lament for Castor's death in Act I (*Tristes apprêts, pâles flambeaux*) is immediately followed by the war-like music that heralds Pollux's arrival.

○ Les Arts Florissants, Christie (Harmonia Mundi HMC 901435.37; 3 CDs).

The one dramatic failure of this opera is that the two brothers are just too good to be true, a drawback compounded on this recording by Howard Crook's rather watery Castor. The recording's strength are its women, with Agnes Mellon particularly convincing in the difficult role of Telaira, and there is some superbly atmospheric orchestral playing, particularly in the overture and in the Hades scenes of Act Three.

ORCHESTRAL MUSIC

As well as writing opera Rameau also wrote for that peculiarly French theatrical hybrid, the opera-ballet, in which each section has a separate plot, and equal importance is given to both song and dance. Rameau's first venture into this genre was *Les Indes galantes* in 1735, a light-hearted work concerned with romance in exotic climes, and reflecting the vogue for the "noble savage" – a concept central to the philosophy of Rameau's fiercest critic, Jean-Jacques Rousseau. The work was so successful that Rameau arranged it for harpsichord and as four orchestral suites, in which form it has become one of his most popular works.

❯ **Suites from Les Indes galantes and Dardanus**: Collegium Aureum (Deutsche Harmonia Mundi 05472 77269 2).

Rameau's selection from *Les Indes galantes* begins with the opera-ballet's gloriously triumphant overture and ends, as the opera-ballet did, with a sombre chaconne. Though recorded in the mid-Sixties the pioneering original-instrument group Collegium Aureum play with an energy and commitment that would put many more recent groups to shame.

INSTRUMENTAL MUSIC

Rameau wrote four books of harpsichord pieces, amounting to sixty-five pieces, of which only books two and three – the best of them – were published during his lifetime. As with Couperin, many of these pieces are fancifully named miniatures, and they are among his most charming creations, less elusive and mysterious than Couperin's but no less beautiful. Among them is a late work, *La Dauphine*, which was extemporized for the wedding of the Dauphin to Maria-Josepha of Saxony, and is full of cascading runs and daring harmonies. Perhaps his finest achievement as a keyboard composer, though, is the glorious *Suite in A major* from the third book – its powerful opening Allemande can stand comparison with the finest of Bach's Allemandes from the English and French suites (see p.14).

◉ **Pieces de Clavecin**: Fuller (Reference Recordings RR27).

The American harpsichordist Albert Fuller is very much a Rameau specialist, having twice recorded the complete works for harpsichord. This recent recording is a selection of some of the finest pieces, including *La Dauphine*, the *Suite in A major* and, most beguiling of all, the tender *La Cupis*, an arrangement of a chamber work. Fuller plays a marvellously generous-sounding instrument, and his manner is notable for the subtlety of its articulation and a broad rhythmic expressiveness that is rare among harpsichordists.

MAURICE RAVEL

(1875–1937)

Nineteenth-century France made a speciality of failing to recognise its homegrown talent (Berlioz being the most spectacular instance of neglected genius), thereby encouraging composers such as Gounod, Massenet and Saint-Saëns to look to Germany – and Wagner in particular – for inspiration. The inevitable consequence of this trend was a reaction against Wagnerism, a reaction which came to a head around the beginning of the twentieth century with the re-emergence of a completely French school of composition. At the head of this resurgence was Debussy; the greatest of his lieutenants was Maurice Ravel.

Ravel's music might at times be redolent of Debussy's later work, but these two composers followed quite different paths. Whereas Debussy pushed his music into a world of extreme formal and tonal ambiguity, Ravel never renounced traditional tonality and form, and cultivated a style that combined the classical with the contemporary. He was fascinated by the grand pianistic tradition of Liszt (as shown by *Gaspard de la nuit*), and even more obviously drawn towards the purity of Rameau and the eighteenth century (as in *Pavane pour une infante défunte* and *Le tombeau de Couperin*), an interesting enough hybrid without the addition of other enthusiasms, such as gypsy music, jazz, Spanish culture and the music of the Far East. This last major influence can be traced to Debussy's encounter with Javanese music in Paris in 1889, a seminal moment from which one can follow the thread of Orientalism through much of France's twentieth-century music, right down to Messiaen and, less obviously, Boulez.

Ravel bound all these strands together with brilliant wit and an unrivalled understanding of orchestration, though his mastery of instrumental colour has sometimes been used as a charge against him – Stravinsky, for example, suggested that something was missing in the substance of a work if the thing you noticed above all was the dazzle of its sound. This is to overlook Ravel's marvellous sense of melody and structure, but it's true that he often expended too much energy refining the surface of his compositions or orchestrating piano works that were already perfect in themselves. Ravel relied excessively on spontaneous inspiration, a precarious thing at the best of times, and perhaps made even more precarious by this perfectionism. As he himself admitted – "I can be occupied for several years without writing a single note . . . one must spend time in eliminating all that could be regarded as superfluous in order to realise as completely as possible the definitive clarity so much desired."

He spent his childhood in Paris, and enrolled at the Conservatoire in 1889. In the course of the next six years he studied with Fauré, among others, and developed a personal style that was characterized above all by unconventional harmonies. His progressiveness offended his conservative elders: in 1901, 1902 and 1903 he entered the Prix de Rome and was failed on each occasion, and his final attempt, in 1905,

HULTON DEUTSCH

caused an outcry when Ravel was eliminated in the preliminaries. This setback did not inhibit Ravel's creativity and the next ten years saw the composition of his greatest works, including the *Rapsodie espagnole*, *Gaspard de la nuit* and *Daphnis et Chloé*. With the outbreak of World War I he tried to enter the services, but neither the army nor the air force wanted him (he was two kilos underweight, and too short), so he became an ambulance driver. He wrote: "They tell me that Saint-Saëns announced that during the war he has composed theatre music, songs . . .If instead he had been servicing Howitzers, his music might have been the better for it."

Ravel, however, did not gain from his engagement in the war, even though his beautiful *Le Tombeau de Couperin* was written as a tribute to the dead. He was released from his duties in 1916 after suffering a complete physical collapse, and the death of his mother shortly afterwards seemed to push him into a slow but inexorable decline. From 1918, with the death of Debussy, Ravel was regarded as France's greatest composer, and was fêted all over Europe, but his creative juices were drying up. The last two decades certainly produced some outstanding works – *L'enfant et les sortilèges*, the *Piano Concerto*, *Tzigane*, the *Violin Sonata* and *Boléro* – but most of his time was spent tampering with earlier compositions. In the last year of his life he was struck by a virulently degenerative brain disease; eventually he could not even sign his name. In December he risked a brain operation, and never regained consciousness.

L'ENFANT ET LES SORTILÈGES

Ravel wrote two operas. The first was *L'heure espagnole* (The Spanish Hour), a one-act comedy which has wonderful rhythmic vitality and orchestral colour, but is ultimately too disorganised to work as a whole. His second venture, written fourteen years later in 1925, is an unqualified success, however. Described as a "lyrical fantasy", *L'enfant et les sortilèges* (The child and the spells), is one of the most entertaining operas written this century. The central character is a spoiled brat who gets his comeuppance when the household objects he has abused –

the sofa, the armchair, the clock and others – come suddenly to life. The trees and animals in his garden are equally hostile, and only when the child attends to a wounded squirrel do they forgive him. He is then returned home and, by implication, restored to innocence. The pictorial clarity of the music is astonishing and, in the garden scene, achieves a ravishing lyricism that is scarcely matched in any other opera.

⊙ Ogéas, Collard, Berbie, Gilma, Herzog, Rehfuss, Maurane, Sénéchal; French Radio Chorus; French Radio National Orchestra; Maazel (Deutsche Grammophon 423 718-2GH).

Lorin Maazel is not renowned for his work in the opera house, but this is a fine performance of Ravel's shimmering score – come the reconciliation he is in his element, revelling in the opulent orchestral sonorities. The cast sings well, with the soprano Francoise Ogéas excelling as the child. A fine introduction to Ravel's music.

DAPHNIS ET CHLOÉ

Daphnis et Chloé, the finest French ballet ever written, was commissioned by the Russian impresario Serge Diaghilev, as was virtually every other decent ballet of the period. Work on the score occupied the composer between 1909 and 1912, the period when Stravinsky was working on another Diaghilev commission, the *Rite of Spring*. The two composers became friends at this point, and Stravinsky was later to remember that Ravel "was the only one to understand the Rite". Like Stravinsky's ballets, *Daphnis et Chloé* now survives not so much in the theatre as in the concert hall, through performances of the two orchestral suites into which Ravel split the ballet. However, the ballet really needs to be heard in its complete form, for *Daphnis et Chloé* is a tone poem in all but name, achieving vivid characterization of the two lovers through adroit orchestration. In Ravel's words: "The work is constructed symphonically, according to a strict tonal plan by the method of a few motifs, the development of which achieves a symphonic homogeneity of style."

⊙ Boston Symphony Orchestra; New England Conservatory Chorus and Alumni Chorus; Munch (RCA 61846-2; with Roussel, *Bacchus et Ariane*).

Charles Munch did not take up conducting until 1932, when he was 41 years old, and within ten years of his debut he was renowned as an inspired conductor of French music. Munch's recording of *Daphnis* is a marvellous example of Euro-American collaboration – in 1955, the date of this performance, no French orchestra approached the standard maintained by the Boston Symphony, but no American conductor approached the stature of Munch, who here achieves remarkable extremes of colour without affecting the intricate musical structure, and without recourse to sentimentality.

PAVANE POUR UNE INFANTE DÉFUNTE

The *Pavane pour une infante défunte* – originally composed for the piano in 1899 but orchestrated by Ravel eleven years later – is typical of his mock-archaic manner. Its sound-world is distinctly eighteenth-century, and as its title implies (*infante* = infanta, the title given to a princess of the Spanish royal family), it recalls the solemn ceremonial dance that was customary at the Spanish court at a time of royal mourning. Popular from its first performance to the present day, it's an extremely tender piece, with an apparent simplicity that belies the demands it makes on the performers – the famous solo horn theme is murderous to play.

○ Philharmonia Orchestra; Cantelli (Testament SBT 1017; with *Daphnis et Chloé* second suite, and other works).

Guido Cantelli, a young conductor whose brilliant career was cut short by a airplane crash in 1956, made a marvellous recording of this brief work in the year of his death. The Philharmonia was at this time one of the greatest orchestras there had ever been, and the horn solo is played beautifully by Dennis Brain, who died in a car crash the following year. It's coupled with a remarkable recording of the second suite from *Daphnis et Chloé*, a performance with range of expression and characterisation even more impressive than Munch attained in his recording of the complete ballet (see above).

LA VALSE

Considering Ravel's anguished state of mind during World War I, it is a wonder that he managed to compose anything. It was largely thanks to the insistent nagging of Diaghilev that he set to work on his "choreographic poem" *La Valse*, which he finally completed in 1920. This is a waltz of sorts, but it's waltz music scarred by the experiences of wartime,

turning the dance form that had recently been the toast of decadent Vienna into a vehicle for biting satire (which gives it a certain affinity with Richard Strauss's *Rosenkavalier*).

◗ Detroit Symphony Orchestra; Paray (Mercury 432 003-2MM; with *Rapsodie espagnole* and other works).
◑ Vienna Philharmonic Orchestra; de Sabata (Nuovo Era NUOV 2219; with *Boléro* and other works).

Most all of Paul Paray's recordings set benchmarks, and his performances of Ravel's music for Mercury are no exception. As with Munch's recordings, the combination of French inspiration and American technique produces outstanding results. It comes coupled with a brilliant version of the *Rapsodie espagnole* (1908), perhaps the most intoxicating product of Ravel's obsession with all things Spanish.

Like Wilhelm Furtwängler – the only conductor with a similarly fanatical following – Victor de Sabata was an inspirational musician who made very few studio recordings, but whose reputation is kept going through live recordings. His searing rendition of *La Valse*, dating from 1953, is as good as you are ever likely to hear, despite the poor sound quality.

A rare recording from the legendary Victor de Sabata

BOLÉRO

In 1928 the dancer Ida Rubenstein (whose troupe first performed *La Valse*) asked Ravel to orchestrate some of Albéniz's piano music as a dance score. Instead he gave her *Boléro*, a piece that made Ravel's name international, and is even better known nowadays, courtesy of Bo Derek's *10* and Torvill and Dean's ice-dance routine. Commenting on its success, Ravel remarked ruefully that he had written only one masterpiece and that there was "no music in it"; Boléro was, he said "orchestration without music". That just about sums up this maddeningly memorable, virtuosic, one-idea creation. It's built from an unwavering repeated phrase in C major, announced and maintained throughout by a snare drum, which the various orchestral instruments join at regular intervals until reaching the famous climax, a quarter of an hour later.

◗ Boston Symphony Orchestra; Munch (RCA 61956-2; with *La Valse*, *Rapsodie espagnole* and other works).

This music is much more difficult to conduct than you might imagine: the hardest part is for the snare-drummer, who must hold a rigid tempo all the way through. The drummer doesn't once lose concentration here, and Munch adopts a well-judged pulse, moulding a wonderfully rich orchestral texture. The performance of *La Valse* on this CD is the best available after the two recommended above

PIANO CONCERTO IN G MAJOR

The G major *Piano Concerto*, one of Ravel's most lyrical and captivating scores, was written in the late 1920s, when jazz was all the rage among the intelligentsia of Paris. The concerto is deeply infused with the idioms of jazz, but unlike Gershwin's *Rhapsody in Blue* (1924) this is a classically organised, three-movement structure, and it's this combination of opposites that gives the music such zest. It begins with a whip-crack then hustles and gambols on towards the pivotal slow movement, whose opening unaccompanied tune evokes Mozart in its purity and Rachmaninov in its breadth. A glittery yet brooding finale, less than half the length of its predecessor, is a perfect conclusion to this work of brilliant contrasts.

◉ Benedetti Michelangeli; Philharmonia; Gracis (EMI CDC7 49326-2; with Rachmaninov, *Piano Concerto No. 4*).

Only one recording of this work is worth buying. Arturo Benedetti Michelangeli, notorious for last-minute cancellations and generally odd antics, is forgiven most of his mercurial behaviour because of the stupendous talents on display here – this is one of the very few records that do justice to his abilities. Especially in the middle movement, he achieves a sonority and expressive range that is simply without equal, and throughout the punchily rhythmic outer movements you're borne along by his panache and unforced wit. He takes the finale at a fittingly brisk pace, but his technical mastery is so perfect that he almost whispers the piano part, barely touching the keys.

STRING QUARTET

Ravel was fast making a name for himself when he began composing the *String Quartet* in 1902, and it was this work – his first and most successful foray into chamber music – that established him as a mature composer when it was premiered two years later. In his autobiography he stated that the *String Quartet* "more than any of my earlier works, was in line with my ideas of musical structure." Indeed, though the enthusiasm of youth is still very much present, the formal poise of the writing is what strikes you above all. Folklore has it that Debussy thought Ravel's quartet bore too close a resemblance to his own, and there are undeniable similarities – both open with a movement in sonata form, for example, and both use the opening theme as the basis for the material of the other movements. However, from the second movement onwards the Ravel quartet displays a rhapsodic, indulgent quality that's miles away from Debussy, and in fact the older composer was a great admirer of the piece; on hearing it for the first time, he wrote to Ravel saying "in the name of God, you must not tamper with this string quartet."

◉ LaSalle Quartet (Deutsche Grammophon DG 435 589-2GGA; with Debussy, *Quartet*).

Some quartets create a more homogenous sound than the LaSalle, but they play with a style and elegance that perfectly captures this music's melancholy. Especially in the muted sections of the second movement, their performance achieves a tranquillity that is inordinately moving.

TZIGANE

Ravel always took a special interest in performers who embodied strong folk traditions, and one of these was the Hungarian violinist Jelly d'Aranyi, whom Ravel heard improvising gypsy music at the home of a friend in 1923, an event that proved to be the inspiration for *Tzigane*. Styled a "rhapsody for violin and piano", it was composed in the following year and dedicated to d'Aranyi, who gave the first performance. The violin part is vividly Hungarian in feeling but its virtuosity also makes a gesture in direction of Paganini – *Tzigane* begins with a fearsome cadenza played solely on the G string, an improvisational-sounding passage that's reminiscent of Paganini's *Variations on a theme from Rossini's Moses*, which is written entirely for the G string. The cadenza culminates with the piano's first entry and the work's main theme (which was heard, in a distended form, in midst of the opening fireworks), setting up a white-hot exchange that continues right to the final bar.

⬤ Vengerov; Vinogradova (Biddulph LAW 001; with works by Schubert, Ernst, Ysaye, Waxman, Tchaikovsky and Debussy).

The boy wonder plays Ravel

Maxim Vengerov was fifteen years old when he recorded this album of violin showpieces, and his playing is some of the most remarkable ever captured on record. When you've got your breath back after his playing of *Tzigane*, listen to his performance of Ysaye's *Third Sonata* – it's the sort of playing that starts you thinking in terms of Faustian pacts.

GASPARD DE LA NUIT

A great deal of Ravel's piano music is light, wistful and undemanding. None of these adjectives applies to *Gaspard de la nuit* (1908), a set of three ferocious and morbid pieces derived from the macabre prose-ballads of Aloysius Bertrand. With its broad washes of tonal colour and its gunfire-rapid repeated notes (a hallmark of Ravel's style), *Gaspard* is a barnstorming addition to the Lisztian repertoire – virtually every major piano competion demands that its entrants risk terminal tendonitis by tackling this piece.

◗ Gieseking (Pearl GEM CD9449 with works by Ravel and Debussy).
◗ Gavrilov (EMI CDM7 69026-2; with other works by Ravel).

Walter Gieseking was renowned for his playing of Ravel's music and made a number of recordings – live and studio – that testify to an extraordinary talent. His 1930 recording of Gaspard is technically incomparable: even on a mono recording, it beguiles and seduces. Gavrilov is less sensitive to the rainbows of colour but, technically, he makes he music ring with energy. He may possess a blistering technique but this performance never degenerates into showing off.

MAX REGER

(1873–1916)

Max Reger was the central figure of the "Back to Bach" movement, and devoted much of his life to the promotion and re-interpretation of Bach and his Baroque contemporaries. However, his neo-classicism was not simply a matter on the resurrection of the old ways of doing thing, no more than the music of his Italian equivalent, Ferruccio Busoni (see p.86) was straightforwardly nostalgic. Reger may have come to dismiss Wagner as "perverted rubbish", but he grew up in his shadow and he remained essentially a Romantic, albeit a Romantic who drew his strength from the great tradition of Bach, Beethoven and Brahms.

Reger's devotion to heavy, Germanic polyphony led to his being labelled "the second Bach", a nickname that had some justice in the case of Reger's organ music, a field in which Bach's influence would have been almost unavoidable. There's also a broad strand of truth to the stereotype of Reger as a rather joyless academic: much of his life was an uneventful succession of teaching posts at Wiesbaden, then Munich and finally Leipzig. But there is more to his music than an obsession with fugues, and the late orchestral compositions in particular are worth a hearing for the way they clothe classical structures in lush, almost Wagnerian orchestration.

THE MUSIC

Reger's finest music is to be found in the *Four Symphonic Poems after Arnold Böcklin* (1913), four well-constructed pieces in which the composer goes some way to betraying his own principles. The influence of the decidedly unclassical Debussy is clear in the harmonies, and the style of Richard Strauss, another bête noir, can be heard in the melodies. Moreover, this is an example of illustrative music, and Reger was forever proclaiming the supremacy of "absolute" music – that is, music that referred specifically to nothing outside itself. Their inspiration comes from paintings by the Swiss artist Arnold Böcklin, whose Symbolist paintings, often showing Romantic landscapes populated by mythical creatures, can be seen as distant ancestors of Surrealism. Reger's interpretation of these images is suitably suggestive: the opening picture of a hermit playing his violin is full of longing and sweet despair, but best of all is Reger's haunting vision of the *Isle of the Dead* – a painting also admired and interpreted by Rachmaninov. The weighted stillness of the scene brings an

outpouring of rich, romantic sound, and the tranquillity of the closing music is some of the composer's finest. An uproarious bacchanal ends one of the composer's most engaging works.

Also enjoyable, in a rather less emotional way, are the classically strict sets of variations that Reger wrote on themes by Hiller, Beethoven and, most famously, Mozart. The first movement of the latter's A major piano sonata forms the basis to Reger's most popular and tuneful score, the *Variations and fugue on a theme of Mozart*, while the *Hiller Variations* (or *Hitler Variations*, as the Proms once advertised them) are his most impressive technical achievement. Bach would have been proud.

◉ **Four Symphonic Poems after Arnold Böcklin**: Concertbegouw; Järvi (Chandos CHAN 8794; with *Hiller Variations*).
◉ **Mozart and Hiller variations**: Berlin Radio Symphony Orchestra; Davis (Philips 422 347-2PH; with Hindemith, *Symphonic Metamorphosis*).

Järvi's account of the *Symphonic Poems* after Arnold Böcklin (part of a general survey of the composer's work on the Chandos label) is splendidly carried off, with the Concertgebouw seemingly committed to rectifying Reger's neglect. Clearly recorded, the performance comes coupled with an adventurous interpretation of the *Hiller Variations*, and makes the best introduction to Reger for anyone who doesn't want to swallow buckets of fugues.

The *Böcklin* pieces are also included on the CD from Colin Davis and the Berlin Radio Orchestra, who give a sympathetic if restrained account of Reger's homage to Mozart. The sound is a little dry but the playing is particularly sweet, and the inclusion of Hindemith's *Metamorphosis* makes this a highly worthwhile recording.

STEVE REICH

(1936–)

Though one of the most influential Minimalist composers, Steve Reich has not been his best publicist, acquiring a reputation for irascibility and moodiness. At one stage Reich was continually contradicting himself in interviews, one minute extolling Minimalism, the next decrying it, at times suggesting that microphones

were the only acceptable electronic aids, while his home studio in Vermont was filled with the latest computers and sampling equipment. Yet for all his "difficultness", Reich's uniquely detailed and ethnic-influenced music is some of the best of the late twentieth century.

Born in New York, Reich was reared on Schubert and Beethoven before encountering

Stravinsky's *Rite of Spring* at the age of fourteen, an event that widened his horizons – soon he was delving into the sounds of African drumming, jazz, the Balinese gamelan and Hebrew chant. He graduated in philosophy at Cornell, progressed to the Juilliard, where he met Philip Glass and Meredith Monk, then went on to study with both Berio and Milhaud. After a spell in San Francisco, where he linked up with Minimalist guru Terry Riley, Reich returned to New York, bought a batch of tape recorders and made *Come Out* (1966), a classic piece of pattern music made out of a single vocal segment ("I had to like open the bruise up and let some of the bruise blood come out to show them") from an interview with a Harlem youth who had been beaten up by racist police.

Continuing to investigate tape-looping and phasing, Reich collaborated with Philip Glass until they had a falling out, then in 1970 went to Ghana on a grant to study the music of the Ewe people. The subsequent *Drumming* (1971), written for bongos, marimbas, voices, glockenspiels, whistle and piccolo, marks the honing of Reich's technique – it's a bright and inventive piece with no melody or changes of rhythm or key, instead using slight changes in timing, pitch and timbre to maintain its momentum. Following on from that, the psychedelic *Music for Mallet Instruments, Voices and Organ* (1973) brought gushing reviews from American writers, and *Music for 18 Musicians* (1974–76) sold like rock music.

Yet Reich's approach had a greater academic seriousness than that of Philip Glass, the other high earner of American Minimalism. Restlessly refining his ideas, he followed the lead of Debussy in studying Indonesian music, and in 1979 went to Israel to study Hebrew chant. In 1983 he utilized the poetry of William Carlos Williams in the hugely symphonic *Desert Music*, then composed the interlocking orchestral piece *Four Sections* (1987) before switching direction again with the award-winning *Different Trains* (1988) for the Kronos Quartet, plus found sounds and voices. His most ambitious project to date is *The Cave* (1993), a four-year work in collaboration with his wife, video artist Beryl Korot, for which he was given a million-dollar grant. Recorded in Israel and America, using the latest in flat-screen video projection, it presented a series of talking heads whose views on Arab or Israeli history were projected onto five large screens, their speeches punctuated by melodies performed by strings, percussion and four singers. It was an enthralling multi-media experience and a new development in Minimalist music, and its success seemed to mellow Reich, who for once smiled in interviews.

THE MUSIC

Two pieces from the 1970s are perhaps the likeliest to make converts to Reich's music. The luminous *Music For Mallet Instruments, Voices and Organ* utilizes marimbas, glockenspiels and vibraphone, augmented by cadences of a female chorus, to achieve an astonishing sound that at once flutters and drones. However, the slightly later *Music for 18 Musicians*, is the classic Steve Reich piece – its cycle of eleven chords over eleven sections is permeated by the rhythms of Africa and Bali, spiced with strains of twelfth-century sacred chant and above all the brassy extremes of jazz. The most accessible of the more recent works – *Different Trains* and *Electric Counterpoint* are available now on a single CD. *Different Trains*, inspired by the holocaust and influenced by Stockhausen's *Gesang der Junglinge*, pits the Kronos Quartet against speech fragments recalling train journeys across Germany and America during World War II. *Electric Counterpoint* displays Reich's instinct for the fluidity of jazz, as Pat Metheny improvises over ten prerecorded guitar and two electric bass parts.

❶ Music for Mallet Instruments, Voices and Organ; The Four Sections: Tilson Thomas; London Symphony Orchestra; Steve Reich & Musicians (Elektra Nonesuch 7559-79220-2).
❶ Music for 18 Musicians: Steve Reich and Musicians (ECM New Series 821 417-2).
❶ Different Trains; Electric Counterpoint: Kronos Quartet; Pat Metheny (Elektra Nonesuch 7559-79176-2).

The lustrous marimbas and glockenspiels of *Music for Mallet Instruments* have been brought into sharper focus by Reich's own digital mixing, while the performance of *The Four Sections* quickly dispels any notion that Minimalism is boring – Michael Tilson-Thomas keeps a grip on the increasing tempo and complexity of the interlocking sections for strings, percussion, winds and brass, prior to unleashing a deafening finale for full orchestra. Rock musicians and jazz maestros such as Norway's Jan Garbarek have long admired and being influenced by the recording of *Music for 18 Musicians*, which is especially memorable for its fluctuating bass clarinets. It has sold over 100,000 copies and is still going strong. Recorded between 1987 and 1988, the *Different Trains* CD is a superb two-setter – Kronos and Metheny are excellent and Bob Ludwig's digital mastering is perfection.

OTTORINO RESPIGHI

(1879–1936)

Such was the success of Verdi and Puccini, and of lesser figures such as Leoncavallo and Mascagni, that by 1900 Italy had almost no composers of instrumental music. A career in music meant a career in opera. The burden of restoring the nation's instrumental tradition fell largley on two men – Ferruccio Busoni (see p.86) and Ottorino Respighi.

Respighi was born in Bologna, where he trained as a violinist. In 1891 he became a student of the composer Giuseppe Martucci (a favourite of Toscanini's) then in 1899 left for St Petersburg, where he began composition lessons with Stravinsky's teacher Rimsky-Korsakov, who heavily influenced his approach towards orchestration. He came back to Italy in 1903 and embarked upon a fairly successful career as a solo violinist, but his rapidly developing interest in Baroque and Classical instrumental music eventually led him to concentrate on writing rather than performing music. In 1913 after a stimulating spell in Berlin, he returned to Rome where he was appointed professor at the conservatory of Santa Cecilia. Nine years later, he became the conservatory's director but resigned within two years in order to devote all his time to composing.

The trouble with Respighi's music is that it wears its influences on its sleeve, and of these influences none is more pronounced than Richard Strauss. The habitual classification of Respighi as the "Italian Strauss" was dismissed by the composer's widow in her biography of her husband, where she stoutly defended his preference for classcial structure. There are indeed many works by Respighi in which he upholds the values of his illustrious predecessors, re-create the logical lines of the eighteenth century, but much of Respighi's neo-classicism amounts to little more than vapid pastiche. For the foreseeable future, the popularity of his over-blown orchestral poems is likely to obscure Respighi's affection for formal clarity.

THE MUSIC

Respighi's most famous compositions are his three technicolour portrayals of Italy's capital city: *Fountains of Rome* (1916), *Pines of Rome* (1924) and *Roman Festivals* (1929). The grandiose and tuneful first part of this "Roman Triptych" is the best, in the sense that it is the most idiosyncratic, even if it does reflect the styles of Debussy, Ravel and, inevitably, Richard Strauss. Melodically, the *Pines of Rome* is heavy going, but the orchestration is vivacious enough to overcome the cumbrousness of the material. The gaudy *Roman Festivals* has been attacked for its fascistic undertones, and it doesn't stand up to comparison with Strauss's earlier treatment of a similar subject in *Aus Italien*.

Respighi's predilection for classical form is perhaps best realised in the *Violin Sonata* of 1916–17, a work championed by many soloists (including Jascha Heifetz), but still little known. Written on a grand scale and demanding a lot of both performers, it is characterized throughout by beautiful melodies, especially in the lyrical opening movement. The finale, a showcase for Respighi's technical dexterity, is a brilliantly written passacaglia, in which a set of twenty variations is built upon a ground first established in a ten-bar bass passage.

○ **Fountains of Rome; Pines of Rome; Roman Festivals**: Montréal Symphony Orchestra; Dutoit (Decca 410 415-2DH).
○ **Violin Sonata**: Chung; Zimerman (Deutsche Grammophon 427 617-2GH; with Strauss, *Violin Sonata*).

There is no better performance of the "Roman Triptych" than Charles Dutoit's. This splendid recording conjures every shade of the score: from the nightingale singing through the pines of the Janiculum, to the thunder of the Roman legions marching down the Appian Way. His tempi are light enough for the thick orchestral treatment not to sound crass, and the Montreal orchestra plays with great passion – if the brass tends to dominate, the imbalance has more to do with Respighi's writing than with Dutoit's control.

The CD from Kyung-Wa Chung and Kristian Zimerman does great service to a pair of unjustly ignored sonatas, giving a highly involved account of Respighi's *Violin Sonata* and a mighty performance of Strauss's opulent work.

═══════ 𝕾𝕾 ═══════

NICOLAI RIMSKY-KORSAKOV
(1844–1908)

Rimsky-Korsakov is honoured as an inspirational teacher and as a fine orchestrator of other composers' music, but of his own compendious output, just a single orchestral score is remembered – *Sheherazade*.

Born into the aristocracy, he received a standard musical education, but his first ambition was to enter the navy. This he did in 1856, aged only twelve. Based in St Petersburg, he was deeply affected by the nationalistic music of Glinka and was encouraged by Balakirev to begin a symphony, which he did, despite his tenuous grasp of the basics of harmony and tonality. In 1865, after two and a half years at sea, he applied himself to the study of theory and resumed work on his symphony; four years later he completed Dargomyzhsky's *The Stone Guest*, his first such second-hand project. In 1871, though still ignorant of the fine details of compositional technique, he was appointed a professor of composition and orchestration at the St Petersburg conservatory, and worked in private to obtain a better knowledge of the subject he was teaching. It was not until 1876, when he began editing a collection of Russian folk songs, that he perfected his technique and developed a genuine musical identity.

From 1882 he began revising Mussorgsky's music (see p.250) and after Borodin's death in 1887 he assisted Glazunov to complete *Prince Igor* (see p.59), a project that coin-

MANSELL COLLECTION

cided with the composition of *Sheherazade*. After attending the first Russian performance of Wagner's *Ring* cycle, he devoted most of his remaining years to opera. These years were interrupted by illness but in 1896 he managed to produce an orchestration and revision of Mussorgsky's *Boris Godunov*. In 1905 he ran head first into the authorities for openly supporting the revolutionaries and the subsequent ban on his music spurred him to compose his last opera, *The Golden Cockerel*. Based upon Pushkin's satirical attack on autocracy, this too was banned and was not performed until the year after his death.

Rimsky-Korsakov's music is famous not so much for what is says but for the manner in which it says it. He was a brilliant orchestrator and contributed as much to the development of the craft within Russia as did Berlioz in France. Like Berlioz he was liberated by his lack of proficiency at the piano, and thought primarily in terms of orchestral textures, developing a style that made adventurous use of primary instrumental colours, progressive harmonies and innovative part-writing. *Sheherezade* is one of the greatest works of nineteenth-century Russia, but ultimately Rimsky-Korsakov's influence is the most important thing. Had it not been for Rimsky-Korsakov, the music of Mussorgsky may have remained unknown, and his efforts to promote Glinka's nationalist ideals were extremely effective. Of those he taught, Glazunov, Prokofiev and Stravinsky were the most significant; the last of the three said of him, "he made me the most precious gift of his unforgettable lessons", and in *The Firebird* (see p.362) produced a powerful testimony to the depth of Rimsky-Korsakov's impact.

SHEHERAZADE

Rimsky-Korsakov's decision to use the *Arabian Nights* as the basis for an orchestral work was symptomatic of the attraction that neighbouring Islamic cultures held for many Russian composers. Each of the "Mighty Handful" (Cui, Balakirev, Borodin, Mussorgsky and Rimsky-Korsakov) wrote orientalist music, and Rimsky-Korsakov's output is particularly dominated by the trend.

Lasting some forty minutes, *Sheherezade* (1888) contains an abundance of beautiful melodies which are carried on a sensual wash of sound. Different moods and pictures are conjured by the music, but the composer denied that *Sheherezade* was a programmatic piece – it was, he insisted, merely a suite of fairy-tale images of the Orient, rather than a sequence of episodes relating to the stories told by the young Sheherezade to delay her execution. The beguiling, sinuous violin solo in the third of the four movements, *The Young Prince and the Young Princess*, is perhaps the most effortlessly beautiful moment in a work which in places sounds like an anticipation of Debussy's hedonistic world.

> ◑ San Francisco Symphony Orchestra; Monteux (RCA 09026 61897-2; with *Sadko* and *Symphony No.2*).
> ◐ London Symphony Orchestra; Mackerras (Telarc 80208; with *Capriccio espagnol*).
>
> Monteux's legendary performance of *Sheherezade*, recorded in 1942, has been released by RCA as Volume Eleven in their huge Monteux Edition. Monteux was born in 1875, and the breathtaking panache, freedom and opulence of this account hint at the orchestral traditions of the age of Rimsky-Korsakov. The accompanying tone poem and symphony are lesser works, but the performances are easily as satisfying. If, however, digital sound is a paramount concern, go for the Mackerras recording, which is stunningly engineered.

JOAQUÍN RODRIGO
(1902–)

Joaquín Rodrigo is another one of twentieth-century music's one-hit wonders, but the beautiful *Concierto de Aranjuez* is quite some hit, brilliantly evoking the sights and sounds of Spain, and pitching the mellow guitar against a full orchestra to create a thrillingly new texture. What is perhaps most impressive of all is that the *Concierto de Aranjuez* is the product of a composer who has been blind from the age of three.

Revealing an innate talent for music in childhood, Rodrigo was sent to study composition with Francisco Antich in Valencia

(1920–23), before becoming a pupil of Dukas at the École Normale de Musique in Paris, where he met and received encouragement from his compatriot Manuel de Falla (see p.130). Following his marriage to the Turkish pianist Victoria Kamhi in 1933, he returned briefly to Spain but then, on receiving a grant, went back to Paris to study musicology. With the outbreak of the Spanish Civil War in 1936 he decided to stay in Paris, returning at the end of hostilities. Rodrigo's politics are something of a grey area. It has been argued by his friends that he was a canny individual who merely paid lip service to Franco's repressive regime; outward signs seem to indicate that his views were in accordance with those of Franco's government, and there is no doubt that he was the musician most favoured by the administration after the premiere of the *Concierto de Aranjuez* in 1940.

Thereafter he was firmly esconced as Spain's leading composer. In 1944 he was appointed music adviser to Spanish Radio, and two years later was appointed to the Manuel de Falla chair, which was created for him at the University of Madrid. Ever since he has led a full life as both an academic and a composer, though he has tended to repeat the musical formula of the *Concierto de Aranjuez* in his later concertos for piano, violin, cello and flute. But, conceding his conservatism in comparison with composers such as Falla, Rodrigo nonetheless did Spanish music an important service by helping to preserve the country's musical identity following the traumas of the Civil War.

THE MUSIC

Rodrigo's nationalism is of a different species from that of Falla, Albéniz and Granados, the big three of modern Spanish music. Whereas they embarked on a deep exploration of the forms of Spanish popular and art music, and transmuted those forms into their compositions, Rodrigo is essentially an impressionist, content to create attractive melodies and rhythms that generally evoke Spain's sunny atmosphere and traditional culture. The *Concierto de Aranjuez* is suffused with the Mediterranean spirit, and an underlying nostalgia for an older and more chivalrous Spain – an element that's particularly marked in the beautifully poised *Fantasia para un gentilhombre*, a fine example of Rodrigo's affection for eighteenth-century forms.

> ◗ **Concierto de Aranjuez; Concierto madrigal; Fantasia para un gentilhombre**: Romero, Romero; Academy of St Martin-in-the-Fields; Marriner (Philips 432828-2).
>
> The Spanish guitarists Pepe and Angel Romero deliver fine performances of three of Rodrigo's most celebrated works – the flamenco quality of Pepe Romero's playing could not be more perfect for the *Concierto de Aranjuez*. The balance between soloists and orchestra is highly satisfying, with every detail finely etched.

GIOACHINO ROSSINI
(1782–1868)

Italian operatic life during the first half of the nineteenth century was dominated by one man – Gioachino Rossini. Between *Demetrio e Polibio*, written before 1809, and *Guillaume Tell*, less than twenty years later, he completed nearly forty operas, taking the first decisive steps towards the establishment of Italian music drama. Donizetti and Bellini worked in his shadow, and it was only when Verdi reached maturity in the late 1850s that Rossini was replaced at the centre of Italian operatic life. His impact upon the development of opera was immense: he was, for example, the first to do away with unaccompanied recitative, thus making the opera a continuous musical fabric, and he was the first to write out all the embellishments for his singers, not leaving anything to chance. But the key to his success was the sheer tunefulness of his

MANSELL COLLECTION

music, a quality which seemed to cause him no effort – "Give me a shopping list and I'll set it to music", he once said.

Praise for Rossini was not universal, however. Berlioz was speaking for many non-Italians when he raged against Rossini's conveyor-belt creations: "Rossini's melodic cynicism, his contempt for dramatic expression and good sense, his endless repetition of a single form of cadence, his eternal puerile crescendo and brutal bass drum, exasperated me to such a point that I was blind to the brilliant qualities of his genius, even in his masterpiece, the *Barber*, exquisitely scored though it is." Making an exception for the enduring popularity of the *Barber of Seville*, Berlioz's opinion has become increasingly common, for Rossini's operas do indeed seem simple after Wagner or Strauss. However, this simplicity is part of Rossini's strength. There is a directness and immediacy to his work that is missing from that of his Italian predecessors and contemporaries, whose plots seem ludicrously entangled alongside Rossini's, and whose characters appear bloodless in comparison.

Rossini was born the son of a trumpeter and a singer. Some time soon after his eighth birthday he composed his first opera and his first commission came before his eighteenth birthday. In 1812 he had a work performed at

La Scala, Italy's most prestigious opera house, and in the following year *Tancredi* and *L'italiana in Algeri* established his name outside Italy. Before long he had been appointed music director of the opera houses of Naples and was producing an enormous amount of music for them, including *Otello* and *Il Barbiere*, *La Cenerentola*, *La gazza ladra* and *Mosè in Egitto*.

In 1822 he married, and soon after visited Vienna where, reputedly, he met Beethoven. Two years later, aged only thirty-two, he moved to Paris, where he composed the epic *Guillaume Tell* (1829). Whether from doubts about his own powers or sheer exhaustion, he composed no more operas. He did write the extraordinary *Stabat Mater*, but for all its acclaim, it did not inspire Rossini to return to full-time composition. Perhaps with the success of Verdi and the advances of Wagner, he thought himself incapable of producing any new opera worthy of his name and reputation.

● **Viva Rossini** (Testament SBT 1008).

This album of classic Rossini recordings from between 1903 and 1940 features performances that put to shame nearly all modern singers, and makes a fine introduction to Rossini's operas. Tito Ruffo's grand and idiosyncratic singing of *Largo al factotum* ("Figaro là, Figaro qua" et cetera) beggars belief, but even more astounding performance is Luisa Tetrazzini's agile singing of *Una voce poco fa* from the same opera. Also on this CD are Giovanni Martinelli and Giuseppe de Luca singing the thrilling Act Two duet from *Guillaume Tell*, plus Enrico Caruso and Francesco Tamagno, Verdi's first Otello.

IL BARBIERE DI SIVIGLIA

Operatic folklore has it that *Il Barbiere di Siviglia*, Rossini's comic masterpiece, was composed in just a fortnight, a feat of which he was certainly capable, though the music is so original and the characterizations so rounded that the tale is unlikely. Nowadays it's one of the most popular Italian operas, but it wasn't an immediate hit – indeed the first performance, in Rome in February 1816, was one of operatic history's greatest disasters. Everything that could have gone wrong did go wrong, and by the second act the music was inaudible above the din of the audience. As the critic Castil-Blaze wrote afterwards wrote afterwards, "All the whistlers of Italy seemed to have given themselves a rendezvous for this performance".

The source of the libretto is a play by Beaumarchais, covering events in the life of the libidinous Duke of Almaviva – the philandering aristocrat of the later Beaumarchais work that became the text for Mozart's *Le Nozze de Figaro* (see p.242). The world of *Il Barbiere* doesn't have the ambiguities and depths of *Le Nozze*, but as a straightforward, life-affirming comic opera it has no equal. Each of its arias is a highlight, and some of them are truly astonishing – Figaro's *Largo al factotum* is of course one of opera's great bravura set-pieces, while Almaviva's *Ecco ridente* is one of the most beautiful things Rossini ever wrote. A characteristic device used to startling effect throughout the opera is the "Rossinian Crescendo", whereby the composer takes a theme and repeats it, each time at a higher pitch and with a larger orchestral accompaniment.

◗ Gobbi, Callas, Alva, Ollendorff, Zaccaria, Carturan, Carlin; Philharmonia Chorus & Orchestra; Galliera (EMI CDS7 47634-8; 2 CDs).

Perhaps the finest studio performance of *Il Barbiere* boasts the sublime partnership of Maria Callas and Tito Gobbi. The latter's Figaro is a deeply personal piece of vocal characterization with a waggish charm that all but overcomes the restrictions of the studio; Callas is only slightly less convincing (but then, so is the role she sings), and Luigi Alva – a marvellous Rossini tenor – sings Count Almaviva with great elegance and charm, although at times he is rushed by the conductor. It may be old-fashioned in its romanticism, but this set has stood the test of time.

LA CENERENTOLA

Stendhal referred to Rossini's music as "seldom sublime, but never tiresome", a description that perfectly fits *La Cenerentola*, a semi-comic homily on the value of true love and the speciousness of rank, inspired by Charles Perrault's *Cinderella*. Perhaps the chief reason for its comparative lack of popularity is the florid writing for the title role, a part that demands the combination of a contralto's range with a coloratura's agility. Once in a while a suitable voice comes along – as has happened recently with the arrival of Cecilia Bartoli – and *La Cenerentola* sneaks back into the repertoire, but it's always going

to be an opera to hear on disc rather than see on stage. In terms of the proportion of time allotted to them, ensembles predominate over arias in *La Cenerentola*, but for all Rossini's concentration on multi-voice writing, the main attraction is the title role, one of the finest female roles in Italian opera.

◗ Simionato, Benelli, Bruscantini, Montarsolo, Carral, Pace; Maggio Musicale Fiorentino Chorus & Orchestra; de Fabritiis (Decca 433 030-2DM2; 2 CDs).
◖ Berganza; Alva; Capecchi; Montarsolo; Guglielmi; Zannini; Trama; Scottish Opera Chorus; London Symphony Orchestra; Abbado (Deutsche Grammophon 423 861-2GH2; 2 CDs).

EMI's studio recording, conducted by de Fabritiis, is a charming and spirited performance, but Abbado's slick recording for DG boasts the incandescent singing of Teresa Berganza, who – unlike Giulietta Simionato for de Fabritiis – transcends mere technical security to give her character life. Abbado and the LSO tend to smash their way through Rossini's score, but for Berganza's singing alone Abbado's recording is worth the money.

GUILLAUME TELL

Like *Il Barbiere*, Rossini's last and grandest opera – *Guillaume Tell* – was not immediately popular, but unlike *Il Barbiere* it has never established a toe-hold on the opera house circuit. The chief reason for this is that *Tell* is very uneven and far too long, as Rossini himself acknowledged: on being confonted by an enthusiast who had recently seen a performance of the second act, the composer replied, "What, the whole of it?" Performed in full, it would last nearly five hours, and it still has lethargic patches in the extensively cut and revised version that's usually performed today. Nonetheless, this serious-minded celebration of Switzerland's great folk hero is worth the effort. Rossini knew well beforehand that it was to be his last opera, and he intended it to be his masterpiece – and in dramatic terms it is, for in its large-scale coherence it looks forward to the through-composed operas of Verdi.

The overture is especially powerful: the very start, scored for cello sextet, is one of Rossini's greatest inspirations but it is the trumpet theme, a third of the way through, that you'll recognize – it was the theme tune for both *The Lone Ranger* and for the *William*

Tell TV series. Act One has an exciting finale but things get even better in the second act, which boasts a glorious aria for the female lead, *Ces jours, qu'ils ont osé proscrire*. Act Three is unbearably dull, but the final act, beautifully introduced by the magnificent tenor aria *Asile héréditaire*, is the opera's crowning glory, culminating in the Swiss nation's prayer of thanksgiving for the liberation of their land.

> ⊙ Milnes, Freni, Pavarotti, Ghiaurov, Tomlinson, Jones, Connell; Ambrosian Opera Chorus; National Philharmonic Orchestra; Chailly (Decca 417 154-2DH4; 4 CDs).

Rossini composed *Guillaume Tell* in France, in French for a French audience, and it should be performed in French if the opera is to receive a fair trial. Due to the absence of any great French singing talent, recent recordings have had to rely upon Italian artists and their dubious pronunciation, or – more usually – on a translation. This set, the finest of the latter category, is very good indeed, boasting an exceptional cast and highly tuned sound. Freni, Pavarotti and Tomlinson are superb, and only Milnes falls short of the high standard.

STABAT MATER

Just as Verdi's *Requiem* was his only major composition during a long period of inactivity, so Rossini's *Stabat Mater* was his first major composition for twelve years and the last he ever wrote. During a journey to Spain in 1831, Rossini was commissioned by Fernandez Varela to set the text of the Stabat Mater. He completed half the score before asking a friend to take over. This friend, Giovanni Tadolini, did as he was asked but ten years later, under pressure from his Parisian publisher, Rossini replaced Tadolini's work with his own. This revised draft was first performed in Paris on January 7, 1842, and was received with wild enthusiasm – an appropriate response to a composition that is not so much devotional music as lyric opera in liturgical attire. Leaving aside considerations of piety, the *Stabat Mater* is brilliantly written and contains some superb vocal music, notably the tenor's melodically sumptuous *Cujus animam* and the unaccompanied quartet *Quando corpus morietur*.

> ⊙ Lorengar, Minton, Pavarotti, Sotin; London Symphony Chorus & Orchestra; Kertesz (Decca 417 766-2DM).

Decca assembled a fine cast for this recording: Pavarotti navigates the D flat at the end of *Cujus Animam* with great flair and is in magnificent form throughout, while Lorengar and Minton tone down their big voices to make light but heartfelt contributions to this remarkable piece of music. The overall performance is directed with equal measures of sobriety and ebullience by Kertesz, and Decca's engineers have produced an even and natural recorded sound.

━━━━━━━━━━━━━━━ 𝄢 ━━━━━━━━━━━━━━━

CAMILLE SAINT-SAËNS
(1835–1921)

A lot of composers began as freakish children, but by any standards Saint-Saëns was an extreme case. As a two-year-old he could read and write, and was picking out melodies on the piano. Shortly after his third birthday he began composing, and by the age of five had given his first piano recital. At seven he was reading Latin, studying botany and developing what was to become an eighty-year interest in lepidoptery. As an encore after his formal debut as a concert pianist, the ten-year-old Camille offered to play any of Beethoven's thirty-two sonatas from memory.

In short, his childhood suggested Mozartian potential, and yet it was a potential that was never realized. Saint-Saëns once remarked that he lived "in music like a fish in water" and that composing was as natural as "an apple tree producing apples". And there lay the problem. As with Mendelssohn, the technique came so easily to him that it virtually extinguished the spark of originality.

That said, for many years he was considered by many to be France's greatest musical revolutionary, though his reputation grew more from his outspoken support of other

GUUS ONG

composers' music – especially Wagner's – than from any work of his own. As well as promoting contemporary music, Saint-Saëns threw his energies into researching the work of his forerunners. Along with Mendelssohn, he was one of the first to re-establish the music of Bach (converting the sceptical Berlioz in the process) and he did much to restore Mozart to his rightful place, being the first to play a complete cycle of the piano concertos. Handel was another unfashionable composer to engage Saint-Saëns' attention, and (as with Berlioz) Gluck held a fascination that lasted most of his life.

By the time Saint-Saëns reached his mid-fifties, the past had won the upper hand over the present. Embittered, ill-tempered and restless, he became the arch-traditionalist, opposing the progressive music of Debussy and Les Six, bellowing outrage at the first performance of *The Rite of Spring*. And yet, for all his reactionary pomposity, he was one of the first neo-classicists, embodying many of the finest traditional qualities of French music – neatness, clarity, elegance and dignity. His best epitaph is the rueful one he wrote for himself – "I ran after the chimera of purity of style and perfection of form".

SAMSON ET DALILA

Of Saint-Saëns' thirteen operas, only *Samson et Dalila* has achieved any lasting popularity. Composed in the 1870s, this retelling of the

Biblical story was originally planned as an oratorio along the lines of Mendelssohn's *Elijah* (see p.229), which Saint-Saëns so admired, but it was cast as an opera on the advice of his librettist. The dramatisation is not the most enthralling example of operatic stagecraft, but *Samson et Dalila* was a huge hit, holding its own for a long time against the tide of Wagnerism then rising in France. Its qualities are modest but genuine: the characters are tightly drawn, the orchestration has real finesse, and both leads are supplied with memorable, tuneful music – the last being the quality that attracted Liszt, who secured the work's first production in Weimar in 1877.

❶ Domingo, Obraztsova, Bruson, Thau, Lloyd, Friedman: Paris Orchestra & Chorus; Barenboim (Deutsche Grammophon 413 297-2GX2; 2 CDs).

Of the two available recordings, Barenboim's account with the Paris Orchestra is the more dramatic. Domingo's statuesque yet lyrical projection makes this one of his finest recorded performances, while Obraztsova is thrillingly dramatic and earthy, giving her role a gravity which, on paper, is almost non-existent. Well recorded and, at mid-price, very good value.

SYMPHONY NO. 3

Saint-Saëns' most popular orchestral work, the *Symphony No. 3*, was dedicated to the memory of Liszt and received its first performance in London in 1886. An upbeat, expressive work that revels in German bombast and French colour, it has stayed in the repertoire mainly on the strength of its last movement, with its resonant organ part – hence its subtitle, "The Organ Symphony". The preceding three movements are less expansive, but the symphony as a whole is still one of the most entertaining written by a French composer, and gives an accurate picture of Saint-Saëns' strengths.

❶ Dupré; Detroit Symphony Orchestra; Paray (Mercury 432 719-2MM; with Paray, *Joan of Arc Mass*).
❷ Preston; Berlin Philharmonic Orchestra; Levine (Deutsche Grammophon 419 617-2GH; with Dukas, *Sorcerer's Apprentice*).

Paul Paray's performance on Mercury is enormously satisfying, even if the recorded sound is not; the structure might be slightly laboured, but balance and overall momentum are brilliantly defined. For a modern recording, Levine's account is over-aggressive but very well engineered, with the last movement in particular a tribute to the wonders of digital recording.

LE CARNAVAL DES ANIMAUX

It is a wonderful irony that Saint-Saëns, a man obsessed with his standing as a serious composer, should now be known chiefly for a piece that was dashed off as a joke. Written to entertain himself and his friends while on holiday in 1886, *Le carnaval des animaux* – his "Grand Zoological Fantasy" – was never intended to be published, and Saint-Saëns forbade its performance during his lifetime. The carnival is in part a musical menagerie, caricaturing some thirteen types of "animal" (including *People with Long Ears* and *Pianists*), of which the thirteenth (*The Swan*), is the best known and most beautiful. It's also a barbed parody of the music of his some of his contemporaries, including Offenbach, Mendelssohn, Berlioz, Rossini and, thankfully, himself.

> ◗ Rogé, Ortiz; London Sinfonietta; Dutoit (Decca 430 720-2DM; with *Symphony No. 3*).

There are over thirty recordings of *Le carnaval des animaux*, most of them sounding very much like each others. Dutoit's performance has the merit of sharpening the satire, while pianists Rogé and Ortiz add to the flair. It's coupled with a meaty version of the proficient, undemanding third symphony.

VIOLIN CONCERTO NO. 3

Composed in 1880 for the Spanish virtuoso Pablo de Sarasate, the *Violin Concerto No. 3* is a stunningly dramatic piece, which opens with one of Saint-Saëns' most striking melodies, a gypsy-like theme on the lowest of the instrument's strings. This hammer blow of an opening leads into a less characterful Adagio, but the finale is a stupendous creation that makes inordinate demands of the soloist.

> ◉ Wei; Philharmonia; Bakels (ASV CDDCA680; with Bruch, *Concerto No. 1*).

Xue Wei's recording comes closest to fulfilling the music's dramatic potential. He uses gut strings, producing a fuller sound than that produced by the routine steel strings, and his playing is the most natural and instinctive performance currently available.

PIANO CONCERTO NO. 2

Saint-Saëns' *Piano Concerto No. 2* epitomizes much of the composer's output, being pleasant on the ear and murder on the fingers. It was also, typically, a quick job – commissioned in 1868 by the great pianist Anton Rubinstein, it was finished in just seventeen days. Unusually for Saint-Saëns, it opens with an unorthodox gesture, a cadenza that runs into a particularly sumptuous first theme. Thereafter things run pretty well to pattern: as with the third violin concerto, the central movement is the work's weak spot, but the Presto is a steamroller of a finale, demanding heroic virtuosity of the soloist.

> ⊚ Biret; Philharmonia; Loughran, (Naxos 8550334; with *Concerto No. 4*).

Idel Biret's enthusiastic account displays great technical assurance and sense of motion, with James Loughran giving solid, if uninspired, support. Similar qualities are brought to bear on the fourth concerto; at budget price, the value is outstanding.

VIOLIN SONATA NO. 1

Most of Saint-Saëns' chamber music is doggedly formulaic, but the *Violin Sonata No. 1* (1885) shows him throwing off the shackles in the last movement, where for once he sets out to thrill. It's a brilliant if technically cruel moto-perpetuo, in which pianist and violinist really have to battle to stay together – an entertaining antidote to Saint-Saëns' habitual propriety.

> ◉ Shaham; Oppitz (Deutsche Grammophon 429 729-2GH; with Franck, *Sonata*; Ravel, *Tzigane*).

Gil Shaham's tone might lack personality but his intonation is faultless, and he and Gerhard Oppitz work extremely well together. The last movement runs just as the composer intended, building to a pace that's just on the civilized side of frenetic.

ERIK SATIE
(1866–1925)

Though dismissed in some quarters as a whimsical lightweight, Erik Satie was one of the most influential figures in twentieth-century French music. Ravel never tired of paying tribute to a man he called simply "the precursor", and the young Debussy (his closest friend) was encouraged by Satie to make the final break with Wagnerism and dispense with the heavy romantic "sauerkraut". Essentially a solitary figure, eking out a living as a pianist in the cafés of Montmartre (dressed always in a grey velvet suit and bowler hat), Satie became famed among the cognoscenti of Paris chiefly for his quirky piano pieces, with their mystifying titles and whimsical performance directions. Compositions such as *Pieces to Make You Run Away*, *Flabby Preludes* and *Bureaucratic Sonata*, published with such unhelpful tips as "Wonder about Yourself" and "Be Clairvoyant", make Satie a forerunner of Dada and Surrealism, while their combination of wistfulness and satirical wit give them a unique – but distinctly French – flavour.

From the mid-1910s Satie was championed by Ravel and by that arch-trend-setter Jean Cocteau, and in turn was unstinting in his support of young musicians, most notably the group known as Les Six, who saw a way forward in his ironic, self-contained miniatures. Sadly, just as his star was really on the rise, his health began to fail him, due in no small part to the strong drink he consumed in vast quantities over the years. He died of cirrhosis of the liver at the age of 59. Among the tributes heaped on him was this one from Darius Milhaud: "The purity of his art, his horror of all concessions, his contempt for money and his ruthless attitude toward the critics were a marvellous example for us all."

PIANO MUSIC

Though he wrote some large-scale pieces – such as the "symphonic drama" *Socrate* and the ballet *Parade* – it's Satie's poignant piano vignettes that are most representative of his art. Despite their frequently absurd titles, these miniatures are often deeply lyrical, with a sound-world derived partly from his interest in the modal music of medieval Christianity. This emphasis on modal techniques and "white-key" harmonies – heard to particularly good effect in the *Sarabandes* (1887), *Gymnopédies* (1888) and *Gnossiennes* (1890), predated Debussy's exploration of such harmonic resources by some fifteen years.

◉ **Avant-dernières pensées and other pieces**: Rogé (Decca 421 713-2).
◉ **Gnossiennes, Gymnopédies and other pieces**: Rogé (Decca 410220-2).

Pascal Rogé's two recordings of Satie's piano music perfectly capture the composer's mixture of knowingness and naïvety, drawing you into this unique sound world in performances that are full of elegant poise. Rogé is just as successful at bringing out the underlying melancholy of a set like the six *Gnossiennes* as he is at catching the sharp wit of a collection like *Veritables preludes flasques*. If you want to pick just one CD as a sampler of Satie's music, go for the collection featuring the *Gnossiennes* and *Gymnopédies*.

ALESSANDRO SCARLATTI
(1660–1725)

Alessandro Scarlatti has become the obscure Scarlatti, but he was a figure of great historical importance. One of the major composers of opera before the generation of Handel and Gluck, he was immensely successful during his lifetime, when numerous editions of his works were published and his operas were frequently produced outside the city by which they were commissioned.

He began his musical studies in Rome with Carissimi (see p.90), under whose guidance he composed his first opera, *Gli equivoci nel sembiante*, in 1679. During the next forty-six years he composed more than one hundred stage works (the precise number isn't known) and became a seminal figure in the world of opera seria – the principal operatic genre of the early eighteenth century. After working for the Queen of Sweden as maestro di cappella, he settled in Naples in 1684, where he stayed until 1702; for the remainder of his life he floated in and out of various court appointments.

Scarlatti established Naples as the centre of Italian operatic life and made several technical advances to the genre, such as his development of the Da Capo aria, his skilful use of instrumental textures, and his adoption of subjects less high-flown than the mythological themes so loved by Monteverdi. Yet he

was not a great innovator – rather, his work looks back to the declamatory Venetian tradition of Monteverdi rather then towards the dramatic school that followed. It was perhaps indicative of a recognition of his fundamentally conservative nature that Scarlatti composed fewer and fewer operas from the 1700s, and the overall pallidness of his style isn't likely to win many admirers nowadays. At the moment there not a single complete Scarlatti opera in the catalogue. If you want a taste of Scarlatti's vocal style at its most attractive, listen to the CD below.

Venere e Adone – Il Giardino d'Amore: Gayer, Fassbaender; Munich Chamber Orchestra; Stadlmair (Archiv 431 122-2AGA).

This mid-1960s recording of Scarlatti's setting of the tale of Venus and Adonis is as gutsy a performance as you could wish for. The tones of the instrumental ensemble might not meet the prim standards of modern Baroque orthodoxy, but the playing is disarmingly fresh and the passionate singing of Catherine Gayer and the great Brigitte Fassbaender make Scarlatti's score sound compellingly red-blooded.

DOMENICO SCARLATTI
(1685–1757)

Although he composed in many genres, Domenico Scarlatti – son of Alessandro – is now known just for his keyboard sonatas. This is scarcely surprising, because between 1719 and his death Scarlatti wrote an incredible 555 of these single-movement works, in one of history's most remarkable musical marathons.

Born in Naples, he studied with his father before moving to Venice some time in the late 1700s. While in Venice he met Handel, whose patron, Cardinal Ottoboni, arranged for a public harpsichord and organ competition between the two composers. Handel was deemed the better organist, while Scarlatti was thought superior on the harpsichord. After working for the Queen of Poland, in 1715 he was appointed music director at St Peter's in Rome, a position he maintained for

four years until he moved to London to work as a harpsichordist in the Italian Theatre.

In 1721 he became court composer to King John V of Portugal, a position whose duties included teaching music to the King's daughter, Princess Maria Barbara. In 1725 he returned to Naples for four years, but then settled in Madrid where he remained in the service of the Princess until three years before his death. His close professional relationship with Maria Barbara inspired him to create the majority of the keyboard works for which he is today exclusively remembered.

THE SONATAS

The keyboard of Scarlatti's day had a far smaller spectrum than the modern piano, but within these confines he created music of extraordinary variety, ranging in character

Scarlatti's sonatas bear no resemblance to the multi-movement form mastered by Haydn, Mozart and Beethoven – to Scarlatti the term "sonata" signified nothing more precise than that a piece was purely instrumental. Scarlatti's one-movement compositions do not develop their material in the organic way that Classical sonatas mould their themes, but rather proceed by the interweaving and juxtaposition of motifs which reappear throughout the sonata. The charm of Scarlatti's melodies, the quick-wittedness with which he conducts his musical arguments, and the quasi-romantic expressive effects he achieves through sharply contrasted motifs, makes these sonatas as absorbing as any instrumental music of the eighteenth century.

> ◐ **Complete Sonatas**: Ross (Erato 2292-45309-2; 34 CDs).
> ◐ **56 Sonatas**: Ross (Erato 2292-45422-2; 3 CDs).
> ◐ **Best Sonatas**: Ross (Erato 2292-45423-2).
> ◗ **The Celebrated Scarlatti Recordings**: Horowitz (Sony SK53460).

Scott Ross died tragically young, but his recordings of the complete Scarlatti sonatas stand as a testament to a brilliantly inventive musician, whose technique constantly transcended the expressive limitations of the harpsichord. Unfortunately, the sonatas are not available on individual CDs, but Erato have released a single disc of the "best" sonatas (a dubious notion with music of such consistent quality) and a three-disc set of fifty-six. Horowitz's performances, part of Sony's Horowitz Edition, highlight the quirkiness of the music and use the piano's full resources to produce textures beyond the scope of the harpsichord. The choice of sonatas is stimulating and the playing is enchanting – this CD is one of the mercurial pianist's greatest successes.

from helter-skelter urgency to the most delicate lyricism. Scarlatti may not possess the depths of his contemporary J. S. Bach, but he boasted a seemingly inexhaustible fertility, and was the first really to explore the limits of what ten fingers could achieve – his music is littered with jumps over two octaves, crossed-hand passages and rapid note repetitions. Indeed like Beethoven, Scarlatti can be credited with the invention of a totally new keyboard technique.

ALFRED SCHNITTKE

(1934–   )

Alfred Schnittke, Russia's most celebrated contemporary composer, is widely seen as the successor to Shostakovich, but the generation gap makes them significantly different musicians. Whereas Shostakovich's music was forged in the heat of the early revolutionary period and tempered in the ice of Stalinism, Schnittke was young during the Kruschev thaw and matured under Brezhnev's stagnation. The other crucial factor in Schnittke's background is that his mother was German and his father German-Jewish – though born in the Volga Republic, he spoke German as his first language and always felt an alien in his native land. Thus it's scarcely surprising that

BETTY FREEMAN/LEBRECHT COLLECTION

if there are any common elements running through his wide-ranging output, they are irony, parody, disguise and wild pastiche. His music can be uncomfortably dissonant and loud, and it does have a tendency to be ramblingly episodic, but Schnittke at his best is one of the wittiest musicians around, and his manifest sincerity has done a lot to secure him a wide following.

Schnittke began his musical studies in Vienna, where his father was posted as a journalist right after the war. The musical traditions of that city – both the classicism of Haydn, Mozart and Beethoven and the fin-de-siècle works of Mahler and Schoenberg – have had an enormous effect on him. In 1948 he settled in Moscow (where he was to stay until moving to Hamburg in 1990), and soon began writing music using serial techniques that were almost obligatory for composers in the West, but led to his marginalization by the Soviet establishment. Few official commissions came his way, and rare performances of Schnittke pieces were packed out, becoming more like socio-political events than concerts. Most of his income came from the cinema (he produced sixty film scores in just twenty years), and his work for directors such as

Elem Klimov and Mikhail Romm, who were to become the leading lights when *perestroika* arrived, helped spread his reputation.

Schnittke's distinctive "polystylism" emerged in the 1970s, with his *Symphony No. 1* (1974) marking a turning point. Since then he has received numerous major international commissions and is still composing with great energy, despite a serious stroke in 1985 and delicate health ever since. *Life with an Idiot*, his eagerly awaited first opera, was premiered in Amsterdam in 1992.

OPERA AND CHORAL MUSIC

Labelled "a requiem for the Soviet Union" by the press, the first production of *Life with an Idiot* was created by a team of people who had all been persecuted by the old regime – writer and librettist Viktor Erofeev, designer Ilya Kabakov, director Boris Pokrovsky, and conductor-cellist Mstislav Rostropovich. The story is transparently allegorical: as punishment for some political misdemeanour, a couple have to share their tiny Moscow apartment with an idiot (a Lenin lookalike in the Amsterdam production) who makes their life a nightmare – he gets the wife pregnant, seduces the husband and then murders the wife and drives the husband into a lunatic asylum. The extraordinarily lewd libretto is a vivid example of post-Soviet kitsch, including wife-beating, sex, abortion and a "chorus of homosexuals".

If this sounds too heavy for you, make a start with the 1983 composition *Seid nüchtern and wachtet (Faust Cantata)*, Schnittke's adaptation of the last chapter of Goethe's *Faust* for soloists, choir and orchestra. Intended as part of a projected Faust opera, this Gothic postmodernist fantasy opens with a liturgical combination of chorus and choir, but with a distant tango beat. The tango comes to the foreground in the climactic scene, where Mephisto describes Faust's blood-spattered room and corpse in a nightmarish monologue. Perhaps most approachable of all is the *Choir Concerto* (1985), a profoundly devotional score using settings of a tenth-century Armenian poet and owing much to the Orthodox choral tradition.

⦿ **Life with an Idiot**: Duesing; Ringholz; Haskin; Rotterdam Philharmonic; Rostropovich (Sony CD52495; 2 CDs).
⦿ **Faust Cantata**: Malmö Symphony Orchestra; DePreist (BIS CD-437; with (K)ein Sommernachtstraum, Ritual & Passacaglia).
⦿ **Choir Concerto**: Danish National Radio Choir; Parkman (Chandos CHAN 9126).

Like much of Schnittke's very theatrical music, *Life with an Idiot* is far better on stage than on disc, but the Rostropovich recording makes the most of the choral interjections and other moments of inventive humour in this uneven score. The conductor also plays the cello a couple of times and gets drawn into the frenetic action to play a sleazy tango on a honky-tonk piano. The BIS recording of *Faust* features a fine Mephisto from the countertenor Mikael Bellini, and is coupled with some of Schnittke's best orchestral music. The Chandos recording of the *Choir Concerto* might lack something of the authentic Orthodox atmosphere, but it comes with a translation of the text, which gives it an edge over the opposition.

ORCHESTRAL MUSIC

Schnittke's landmark *Symphony No. 1* was premiered by Gennadi Rozhdestvensky – a consistent promoter of his music – in 1974 in Gorky, an emblematically out-of-the-way venue for this crazed mish-mash of a work. "The First Symphony is the central work for me," says the composer, "because it contains everything that I have ever had or done in my life, even the bad and the kitschy as well as the most sincere . . . all of my later works are its continuations and are determined by it." Featuring theatrical entrances and exits for the orchestral players, free-jazz improvisation and undigested fragments from the classics, it's a raucously eclectic piece. By contrast, the consistently powerful second symphony – actually a mass rather than a symphony – was inspired by Austria and by Bruckner in particular; permeated by bell sounds and sonorous choral writing, it's a far more homogenous work than its predecessor. The *Concerto Grosso No. 1* is quintessential Schnittke polystylism, with frenzied excerpts of Vivaldi, dissonant outbursts and a tango for harpsichord and violins; it has its moments, even if it doesn't quite add up. The *Viola Concerto*, by contrast, is romantic and expressionistic: its two slow outer movements enclose a frenetic central section at the centre of which comes a moment of uneasy repose, with the viola playing a simple classical melody over a piano accompaniment. It's not easy listening, but in the right hands it's a mightily impressive piece.

⦿ **Symphony No. 1**: USSR Ministry of Culture Symphony Orchestra; Rozhdestvensky (Melodiya SUCD10-00062).
⦿ **Symphony No. 1**: Stockholm Philharmonic Orchestra; Segerstam (BIS CD-577).
⦿ **Symphony No. 2**: Leningrad Philharmonic Symphony Orchestra; USSR Ministry of Culture Chamber Choir; Rozhdestvensky (Melodiya SUCD 10-00063).
⦿ **Concerto Grosso No. 1**: Kremer; Grindenko; Chamber Orchestra of Europe; Schiff (Deutsche Grammophon DG 429 413-2; with *Quasi una sonata* & *Moz-Art à la Haydn*).
⦿ **Viola Concerto**: Rostropovich; London Symphony Orchestra; Bashmet (RCA RD60446).

Rozhdestvensky, the work's dedicatee, conducts the most committed CD performance of the *Symphony No. 1*, but the BIS version is more readily available and better recorded. The second symphony works far better on CD and is given a splendidly atmospheric reading by Rozhdestvensky, who conducted its premiere in 1980; this is one of the few performances of a Schnittke work that draws you into the music rather than making you wonder what trick he's going to pull next. However, if you prefer the eclectic Schnittke, the best basic introduction is the CD of the *Concerto Grosso No. 1*, which gets ideal performances from Gidon Kremer and Tatiana Grindenko; it's combined with *Quasi una sonata*, a strenuous rearrangement of his second violin sonata, and

Moz-Art à la Haydn, a more playful reworking of Mozart. The *Viola Concerto*, one of Schnittke's most Mahlerian scores, is given a definitive performance by Yuri Bashmet, for whom it was written.

CHAMBER MUSIC

Schnittke's chamber music generally shares the multi-stylistic character of his large-scale pieces, and the most evocative of these chamber works is the *Piano Quintet* of 1976. Written in memory of his mother, it juxtaposes episodes of tortured longing with a bittersweet waltz, using conflicting elements to construct a statement that is imaginative and haunting. The most often performed Schnittke string quartet is his third (1983), which contains gestures to Lassus, Beethoven and Shostakovich, while the *Piano Quartet* of 1988 is a crazed reworking of Mahler.

◉ Piano Quintet; Piano Quartet; String Quartet No. 3: Borodin Quartet; Berlinsky (Virgin VC 7 91436-2).

This disc is highly recommended as a first step into Schnittke's music. The Borodin Quartet have a close relationship with the composer (they premiered his first quartet in 1966), and here they give glorious performances of three of his finest chamber works.

ARNOLD SCHOENBERG
(1874–1951)

In 1909 Arnold Schoenberg wrote his *Three Pieces* for piano, Op. 11. It was perhaps the single most significant composition of the twentieth century, for this was the first wholly atonal piece of music. Schoenberg prefered the term "pantonal" but the words define the same thing – the rejection of tonal centres, of key signatures and of traditional harmony. In short, the techniques of musical expression as they had been understood for hundreds of years were abandoned in favour of an ideal in which all the notes of the chromatic scale were assigned equal weight. As might be imagined, this brought the heavens down upon Schoenberg's head.

Born in Vienna to Jewish parents (his father was born in Hungary, his mother was Czech), Schoenberg first learned the violin and cello, and taught himself music theory until 1894, when he took composition lessons from Zemlinsky (see p.421), who was only two years Schoenberg's senior. During these early years Viennese musical life was still riven by the Wagner versus Brahms debate, even though Wagner had been dead for more than ten years, and from the very beginning Schoenberg's loyalties were with Wagner. By the age of twenty-five he had seen each of Wagner's major opera's more than twenty times, perhaps. Although his very earliest compositions reflect an admiration for Brahms's classical discipline, in 1899 Wagner's influence overtook Schoenberg completely, and he embarked upon a series of opulent late-Romantic scores, beginning with the string sextet *Verklärte Nacht*. The following year he began composing what was to be his most grandiose work, *Gurrelieder*, and with the first part of this gigantic project under his arm he applied for a teaching post in Berlin. With Strauss's recommendation he was accepted at the Stern Conservatory, where he stayed for three years, a period during which he composed his Straussian *Pelleas und Melisande*.

Whereas Strauss and Pfitzner seemed content to live on the legacy of Wagner, to Schoenberg it seemed evident that a point of crisis had been reached, that Wagnerian chromaticism had exhausted the conventional vocabularies without offering any way forward. In the mid-1900s Schoenberg set off along his own path, developing a personal style from which he gradually purged the chromatic indulgences of *Gurrelieder* in favour of a more economical language. With the *String Quartet No. 2*, written in 1907, he

LEBRECHT COLLECTION

came to the brink of composing music that was in no key, and with the *Three Pieces* of 1909 he finally made the complete break with tonality.

By the following year, Schoenberg and Strauss (from whom he was now estranged) were Europe's pre-eminent enfants terribles, but whereas Strauss was fabulously success-ful, Schoenberg was the subject of venomous abuse – though he received staunch support from his pupils Anton Webern (see p.413) and Alban Berg (see p.42), the other key members of what came to be called the Second Viennese School. The Viennese premiere of the atonal *Pierrot Lunaire* in 1912 provoked outright hostility, in marked contrast to the premiere of the luscious *Gurrelieder* later the same year, which was an unqualified success. Had Schoenberg arrived on the scene as a fully-fledged atonalist, nobody would have given him the time of day, but the undeniable mastery displayed in such works as *Gurrelieder* was at least to earn him an audience, albeit an uncomprehending one. To steal a joke used in another context by

Pierre Boulez, the critics had respect for Schoenberg's mind, but they hated what it thought.

Schoenberg served in the ranks during World War I, and immediately after the war he returned to Vienna, where he, Berg and Webern organized and played in concerts of new music, events from which the critics of the Viennese press were barred. He composed little until 1924, when he announced his re-emergence with the creation of twelve-tone serialism, the method by which he brought order to the potential chaos of atonalism. Whereas pure atonalism had given the composer freedom to select notes at will from the entire chromatic scale, the twelve-tone technique showed how entire compositions could be built around an ordained sequence of twelve notes, from which all the piece's motifs and chords could be derived, by superimposition, inversion, reversal and other procedures. In effect, the tone-row provided a democratized replacement for the conventional harmonic scale.

In 1925 he moved back to Berlin, where he taught composition at the Academy of Arts, but with the advent of Nazism he was dismissed from his post. Schoenberg left Germany and in 1933 emigrated to the United States, where he began spelling his name "Schoenberg" rather than the Germanic "Schönberg". He settled in Los Angeles, where from 1936 he taught at UCLA. In the remaining years of his life his devotion to serialism sometimes wavered, and he produced a lot of generally unremarkable new music during this period, in addition to revis-ing earlier scores. In 1944 he applied for a Guggenheim grant to allow him to complete his opera *Moses und Aron*, which he had begun in 1930; his application was refused, and he died leaving the third act incomplete.

Schoenberg is one of the most remarkable figures in the history of music, as inspira-tional in his dedication to his art as in his published work. Driven by an inner compul-sion to create new foundations for western music, he was spurred to ever greater deter-mination by the hostility he encountered. In 1947 he accepted an award from the American Academy of Arts with the words:

"That you should regard all I have tried to do in the last fifty years as an achievement strikes me as in some respects an overestimate. My own feeling was that I had fallen into an ocean of boiling water; and, as I couldn't swim and knew no other way out, I struggled with my arms and legs as best I could . . . The credit must go to my opponents. It was they who really helped me." He was a modest man, but had no illusions as to his significance. When he was in the army, someone asked him if he was the composer Arnold Schoenberg. He replied, "Someone had to be."

CHORAL AND STAGE WORKS

Of all Schoenberg's choral works, the most important is the mighty *Gurrelieder*, perhaps the greatest Austro-German choral composition of the twentieth century. After Mahler's *Symphony No. 8* it requires the largest forces of any concert work, and each of Schoenberg's subsequent stage works also demands a large-scale orchestra. However, these later pieces – *Ewartung*, *Die glückliche Hande*, *Von Heute auf Morgen* and *Moses und Aron* – are of completely different character from *Gurrelieder*, for they all come after his shift into atonality. Lyricism and melody are not wholly absent from the stage works (indeed, *Ewartung* is littered with moments of lush expressionism), but on the whole they are challengingly austere and aggressive. The orchestra is heavily sub-divided, so that often only a few instruments are playing at any one time, while the vocal parts are typified by extreme leaps and the use of *Sprechstimme*, a style of declamation that is midway between speech and song (Berg's *Wozzeck* is the finest example of the technique). *Ewartung* and *Moses und Aron* are justifiably the two stage pieces that receive most frequent performances.

GURRELIEDER

Of all Schoenberg's scores, none has won such wide popularity as *Gurrelieder* (Songs of Gurre) – there is even a world-wide Gurrelieder Society. Its success has as a lot to do with its scale, for *Gurrelieder* is a work that blasts you out of your seat. Deploying a veritable army of players, it calls for at least seventy strings, four choirs, five soloists, a narrator, eight flutes, ten horns, seven trumpets, seven trombones, five tubas, four harps, six percussionists and iron chains – and that isn't a full tally.

Schoenberg started it in 1900 but didn't complete the orchestration until 1911. Thus when it was first performed in 1913, conducted by Franz Schreker (see p.315), audience and critics were astonished to hear such lush expressionism from a composer who was by then immersed in work that denied everything that *Gurrelieder* stood for. Based upon a poem by the Danish romantic Jens Peter Jacobsen, the ninety-minute work dramatises the love between King Waldemar and Tove, resident of Castle Gurre. Set in the fourteenth century, it's a tale that would have appealed to Wagner, and indeed the music of *Gurrelieder*, though in part a homage to Strauss, is especially indebted to Wagner, whose *Tristan and Isolde* is the prototype for the febrile emotionalism of Part One. This section is dominated by a long and luxuriant duet for Waldemar and Tove, which is interrupted after each verse by sumptuous orchestral commentaries, and is followed by the murder of Tove and a lament for her, sung by a wood dove. Part Two sees Waldemar cursing his fate (combative relationships with the deity were to recur in Schoenberg's work), but Part Three builds to a final, pantheistic chorus of outrageous, wondrous dimensions.

Schachtschneider, Borkh, Topper, Engen, Fehenberger; Bavarian Radio Chorus & Orchestra; Kubelik (Deutsche Grammophon 431 744-2GC2; 2 CDs).

Considering how expensive it is to record, there's a surprisingly large number of CDs of *Gurrelieder* in the catalogue. Best of them is Kubelik's transcendental account, on a superbly engineered live recording that is now available at mid-price. Most conductors adopt desperately analysed tempi that fail to capture any of the frenzy of the first part and allow the music to sink into pomposity at the conclusion. Kubelik keeps an iron grip and pushes the score along where it most needs it. He achieves a fine balance that prevents the chorus and orchestra from dominating his soloists, amongst whom Inge Borkh, one of the century's greatest dramatic sopranos, is pre-eminent.

ERWARTUNG

Ewartung (Expectation), for soprano and large orchestra, is a thirty-minute monologue of gruelling concentration. Schoenberg wrote it in 1909, soon after the Op. 11 piano pieces, and *Ewartung* shows him applying the techniques he had developed in those atonal miniatures to a large, dramatic structure. Though moments of tonality and tantalising classical motifs do punctuate the score, it's essentially a stream of dreamlike images and jagged musical gestures, creating a terrifying image of a mind gripped by unmitigated fear.

The plot, if that is the right word, was created by Marie Pappenheim, a young doctor and poet, and is a typical product of Freud's Vienna. A lone, unnamed woman is seen wandering at night through a forest which may be real or may be the landscape of her subconscious. The woman is searching for her lover, whose corpse she stumbles across fairly early in the work; leaving unanswered the question of the motive and identity of the murderer, the rest of *Ewartung* is given over to the woman's disjointed, distracted recollections of their life together. Vocally, the work is a tour de force, demanding a singer with a capacity for both tenderness and hysteria, as well as lungs strong enough to keep going without a break for over half an hour.

⦿ Norman; Metropolitan Opera Orchestra; Levine *
(Philips 426 261-2; with cabaret songs).

Levine's performance of this dense score is a revelation, unleashing tremendous power at the climaxes as well perfectly controlling the orchestra in the delicate, introspective passages. The disc is dominated, however, by a fearful performance from Jessye Norman – this is perhaps her greatest half-hour on record. The skittish, fragile cabaret songs are less suited to her massive voice, but she succeeds in bringing a smiling quality to the frequently witty texts. The recording is ideal.

MOSES UND ARON

An unresolved need for communication with God was central to Schoenberg's artistic personality, and for most of his life he was racked by the problems of self-knowledge and religious belief. His conversions to and desertions of Judaism were indicative of the anguish he suffered, and in his last opera, *Moses und Aron*, he wrestled with the issue of humanity's inability to deal with absolute truth, as given to Moses by God. The work was left incomplete at his death, not because of the shortage of time, but because Schoenberg found it impossible to find music for the final act, in which Moses berates Aaron for his devotion to the Image rather than to the Idea.

Moses und Aron is Schoenberg's largest staged work and the most complete dramatic expression of serialist techniques. The deeply philosophical libretto – written by the composer – is set to music of such complexity that Schoenberg doubted that a performance would be possible. The work is too hieratic to be completely successful on stage, but for all the difficulty of the music, the emotional power of *Moses und Aron* is as direct as anything by any of Schoenberg's more traditional contemporaries. The baritone role of Moses is written in *Sprechstimme* while Aron's part is fully scored for a very high tenor – as far from the style of Moses as could be imagined. An almost delirious intensity is generated by the resulting range of expression in their exchanges. The longest, most significant and most accessible scene comes in the second act, where Aaron leads the people to reject Moses (who is on the mountain top communing with God) and descend into an orgy of debauchery, for which Schoenberg wrote music of sumptuous colour.

⦿ Mazura, Langridge, Haugland, Bonney, Zakai; Glen Ellyn Children's Chorus, Chicago Symphony Chorus; Chicago Symphony Orchestra; Solti (Decca 414 264-2DH2; 2 CDs).

Solti's recording is a brilliantly sung and recorded performance of great dramatic punch. Franz Mazura as Moses and Philip Langridge as Aron are both excellent, and there's a notable contribution from Barbara Bonney, who sings the role of the Young Girl.

ORCHESTRAL WORKS

It was his orchestral music that first earned Schoenberg his reputation as a dangerous radical. The premiere of the "tuneless" *Five Orchestral Pieces* caused an outrage at its first performance, as did the later *Variations for Orchestra*, an uncompromising example of fully developed serialism. To appreciate the origins of these works you should approach them via his early *Pelleas und Melisande*, which shows Schoenberg at his most romantic. These three works represent only a small selection of Schoenberg's orchestral output, but they will give you an excellent introduction to the composer's range.

PELLEAS UND MELISANDE

Debussy wrote his *Pelléas et Mélisande* in the mid-1890s; though unaware of Debussy's opera, Schoenberg also considered writing a stage work based on Maeterlinck's play at this time, but in 1902 he decided instead to turn the story into a symphonic poem. Whereas Debussy's opera is all about understatement and implication, Schoenberg's music is a tightly strung, blatantly hedonistic piece, explicitly portraying Melisande's illicit love for her brother-in-law – the love duet in particular is breathtakingly effective, containing some brilliantly dramatic counterpoint. In places *Pelleas und Melisande* does suggest that Schoenberg's grasp of the technicalities of orchestration was not yet complete, yet Schoenberg's only symphonic poem is obsessively involving, and contains some of the most erotic music ever written. Wagner would have been proud.

⦿ Vienna Philharmonic Orchestra; Böhm (Deutsche Grammophon 435 323-2GWP; with Strauss, *Tod und Verklärung*).

Böhm's *Pelleas und Melisande*, recorded live in June 1969, is a performance of strict discipline and revelatory clarity, imposing a sense of order on the rich, sometimes over-ambitious orchestrations. The conductor's enthusiasm for the music results in committed and responsive playing from the orchestra and while the recording gives too much prominence to the wind and brass, the sense of occasion is more than worth the imbalance. The accompanying *Tod und Verklärung* is superb, making this a very special recording indeed.

FIVE ORCHESTRAL PIECES

Composed in the annus mirabilis of 1909, the *Five Orchestral Pieces* shows Schoenberg moving away from the tonal manner of *Pelleas* and into the free-floating world of atonalism, yet this is not a schism so much as a transition. The rather unwieldy orchestrations betray an affinity with the fin-de-siècle aesthetic of *Pelleas*, as do some of the titles

originally appended to each of the five pieces: *Premonitions*, *Yesteryears*, *Summer Morning by a Lake*, *Peripetia* and *The Obbligato Recitative*. The first of the set is an obscurantist composition that might frighten you off, but the second piece is a restrained and essentially Romantic episode which in turn leads into the extraordinary *Summer Morning by a Lake*, the work's high point. Here Schoenberg explores the possibilities of what was termed *Klangfarbenmelodie* ("sound-colour melody"), in which a melodic effect is transformed simply by changing the timbre of a single note or a simple harmony. Just as colour can alter the eye's perception of an object's shape, so a chord or run of notes is here modified by playing with its tone-colour. The tranquillity of this third movement is extremely affecting, and its stylistic impact upon Webern and subsequent generations is incalculable.

⦿ London Symphony Orchestra; Dorati (Mercury 432 006-2MM; with orchestral works by Schoenberg, Webern and Berg).

This is an amazing recording from one of the century's most perceptive conductors. Aware of every inflection of the music's colour and internal shape, Dorati makes the most of Schoenberg's orchestration; combined with other fine examples of the Second Viennese School, this brightly engineered recording serves as an excellent starting point for atonal orchestral music.

VARIATIONS FOR ORCHESTRA

The *Variations for Orchestra*, Schoenberg's most successful orchestral application of twelve-tone method, was premiered by Wilhelm Furtwängler on December 3, 1928, and prompted such tumultuous scenes that the concert came close to being abandoned. Nonetheless the critic Max Marschalk was moved to comment – "Schoenberg convinces us with the *Variations* that he has succeeded in discovering new vistas in music in which we can feel comfortably at home . . . The music he presents in the *Variations* is without precedent." This is not strictly true, for Schoenberg had created his own precedents, but this music certainly did mark a new direction in its rigorous formal cohesion. You cannot hear the variations taking place – Schoenberg himself said that this was impossible – but you can detect an underlying momentum generated by the music's complex rhythmic patterns, and the rich orchestral detail builds to a climax fulfilling as that of any conventional variation sequence. The more often you listen to this piece, the more easily you'll be able to follow the many layers of which it is constructed and so appreciate its fundamentally classical architecture.

◗ Berlin Philharmonic Orchestra; Karajan (Deutsche Grammophon 415 326-2GH; with *Verklärte Nacht*).

Karajan's finely crafted performance of this extraordinary unbroken twenty-five-minute score is extremely persuasive. There is no question but that this is difficult stuff, yet Karajan's subtle and highly imaginative approach allows the music's lines to appear clearly, and the resonant recording brings out the richness of Schoenberg's textures.

CHAMBER AND PIANO MUSIC

Schoenberg's string quartets and his piano music comprise two categories of his output within which you can clearly trace the dominant pattern of his career, from chromatic Romanticism through atonality to serialism. Besides these works, one other piece is essential listening – the string sextet *Verklärte Nacht*, the composer's most seductive creation.

VERKLÄRTE NACHT

Verklärte Nacht (Transfigured Night) was one of Schoenberg's earliest pieces and it gave him his first taste of success when it was performed in 1903, four years after its composition. It was liked both by the public and by its creator, who produced orchestrated versions of it in 1917 and 1943, each of which proved as popular as the orginal sextet.

Verklärte Nacht was written shortly after Schoenberg's immersion in the symbolist poetry of Richard Dehmel, whose words he used for a set of early songs. The Dehmel poem that specifically inspired the sextet concerned a woman racked by guilt and fear, like the figure portrayed in *Ewartung*. However, whereas *Ewartung* ends in unease, *Verklärte Nacht* ends with a resolution: she confesses to her lover that she is pregnant by another man; he replies that through their

love the child will be born his, and thus their situation is transfigured. However, no knowledge of this premise is really necessary to enjoy a piece of music that's a peak of late-Romantic expressionism. Schoenberg here achieves a sort of reconciliation between Brahms and Wagner: the lyricism, instrumentation and simple tunefulness of *Verklärte Nacht* reflect the influence of the former, while its chromaticism and overall construction bear the marks of the latter.

◉ Raphael Ensemble (Hyperion CDA66425; with Korngold, *Sextet*).

The Raphael Ensemble deliver a pulsating but sensitively drawn performance, in which the intricately balanced counterpoint is made to sigh with erotic yearning – in the final part, introduced by the second cellist's beautiful solo theme, the music seems about to burst its banks. Coupled with Korngold's equally sumptuous *Sextet*, this well-engineered and finely annotated set should be in any basic CD library.

STRING QUARTETS

Schoenberg's *String Quartet No. 1* of 1905 is a Brahms-like piece, forward-looking in the sense that it is written as a single extended movement, but basically conservative in its language. In extreme contrast, the third and fourth quartets (1927 & 1936) are thoroughgoing serial works. Bereft of anything that could be termed conventional melody, they are immensely intellectual pieces that should not be approached until you've become familiar with the earlier works – and, preferably, also done a fair amount of background reading. The *String Quartet No. 2* (1907) is the one most likely to excite you if you're coming fresh to Schoenberg. In the last two movements this amazing quartet steps over the line into the shifting, eerie soundscape of atonality, a move announced by a soprano soloist who sings Stefan George's prophetic words – "I breathe the air of other planets". More than any other of Schoenberg's works, the *String Quartet No. 2* dramatizes the transition from the old to the new.

◗ La Salle Quartet; Price (Deutsche Grammophon 419 994-2; with quartets by Berg and Webern; 4 CDs).

These 1971 recordings by the La Salle Quartet of the complete Schoenberg, Berg and Webern string quartets remain unsurpassed, and one of the highlights is the account of the *String Quartet No. 2*, which is blessed by the ecstatic voice of Margaret Price. These committed and winning performances are well recorded and come with an exemplary explanatory booklet. Unfortunately, the four discs are not available separately but as an introduction to the Second Viennese School this set is unbeatable.

PIANO WORKS

Schoenberg was not a pianist and composed very little for the instrument – indeed he published only six works for solo piano. However, no part of his oeuvre provides so complete and so concise a survey of the composer's development.

The unpublished *Piano Pieces* of 1894 suggest nothing of the direction in which Schoenberg was to move, and they have a clumsy, slightly embarrassed feel, as if he were intimidated by his great precursors. He did not compose for the solo piano again until 1909 when he produced the epoch-making atonal music of the *Three Piano Pieces* Op. 11. The first of this set is constructed as a set of variations, but in the absence of a home key it's impossible for the untrained ear to perceive the structure in the way it could perceive the musical argument of, say, Beethoven's *Diabelli Variations* or Bach's *Goldberg Variations*. What the *Three Piano Pieces* is working towards is a sound-world that denies the sense of closure and hierarchy that the major and minor scales create, the sense that some episodes in a piece are more important than others. This movement towards an open-ended music in which every statement has equal space is furthered by the aphoristic *Six Little Piano Pieces* Op. 19 (1911), which rejects all motivic development in favour of a reliance upon tonal colour and vertical relations between the notes, proceeding through clusters of tones that obey no other logic than Schoenberg's intuitive sense of what works. As they did at the time of their creation, these pieces still attract dissent: some people find them insubstantial and uncomfortably dissonant, but others regard them as masterpieces of expressive concision, in which everything happens in the present tense.

The next piano work, *Five Piano Pieces* Op. 23, concludes with a waltz (undanceable, needless to say) whcih was the first published example of rigorous serial music. The *Piano*

Suite Op. 25, a distant relative of the Baroque suites of Bach and his contemporaries, shows Schoenberg further refining the twelve-tone method, which he once declared – rashly, it turned out – would "assure German music of its pre-eminence for the next century". The two *Piano Pieces* of Op. 33, written while Schoenberg was at work on *Moses und Aron*, show the twelve-tone technique at its most polished. With all this twelve-tone music you'll need a lot of research behind you if you're to appreciate the formal intricacies; as with so much modernist art, its creator expects its recipients do to almost as much work as he did. This is not to say, however, that the non-specialist should stay away, for the radical dynamic shifts, eventful rhythmic changes and startling juxtapositions of tones within these small-scale pieces make them as engrossing, if not as comforting, as any Chopin study or Schumann miniature.

◗ Pollini (Deutsche Grammophon 423 249-2GC).

Pollini's recording of the complete published piano music is a magnificent achievement. As ever he is technically in a class of his own, and nobody has ever matched the intellectual and emotional cohesion he brings to this music. If anyone tells you that Schoenberg is all about composing by numbers or by random selection, just listen to this CD – Pollini reveals the passion behind the method.

POLYGRAM

Maurizio Pollini

FRANZ SCHREKER

(1878–1934)

In the 1910s Franz Schreker was regarded as the third member of German music's avant-garde triumvirate, alongside Richard Strauss and Arnold Schoenberg. Nowadays he has become little more than a footnote to the history of modern music, even though his operas – especially *Der ferne Klang* – are among the most intriguing works of the early twentieth century. Drawing on the music of Richard Strauss and Debussy, Schreker creates a sound-world of ever-changing moods and colours, a style perfectly suited to the post-Freudian psychology of his subjects.

Schreker was born in Monaco to Austrian parents. The family returned to Vienna, where at the age of fourteen he gained a scholarship to enter the conservatory. Remaining in the city after his graduation, he devoted himself to composition, and didn't have to wait long for his breakthrough. His first success came in 1908 with *Der Geburtstag der Infantin*, a ballet based on Oscar Wilde's *Birthday of the Infanta*; four years later the premiere in Frankfurt of the first of his major operas, *Der ferne Klang*, established his reputation as a leading modernist. Alban Berg and Arnold Schoenberg both greatly admired it – indeed Alban Berg made a piano reduction of the score.

During World War I he wrote two operas, *Die Gezeichneten* and *Der Schatzgräber*, which were performed when hostilities had ceased. By 1920, installed as director of the Hochschule für Musik in Berlin, he had achieved a position of great influence, and was acclaimed as one of the country's finest composers. But from then on his life went into swift decline. By the mid-1920s his opulent style was rapidly going out of fashion, as the "new realism" of musicians such as Kurt Weill (see p.415) began to gain ground. He produced four more operas but his later works were not well received, even though they were championed by the great conductors Otto Klemperer and Erich Kleiber. Then came the Nazis. The victim of anti-Semitic demonstrations, Schreker was forced to resign his position in 1932; two years later, a broken man, he died of a heart attack.

THE OPERAS

Two Schreker operas receive occasional performances today, chiefly because they are fine examples of his ability to conjure marvellous textures from a large orchestral palette. *Der ferne Klang* (The Distant Sound) is in fact about a magical sound, which haunts a young musician named Fritz and acts as a motif throughout the piece. In a plot typical of Schreker's taste for the mystical and the erotic, Fritz abandons his lover, Grete, to go in search of the sound; she falls into prostitution, but they are finally re-united as Fritz is dying – whereupon he realizes that the "distant sound" is the motif of love. It's an accomplished piece of musical Expressionism, with several luscious orchestral passages (the opera calls for off-stage ensembles in addition to the main orchestra), and some powerful set pieces, notably the final duet.

Die Gezeichneten (The Stigmatized Ones) is an even stronger brew. After the success of *Der Geburtstag der Infantin*, Alexander Zemlinsky asked Schreker to write him a libretto for an opera based on the same Oscar Wilde story. Zemlinsky did produce an opera of *Der Geburtstag* (see p.421), but he had to go elsewhere for his text, as Schreker became so fascinated by Wilde's theme that he composed his own exploration of it. Set in sixteenth-century Genoa, *Die Gezeichneten* is a tale of erotic obsession, physical deformity, self-sacrifice and madness, carried by some of Schreker's most lyrical, richly chromatic music.

◉ **Der ferne Klang**: Moser, Schnaut, von Halem, Nimsgern; Berlin Radio Symphony Orchestra; Albrecht (Capriccio 60024-2; 2 CDs).
◉ **Die Gezeichneten**: Schmiege, Cochran, Cowen; Dutch Radio Philharmonic; de Waart (Marco Polo 8.223328/30; 3 CDs).

These two performances are the best available introductions to Schreker. Both sets suffer from a somewhat shrill soprano, but this is partly due to Schreker's Expressionist music, and the casts are otherwise good, with especially fine singing from the men in *Der ferne Klang*. Albrecht also gets a better performance from his orchestra, and superior recording quality too.

FRANZ SCHUBERT
(1797–1828)

The neglect that Schubert suffered for most of the nineteenth century now seems incredible. None of his symphonies was performed during his lifetime and not one was published until some fifty years after his death. In 1827 a music dictionary was published in which Schubert's name did not so much as feature once. A century later, another book attacked him as a "conventional music-machine, contentedly turning out work after work, day after day". A partial explanation for this situation is that – unlike Beethoven or Mozart – Schubert was not a virtuoso musician, and he found no other means of promoting himself. Ironically, however, his unfettered talent for melody and his attachment to classical forms also contributed significantly towards his neglect. In the high Romantic period, when density and ambiguity were the order of the day, Schubert's lucid and tuneful music was often dismissed as the product of a naïve mind. But even in the area of his output where melody predominated – his Lieder (songs) – there is so much more to his work than mere tunefulness. During a life of less than thirty-two years he composed over six hundred songs, and no other composer had ever displayed such an ability to match music to poetry so closely that the words seem to have been written expressly for this purpose. He remains the greatest of all song-writers, but that is not the limit of his achievement, for in his late chamber music, piano sonatas and symphonies Schubert created works that mark him down as the first great Romantic. The progressive element to this late music suggests that, had he lived longer, he would have gone on to produce music of daunting originality. The epitaph on his monument in Vienna says as

MANSELL COLLECTION

much: "The art of music here entombed a rich possession, but even fairer hopes".

He was born in Liechtenthal, a suburb of Vienna, and at the age of nine or ten was sent to study with the local church organist, Michael Holzer. As Holzer later wrote: "If I wished to instruct him in anything fresh, the boy already knew it. So I gave him no actual tuition but merely talked to him and watched him with silent astonishment." Another man who briefly instructed the boy stated "I can't teach him anything else; he's learned it all from God himself." Every moment Schubert had to himself was spent composing, and in 1812 he was accepted as a student by Salieri, under whose guidance he composed his first symphony. Two years later, to Salieri's astonishment, the seventeen-year-old presented him with the 341 pages of his fully orchestrated first opera. (Despite repeated attempts mastery of operatic form was always to elude him.) On October 19, 1814, Schubert wrote his setting of Goethe's poem *Gretchen am Spinnrade* (Gretchen at the Spinning Wheel), the first of a flood of sublime miniatures. For Schubert, composing was a natural function. On the first anniversary of *Gretchen am Spinnrade* he composed no fewer than eight songs in the one day, and in the course of 1815 he produced some 144 songs. The following year he completed a four-movement quartet in less than five hours.

From 1814 to 1817 he worked in his father's school, spending all his time writing – any student who interrupted him received short shrift. Towards the end of this period he began to make friends with some of the city's most prominent artists and thinkers, forming the closest ties with the poet Mayrhofer and the operatic baritone Michael Vogl, for whom he composed many of his greatest songs. Although his music was now sporadically performed in concert as well as at private "Schubertiades", Schubert was regarded as an esoteric taste and he was in desperate need of money, as he was to be throughout his life.

In 1818 he moved to Johann Esterhazy's summer residence, where he taught the count's two daughters. Upon his return the following year he took rooms with Mayrhofer and a man named Joseph Huttenbrenner, who proceeded to devote himself to the composer, collecting and catalogueing his music. The following year was very productive, especially the carefree summer months, which inspired him to compose the *Trout Quintet*. In 1821 the song *Erlkönig* was published by Diabelli – his first published composition – and in the same year he sketched, but never orchestrated, a seventh symphony. His eighth symphony, composed the year after, was also left incomplete.

At some point Schubert contracted syphilis, and in 1823 his health began to fail, resulting in his admission to the Vienna general hospital. However, his illness and subsequent depression did nothing to inhibit his creativity and while in hospital he composed the first songs of the cycle titled *Die Schöne Müllerin*. In 1825 he and Vogl spent five months touring Austria, in the course of which he is said to have composed a symphony, though no trace of the work has ever been found. At some point during the next two years Schubert met Beethoven but there are no reliable details. He did, however, definitely visit him on his death bed and is known to have been one of the torchbearers at Beethoven's funeral on March 29, 1827. His last two years saw the creation of his finest works: the *Quintet in C major*, the *Winterreise* song cycle, the last three piano sonatas and his final symphony. In March 1828 he gave a concert of his own music; the Viennese turned out in force, but not a single music critic attended. On November 19 he died. His brother interpreted his dying words as a wish to be buried near Beethoven, and so he was; in 1888 both bodies were exhumed to be placed in the Zentralfriedhof in Vienna, where they now lie side by side.

SYMPHONIES

Schubert lived beneath Beethoven's shadow all his life and yet his symphonies owe less to Beethoven's style than you might expect. Devoid of the Promethean defiance so common to Beethoven's works, they generally have a lightness, openness and thematic profusion that owes more to Haydn and Mozart than to Beethoven. However, while it's true that Schubert's symphonies as a whole are not as individualistic as his smaller-scale works, the last two symphonies display an approach to orchestral colouring that looks forward to the expansive symphonies of the mid-nineteenth century – the opening of the *Unfinished Symphony*, for example, is more Romantic than Classical in feel. As with all his works, the symphonies are dominated by a succession of seraphic melodies, but unlike the highly melodic symphonies of Schumann and Mendelssohn, Schubert's are never facile, and their range of emotion, from capricious gaiety to the deep melancholy, marks them out as one of the great cycles of the century.

The numbering of Schubert's symphonies can be confusing, as *Symphony No. 7* was never orchestrated by Schubert (though others had a go). Thus, although Schubert composed nine symphonies, only eight are played and some authorities label *Symphony No. 8* (the *Unfinished*) as *Symphony No. 7* and *Symphony No. 9* (the *Great*) as *Symphony No. 8*.

⦿ **Complete Symphonies**: Concertgebouw; Harnoncourt (Teldec 4509-91184-2; 4 CDs).

Hamoncourt's Beethoven cycle reaped every award on offer, but his Schubert set is far better. The rigid didacticism that marred the Beethoven cycle is here replaced by refreshingly instinctive conducting that is at once lyrical and brisk. If you've heard more traditional recordings, the light-footed delicacy of the much-reduced Concertgebouw orchestra might surprise you, but nothing is done merely to surprise. These performances probably come as close as possible to how Schubert might have heard his symphonies. The only negative point is that the sleeve-notes are appallingly pretentious.

SYMPHONY NO. 5

Schubert's first six symphonies were written between 1813 and 1818. The most popular of these is *Symphony No. 5* (1816), a symphony of Mozartian orchestral and architectural scale, but with a personality that is definitely not of Mozart's period. The exquisite slow movement, characterized by poignant, uniquely Schubertian key modulations, features a magical duet between the strings and wind section near the end, while its coda is perhaps the most affecting conclusion in all his symphonic music. He had attained the grand age of nineteen when he completed this masterpiece, and its captivating finale embodies all the optimism and clear-sightedness of youth.

⦿ San Francisco Symphony Orchestra; Blomstedt (Decca 433 072-2DH (with *Symphony No. 8* and *Rosamunde Overture*).
◗ Royal Philharmonic Orchestra; Beecham (EMI CDM7 69750-2; with *Symphonies Nos. 3 & 6*).

Blomstedt's account is marked by finely judged balance and exquisite melodic colour, best shown in the slow movement, where a beguiling attention to detail creates a chamber-like intimacy. It's coupled with an excellent version of the eighth symphony (see below), whereas Thomas Beecham's venerable and vivacious mid-price set comes with the weaker third and sixth symphonies.

SYMPHONY NO. 8

Schubert's *Symphony No. 8* was composed in 1822, and then abandoned for reasons about which one can only speculate. It may be that he was simply unable to find the inspiration to continue with the last two movements or, more likely, that he was repulsed by the symphony's association with the painful events that had accompanied its composition – arguments

with Vogl, a regrettable publishing agreement, and the emergence of the symptoms of syphilis. Its truncated form has been no handicap to success, however, and this is now the best-known of all Schubert's orchestral music.

The first movement is ushered in by the basses, playing a darkly hued theme of ominous power. This leads to a gentle rustle of strings over which an intensely yearning theme is played by oboe and clarinet in unison; then the movement's dominant idea is introduced, in the shape of a sweeping melody which, for extra weight, is given over to the cellos. It is one of the most profound openings in all symphonic music. The second movement is an open-air episode, in which the first movement's intimations of doom are transformed into radiant optimism. With this movement Schubert showed himself to be a master of orchestration as well as of symphonic form. From here on, no-one could categorize him as a song writer with unseemly aspirations.

⦿ Vienna Philharmonic Orchestra; Kleiber (Deutsche Grammophon 415 601-2; with *Symphony No. 3*).
⦿ San Francisco Symphony Orchestra; Blomstedt (Decca 433 072-2DH; with *Symphony No. 5* and *Rosamunde Overture*).

Carlos Kleiber's recordings are self-recommending: unwilling to tackle any piece of music without thoroughly thinking it through, he goes into the studio very rarely, and always obtains thrilling results. This account of the *Unfinished* is the most dramatic on record, highlighting the dynamic contrasts without impeding the flow. It's coupled with a quicksilver interpretation of the third symphony.

Blomstedt concentrates on the essentially lyrical nature of the *Unfinished* – nothing is forced and everything has its place. Something of the composer's contradictory psychology might be missed, but this is immensely accomplished playing, and it comes with the best available version of the fifth symphony.

SYMPHONY NO. 9

Schubert's orchestral masterpiece is the mighty *Symphony No. 9*, better known as the *Great*. It was written in the year of his death for the Gesellschaft der Musikfreunde (Society of Friends of Music), who found the music too difficult for their tastes. The spurned manuscript went missing for a number of years until Schumann found it in 1838, whereupon he sent it to Mendelssohn, who gave the symphony its premiere in Leipzig on March 21, 1839.

Schubert's slow movements are frequently the high points, and the blissful, ardent slow movement of the *Great* is very special indeed. Schumann, for one, admired this movement immensely, extolling its "heavenly length". He was especially taken by the section leading towards the recapitulation of the main theme, when the horn plays a series of delicate repeated notes – the instrument, Schumann said, was "calling as though from . . . another sphere. Everything else is hushed, as though listening to some heavenly visitant hovering around the orchestra". The symphony as a whole is characterized by an exceptional rhythmic energy, while his radically advanced orchestration places much greater weight on the brass sections, anticipating the bias of much Romantic orchestral music. In brief the *Great* is Schubert's longest, most demanding and most eloquent symphony.

○ Berlin Philharmonic Orchestra; Furtwängler (Deutsche Grammophon 427 781-2GDO (with Weber, *Overture to Der Freischütz*).
◉ North German Radio Symphony Orchestra; Wand (RCA RD60978).

Furtwängler's vision and discipline bring a dimension to this music that few other conductors have realized on disc; recorded live in 1942, this is a performance of extreme emotional intensity, in which the shadow of world conflict looms large. Gunther Wand's recording with the North German Orchestra is a good modern alternative; his players might respond with less character and immediacy than do Furtwängler's, but the sound and balance are considerably better.

CHAMBER MUSIC

Schubert composed an astonishing amount of chamber music and nearly all of it justifies the use of superlatives. As a body of work it is marked above all by a vein of intensely lyrical melody, but the later chamber music is marked by a strengthening of resources on several fronts. Increasing chromatic boldness and a greater flexibility of form are notable in these works, as are a scrupulous attention to the details of instrumentation, a more aggressive use of rhythm, and a sometimes overwhelming sense of urgency – not even Beethoven conveys the implacable momentum that runs through Schubert's last chamber pieces.

QUINTET FOR PIANO AND STRINGS – THE TROUT

In 1819, during a walking tour with Michael Vogl in upper Austria, Schubert stayed in Vogl's home town of Steyr, a place he thought "inconceivably lovely". Here the two men met a wealthy patron of the arts named Sylvester Paumgartner, who asked Schubert to compose a work for one of his musical gatherings. Paumgartner made some stipulations: the piece should employ the same instrumentation as Hummel's *Quintet* (piano, violin, viola, cello, double bass) and at least one of the movements should be a theme and variations based upon Schubert's song *Die Forelle* (The Trout). The resulting *Trout Quintet*, completed the following year, is an irresistibly good-natured piece of music, and there is no better introduction to Schubert. The dramatic Allegro, soulful Andante, lively Scherzo, rippling variations and gypsyish finale all display a staggering wealth of invention and thematic contrast. The piano part is marvellously integrated with the textures of the strings, with a high, lightly written role that beautifully balances the weight of the double bass.

◉ Jandó, Tóth, Kodály Quartet (Naxos 8550658; with *Adagio* and *Rondo concertante*).

The Kodály Quartet have produced a succession of excellent recordings for Naxos (notably their Haydn series), and Jenö Jandó has recorded dozens of fine performances for the budget label. In 1992 they came together with István Tóth to make this warm and effulgent version of the *Trout*. Star-name recordings are frequently dominated by an overbearing pianist but Jandó and the Kodály Quartet are brilliantly coordinated in their light-footed approach. A charming recording, and astonishing value.

THE OCTET

Schubert's serenely confident *Octet* is doubly unique: it is is his only work for eight players, and no other major composer has written for the same combination – two violins, viola, cello, bass, clarinet, horn and bassoon. It was commissioned by a Viennese nobleman named Ferdinand Troyer, a fine clarinettist, who wanted a companion piece to Beethoven's *Septet*, a work of immense popularity at the time. Schubert completed his commission on March 1, 1824, but it was not performed until 1827 and did not appear in print until twenty-six years later.

The *Octet*'s six movements last over an hour, but the piece is so light-hearted that the time flies past. Similarities between Beethoven's and Schubert's works are few, and the only real acts of homage are Schubert's imitation of Beethoven's use of folk-based variation form for the fourth movement, and the use of a slow introduction to the finale – exactly eighteen bars in length, just like Beethoven's. Highly appealing is Schubert's delicate, unfussy counterpoint and, as ever, his concentration upon song-like melody, but the most remarkable feature of the *Octet* is his effortless unification of the potentially disparate instrumental colours, with the clarinet and violin taking the dominant roles.

◗ Vienna Octet (Decca 421 155-2DM; with Mozart, *Divertimento*).

There are a number of fine *Octet* recordings, but the Vienna Octet's performance is perhaps best suited to the music's optimistic nature, and their attention to ensemble playing produces an endearing through-flowing momentum. Excellently recorded and, at mid-price, good value.

STRING QUARTET NO. 14 – DEATH AND THE MAIDEN

On March 31, 1824, Schubert wrote to a friend that he was "the most unhappy and wretched creature in the world". A few days before sending this letter, he had completed his first piece of chamber music for over three years – the two quartets in A minor and D minor. The latter is perhaps his greatest quartet, chiefly on account of its harrowing emotional honesty, which reaches an almost unendurable pitch in the second movement, a set of variations based upon Schubert's song *Der Tod und das Mädchen* (Death and the Maiden). The quartet is characterized by its unrelenting rhythmic force, which is introduced by the opening movement's principal theme, then carried by the desperate song of the variations, which is in turn followed by a grim Presto. A tragic, unfathomable piece, Schubert's *Death and the Maiden* is one of the key works of the quartet repertoire.

● Vermeer Quartet (Teldec 9301-74783-2; with *Trout Quintet*).

The Vermeer Quartet's highly committed version of *Death and the Maiden* has a gutsy, often pugnacious sound, which is not to say that the playing is insensitive in any way – indeed they bring unsettling pathos to the variations. The final movement, however, shows them at their best, attacking the score with chilling but entirely suitable violence. The recording highlights the lower frequencies, a balance that well suits the Vermeer's dark timbres.

PIANO TRIO NO. 1

The first of Schubert's two piano trios, probably composed in 1827, is one of his most ripe creations. Stuffed with long melodies of effortless lyricism, it is a perfectly balanced composition – whereas Beethoven's trios give preference to the piano part, each of Schubert's three players is accorded an equal bite of the very sweet cherry. All four movements are immensely attractive but the second is its finest: a journey of musical discovery, it begins with one of the most marvellous of all his tunes, played first by the cello over rippling triplets and then by the violin.

● Trio Zingara (Collins 1215-2; with *Notturno* and *Trio Movement*).

The Trio Zingara have produced a sumptuous, romantic vision of the score. This is a fluent, instinctively balanced account, boasting some wonderfully sweet playing from the cellist Felix Schmidt.

STRING QUINTET

Schubert's *String Quintet* in C major, his greatest chamber work, was also his last – on October 2, 1828, just seven weeks before his death, the composer wrote to a friend that he had "finally turned out" a quintet. Rather than compose for a string quartet plus extra viola, which is the conventional set-up for a string quintet, Schubert scored his work for an extra cello, thus creating a darker, more sonorous tone for this tragically beautiful music. Every moment is magnificent – no other composer could surpass the lyricism of the cello duet in the opening movement, the simple grace of the third movement and the rhythmic bite of the finale. But the emotional centre of gravity is the Adagio, a desperately poignant, valedictory statement.

🔵 Lindsay Quartet, Cummings (ASV CDDCA537).

This wonderful performance is courageously restrained, with none of the extravagant emotionalism that mars many other recordings. Delicate yet full of intense contrasts, this understated account does full justice to Schubert's masterpiece.

SONGS

Schubert's *Gretchen am Spinnrade*, written at the age of seventeen, announced the arrival of a songwriter of preternatural abilities. Nobody previously had brought such complexity to this salon genre. In *Gretchen am Spinnrade* the piano is not a mere accompaniment to the singer, it's a protagonist in its own right, playing its part in the creation of the emotional drama. Through the music you hear the motion of the spinning wheel and sense every fluctuation of Gretchen's ever-changing emotions, which build to a crisis at the extraordinary moment when the wheel stops, only to begin again as she recovers herself. Goethe, on whose poem the song is based, disapproved of the prominent piano part and felt that Schubert's harmonic style was too bizarre; he returned the manuscript, unimpressed. However, the poet later had a change of heart regarding Schubert's songs. In 1830 he heard *Elkönig* performed by Wilhelmine Schröder-Devrient (one of Wagner's favourite singers), and was moved to remark – "I saw this composition once before, when it did not appeal to me at all; but sung in this way the whole shapes itself into a visible picture."

More than anything else by the composer, Schubert's songs live or die with the talents of their performers. They are fragile creations that require singers capable of balancing characterization and vocal beauty, and a pianist who knows when to step into the limelight and when to withdraw. An extraordinarily high proportion of Schubert's six hundred songs are characterised by both memorable melody and an acute sensitivity to the text's nuances of mood – Schubert strove to capture the overall meanings of a poem, rather than elucidate its word-by-word progress. If you want to start at the top before venturing in the vast terrain of Schubert's song catalogue, listen first to the three major cycles: *Die schöne Müllerin*, *Winterreise* and *Schwanengesang*.

🔵 The Song Cycles: Souzay; Baldwin (Philips 438 511-2; with 29 other songs; 4 CDs)
🔵 Lieder: Fischer-Dieskau, Moore (Deutsche Grammophon 437 214-2GX21; 21 CDs).
🔴 The Hyperion Schubert Edition: Graham Johnson (Hyperion; 36-CD series).

Gérard Souzay was perhaps the most complete Lieder singer of the century, easing the words from the score so that one is drawn into Schubert's beautiful world, rather than pushed. His voice was so flexible that he could shift from dark bass-baritone to light bari-tenor in the turn of a page, and his expressive range was incredible, unerringly finding the right shade or colour for each particular phrase without over-dramatizing the sentiment. Souzay's recordings of the Schubert song cycles are now available in a four-disc mid-price set from Philips, which also includes nearly thirty of Schubert's best individual songs. There is no finer set.

Dietrich Fischer-Dieskau, the most popular of all Lieder singers, has a declamatory and forceful style that is utterly unlike Souzay's. Nobody has lived with Schubert's songs for as long as Fischer-Dieskau, and he has produced scores of recordings of them, often returning to the same pieces several times, invariably bringing something new to them on each occasion. Deutsche Grammophon's colossal budget-price boxed set is a splendid testament to a great artist, and includes nearly all of Schubert's songs. The 21 CDs are also available in three volumes, covering the periods 1811–17 and 1817–28, with the three cycles comprising the third volume. Some of Fischer-Dieskau's finest single-CD recordings are recommended below.

Once you've become engrossed in Schubert's songs – and this is one of those areas of classical music, like the operas of Wagner, that does tend to breed obsession – you should get to know the wonderful Hyperion series. Under the guidance of pianist Graham Johnson, who provides capacious and highly intelligent anotation to each CD, Hyperion have set out to record all Schubert's songs before the bicentenary in 1997. The novelty of this series is that the songs are grouped not chronologically but by theme, with singers selected for their suitability for each group of songs (not even Souzay or Fischer-Dieskau is right for every song). Thus Arleen Auger's recital concentrates on songs with a theatrical connection, Brigitte Fassbaender has made a set of songs about death, and Thomas Hampson has contributed a recital on the theme of the ancient world. This is one of the most stimulating recording projects of the post-war era.

DIE SCHÖNE MÜLLERIN

Goethe inspired many of Schubert's finest songs, but two of the great song cycles are settings of texts by the irredeemably second-rate Wilhelm Müller, an archetypal maudlin, self-dramatizing Romantic hack. In 1823 Schubert applied his alchemical skills to twenty poems by Müller, and transformed the poetic dross into *Die schöne Müllerin* (The Fair Maid of the Mill), a supreme example of how Schubert's music could create depths of which the writer was only dimly aware. Evoking both the solitude and the sociability of the rural world, *Die schöne Müllerin* is the most out-going of the song cycles, but its unhappy denouement foreshadows the world of *Winterreise*.

❯ Fischer-Dieskau, Moore (EMI CDC7 47173-2)
❯ Souzay, Baldwin (Philips 438 511-2; 4 CDs; with other cycles and songs).

Fischer-Dieskau has recorded this cycle several times. Of his three versions with Gerald Moore, this 1961 account is the best as a first-time buy. His partnership with Moore produces some dramatically spontaneous singing and his wonderfully crafted voice comes into its own in the more sombre songs (he is slightly uncomfortable in the lighter, less furrowed works). Another masterpiece of interpretive singing is Souzay's account, included in the Philips boxed set.

WINTERREISE

The composition of *Winterreise* (Winter Journey) dominated the last two years of Schubert's life. He started it in 1827 after hearing that he had failed to secure a court chapel appointment, a disappointment that intensified an already bleak depression. Again using words by Müller, he composed music of such awful despair that it seems to have worsened his psychological state. Nonetheless he pushed ever onwards, believing that *Winterreise* would one day be regarded as his greatest achievement, as it now is by many people. *Die schöne Müllerin* ended in gloom, a mood that *Winterreise* takes up at the outset. Its protagonist is an outcast lover on the verge of breakdown, and the twenty-four songs follow his lonely peregrinations through a snow-bound landscape; the sequence has flashes of weak consolation, but its general progress is a descent into desolation.

◉ Fischer-Dieskau, Brendel (Philips 411 463-2PH).
◉ Schreier, Richter (Philips 442 360-2).

Fischer-Dieskau's dark intensity is best suited to these heavy-hearted songs, and he brings terrible poignancy to the plight of the friendless wanderer. This is perhaps the finest of all Fischer-Dieskau's Schubert recordings. Some people, however, find that a baritone voice rather overdoes the gloom of *Winterreise*, and that a tenor actually enhances the

Souzay's Schubert, one of the best introductions to the composer

drama through the contrast between vocal tone and meaning. Peter Schreier's live recording, accompanied by the ever-thoughtful Sviastoslav Richter, is a most persuasive argument in favour of the tenor approach.

SCHWANENGESANG

The fourteen songs of the aptly named *Schwanengesang* (Swan-Song) were not conceived as a cycle by Schubert, but were schakled together after his death by the publisher Haslinger. The verses of three young poet – Heine, Rellstab and Seidl – were used, and while there is no unifying theme, Schubert's selection and setting creates a coherent psychological landscape. *Schwanengesang* isn't coloured by the unremitting grief of *Winterreise*, but the mood is fairly sombre, and even in the joyously lyrical outburst, the shadow of woe is usually in the background.

◉ Souzay, Baldwin (Philips 438 511-2; 4 CDs; with other cycles and songs).
◉ Fassbaender, Reimann (Deutsche Grammophon 429 766-2; with five other songs).

The best *Schwanengesang* is Souzay's astonishing account on Philips. Dalton Baldwin was a superb Lieder pianist, and here his uncanny understanding of tempo rubato produces the most amazing results, moulding each phrase to wonderful effect. This is one of the most profound examples of Lieder singing ever recorded. Of the versions available on a single disc, the most challenging is the one from Brigitte Fassbaender, who packs more incident into these micro-dramas than anyone else.

PIANO MUSIC

Schubert wrote some twenty-one piano sonatas and was the last great composer for whom the sonata was the primary genre of piano music. His loyalty to the form goes some way to explain his neglect in the era of Chopin, Liszt and Schumann, for whom the traditional imperatives of the sonata made it less attractive than the étude, prelude and other vehicles for spontaneous-sounding expression. However, Schubert's relationship to the sonata tradition was not one of straightforward allegiance. Most of his piano sonatas – especially the last three – display a flexibility of structure and an adventurous handling of harmony and tone that you won't find in their predecessors. Schubert is even more plainly seen as a Romantic composer in the *Wanderer Fantasy* and the two sets of *Impromptus*, pieces in which he places the minimum of formal constraints on his melodic expansiveness.

THE WANDERER FANTASY

Comprising four movements to be played without a break, the *Wanderer Fantasy* of 1822 is at once a homage to the classical sonata and a subversion of it. The overall shape resembles that of the great Beethoven sonatas, but it is used to contain quasi-improvisatory elements which, as it were, break down the ordained structure from inside. Thus the second movement is a set of variations that sounds more like a sequence of impressionistic mood pieces, while the finale opens as a fugue that evolves quickly into a blazing outbreak of unfettered passion. A degree of formal unity comes from the motif with which the fantasy opens, for it provides the basic material from which all the subsequent major themes are constructed. In the second movement this motif becomes recognizable as a theme from Schubert's song *Der Wanderer*, a link that introduces a Schumann-like element of autobiographical confession. The array of free-ranging ideas within a plan of overarching unity marks the *Wanderer Fantasy* as an ancestor of Liszt's B minor sonata.

◉ Pollini (Deutsche Grammophon 419 672-2; with *Piano Sonata in A minor* Op. 42).

Pollini's version of the *Wanderer* is an ideal performance: highly charged but not reckless, tautly structured but not inflexible. It's coupled with the virtuosic *Piano Sonata in A minor*, written three years after the *Fantasy*, and showing a similarly ambivalent attitude towards sonata form. It's the finest of Schubert's sonatas before the final three, and Pollini gives a quite magnificent account of it.

IMPROMPTUS

Schubert once wrote to his father "people assured me that the keys became singing voices under my hands", and nowhere is the vocal nature of his piano writing more evident than in the two sets of four *Impromptus* he composed in the last year of his life. Perhaps best described as large-scale minatures, these brief but expansive pieces have the appearance of spontaneous personal utterance, veering from one mood to another with all unpredictability that the title "Impromptu" suggests. The second set has sometimes been read as a loose-limbed sonata: it certainly is not one in any conventional sense, but certainly there's a sense of interconnection to the sequence, which culminates in a fierce, scherzo-like episode. In their roaming exploration of fleeting emotion and piano texture, the *Impromptus* are Schubert's most direct connection to the music of Chopin, Schumann and Liszt.

◉ Perahia (CBS CD37291).

Perahia's recording of the *Impromptus* was deservedly hailed as a classic on the day of its issue, in the mid-1980s. Elegant and perfectly paced, Perahia's playing is so subtle and profound al that you are left with something different after every hearing.

THE LAST SONATAS

The last three sonatas – *No. 19* in C minor, *No. 20* in A major and *No. 21* in B flat major – were all composed around the same time as the *String Quintet*, and Schubert died two months after finishing his work on the last of the group. Comparison with Beethoven's final sonatas are inevitable, and to an extent the comparison is just: like Beethoven's last five, these works are overcast by the imminence of death, and they represent the furthest extremity of the composer's keyboard music in more than a merely chronological sense.

But whereas the late Beethoven sonatas are marked by a desperate need to communicate, to arrive at a means of conveying something that ultimately eludes expression, the Schubert sonatas look inward, constantly repeating and reformulating themes as if they were persistent memories. Deep pessimism pervades this music – the Andantino of *Sonata No. 20*, for example, is built on a melody that returns again and again to the same single note, as if to an assuageable pain, and is then interrupted by a terrifying outburst of splintered motifs within which no melody can be found. The late sonatas are long musical soliloquies in which the forceful direction of Beethoven's music is replaced by structures that seem to circle round their subjects without ever coming to rest. This is not to say that these works are in any way self-indulgent or prolix. It is rather that the conventional perception of linear time is here suspended. The philosopher Theodor Adorno summarized what is astounding about these three sonatas when he talked about their "landscape-like quality"; they do indeed define an emotional terrain that is unique to Schubert.

⊙ **The Late Piano Sonatas**: Pollini (Deutsche Grammophon 427 327-2GH; with *Drei Klavierstücke* and *C minor Allegretto*; 2 CDs).

This rapt, anguished and self-absorbed music requires more than just sensitivity to each inflection – it requires the application of an analytical mind to bring out the essential cogency of the longer spans. So perfectly judged are the tempi, tone and weight of Maurizio Pollini's performances that there's always a point to each repetition; what can seem like meandering diversions in other hands here come across as essential qualifications and revisions. These superb accounts are coupled with four late Schubert miniatures, each as melancholy as the sonatas; the set is also available as two separate CDs.

ROBERT SCHUMANN

(1810–1856)

Robert Schumann died a failure in his own eyes, yet he occupies a key positions in the music of the nineteenth century. The first Romantic with a deep knowledge of literature and philosophy, Robert Schumann saw it as his mission to fuse all the arts in music that spoke profoundly of its creator. He once wrote: "I am affected by everything extraordinary that goes on in the world and think it over in my own way . . . then I long to express my feelings and find an outlet for them in my music: a poem, something infinitely more spiritual, the result of poetical consciousness." His music came to be the confessional for his inner life. Schumann composed four symphonies and some fine chamber music, but it is his transparently candid piano works that truly reveal this enigmatic, complex composer. Despite his respect for classical forms (he was in awe of Beethoven), Schumann was quick to break away from them, creating instead music which reads like the pages of a diary – fragmented, condensed and profuse in invention. Schumann's compositions have a uniquely changeable emotional climate, shifting from passion to nostalgia, or from pain to ingenuous optimism, in the passage of a moment.

He was a middle-class boy from the provinces, born in Zwickau, Saxony, in 1810. His father, a bookseller and novelist, died in 1826 whereupon Robert's sister committed suicide, an event from which he never recovered. He enrolled at Leipzig University to study law, enjoyed the good life and the customary Grand Tour of the continent, and was told by his professor that he had no talent whatsoever. Yet he continued with his musical studies under Friedrich Wieck, a notable teacher in whose house he took lodgings. There he met Wieck's daughter Clara, a nine-year-old who was already showing signs of extraordinary ability as a pianist. Robert's own hopes of becoming a virtuoso were soon wrecked by the crippling of his left hand – ostensibly the result of a machine designed to strengthen his fourth finger, but more likely due to poisoning by the mercury he took when he realized he had syphilis ("My whole house is like a chemist's shop" he told his mother). Fortunately he had already begun to show talent as a composer.

His Opus 1 *Variations* derived their central motif from the letters of the surname of Meta Abegg, an early love. Schumann would often use such codes to devise thematic fragments, which he then developed into musical dialogues between imagined characters who reflected the ambivalences of his nature. In Jean-Paul's novel *Die Flegejahre* (Years of Indiscretion) he came across Walt and Vult, introvert and extrovert, from whom he derived his two creative demons, christened Florestan and Eusebius. The personae of Florestan and Eusebius recur in his work "in order to express contrasting points of view about art", as the composer explained, since he perceived music as having the cut-and-thrust of Hegelian dialectic. Then there was the Davidsbund (The band of David), a fictitious band of musicians at war against the artistic philistines; their names swarm through his scores and their signatures peopled the pages of Neue Zeitschrift für Musik, an iconoclastic musical journal of which Schumann was editor.

The 1830s began with the "Abegg" variations and produced most of his finest music: *Papillons, Carnaval, Davidsbündlertänze, Fantasiestücke*, the piano sonatas, *Kinderszenen*, the *Fantasia in C major*, the beginnings of the *Études Symphoniques*. Yet it was also a decade of despair, for his attempts to marry Clara were blocked by her father. There were good reasons for the obstructiveness: Clara's blossoming career (unquestionably sacrificed in later years by the demands of life with Schumann); the frivolities of a young man who showed little sign of being able to establish a serious career. In 1840 Schumann won legal action to overturn Wieck's veto and the couple were married one day before Clara's twenty-first birthday.

In 1840 Schumann composed two great song cycles, *Dichterliebe* and *Frauenliebe und -leben*, both relate to his feelings for Clara. The following year his first symphony appeared, then in 1843 Mendelssohn offered

MANSELL COLLECTION

him a piano professorship at the new Leipzig conservatory. But Schumann's manic-depression was now taking the form of increasing bleakness of vision and creative sterility, and led to serious breakdowns. He resigned and moved to Dresden, but Clara's triumphant concert tours, triumphs for herself as a concert-artist, only emphasized how widespread indifference to her husband's music had become. He lacked the training to dash off musical money-spinners: operas, festival canatas, frothy salon-pieces. His spell as conductor in Leipzig, beginning 1850, ended in recriminations and disaster. In 1854 he attempted suicide by throwing himself in the Rhine and was committed to an asylum near Bonn. There he died in July 1856, in the final ravages of tertiary syphilis, having starved himself through depression.

Of all great composers, Schumann is perhaps the worst represented by the CD catalogue. There have been some wonderful recordings over the years – Artur Rubinstein's 1960s interpretations of *Carnaval* and the *Fantasiestücke*, for example, or Murray Perahia's brilliant debut recording of the *Davidsbündlertänze* and *Fantasiestücke*. None of them is available at the moment. You can get hold of Perahia's versions of *Papillons* and the *Études*

Symphoniques, but only if you invest in an eleven-disc set of Perahia recitals. It's a similar situation with Horowitz's performances of Schumann, which are only available packaged with other music in volumes 1, 3, 4 and 7 of Sony's *Horowitz Complete Masterworks* set – a fascinating series, but someone coming new to Schumann might not want to buy two hours of additional music just to hear Horowitz play ten minutes of Schumann. Deutsche Grammophon have issued a mid-price four-disc survey of Schumann's piano music played by Wilhelm Kempff, a set that has many high-points (eg a very fine *Carnaval* and a superb *Davidsbündlertänze*), but in places misses the evanescent quality of the music. If you want to familiarize yourself with the range of Schumann's output, buy the Kempff set. If you want the very best, however, keep an eye out for Perahia and Rubinstein reissues, and in the meantime take your pick of the CDs selected below.

SYMPHONIES

Schumann for years tinkered with sketches for a major orchestral work, but like Brahms he lacked the courage to pursue them further. His discovery of Schubert's ninth symphony gave him the encouragement to try again, and in January and February of 1841 he wrote his *Spring Symphony*. It's an exuberant work, as indicated by the titles Schumann originally gave to its four movements – *Spring's Awakening*, *Evening*, *Merry Playmates* and *Full Spring*. The second symphony, written in the wake of a nervous breakdown in 1845, is the darkest, most conventional and least popular of the cycle, but the third, the *Rhenish*, is his most joyous and spontaneous. Conceived as a celebration of the landscape, legends and history of the Rhineland, it progresses from a thrilling, syncopated opening to a stately polyphonic finale that was inspired by a Mass Schumann saw in Cologne Cathedral – he marked it to be played "In the manner of an accompaniment to a solemn ceremony." The *Symphony No. 4*, written in 1841 but massively revised in 1852, is an extremely intense work, and is of revolutionary originality, being through-composed as one seamless development – almost every significant theme

is generated by the motifs that appear in the slow introduction to the opening movement.

It has to be admitted that Schumann's symphonies are not masterpieces of orchestration. Schumann's first thoughts came to him as piano music, and his efforts to reorchestrate them invariably make them more opaque. It may be that he was deliberately making the music easier for inept orchestras and conductors (Schumann had experience of both), but whatever the reason, they sometimes sound clumsy and clotted. For all that, they are essential to a full understanding of the composer, and there's a great deal in the symphonies to dispel the myth that Schumann's final years were a period of unmitigated decline.

⊙ Staatskapelle Dresden; Sawallisch (EMI CMS 7 64815 2; 2 CDs).
◗ Berlin Philharmonic Orchestra; Karajan (Deutsche Grammophon 429 672-2; 2 CDs).

Honours are divided between these two sets, for Sawallisch's pace and Karajan's characterization each brings rewards. Sawallisch's euphoric vitality wins the day in the first and most famous symphony, whereas Karajan's account of *No. 2* has a Bruckner-like breadth that makes you wonder at the work's neglect. The differences are encapsulated by the fourth, where Sawallisch moves like a fast wave, while Karajan gathers his resources towards an inexorable climax.

PIANO CONCERTO

In 1841 Schumann composed a single-movement piece for piano and orchestra, "something between a symphony, a concerto and a large sonata." When it was turned down by the publishers, he decided to transform it into a full-length concerto, but it was not until 1845 that he completed its intermezzo and finale, extracting the motifs for both added movements from the woodwinds' opening theme. Liszt called the end result "a concerto without piano" and, anticipating its rejection, Schumann had declared he was unable to write a display piece. It certainly is not a vehicle for hair-raising virtuosity, but the concerto is a supremely eloquent piece, placing its emphasis on intimate dialogue between the soloist and orchestra. Its most obvious antecedents are Beethoven's fourth concerto; its descendants are the concertos of Brahms, and especially the concerto by Grieg.

● Kovacevich; BBC Symphony Orchestra; Davis (Philips 412923-2; with Grieg, *Piano Concerto*).
● Perahia; Symphonie-Orchester des Bayerischen Rundfunks; Davis (Sony SK44899 with Grieg *Piano Concerto*).

These two performances get to the heart of the music, each in its own way. Perahia is the more impulsive – this is a performance of surprising understatements and quick asides, building up effects and then redefining them. Kovacevich is less extrovert, with a closer rapport between soloist and orchestra; without resorting to forcefulness, he gives back-bone to a concerto that can easily fall apart. Yet Perahia's wit, his range and sense of adventure, are a delight – and Sony's recording is seventeen years younger. Buy both.

PAPILLONS

Schumann once referred to himself as a chrysalis, and he spoke of his initial inspirations as butterflies – motifs which appeared and then as suddenly disappeared in a flitter of colour and uncertain shape. The image is perfectly suited to the Opus 2 *Papillons*, which were written as a suite of twelve waltzes inspired by *Die Flegeljahre* (see above). Beginning with a motif that fades past vanishing point at its end, *Papillons* contains the most capricious and diaphanous music Schumann wrote, a supreme instance of art concealing art: completed in 1831, they represent three years of intermittent but intense work, distilling countless sketches and rearrangements.

● Ashkenazy (Decca 414 474-2; with *Études Symphoniques* and *Arabeske*)

With Perahia's wondrous account only available in Sony's huge boxed set, Ashkenazy's performance of *Papillons* is the obvious first choice. Ashkenazy finds the resilience of these pieces as well as their lightness, through playing in which subtlety and vigour are well matched. It's coupled with a good, meaty version of the *Études Symphoniques*.

PIANO SONATAS

Schumann's three sonatas were all started in the same year, 1833, but were completed at intervals over the next five years – the first in 1835, the second in in 1836, the third in 1838. Shortly after finishing the last one, Schumann thus expressed his thoughts on the sonata as a genre: "it seems that the form has outlived its life cycle. This is of course in the

natural order of things: we ought not to repeat the same statements for centuries, but rather to think about the new as well. So let's write sonatas or fantasies" – adding the comment, "what's in a name?" In essence, Schumann's sonatas are fantasies braced by a desire to live up to the example of Beethoven's sonatas. They are not as episodic as his other major works for solo piano (there are, for example, numerous motivic links between the movements), but neither do they adhere to the principles enshrined in the great Germanic tradition – in the *Sonata No. 1*, for example, the four movements are so disparate that really there's no reason why the work couldn't just as easily have been six movements long, or three or five. With their sudden changes of key, dramatic thematic transformations, and juxtaposition of rapt self-absorption with outbreaks of expansive emotion, the sonatas are quintessential Romantic piano music. The first two are more rewarding than the third – a revision of an earlier work, it is far less frequently recorded.

● **Sonata No. 1**: Pollini (Deutsche Grammophon 423 134-2: with *Fantasia in C major*).
◐ **Sonata No. 2**: Argerich (Deutsche Grammophon 437 252-2; with Liszt, *Sonata in B minor*; Brahms, *Rhapsodies*).

Lesser players can make the first sonata sound like nothing more than a stream of fugitive ideas, but Pollini's precise articulation and his sense of overall form ensure that the music's impetuousness never degenerates into incoherence – every gesture has a context. In the second sonata, Martha Argerich gives a performance of fearless virtuosity: whole passages of notes are at once perfectly transparent yet gorgeously coloured, and there's a sense of tightly disciplined improvisation about the entire piece.

CARNAVAL

Carnaval is the Schumann piece in which spontaneity, invention and superlative technique coexist most vividly. Written in September 1834, *Carnaval* is a series of tableaux, a masked ball in which one character after another takes centre-stage. It was described by the composer as "Little scenes on four notes", a reference to the exercise in creative cryptography by which Schumann proclaimed his love for Ernestine von Fricken through the music. The letters ASCH, which spell Ernestine's birthplace as well as a fragment of his own name, translate in German musical notation into the notes A, E flat, C and B. Permutations of these notes litter the entire score, generating the themes for the Carnival characters, some of them historical (Chopin and Paganini), others folkloric (Pierrot and Harlequin), and others incarnations of Schumann's various personae (Florestan and Eusebius). It concludes with a *March of the Davidsbündler*, in which the Philistines are put triumphantly to flight.

⏵ Barenboim (Deutsche Grammophon 431 167-2; with *Kinderszenen* and *Faschingsschwank aus Wien*).

An excellent deal from Deutsche Grammophon, with Daniel Barenboim playing not only *Carnaval* but also a sensitive *Kinderszenen* and the under-rated *Faschingsschwank aus Wien*. It's not the subtlest presentation, nor the most charming, but there's a big personality at work here, and at modest price this CD makes a splendid introduction to Schumann.

DAVIDSBÜNDLERTÄNZE

Written three years after *Carnaval*, the *Davidsbündlertänze* (Dances of the band of David) is an assembly of eighteen mood-pieces that epitomize the multifariousness of Schumann's art. The sequence begins with a musical motto composed by Clara, and most of the dances use this motto's interval of a falling second as their starting point. Schumann attached a traditional poem as the epigraph – "In all and every time, pleasure and pain are linked" – and each of the pieces bears a phrase sketching the atmosphere: "Rather cockeyed . . . wild and merry . . . as if from afar". If you don't find the *Davidsbündlertänze* irresistible, you're not going to get on with Schumann.

⏺ Ashkenazy (Decca 425 109- 2DH; with *Fantasiestücke*)

Ashkenazy's performance is fervent and brightly characterised, even if it doesn't match the standards set by Perahia's deleted set – or indeed Kempff, on his four-disc compilation. With it comes a version of the Opus 12 *Fantasiestücke* which is as good as most in the catalogue.

FANTASIESTÜCKE

The Opus 12 *Fantasiestücke* (there's another, less interesting *Fantasiestücke* set, Op. 111) was composed between May and July 1837, shortly after Clara had returned all

Schumann's letters. The ever-volatile composer dedicated the work to a Scottish pianist by the name of Roberta Laidlow. The *Fantasiestücke* catches the fragility of inspiration, which Schumann felt sprang from hidden depths to vanish as consciousness was reached, and the titles of its chimerical scenes evoke the higher realities of Romanticism – the worlds of night, twilight and dreams. Some of Schumann's most touching and delicate writing is here: *Warum* (Why?), for example, in which the music is the subject of momentary dialogue rather than formal development, or *Des Abends* (Of the evening), which moves into unexpected keys to create a sense of revelation within stasis.

⏺ Brendel (Philips 411 049-2; with *Fantasia*).
⏺ Rubinstein (RCA 09026 61160 2; with pieces by Beethoven, Chopin and Debussy).

The Brendel recording is more than adequate, though his approach is a little too unbending to make it an unqualified recommendation. Rubinstein's account is a live recording made towards the end of his life; his command of the ebb and flow of musical phrases is as alluring as ever it was, but the precision isn't perfect, and the recording quality is pretty lousy. In short, these two CDs are fair enough stopgaps pending a reissue of Rubinstein's studio version or the one from Murray Perahia.

KINDERSZENEN

Written in February 1838, *Kinderszenen* (Scenes from Childhood) was suggested by Clara's comment that Schumann sometimes seemed to her like a child. These tiny, exquisite pieces are very much the recollection of an adult, yet one whose affinity with the innocence and vulnerability of childhood was painfully acute. *Kinderszenen* opens with *Of Strange Lands and People* (the storyteller's "once upon a time") and progresses through evocations of emotions in their purest state, until at last the adult steps forward in *The Poet Speaks* (the titles of the episodes suggested themselves after the music was written). Trance-like and apparently artless, *Kinderszenen* contains moments of disarming enchantment: the floating syncopations of *Almost Too Serious*, for instance, or the phrase with which *Entreating Child* opens and closes, so that the piece ends as it began, and hangs quizzically in space.

● Horowitz (Sony S2K 53457; with pieces by Chopin, Rachmaninov, Liszt, Beethoven, Schubert, Debussy and Scriabin; 2 CDs).
● Argerich (Deutsche Grammophon 410 653-2, with *Kreisleriana*)

Kinderszenen is the perfect conjunction of naivety and experience, and to conjure it up you need to be a master of fleeting effects. Vladimir Horowitz has this quality in abundance, but also brings a higher cohesion to the music. Of the versions issued on a single disc, the best is from Argerich, a more straightforward reading yet deeply astute.

FANTASIA IN C

In 1838 Schumann wrote to Clara: "I have just finished a fantasy in three movements that I sketched in all but the detail in June 1836. The first movement is, I think, the most passionate thing I have ever composed – a deep lament for you." Possibly so, but the work's origins lie in an attempt to raise funds for a monument to Beethoven. Schumann thought he could contribute best with a commemorative sonata, and the original titles of its movements are suitably redolent of tribute: *Ruins*, *Triumphal Arch* and *Wreath of Stars*. The *Fantasia* has Beethoven-like drive and verve, and indeed draws part of its thematic material from a Beethoven song. But if its march – "it makes me hot and cold all over" Clara wrote – is worthy of Beethoven's *Hammerklavier* (see p.37), its ardent and tender finale reveals a different, more diffused world. In the words of the philosopher Theodor Adorno, it seems to "open upon an undefined vastness." Subtle chromaticism, cross-rhythms, syncopation, counter-melodic chords and a host of other stylistic subtleties give substance to the Schiller quotation that Schumann appended to the score: "Through all sounds in the coloured earthly dream resounds a quiet sound drawn for him, who secretly listens."

● Horowitz (Sony S3K 53461; with pieces by Bach/Busoni, Scriabin, Chopin, Debussy and others; 3 CDs).
● Pollini (Deutsche Grammophon 423 134-2, with *Sonata No. 1*).
● Perahia (Sony MK 42124, with Schubert, *Wanderer Fantasy*).

Horowitz's recording is a document of one of the major concerts of the 1960s, his return to the platform after years of fearful introspection. The first movement is mercurial and dynamic, with the left hand providing surging motive force (a technique that became a mannerism in later years), while in the finale he creates a weightless shimmer of sound. Playing with the composure that almost flawless technical reserves make possible, this is Horowitz at his best.

Two other major accounts are available on a single CD. Pollini's impeccably judged performance is coupled with the finest version of the first sonata, while Murray Perahia's characteristically poised and fresh interpetation is combined with a splendid *Wanderer Fantasy*.

ÉTUDES SYMPHONIQUES

They *Études Symphoniques* began life in 1834 simply as variations on a theme written by Ernestine von Fricken's father. After years of dogged gestation, they emerged in 1852 as one of the cornerstones of Romantic piano literature, a dazzling exposition of the "symphonic" possibilities of the instrument for blending, contrasting and superimposing timbres. The variation technique still forms the structural armature of the *Études Symphoniques*, but at the heart of this work is the exhilaration of experiment – of clarifying dense planes of polyphony, presenting themes against a background of tonal reverberation (in a way that anticipates Debussy), exploring the borders of sound and silence.

● Richter (Olympia OCD 339).
● Pollini (Deutsche Grammophon 410 916-2; with *Arabeske*).

Richter thinks through the organic structure of this music in playing of extraordinary richness and power; there's an unflagging urgency to this account, yet Richter never loses the crucial sense of private meditation. This is performance which thinks on the move. Pollini's version doesn't project quite the same degree of personal commitment, but it has an even greater analytic rigour and range of tone. He couples it with a touching account of *Arabeske*, a marvel of considered innocence.

DICHTERLIEBE

Dichterliebe takes its text from Heinrich Heine and introduces to German song a new mingling of sentiment and irony, much as Heine's poems had done for German verse – this is a world of disillusion in which nature acts as an adjunct and reflection to a bittersweet love-story. *Dichterliebe* takes the song to a higher level of evolution: the piano here becomes an equal partner with the singer, appearing sometimes as combatant, sometimes as commentator, and is given long solo preludes and postludes which add an extra dimension to the possibilities of the genre. In a sense *Dichterliebe* is a continuation of Schumann's character-pieces for piano, adding a second layer of tone-colour, liberating the lyrical element and defining the emotional content more precisely. They offer, as the composer put it, "a deeper insight into my inner musical workings."

Wunderlich; Giesen (Deutsche Grammophon 429 933-2; with Schubert and Beethoven songs).
Fischer-Dieskau; Brendel (Philips 416 352-2, with *Liederkreis*).

Fritz Wunderlich, one of this century's finest tenors, made his recording in 1966, shortly before his premature death. His singing is richer than Fischer-Dieskau's, and smoother too, but Fischer-Dieskau has a greater perception of dramatic narrative, and in Alfred Brendel he has a creative partner rather than a mere accompanist. Ideally you should have both versions, for Wunderlich's youth and freshness, and for the valedictory power and anger of Fischer-Dieskau.

HEINRICH SCHÜTZ

(1585–1672)

Heinrich Schütz was the greatest German composer before J. S. Bach, a status that has a lot to do with the four years he spent in Venice, assimilating the polychoral style of Giovanni Gabrieli (see p.136). Schütz took this resonant style back to Germany, where he applied it to the texts of the Lutheran Church to produce some of the most powerful and pious music of the seventeenth century.

Schütz was born in Kostritz in Saxony into a family of legal officials. He began studying law at Marburg University in 1608, but was encouraged to turn his attention to music by the Landgrave of Hesse, who sponsored his studies in Venice. Schütz returned in 1612 and was made organist at the Landgrave's chapel at Kassel before being poached by the more powerful, but less sympathetic, Elector of Saxony at Dresden. He was officially appointed the Elector's Kapellmeister in 1618, the same year that the Thirty Years War broke out – a religious conflict that was to devastate northern Europe.

In 1628 Schütz returned to Venice to recruit new musicians for Dresden and to familiarise himself at first hand with the new style of Monteverdi. To escape further the ravages of the war, which had severely depleted the musical forces at Dresden, Schütz requested extended leave of absence,

and between 1633 and 1635 he was at Copenhagen reorganizing the court chapel there. Back in Dresden his duties at the court became increasingly onerous, but the Elector was not prepared to pension him off, and much of Schütz's time was spent petitioning for funds to pay the few court musicians who remained. He finally retired when he was 72, to his sister's house at Weissenfels, where he spent the final years of his life occasionally composing but mostly studying and reading the Bible.

SACRED MUSIC

Schütz wrote several operas, including the first ever written in German (*Dafne*), but none has survived. Nowadays he is entirely known as a composer of a large body of magnificent sacred music. Though his sixty-five years as a composer were marked by some quite radical changes of style, notably the shift from the monumental choral works such the *Psalmen Davids* (1619) to the more intimate madrigalian style of the *Cantiones Sacrae* (1625), there is nonetheless a consistent tone of grave solemnity that runs through most of his sacred works, punctuated by many dramatic and highly expressive moments.

One of Schütz's greatest works is the *Musikalische Exequien* of 1636, a Lutheran

Requiem composed for the funeral of one of Schütz's early benefactors, Prince Heinrich von Reuss. The Prince had specified that certain texts should be inscribed on his coffin, and that these should be set to music for performance at his funeral. Schütz assigns these contemplative words to his soloists, and inserts them within a setting of the Kyrie, sung by a chorus. This is followed by a choral motet and culminates in an extraordinarily powerful setting of the Nunc Dimittis in which a spectral-sounding reduced choir periodically interrupts the main chorus with the words *Selig sind die Toten, die in dem Herren sterben* (Blessed are the dead who die in the Lord).

◉ **Musikalische Exequien, Motetten und Konzerte**: The Monteverdi Choir; English Baroque Soloists, His Majesties Sagbutts and Cornetts; Gardiner (Deutsche Grammophon Archiv 423 405-2).

This is a wonderful selection of some of Schütz's most startling and intense music, featuring the *Musikalische Exequien* and four short motets which are remarkable for the richness of their sonority. One of them, *Auf dem Gebirge* (In the mountains), has a spine-tinglingly mysterious opening in which the overlapping vocal lines of two counter-tenors seem to float across the dark, stolid tones of the sackbuts (early trombones). It is these subtleties of colouration that give so much of Schütz's music its power, and John Eliot Gardiner is brilliant at balancing and controlling his forces to bring out the finest gradations of light and shade. In the more complex *Musikalische Exequien* the amazing variety of vocal and instrumental combinations is handled with a remarkable assurance.

ALEXANDER SCRIABIN
(1872–1915)

Alexander Scriabin was the embodiment of E.T.A. Hoffman's dictum: "Only in the truly Romantic does comedy mix so fittingly with tragedy that both are fused in a total effect". Scriabin's egomaniacal delusions – sustained by the attentions of countless adoring aunts, wives, lovers and nurses – grew to a grandiosity unrivalled even in the history of music. He came to believe that he was one with God and that he would ultimately be absorbed into the rhythm of the universe, becoming a revivifying deity who would one day unite the world. Grand ambitions for someone who died from a septic boil on his lip. However comical his writings and beliefs, there is no question about the merits of Scriabin's music. He lived out the transition from Romanticism to modernism, initiating a musical language that moved decisively towards a break with tonality. Only slightly less radical than Schoenberg or Debussy, he could have become one of the indisputed greats had he not died so young.

He was Rachmaninov's immediate contemporary, attending the same class and graduating from the Moscow conservatory in the same year. Like Rachmaninov he was a virtuoso pianist. But whereas Rachmaninov remained an ardent traditionalist, Scriabin quickly arrived at conclusions that placed him at the forefront of contemporary musical thought. His earliest piano music reflected his obsession with Chopin, although there are certain hints at what was to come. The *Sonata No. 1* bore reflections of Rachmaninov,

GUUS ONG

Prokofiev and early Stravinsky, but by the *Sonata No. 3* his style was clearly shifting towards the shimmering exoticism with which he is now associated. The breakthrough came in 1907 with the completion of his *Sonata No. 5*, a single-movement work of extreme difficulty and tonal dissolution.

From then on, Scriabin's musical experimentation led him as far away from his peers as could be imagined, while his extreme hypochondria and his fascination with his own personality assumed Wagnerian dimensions. Egocentric and amoral, he justified his actions with careless ease: when he left his wife for a pupil, he informed the distraught woman that he was doing so "as a sacrifice to art". In 1909 Scriabin unveiled a project more ambitious than anything Wagner ever dreamed up. The *Mysterium* was an extraordinary, cataclysmic idea, synthesizing all the arts and senses into a extravaganza involving a "colour organ", pianos, a huge orchestra, choirs, dancers, "visions" and clouds of perfume. His friend and publisher, the conductor Serge Koussevitsky, bought the rights. Scriabin designed a temple to be built in India expressly for the performance of the *Mysterium*, and in preparation for the great day bought himself a sun hat and a book on Sanskrit grammar. The project died with him.

THE SYMPHONIES

Completed in 1900, Scriabin's *Symphony No. 1* shows him thinking in typically immodest terms: lasting fifty minutes, it's in six movements, the last of which boasts a chorus and soloists singing "visionary" texts of his own writing. The circulation and repetition of thematic ideas is used to bind together the work's ambitious length, and Scriabin's extensive use of triple time (finally broken in the finale), progressive tonality and highly dramatic melody all contribute towards a sweeping fluency that makes this one of the most powerful of all Russian Romantic symphonies.

The *Symphony No. 2*, composed the following year, is the same length as the first and is similarly marked by religio-mystical inebriation, but it is neither as bombastic nor as engaging. It's chiefly of interest for its orches-

tration, for in its use of bold instrumental colour and its quotation of birdsong it looks towards the style of Messiaen, another composer for whom music was an aspect of the spiritual world.

The extra-musical dimension of the *Symphony No. 3* or *Divine Poem* (1904) was helpfully summarized by its composer: "The *Divine Poem* represents the evolution of the human spirit which, freed from the legends and mysteries of the past that it has summoned and overthrown, passes through pantheism and achieves a joyful and exhilarating affirmation of its liberty and its unity with the universe." As you may imagine, this is his most opulent creation. There is a conservative, formal architecture beneath the gorgeous, kaleidoscopic orchestral colour, but really it's best to treat the *Symphony No. 3* as an aural wallow.

Symphonies Nos. 1–3: Myers, Toczyska; Philadelphia Orchestra; Westminster Chorus; Muti (EMI CDS7 54251-2; 3 CDs; with *Poem of Ecstasy* and *Prometheus*).

Muti's is the finest available set, for he gives wonderful cogency to these massive works. The Philadelphia Orchestra plays with bright and responsive enthusiasm, while the solo soprano and tenor in the last movement of *Symphony No. 1* give suitably ecstatic performances. The symphonies are coupled with the *Poem of Ecstasy* and *Prometheus*, the first of which is the finest of Scriabin's four tone poems. Written between 1905 and 1908, it's a masterpiece of orchestration and harmonic modulation, with shifting sound colours that reflect the composer's intense interest in Debussy's music.

PIANO CONCERTO

Scriabin's *Piano Concerto* is the most neglected of major Romantic concertos, presumably because it requires a very large and expensive orchestra and makes savage demands on the soloist. Completed in 1898 and scored in three lush movements, it's an extended piece of fin de siècle opulence, whose textures recall Rachmaninov or, in the last movement, Tchaikovsky. Full of bewitching melody and counterpoint, this is Scriabin's most accessible work for orchestra.

Ashkenazy; London Philharmonic Orchestra; Maazel (Decca 417 252-2DH; with *Prometheus* and *Poem of Ecstasy*).

Ashkenzay's mid-1970s recording with Lorin Maazel still makes the most convincing argument for Scriabin's concerto. Ashkenazy moves unscathed through the work's technical minefields, and if Maazel's grip on the orchestra is not always as tight as it might be, he does produce some wonderfully luscious sonorities. This CD, including Maazel's equally grand readings of the *Poem of Ecstasy* and *Prometheus*, is the finest introduction to Scriabin.

PIANO SONATAS

Scriabin's extensive output for piano is dominated by his sonatas, which cover his entire creative life: he wrote his first (unnumbered) sonata in 1892, and his last in 1913. The first four of the ten numbered sonatas are for the most part routinely Romantic, relying heavily on the legacy of Chopin and featuring a lot of aimless, overripe material. As examples of turn-of-the-century expressionism they are of some interest, but the *Sonata No. 5* (1907) is extremely interesting in itself. A brooding creation, it poses severe musical challenges, not least the dissonant, violent introductory bars, in which the music rises from the growling bass to the uppermost reaches of the keyboard in a startling flash of inspiration. From this work onwards, the sonatas become increasingly fiendish in their technical difficulty, exploring every recess of piano sonority. Scriabin's extremely complicated chromaticism – effectively border-line atonalism – reaches its expressive extreme in the so-called *Black Mass Sonata* and in its successor, the tenth. Concentrating myriad themes into the span of a single, multi-layered movement, these last two sonatas are as scintillating as the virtuosic piano works of Liszt.

◑ Ashkenzay (Decca 425 570-2DM2; 2 CDs).

Vladimir Ashkenazy's cycle of the ten sonatas, recorded in the 1970s, set the standards against which all other performances have been judged. His percussive, frequently belligerent tone is ideal for Scriabin's Mephistophelean music, and the recorded sound is excellent.

DMITRI SHOSTAKOVICH
(1906–1975)

Dmitri Shostakovich died in 1975, four years after Stravinsky, and was the last composer whose qualities were acknowledged throughout the western world, in both the modernist and the traditionalist camps. Within weeks of his death, memorial concerts were held throughout the world and he was being celebrated as the finest composer of the century. For many that claim still holds true, and even among those who rate him not quite so highly, none would argue that he is one of modern music's most fascinating characters. Unlike Prokofiev, who grew up and was educated in Tsarist Russia, Shostakovich spent his entire life under the Soviet system, and he was the first successful composer to emerge because of and not despite the Communist regime.

Shostakovich was taught initially by his mother, but his first major musical influence came from Glazunov, who encouraged the boy when he entered Petrograd (St Petersburg) conservatory in 1919. Four years later Shostakovich graduated from Glazunov's piano course and began giving concerts. In 1926, his diploma work – the *Symphony No. 1* – was performed in Moscow and Leningrad (the renamed Petrograd), earning the composer international fame before his twenty-first birthday. The idealistic Shostakovich believed that it was his responsibility to serve the state as an artist, and he settled down to composing "realist" music, albeit with a progressive edge. He was impressed by much of the music of the Second Viennese School and by Berg's *Wozzeck* in particular, and developed an eclectic style that was rooted in tonality yet incorporated some more abrasively Germanic and avant-garde tendencies. His mission was to produce work that was accessible without being regressive, and it was to bring him into

MARY EVANS PICTURE LIBRARY/IIDA KAR

conflict with the musical arbiters within the government.

Two years after the successful 1934 premiere of his opera *Lady Macbeth of the Mtensk District*, the work was savaged in *Pravda*, where an article titled "Chaos instead of Music" deplored *Lady Macbeth* for its "confused stream of sounds" and "petty bourgeois sensationalism". The state made it clear that "Soviet art can have no other aim than the interest of the people and the state" and while Shostakovich sympathized in part with these vague dictates, he was appalled by the extremes to which the state was willing to go. When you have a country of over 180 million people, speaking 108 different languages, it is hard to find a common musical ground, but Shostakovich was relentless bullied for his deviations from the ill-defined path of Socialist Realism.

From 1938 until 1955 Shostakovich devoted himself chiefly to symphonic music, and also began his vast cycle of string quartets. Notably, he produced nothing for the stage. During the siege of Leningrad in 1941 he fought fires and helped the wounded, then in 1943 he settled in Moscow, where he was appointed a professor of composition at the conservatory. Even though he toed the party line with humiliating obedience, Shostakovich still fell foul of the government in 1948, when he and many other prominent Russian composers were singled out and denounced for "formalism" and the creation of "anti-people art". He was dismissed from his teaching post, and subsequently composed almost nothing but film scores and patriotic music until after Stalin's death in 1953. The last twenty years of his life were much calmer: free from state intrusion, he produced some particularly fine music, and saw the first performance of several major pieces written during the Stalinist repression. One of his most consistent pleasures in later years was his friendship with Benjamin Britten and the group of Russian musicians for whom he composed, including Nikolayeva, Oistrakh and Rostropovich.

Shostakovich's style is heterogenous yet immediately recognizable, combining the three strands of "high-spirited humour, introspective meditation and declamatory grandeur", in the words of musicologist Boris Schwarz. As Schwarz goes on to say, in much of his music Shostakovich allows one of these elements to prevail, and the result can be monotonous and wearisome. But in his greatest works, notably the symphonies and string quartets, he encompasses exceptionally wide emotional extremes, juxtaposing tragic intensity and grotesque wit, sublimity and banality, folksy jauntiness and elemental darkness, in a manner that recalls Gustav Mahler, a composer he especially admired

LADY MACBETH OF THE MTENSK DISTRICT

The greatest of Shostakovich's four full-length operas, *Lady Macbeth of the Mtensk District* (usually abbreviated to plain *Lady Macbeth*) was heralded as a work of great power and originality after its premiere in Leningrad on January 22, 1934. Productions outside the Soviet Union soon followed, but in December 1935 Stalin himself went to see the show. The result was a *Pravda* editorial decrying this "fidgety, screaming, neurotic music" and deriding the composer for sympathizing with a thoroughly wicked heroine – a bored adulteress who murders her husband, is exiled to Siberia with her lover, and ends up committing suicide. The authorities entirely missed the opera's mordant social satire, and demanded a revision; Shostakovich duly toned down what he termed the "animal eroticism" of *Lady Macbeth*, and the work re-emerged in 1956 under the new title *Katerina Izmaylova*.

The strength of *Lady Macbeth* is the orchestral score, a brilliantly garish creation of primary colours, cruelly driving rhythms and wild dissonances. It can be difficult listening even for modern audiences, but as a piece of sustained and intense dramatic writing *Lady Macbeth* warrants comparison with *Wozzeck*. Characterization and mood are created chiefly by the orchestra rather than by the vocal roles, for Shostakovich rarely wrote well for the voice. Perhaps that is one of the chief reasons why he never composed the

rest of his planned tetralogy of operas about women, a cycle that was intended to end with a work concerning a hard-working employee of the Dnieper hydroelectric installation.

⚫ Vishnevskaya, Gedda, Petkov, Krenn, Tear, Valjakka; Ambrosian Opera Choir; London Philharmonic Orchestra; Rostropovich (EMI CDS7 4995-2; 2 CDs).

Rostropovich might have a general tendency to be careless and lumbering, but here he gets it right, extracting vivid performances and generating a real erotic charge. The cast includes Rostropovich's wife, Galina Vishnevskaya, and the incomparable Nicolai Gedda.

THE SYMPHONIES

From the daring precosity of the *Symphony No. 1* (1923–24) to the anguished bitterness of the *Symphony No. 15* (1971), Shostakovich's symphonies display a range unequalled by any other modern cycle. His style, however, was consistent from the *Symphony No. 4* onwards: characterized by a peculiar harmonic language that borrowed much from Prokofiev and Russian folk-song, and by a distinctive rhythmic manner and a fixed sense of orchestration, his music can be identified within a matter of bars. As the bulk of his symphonic work is carved from the same rock, you need only sample the three we've picked out to gauge whether or not Shostakovich is to your taste.

Shostakovich began the *Symphony No. 5* a year after *Pravda* had mauled *Lady Macbeth*, and the work was premiered on November 21, 1937, bearing the subtitle "A Soviet Artist's Practical Creative Reply to Just Criticism". It was a sensational success, for in accordance with the Politburo's dictum that "all aspects of music should be subordinated to melody and such melody should be clear and singable", Shostakovich produced a work bursting with tunes. The treatment is considerably less bombastic than its immediate precursor, but the symphony is still constructed along grand lines – though the composer may have intended a degree of irony to some of its more histrionically tragic moments.

The perpetually popular *Symphony No. 7*, known as the *Leningrad Symphony*, was written very quickly during the siege of that city in 1941, and is a relentlessly bleak evocation of war. Intended to "inculcate the pictures of heroic deeds", this is as close as Shostakovich ever came to writing purely programmatic music. You'll get the taste of this savagely communicative piece right from the first movement, where the "Invasion" theme slowly and obsessively builds to a shuddering climax of repetition.

Shostakovich's *Symphony No. 10* was performed soon after the death of Stalin, and the bleak power of the first three movements might be taken as a commentary on the dark age that had just passed. The finales of Shostakovich's previous symphonies had been problematic, as the composer had to take note of the official preference for upbeat endings; *Symphony No. 10* concludes with a lightening of the mood which slightly dissipates the momentum, but overall the final movement is better integrated into the grand scheme. The tenth is perhaps the finest of his symphonies.

> ● **Symphony No. 5**: London Philharmonic Orchestra; Haitink (Decca 410 017-2DH).
> ● **Symphony No. 7**: London Philharmonic Orchestra; Haitink (Decca 417 392-2DH2).
> ● **Symphony No. 10**: Leningrad Philharmonic Orchestra; Mravinsky (Saga SCD 9017).
> ◗ **Symphony No. 10**: Leningrad Philharmonic Orchestra; Mravinsky (Erato 2292-45753-2).

Bernard Haitink has recorded a fine cycle of the complete Shostakovich symphonies. His account of the *Symphony No. 5* is one of the highlights. Where other conductors have tried to project its despair through indulgent speeds and other sentimentalizing tricks, Haitink is powerfully steady and dignified. The sound is at times cloudy, but the lack of clarity particularly suits the third movement, the opening of which is one of Shostakovich's most heartrending creations. Haitink's performance of *Symphony No. 7* is hard-driven but expressive. Especially in his development of the "Invasion" theme, his control of the pace and orchestral forces is most impressive, and the climax of the first movement is something to behold.

As principal conductor of the Leningrad Philharmonic, Evgeny Mravinsky gave the first performances of Shostakovich's fifth, sixth, eighth, ninth and tenth symphonies, and his Shostakovich recordings are thus uniquely authoritative, if a bit too stern for some tastes. That said, his two available readings of the *Symphony No. 10* are very different. The Saga version was recorded live in 1954 (the year after he gave the first performance) and is an oppressive view of the score, savage in its lack of compromise and really quite disturbing. The later performance was recorded – again live – in 1976 and boasts better sound and tighter playing from the orchestra, but it is excessively hard and devoid of compassion. The earlier performance is closer to the composer's intentions, but beware the sound quality.

THE VIOLIN CONCERTOS

Shostakovich composed two violin concertos, both of them written for and first performed by David Oistrakh, one of the century's finest violinists. The better is the first, which was composed in 1947–48 but remained unperformed until 1955, and was perhaps altered during the intervening years. This concerto features some of the finest music ever written for the violin, and in its second movement Shostakovich created his most beautiful concerto episode – a deeply spiritual Adagio, in which the timpani announce a regular rhythmic pattern against which the soloist plays a desperately mournful lament. The concerto as a whole is a multi-faceted work of great difficulty for the soloist but of complete immediacy for the listener.

> ● Mordkovitch; Scottish National Orchestra; Järvi (Chandos CHAN8820).

The legendary 1956 recording with Oistrakh is no longer available – the best substitute is this version by Lydia Mordkovitch, one of his pupils. Mordkovitch produces a shuddering sonority that spans a massive emotional range – the Passacaglia in particular is almost unbearably intense, reaching a pitch that is normally well beyond the reaches of studio recording.

THE PIANO CONCERTOS

Shostakovich's first piano concerto, written in 1933, is scored for strings, piano and solo trumpet, a combination as unusual as the concerto's form, which consists of four through-flowing movements which sound like just one. It's always been a popular work, chiefly because of its plenitude of uplifting tunes and its frequent, provocative changes of mood. The second concerto, written for his son Maxim in 1957, is for the conventional combination of instruments, and is a lighter work than its predecessor, doubtless due to the composer's relief at the demise of Stalin. Like the *Violin Concerto No. 1*, it has a slow movement of exquisite pathos; the last movement – as with so many of Shostakovich's finales – is disappointingly flippant, but the concerto is well worth a listen for the Andante alone.

> ◗ Alexeev, Jones; English Chamber Orchestra; Maksymiuk (Classics for Pleasure CFP4547; with *The Assault on Beautiful Gorky*).

Dmitri Alexeev's playing might be a bit too rushed in places, but this is the best available coupling of both concertos, and as a bonus it comes with a fine mini-concerto taken from one of the composer's many film scores.

THE STRING QUARTETS

Shostakovich wrote fifteen symphonies and fifteen string quartets, but the numerical equality might be misleading – he didn't compose his first quartet until 1938, when he had already completed his fifth symphony, and waited another six years before embarking on the second. Each of the quartets displays an understanding of the interrelationship of string instruments that is as fine as that shown by Schubert or Beethoven, and as with the Beethoven quartets these pieces are a vehicle for composer's most intimate utterances. In comparison with Bartók's quartets, the century's other great cycle (see p.21), Shostakovich's are extremely melodic and direct, sometimes to the point of obviousness, but his gift for the unexpected turn of phrase is evident in every one.

Two of the finest of this astonishingly sustained sequence are the first and the eighth quartets. The former contains some gorgeous melodic writing, particularly in the second movement, which possesses the sort of tune that sets you thinking of divine inspiration. The latter was written in 1960 but was inspired by the firebombing of Dresden, a disaster that was also a source for Strauss's *Metamorphosen*. Unlike *Metamorphosen*, however, this is a bleak creation that offers no sense of hope or reconciliation. Written "In Memory of the Victims of Fascism and War", it's also a coded autobiography, for the music quotes from Shostakovich' own *Piano Quintet* and from *Lady Macbeth*, while the dominating theme is his musical "signature" D-S-C-H (D-E flat-C-B), which he also used in the *Symphony No. 10* and in other places.

◗ **Complete string quartets**: Borodin String Quartet (EMI 7243 6 65032 29; 6 CDs).

This set of live recordings is one of the finest examples of quartet playing. The Borodin Quartet create an atmosphere that can only come from the presence of an audience, but they produce the sort of technical perfection that usually requires the assistance of studio engineers. More than the symphonies, these works demand to be heard in their entirety, but each of the six discs that make up the set is available separately.

PRELUDES AND FUGUES

Shostakovich's penchant for musical "signatures" derived from his study of the music of Bach, who wrote pieces in which the notes signified by the letters of his name were used as thematic material. A more interesting product of his immersion in Bach was the *24 Preludes and Fugues* Op. 87, which was written in 1950–51 for Tatiana Nikolayeva. Comprising a prelude and fugue in each key, this huge composition mirrors the structure of the *Well-Tempered Clavier*, but this music is a world away from the decorum of the Baroque era. These are intensely personal pieces, covering an emotional spectrum almost as wide as that of the quartets. From the simplicity of the first in C major to the quasi-symphonic grandeur of the last in D minor, the *Preludes and Fugues* bare the composer's soul with uncompromised honesty.

◉ Nikolayeva (Hyperion CDA66441/3; 3 CDs).

It was a Bach recital by Tatiana Nikolayeva that gave Shostakovich the idea of writing the *Preludes and Fugues*, and she advised him throughout its composition. Unrecognized outside Russia until only a few years before her death in 1993, Nikolayeva was a brilliant pianist who combined a sparkling unpredictability with a powerful technique. Powerhouse pianism is required by these demanding scores and she plays them as if her life depended on it. A superb document and a lasting testament to a great musical personality.

Tatiana Nikolayeva

JEAN SIBELIUS

(1865–1957)

Nineteenth-century Finland was a Grand Duchy of Tsarist Russia, ruled by the Swedish-speaking minority. It was one of Sibelius's greatest achievements to reassert Finnish culture as something distinct from that of both Russia and Scandinavia. Sibelius became the cultural figurehead of Finnish nationalism, a status he achieved largely through writing some of the greatest symphonic music of the nineteenth and twentieth centuries.

Johan (later Jean) Julius Christian Sibelius was born into a Swedish-speaking doctor's family in a small town in southern Finland, but spent much of his school life in a Finnish-speaking environment. He was composing by the age of ten and at first saw his future as a violinist, though he entered Helsinki University to study law, before turning to music when he came under the influence of Ferruccio Busoni (see p.86), then

on the university's staff. Sibelius continued his musical studies in Berlin and then in Vienna.

Returning to Finland in 1891, he completed his first major work, the choral symphony *Kullervo*, the first of many compositions based on the mythology of the Finnish national epic, the *Kalevala* – the closest Finnish equivalent to the Arthurian legends of Anglo-Celtic culture, or the Nordic legends of Scandinavia. His *Symphony No. 1* (1899) consolidated a reputation in his home country, which had already honoured him with a small pension for life, partly as recompense for his not getting the post of director of music at Helsinki University. His fame now spread abroad and several ensuing works were first performed in Berlin, including the *Violin Concerto* (1903–05), which was given its premiere under Richard Strauss.

The first decade of the century also saw Sibelius develop a more personal style, away from the Tchaikovsky-inspired early symphonies towards something sparer, more refined and more organic in structure. When cancer of the throat was diagnosed in 1908, depriving him of his beloved tobacco and alcohol, he responded by darkening and paring down his style even further, a process clear in works such as the *Symphony No. 4* (1911). Further deprivation was to come: the outbreak of World War I obliterated his income from royalties, then an attempted Communist coup in Finland – which had achieved independence in the wake of the Russian Revolution – forced Sibelius to leave his home in the forests to the north of Helsinki.

After the war Sibelius composed the last two of his seven symphonies and the great tone poem *Tapiola* (1926). The following year, with restored royalties and his state pension giving him a secure future, he simply retired from composing and conducting, and for the next twenty years kept the musical world waiting for an eighth symphony that never materialized.

ROYAL COLLEGE OF MUSIC

SYMPHONIES

Sibelius is the most original symphonist since Beethoven, in that he found unique solutions to the problems of symphonic form. The earliest work is a fairly traditional nineteenth-century Romantic symphony, but Sibelius soon went on to develop a highly complex structural approach, in which the music was conceived in terms of a great arch. As broad generalization, the mature symphonies of Sibelius progress from scattered and fragmentary ideas into fully formed themes and sections, as if the compositional process were happening in the presence of the audience. The high point of this process is the *Symphony No. 7*, where Sibelius manages to combine the usual four movements into a single continuity, in which it is impossible to tell where one section ends and another begins.

⏺ **Complete Symphonies**: Philharmonia Orchestra; Ashkenazy (Decca 421 069-2; 4 CDs).

Complete sets of the symphonies have proliferated recently; each has its merits, but Vladimir Ashkenazy's mid-price cycle with the Philharmonia offers the most consistent rewards – indeed several of his performances are first-choice recommendations for single symphonies (see below).

SYMPHONY NO. 1

Sibelius was still under the influence of Tchaikovsky when he wrote his first symphony, but these Russian overtones co-exist with assuredly individualistic orchestral textures and themes. At the very opening, for example, in a highly original stroke, a clarinet over a gentle timpani roll introduces the main theme, which achieves its apotheosis at the climax of the finale. An emphatically rhythmic Scherzo reveals the influence of Bruckner, a composer whose music he had first encountered in Vienna in 1890.

⏺ Philharmonia Orchestra; Ashkenazy (Decca 414 534-2; with *Karelia Suite*).

Ashkenazy is the ideal interpreter here, finding the perfect balance between the work's Russian facets and its less conventional elements. The Philharmonia's playing is typically full-blooded and the recording one of the Decca label's warmest.

SYMPHONY NO. 2

The *Symphony No. 2* (1901) marks a transition between the youthful and the mature Sibelius. Much of it was composed in Italy, and the Russian influence has here been replaced by something more southern in feeling: its textures are more open and its thematic writing more ingratiating. That said, it does offer a "big tune", that most Russian of concepts, at the crowning point of the finale.

⏺ Gothenburg Symphony Orchestra; Järvi (BIS-CD-252; with *Romance in C*).

Neeme Järvi's recording with the Gothenburg Symphony Orchestra is the most thrilling available – full of energy yet alert to the demands of its formal structure.

SYMPHONY NO. 3

Perhaps because it lacks the broad sweep of the earlier symphonies, *Symphony No. 3* (1907) is one of Sibelius's least-known symphonies, which is a pity given its many attractions. It shows Sibelius moving in a new direction, with restraint, subtlety and clarity of texture the most obvious characteristics. The orchestra is now relatively small and the strings dominate the presentation of the main thematic material.

⏺ Philharmonia Orchestra; Ashkenazy (Decca 414 267-2DH; with *Symphony No. 6*).

Ashkenazy has the measure of this work, achieving an inexorable sense of its momentum, with the strings of the Philharmonia producing a rich and finely articulated sound.

SYMPHONY NO. 4

The increasing austerity and reduction of scale is even more marked in the *Symphony No. 4*, a work that can be seen as Sibelius's risposte to the megalomaniac tendencies of Bruckner and Mahler. Sibelius's fear of death (more specifically, his fear of a recurrence of cancer) seems to be another strong factor in this symphony, which is characterized by a generally grey orchestral palette and an emphasis on themes and harmonic relationships based on the tritone, a musical interval traditionally called upon to represent the devil or other sinister concepts – as in Liszt's *Mephisto* waltzes and Saint-Saën's *Danse macabre*.

◗ Philharmonia Orchestra; Ashkenazy (Decca 430 749-2; with *Symphony No. 5*).

Vladimir Ashkenazy conveys the fatalistic mood perfectly, in an atmospherically recorded account that never resorts to mere colourising at the expense of pace and direction.

SYMPHONY NO. 5

The *Symphony No. 5* is one of Sibelius's most original reworkings of symphonic form and he had great difficulty in getting it completed to his satisfaction: he withdrew it after the premiere in 1915 (to celebrate his fiftieth birthday) and the final version didn't appear until 1919. Originally it was in four movements, but during the revision he merged the first and second into one, with a transition passage that miraculously glides from one into the other (given the right conductor). The formal concision of the fifth is astonishing – a horn call at the start of each movement defines a chord that then becomes the basis for that movement's material.

After the pessimism of *No. 4* this symphony is one of his most heroic and confident statements, with a triumphant finale whose main theme was memorably described by the writer Donald Tovey as "Thor swinging his hammer" – it culminates in a series of crashing chords that will have you on tenterhooks for the final cadence.

◗ City of Birmingham Symphony Orchestra; Rattle (EMI 7 64112 2; with *Symphony No. 7*; *Nightride & Sunrise*; *Scene with Cranes*).

Simon Rattle has recorded the work twice, once with the Philharmonia and later with the CBSO. Both versions display a refinement and structural integrity that are rarely found elsewhere, but given that it is coupled with his equally top-rated performance of the *Symphony No. 7*, the CBSO version is the one to have.

SYMPHONY NO. 6

The *Symphony No. 6* (1923) is another restrained work, which seems to combine the sound worlds of the third and fourth symphonies, though it was actually conceived alongside the fifth – Sibelius even sketched passages for one that ended up in the other. The music is based on modal rather than traditional tonal harmonies and melodic lines, and the effect of this procedure on the work's

mood is well summed up in Sibelius's suggested motto: "When shadows lengthen".

◗ Philharmonia Orchestra; Ashkenazy (Decca 414 267-2DH; with *Symphony No. 3*).

Vladimir Ashkenazy's subtly hued Philharmonia performance is a worthy coupling to his account of the third symphony.

SYMPHONY NO. 7

After the formal experiments of *Symphony No. 5*, Sibelius finally went the whole hog and created a one-movement symphony that contains all the traditional four-movement symphony's characteristics of contrast and development. It's perhaps the greatest of all his works: extraordinarily fluid, expressive and even epic in character, and yet in its concision and brevity (it lasts twenty minutes) anticipating the structural rigour of Webern.

◗ City of Birmingham Symphony Orchestra; Rattle (EMI 7 64112 2; with *Symphony No. 5*; *Nightride & Sunrise*; *Scene with Cranes*).
◗ Philharmonic Orchestra; Beecham (EMI CDM 7 63400-2; with *Pelléas and Melisande*; *The Oceanides*; *Tapiola*).

Simon Rattle again excels in this most complex of works; the performance is seamless and the playing of the CBSO as fine as any. Thomas Beecham's classic account is coupled with *Tapiola* (see below) and all but one of the nine movements of *Pélleas and Melisande*, an orchestral suite extracted from music Sibelius wrote for a production of Maeterlinck's play in 1905. It makes an earthy counterargument to Debussy's better-known evocation of Maeterlinck's world.

VIOLIN CONCERTO & ORCHESTRAL WORKS

Though Sibelius's music is dominated by his symphonies, these are by no means the sum of his orchestral output. In addition to his great *Violin Concerto*, he wrote a string of symphonic poems that are formally just as original as the best of the symphonies, and make especially vivid use of the orchestra to conjure up the atmosphere of the northern forests and Finland's mythical tales. There is also a wealth of music for the theatre, and orchestral pieces composed for specific occasions, of which the best known is *Finlandia*.

VIOLIN CONCERTO

Sibelius's *Violin Concerto* is now acknowledged as one of the top half-dozen concertos in the repertory, but its reputation was not won immediately. By the time of its premiere in 1904 Sibelius already had two symphonies behind him, and he expected the concerto to get the same sort of acclaim. In the event, Karl Flodin, the country's most prominent music critic, pronounced it "a mistake", partly because the soloist made such a mess of the numerous tricky episodes in the work – the first movement has two full cadenzas, for example, instead of the regulation one. Flodin had a few misgivings about the structure as well, and Sibelius seems to have taken these to heart, for in the following year he unveiled a smoother and trimmer version that was about five minutes shorter than the orginal. Boldly Romantic, culminating in a lumbering finale which has been likened to polar bears dancing in the snow, this second draft is the version that is now almost invariably played.

⊙ Kavakos; Lahti Symphony Orchestra; Vänskä (BIS CD-500).

⊙ Mintz; Berlin Philharmonic Orchestra; Levine (Deutsche Grammophon 419 618-2GH; with Dvořák, *Violin Concerto*).

Greek violinist Leonidas Kavakos gives fine performances of both versions of the concerto: the playing of the little-known soloist and orchestra is equal to anything produced by bigger-name artists, and has the added fascination of giving insight into Sibelius's creative processes. If you just want the "authorized" version, go for the lush Shlomo Mintz recording, which is coupled with an outstanding version of the Dvořák concerto.

KULLERVO

Kullervo was classified by Sibelius as a choral symphony, but could be more accurately described as a symphonic poem, since its form is determined by a literary source – the five movements depict the exploits of the eponymous mythological hero of the *Kalevala*. Preceding his first "abstract" symphony by some eight years, it was *Kullervo* that first brought Sibelius to prominence in Finland. Sibelius himself withdrew it after the premiere, and it was not performed again until after his death, but it's well worth hearing – it could have been written by no-one

else, and its importance to his development is crucial.

⊙ Mattila, Hynninen; Gothenburg Symphony Orchestra; Järvi (BIS CD313).

Neeme Järvi's is the most successful of the handful of recordings in the catalogue: the choral and solo singing is dramatic and the whole is spectacularly recorded.

KARELIA SUITE AND FINLANDIA

Karelia, a region that spreads over eastern Finland and into neighbouring Russia, is the heartland of Finnish culture. In 1892 Sibelius wrote music to accompany a student production of scenes based upon its history, and the rousing three-movement *Karelia Suite* evolved from this music as a separate concert work. Sibelius's other well-known piece of nationalist banner-waving, *Finlandia*, evolved in a similar way. Originally written to accompany a series of tableaux staged in Helsinki in 1899, representing events in Finnish history, the show was put on in the guise of a charity event, but was designed to encourage anti-Russian sentiment. First known under the title *Finland Awakes*, it struck an immediate chord – so much so that the authorities banned people from whistling its melodies in the streets.

◗ Philharmonia Orchestra; Ashkenazy (Decca 417 762-2; with *Tapiola* and *En Saga*).

Ashkenazy is first choice in both these works: in *Karelia* the outer movements in particular have great sweep, while the performance of *Finlandia* is the most stirring available, with a ripe recording and a particularly pungent sound from the Philharmonia's tuba. It's coupled with good performances of *Tapiola* (see below) and *En Saga* (A Saga), a generalized evocation of the spirit of the Nordic sagas, written in 1893 and revised in 1901.

LEMMINKÄINEN SUITE

The *Lemminkäinen Suite* (1895), also known as *Four Legends*, is another early work based on the *Kalevala*. It's best known for its second movement, *The Swan of Tuonela*, in which a cor anglais, singing mournfully over sombre string and low wind harmonies, evokes the swan gliding on a dark river. The excerpt is heard far more often on its own than in its original context, but the other three movements are equally worth getting to know for Sibelius's distinctive way of creating drama and atmosphere.

🔘 **Lemminkäinen Suite**: Gothenburg Symphony Orchestra; Järvi (BIS CD294). 3x
🔘 **The Swan of Tuonela**: Berlin Philharmonic Orchestra; Karajan (Deutsche Grammophon 413 755-2; with *Finlandia*; *Valse Triste*; *Tapiola*). 3x

Neeme Järvi conducts a particularly satisfying performance of the whole suite, with the Gothenburg Symphony Orchestra warmly recorded. If you just want the highlight, go for the Karajan version, which boasts the peerless string tones of the Berlin Philharmonic.

THE TEMPEST AND TAPIOLA

Sibelius composed a fair amount of music for theatrical productions (in those days many theatres had orchestras), and his finest piece of theatre music was his last, written for a production of Shakespeare's *Tempest* in Copenhagen in 1926. Beginning with a wonderful evocation of the storm, cleverly composed almost entirely of held chords and swishing cascades of chromatic scales, it consists of over thirty separate numbers, including character studies and settings of the play's songs. Written immediately after *The Tempest*, *Tapiola* was Sibelius's last work, and it's one of his greatest. Inspired by Tapio, the ancient Finnish god of the forest, this symphonic poem – like the early *En Saga* – is a broadly pictorial and atmospheric composition, rather than a musical depiction of a specific train of dramatic events. It's as tautly conceived as any of his symphonies and as evocative in its tone-painting as anything in his entire oeuvre.

🔘 **The Tempest**: Tiihonen, Paasikivi, Hirvonen, Kerola, Keinonen; Lahti Opera Chorus & Symphony Orchestra; Vänskä (BIS CD581).
🔘 **Tapiola**: Gothenburg Symphony Orchestra; Järvi (BIS CD312; with *Pohjola's Daughter*; *Rakastava*; *Impromptu*).

There have been several recordings of the suites compiled from Sibelius's full score of *The Tempest*, but none matches the magnificence of the BIS recording of the complete music. The epic northern landscape is marvellously conjured up in Järvi's Gothenburg account of *Tapiola*, which is couple with a luscious version of *Pohjola's Daughter* (1906), another Kalevala-inspired tone poem. Sibelius's command of the orchestra was never more clearly revealed than in this piece, and Järvi's stunning recording does full justice to its wide-ranging and sumptuous use of orchestral colour.

ROBERT SIMPSON
(1921–   )

Born in the same year as Macolm Arnold (see p.5), Robert Simpson is another British composer whose musical ideals are staunchly traditional. In defence of his antipathy to modernism he has asserted that "contact with durable human instincts is more vital than tagging onto fashions". As a young man he composed a piece in which he experimented with serial techniques, but since completing his first symphony while studying at Durham University he has never strayed from the language of tonality.

String quartets and symphonies comprise the nucleus of his output, but it's in the latter that Simpson's character most obviously reveals itself. The principal influences on these works are Beethoven, Bruckner and Nielsen (he has written perceptive books on the symphonies of all three), and they tend to follow a firm thematic and tonal plan, in the approved manner of the nineteenth century. Simpson's well-constructed musical architecture attempts, he has said, "to express human force by means of positive musical development". It must be said that to an untrained ear such development can be elusive, and comparisons with Beethoven might seem eccentric. Nonetheless Simpson's striving for "maximum human power" can produce startlingly immediate effects, not least through his gift for deeply considered melody.

THE MUSIC

Of the Simpson compositions currently in the catalogue, the *Symphony No. 6* and *String Quartet No. 1* offer the clearest and most entertaining introduction to the composer. The *Symphony No. 6* was written in 1977 for a gynaecologist friend who suggested that Simpson compose a symphony that grew from basic melodic cells in a manner analogous to the development of a living being, an idea that Simpson, who was trained in medicine, found very appealing. The huge, unbroken symphony is lush and heavily contrapuntal, and could be taken as the embodiment of Nielsen's view that music "is the sound of life". Simpson's *String Quartet No. 1* is his most traditional and the easiest to digest at one sitting. Full of well-extended and devel- oped melody, it was begun at the same time as the masterly first symphony (no recording of which is available) and was completed in 1951.

> ● **Symphony No. 6**: Royal Liverpool Philharmonic Orchestra; Handley (Hyperion CDA66280; with *Symphony No. 7*).
> ● **Quartet No. 1**: Delmé String Quartet (Hyperion CDA66419; with *Quartet No. 4*).

Simpson is fortunate in having the support of Hyperion, who to date have recorded six of his ten symphonies and fourteen of his fifteen quartets. Vernon Handley has conducted all the symponies, and his performance of the sixth with the RLPO is typically energetic and well-balanced; coupled with the seventh symphony, this is the most obvious recommendation for a first foray into Simpson. The Delmé Quartet has recorded a large proportion of Simpson's quartets on Hyperion, and their enthusiastic performance of the *Quartet No. 1* brings much to music that demands a lyrical yet rhyth- mically pungent approach.

BEDŘICH SMETANA
(1824–1884)

Czech classical music did not spring into existence with the arrival of Bedřich Smetana – Prague, after all, was one of the great musical centres of the eight- eenth century. However, Smetana almost single-handedly established Czech musical nationalism, being the first to integrate folk- based material into his compositions. His music may reflect a prominent Germanic influence – hardly surprising considering that he spent his formative years under Austrian rule – but his impact upon the more overtly nationalistic Dvořák, Janáček and Martiny is incalculable.

Born in Bohemia, the son of a brewer, Smetana showed incredible ability as a child: he was playing in a string quartet from the age of five and three years later produced his first symphony. He was educated at the Proksch Institute in Prague, where he wrote some Lisztian tone-poems that received little recog- nition. Obliged to teach in order to make ends meet, he was almost penniless when Liszt

GUUS ONG

prompted him to try his fortune in Sweden, away from the oppressive atmosphere of Austrian-ruled Prague. From 1856 to 1861 he lived in Gothenburg and it was there that he composed his first successful symphonic poem, *Richard III*; written as a tribute to Liszt, it was heavily Romantic and Germanic, giving no hint of a Czech national style.

In 1861, with the easing of the Austrian regime, Smetana returned home. His financial instability forced him to tour as a pianist for a while, but exciting possibilities appeared with the opening in 1862 of the Provisional Theatre, Prague's first theatre built exclusively for Czech use. Four years later Smetana's first opera, *The Brandenburgers in Bohemia*, was performed there, and its success led to Smetana's appointment as the theatre's chief conductor. Later the same year, a draft of Smetana's most remarkable opera, *The Bartered Bride*, received its premiere at the Provisional, but it was the performance of the definitive three-act version in 1870 that effectively created a Czech national opera.

It was to prove the apex of his public career. His subsequent operas were attacked for their Wagnerian tendencies, and Smetana's enemies plotted for his removal. In the event, he was forced to resign in 1874 when he went deaf as a result of syphilitic infection. He continued to compose (*Má Vlast*, his best-known work, comes from this period), and he became recognized as something of a national institution, but Smetana's life ended tragically. Suicidally depressed and ravaged by syphilis, he eventually went mad, and was committed to Prague's lunatic asylum early in 1884. He died in May, and was buried with full Czech honours.

THE BARTERED BRIDE

The Provisional Theatre was not the best-appointed opera house in Europe. Bewailing its meagre facilities, Smetana wrote: "How can we possibly play opera in a house as small as ours? In *Les Hugenots*, the armies barely number eight on each side . . . and thus provoke laughter. The singers are pressed so close together in the foreground that everyone must be careful not to hurt his neighbour when he turns." Yet it was in this theatre, in 1866, that *The Bartered Bride* heralded the birth of Czech opera.

Smetana later wrote that he had composed *The Bartered Bride* "out of spite, because I

was accused after *The Brandenburgers* of being a Wagnerian who was incapable of writing anything in a lighter vein." Even though he was working on *The Bartered Bride* some time before *The Brandenburgers* was staged, there is something to Smetana's claim, for the style of this opera is indeed unlike the declamatory Wagnerian manner of *The Brandenburgers*. Set in a Bohemian village, *The Bartered Bride* is an engagingly direct love story in which boy gets girl after just the right amount of comic misunderstanding, and the music is full of broad strokes and bold contrasts, with plenty of Czech "numbers", such as drinking-choruses and polkas, to keep things moving. An equally important aspect of *The Bartered Bride* is Smetana's vivid characterization. Each of the leads is assigned clearly recognizable musical features that are maintained throughout the opera, and Smetana brilliantly uses key signatures to reflect their changing moods.

⬤ Benacková, Dvorsky, Kopp, Novák; Czech Philharmonic Orchestra & Chorus; Kosler (Supraphon 103511-2; 3 CDs).

Many recording of *The Bartered Bride* use a translated libretto, but Smetana's operas lose much of their musical style if not performed in Czech. The earthy qualities of the original are best heard in Supraphon's excellent recording under Zdenek Kosler with the then fabulous Czech Philharmonic. Lyrical central performances from soprano Gabriela Benacková and tenor Peter Dvorsky, together with some exemplary chorus work, make this a highly entertaining production.

MÁ VLAST

The six symphonic poems of *Má Vlast* (My Homeland) were begun in 1872 and completed a full seven years later, but at the end of this process he had created his fullest expression of the Czech national spirit – although, ironically, the principal theme of *Vltava*, the second and most famous of the six, is a derivation of a Swedish rather than a Czech folksong. Characterized by expansive melodies and dramatic rhythms, *Má Vlast* presents a vision of Czech legend, history and landscape, packing an incredible array of battles, celebrations and other scenes into fifty minutes' music. Specifically, the first section is a graphic description of the river flowing through Prague, the second is a portrait of the Czech countryside, and the remaining four refer to episodes from Czech history, making repeated use of a nationalist hymn in the last two sections. It's heroic, astonishingly well-crafted music, meriting comparison with the orchestral poems of Liszt – Smetana's inspiration – and Richard Strauss.

◗ Boston Symphony Orchestra; Kubelik (Deutsche Grammophon 429 183-2GGA).

◎ Czech Philharmonic Orchestra; Kubelik (Supraphon 111208-2).

Rafael Kubelík's two recordings of this masterpiece of orchestral virtuosity are both essential listening. The earlier account, with the Boston Symphony, boasts the most luscious instrumental sonorities and strongest rhythmic bite but the studio recording is slightly dry and over-precise. Kubelík's second recording was made on the occasion of his return to Prague to conduct the Czech Philharmonic after a break of many years. The reunion inspired conductor and orchestra to put on a display of explosive emotional exuberance, captured on a recording of excellent quality. The playing may be rougher than the Boston version, but few CDs transmit such a sense of occasion.

STRING QUARTETS

The first of Smetana's two stupendous string quartets was composed in 1876, two years after he had gone deaf from the disease which eventually was to kill him. Subtitled "From my life", the *String Quartet No. 1* is Smetana's autobiography in music; as he put it himself, the four movements comprise a "recollection of my life and the catastrophe of total deafness". The folk rhythms and rustic harmonies are allied to a heightened comprehension of the instruments' expressive potential, a development which, as with Beethoven, was surely connected with the composer's isolation. In a moment of desperate poignancy, the end of the jaunty last movement is interrupted by a shattering, dissonant high E on the first violin. This is the note which tormented the composer in his deafness; Smetana grimly referred to it as his "little joke".

The *Quartet No. 2* is not blatantly autobiographical, but the music does relate to the suffering of his later years, and its bittersweet themes can be deeply distressing. It was composed in 1882, when Smetana's mind was in such a state that he found concentration all but impossible, and he would frequently forget a theme within seconds of writing it down. The movements are therefore episodic and brief, but they constitute an amazingly advanced essay in the form. Schoenberg judged that in its treatment of rhythm, harmonic obscurity, melodic richness and tendency to terseness, Smetana's *Quartet No. 2* was decades ahead of its time.

◎ Talich Quartet (Collins 13232; with Suk, *Meditation on an old Czech hymn*).

The Talich Quartet produce astonishingly imaginative performances that project all the composer's anxiety into a world of sumptuous colour. Perfectly recorded, and coupled with Suk's haunting *Meditation on an old Czech hymn*, this is one of the most rewarding CDs of Smetana's music.

ETHEL SMYTH

(1858–1944)

Fifty years after her death, Ethel Smyth is finally beginning to achieve the attention she deserves, although only a few works are currently available on CD. The daughter of an army general, Smyth was a quite extraordinary woman, who refused to conform to the behaviour expected of her class and gender. She was determined to study music at a time when professional careers for women were frowned on, campaigned vigorously for women to be allowed into professional orchestras, and flung herself into the fight for universal suffrage. Above all, she fought with a most unladylike tenacity for recognition as a composer, and for performances of her powerfully vital music.

After a fierce battle with her family, Smyth went to Leipzig to study composition. Her first works, chamber music and songs, were published and performed there, and show a decidedly Germanic tone. On her return to England she had a few successful performances of works such as the turbulent *Overture to Anthony and Cleopatra* (1890) and her *Mass in D* (1891), but she found it difficult to interest most conductors and promoters in such large-scale music. Women were thought to be incapable of producing complex compositions, being expected to write nothing but pretty songs and delicate piano pieces. Undaunted, Smyth turned to opera, the most complex of all musical genres. She realised that new operas had little chance of success in Britain, and her first two operas, *Fantasio* (1892–94) and *Der Wald* (1899–1901), were written with German libretti and first performed in Germany. In 1902 *Der Wald* was given a well-received British premiere and Smyth started work on her greatest opera, *The Wreckers*, which was first performed in Leipzig in 1906. A tragic story of two lovers who defy the Cornish fishing community in which they live and are then sentenced to death, *The Wreckers* is a thrilling work, Wagnerian in its orchestration and use of leitmotifs, and full of passionate vocal writing and powerful evocations of the treacherous Cornish coast.

After devoting two years to the Pankhursts' militant suffragette campaign, including a few weeks in Holloway prison for throwing a stone through the window of the Colonial Secretary's house, Smyth went to Egypt to write the most frequently performed of all her operas, *The Boatswain's Mate* (1913–14), a comic opera with a decidedly feminist theme – Mrs Waters, the strong-willed heroine, constantly outwits a bumbling suitor who is determined to prove that she needs a man to protect her. Smyth also wrote two other operas, *Fête Galante* (1922), a neo-classic "dance-dream" set in the eighteenth century, and another comic opera *Entente Cordiale* (1925); works in other forms included the lively unaccompanied chorus *Hey Nonny No* (1911), the beautiful orchestral songs *Three Moods of the Sea* (1913), and *The Prison* (1930), an intense work for soloists, chorus and orchestra, setting a metaphysical poem

by her only male lover, Harry Brewster. Smyth had realised that she was beginning to lose her hearing during the 1910s, and although she continued to compose, in later life she concentrated more on her nine volumes of memoirs and essays, in which she expressed her views on subjects ranging from women's creativity to golf and sheep-dogs.

THE MUSIC

At the time of going to press, a new recording of *The Wreckers* from the Conifer label has just been announced. Until it appears, the only readily available large-scale work by Ethel Smyth is the *Mass in D* (1891), which was written while Smyth was infatuated with the devoutly Catholic Pauline Trevelyan, and first performed in January 1893 after intense lobbying by Smyth's aristocratic friends, such as the Empress Eugènie, widow of Napoleon III. The audience and most of the critics were impressed but the work was not performed again until 1924, which was unfair, for it's a compelling piece, from its sombre opening to the expansive exultation of the final Gloria.

Most of Smyth's chamber music was written while she was at Leipzig in the 1880s, and the best of her work from this period is represented by the *String Quintet* (1883), an energetic item with a beautifully poignant slow movement, and the impressive four-movement *Violin Sonata* (1887), which a contemporary reviewer found "deficient in the feminine charm that might have been expected of a woman composer". The *String Quartet* is one of her pieces of instrumental chamber music written after she had left Leipzig. The first two movements were written in 1902 but not performed until 1912, when they were heard at the first public concert of the Society of Women Musicians. On hearing them, Smyth decided to complete the work by adding two more movements, an expressive Andante and the exuberantly contrapuntal finale.

In the 1900s, when Smyth spent much of her time in France, her music began to depart from the Germanic tradition of her earlier works. This is reflected in the *Four Songs* of 1907, sensuous settings of French poems for mezzo-soprano accompanied by flute, harp, string trio and percussion; they were immediately successful and were admired by Debussy, who heard them played at a private party in London. The militant side of Smyth is displayed by her *Three Songs* (1913), for voice and piano, which were written while Smyth was involved in the suffragette campaign. The second of the trio, *Possession*, is a heart-felt love song dedicated to Emmeline Pankhurst, while the third, *On the Road*, is a rousing piece about the fight for freedom, incorporating her *March of the Women*.

> ◉ **Mass in D**: Harrhy, Hardy, Dressen, Bohn; Plymouth Music Series Chorus & Orchestra; Brunelle (Virgin VC7 59022-2; with other works by Smyth).
> ◉ **String Quintet; Cello Sonata; Violin Sonata; String Quartet**: Fanny Mendelssohn Quartet; Dutilly (Troubadisc TDCD 03; 2 CDs).

> ◉ **Four Songs; Three Songs; Double Concerto for violin and horn**: Paulsen, Eggebrecht-Kupsa (Troubadisc TRO-CD 01405).

Philip Brunelle conducts a spirited performance of the *Mass* on a CD that offers the added bonuses of Mrs Waters' aria *What if I were young again* from *The Boatswain's Mate* (1916) and Smyth's suffragette anthem *The March of the Women*, which she conducted with her toothbrush from her cell in Holloway.

Despite some slightly underpowered performances, the two-CD set from Troubadisc provides the best introduction to hear Smyth's early chamber works and the later *String Quartet*. On the other Troubadisc CD the American mezzo-soprano Melinda Paulsen gives a much better performance of the *Four Songs* than of the later English set, which lack power and conviction. Although it is interesting to hear the late *Double Concerto*, it is a shame that it is given in the composer's arrangement for piano rather than with the original orchestral accompaniment.

KARLHEINZ STOCKHAUSEN
(1928–   )

I n today's global village of information highways and cultural cross-pollination, no composer occupies so pivotal a place as Karlheinz Stockhausen, who way back in the 1960s was predicting "a music of the whole world". The iconic figure of postwar highbrow modernity, he has been admired by people right across the musical spectrum: Frank Zappa and a generation of German progressive rock musicians like Tangerine Dream looked up to him, as did John Lennon – the single *Strawberry Fields* as well as chunks of *Sergeant Pepper* were directly influenced by Stockhausen's electronic music of the 1950s. As the first electronic studio composer, he is revered by the newest generation of rock and pop producers, whose computer processes and sampling techniques owe much to Stockhausen's pioneering efforts.

Brought up in the environs of Cologne, Stockhausen spent his earliest years on the move, following the wanderings of his schoolteacher father, while absorbing music from his mother – who played piano and sang –

and from the new media of radio and gramophone. The war shattered his childhood: his mother, who had been recuperating in a mental home, fell victim to the Nazi's inhuman euthanasia programme; his father was reported missing, and was never seen again. Conscripted as a stretcher-bearer the orphaned Stockhausen witnessed the most brutal carnage, and many times came within an inch of losing his life. By the war's end he had become a devout Christian, and was playing jazz piano for American GIs to finance his courses at Cologne's music school and university, where he studied German literature, philosophy, piano and musicology.

Under the influence of Schoenberg and the cell-like writing of Anton Webern (see p.413), Stockhausen composed some brilliant serial pieces, including *Choral* (1950), a haunting evocation of the bleak North Rhine landscape. By the following year he was attending new music courses in Darmstadt, where he was entranced by the work of Olivier Messiaen (see p.231), with whom he then studied in Paris – and by whom he was

STOCKHAUSEN-VERLAG

Karlheinz Stockhausen, photographed at work in 1958

promptly proclaimed a genius. There he also met Pierre Boulez (see p.61) and Pierre Schaeffer, who were working on innovative forms of tape composition at the studio of ORTF radio.

Fascinated by Messiaen, Stockhausen – like Boulez – went on to advocate a music of "total serialism", where every element would be determined by impersonal parameters. Performances of his work at Darmstadt were greeted with shock and dismay, as audiences struggled with music that just seemed to consist of an amorphous blob of notes, lacking any discernible melodic or rhythmic sense. In 1952–53 he spent three months in Paris splicing and processing two minutes and twenty seconds of taped "concrete" sounds (ie "real" sounds). On its presentation to Schaeffer, the resulting *Etude* was dismissed as sheer folly, but at the age of twenty-four

Stockhausen was offered a job at the WDR radio station in Cologne to continue his search for a "pure electronic music". Later in 1953 he went on to create *Studie I*, the first piece of music constructed entirely of sine waves.

Stockhausen tirelessly experimented with white noise, feedback and chance operations, stimulated by his studies in phonetics and communications science at Bonn university. From this period came *Gruppen* for three orchestras, a piece that moved music through space as well as time, but the great work was the thirteen-minute *Gesang der Jünglinge* (Song of the Youths) for boy soprano and electronic sound, a tour de force which took more than a year to create in the primitive Cologne studio. Its debut at WDR caused as much uproar as Stravinsky's *Rite* had done, for the audience were made to sit down and experience a performance of this "electronic space music" through loudspeakers alone. Fame quickly spread, as people such as Ligeti (see p.196) made pilgrimages to Cologne to see the inspirational German inventor.

Stockhausen's career now entered a stage of consolidations and expansions. *Kontakte* (1960) pushed the tape machine to its limits; *Momente* (1962) for choral groups and instrumentalists applied to acoustic instruments his electronic discoveries about the importance of such elements as sound-colour and silence-duration; in 1966, after a visit to Japan, he wrote *Telemusik*, a meta-collage of ethnic musics; and his openness to world music was further explored in *Stimmung*, a choral work inspired by Aztec and Maya mythology. Everything he saw, heard or in any way experienced – however trivial – was assimilated into a continuous production system in which events were meticulously annotated, logged and transcribed into music. Stockhausen's presentation of a thousand hours of "musical space travel" at the Osaka Expo of 1970 was a typically audacious project.

The apotheosis of Stockhausen's inexhaustible ambition came in 1977, when he announced the genesis of the twentieth century's closest equivalent to gigantic musical projects of Wagner. He had set himself the task of creating a Gesamtkunstwerk titled *Licht* (Light), a seven-part opera (one for each day of the week) for solo voices, solo instruments, solo dancers, choirs, orchestras, dancers, mimes and electronics. To date, four sections have been completed – *Donnerstag* (Thursday; 1978–80), *Samstag* (1981–83), *Montag* (Monday; 1984–88) and *Dienstag* (Tuesday; 1977 & 1988–91). *Freitag* (Friday) will be premiered in March 1995 in Leipzig, and the project is intended to be presented in its entirety at the dawn of the new millennium.

THE MUSIC

In 1991 Stockhausen returned to WDR to digitally remaster his entire 205-composition oeuvre on CD. The dazzlingly remastered works are now being issued by Stockhausen-Verlag, a company based at the composer's self-designed house in Kürten, and you can only get hold of them direct from there – the address for CDs, stock lists and other publications is Stockhausen-Verlag, Kettenberg 15, 51515 Kürten, Germany. Together with Stockhausen's own incisive insights into his music and life, detailed in his six-volume *Texte zur Musik* (excerpts translated as *Towards a Cosmic Music*, published by Element), the Stockhausen-Verlag series will amount to a definitive career statement. We've selected the three releases that make the best introduction to Stockhausen's vast output, plus one of the few Stockhausen CDs from other companies.

⊙ **Chöre für Doris; Choral; Drei Lieder; Sonatine; Kreuzspiel**: Stockhausen; Choir of North German Radio; German Symphony Orchestra; London Sinfonietta; Jacobeit; Anderson (Stockhausen Complete Edition CD1).

These are core early works, written in 1950 and 1951. The Baudelaire-based *Drei Lieder*, for alto voice and chamber orchestra, earned him a first-class degree at Cologne. *Chöre für Doris* and *Choral* both convey a profound Christian belief, with the latter's twelve-tone style revealing a masterly understanding of volume and cadence. *Sonatine*, for violin and piano, is Stockhausen's farewell to serialism, while *Kreuzspiel*, for oboe, bass clarinet, piano and three percussionists, marks the blossoming of Stockhausen's distinctive voice, with its spatial sound and seemingly disconnected notes. The performances by the London Sinfonietta, recorded in 1973, are unbeatable.

⊙ **Elektronische Musik** 1952–1960: Stockhausen (Stockhausen Complete Edition CD3).

Backed by a superb 134-page booklet, this is probably the best Stockhausen disc available. *Etude* (1952) is the three minutes of spliced tape that so incensed Schaeffer that he sent Stockhausen packing from Paris. *Studie* (1953–54), a huge spectrum of synthesized sounds using sine-wave generator and tape recorder, was the first electronic score ever published, but even this can't match the impact of *Gesang der Jünglinge* (1956), a piece that echoes around much contemporary electronic music. Part of a projected but never completed Mass, it matches a boy soprano's voice to every conceivable type of electronic sound. *Kontakte* (1960), the latest work on the CD, displays a brilliant understanding of the possibilities inherent in tape loops, and still sounds adventurous.

⊙ **Stimmung**: Singcircle (Hyperion CDA66115).

Bewitched by Maya temples and ancient Aztec culture after a trip to Mexico in 1968, Stockhausen returned to Connecticut to create *Stimmung* (Tuning), a hypnotically static work for unaccompanied voices, in 51 brief sections. Using only the overtones of B flat, the six singers recite and transform speech sounds based on various "magic names" (mostly gods and goddesses) and erotic texts. This brilliant version comes from 1983. The Stockhausen Complete Edition recording of

Stimmung (CD12; 2 CDs) contains two slightly different performances of the piece; both are outstandingly performed by the vocal group that gave the first performance, but non-aficionados are better advised to go for the single-CD Hyperion account.

● **Tierkreis; Musik im Bauch**: Les Percussions de Strasbourg (Stockhausen Complete Edition CD 24).

One of Stockhausen's most accessible works, this twelve-part dedication to the Zodiac is available in two versions: Stockhausen Complete Edition CD 35 contains a chamber version for clarinet, flute, trumpet and piano, but the CD 24 version is even more beguiling, as it's played on music boxes from the Reuge factory in Switzerland. It's coupled with *Musik im Bauch*, a music-theatre piece which similarly reveals the more playful side of Stockhausen.

ALESSANDRO STRADELLA
(1644–1682)

Alessandro Stradella was a notorious womanizer whose sexual adventures led to his murder in Genoa at the age of thirty seven. This has tended to obscure the fact that he was also a notable composer of opera and oratorios – one of the latter, *San Giovanni Battista*, being among the most dramatically compelling works of the seventeenth century. In both his oratorios and his purely instrumental works Stradella was one of the first composers to employ the concerto grosso form, in which the music was divided between the full ensemble and a smaller group within it, for the purpose of dramatic contrast.

Stradella was born in Rome into the minor nobility, a distinction that allowed him entry into exalted aristocratic circles. His patrons included the powerful Colonna and Pamphili families as well as Queen Christina of Sweden, who was living in Rome in voluntary exile and in whose household Stradella served from the age of fourteen. In 1669 the discovery of his involvement in a plot to embezzle money from the Church forced him, briefly, to leave the city although he returned in time for the opening of a new theatre, the Teatro Tordinona, which was to perform several of his works.

In 1673 in Florence he attempted to abduct a young nun, Lisabetta Marmonari, who had been the object of his attentions for several years. Four years later in Venice, having been hired by Alvise Contarini to give music lessons to his young mistress, Stradella instead eloped with her to Turin. An incensed Contarini pursued the couple and eventually two of his hired thugs left Stradella seriously wounded after a murder attempt. He fled to Genoa early in 1678, but four years later yet another amorous involvement with a high-ranking lady led to his assassination at the hands of a hired killer in the city's main square.

SAN GIOVANNI BATTISTA

San Giovanni Battista was written for the Confraternity of Florentines in Rome, who in 1675 – declared a Holy Year by the Pope – commissioned fourteen oratorios on the subject of their patron saint, Saint John the Baptist. Stradella's is a masterpiece of

Minkowski's ground-breaking account of San Giovanni

dramatic sophistication, with fully rounded characters, a huge range of emotions and a remarkable immediacy that's increased by the fact that the text is in Italian rather than Latin. Though San Giovanni is the protagonist, it is the corrupt and incestuous court of Erode (Herod) that generates the piece's psychological complexity. Stradella is helped by his librettist, who maintains the tension by dispensing with a narrator, but it is the music that builds up the atmosphere of degeneration and moral panic. In several arias Stradella seems to anticipate Handel's florid lines, but he doesn't have Handel's tendency to spin out the luxuriant moments at the expense of dramatic momentum – the mood often changes here within the space of a single aria. Thus when Erodiade (Salome) makes her request for the death of San Giovanni, she begins her exchanges with Erode nervously,

becoming insinuating then petulant, and finally pleads with him in a beguilingly beautiful aria, *Queste lagrime*. Only Monteverdi's *L'Incoronazione di Poppea* (see p.238) creates such a splendid frisson from the apparent triumph of evil.

● **San Giovanni Battista**: Bott, Lesne, Huttenlocher, Batty, Edgar-Wilson; Les Musiciens du Louvre; Minkowski (Erato 2292457392).

This performance is exceptionally well cast, with an emphasis on characterful rather than merely beautiful singing. Indeed the Erode of Phillippe Huttenlocher (bass) is a little woolly-sounding, but this defect is more than compensated for by the convincing way he projects the tyrant's mixture of bluster and fearfulness. Gerard Lesne (counter-tenor) as San Giovanni gives an equally convincing interpretation, with an incisiveness of tone that admirably conveys the incorruptible authority and dignity of the saint, while Catherine Bott's rendition of the demented aria *Su, coronatemi* (Come now crown me) is one of the highlights of the disc.

THE STRAUSS FAMILY

When Johann Strauss died in 1849 at the age of forty-five, a Viennese obituarist suggested that the city should mourn not just because a great man had gone but because once again Vienna's resident genius had been struck down prematurely. Fifty years later the same writer made the same claim for Johann Strauss the Younger (1825–99), and again incited outrage at the idea that waltz-manufacturers should command as much respect as Schubert, or indeed any composer of symphonies and sonatas. Admirers of the Strauss family still face an uphill struggle to convince people that their music is anything more than the froth of Viennese high society, but it's a mistake to patronize the talent required to write hundreds of memorable pieces within the extreme technical limitations of the waltz. Strauss senior's compositions may often have been convention-bound and short-winded, yet in his flamboyant *Radetzky March* he produced a work that became the very symbol of Habsburg military might, just as his son's

GUUS ONG

Johann Strauss the Younger

Blue Danube was to epitomize the glittering hedonism of imperial Vienna.

In addition to the two Johanns there was also a Josef (Johann the Younger's brother), who composed some 280 pieces, but couldn't match the fertility of his sibling, the so-called "Waltz King". Johann Strauss the Younger set the standards for every writer of "light" music in the next half-century, not just by enriching the Viennese waltz and other dance forms, but also through the creation of *Die Fledermaus* (The Bat), a magnificent operetta that has a claim to be his finest composition. Nobody would make out that there is any great depth here, but Johann the Younger has few rivals as uncomplicated melodist and orchestrator, and his music has retained the nostalgic attraction to which the obituary referred when it called him "the last symbol of cheerful, pleasant times".

DIE FLEDERMAUS

Premiered in 1874, *Die Fledermaus* is a brilliantly clever commentary on Viennese moral laxity, cloaked in sparklingly tuneful music that made it an instant hit – by the end of the decade, it was playing in some 170 theatres. On paper the plot is complicated to the point of unintelligibility, but on stage this tale of infidelity, mistaken identity and excessive champagne consumption works as well as any piece of music theatre. Offenbach's witty, hedonistic operettas obviously influenced the musical style of *Die Fledermaus* but Strauss's quintessentially Viennese decorum softens the edge of the satire. The most important stage work of its sort ever written, *Die Fledermaus* established a tradition that saw its apogee in the works of Lehár, and Richard Strauss paid homage to its waltz rhythms in *Der Rosenkavalier*.

⊙ Varady, Popp, Prey, Kollo, Weikl, Rebroff, Kusche, Gruber, List, Muxeneder; Bavarian State Opera Chorus & Orchestra; Kleiber (Deutsche Grammophon 415 646-2GH2; 2 CDs).

For its flair and wit, Carlos Kleiber's superbly conducted performance of *Die Fledermaus* is the obvious choice – the reclusive, semi-retired Kleiber the most remarkable Strauss conductor of the present generation, and there is no conductor alive today who's able to get such downright erotic sounds out of an orchestra. His cast isn't ideal, but Hermann Prey gives one of the best performances of his career, and Julia Varady and Lucia Popp are very, very good – their singing

of Act One's *So muss allein ich bleiben* is completely wonderful.

THE DANCE MUSIC

Johann I's *Radetsky March* is played every year at the New Year's Day concert at the Vienna Musikverein, an outbreak of white-tie jollity to celebrate the city's kings of dance music. Leaving aside the *Radetzky March*, however, it's Johann II's waltzes that dominate the dynasty's output, and pieces such as *Thunder and Lightning*, *Vienna Blood*, *Acceleration*, *Tales from the Vienna Woods* and *The Blue Danube* are among the best-known tunes of the nineteenth century. (*The Blue Danube* has now been recorded more than seventy times, putting it in the same league as many of Beethoven's symphonies.) Strauss once claimed that he merely took over the waltz form from his father, and indeed the structure of Johann II's waltzes is similar to the later works of his elders: slow introduction, five repetitions of the waltz and a quick coda. However, Johann II greatly increased the length of the central sections, introduced a greater sense of homogeneity to the whole piece, and enhanced the textural complexities, which makes his waltzes much more satisfying as concert music. But ultimately, of course, this is music to move to. If you don't have a ballroom at your disposal, sample the following CDs sparingly, because you can only listen to so many waltzes before going berserk. Taken in measured doses, however, they'll cheer you up in almost any circumstances.

⊙ **New Year's Day Concert 1989**: Vienna Philharmonic Orchestra; Kleiber (Sony SX2K 45564; 2 CDs).
⊙ **New Year's Day Concert 1992**: Vienna Philharmonic Orchestra; Kleiber (Sony SK 45808).
⊙ **Strauss Waltzes and Polkas**: Vienna Philharmonic Orchestra; Krauss (Biddulph WHL001).

Naturally, for such spontaneous music, live recordings are preferable to studio efforts, and Kleiber's two New Year's Day concerts in Vienna are as witty and thrilling as could be wished for, with the conductor teasing the orchestra into giving him ever more sparkle and zest. The only studio sessions to match the vivacity of Kleiber's live sets are Clemens Krauss's mercurial performances from the 1940s; the sound quality is poor but the conductor's freedom and enthusiasm compensate for any such considerations.

RICHARD STRAUSS

(1864–1949)

In the years after the death of Wagner it was Richard Strauss who carried the banner of German music into the twentieth century. He was the last great German Romantic, but the trajectory of his career was more convoluted than such a definition suggests. Having burst onto the scene as the composer of feverishly ardent orchestral pieces, he went on to produce operas as progressive and discomforting as any of their time, before switching to decorous, slightly decadent and often ironic conservatism. However, through each phase of Strauss's long life, from the sweeping indulgence of *Don Juan* to the delicate eighteenth-century charm of *Capriccio*, there runs a fundamentally consistent harmonic and melodic style, marked above all by a Mozartian tunefulness. Like Mozart, Strauss possessed an amazing technical facility, and his abilities did some-

times lead to passages of weightless note-spinning, but he was constitutionally incapable of writing anything slipshod or unenjoyable. Often depicted as the traditionalist opponent of modernism, even the epitome of bourgeois complacency (few composers ever enjoyed Strauss's financial success), he has now come to seem like a prophet of the postmodern age, in which irony and pastiche are perceived as radical procedures.

He was born in Munich, the son of the principal horn player in the Bavarian Court Opera, who instructed him in music's fundamentals. He took piano lessons from the age of four, began composing two years later and, requiring no formal musical tuition, received a traditional, rounded education. After the composition of his Brahmsian *Symphony No. 1* in 1880, Strauss scored

POPPERFOTO

something of a success with his *Serenade* for wind instruments, which in turn induced Hans von Bülow to commission a suite from him in 1882. By 1885 he has succeeded von Bülow as principal conductor at Meiningen, a post he left the following year to journey to Italy, where he composed his first symphonic poem, *Aus Italien*. Upon his return, he was appointed conductor at the Munich Opera.

Having achieved provincial success as a conductor, Strauss struck international success as a composer in 1889 with *Don Juan*, a flamboyant tone poem that established him as the most exciting composer in Germany, a position secured by a string of virtuosic orchestral pieces written between 1895 and 1899. During the next six years he concentrated chiefly on conducting, though in 1901 he produced his first successful opera, *Feuersnot*. In 1905 he shocked audiences with his interpretation of Oscar Wilde's *Salome*, then four years later repeated the outrage with *Elektra*: both works were decried for their moral corruption, while the music was deemed dissonant and unintelligible. After *Elektra* it seemed inevitable that Strauss would cross over into outright atonality, but *Der Rosenkavalier*, composed only two years later, turned out to be a sumptuously tonal and charmingly elegant comedy. The volte-face caused much consternation, but *Der Rosenkavalier* established itself immediately as his operatic masterpiece, and its reputation has remained intact ever since.

In 1915 Strauss completed *Ein Alpensinfonie*, which, with the exception of *Metamorphosen* and the *Four Last Songs*, turned out to be his last large-scale non-operatic work. From then on, having completely mastered his craft, Strauss settled into the composition of opera, never looking back to the extremes of *Elektra*, never tempted by the formal innovations of Schoenberg and the Second Viennese School. Living in a plush villa in Garmisch, not far from Munich, Strauss wrote prolifically and was amply rewarded for his work, but a problematic chapter in his life began in 1933, when the Nazis appointed him President of the Reichsmusikkammer, a job that effectively made him the national representative of German music. For two years he seems to

have been content to fulfill the function required of him, disengenuously maintaining the belief that he could serve German music in the Reich without serving the Reich itself. However, two years later he had to choose between loyalty to the abstraction of German culture and loyalty to a Jewish individual, the writer Stefan Zweig, with whom he was working. He refused to condemn Zweig, was removed from his post, and from that point on was merely tolerated by the Nazis. He remained in Germany until the war's end, when he was investigated as a Nazi collaborator, and acquitted. In 1947 he took his first flight in an aeroplane to travel to London, where he was honoured as the greatest living German composer. Strauss died in his villa shortly after celebrating his eighty-fifth birthday.

OPERA

The major part of Strauss's life was dedicated to opera and of all twentieth-century operatic composers only Puccini could match his fluency. His first opera, *Guntram*, was a Wagnerian experiment, interesting solely for one glorious tune in the final act. Similarly, his Bavarian folk-tale *Feuersnot*, though showing Strauss's ever increasing understanding of the orchestra and human voice, is little more than a Wagnerian homage. With *Salome* and *Elektra* he arrived at a unique expressionistic style, to which he returned – after the recidivistic *Der Rosenkavalier* and his delightful chamber opera *Ariadne auf Naxos* – in the extremely complicated and not altogether successful symbolist drama, *Die Frau ohne Schatten*, composed in 1919. After *Die Frau* Strauss produced nothing of comparable quality until 1933 when he wrote *Arabella*, a work along the same mock-classical lines as *Rosenkavalier*. Five years later came *Daphne*, followed in 1942 by his fifteenth and final work for the stage, *Capriccio*.

The vividness of characterization in Strauss's work is partly attributable to the quality of the writers with whom he collaborated. Of all these librettists the greatest was Hugo von Hofmannsthal, with whom Strauss established a relationship as productive as that of Mozart and da Ponte: four of the five operas they produced together – *Elektra*, *Der Rosenkavalier*, *Ariadne auf Naxos* and *Arabella* – represent the pinnacle of Strauss's operatic art. Precise delineation of character is only part of the appeal of Strauss's operas, however, for they provide some of the most hedonistic pleasures to be found in twentieth-century music. Above all, they are typified by lushly expressive harmony, elastic and extended melody, ingenious orchestrations and an unrivalled understanding of the female voice.

SALOME

It was the premiere of *Salome* on December 1905 that catapulted Strauss into superstardom. Oscar Wilde's drama, originally in French, translated into German by Hedwig Lachmann and cut into shape by Strauss himself, formed the basis for the shocking libretto. Herod arrests and jails John the Baptist (Jokanaan), who then rejects the advances of Salome, Herod's step-daughter. Salome performs the Dance of the Seven Veils for Herod on condition that he give her anything she asks for. Herodias, her mother, tells her to ask for the head of Jokanaan. The severed head is brought out on a platter and in a final scene of immense length and power, she kisses its lips. In disgust, Herod has her crushed to death.

Salome is an intoxicating evocation of depravity and madness. The headily erotic decadence of the narrative is conveyed by music of unprecedented colour, and Strauss's portrayal of Herodias's necrophilic daughter is of awesome emotional strength. Strauss described the title part as a role "for a sixteen-year-old-girl with the voice of Isolde" and this is indeed one of the most demanding soprano roles, as Salome is rarely off stage during the continuous ninety minutes of the opera. Though *Salome* is not imitative of Wagner in the way Strauss's earliest efforts were, this through-composed opera still owes much to Wagner in its use of the orchestra (which is dominant throughout), in its system of leitmotifs and in its vocal writing, which alternates between declamation and sustained melodic lines of thrilling richness.

Birgit Nilsson, the scariest Salome

⊙ Nilsson, Hoffman, Waechter, Stolze, Veasey; Vienna Philharmonic Orchestra; Solti (Decca 414414-2; 2 CDs).

Birgit Nilsson's Salome generates the sort of tension more commonly found in the theatre than on record, while Eberhard Wächter is a grand but lyrical Jokanaan and Gerhard Stolze is a revolting Herod. Solti's conducting is the best testimony to his gift for Strauss's music, and the Vienna Philharmonic make an indecently sumptuous sound, revelling in the sweatiness of Strauss's colossal score. A legendary performance, tightly recorded.

ELEKTRA

Elektra (1909) was the first Strauss opera with a text by Hofmannsthal, who here provided Strauss with a libretto (based on his own play) that remains one of the greatest of all operatic texts. The immediacy of Elektra's hatred for her mother Klytemnestra, her love for her brother Orestes and her disgust with her sister Chrysothemis inspired Strauss to heights even he could never equal. Elektra's savage desire for her mother's death (in revenge for Klytemnestra's killing of Agamemnon, Elektra's father) is realised in a characterization of chilling dramatic depth and though all the characters are essentially grotesque, Klytemnestra, for whom Strauss composed his only atonal music, is the most disgusting creation in his entire output. Orestes is the opera's weakest portrayal but his contribution is of little relevance until the climax.

This astonishing one-act opera is sumptuously Romantic yet dissonant, so that its dozens of melodies are not immediately apparent, but rather blossom to surface as your ear becomes accustomed to the textures. The first audiences had problems with Strauss's complicated and heavy counterpoint, his virtuosic orchestrations and his insistent use of polytonality, but the superb vocal writing quickly made it a soprano's favourite. Especially memorable are Elektra's and Chrysothemis's monologues, the recognition scene between Elektra and Orestes, and the final duet for the two sisters, when Elektra performs a hysterical, fatal victory dance.

🌓 Borkh, Madeira, Schech, Uhl, Fischer-Dieskau; Dresden Staatskapelle Chorus & Orchestra; Böhm (Deutsche Grammophon 431 737-2; 2 CDs).

Jean Madeira in suitably fragile as Chrysothemis and Fischer-Dieskau copes well with Orestes' extended range but it is the instinctive partnership between Borkh and Böhm that marks this performance out as the finest on record. Inge Borkh is just about perfect in the title role, producing a fearsome mixture of hysteria, compassion, love and vehement determination. Böhm's tempi are very quick, creating a momentum that is only briefly stilled in the magical recognition scene, and yet this is performance that makes much of the sweeping Romantic gestures. The Staatskapelle are in superb form and the recording is as realistic as can be imagined.

DER ROSENKAVALIER

After the excesses of the one-act shockers, Strauss and Hofmannstahl turned in 1911 to Mozartian comedy with *Der Rosenkavalier*, which has always been the most popular Strauss opera. Subtitled "a comedy for music", it is set in Vienna in the middle of the eighteenth century, and adopts a neo-classical framework for its bitter-sweet tale of romantic love, in which Baron Ochs (a "rural Don Giovanni" in Strauss's words), intends to marry the young Sophie, but is thwarted when she ends up falling for Octavian, the lover of the Marschallin and the "Rose Cavalier" of the title. In the end the young lovers are

united, and the ageing Ochs and Marschallin withdraw from the scene. Boasting a subtle and clever libretto, and Strauss's most delicate and seductively tuneful score, *Der Rosenkavalier* is a perfect combination of good humour, high farce, deep sentiment and pleasant sentimentality. The smoothness of the dramatic action, the fullness of characterization and the graceful profusion of melody make *Der Rosenkavalier* a worthy homage to the art of Mozart.

Central to *Der Rosenkavalier* are its waltzes, which are derived from the music of Schubert, Lanner and Johann Strauss the Younger, but are treated in so refined a way as to cheat the ear into believing thye could have been a feature of eighteenth-century musical life. The enchanted atmosphere of these waltzes is sustained in moments of intense lyrical beauty: the tenor's "Italian" aria and final scene of Act One, the presentation of the rose in Act Two and the famous final soprano Trio of Act Three are among the most overwhelmingly beautiful music composed this century.

🌓 Schwarzkopf, Ludwig, Stich-Randall, Edelmann; Philharmonia Orchestra; Karajan (EMI CDS7 49354; 3 CDs).
⚫ Crespin, Minton, Donath, Wiener; Vienna State Opera; Solti (Decca 417 493-2; 3 CDs).

Schwarzkopf was famous in two of the principal female leads in *Rosenkavalier* but it was with the Marschallin that her name was most frequently associated. For Karajan's first account of the opera Schwarkopf, Christa Ludwig (Octavian) and Theresa Stich-Randall (Sophie) produced an ensemble performance of indescribable humanity. Otto Edelmann as the bumbling Baron Ochs is also splendid and Nicolai Gedda gives a charming account of the Act One tenor aria. Karajan presides over the glowing pit of sound with extreme sensitivity to the individual qualities of his singers' voices. Good sound for 1957.

Solti's version has better sound but has an over-inflated view of some of the more purple passages. Régine Crespin makes a touching Marschallin, Yvonne Minton is a full-voiced Octavian, and the lecherous Baron Ochs is the brilliantly characterized by Otto Wiener.

ARIADNE AUF NAXOS

Ariadne auf Naxos (1916) is Strauss at his most economical, using a chamber-sized orchestra for large-scale effects. The opera began as an entertainment to follow a production of Molière's play *Le Bourgeois Gentilhomme*; Strauss then revised it, adding a prologue showing preparations for the performance of the opera in a Viennese nobleman's home. To save time before his big fireworks display, the patron insists that the opera be played simultaneously with a *commedia dell'arte* piece, and the ensuing mix-ups provide plenty of opportunities for musical pastiche and musings on the nature of operatic art. Containing lyrical outpourings for the soprano lead, interspersed with comic scenes and arias for the burlesque troupe, *Ariadne auf Naxos* is an entertainingly self-referential musical hybrid.

> ◗ Janowitz, King, Geszty, Zylis-Gara, Prey; Dresden State Opera; Kempe (EMI CMS 7 64159-2; 2 CDs).

Kempe's performance is a joy from beginning to end. The orchestra is superb in this often subtle score, and Gundula Janowitz is a searing Ariadne, supported by a fine cast of Dresden regulars such as Peter Schreier and Hermann Prey.

ARABELLA

Strauss and Hofmannsthal returned to Viennese social comedy with *Arabella* (1930–32), their last collaboration. There are considerable atmospheric and musical similarities between *Der Rosenkavalier* and *Arabella* (waltzes are prevalent in both, for instance), but the latter, set during a carnival in the middle of the nineteenth-century, has closer affinities with the world of operetta than with Mozart. An impoverished noble family seeks a suitor for their elder daughter, Arabella. To save the expense of having two debutante daughters, the younger, Zdenka, is kept dressed as a boy. Zdenka impersonates Arabella in order to win the man of her dreams, Matteo, one of Arabella's suitors. Arabella is wrongly accused of infidelity by an eligible character called Mandryka, but Zdenka confesses and there follows a double engagement and happy ending.

Critics tended to react to Arabella as though it were just a weak imitation of *Rosenkavalier*, and certainly the characters are less immediate in the later work. On the other hand, the orchestration is irresistibly luscious and the vocal writing is amazingly opulent, especially for the women, as with

Rosenkavalier. Supreme among its many memorable episodes are the Act One duet between Arabella and Zdenka and the confession of love between Arabella and Mandryka, but the dreamy melodic invention never really flags at any point.

> ◗ della Casa, Rothenberger, Fischer-Dieskau, Uhl; Bavarian State Opera Chorus & Orchestra; Keilberth (Deutsche Grammophon 437 700-2; 3 CDs).

Lisa della Casa recorded the role of Arabella twice: in the studio with Solti in 1957 and live with Keilberth in 1963. The latter is miraculous. Della Casa is in incandescent form, producing impeccably seamless yet varied tone in a performance that is tearful with emotion; her duet with Fischer-Dieskau is the most ravishing declaration of love you'll ever hear. Much of the glory should go to Keilberth, whose effortless conducting encourages all the singers to revel in their wonderful music: his tempi veer from fast to snail's pace and yet they always flow with the music.

CAPRICCIO

Capriccio (1942), Strauss's farewell to opera, is explicitly about that art form. The complicated but highly engaging libretto, written with the conductor Clemens Krauss, addresses the problem of the precedence of words or music in opera, a dilemma presented as an argument between a poet and musician, who are competing for the hand of a Countess. In acknowledgement of the symbiotic relationship between music and text, the question is left hanging, and the Countess's concluding monologue sees her undecided between her suitors.

Strauss labelled *Capriccio* "no work for the public, only a fine dish for connoisseurs", but there's more than a touch of weary irony here. The subtitle – "conversation piece for music" – tells you what's in store in a work in which the dramatic pulse of Strauss's earlier operas has been replaced by something more cerebral and considered. The composer who had represented the last flourishing of Romanticism here ends his operatic career with a statement of calm resignation, in music decorated with Rococo touches and witty musical parodies.

> ⦿ Janowitz, Fischer-Dieskau, Schreier, Prey, Troyanos, Auger; Bavarian Radio Orchestra; Böhm (Deutsche Grammophon 419 023-2; 2 CDs).

Böhm was a close friend of Strauss, and this recording reveals the depth of his affinity with his music. He was fortunate in having one of the best-ever Strauss casts: Gundula Janowitz's Countess is effortlessly convincing, and Hermann Prey as the poet treats his performance almost as an extended song recital. This sense of intimacy is maintained throughout, and the final scene in particular has a translucent delicacy.

ORCHESTRAL MUSIC

Strauss first achieved fame for his mastery of the orchestra, as demonstrated in the set of massive tone poems he produced in the last years of the nineteenth century: principally *Don Juan*, *Tod und Verklärung*, *Till Eulenspiegel*, *Also Sprach Zarathustra*, *Don Quixote* and *Ein Heldenleben*. Notable for their flamboyant gestures, complicated counterpoint and remarkable melodies, these pieces are the lineal descendents of the tone poems of Berlioz and Liszt, but their musical stories are even more expansive and dramatic. The expressive, pictorial and narrative elements of these orchestral works paved the way for his operas, and once he had embarked on his operatic career Strauss rarely returned to purely instrumental composition. However, towards the end of his life he created possibly his finest orchestral work, *Metamorphosen*, then brought the full panoply of his orchestral skills to bear in his valedictory *Vier letzte Lieder* (Four Last Songs).

DON JUAN

Don Juan set the musical world on fire in 1888. In less than twenty minutes of music Strauss showed himself to be both a classical master of his craft and a radical innovator, for the demands upon the orchestra (especially the horns) were more strenuous than anything even in Berlioz, and the sheer scale and drama of the scoring was shocking. The piece recounts the loves and losses of the amorous Don Juan, who is characterized throughout the score by a horn call of Wagnerian intensity. Some gushingly exciting string writing leads to a love scene in which the oboe solo prefigures many of the sentimental tunes that were to come in Strauss's operas. The finale, leading the anti-hero's damnation is a blazing crescendo that will knock your socks off.

Berlin Philharmonic Orchestra; Furtwängler (Deutsche Grammophon 427 782-2; with *Sinfonia Domestica*).

San Francisco Symphony Orchestra; Blomstedt (Decca 421 815-2; with *Ein Alpensinfonie*).

Furtwängler's 1947 recording of *Don Juan* is just about ideal. The power and sweep of his vision and the incredible passion with which he concludes the work has no comparison on disc. Herbert Blomstedt's modern and solid account for Decca is coupled with an unbeatable performance of the *Alpine Symphony* (1911–15), not the tautest of Strauss's orchestral works, but featuring a lustrous depiction of the dawn.

EIN HELDENLEBEN

When *Ein Heldenleben* was premiered in 1899 it caused a sensation, not because of its musical audacity but because of the arrogance of a composer who, at the age of thirty-five, could present the world with an autobiographical piece titled "A Hero's Tale". There's no point trying to argue away Strauss's overweening self-belief – he did, after all, once remark that he found himself "every bit as interesting as Caesar or Napoleon". The music itself, however, is a vigorous affirmation of life, realised in orchestration of sensational colour and imagination. The hero battles against the critics, who are portrayed by a bleating and dissonant wind section, and is both soothed and frustrated by his wife, depicted by the lead violin. His victory is hailed in "The Hero's Works of Peace", an eight-minute section in which Strauss packs in some thirty excerpts from his own catalogue, including all his other tone poems. "The Hero's Retirement from the World" ends the work: its tender duet for horn (himself) and violin (his wife) is perhaps the most beautiful bit of music outside his operas.

Vienna Philharmonic Orchestra; Krauss (Decca 425 993-2; with *Don Juan*).

Chicago Symphony Orchestra; Reiner (RCA 09026 60929-2; with *Also Sprach Zarathustra*).

These two superlative recordings both come from conductors who knew the composer well. Clemens Krauss, Strauss's helpmate on *Capriccio*, gives a splendidly tight performance that's notable above all for its irridescent instrumental textures; the only drawback to this marvellous disc is the inconsistent violin playing of Willi Boscovsky. Fritz Reiner, conducted the first Dresden performance of *Die Frau ohne Schatten*, gives a reading that is generally more muscular and hard-driven (the battle scene is suitably cacophonous), without being brutal. He brings out the part-writing with exemplary lucidity, and in the final part he employs the sweetest of tones to create a great Romantic wash of sound. Reiner's *Heldenleben* comes with a dynamic version of *Also Sprach Zarathustra*, a piece of music now known the world over as the theme from *2001, A Space Odyssey*.

METAMORPHOSEN

Strauss spent much of his life expressing the emotions of others; in *Metamorphosen* he expressed himself, pouring out his grief over the destruction of Dresden, Weimar and Munich in 1945. As he wrote shortly after: "history is almost entirely an unbroken chain of acts of stupidity and wickedness, every sort of baseness, greed, betrayal, murder and destruction. And how little those who are called upon to make history have learned from it." A single movement for twenty-three strings, *Metamorphosen* is based upon a motif taken from the funeral march of Beethoven's *Eroica*, and as the piece progresses its emotional state is transformed from grief-striken sombreness to grudging reconciliation, via music of the most trenchant anger.

◉ Berlin Philharmonic Orchestra; Furtwängler (Music & Arts CD719; with works by Debussy, Ravel and Honegger).
◉ London Festival Orchestra; Pople (ASV CD DCA 743; with Schoenberg, *Verklärte Nacht*).

Furtwängler's live Berlin performance from shortly after the war is possessed of a staggering emotional directness. He wrings every last drop of pathos from this awesome score and yet does it by adopting what might be regarded as excessively quick tempi. The recorded sound is offputting but no other performance comes so close to the work's desperation. Alternatively, Ross Pople's recording is extremely well played and the recorded sound just about the finest available. Tempi are slower and accents less pronounced, but his approach is still highly successful.

FOUR LAST SONGS

Like Grieg, Strauss learned most about the quality and capacity of the female voice from his wife, for whom he wrote a great deal of music, including his finest group of chamber songs, the four Op. 27, which were composed as a wedding present for her. The great majority of his two hundred songs are for soprano, and Strauss ended his life as a composer with a grandiloquent piece for soprano and orchestra, the *Four Last Songs*. They were not composed as a cycle – after Strauss's death, his publisher brought them together, gave them an opus number and saw to their first performance – but they indubitably work as one, for they share a mood of autumnal peace and absolute honesty in the face of death, and the music is of a consistent simplicity and clarity. After settings of three poems by Heine, the *Four Last Songs* concludes with a text by Eichendorff, *Im Abendrot* (At Sunset), where Strauss alters the last line from "Is that perhaps Death?" to "Is this perhaps Death?" This final song portrays an ageing couple watching the setting sun: as they close their eyes, their lives end to the sound of trilling flutes, signifying skylarks and the liberation of their souls. Some might find it maudlin, but for many people it's an acutely moving conclusion to one of the most intriguing careers in the history of music.

◗ della Casa; Vienna Philharmonic Orchestra; Böhm (Decca 425 959-2; with excerpts from *Arabella, Ariadne auf Naxos & Capriccio*).
◗ Janowitz; Berlin Philharmonic; Karajan (Deutsche Grammophon 23 888-2; with *Metamorphosen & Oboe Concerto*).

Della Casa's recording of the *Four Last Songs* is the finest ever made. Her limpid, tranquil tone is beautifully supported by Karl Böhm, who prevents the music from descending into sentimentality. A dry-eyed and dignified account, this recording is a wonderful testament to all those involved. Gundula Janowitz's is another famous account: her voice is creamier and her approach a touch more self-indulgent, but it's still splendid.

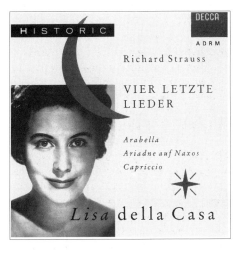

Lisa della Casa – the perfect voice for Strauss

IGOR STRAVINSKY

(1882–1971)

Like his friend Pablo Picasso, Igor Stravinsky became a modernist icon, an artist as well known to the general public as he was to the cognoscenti. And as with Picasso, people were never quite certain what Stravinsky was going to do next. He made his name with *The Firebird*, *Petrushka* and the *Rite of Spring*, Dionysian masterpieces that shocked and enthralled their first audiences. He then rejected the legacy of Romanticism and went into a neo-classical phase, an audacious change of direction, but not quite as extraordinary as the last volte-face of his career, when, in ripe old age, he threw in his hat with the serialist enemy. However, through all his metamorphoses Stravinsky remained a classicist at heart. Above all other things he loved precision, order and structure, and all his works have a consummate sense of poise. The Swiss writer C. F. Ramuz, who collaborated with Stravinsky on *L'Histoire du Soldat*, once wrote: "His writing desk resembled a surgeon's instrument case. Bottles of different coloured inks in their

ordered hierarchy each had a separate part to play in the ordering of his art . . . One was reminded of the definition of St Thomas: beauty is the splendour of order."

Stravinsky's early years gave little hint of the enfant terrible to come. Born near St Petersburg, he was a musical child and diligent student, but on the advice of his parents he studied law, thinking that profession a safer bet than a life devoted to music. In 1903 his encounter with the great pedagogue Rimsky-Korsakov (see p.295) changed the direction of his life. Rimsky took on Stravinsky as a private pupil, and Stravinsky soon resolved to try to make it as a composer, albeit against his teacher's advice.

By a stroke of good fortune Russia's leading impresario, Serge Diaghilev, happened to catch his first mature compositions – *Scherzo fantastique* and *Feu d'artifice* – at a St Petersburg concert in 1909, and promptly asked Stravinsky to write two numbers for a ballet he was producing. Stravinsky acquitted himself so well that Diaghilev commissioned

HULTON DEUTSCH

from him a score for his new Paris-based dance troupe, the Ballets Russes – and, as Diaghilev had predicted, the *Firebird* made Stravinsky famous overnight. Knowing that he was on to a good thing, Diaghilev persuaded Stravinsky to write an even more exotic Russian-style ballet for the next season. The result was *Petrushka*, a work which caused a stir with its daring polytonality and tart rhythms. This was nothing compared to the impact of Stravinsky's next ballet, the *Rite of Spring*. A score of unprecedented rhythmic and harmonic ferocity, it caused a riot at its premiere on May 29, 1913, and established Stravinsky as the prince of the avant-garde.

During World War I Stravinsky and his family found refuge in Switzerland, where wartime deprivation obliged him to think in terms of writing for small ensembles. *Les Noces* (1913–17) and *L'Histoire du soldat* (1918) showed Stravinsky developing leaner textures, and he spoke of the latter as his "final break with the Russian orchestral school". With the coming of peace in 1918, Stravinsky and his family settled in Paris, where the composer took up French citizenship. (Their planned return to Russia became impossible after the Communists confiscated their property and blocked Stravinsky's royalties.) At the behest of Diaghilev, Stravinsky began fashioning music for a ballet called *Pulcinella* (1920) out of some pieces by the eighteenth-century composer Pergolesi, a commission that marked the beginning of his neo-classical phase. Whereas Schoenberg devised the twelve-tone method as a modernist discipline to supplant the prescriptions of the past, Stravinsky reinvented the past, using its conventions as vessels for modern ideas. His neo-classicism was immensely fluid, adapting Handel and Gluck for *Oedipus Rex* (1927), Mozart in *The Rake's Progress* (1951), but running through most of his work for the next thirty years was an emphasis on classical elegance and clarity.

By the end of the 1930s Stravinsky was tiring of Europe: his wife and a daughter had both died of tuberculosis, war was once again about to break out, and the French critics who had once vilified *The Rite* were now carping about his supposed sell-out to neo-classicism. The USA seemed the obvious place to go: he had wealthy admirers there, and the conductor Serge Koussevitsky was proving a hugely influential champion of his work, having already commissioned the *Symphony of Psalms* for the fiftieth anniversary of the Boston Symphony Orchestra. In 1939 he made the move, taking with him his mistress, the painter Vera de Bossett, whom he married the following year. In 1940 Stravinsky and his family settled in Hollywood, where the cell of exiled European artists included Arnold Schoenberg, whom Stravinsky seems to have avoided.

During the 1940s he composed some magnificent neo-classical works, including the *Symphony in C* and *The Rake's Progress*, but then came his dramatic conversion to the serialist cause. The young American conductor Robert Craft discreetly introduced him to various key serial works, and Stravinsky became particularly taken with the crystalline scores of Anton Webern, declaring that "the serial composers are the only ones with a discipline that I respect". He now turned to twelve-note techniques with characteristic inventiveness and a vigour that was typified by the creation of the astringent *Agon* (1957) at the age of seventy-five. By now, such was Stravinsky's reputation that each new work was guaranteed several performances and a recording, however prickly its music language. In his last decade he achieved a degree of celebrity unmatched by any composer since Mozart, being fêted by Pope John Paul XXIII, by the Kennedys and, in a triumphant visit to Russia in 1962, by Nikita Kruschev. He died in New York on April 6, 1971, and was buried where he had asked to be – near to his old comrade Diaghilev, on Venice's cemetery island of San Michele.

○ The Igor Stravinsky Edition (Sony SX22K 46 290; 22 CDs).

Towards the end of his life Stravinsky gave a lot of his time to conducting and supervising performances of his works. Sony have gathered all of Stravinsky's performances of his own music, supplemented by recordings of those pieces he didn't conduct himself, into this immense set, which is available as one box of twenty-two CDs, or as twelve separate volumes. It has to be said that Stravinsky was not an outstanding conductor, and there are better recordings of much of his music, but this is nonetheless a great historical document – and Stravinsky's output was so vast that in several instances the Stravinsky edition offers the only opportunity of getting to know a piece on disc.

OEDIPUS REX

Based on Sophocles's most famous tragedy, Stravinsky's *Oedipus Rex* (1927), is a semi-abstract, ritualistic music drama that narrates its events in the simplest, starkest terms. The sense of Oedipus's story as the exemplar of inexorable fate is enhanced by the absolute detachment of the presentation, in which the arias and choruses are punctuated by short and simple texts delivered in French by a narrator who stands apart in modern clothes from the rest of the costumed cast, who are themselves not empowered to act or express any individuality. For the text of the vocal parts, Stravinsky and his collaborator Jean Cocteau settled on Latin as "a medium not dead, but turned to stone, and so monumental-ized as to have become immune from all risk of vulgarization". Narrative momentum and cohesion is created above all by the music: the drama of Oedipus Rex is static, but the score is awesomely powerful. This is also one of the most impressive displays of Stravinsky's allu-sive neo-classical technique, with its evoca-tions of such composers as Monteverdi, Handel, Mussorgsky and Verdi.

⊙ Cole, von Otter, Estes, Sotin, Gedda, Chereau; Eric Ericson Chamber Choir; Swedish Radio Symphony Orchestra & Chorus; Salonen (Sony SK48057).

The Swedish whizzkid Esa Pekka Salonen conducts the finest account of Stravinsky's opera-oratorio yet committed to disc. It is gripping from the first bar to the last, with the chorus and top-class singers as incisive as the orchestra.

SONY

Esa Pekka Salonen

THE RAKE'S PROGRESS

Stravinsky's only full-length opera was inspired by Hogarth's *Rake's Progress*, and its libretto (by W. H Auden and Chester Kallman) fleshes out the story told in Hogarth's prints, charting Tom Rakewell's descent through dissipation into madness. Appropriately enough, the musical language of this eighteenth-century morality tale is heavily indebted to Mozart – *The Rake's Progress* is constructed from solo and ensemble numbers which are accompanied by a small orchestra and strung together by recitatives accompanied by harpsichord. Needless to say, this is not an archaeological reconstruction of Hogarth's period but is rather a bitingly ironic work, in which the music's anachronisms mirror the moral discontinuites of Tom's career. Almost every-thing in this appears in quotation marks, so to speak, and its libretto – by W. H. Auden and Chester Kallmann – is perhaps the richest operatic text of this century. Dylan Thomas, after hearing the opera's first performance in Venice on September 11, 1951, was moved to remark that "Auden is the most skilful of us all". The opera demands a little effort but it does include some episodes of extraordi-nary directness: the final scene in Bedlam is saturated with desperate tragedy, and Anne Trulove's farewell to Tom is probably Stravinsky's most tender creation.

⊙ Langridge, Pope, Ramey, Walker, Dobson, Varnay; London Sinfonietta Chorus; London Sinfonietta; Chailly (Decca 411 644-2DH2; 2 CDs).

This brilliantly cast recording of the *Rake* has no equal. Philip Langridge's colourful characterization brings Tom's fall from grace to startling life, and Cathryn Pope is no less aware of her role's dimensions – the final scene is given an aching sense of pathos. The lively London Sinfonietta respond enthusiasti-cally to Chailly's light-footed direction, and the recording is clear and well balanced.

THE FIREBIRD

The Firebird (*L'Oiseau de feu*) is a straightfor-ward fairy tale, in which the Firebird helps a young prince to rescue a beautiful princess from an evil ogre, and in the process win her heart. Aspects of its musical language would have been familiar to its first Parisian audience in 1910, for Stravinsky borrows much from his teacher Rimsky-Korsakov, for example in his use of chromaticism for the ballet's magic creatures and of a modal-diatonic style for the mortals. Knowledgeable onlookers, however, realized that there was something much deeper here than another piece of Rimsky-style exoticism. Debussy for one was thrilled by its latent barbarism, and revelled in its "unusual combinations of rhythms".

🔘 Chicago Symphony Orchestra; Boulez (Deutsche Grammophon 437 850-2; with *Four Études; Fireworks*).

Boulez's second recording of the Firebird is as colourful and vivid as his original version, but even more tightly focused. The playing of the Chicago Symphony is characterized by great finesse and power.

PETRUSHKA

To quote Stravinsky, the central figure of *Petrushka* is "the immortal and unhappy hero of every fair in all countries"; more specifically, he's a "puppet, suddenly endowed with life, exasperating the patience of the orchestra". On June 13, 1911, the title role was danced by the legendary Nijinsky, ensuring that what was happening on stage was as remarkable as what was coming out of the orchestra pit. The ballet's burlesque and parodic elements are heightened by ever-shifting rhythms and a startling polytonal harmonic language – the juxtaposition of the two unrelated keys of C major and F sharp major in one section is typical of Stravinsky's brazen innovation. These advanced musical devices, which are primarily used for the appearances of Petrushka himself, are contrasted with the predominantly diatonic harmonies of the vivid crowd scenes.

🔘 Minnesota Symphony Orchestra; Dorati (Mercury 417 758-2DM; with *Rite of Spring*).

As with his performance of *The Rite* (see below), Dorati gives a blazingly urgent reading of Stravinsky's second seminal ballet.

THE RITE OF SPRING

The idea for the *Rite of Spring* (*Le Sacre du Printemps*) came to Stravinsky several years before he actually wrote it, as he was later to recount. "One day, when I was finishing the last pages of the *Firebird* in St Petersburg, I had a fleeting vision . . . I saw in my imagination a solemn pagan rite: sage elders, seated in a circle, watched a young girl dance herself to death. They were sacrificing her to propitiate the god of spring". In 1913 he unleashed the visceral music that this vision prompted, and the result was the most notorious premiere in the history of modern music. The catcalls started only seconds after the music, and soon Debussy was pleading vainly for people to calm down, while Ravel yelled "Genius, genius!" in the midst of fist-fights and screams of abuse so loud that the dancers were unable to hear the orchestra.

It is not difficult to understand why *The Rite of Spring* had such a profound effect. Written for a huge orchestra, it's unrelentingly barbaric in its dissonances and asymmetrical rhythms, jolting the listener into attention from first to last. *The Rite*'s defining quality is its thumping, irregular pulse, a rhythmic propulsion achieved through frequent changes in time signature – sometimes, as in the Sacrificial Dance, in every successive bar.

🔘 Minnesota Symphony Orchestra; Dorati (Mercury 417 758-2DM; with *Petrushka*).

Dorati's fiery temperament made him an ideal interpreter of the *Rite* and his various studio recordings of the work have never been bettered. The finest of all is the recording he made for Mercury: fast, furious and dangerous, this account lets you hear what Stravinsky wanted you to hear – "the whole earth cracking". Including Dorati's fire-breathing *Petrushka*, this disc is extraordinarily good value.

PULCINELLA

The ballet *Pulcinella*, written in 1920 for Diaghilev and the choreographer Massine, inaugurated Stravinsky's neo-classical period. Stravinsky's source material was a mélange of operas, cantatas, trio-sonatas and other pieces by Pergolesi (see p.265), which he turned into the music for a commedia dell'arte story. Although the orchestration of *Pulcinella* recalls a lean, eighteenth-century ensemble, Stravinsky gives Pergolesi's original melodies a modernist spin through a range of devices. The harmonies of *Pulcinella* are decidedly non-authentic, its rhythmic accents shift about ceaselessly, while its melodies sometimes seem to start in mid-stream, or stop short of a satisfactory resolution. The whole effect of *Pulcinella* is of an oscillation between passages of giddy energy and elegant if tentative repose.

⊙ Murray, Rolfe Johnson, Estes; Ensemble Intercontemporain; French National Orchestra; Boulez (Erato 2292-45382-2; with *Le chant du rossignol*).

As a young man Pierre Boulez was fond of heckling at premieres of new works from Stravinsky, in his capacity as standard-bearer of the avant-garde. He went on to become one of the finest conductors of twentieth-century music, and this meticulously lucid and sprightly reading of *Pulcinella* is a marvellous example of Boulez's ability to think himself into an aesthetic that is miles away from his own.

AGON

Completed in 1957 for George Balanchine's New York City Ballet, *Agon* is as abstract a dance piece as it's possible to write. The title means "contest" in Greek, and the work is can be read as a kind of dialectic between tradition and modernity. Starting with neoclassical fanfares, it becomes increasingly chromatic until it reaches fully fledged serialism, then at its conclusion returns to the tonal fanfares. Along the way you'll hear some of the finest dance music written this century, and if any single piece is going to convince you that serialism does not have to be hard work, *Agon* is it.

☽ Los Angeles Festival Symphony Orchestra; Stravinsky (Sony SM3K 46292; 3 CDs; with *Apollon musagette* and other ballets).

Agon is strangely under-represented in the CD catalogue – the only decent version is this one, made by the composer in the year of its premiere, and packaged in a three-CD set of the later ballets as part of Sony's monumental Stravinsky Edition. Stravinsky was sometimes a poor interpreter of his own music, but this is an assured and atmospheric account, theatrical without being mannered.

SYMPHONY OF PSALMS

The *Symphony of Psalms* (1930) is symphonic only in the loosest sense of the word, for in its treatment of chorus and orchestra it looks back to the choral works of the Baroque period rather than to archetypal classical models. Dedicated "to the glory of God", it was written not long after Stravinsky's conversion to Christianity and is imbued with the intensity of the first flood of faith. The Latin

texts of the three movements are taken from the Psalms, which the composer saw as "poems of exultation, but also of anger and judgement", and he responded with music in which self-expression is expunged in favour of humble devotion. The sound-world of *Symphony of Psalms* is austere, due in large part to the absence of the "warm" sonorities of the violin, viola and clarinet.

⊙ Suisse Romande Chamber Choir & Orchestra; Järvi (Chandos CHAN 9239; with *Concerto for Piano and Wind Instruments*; *Symphony in C*).

Järvi gives a performance of breathtaking beauty and power, inspiring his choral singers to pinpoint precision of ensemble. This is a strongly characterized reading, enhanced by first-rate recording quality.

SYMPHONY IN THREE MOVEMENTS

The *Symphony in Three Movements* (1943–45) was described by Stravinsky as his "War Symphony", and it is indeed one of the most significant compositions to come out of World War II – although unlike the war music of Prokofiev, Shostakovich and Richard Strauss, the *Symphony in Three Movements* reflects images seen on newsreels, rather than the direct experience of a country ravaged by armies. Stravinsky's hallmark techniques – prominence of wind instruments, rapid changes of time signature, astringent harmonies – are all employed to telling effect, and Stravinsky's loathing of fascism is nowhere better depicted than in the third movement, with its relentless march rhythms and sharp brass-band orchestration.

⊙ Berlin Radio Symphony Orchestra; Ashkenazy (Decca 436416-2 DH; with *Symphony in C*; *Symphony of Wind Instruments*).

Ashkenazy brings a jagged intensity to the *Symphony in Three Movements*, and the Berliners play with great precision and flair. The fill-up items are just as good, and the sound quality is finely detailed.

PIANO MUSIC

Stravinsky was a very accomplished pianist and composed a fair amount of music for the instrument, the best known being his stupendous arrangement of three movements from

Petrushka for Artur Rubinstein. Of the other, woefully overlooked piano pieces, the best are the two piano sonatas, the *Four Études* and the offbeat *Circus Polka*

The heavily Romantic early sonata was composed under Rimsky-Korsakov's guidance in 1903–04, and is extremely similar to the first sonatas of Rachmaninov, Prokofiev and Scriabin. The other sonata, written twenty years later, is also highly entertaining but in a rather more different manner – it's a fiendishly difficult piece, in places giving every finger its own clearly delineated role in the musical texture. The *Four Études* (1908) are just as difficult to play, with their complex rhythmic and polytonal experiments. They are by no means esoteric compositions, however. On the contrary, they are light, tuneful and immensely witty – the performer is the one who suffers, not the listener. Stravinsky at his wittiest appears in the *Circus Polka* of 1942, a piece commissioned by the Barnum and Bailey Circus, who wanted a work that could be danced by the troupe's elephants. Originally written for orchestra, it was later made into a wonderfully effective showpiece for piano.

◉ Three Movements from Petrushka: Pollini (Deutsche Grammophon 419 202-2GH; with music by Prokofiev, Boulez and Webern).
◉ Sonatas; Four Études; Circus Polka; Serenade; Tango; Piano Rag Music; Scherzo: Sangiorgio (Collins 13742).

Maurizio Pollini's recording of the *Three Movements from Petrushka* is a bewilderingly brilliant performance, taking the music at a speed that defies belief. Coupled with equally stunning accounts of other key twentieth-century piano pieces, this is Desert Island Disc material.

Victor Sangiorgio's recording of most of Stravinsky's piano compositions was one of the most entertaining piano CDs released in 1993. His understanding of the composer's orchestral style of writing and his affinity with Stravinsky's humour are apparent in every item, and his technique allows him to navigate easily this often horrendously difficult music. The recital is excellently recorded and well annotated.

═══════════════ ♭♮ ═══════════════

JOSEF SUK
(1874–1935)

Before he had reached the age of twenty, Josef Suk was being hailed as the musical heir of Antonín Dvořák, his father-in-law and teacher. He did indeed produce work that was remarkably similar to Dvořák's – the light-hearted and tuneful *Serenade for Strings* of 1892 shows a direct influence, for example. Yet the resemblances are less important than the differences between Dvořák and a composer he once accused of writing too much in the melancholic minor keys. Suk's music has amost nothing of the joyful pastoralism that's so common to Dvořák, and in his orchestral pieces – in particular *Asrael* – Suk's use of huge orchestral forces to create vast expressions of anguish suggest closer affinities with Mahler.

Suk received his first lessons from his father, a schoolmaster and choir director in Bohemia. In 1885 he entered the Prague conservatory where, three years later, he began studying chamber music with the cellist Dennis Wihan – a friend of both Dvořák and Richard Strauss. After six years he graduated but remained at the conservatory for a further year in order to pursue his lessons with Wihan and begin studies with Dvořák. It was at this time that Suk joined the Czech Quartet, an ensemble with whom he was to play some four thousand concerts until his retirement in 1933. In 1898, he married Dvořák's daughter Otilie, and was by then acknowledged as one of the most important Czech composers.

However, he never really established himself outside his native country and for the rest of his life he remained something of a peripheral figure, bathing in the light shed by his father-in-law more than in the glory of his own reputation. Nowadays, although sporadic attempts are made to bring his music to wider audiences, he is still widely known for just one work.

ASRAEL SYMPHONY

Suk was at his best working on a large scale, and his most popular work, the massive symphony of mourning called *Asrael*, is the finest example of his expressive, late Romantic style. Taking its title from the name of the Islamic angel of death, the symphony was written in response to the death of Dvořák in 1904 and the death of Suk's own wife a year later. The five-movement symphony, with its concentration of slow movements, is saturated with a sense of loss, conveyed in music of cathartic intensity – in the depths of his grief, Suk wrote that he was "saved by music". Though to an extent indebted to Mahler in its funereal idiom and to Strauss in its orchestration, *Asrael* is one of the finest orchestral works of its time.

⦿ Royal Liverpool Philharmonic Orchestra; Pešek (Virgin VC7 91221-2).

The *Asrael* Symphony has found considerable popularity in recent years and a number of recordings are now available. Libor Pešek's account with the RLPO makes a convincing case for this mighty work: his tempi brings heart-rending gravity to the symphony, and the work's plush sonorities are given fabulous colour and shape.

ARTHUR SULLIVAN
(1842–1900)

"They trained him to make Europe yawn" ran George Bernard Shaw's obituary of Arthur Sullivan, referring to music that has now been forgotten, despite Sullivan's angst at not being able to devote more time to it. But Arthur Sullivan hangs on as the composing half of Gilbert and Sullivan, creators of a uniquely English blend of social satire, burlesque and sophisticated musical parody.

He was born in Lambeth in 1842, and was accepted into the Royal Academy of Music in 1856. Studies at the Leipzig Conservatory between 1858 and 1861 culminated in a performance of his Mendelssohnian overture to *The Tempest*. He wrote a ballet and in 1867 visited Vienna, where he discovered a lost Schubert score, which did his credentials as a serious musician no harm at all. In the same year he met W. S. Gilbert.

The first fruit of their partnership, *Thespis*, closed to mixed reviews, and Sullivan returned to teaching and religious composition – including the hymn *Onward Christian Soldiers*. His permanent reunion with Gilbert was brought about by the impresario Richard d'Oyly Carte, who suggested the plot of what became *Trial by Jury* (1875), a work so successful that a string of collaborations followed, including *The Sorcerer* (1877), *HMS Pinafore* (1878), *The Pirates of Penzance* (1880), *Patience* (1881), and *Iolanthe* (1882).

In 1882 Sullivan was knighted. Honours notwithstanding, his frustration at his diet of musical frivolity came to a head with *Princess Ida* (1884), and off he stormed to tour Europe. Carte negotiated a truce between him and Gilbert, and after a lot more bickering *The Mikado* took shape. It was, in the view of Ethyl Smyth (see p.345), their masterpiece; within four years *The Gondoliers* and *The Yeomen of the Guard* were to follow.

A quarrel and lawsuit between Gilbert and Sullivan in 1890 was later patched up, but it ended their creative streak. Sullivan died ten years later, in his own estimation a shadow of what he should have been. A jaunty *Symphony in E* hints at what he might have achieved, had Gilbert never turned up. As it is, he's forever shackled to Gilbert, with whom he created a sequence of crisp, witty and untranslatable works of art. Sullivan represents the acceptable face of Little Englandism.

HMS PINAFORE AND THE MIKADO

Sullivan never wrote sprightlier music, and Gilbert rarely wrote better lines, than for *HMS Pinafore*, a brisk satire on social divisions. At the centre of the machinations are humble seaman Ralph Rackstraw and Captain Corcoran, who have to swap places instantly when it turns out that they were mixed up as toddlers. This changes the context for three romantic entanglements: Ralph's love for Josephine, Corcoran's daughter (which he dared not announce); Josephine's love for Ralph (which she'd suppressed out of snobbery); and the loveless engagement which is being manoeuvred between Josephine and the talentless "Ruler of the Queen's Navee", the Rt Hon Sir Joseph Porter, KCB.

Librettist and composer were at their most epigrammatic and imaginative in *The Mikado*, which was their longest-running show. A hugely popular exhibition of Japanese products in Knightsbridge suggested the setting, but the work's orientalism is only skin-deep: the absurdly convoluted tale, tying together such characters as Ko-Ko the Lord High Executioner, Pooh-Bah "the Lord High Everything Else", the wandering minstrel Nanki-Poo and the lovely Pitti-Sing ("Pretty Thing" in baby talk), is a satire aimed at the absurdites of British society. The wit of Sullivan's music can be gauged by the fact that *The Mikado* manages to incorporate a genuine Japanese tune (used for the entrance of the Mikado himself), an English madrigal and a Bach fugue, and still sounds completely coherent.

> ◗ **HMS Pinafore**: Reed, Skitch, Round, Adams, Hindmarsh, Wright, Knight; D'Oyly Carte Opera Chorus; New Symphony Orchestra of London; Godfrey (Decca 414 283-2; 2 CDs).
> ● **The Mikado**: Adams, Johnson, Suart, Van Allan, Folwell, McLaughlin, Howells, Watson, Palmer; Orchestra and Chorus of Welsh National Opera; Mackerras (Telarc CD-80284).

Isadore Godfrey creates a *Pinafore* of great pace, with comically effete top brass and excellently performed spoken dialogue. Inclusion of the spoken parts isn't so important with *The Mikado*, so the best recording to go for is Mackerras's performance of the edited score: this the freshest version you'll find, alert yet relaxed, serious without being stolid.

━━━━━━━━━━━ ♮ ━━━━━━━━━━━

KAROL SZYMANOWSKI
(1882–1937)

Karol Szymanowski, the most prominent Polish composer of the twentieth century, is comparable to Bartók in the way he forged a distinctive style out of the folk music of his native land, but there's another important component to his achievement. Many of his visionary scores constitute a personal celebration of Dionysus and ecstatic love, exemplified by works such as the opera *King Roger*, *Symphony No. 3 – Song of the Night* and the two violin concertos, all of which create an opulent soundworld full of yearning melodies and filigree decoration. If any music could be said to be heavily perfumed, it's Szymanowski's.

Szymanowski was born in Tymoszówka in the Ukraine, to a musical family whose life seems to have been a continuous round of dances, plays and music. The poet Jarosław Iwaszkiewicz, with whom Szymanowski later worked on *King Roger* and the ballet *Harnasie*, left accounts of the elaborate fancy-dress balls for which Karol and his elder brother Felix composed the music. Of the five children in the family, three went on to become professional musicians – his sister Stasia became an opera singer and starred as *Roxana* in the first performance of *King Roger*.

Yet in his early years Szymanowski found little to inspire him in Poland, a country then partitioned between Germany, Russia and the Habsburg Empire. His musical interests lay with foreign composers such as Richard

Strauss, Debussy, Scriabin and Stravinsky, and he felt a deep affinity with Italy, Sicily and North Africa, regions he explored in 1911 and 1914 with Stefan Spiess, probably his lover. The cultures of ancient Greece, Norman Sicily and the Arab world had a huge and lasting impact on his music.

World War I and the Russian Revolution completely overturned Szymanowski's world – the house at Tymoszówka was destroyed by the Bolsheviks in 1917, and he was unable to compose amidst the upheaval. Instead he wrote a novel called *Efebos*, "in order to exorcise the black pit of an endless succession of days, weeks and months . . . by a magical vision of Italy." The book was also an exploration of homosexual love and Szymanowski didn't want it published during his mother's lifetime; the manuscript was kept by Jarosław Iwaszkiewicz and was destroyed by fire in Warsaw in 1939.

An independent Poland emerged out of the chaos of World War I, and like many Polish intellectuals Szymanowski was determined to create a truly national art. In the exotic pieces for which he first gained international recognition – works such as the *Symphony No. 3*, the *Violin Concerto No. 1* and *King Roger* – he resisted using folk material out of a fear of its limitations ("Poland's national music should not be the stiffened ghost of the polonaise or mazurka" he wrote). However, in the early 1920s a meeting with Stravinsky and the direct experience of *Le Sacre de Printemps* and *Les Noces* showed him a way to use folk elements in a completely unsentimental way.

During the 1920s he spent more and more time in Zakopane, at the heart of a distinctive folk culture of the Tatra mountains. A key member of the group of prominent intellectuals who called themselves "the emergency ambulance service of Tatra culture", Szymanowski befriended the Obrochta family – one of the leading bands of village musicians – and began to notate the strange and idiosyncratic sounds of *gorale* (highland) music. In the words of a surviving member of the Obrochta clan: "Szymanowski went everywhere searching for music . . he always had a note-pad with him". The main work to come out of this research was the ballet *Harnasie* (1923–31), a tale of highland brigands culminating in a village wedding, a score which includes many genuine *gorale* dances. Alongside *Harnasie*, Szymanowski worked on his austerely beautiful *Stabat Mater* (1926), a piece that uses the ancient traditions of Polish church music, but in a much less self-conscious and bombastic way than *Harnasie* uses folk melodies.

During the last decade of his life Szymanowski took over the directorship of the Warsaw conservatory but suffered increasingly from health problems as the first signs of tuberculosis appeared. This was not a fruitful period as a composer, but he completed two major works, the *Symphonie Concertante* for piano and orchestra and the second violin concerto, both of which have characteristics of Polish folk music, combined with the lush exoticism of his earlier style. His last years were a sad story of failing health, financial hardship and neglect in Poland, but at least he had growing success abroad – *King Roger* was triumphantly received in Prague and *Harnasie* likewise in Paris. Szymanowski died in a sanatorium in Lausanne and received a huge state funeral in Kraków, with the Obrochtas playing beside his tomb.

KING ROGER

The opening of *Król Roger* (1924) is one of the most extraordinary of any opera. The curtain rises on a service in the Palermo cathedral during the twelfth-century reign of King Roger, as choral music evokes clouds of incense and glistening mosaics. A mysterious shepherd arrives to preach a new faith of ecstasy and love ("My god is as young and beautiful as I am") – he is the embodiment of the union between Christ, Dionysus and Eros, a mystical idea sketched by Szymanowski in his novel *Efebos*. Roger's wife Roxana and many of his subjects find the shepherd's message intoxicating, and the opera culminates in a ritual in an ancient Greek theatre: the shepherd is transformed into Dionysus, while Roger – also transformed by the experience – salutes Apollo and the rising sun.

The opera is rarely performed, perhaps because it is essentially contemplative rather than dramatic. The music, though, has some breathtaking set pieces – the opening

Karol Szymanowski KönigRoger op.46
Król Roger · King Roger · le Roi Roger

The most recent recording of Szymanowski's opera

religious service, the arias of the shepherd and Roxana, a wild Dionysiac dance and the final hymn. Szymanowski was working on the score just after hearing Ravel's *Daphnis et Chloé* in America, and it shows the composer indulging in orientalist fantasy at its most full-blown.

⊙ Hiolski, Rumowska, Pustelak; Choir and Orchestra of the Teatr Wielki, Warsaw; Mierzejewski (Olympia OCD 303; with *Harnasie*; 2 CDs).
⊙ Skulski, Zagórzanka, Kowalski; Choir and Orchestra of the Teatr Wielki, Warsaw; Satanowski (Koch Schwann 314 014; 2 CDs).

The Olympia recording was made in 1965 but stands up very well, with an incredible sense of awe and spectacle in the opening scene. What's more it comes with a decent performance of *Harnasie* as a fill-up. The Schwann recording from 1988 is technically superior, with a much greater dynamic range, and it does have the advantage of a libretto, but it misses the theatrical and dramatic quality of the older version.

HARNASIE

Szymanowski is sometimes called the Polish Bartók, but he's far less rigorous and economical with his material, favouring a more rhapsodic and colourful approach. Typical of Szymanowski's style is *Harnasie*, his most ambitious attempt at reworking highland folk music in symphonic form. The music is scored for a massive orchestra plus tenor soloist and chorus, which often seems overblown for melodies and dances that belong to a small village ensemble, but there is no

denying its vigour and local colour, with the orchestra recreating the typical melodies and harmonies of *gorale* music.

⊙ Choir and Orchestra of the Teatr Wielki, Warsaw; Satanowski (Koch Schwann 311 064).

This wonderfully clear and vivid recording of Szymanowski's ballet is coupled with another interesting ballet score, *Mandragora*. There is an alternative version of *Harnasie* coupled with *King Roger on Olympia* (see above), but it's more heavy-handed than this one.

STABAT MATER

Szymanowski made a study of sixteenth-century Polish church music in preparation for writing the *Stabat Mater*, and the results are plain in the simplicity and purity of the piece, which makes an interesting counterweight to the lush scores of *King Roger* and *Symphony No. 3*. Gone is the over-chromatic harmony that dominates so much of his earlier work, replaced by simpler chords and finely placed tensions and dissonances. Szymanowski was not a religious man, and perhaps his indifference to the established church helped him to maintain the detachment that makes this his masterpiece. Szymanowski described the work as a peasant requiem (the text is in Polish, not Latin), and it has the same qualities of naïve directness as the paintings that adorn some of the ancient wooden churches of southern Poland.

⊙ Szmytka, Garrison; City of Birmingham Symphony Orchestra; Rattle (EMI CDC5 55121-2; with *Symphony No. 3*).

The *Stabat Mater* contains some of Szymanowski's most beautiful music and this is the finest recording of it. The opening of the last movement, for instance, with the soprano solo rising from soft dissonances with the clarinets to a glowing major chord with the chorus, is a sublime moment. If this can't win new fans for Szymanowski, nothing can. Rattle controls the ebb and flow perfectly, moving from rapt intensity to outbursts of passion.

SYMPHONY NO. 3

Szymanowski's *Symphony No. 3*, subtitled *Song of the Night* (1916) is the most lavish of his large-scale compositions. Fascinated by eastern mysticism, he turned for inspiration to the writings of the thirteenth-century Persian poet Jelal-ad-din Rumi, the founder of the Mevlevi (or Whirling Dervishes). Like other Sufi sects, the Mevlevi strove to attain an ecstatic relationship with God, and the poem from which *Symphony No. 3* is derived is typical of their art, celebrating the beauties and mysteries of an eastern night. Szymanowski was no Persian scholar, but his instinctive response to this text produced an opulent, intoxicating score full of langour and intense emotion.

> ◉ City of Birmingham Symphony Orchestra; Rattle (EMI CDC5 55121-2; with *Stabat Mater*).

Simon Rattle – Szymanowski's most persuasive advocate

All Szymanowski's colouristic effects shine through on this wonderful recording, particularly the languorous melodies on the solo violin and the glittering flashes on piano, harp and percussion. After this performance you can understand Lutosławski's comment that listening to this music was like opening a gate onto a fantastic, intoxicating garden.

VIOLIN CONCERTOS

Along with the *Stabat Mater*, the violin concertos are probably the place for the Szymanowski novice to start. The first was written in 1916 and was inspired by a poem titled *May Night*, a fervent evocation of love amid the rich fecundity of nature. In this rhapsodic one-movement fantasy the solo violin part is characterized by filigree decoration or swooning melodies in a very high register, whereas in the second concerto (1933) – another one-movement piece – the solo writing is earthier and leaner, perhaps reflecting Szymanowski's immersion in Polish folk music. Both works show Szymanowski at his most sensuous and seductive.

> ◉ Juillet; Montreal Symphony Orchestra; Dutoit (Decca 436 837-2; with Stravinsky, *Violin Concerto*).
> ◉ Wiłkomirska; Warsaw National Philharmonic Orchestra; Rowicki (Polskie Nagrania PNCD 064; with other Szymanowski pieces for violin and piano).

The superb quality of the Decca CD, conducted by Charles Dutoit, is evident from the opening of the first concerto, which reveals every detail of the shimmering flutes and strings. Throughout the recording the wonderful clarity reveals just how remarkable the textures of these pieces are, and the soloist, Chantal Juillet, is very fine. The older recordings on Polskie Nagrania can't match the technical standards of the Decca disc, but the lyrical intensity of Wanda Wiłkomirska is the trump card here.

THOMAS TALLIS
(1505–1585)

Tallis's powerful but ethereal sacred music was written during one of the most turbulent periods of English history. Each of the four Tudor monarchs whom he served possessed widely different attitudes to religious affairs. This not only meant that he was forced to write sometimes in Latin and sometimes in English, but also resulted in regular changes of musical style. His earliest music adopts a peculiarly English, florid style of polyphony, quite similar to Taverner (see p.372); then during the reforms of Edward VI he was obliged to write much more simple and direct music in line with the rationalization of the liturgy; finally in Elizabeth I's reign he developed a tighter and more lucid polyphonic manner, one which became increasingly sensitive to the meaning of the words being set.

Next to nothing is known of Tallis's early life, but in 1540 his livelihood was directly influenced by the volatile religious climate when he lost his job as organist at Waltham Abbey, following the abbey's dissolution. He received twenty shillings payment and a further twenty shillings as compensation. After brief employment at Canterbury Cathedral, Tallis joined the royal household in 1543 as a Gentleman of the Chapel Royal, a position he maintained until his death. His duties as composer and organist earned him significant rewards from his royal patrons: in 1557 Queen Mary granted him a twenty-one-year lease on a lucrative property in Kent and in 1575 Queen Elizabeth gave him, and his younger colleague William Byrd (see p.87), the exclusive right to print and publish music. Their first publication, which came out in the same year, was the *Cantiones Sacrae*, a collection containing seventeen Latin motets by each composer. It was not a financial success, and the two men petitioned the Queen as a result of which they were granted a joint lease on another property. Tallis died in 1585 and was buried in the church of St Alphege at Greenwich.

SACRED MUSIC

Among Tallis's most celebrated works are the two settings of the *Lamentations of Jeremiah*, sombre and heart-felt works that convincingly express the spirit of their melancholy words, and the extraordinary and unforgettable motet, *Spem in Alium*, for five eight-part choirs. Possibly written for the fortieth birthday of either Queen Mary or Queen Elizabeth (no-one knows for sure), *Spem in Alium* uniquely combines complex and delicate polyphonic writing with clamorous tutti passages, and is one of the greatest achievements of all English music.

◉ **Spem in Alium and other music**: Winchester Cathedral Choir; Hill (Hyperion CDA 66400).

This recording, which contains both *Spem in Alium* and the *Lamentations of Jeremiah*, is remarkable for two reasons: firstly the choir of Winchester Cathedral is outstanding, and secondly the resonant acoustic of the vast cathedral adds an extremely dramatic quality to the sound. The opening of *Spem in Alium*, with its gradual accumulation of voices from just one voice is particularly thrilling. In the lighter-textured five-part motets, especially the austere first setting of *O Salutaris*, there is a quality of rapt concentration in the singing that perfectly matches the directness of the music.

JOHN TAVENER
(1944–   )

If John Tavener seemed unexcited by the 1993 chart success of his sumptuous work for solo cello and strings, *The Protecting Veil*, it's hardly surprising – he has seen it all before, and it turned sour the first time round. Back in 1968 the critics pronounced Tavener the new composer to watch; the *Guardian* described the premiere of Tavener's *In Alium* as "nothing less than a musical love-in"; he found himself courted by the Beatles to record for their Apple label; London's Trinity College of Music invited him to join their staff as a Professor of Composition; and to cap it all, Covent Garden commissioned him to write a full-length opera, on the recommendation of Benjamin Britten. The pressure soon began to tell, and by the early 1970s Tavener was finding that it took a progressively longer time to compose each work, and there were worrying "dry" periods. He was in danger of burning out. Salvation came in the shape of the Russian Orthodox Church.

Ever since Tavener converted to the Orthodox church in 1977, he has held the view that art is inseparable from religion – "iMusic is a form of prayer, a mystery." His fervent spirituality was not the result of some blinding revelation – on the contrary, he has been concerned with such things from the start. As a boy of twelve he was profoundly influenced by a broadcast of Stravinsky's *Canticum Sacrum*, a remarkable synthesis of ancient and modern, Eastern and Western, sacred and secular, with which he felt an instant affinity. His parents brought him up a Presbyterian and some of his earliest compositions were written for that church. Apart from the works produced in the late 1960s, when he became something of an apostle of flower-power, Tavener has devoted himself to exploring the connection between art and the sacred.

Despite a conventional British musical training, Tavener is by his own admission "not very interested in Western art music", reserving special disdain for "angst-ridden serial music". Tavener instead looks for inspiration to Greek, Persian, Indian and Sufi music, exotic languages from which he has distilled a style that conveys spiritual depth through simple textures and forms. His music is non-developmental – "iconic" is his preferred term. For Tavener "the icon is the supreme example of Christian art", and the severe shapes and limited colours of a Byzantine icon are, in his view, analogous to the spartan means by which his music seeks to inspire a sense of spiritual wonder.

Tavener has his detractors, for whom his static simplicity is merely musical illiteracy, but he's become one of the most frequently performed living composers, and recordings of his works are selling in vast numbers. For the time being, at least, the unashamedly backward-looking music of Tavener, like the similarly devotional works of Gorécki (see p.150) and Pärt (see p.262), seem to have struck a chord among people seeking refuge from postmodern neurosis.

MARY OF EGYPT

Barely a month goes by in which there is not a Tavener premiere or new recording, and he now has so many published works in the catalogue that it's hard to believe that he ever suffered from writer's block. If one work could be said to sum up his achievements so far, it's the mesmeric *Mary of Egypt*, possibly the most unoperatic opera ever written. Expect no grandiloquent gestures, scenes of ornate spectacle or showy arias, for this is a piece of music theatre in which dramatic movement takes second place to deeply contemplative reflection. Like most of Tavener's music of the last decade, *Mary of Egypt* is a modal composition based on medieval models – specifically, its musical source material is a Byzantine Lenten hymn, *Awed by thy beauty*, which, with its simple stepwise vocal writing, gives the opera a sense of intense, calm joy.

○ Rozario, Varcoe, Goodchild; Choristers of Ely Cathedral, Britten-Pears Chamber Choir, Aldeburgh Festival Ensemble; Friend (Collins 7023-2; 2CDs).

This live recording of the 1992 Aldeburgh premiere production was clearly a labour of love for all concerned. Lionel Friend's interpretation is memorably atmospheric, pinpointing each minute advance in the story with the utmost subtlety. The soloists are simply outstanding, while the contributions from the Ely choristers and chamber choir are beautifully understated and haunting. The CD includes an illuminating interview with Tavener on the subject of the opera.

JOHN TAVERNER
(c.1490–1545)

John Taverner was the outstanding talent of pre-Reformation English music and one of the greatest of all polyphonists. To a large extent his music was the culmination of an extremely rich English polyphonic tradition which employed highly florid vocal writing and a variety of contrasted voice combinations within the same piece. To this tradition Taverner added the continental device of imitation, whereby a phrase sung by one voice would be repeated by another, thus giving his works a greater sense of shape and direction than those of his English predecessors.

Taverner was probably born in Lincolnshire: the earliest record of his musical activities is in 1525 as a lay clerk at the collegiate choir of Tattershall, northwest of Boston. The following year, on the recommendation of the Bishop of Lincoln, he was appointed choirmaster to the newly founded Cardinal (later Christ Church) College, Oxford. This was a prestigious position but a short-lived one, due to the fall from power in 1529 of the college's founder, Cardinal Wolsey. The year before that, Taverner was briefly arrested for his involvement with a group sympathetic to Lutheranism, an incident treated with leniency at the time, but which gave rise to the legend that Taverner eschewed both Catholicism and music to dedicate his remaining years to the destruction of the monasteries. This is the subject of Peter Maxwell Davies's 1970 opera on the life of the composer, but the truth seems to be rather less dramatic. Taverner returned to Lincolnshire to become a lay clerk and possibly choirmaster at the church of St Botolph's at Boston. Once again it was not an appointment that he held for long – this time he left because of the collapse of the guild that paid his wages. From 1537 his musical activities seem to have ceased and the rest of his life was spent in the role of a well-to-do local dignitary, one well enough regarded to be honoured at his death with burial beneath the tower of St Botolph's church.

SACRED MUSIC

Eight of Taverner's Masses have survived, of which the most beautiful is the early six-part *Missa Gloria Tibi Trinitas*. This employs a plainsong cantus firmus which is located in the alto part, thus making it more audible than usual since only the treble part is higher. The work is remarkable for its variety and for the liveliness of its counterpoint – there are several moments of richly florid writing, notably near the beginning of the Credo, when the treble line weaves ever more complex patterns above the bass part. Its most famous section, the *In Nomine* from the *Benedictus*, was used by subsequent English composers from Tallis to Purcell as the thematic material from which to write short pieces for viol consorts, which were duly known as "in nomines".

⊙ **Missa Gloria Tibi Trinitas; Leroy Kyrie; Dum Transisset Sabbatum**: The Tallis Scholars; Phillips (Gimell CDGIM 004).

The Tallis Scholars bring to the *Missa Gloria Tibi Trinitas* their customary precision and textural clarity, but with a greater degree of flexibility and warmth than is usual. The intimacy of the reduced voice passages is well contrasted with the radiant sound produced by the full choir, for instance in the Gratias agimus section of the Gloria. Occasionally the incisiveness of the female voices in the upper parts brings a slightly top-heavy quality to the sound, but this is a small distraction. The other two works included on the disc are less animated, both being made up of smoother, more drawn-out phrases which produce an altogether more solemn and serene impression.

PYOTR IL'YICH TCHAIKOVSKY
(1840–1893)

If any one composer can be said to encapsulate the essence of Russianness, it is Pyotr Il'yich Tchaikovsky, and yet he was the one major composer of nineteenth-century Russia who cannot be bracketed with the Russian nationalist school. Although he associated with prominent nationalist figures, particularly Balakirev, Tchaikovsky followed a fiercely independent path, and he paid heavily for his determination to be true to himself above all else – few major artists have ever suffered the sort of critical savaging that

HULTON DEUTSCH

entered the city music conservatory to study with Anton Rubinstein, a composer and stupendous pianist. In 1866 he went to Moscow, where Anton's brother Nikolai appointed Tchaikovsky professor of harmony at the conservatory.

In Moscow he came into contact with Rimsky-Korsakov and his cabal of young nationalists, and for a short while Tchaikovsky was swept up by their enthusiasm for Russia's folk heritage. He even composed a nationalist symphony – the *Symphony No. 2*, known as the *Little Russian* – but it was not long before his cosmopolitan instincts prevailed. By the time of the first performance of his *Piano Concerto No. 1* in 1875 he had created a style that was strongly individual while being equally accessible to any audience raised on the wider European tradition – indeed, the concerto at first found greater acclaim abroad than at home.

In 1877, seeking refuge from his own homosexuality (homosexual acts were punishable by death in Russia), Tchaikovsky married a besotted pupil named Antonina Milyukova, a young woman with more than her own share of psychological problems. It was an unmitigated disaster: they separated within nine weeks, and Tchaikovsky fell into a suicidal depression. He was saved by the remarkable Nadezhda von Meck, a wealthy widow who had been impressed by some of his early music and who now commissioned Tchaikovsky to produce some violin and piano arrangements of his own works. Thus began a relationship that lasted fourteen years, during which time they never once met. She supplied Tchaikovsky with a generous annuity so that he could concentrate on composition, and that is exactly what he did, dedicating his *Symphony No. 4* to von Meck in 1878 and completing his opera *Eugene Onegin* in 1879.

By the 1880s his music was being played as far afield as the USA, and by 1885 he had made enough money to buy himself a country estate at Klin. He lived there in complete isolation until 1887, when he ventured back to Moscow to make his debut as a conductor. In this capacity he toured Europe in the following year, and then in 1889 he moved to Florence, where he composed what is prob-

was meted out to Tchaikovsky. Nowadays it's difficult to understand why his music aroused such antipathy, for Tchaikovsky is the most powerful and direct of composers: characterized above all by its tunefulness and sweeping orchestral sound, Tchaikovsky's music appeals directly to the heart. Certainly he was prone to bombastic gestures and sentimentality, but these weaknesses are the obverse of his chief strength, which is his sincerity. The emotional fluctuations and contradictions of his work reflect the turbulence of an extraordinary life.

Tchaikovsky was born some six hundred miles east of Moscow in the provincial town of Votkinsk, where his father was a mining engineer. His formal tuition began at home, where his parents played him pieces by Mozart, Bellini and Rossini, and gave him lessons in piano and music theory. In 1848 the family moved to St Petersburg, and in 1850 he was sent to a boarding school in the city; nine years later, after intensive and extended law studies (and the death of his mother, a trauma that was to scar him for the rest of his life) he found employment at the Ministry of Justice. Aged twenty-two he left the ministry and ably his greatest opera, *The Queen of Spades*. The work's triumph was marred by the breakdown of his relationship with von Meck, but although he was deeply distressed by their falling out, he made an incredibly successful visit to the USA in 1891, conducting at the opening night of what was to become Carnegie Hall. "I am a much more important person here than in Russia", he wrote, bewildered by his reception.

In 1893 his achievement was recognized in France, where he was elected a member of the Académie Française, and England, where Cambridge University awarded him an honorary doctorate. In August he completed his *Symphony No. 6*, the *Pathétique*, a creation that typifies the work of a composer who poured the whole of his life into his music. It was premiered in St Petersburg on October 28; nine days later he was dead.

The circumstances of Tchaikovsky's death remain controversial to this day. The official version was that he had died from cholera after drinking unboiled water. Many people surmised that Tchaikovsky had hoped this reckless act would bring about his death, but in the 1970s a Russian scholar produced a new account of Tchaikovsky's last days, a version which, it was claimed, established suicide as the incontrovertible cause of death. Shortly before his death, the story goes, Tchaikovsky had been caught *in flagrante* with a nephew of a high-ranking official. Tchaikovsky's law-school colleagues, determined to avert a scandal that would reflect badly on them, summoned Tchaikovsky before a "court of honour" on October 31 and ordered him to commit suicide. Two days later, he took arsenic.

OPERA

Tchaikovsky's operas are the distillation of what he termed his "lyrical idea", the notion that everything can be characterized or made real through melody. His technique was always at the service of melody, and his music was first and foremost conceived for the voice – whether or not it was actually written for voice, all his music can be sung. Tchaikovsky was not, however, an effortless

tune-writer in the manner of Mendelssohn or Strauss. He worked hard at honing his skills, making an intensive study of his European precursors, not just as a student in Russia, but also in later life as a touring celebrity. For his operatic music Tchaikovsky immersed himself in Italian bel canto as well as in the operas of Mozart, and the breadth of Tchaikovsky's schooling is a major distinction between him and his Russian contemporaries. He wrote no fewer than ten operas, though only two of them have found a regular place in the repertory – *Eugene Onegin* and *The Queen of Spades*.

EUGENE ONEGIN

In May 1877, Tchaikovsky received an unsolicited letter from Antonina Miklyukova, professing her love. Later that month, a friend suggested to Tchaikovsky that he make an opera of Pushkin's great verse-novel *Eugene Onegin*. Initially unconvinced of the poem's suitability as a libretto, he came to the passage where Tatyana, the heroine of the story, writes a letter to Onegin, in which she expresses her love for him. Tchaikovsky began to write a setting of the letter scene, and by July, when he married Antonina, he had already completed two-thirds of the opera.

The relationship was calamitous, and the misery it caused him delayed completion of the opera until 1879, yet *Eugene Onegin* contains some of the composer's most graceful, untroubled music. Where Pushkin's poem had explored at length the social and moral discrepancies between the world of Tatyana, the country girl, and that of the aristocratic Onegin, Tchaikovsky keeps the spotlight on their aborted relationship. Onegin spurns Tatyana, then flirts with her sister at the party to celebrate the sister's engagement to Lensky. When Lensky protests, Onegin reluctantly fights a duel, in which Lensky is killed. Six years later Onegin returns from abroad to find Tatyana married. Realizing he loves her, he tempts her to leave with him, but eventually she rejects him.

Lensky is a particularly fine tenor role (his aria is one of the work's highlights) and Onegin is delineated with great subtlety, but it is the characterization of Tatyana that is the making of this opera. There are few more realistic or sympathetic heroines, and her "Letter Scene" is just about the most moving quarter-hour that Tchaikovsky ever devised.

> ⊙ Allen, Freni, von Otter, Schicoff; Staatskapelle Dresden; Levine (Deutsche Grammophon 423 959-2; 2 CDs).

Levine's thrilling account for DG is the most impressive modern recording. Thomas Allen's Onegin is a perfectly shaped performance and the surprise casting of Mirella Freni works amazingly well – she is able to convey the requisite youthfulness for her first meeting with Onegin just as clearly as the maturity needed for their final confrontation, and her "Letter Scene" is particularly well drawn. The Dresden orchestra play with great fervour and the smaller roles are played with similarly convincing commitment.

THE QUEEN OF SPADES

The Queen of Spades (sometimes translated as *Pique-Dame*) is also based upon a story by Pushkin. Its protagonist is a young army officer named Hermann, who is trying to discover a secret to success in gambling, a secret known only to the Countess who is the grandmother of Lisa, the woman he loves. He breaks into the Countess's room at night in order to attain the secret of the "three cards", but so terrifies her that she dies of shock. The Countess returns as a ghost and tells Hermann the secret. He abandons Lisa (who drowns herself), and takes to the gambling rooms ready to make his fortune. However, the Countess reappears and, in revenge, drives Hermann into killing himself.

The opera was premiered in St Petersburg in 1890, over ten years after *Onegin*, by which time Tchaikovsky's technique had become far more sophisticated. In *The Queen of Spades* he combines nineteenth-century realism with the elegance of Mozart's world and the Rococo style of Catherine the Great's St Petersburg. Indeed, a generalized longing for the past permeates the score. The focus upon Fate – a recurrent idea in Tchaikovsky – is handled brilliantly, with the "three cards" motif strongly colouring the work's fabric. The roles of Hermann (a high, dramatic tenor) and the Countess (a dark and noble contralto) interact in some immensely impressive scenes – especially the blood-curdling episode where Hermann is confronted by the ghost of the Countess. But *The Queen of Spades* is littered with memorable moments; as he wrote to his brother (his co-librettist) – "Unless I'm terribly mistaken, the opera is a masterpiece".

> ⊙ Freni, Atlantov, Hvorostovsky, Forrester, Boston Symphony Orchestra, Ozawa (RCA 09026 60992-2; 3 CDs).

This is perhaps Ozawa's finest achievement on record. His direction is tight but flexible, the Boston Symphony makes a wonderful sound, and the cast is sensational. It's headed by the mighty Vladimir Atlantov as Hermann – frequently over the top but always powerful and committed. Freni was too old to be playing Lisa as Tchaikovsky intended her but she is still in glowing voice, while Margaret Forrester gives a fine portrayal of the Countess. Excellent recorded sound.

BALLET

Russian ballet music before Tchaikovsky was vapid stuff, amounting to little more than background music for displays of the dancers' qualities. Tchaikovsky introduced a greater range of rhythms, an increased richness of melody and orchestration, and above all gave the ballet a sense of symphonic construction – in short, he gave respect to ballet music as an art form. Classical ballet owes more to Tchaikovsky than to any other composer, and if *Swan Lake*, *The Sleeping Beauty* and *The Nutcracker* met with little more than polite approval during Tchaikovsky's lifetime, they are now the world's most frequently performed dance scores.

> ◑ Ballet Suites; Berlin Philharmonic Orchestra; Rostropovich (Deutsche Grammophon 429 097-2GGA).

This recording of the suites from *Swan Lake*, *The Sleeping Beauty* and *The Nutcracker* is a bargain at mid-price. Rostropovich is not the greatest conductor who ever lived but he is given ravishing support from the Berlin Philharmonic, and both he and the orchestra clearly enjoy every minute of the music.

SWAN LAKE

Tchaikovsky was commissioned to write *Swan Lake* at the end of May 1875 by the Imperial Theatre. He gladly accepted the work, partly because of his poor financial situation, and partly because, as he wrote to Rimsky-

Korsakov, "I have long had the wish to try my hand at this kind of music." Tchaikovsky duly produced the first ballet that had overall musical coherence, for rather than being the customary series of dances strung together by the vaguest of plots, *Swan Lake* is constructed of extended quasi-symphonic movements, unified by a system of themes and key structures. Tchaikovsky's brilliantly orchestrated musical narrative flows perfectly, and features more memorable tunes than any of the composer's other scores. The first production was nonetheless a resounding failure. Petipa, the pre-eminent choreographer of his day, and Drigo, a ballet composer of the old school, then set about revising the work, but it was still considered undanceable. Time has told a different story.

⊚ Philharmonia Orchestra; Lanchbery (Classics for Pleasure CD-CFPD 4727; 2 CDs).

John Lanchbery, a ballet conductor who worked frequently with Fonteyn and Nureyev, made this budget-price recording in 1982, and it remains the best version on record. This is a delicate, flowing performance with fine orchestral playing and a spacious dynamic range that highlights even the subtlest of touches.

THE SLEEPING BEAUTY

Tchaikovsky's second ballet is a work of his maturity, coming between the fifth and sixth symphonies. It was premiered in 1890, with choreography by Petipa, and this time Tchaikovsky had learned his lesson – he allowed Petipa to guide him, section by section, through the ballet's composition. (On certain occasions Petipa would go so far as to specify the number of bars required.) Unlike its predecessor, *The Sleeping Beauty* is a happy-ending tale, but for all the sweetness of the story line, this is Tchaikovsky's finest ballet, for if *Swan Lake* marked the establishment of a symphonic style of ballet music, *Sleeping Beauty* went a stage further – it was even attacked at the time for being "too symphonic". Elaborately constructed, it contains movements within movements that are, effectively, miniature concertos for the orchestral section leaders.

➊ Concertgebouw, Dorati (Philips 420 792-2PH3; 3 CDs).

Antal Dorati's recording of the complete *Sleeping Beauty* is magnificently coherent. Dorati's aggressive manner and almost impatient tempi, exemplified by his performances of music by Stravinsky, is a gift to music that can easily become sickly sweet.

THE NUTCRACKER

The Nutcracker, based on E. T. A. Hoffmann's story of a little girl and her Christmas presents, was written at the end of Tchaikovsky's life but it reflects nothing of his misery or self-hatred – rather it evokes a world of innocence where everything is as it should be. Again, Petipa worked closely with the composer on the production of a detailed scenario, and much of Hoffmann's ironic juxtaposition of reality and fantasy was lost in the process. Yet this is still an enchanting work, containing many of Tchaikovsky's best-loved tunes – notably the *Sugar-Plum Fairy*, which includes music for the celesta, a new instrument that Tchaikovsky was desperate to keep secret from his rivals, in particular Rimsky-Korsakov. The celesta's finest hour was to come courtesy of Bartók (see p.20).

➊ London Symphony Orchestra; Dorati (Mercury 432750-2MM2; with *Serenade*; 2 CDs).

The Nutcracker is shorter and considerably less ambitious than *Sleeping Beauty*, but it is in no way lacking in drama or colour. Dorati's calm direction is perfectly delicate but he produces a wash of sound such as few have achieved on record. A wonderful, superbly engineered recording.

SYMPHONIES

Tchaikovsky viewed the symphony as the mould into which to pour his most profound thoughts and feelings, and his seven completed symphonies are the emotional graph of a lifetime, from the relative calm of the *Symphony No. 1* (*Winter Daydreams*) to the desolation of the *Symphony No. 6*, the *Pathétique*. (The seventh bears the title *Manfred* rather than a number.) They are uniformly revealing but not uniformly excellent. The first three have plenty of Tchaikovsky's outgoing melodies and thrilling rhythms, but they also have slack episodes that you won't find in the last three numbered symphonies. This trio represents a high-point of the Romantic symphony.

⊙ **Complete Symphonies**: Oslo Philharmonic
Orchestra, Jansons (Chandos 8672/8; 7 CDs).

Mariss Jansons' survey of Tchaikovsky's symphonies is a
remarkable achievement, bringing something fresh to each
one. He and the Oslo players give a sense of conviction to the
early symphonies that is lacking from the majority of alternative
versions, and with the late masterpieces they are at least the
equal of any rivals. These fine recordings are available on separate, full-price discs, or as a specially reduced set – in the latter
format they represent a very rewarding investment.

SYMPHONY NO. 4

The composition of the *Symphony No. 4* was
interrupted by the breakdown of
Tchaikovsky's marriage and by a consequent,
pathetic attempt at suicide – he waded into a
river, hoping to catch pneumonia. Yet when
he completed the piece in December 1877,
he was convinced that it was his greatest
work: "in technique and form it represents a
step forward in my development, which has
been proceeding extremely slowly." The
fourth symphony shows a greater control of
the orchestral palette, and a stronger grasp of
the means of integrating melodic material into
an overall structure. The first movement is an
expansive conception, dominated by a bleak
"Fate" motif that colours the entire movement, while the second is a mournful song of
poignant beauty. The third movement features
some amazingly original scoring for plucked
strings, but it is the charging, ebullient finale
that justifies the use of superlatives – incorporating variations on a Russian folk song,
this is the composer's most exciting
symphonic invention, ending in a torrent of
enthusiasm after the violent incursions of the
"Fate" motif.

⊙ Chicago Symphony Orchestra; Solti (Decca 430 745-2DM; with *Romeo and Juliet*).

The best alternative to the Janson recording (see above) is
Solti's thumping account for Decca, which makes a good case
for the work's grander aspects even if it misses something of
the delicacy.

SYMPHONY NO. 5

Tchaikovsky wrote of the *Symphony No. 5*
(1885): "I have become convinced that the
symphony is unsuccessful. There is something repellant about it, a certain patchiness,

insecurity and artifice . . . All this causes me
a keen torment of discontent . . . it is all most
distressing." This certainly is a distressing
work, but chiefly because of its unguarded
candour rather than because of any compositional failings. Fate is more cruel and implacable in this symphony than it was in its
predecessor: it begins in despairing mood,
and the frequent, massive emotional climaxes
generate a sense of hysteria that rarely
featured in the fourth. The symphony's "Fate"
motif destroys even the songlike melody of
the slow movement, and only at the close of
the finale does the tragic atmosphere lift –
even then, you feel it's a case of putting a
brave face on things.

⊙ London Symphony Orchestra; Dorati (Mercury 434
305-2MM; with *Marche Slave* and excerpts from *Eugene
Onegin*).

Dorati's discipline prevents the emotional climate of the
symphony from becoming too oppressive, and the potentially
cloying textures are balanced with precision and imagination.
The first four movements are evenly paced, but the finale is
driven with an insatiable energy that is well served by a clear
and resonant recording.

SYMPHONY NO. 6 –
THE PATHÉTIQUE

"I give you my word of honour that never in
my life have I been so contented, so proud, so
happy in the knowledge that I have written a
good piece." Within months of writing this to
his publisher, Tchaikovsky was dead, possibly pushed towards suicide by the hostile
reception accorded to his *Symphony No. 6*.
The title *Pathétique* was added by the
composer's brother, and is undeniably appropriate to a work which, despite a number of
positive interludes and beautiful thematic
writing, is overwhelmingly melancholic.

Although the opening movement contains
one of Tchaikovsky's loveliest themes, a
sense of intense internal struggle is conveyed
by extremes of dynamics – no previous
symphony had displayed such violent ranges
between soft and loud. The second movement
is a ghostly piece written in a rhythm that
seems to be imitating a waltz but never quite
becoming one. In the third movement a hectic
march takes over, but any hints of momentary
triumph are soon dispelled. Unusually the

symphony ends with a slow movement, and it's the most anguished music Tchaikovsky ever composed – the emotional weight of this Adagio becomes ever more burdensome until, breaking down with grief, the music disappears into the darkness from which it emerged.

⊙ Russian National Orchestra; Pletnev (Virgin VC7 91487-2; with *Marche Slave*).

The pianist Mikhael Pletnev's transition to conducting began with this staggering performance of the *Pathétique*, in which he achieves a perfect balance of strength and pathos. The orchestra's playing is breathtakingly urgent and the expressive range truly harrowing. Ideally recorded.

CONCERTOS

Tchaikovsky composed five concertos: three for piano, one for violin and the *Variations on a Rococo Theme*, which is for cello in all but name. The *Violin Concerto* and *Piano Concerto No. 1* are particularly grand conceptions, boasting an exceptional orchestral expertise in addition to the customary large-scale emotionalism. The second and third piano concertos, on the other hand, have never really entered the repertoire, while the *Rococo Variations* is a pale neo-classical piece that only gets an airing when the concertos by Dvořák and Elgar have been played into the ground.

PIANO CONCERTO NO. 1

Many of Tchaikovsky's best-known works received a rocky ride, but none came in for as much flak as the *Piano Concerto No. 1*, which Nikolai Rubinstein, the intended dedicatee, pronounced "worthless, unplayable and clumsy". He went on to declare the concerto so bad that it was not worth the effort of revision. Rubinstein later grandly agreed to play it on condition that Tchaikovsky changed the work to suit his requirements, but by this stage Tchaikovsky had re-dedicated the piece to his lifelong friend Sergei Taneyev. Tchaikovsky then changed his mind once more and replaced Taneyev's name with that of the German conductor Hans von Bülow, who cheerfully agreed to take on the responsibility for the premiere, which took place on October

13, 1875 in Boston. It went down a storm in the USA (though not at first in Russia), and in time even Rubinstein came to love it.

No-one would argue that it's the most coherent of concertos – there's little discernible link between the opening movement and what follows, and the last movement is anticlimactic. But Germanic rigour is not what Tchaikovsky is about, and the heroic bravado and typically Russian "big tunes" of the *Piano Concerto No. 1* have made it one of the most popular concertos. Incidentally, its most famous flourish, the grandiose piano chords which accompany the opening melody, was in large part the creation of one Alexander Siloti (cousin and teacher of Rachmaninov), who helped arrange the score for its third edition. Siloti suggested that the repeated chords of Tchaikovsky's original be replaced by chords that covered the whole of the instrument's range; to his immense credit, Tchaikovsky agreed, thereby creating one of classical music's great attention-grabbing effects.

◗ Horowitz; NBC Symphony Orchestra; Toscanini (RCA GD 87992; with Beethoven, *Piano Concerto No. 5*).
⊙ Argerich; Royal Philharmonic Orchestra; Dutoit (Deutsche Grammophon 415 062-2; with Prokofiev, *Concerto No. 3*).

Toscanini, conductor of his son-in-law's great Tchaikovsky No. 1

In 1943 Vladimir Horowitz and his father-in-law Arturo Toscanini gave a performance of Tchaikovsky's *Piano Concerto No. 1* at the Carnegie Hall, to raise money for the war effort. Financially and artistically it was a stunning success. Ignore the constricted sound quality – this is the performance of a lifetime, bursting with energy and old-fashioned virtuosity, and there has never been a recording to compare with it. Of modern interpretations, Martha Argerich's more thoughtful, less frenetic partnership with Charles Dutoit is the best of the bunch.

VIOLIN CONCERTO

The history of Tchaikovsky's *Violin Concerto* is somewhat similar to that of the *Piano Concerto No. 1*. Written in just one month in 1877, it was intended for the violinist Leopold Auer (Heifetz's teacher), who promptly refused to perform it when he saw the difficulty of the solo part. Instead, it was Adolf Brodsky who gave the premiere in Vienna on December 4, 1881. Europe's pre-eminent music critic, Eduard Hanslick, was in the audience – "stinking music" was his verdict. The reaction was hardly unexpected, for the conservative Wagner-hating Hanslick was Brahms's biggest fan, whereas Tchaikovsky loathed everything that Brahms stood for – indeed, Tchaikovsky had been singularly unimpressed by the Brahms violin concerto, which had appeared in 1879. The two concertos are in the same key (the same key as Beethoven's masterpiece), but that's where the resemblance ends. Whereas tension and constraint are essential Brahms, Tchaikovsky creates a largely effortless, song-like part for the violin, while the orchestral score is packed with rumbustious energy and bold melodies. If the Brahms concerto is like a well-scripted dialogue, the Tchaikovsky is more like an uninhibited duet for soloist and orchestra.

> ◉ Heifetz; London Philharmonic Orchestra; Barbirolli (Biddulph LAB026; with works by Wieniawski, Glazunov and Sarasate).
> ◉ Gitlis; Vienna Pro Musica Orchestra; Hollreiser (Vox Legends CDX2 5505; with concertos by Mendelssohn, Sibelius and Bartók; 2 CDs).
> ◉ Wei; Philharmonia; Accardo (ASV CDDCA 713; with other Tchaikovsky violin works).
> ◉ Mullova; Boston Symphony Orchestra; Ozawa (Philips 416 821-2; with Sibelius, *Violin Concerto*).

Heifetz recorded the work a number of times but the finest version is his first, made in 1937. With Barbirolli's sympathetic, flexible accompaniment, Heifetz hurls himself into the score,

producing an extraordinarily exciting sound. Less flashy but no less convincing is the account by the eccentric Frenchman Ivry Gitlis, made in the 1950s. Projecting the most remarkably smooth phrasing and sense of style, this is violin playing quite unlike anything else on disc.

Two modern recordings make outstanding alternatives to the pyrotechnics of Heifetz or the beguiling sweetness of Gitlis. Xue Wei's account is an immensely sensual performance under the direction of fellow violinist Salvatore Accardo, who allows his soloist as long a rein as he wants. Viktoria Mullova's thrilling interpretation is distinguished by ringing tone, impeccable technique and Russian flair; one of her first projects for Philips after winning the Tchaikovsky competition, it comes generously coupled with an equally fine account of Sibelius's concerto.

CHAMBER MUSIC

In the eyes of many of the Russian intelligentsia, chamber music was almost as trivial a genre as ballet, but Tchaikovsky created some fine work in this field, even without a strong indigenous tradition to support him. It's in his chamber music that Tchaikovsky's style is most clearly indebted to the great Germans, and to Brahms in particular, but as with everything he wrote, the overriding tone is quintessentially Russian. The three string quartets represent the best of his chamber music, and the sextet entitled *Souvenir de Florence* is also a splendid creation; his *Piano Trio* has quite a few admirers, but newcomers to Tchaikovsky are likely to find it a turgid exercise.

STRING QUARTETS

The *String Quartet No. 1* (1871) is Tchaikovsky's most attractive chamber work. The majority of the music is jauntily lyrical and folk-inspired, free of the melancholy and fatalism so common to Tchaikovsky. That said, its reputation rests on its incredibly mournful second movement, the Andante cantabile, which has become one of his most popular pieces – both in its original form and in orchestral transcription. The *Quartet No. 2*, written three years later, lacks the unity of the first and is notably less tuneful. The *Quartet No. 3* (1876), although well constructed, seems to strain for originality, and it is uncomfortably dominated by the first violin, no doubt in response to the death of the violinist Laub, the dedicatee of the quartet.

◗ Borodin Quartet (Melodiya 74321182902; with *Souvenir de Florence*; 2 CDs).

The Borodin Quartet, widely acknowledged as one of the greatest chamber ensembles of the twentieth century, made these recordings between 1965 and 1980. The performances of the quartets approach perfection, especially the *Quartet No. 1*, and their account of the *Souvenir de Florence* sextet, with Rostropovich as the second cellist, is similarly superb, combining a supple instrumental balance and extraordinary fluidity of melodic line. Excellent sound quality and excellent value.

GEORG-PHILIPP TELEMANN

(1681–1767)

Telemann was the greatest German composer of the first half of the eighteenth century – at least that's what they thought in Germany at the time. Nowadays his friend and colleague J. S. Bach, who became cantor at Leipzig only because Telemann turned it down, is regarded as infinitely superior, while Telemann is treated as an over-productive and superficial also-ran. He was certainly incredibly prolific, writing among other things about forty operas, forty-six Passions and five complete cycles of cantatas for the Lutheran liturgical year. And there's some justice to the charge of superficiality – able to write in pretty well any style that was demanded of him, he wrote no single work that stands out distinctly as his own. Yet at its best, the music of Telemann has a bright melodiousness that looks forward to that of Haydn and Mozart.

Telemann was born at Magdeburg into an affluent middle-class background. Both his father and his brother, like several of their ancestors, were clergymen, and despite showing musical aptitude from an early age (he wrote his first opera aged twelve), Georg Philipp was intended for a similarly respectable career. In 1701 he went to the University of Leipzig to study law, but once his musical talents were discovered by others, it was impossible for him to do anything else. He founded the Collegium Musicum (a society that gave public concerts, and which Bach later directed), became organist of the Neue Kirche, then director of the Leipzig Opera, and so dominated the city's musical life that its ostensible music director, Kuhnau, started

to become extremely irritated. Telemann left Leipzig in 1705, and after positions at Sorau and Eisenach became music director of the city of Frankfurt, and Kapellmeister of the Barfusserkirche (church of the Barefoot Friars). He was there for nine years, from 1712 to 1721, before being invited by the city of Hamburg to be cantor of the Johanneum, the grammar school, and to be responsible for music at the city's five principal churches. A dispute with the civic authorities led to his applying for the Leipzig cantor's job in 1722, but things were patched up (his salary was increased) and he remained at Hamburg until his death, when he was succeeded in the post by his godson, C. P. E. Bach (see p.6).

CHORAL MUSIC

Telemann's prodigious output as a cantata composer is not quite so impressive once you realize that he was mostly writing solo cantatas, and not complex large-scale works like Bach's cantatas. Yet he did write plenty of big choral works, and among the most interesting of these is the oratorio, the *Hamburgische Kapitansmusik*, written to celebrate the centenary gala dinner of the Hamburg civic militia. The breezy and idiomatic text, which finally exhorts everybody to enjoy their food, is Telemann's own. Its recitatives, arias and chorales evoke an atmosphere that is sometimes solemn but more often festive, and at times sounds very close to Handel. There is also a distinctly Handelian feel to the delightful *Magnificat in C*, an early work probably written when Telemann was still a student in Leipzig.

⦿ **Magnificat in C; Hamburgische Kapitansmusik 1730**: van der Sluis, Pushee, Jochens, Langshaw, van der Kamp; Alsfelder Vokalensemble; Barockorchester Bremen; Helbich (CPO 999 109-2).

Both works get highly spirited and engaging performances on this CD, with outstanding contributions from the soloists. The *Magnificat* is more obviously appealing and contains some extremely beautiful arias, notably the alto's *Quia respexit* and the soprano's *Et misericordia*. The *Hamburgische Kapitansmusik* is very much more light-hearted, with several light and bouncy choruses, including a delightful Chorus of the Joyful, which the Alsfelder Vokalensemble bring off with real aplomb.

ORCHESTRAL MUSIC

In Telemann's time the dominant orchestral forms were the concerto and the orchestral suite, which was made up of a French-style overture and a series of formalized dance movements. One of Telemann's employers, Count Erdmann II of Promnitz, distinctly favoured the French style of music and Telemann consequently composed several suites for him. It was while at the count's court at Sorau that he came into contact with the indigenous music of Upper Silesia, and folk elements – both rhythmic and instrumental – became a feature of his music throughout the rest of his career. In his concertos the influence is more Italian than French, with the model of Vivaldi particularly apparent in the way he frequently employs quite strange combinations of instruments as the solo group.

⦿ **Concerto in D major; La Bouffonne Suite; Grillen-Symphonie; Alster-Ouverture**: Collegium Musicum 90; Standage (Chandos CHAN 0457).

This is a disc that really shows off Telemann's versatility, from the rather formal and slightly bland elegance of the *Bouffonne Suite* to the inspired and bizarre scoring of the delightful *Grillen-Symphonie*, in which a double-bass, a piccolo and a chalumeau (a clarinet-type instrument) combine with a string quartet to startling effect. Best and most striking of all is the *Alster-Ouverture*, a piece of light-hearted scene-painting with one movement of weird harmonies and unexpected key changes representing the music of the local peasantry while another, full of spikey dissonances, conjures up the sounds of frogs and crows. Utterly compelling, and played with much spirit and enthusiasm by Collegium 90.

CHAMBER & INSTRUMENTAL MUSIC

Telemann published an enormous amount of chamber music for a wide range of musical combinations and in several different styles, including sonatas, quartets and Corellian trio sonatas. Much of it was aimed at amateur players and was not especially difficult. For this reason it was highly successful and his fame became so widespread that when his largest collection of chamber music, *Musique de table*, was published in 1733, 52 of the 206 subscriptions came from abroad. The predominant style is what the eighteenth-century dubbed "galant", meaning music in which simple melodies and clear textures convey a mood of easy-going elegance and charm.

Of the relatively small amount of instrumental music that Telemann wrote, the *Twelve Fantasies* for flute and the *Twelve Fantasies* for solo violin are outstanding. The latter pieces invite comparison with J. S. Bach's slightly earlier works for solo violin, but Telemann's approach is rather different. Though the first six fantasies have contrapuntal elements, including fugues, they don't have Bach's sense of organic development, placing more emphasis on contrast between the movements. Fantasies six to twelve are in more of a galant style, full of delightfully bright and sprightly melodies. They have neither the emotional range nor the musical complexity of Bach's solo violin pieces, but these are among Telemann's most personal and rewarding works.

⦿ **Chamber Music**: Ensemble Florilegium (Channel Classics CCS 5093).
⦿ **Twelve Fantasies for Violin**: Homburger (Maya MCD 9302).

The Ensemble Florilegium disc is a fine selection of consistently first-rate and beautiful music, even though much of it recalls other composers. Four of the five works use a recorder or flute to carry the melody, the exception being the *Sonata in F major*, an uncannily accurate evocation of Corelli's chamber music. Other highlights are the stately elegance of the *Sixth Paris Quartet*, and the nervous intensity of the A minor concerto's opening movement – wonderfully atmospheric music, and this time sounding like nobody else.

Homburger plays the *Fantasies* in a fairly resonant church acoustic, which creates a warm and spacious ambience around the violin sound. Her playing is lively but controlled, and communicates the music's passion without recourse to histrionics. The faster movements are played with particular stylishness, full of verve and with a strong and penetrating tone.

MICHAEL TIPPETT

(1905–)

HULTON DEUTSCH

Michael Tippett was nearly thirty years old when Elgar died, yet he is more a modern composer than his immediate contemporaries Walton and Britten. A late starter, he did not produce his first recognized score until he was thirty, and attracted virtually no public attention until he was nearly forty. When he did, however, his neo-romantic notions of self-expression attracted considerable, if far from universal, enthusiam. Tippett belongs to no category except his own. On the one hand he has little sympathy with the ideas of modernity represented by atonalism or minimalism, but on the other he writes music that is less accessible than that of traditionalists such as Arnold or Simpson. In short, he exemplifes the dauntless, sometimes eccentric individualism that some regard as a defining characteristic of the English.

He did not begin to study music until he was eighteen years old, but then applied himself vigorously to the mechanics and fundamentals of composition, continuing his studies at the Royal College of Music. After that he became a schoolmaster and conductor, but his life story has been a generally uneventful chronicle of devotion to his music – unless you count his imprisonment during World War II, a result of his pacifist beliefs. Tippett's beliefs play a conspicuous part in much of his work, and it has to be admitted that his operas and choral music are, for the most part, dogged by impossibly pretentious and naïve libretti of his own creation, while his striving to appear topical can lead to embarrassing misjudgements. His 1988 opera *New Year*, for example, contains a lot of hippyish nonsense about time-travel, and features a "rap" routine that is possibly the most excruciating episode in modern music. With that proviso, the music of Michael Tippett constitutes one of the more interesting twentieth-century re-interpretations of the classical tradition. Unlike many composers who set themselves against the avant-garde, he has never ceased to develop, and there's genuine originality both in his rhythmic language and his complex tonal harmony.

KING PRIAM

Tippett's breakthrough opera was *The Midsummer Marriage* (1955), a typically ambitious re-working of the myth of the Fisher King. It was not, however, a wholehearted success, for several critics complained of its tendency to longwindedness. Tippett's response was the bracingly austere and intense *King Priam* (1962), his finest opera. Like Berlioz's *Les Troyens*, *King Priam* takes its material directly from Homer's *Iliad*, but there are no further similarities between Berlioz's heroic production and Tippett's pared-down study of what he has termed "the mysterious nature of choice". *King Priam* has a sparser orchestral score, a more declamatory vocal style and a more strident harmonic base than *The Midsummer Marriage*, and is perhaps not as immediately accessible. On the other hand, the dramatic structure is far tauter, and the opera has some marvellous dramatic moments, such as the tender lament of Achilles and Priam over the body of Hector, at the close of the first act.

● Bailey; Harper; Allen; Palmer; Langridge; Minton; Tear; Roberts; Murray; Wilson-Johnson; London Sinfonietta Chorus; London Sinfonietta; Atherton (Decca 414 241-2LH2; 2 CDs).

Atherton's conducting is reliable rather than revelatory, but this *King Priam* features perhaps the best available cast. Norman Bailey and Robert Tear are notably fine as Priam and Achilles.

ORCHESTRAL MUSIC

The most successful and popular of Tippett's works for full orchestra is his *Fantasia concertante on a theme of Corelli*, commissioned by the Edinburgh Festival in 1953 to celebrate the tercentenary of Corelli's birth. Taking as its base a theme from Corelli's Concerto Grosso Op. 6 No. 2, it's a staunchly neo-classical composition, but is far from being a simple pastiche of its primary source – indeed, the central section could well be by Puccini. The *Fantasia*'s Italianate tone sometimes gets smothered beneath Tippett's extemporizations, but on the whole this is a very entertaining piece.

Tippett's other major orchestral work from this period is the *Piano Concerto*. In the composer's own words, this piece "had its precise moment of conception years before, when I was listening to a rehearsal of Beethoven's Fourth Piano Concerto with Gieseking, who had just returned to England after the war. I felt moved to create a concerto in which once again the piano might sing." The first of the three movements (the longest at around fifteen minutes) sets smooth-flowing lines of melody against agitated orchestral effects, creating an engaging sense of momentum. Overall the concerto is a heavily contrapuntal composition, but in the slow movement it approaches a more rhapsodic sense of form; the last movement is basically an orchestral rondo, culminating in a marvellous duet for piano and celesta.

> ◗ **Fantasia Concertante on a Theme of Corelli; Piano Concerto**: Bath Festival Orchestra; Philharmonia; Ogdon; Menuhin; Masters; Tippett; Davis (EMI CMS 7 63522-2; 2 CDs; with *Concerto for Double String Orchestra; Piano Sonatas Nos. 1 & 2; String Quartet No. 1*).

The composer's own recording of the *Fantasia Concertante* is easily the finest, with exemplary lightness and clarity. The leading violins of Yehudi Menuhin and Robert Masters play extremely well, while the enthusiastic Bath Festival Orchestra delivers a crisp and well-balanced performance. John Ogdon's playing of the *Piano Concerto* is exceptional, and Colin Davis, a renowned interpreter of Tippett's music, conducts this piece with real energy – the sharply defined colours of the finale are especially marvellous. This double CD set, containing fine performances of four other Tippett compositions, is the best way to familiarize yourself with his range.

STRING QUARTETS

Spanning his entire creative life, Tippett's five string quartets allow you to chart the evolution of his distinctive style, an essentially contrapuntal technique, in which the example of Beethoven's chamber music is never too far away. The first three are the most appealing, especially the tuneful *Quartet No. 1* of 1935 (the first piece Tippett was prepared to acknowledge), which successfully reconciles the influences of Sibelius, Beethoven and English folk song. The second and third quartets, dating from 1942 and 1946, are grandly expressive creations, distinguished by close attention to the textures and intricacies of part-writing – three of the movements of *Quartet No. 3*, for example, are fugal in structure. The last two quartets are more problematic. The *Quartet No. 4* is an abrasive piece that illustrates a somewhat banal cradle-to-grave programme (also the theme of the *Symphony No. 4*), while *Quartet No. 5* was not at all well received when it was premiered in 1991, the concensus being that it amounted to little more than a rehash of late Beethoven.

> ◗ **String Quartets Nos. 1–4**: (Collins 7006-2; 2 CDs).

The Britten Quartet's survey of the first four quartets is unmatched for its quality of playing, originality of insight and clarity of sound. The music (especially the last quartet of 1974) can seem unapproachable at first, but repeated listening brings lasting rewards.

VIKTOR ULLMANN

(1898–1944)

I n 1938, mirroring the infamous Munich exhibition of *Entartete Kunst* (Degenerate Art), the Nazis organized an exhibition of *Entartete Musik* in Düsseldorf, where the public was invited to sneer at recordings of the offending creations. "Degenerate" in this instance meant anything vaguely avant-garde, anything with jazz or black-American associations, and absolutely anything written by a Jew. Black-listed composers such as Korngold, Schoenberg, Weill, Zemlinsky and Hindemith soon emigrated; some of the lesser-known were to endure marginalization and neglect, but at least they escaped with their lives. Others, such as Hans Krása, Erwin Schullhof and Viktor Ullmann, were not so lucky. A generation of composers was annihilated by the Nazis, and it's only in recent years that their music has been rediscovered, so that at last we can assess the true history of twentieth-century music in central Europe.

Ullmann was born into a German-speaking family in Teschen (now Těšín) on the Moravian-Polish border, but received his musical education in Vienna, where he joined Schoenberg's composition class in 1918. Schoenberg, Zemlinsky and Berg all became personal friends and strong influences, though Ullmann's highly chromatic music resisted the atonality of the Second Viennese School and always retained a strong tonal centre. In the 1920s he worked as assistant to Zemlinsky in Prague, then took up posts in Aussig and Zurich before giving up his musical career to run the Anthroposophic Society's bookshop in Stuttgart, devoting himself to the dissemination of Rudolf Steiner's philosophy of self-knowledge. Hitler's rise to power forced him back to Prague in 1933, but it was to prove a temporary haven.

After the Nazi occupation of Prague it is thought he tried, but failed, to emigrate. Soon after he was sent to the Jewish ghetto established by the Nazis in the town of Terezín, otherwise known as Theresienstadt. On his arrival in September 1942, Ullmann was excused the customary work assignment and asked to organize concerts and musical activities. He wrote reviews and set up a group to give performances of works by Terezín composers – Gideon Klein, Hans Krása, Pavel Haas and Ullmann himself – as well as by Mahler, Schoenberg and Zemlinsky. During his two years in Terezín, Ullmann was more prolific than at any other time in his life, writing three piano sonatas, the beautiful *String Quartet No. 3*, several songs and orchestral scores, and perhaps his most remarkable work, the satirical opera *Der Kaiser von Atlantis*. In October 1944, not long after the first performance of *Der Kaiser* had been banned by the SS, Ullmann and the majority of the composers and musicians in Terezín were transported to the gas chambers of Auschwitz.

DER KAISER VON ATLANTIS

Ullmann wrote two operas in Prague immediately before the war, *Der Sturz des Antichrist* (The Fall of the Antichrist) and *Der*

zerbrochene Krug (The Broken Jug), but his most remarkable work, *Der Kaiser von Atlantis* (The Emperor of Atlantis) was written in the appalling conditions of the Terezín ghetto and designed for performance there.

The opera portrays a mad, paranoid Emperor, fighting wars on all fronts until Death, "an old-fashioned craftsman of dying", refuses to work any longer, in protest at the infernal mechanization of killing. With the sick and wounded now condemned to live on in agony, the Emperor pleads with Death to return to work, but he will do so only on one condition – that the Emperor agrees to be his first victim. The Emperor's demise in the final scene echoes the Nazi defeats on the eastern and western fronts.

Der Sturz des Antichrist had foundered because the antichrist could have been interpreted as a reference to Hitler, and *Der Kaiser* similarly fell foul of the authorities – the opera was rehearsed up to the dress rehearsal, but then banned after the slow-witted SS officers at last saw it as a satire of their leader. Whereas *Der Sturtz* remains unperformed to this day, *Der Kaiser von Atlantis* was premiered in 1975, proving to be a very powerful work on stage. Ullmann's score is an eclectic mixture of cabaret music, pastiche (there is a daring send-up of the German national anthem), operetta and lush Romanticism, for a band that includes saxophone, banjo and harmonium. Death is depicted in music of ecstatic beauty, dripping with sumptuous harmonies – not a fearsome character, but a reliable and faithful friend, merciful and welcoming. The ultimate message is one of hope mingled with resignation, as Death himself declares: "It's not the other side we need fear, but rather this world that is veiled in darkest shadow."

🔘 Mazura, Kraus, Berry, Vermillion; Leipzig Gewandhaus Orchestra; Zagrosek (Decca 440 854-26).

This premiere recording in the Decca Entärtete Musik series is welcome but flawed, in that it misses the subversive cabaret element of the piece. Franz Mazura as the MC figure doesn't give the part the slick edge it needs, and Walter Berry is a bit unfocused as Death. However, the Emperor's farewell is brilliantly performed by Michael Kraus, and the closing chorale is very moving.

ORCHESTRAL WORKS

Ullmann wrote some impressive orchestral pieces before the war, including the uncompromising *Variations and Double Fugue on a Piano Piece of Schoenberg* (1934) and the powerfully lyrical *Piano Concerto* (1939). As with his operas, though, the extremity of Terezín produced his finest work.

The manuscript of Ullmann's *Piano Sonata No. 7*, which he completed only a few weeks before he was transported to Auschwitz, was covered with notes for its orchestration into a symphony. Now completed by the German composer Bernhard Wulff, this *Symphony in D* is a final summation of Ullmann's savagely curtailed career – including a quotation from *Der Sturz des Antichrist* and a waltz from Heuberger's operetta *Der Opernball*, which Ullmann worked on in Prague, it ends with an impressive *Variations and Fugue on a Hebrew Folksong*. The source tune for this resilient final movement, a Zionist song which would have been familiar to many inmates of Terezín, is transformed into a Czech Hussite hymn whose message of national liberation would also not have been lost on the symphony's intended audience.

🔘 **Symphony in D; Piano Concerto; Variations and Double Fugue on a Piano Piece of Schoenberg**: Richter; Brno Philharmonic; Yinon (Bayer BR 100 228).

This premiere recording of the *Symphony in D* reveals it as a very fine work indeed. The conductor, Israel Yinon, keeps a grip on the symphony's very fluid scoring, in which melodic fragments dart from one instrument to another. This recording includes the *Variations and Double Fugue on a Piano Piece of Schoenberg* and the *Piano Concerto* – the latter given a fine performance by Konrad Richter, who finds just the right balance of power and gentle lyricism. This is the best all-round CD of Ullmann's works.

CHAMBER MUSIC

Ullmann's most accomplished piece in Terezín, and the one most likely to enter the standard concert repertoire, is the *String Quartet No. 3*, which was written in January 1943 although it isn't known whether it was ever performed in Terezín. It has a beautiful lyrical opening tinged with a melancholy typical of his Viennese background, while in the slow movement he ventures into the world of Schoenberg and Berg with a twelve-note motif, though he always retains an underlying sense of tonality. Ullmann's seven piano sonatas – three written in Terezín, four before his incarceration – are of more specialized interest, but they show him as a distinctive voice in the central European musical tradition. The writing can seem a little indigestible at first, but it mellows on further listening.

○ **String Quartet No. 3; Piano Sonatas Nos. 5–7**: Group for New Music; Kolben; Kraus (Koch International 3-7109-2).
○ **Piano Sonatas Nos. 1–4**: Kraus (Edition Abseits EDA 005-2).

The Koch CD – Volume I in the company's Terezín Music Anthology – presents Ullmann's chamber music from Terezín in very fine performances. In the luscious opening of the quartet the independent lines of the four instruments are beautifully blended, the melodic lines moving effortlessly from one player to another. Edith Kraus, who plays the sixth sonata, premiered this piece in the ghetto, and it's the most attractive of the three sonatas on this disc (the seventh sounds a bit awkward once you've heard its orchestrated version, the *Symphony in D*).

Kraus's recording of the intense and knotty early sonatas – a comprehensive survey of the pre-Terezín compositions – shows clearly Ullmann's orientation towards Viennese music, in contrast to the folk-influenced style of his Czech contemporaries. That said, the second sonata includes a fine set of variations on a Moravian folk song that was collected by Janáček.

EDGARD VARÈSE
(1883–1965)

As early as 1917 Edgard Varèse spoke of instruments which could offer "a whole new world of unsuspecting sounds", foreshadowing the use of synthesizers and computers in contemporary music. He devoted his life to new ideas, new instruments and new music, and though his output is fairly meagre by comparison with many of this century's great innovators, he was to be a prime influence on the post-war avant-garde.

Of Franco-Italian parentage, Varèse had already written an opera by the age of eleven, but studied maths and science when he went to the university of Turin. By 1909 he was in Berlin, where he became friends with Busoni (see p.86), then he moved on to the Paris, where he studied at the Conservatoire, impressed Debussy and met Apollinaire, Satie and Jean Cocteau. He was present at the riotous premiere of the *Rite of Spring*, a work with which he felt an immediate sympathy – the audience around him screamed abuse at the stage, but Varèse remarked "The music seemed very natural to me."

Conscripted in 1914, he was discharged through illness and escaped to America the following year. Varèse's arrival in New York

– where he was to spend the rest of his life – was the start of his career as an evangelist for new music. He organized an International Composers Guild for the presentation of works by Schoenberg, Stravinsky and Webern, and his first major composition, *Amériques* (1922), displayed his espousal of Stravinsky's anti-Romantic intensity, using plentiful brass and woodwind to invoke the pounding presence of the new world and the thrill of discovery. "I refuse to limit myself to sounds that have already been heard," he declared. After labouring for years on *Arcana*, a huge work for 120 musicians but no string sections, his search for new sonorities led to *Ionisation* (1933), in which sirens, anvils, gourds and sleigh bells compete for attention.

In the 1930s and 1940s he explored the sonic potential of various electro-mechanical devices and new instruments such as the ondes martenot – an invention exploited most effectively by Messaien (see p.231). In the 1950s Varèse went on to compose *Deserts* (1954), a pioneering work for magnetic tape, and to collaborate with Xenakis (see p.419) on the *Poème Electronique* for the World's Fair of 1958. He died seven years later, hailed as a visionary by Stockhausen, the composer whose work did most to realize Varèse's vision of an electronic future.

THE MUSIC

Varèse's most famous work is *Ionisation*, a six-minute piece scored for 25 different percussion instruments; it was written well over half a century ago, but its contrast of "primitive" tones with the more "civilized" celeste and piano still sounds spontaneous and fresh. However, *Octandre* (1923) is an easier way into Varèse, as it is scored for a less aggressive ensemble of horns and wood-winds, and is divided into three compact movements within which the music flows like water. To get an idea of Varèse's range – he's not the one-man noise factory he's made out to be in certain quarters – you should get to know *Arcana*, a rich orchestral score that is

generated from a single melodic line, and *Density 21.5* for solo flute, a piece that reveals a quieter, more contemplative side to the composer.

You can sample all these pieces, as well as his seminal *Amériques*, on the CD reviewed below; for those who want to explore more of Varèse's output, Erato are recording the complete works with Kent Nagano and the Orchestre National de France, but the series has only just got under way.

⊙ **Amériques; Arcana; Density 21.5; Intégrales; Ionisation; Octandre; Offrandes**: Boulez; New York Philharmonic & Ensemble Intercontemporain; Beauregard; Yakar (Sony SMK 45844).

This is a great disc from the man who made a name for himself as a conductor by performing Varèse in New York in the 1970s. The CD is a substantial expansion of the 1977 CBS recording of *Ionisation*, and its high-definition remastering lends Varèse a deeper, more detailed sound than the vinyl had. Absolutely essential.

═══ ♫ ═══

RALPH VAUGHAN WILLIAMS
(1872–1958)

With his friend and colleague Gustav Holst, Vaughan Williams spent many years researching and cata-loguing English traditional songs that had never previously been written down, thereby spurring a resurgence in English music comparable to the similar folk-inspired movements within Russia and central Europe. He remains, with Purcell and Elgar, one of England's most popular composers, thanks to music that is affirmatively humanistic and insular, however unfashionable such attitudes may have become. "Why need music be origi-nal to be enjoyed?" he once demanded.

Vaughan Williams was a late starter. In 1897, after graduating from the Royal College of Music, he went to Germany, where he stud-ied with Bruch, and as late as 1908 he moved to France to take much-needed lessons in orchestration from Ravel. Both men influ-enced him enormously and, upon his return to

England, he settled down to composition, producing at the age of thirty-nine his most successful work – the *Fantasia on a Theme by Thomas Tallis*. By 1914 he had produced a considerable body of music, including two symphonies, and was beginning to find an audience. After World War I – during which he served in the medical corps and the artil-lery – he threw himself into musical activity, not just composing but also conducting the Bach Choir and Handel Society, and teaching at the Royal College.

During the 1920s his music began to be heard overseas, with notable performances of his work being given in Salzburg, Venice, Prague and Geneva. By the middle of the following decade he was established as the figurehead of English music, and was very much in demand as a conductor of his own work. His recordings – notably his 1937 version of the *Symphony No. 4* – testify to a

symphonies, and as an expression of religious faith it won't leave anyone completely unmoved. Don't start here, but if you want to understand the world-view of Vaughan Williams you should certainly tackle it. As the composer wrote – "It's not like the operas they are used to, but it's the sort of opera I wanted to write, and there it is."

Noble, Herincx, Partridge, Lloyd, Hodgson; London Philharmonic Chorus & Orchestra; Boult (EMI CMS7 64212-2; 2 CDs).

The *Pilgrim's Progress* is not an especially dramatic work, but Adrian Boult engineers some wonderfully luxurious orchestral playing, and his cast is excellent, especially John Noble and Raimund Herincx. The chorus work – of crucial importance in this opera – is also outstanding.

SYMPHONY NO. 5

The *Symphony No. 5* was commenced in 1938, while he was at work on *The Pilgrim's Progress*. Beginning to doubt that he would ever complete his magnum opus, he used some of the opera's material for the symphony, which he completed in 1943 but then revised in 1951. The final version is the best of Vaughan Williams's nine symphonies. The first movement begins with a particularly haunting idea, stated softly by the horns, which is followed by ominously shifting music that foreshadows what's to come beyond the ghostly, muted Scherzo. Everything is leading towards the huge span of the wonderful slow movement, where Vaughan Williams introduces overwhelmingly emotive solos for oboe and violin. Its mood of reverence extends to the finale, a harmonic and rhythmic kaleidoscope that builds to an exalted climax before subsiding into a quietly contemplative state.

Philharmonia, Slatkin (RCA RD60556; with *Symphony No. 6*).

Slatkin's performance of the *Symphony No. 5* stands out from the rest of his Vaughan Williams symphonic cycle. The scale and sense of structure are brilliantly handled and the Philharmonia play with absolute conviction – there are few more moving accounts of the slow movement and the finale is realized with heartbreaking restraint. It's coupled with a similarly urgent and well-recorded account of the sixth symphony, a work that clearly bears the marks of the war years.

greater talent than he would have admitted. He once began a concert saying "You start and I'll follow", a self-deprecating joke typical of a man who modestly defined his role with the words – "the composer must not shut himself up and think of art; he must live with his fellows and make his art an expression of the whole life of the community."

THE PILGRIM'S PROGRESS

Vaughan Williams spent more than half his life on *The Pilgrim's Progress*, a four-act opera derived from John Bunyan's moralistic allegory, with additional texts from the Bible. It began life in 1906 as a piece of incidental music for a semi-amateur stage adaptation of the novel, and was premiered in its entirety at Covent Garden in 1951. One critic described it as an "aftermath", and there was little enthusiasm elsewhere for a work that was held to have been flawed by its long gestation. Progressing by means of tableaux which present salient scenes from the book, *The Pilgrim's Progress* is not the most fluid of operas, and Vaughan Williams's vocal style was never as assured as his way with the orchestra. Yet moments such as the depiction of Vanity Fair or the arrival at the Celestial City are as impressive as anything in the

OBOE CONCERTO

Vaughan Williams's *Oboe Concerto*, written for Leon Goosens in 1944, resembles the *Symphony No. 5* in mood, and may even contain material that was discarded from the symphony, having been discarded from *The Pilgrim's Progress*. Scored for strings and oboe, the concerto makes marvellous use of the solo instrument's lyrical, somewhat mournful qualities, though the work's dominant movement is the finale, which is characterized above all by its capricious virtuosity.

> ◗ Cantor; London Symphony Orchestra; Judd (Pickwick MCD 59; with Strauss, *Oboe Concerto*).

This is the most simple and unaffected of a number of good recordings. Judd's tempi avoid self-indulgence, the accompaniment is bright and well forward, and Cantor produces a wonderfully vocal oboe tone. This truly involved performance is excellently recorded and its coupling, Strauss's autumnal concerto, makes a highly illuminating comparison.

FANTASIA ON A THEME BY THOMAS TALLIS

Termed a "Jacobean Fantasy" by the composer, the *Fantasia on a Theme by Thomas Tallis* (1910) is Vaughan Williams's homage to the music of Renaissance England. Specifically it grew out of his work editing the English Hymnal, in the process of which he came across a melody that Thomas Tallis had written as a Psalm setting in 1567. Vaughan Williams took this basic theme and developed it into music that is both intensely devotional and sumptuously romantic. Commissioned for the Three Choirs Festival in Gloucester, the *Fantasia* is scored for two string orchestras, the smaller of which was arranged to produce an antiphonal effect, even in acoustics less resonant than the cathedral in which it received its first performance. The *Fantasia* also assigns separate parts to a string quartet, and the numerous independent voices confused many of those present at the premiere – one critic called it "a queer, mad work by an odd fellow from Chelsea". He was probably in the majority, but the work soon secured Vaughan Williams's place as the spiritual leader of English music, and nowadays it's by far the best known of all his works.

> ◉ New Queen's Hall Orchestra; Wordsworth (Argo 440 116-2; with *The Lark Ascending*, *Five Variations on Dives and Lazarus*, and *Fantasia on "Greensleeves"*).

This account, played on period instruments and supposedly in period style, has a uniquely sweet sound, and conductor Barry Wordsworth encourages just about the right amount of gushing. Including performances of three other immensely engaging orchestral pieces, this well-engineered CD makes a perfect introduction to Vaughan Williams.

GIUSEPPE VERDI
(1813–1901)

Verdi's operas are paragons of high Romanticism, with their lavish emotionalism, demanding vocal and instrumental writing, complex plots, high-voltage characterizations and so forth. Yet political engagement was not a notable feature of the lives of most Romantic composers, and Verdi was a supremely political artist. In the aftermath of the Napoleonic wars, Italy was divided into a mosaic of kingdoms and duchies, a situation that prevailed for most of the century, in the face of a burgeoning movement for national unification. Many of the plots of Verdi's earlier operas can be read as allegories related to the aspirations of the Italian people – the well-known *Chorus of the Hebrew Slaves* from *Nabucco* struck a particular chord in an audience living under the rule of countless princelings and foreign oppressors.

Censorship was a bugbear: although Verdi managed to smuggle a topical message into such works as *Nabucco* and *La battaglia di Legnano*, where centuries of history provided a disguise of sorts, in other instances his plots had to be tampered with in order to ensure performance. Such interference achieved nothing, however. As the nationalist movement gathered force in the 1850s and 1860s, and Victor Emmanuel, liberal ruler of Piedmont, became the popular choice for king of united Italy, the chant "Viva Verdi!" was heard at performances of his work and on the streets – the composer's name being also an acronym for "Vittorio Emmanuele, re d'Italia" (Victor Emmanuel, King of Italy). Verdi himself came to be seen as a figure-head for the unification movement, and once the goal had been achieved he became an active politician, and was elected to the Italian senate in 1874.

There is little in Verdi's early upbringing that foreshadows the cosmopolitan operatic master. His parents ran a village inn in the northern plains of Parma, and everything about his education and early life suggests provincialism. After private studies in Milan (he failed to gain entrance to the city's conservatory) he returned to his home area as music director for the town of Busseto, where he yearned to get back to the Lombard capi-tal. In the end he found it impossible to stifle his ambition to see an opera of his performed at La Scala: in 1839 he resigned his post in Busseto and headed with his family back to Milan. He was fortunate in that his first opera, *Oberto*, was almost immediately accepted for performance, even though his previous compositions of any consequence amounted to just a few academic exercises and liturgical works. *Oberto* was first heard in November of the same year, and it made the Milanese public sit up and take notice of the ambitious twenty-six-year-old.

His second opera, *Il Giorno di Regno* (1840), was a flop, but two years later he produced *Nabucco*, which really saw his career take off. In the wake of its success came a steady stream of commissions from other Italian cities and from abroad, resulting in thirteen operas in just eight years: *I Lombardi alla prima crociata* (1843), *Ernani* (1844), *I due Foscari* (1844), *Giovanna d'Arco* (1845), *Alzira* (1845), *Attila* (1846), *Macbeth* (1847), *I Masnadieri* (1847), *Jérusalem* (1847), *Il Corsaro* (1848), *La Battaglia di*

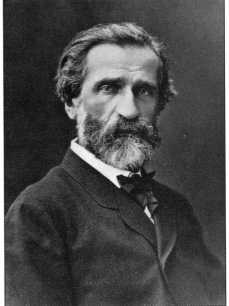

MANSELL COLLECTION

Legnano (1849), *Luisa Miller* (1849) and *Stiffelio* (1850). By the end of this sequence his mastery of the operatic stage was well established and he had earned so much money he could have retired had he wished. The pace of composition relaxed in the 1850s, but it was in this period that Verdi wrote his most popu-lar operas, beginning with the trio of *Rigoletto* (1851), *Il Trovatore* (1853) and *La Traviata* (1853), followed by, among others *Simon Boccanegra* (1857), *Un Ballo in Maschera* (1859), *La Forza del Destino* (1862), *Don Carlos* (1867) and *Aida* (1871).

There then followed a gap of some fifteen years before the premiere of another Verdi opera, a phase during which he composed his only non-operatic work of any standing, the *Requiem* (1874), and otherwise concentrated on revising some of his earlier works, when-ever new productions or new translations of the libretto brought an opportunity to tighten up structure or expand scenes. *Macbeth*, *La Forza del Destino*, *Simon Boccanegra* and *Don Carlos* were all overhauled at this time. The revised *Boccanegra* benefited from the involvement of the poet and composer Arrigo Boito, who provided the librettos for Verdi's last two operas, *Otello* (1887) and *Falstaff* (1893). His final years were spent on more religious music, the *Four Sacred Pieces*, and masterminding the foundation of the Casa di Riposa, a retirement home for musicians in Milan, funded by his royalties. He died of a stroke in January in 1901 and was buried in the grounds of the Casa di Riposa; a quarter of a million people attended his funeral cortège.

THE OPERAS

Verdi's fame rests as much on his stagecraft as on his music, for with Verdi, more than with any of his Italian predecessors, drama and music are fused into an indivisible entity. It's an indication of the speed of his advances that in his youth Rossini's operas were all the rage, with their concentration on vocal display and decoration at the expense of expressiveness. By the 1830s the trend had shifted, as more dramatic operas of Bellini (see p.39) and Donizetti (see p.114) swept Rossini's style aside, displacing light-hearted comedy with tragedies of star-crossed lovers and grandiose historical settings. During his time studying in Milan, Verdi had a subscription seat at La Scala and thus became thoroughly conversant with all the latest developments.

Accordingly, even his earliest operas revealed a mature knowledge of what was possible on stage. Admittedly, in his earlier work the style is not always up to the demands of the drama: *Macbeth*, for example, for all its wonderful tunes and its dramatic speed, often resorts to rum-tum-tum accompaniments that suggest comedy more than tragedy. It's a stylistic mannerism that even affects mature works such as *La Traviata* and *Rigoletto*, but the late works are masterpieces of consistency and continuity – by the time he came to write *Otello* and *Falstaff*, he could make each act a continuous flow from which it is virtually impossible to extract individual arias without destroying their meaning. By this stage, too, Verdi's music had gained a much broader harmonic vocabulary, with more subtlety and ease than the rather four-square harmonic language of the early works. And of course, one skill he always displayed in profusion was his talent for melody, and it is the striking originality of Verdi's arias and choruses that have made him, with Puccini, the most popular operatic composer in history.

MACBETH

In total Verdi wrote twenty-eight operas, but fewer than half of these are in the regular repertory, though several of the earlier works are often revived for one-off productions. Of his first sixteen, only *Macbeth* has a secure place in the opera houses, and that's because it sits head and shoulders above its contemporaries following Verdi's revision of it in 1865. None of the early pieces conveys the sense of drama of Verdi's first encounter with Shakespeare, a writer who was to inspire his two greatest works at the opposite end of his career. As with all these products of what he termed his years as "a galley slave", the music sometimes seems incongruously upbeat, but there is an intensity to the arias and choruses of this opera which makes it worth investigation after you've heard Verdi in his prime.

🎵 Milnes, Cossoto, Raimondi, Carreras; Ambrosian Opera Chorus; New Philharmonia, Muti (EMI CMS 7 64339 2; 2 CDs).

Macbeth has been particularly successful on disc, but Muti's is first choice for fitting on to two mid-price discs and for its unwavering drama and musicality. Sherrill Milnes and Fiorenzo Cossotto are grippingly powerful as Macbeth and his wife, and Muti inspires concentration from all involved.

Sherrill Milnes smoulders as Macbeth

RIGOLETTO

Rigoletto was the work that revealed Verdi's operatic maturity, and it's always been one of his most popular. The tragic tale of the cursed hunchback jester Rigoletto, the heinous Duke of Mantua, and Rigoletto's daughter Gilda, was based on Victor Hugo's *Le roi s'amuse*, but thanks to the Venetian censors the action had to be moved from the French royal court to the sixteenth-century ducal court of Mantua. This was admittedly closer to home for its audience, but at least the setting didn't depict a womanizing monarch – Venice was at that time ruled by the monarchist Austrians. *Rigoletto* is an immensely accessible opera, moving swiftly and coherently through a series of memorable arias, choruses and confrontations. Yet it's also a very dark work: Gilda sacrifices her life to the philandering duke, whose role is assigned to a tenor, normally the voice of the good guy. The villain gets the opera's best tune as well – *La donna è mobile* (Women are fickle).

> ◉ Gobbi, di Stefano, Callas; La Scala Chorus & Orchestra; Serafin (EMI CDS 7 47469 8; 2 CDs).
> ◉ Agache, Leech, Vaduva; Welsh National Opera Chorus & Orchestra; Rizzi (Teldec 4509-90851-2; 2 CDs).

Serafin's recording is a classic, with three of the greatest exponents of the main roles in Tito Gobbi's Rigoletto, Giuseppe di Stefano's Duke and, above all, Maria Callas's touching Gilda. For a modern stereo account, Rizzi's recent recording is almost as good, and is a safe bet for those who find Callas's voice unattractive, despite its dramatic qualities.

IL TROVATORE

Best known for its supposedly incomprehensible plot, *Il Trovatore* (The Troubadour) is another fast-moving drama of revenge with a parent-child relationship at its centre, this time one of mother (Azucena) and supposed son (Manrico, the troubadour of the title). In some ways the opera backslides into pre-*Rigoletto* free-standing musical forms, in that the arias tend to hold up the action rather than move it on. Nonetheless the characterization is strong, and there is novelty in making a mezzo-soprano (Azucena) the centre of attention rather than a soprano, just as the baritone had usurped the lead role from the

more glamorous tenors in *Rigoletto* and *Macbeth*. *Il Trovatore* too has one of Verdi's big tunes – this time the *Anvil Chorus*.

> ◉ Plowright, Domingo, Fassbaender; Rome St Cecilia Academy; Giulini (Deutsche Grammophon 413 355-2; 3 CDs).

This is a red-blooded performance, with a richly detailed characterization of Azucena from Brigitte Fassbaender, a fine Manrico in Plácido Domingo and a touching Leonora (Manrico's lover) from Rosalind Plowright.

LA TRAVIATA

After a pair of operas with historic settings, Verdi wrote one placed in his own time. *La Traviata* (The Fallen Woman) is based on Alexandre Dumas the Younger's play *La dame aux camélias*, about a consumptive "society hostess" (Violetta) whose love for upper-class Alfredo provokes the disapproval of his class-conscious father, Germont. After the costume melodrama of *Rigoletto* and *Trovatore*, *Traviata* is a much more intimate piece, played out among the three principals against a high-society background. Nowadays this is perhaps Verdi's most popular opera, yet initially it was one of his few flops, though the reasons for its failure are to be found in the inadequacy of the original casting (including an implausibly unfrail Violetta) and in the fact that the director had for no obvious reason set it in the eighteenth rather than the nineteenth century. The role of Violetta is one of the most demanding in the repertoire, and there's scarcely a high-profile soprano who hasn't at some time in her career had a go at one of her poignant arias.

> ◉ Gruberova, Shicoff; London Symphony Orchestra; Rizzi (Teldec 9031-76348-2; 2 CDs).

This was Carlo Rizzi's first operatic recording and immediately went to the top of the pile. There is a refinement in the playing of the London Symphony Orchestra rarely found among its rivals, and the cast has only one weak link, with Neil Shicoff a rather rough-edged Alfredo.

SIMON BOCCANEGRA

Simon Boccanegra explores one of Verdi's favourite themes, the conflict between the private and public faces of rulers. Here the arena is fourteenth-century Genoa, where the action centres on the clash between its lowly born doge (Boccanegra) and the nobility (represented by Fiesco), with the complication that Boccanegra has fathered a daughter (Amelia) with Fiesco's daughter. The opera was not a great success when first staged, but was improved immeasurably in Verdi's 1881 revision and, although it is an opera perhaps more admired than loved, it comes close to the final Shakespearean operas in its scale and dramatic characterization – and it does have some of Verdi's most glorious duets.

◉ Cappuccilli, Freni, Carreras, Ghiaurov; La Scala Chorus & Orchestra; Abbado (Deutsche Grammophon 415 692-2; 2 CDs).

Made in 1977 and based around a La Scala production, this is a classic among modern Verdi recordings. The sound is warm, and it makes the most of the moments of high drama, with Piero Cappuccilli an intense, touching doge and Mirella Freni a fresh-sounding Amelia.

UN BALLO IN MASCHERA

Verdi had to change many things in his operas to suit the censors, and this happened most famously with *Un Ballo in Maschera* (A Masked Ball). It was originally based on a fictionalized account of the assassination of King Gustavus III of Sweden at a court ball in 1789, but the very idea of a king's murder being portrayed on stage was anathema to the Neapolitan censors. The action was duly transferred to Boston before the American War of Independence, with the king becoming Riccardo, the English governor. It is still performed in both versions – only the characters' names are different.

History records the incident as a motiveless killing by one of Gustavus's officers, but Verdi's opera suggests that Gustavus was killed in revenge for seducing the officer's wife (despite the historical evidence that his proclivities led elsewhere), and also throws in a few extra characters in the form of Oscar, the king's page, and the witch Ulrica, who foresees the murder. Much of the music emphasizes the dark inevitability of the king's fate, but the grimness is leavened by the mischievous character of Oscar (a soprano role), and by some wonderful ensembles and love duets.

◉ Price, Pavarotti, Bruson, Gruberova; National Philharmonic Orchestra; Solti (Decca 410 210-2; 2 CDs).

This set is dominated by the glorious singing of Margaret Price as Amelia, though Pavarotti too is in his prime as the king. Solti's conducting is less pugnacious than usual and brings out the score's lighter textures and moods to perfection.

LA FORZA DEL DESTINO

La Forza del Destino (The Force of Destiny) is another of Verdi's turbulent family dramas: the central character, Don Carlo, is tracking across country after country in pursuit of Don Alvaro, who has eloped with his sister, Leonora, and accidentally killed their father. He then unwittingly befriends the man he is seeking, ensuring calamity on all fronts. The opera was written to a commission from St Petersburg in 1862, but seven years later Verdi revised the ending and other passages for performances in Milan; it is this marginally less bleak version which is most often heard today. The time-spread of the action gives *La Forza del Destino* a rather disjointed narrative, and Verdi's use of recurring motifs (such as the fate themes in the well-known overture) doesn't create a cohesion comparable to that of Wagner's developmental leitmotifs, but it's an intriguing experiment in through-composed opera. It's not the place to start with Verdi, but you'll appreciate its boldness after you've heard his later work.

◉ Price, Domingo, Milnes; London Symphony Orchestra; Levine (RCA RD81864; 3 CDs).

La Forza del Destino is an expansive work, and James Levine has the skill to mould such an epic into a satisfying whole. There's sumptuous singing from Leontyne Price as Leonora and sterling tone from Domingo as Alvaro.

DON CARLOS

Verdi's next opera – a work on an even larger scale – was originally composed in French for Paris; hence the existence of two versions, the French-language *Don Carlos* and the Italian-language *Don Carlo*. Like *Un Ballo in Maschera*, its starting point is a fictional account of events in the lives of historical figures. Here Verdi adapts Schiller's play about the sixteenth-century Spanish king Philip II and his son Don Carlos, whose fateful love for his young stepmother, Elisabeth, leads to his downfall. The welter of political intrigue and emotional drama is most effective in the five-act French version, from which Verdi later excised some scenes crucial to the dangerous relationship between Don Carlos and Elisabeth.

> ◉ **Don Carlo**: Domingo, Caballé; Royal Opera House Chorus & Orchestra; Giulini (EMI CDS 7 47701 8; 3 CDs).
> ◉ **Don Carlos**: Domingo, Ricciarelli; La Scala Chorus & Orchestra; Abbado (Deutsche Grammophon 415 316-2; 4 CDs).

Giulini brings out the fervour of this glorious score with an unfailing sense of pace and drama; Abbado's recording of the French version, which also boasts an appendix of variant versions and additions, is less successful as an overall experience, though Domingo is arguably in better voice here than in the Giulini performance. Otherwise the strong casts are on a par with one another.

AIDA

In 1869 the opening of the Suez Canal was celebrated by, among other events, the inauguration of the Cairo Opera House. The opera chosen to open the first season was *Rigoletto*, and such was it success that it was decided to commission a new opera specifically for Cairo. Thus was born *Aida*, the spectacular successor to *Don Carlos*. Associated above all with its *Triumphal March*, it is regularly subjected to the most lavish treatment that stage technicians can muster – every year in Verona, for example, the Roman amphitheatre is turned into a replica of Pharaonic Egypt for a cast-of-thousands production of *Aida*. But, as with *Don Carlos*, the spectacle is really nothing more than a backdrop to an intense emotional drama. In essence, *Aida* is another of Verdi's tragedies of divided loyalty, focusing on the Ethiopian slave girl Aida, daughter of the captured Ethiopian king, and her love for the Egyptian Captain of the Guard, Radames.

> ◗ Freni, Carreras, Baltsa; Vienna Philharmonic Orchestra; Karajan (EMI CMS 7 69300 2; 3 CDs).

The second of Karajan's two recordings of Aida encompasses both the grandeur and excitement of the big public moments and the intimacy of the real drama beneath. His cast is equal to the conception, with José Carreras an ardently youthful Radames, Mirella Freni spinning out beautiful lines as Aida and Agnes Baltsa sonorous as her rival in love, Amneris.

OTELLO

In 1879 Verdi began to sketch an opera based on Shakespeare's *Othello*, a project that was to take more of his time than any of his other works. *Otello* was completed in 1886, some sixteen years after *Aida*, and shows Verdi achieving an extraordinary level of dramatic sophistication. This opera marks the culmination of the evolutionary development of the perfectly through-composed Italian opera (German opera already had Wagner), in which each act is a continual dramatic sweep within which the set pieces are intrinsic parts of the whole, intensifying the action rather than arresting it.

Some of this credit for *Otello*'s economy must go to Verdi's librettist Boito, who ditched the entire first act of Shakespeare's play to create a piece that focuses entirely on the characterization of the central trio, giving greater prominence to Iago than accorded by Shakespeare – indeed for years Boito and Verdi used the working title *Jago*.

> ◗ Domingo, Scotto, Milnes; National Philharmonic Orchestra; Levine (RCA GD82951; 2 CDs).

This recording was made in 1977, when Domingo, now established as the greatest modern exponent of the role, was still relatively fresh to it. His ardour is matched by the vibrant account of the score from James Levine, while Renata Scotto and Sherrill Milnes respond with character and power to their roles as Desdemona and Iago.

FALSTAFF

Rossini once remarked that Verdi was "too melancholic and serious" to write a comedy. Verdi's riposte came right at the end of his life – premiered in 1893, the composer's eightieth year, *Falstaff* displays the wit and joie de vivre of a work created by a man half Verdi's age. He and Boito concentrate almost exclusively on the Falstaff of *The Merry Wives of Windsor*, and the fat knight's forlorn attempt to seduce Alice Ford and Meg Page simultaneously, with inevitable consequences. *Falstaff* has the formal perfection of *Otello*, yet was not immediately as successful – whereas the audience had packed the streets outside Verdi's hotel after the premiere of the latter, at the opening night of

Falstaff the atmosphere was one of deep respect rather than spontaneous joy. It was mainly due to the efforts of Toscanini, who conducted the work in opera houses all over the world, that *Falstaff* achieved its due acclaim as one of Verdi's masterpieces.

⏺ Gobbi, Schwarzkopf; Philharmonia Chorus & Orchestra; Karajan (EMI CDS 7 49668; 2 CDs).

After the heaviness of *Aida* and the power of *Otello*, *Falstaff* requires an almost Haydn-like lightness of touch and this it receives in Karajan's classic first recording – one of the very first stereo recordings in the mid-1950s. Tito Gobbi was the greatest Falstaff of the age and he is joined by equally distinguished colleagues, including Elisabeth Schwarzkopf as Alice, Anna Moffo as Nannetta and Rolando Panerai as Ford. But the most impressive feature of this historic set is the superbly fleet-footed playing of the Philharmonia, dampened only by the lack of bloom in the recording.

KARAJAN
Verdi
FALSTAFF
GOBBI · SCHWARZKOPF
MERRIMAN · BARBIERI
MOFFO · PANERAI · ALVA
Philharmonia Chorus
Philharmonia Orchestra
EMI

It's not over until the fat boy sings – Gobbi has fun as Falstaff

THE REQUIEM

Apart from a string quartet, Verdi composed just one non-operatic work of consequence: his massive *Requiem*, written in 1873–74 in memory of the nationalist Italian writer Alessandro Manzoni. Verdi never had a particularly strong Christian faith, but intimations of mortality prompted a number of sacred works in his last years, notably the *Four Sacred Pieces*. However, none of these pieces stands up to comparison with the lavish *Requiem*, the most ambitious sacred work of the late nineteenth century. Hans von Bülow described it as Verdi's "latest opera, in church vestments", and indeed if you take Bach and Mozart as your standards, you'll find the Verdi *Requiem* more religiose than religious. Operatic gesture is never far from the surface and indeed irrupts into the foreground on more than one occasion, for example in the terrifying drama of the Dies Irae and in the aria-like lyricism of some of the solos.

⏺ Dunn, Curry, Hadley, Plishka; Atlanta Symphony Chorus & Orchestra; Shaw (Telarc CD80152; with various opera choruses; 2 CDs).
⏺ Schwarzkopf, Ludwig, Gedda, Ghiaurov; Philharmonia Chorus & Orchestra; Giulini (EMI CDS 7 47257 8; with *Four Sacred Pieces*).

Robert Shaw was Toscanini's choral assistant and his account of the *Requiem* reveals his mastery in this territory, with superb choral singing, excellent young soloists who avoid the histrionics of some their seniors, and alert orchestral playing. Comparable as a performance, but showing its age as a recording, is Giulini's account from 1963, in which the monumentalism of the orchestral music is eloquently contrasted with the limpidly beautiful solo singing.

𝄞

TOMÁS LUIS DA VICTORIA
(1548–1611)

Of all the great polyphonists of the sixteenth century, it was Victoria who wrote most powerfully. Whereas the music of his contemporary Palestrina (see p.260) creates a mood of serene repose and contemplation, Victoria transforms the polyphonic technique into a vehicle for more fervent and passionate feelings, ones that suggest a direct and personal relationship with God. It is a quality that has its roots in a particularly Spanish form of Catholicism, an intense piety that can be found in the writings of the mystic Saint Teresa of Ávila (whom Victoria probably knew), and in the visionary paintings of El Greco.

Victoria was born at Ávila, where he later served as a chorister at the cathedral and attended the Jesuit school of San Gil. Around 1565, with King Philip II as his benefactor, he was sent to Rome to complete his education at another Jesuit institution, the Collegium Germanicum. While there he would almost certainly have come into contact with Palestrina, who may even have given lessons to the young man. Victoria held several important positions during his time in Rome, culminating in that of maestro di cappella at the Collegio Germanico (1573–78). Ordained a priest in 1575, he joined the community of Filippo Neri, the creator of the oratorio form; this community was based at the church of San Giralmo della Carità, where Victoria held a chaplaincy from 1578 until 1585.

In the mid-1580s he expressed a wish to return to Spain and was made the personal chaplain to Philip II's sister, the Dowager Empress Maria, who was then living in retirement at the Convent of the Descalzas Reales in Madrid. He returned just once to Rome, between 1592 and 1594, to supervise the printing of his works and to attend the funeral of Palestrina; otherwise he remained in Madrid, serving the Empress until her death in 1603, after which he continued at the convent until his own death eight years later.

SACRED MUSIC

Compared with Palestrina, Victoria's output is extremely small but it has a far wider emotional range, from the rapturous opening of the motet *O Quam Gloriosum* to the dark intensity of the *Tenebrae Responsories*. His greatest work is the *Requiem*, which he wrote for the Dowager Empress Maria in 1603, a piece which includes music for both the Mass of the Dead and the services that preceded it. Though at times solemn, there is nothing gloomy about this music. Its greatest moments – the swelling chords that open the Kyrie, the hushed intensity of the motet *Versa est in luctum* – rather give an impression of joyful acceptance and spiritual aspiration.

● **Requiem**: Westminster Cathedral Choir; Hill (Hyperion CDA 66250).
● **O Quam Gloriosum (mass & motet); Missa Ave Maris Stella**: Westminster Cathedral Choir; Hill (Hyperion CDA 66114).

The reputation of the Westminster Cathedral Choir received a major boost with their recordings of Victoria in the late 1980s. Intensely committed and sharply focused, these performances convey with complete conviction the spirituality of this music – a quality augmented by the cavernous acoustic. In the *Requiem*, to give some idea of the liturgical context, the recording has included some of the plainsong material that would have been sung with it. Surprisingly the *O Quam Gloriosum Mass* does not quote from the glorious opening phrase of the motet on which it is based (included on the disc), but it does have the same rapturous energy and variety – joyful in the *Gloria*, reverent in the *Benedictus*. The *Missa Ave Maris Stella* is more obviously soulful, and contains at the close of the second *Agnus* setting one of the most delicate moments in all Victoria's music.

═══════════════ ♬ ═══════════════

HEITOR VILLA-LOBOS
(1887–1959)

Heitor Villa-Lobos was living proof that you do not need a conventional musical education to become a composer. He received most of his music lessons from his amateur cellist father, then taught himself to play many other instruments besides, including the guitar, on which he gained a remarkable facility. His close friend and compatriot, the conductor Burle Marx, once asked Villa-Lobos if there was anything he did not play. "Only the oboe," was the reply; but when the two men met again soon afterwards, Villa-Lobos was already well on the way to mastering the instrument. Villa-Lobos became Brazil's leading composer partly because his lack of academic training made him remarkably free-ranging in his approach to composition and in his selection of source material.

On his father's death, instead of pursuing the medical career his mother wished for, he preferred to spend his time playing guitar with the street-bands of Rio, and for several years lead a dissipated Bohemian life. In his late teens and early twenties he undertook a long tour of Brazil to research its folk music. Villa-Lobos was fond of telling Rio's chattering classes that during his travels he had been captured by cannibals, who spared him only because of his musical capabilities; more plausibly, he claimed that the map of Brazil was his first harmony book. On returning to Rio he enrolled at the National Music Institute to further his technical studies, but soon found the atmosphere stifling, and decided to abandon his training in midstream. However, he gained the respect of the teaching staff, who continued to provide help, support and advice after he had left.

Although money was hard to come by, he spent the next few years building up a strong local reputation, and caused a sensation when his compositions were performed at a series of concerts in Rio in 1915. With scant concern for academic niceties, he had amalgamated a vast range of material into music that was eclectic and original. Indigenous Brazilian music went into the mix alongside Wagner, Puccini, Debussy, Chopin, Stravinsky, Gregorian chant, Palestrina and Johann Sebastian Bach, the musician who meant most to him.

The pianist Artur Rubinstein, on hearing some of the composer's work in Brazil in 1919, helped persuade wealthy patrons to sponsor Villa-Lobos' first journey to Paris in 1923. Parisian audiences immediately warmed to his music, and he was fêted by the press and artists of all descriptions, including people of widely different temperament from his own, such as Edgard Varèse (see p.387). On returning to Brazil he became a figurehead for young musicians. In 1930 he was appointed director of the National Music Academy and two years later he was given charge of the country's music education. In 1942 Villa-Lobos founded the Conservatorio National de Canto Orfeonico, with the aim of providing music teachers for Brazilian schools. Leaving aside the merits of his compositons, as a pedagogue and administrator, as well as folklorist and musicologist, Villa-Lobos made an incalculable contribution to Brazilian music.

THE MUSIC

Villa-Lobos wrote music at all hours of the day and night, wherever he happened to be, jotting down ideas as they occurred to him, and rarely bothering to revise them. Thus his output is immense (around 1500 officially listed works) and highly uneven. At his best he achieved a romantic, strongly coloured amalgam of indigenous Brazilian music and the classical tradition of Western Europe, and nowhere is this better demonstrated than in his remarkable *Bachianas Brasileiras*, little suites that fuse the style of Bach with the idioms of Brazilian folk music. The seductive soprano part in *Bachianas Brasileiras No. 5* has made it Villa-Lobos's most recorded piece. His fourteen *Chôros* are more populist but no less groundbreaking, representing, to quote the composer, "A new form of musical composition, synthesizing different types of Brazilian, Indian, and popular music". A *chôro* is a traditional Brazilian serenaders' ensemble of wind instruments and strings, but Villa-Lobos' *Chôros* have extremely varied orchestration, ranging from a single guitar to a double orchestra.

⦿ **Bachianas Brasileiras Nos. 1 & 5; Suite for voice and violin; arrangements of Bach preludes and fugues**: Gomez, Manning; Pleeth Cello Octet (Hyperion CDA 66257).
⦿ **Bachianas Brasileiras No. 6; Chôros No. 2 and other works**: Bennett, King, Black, Knight, O'Neill, Tunnell, Weinberg (Hyperion CDA66295).

These two CDs from Hyperion make an excellent introduction to the music of Villa-Lobos. Jill Gomez is in ravishing voice on the first set, and the Pleeth Cello Octet provide a winning combination of expressive power and voluptuousness in the *Bachianas Brasileiras No. 5*, with Peter Manning giving warm and characterful support in the Suite. Completing a fascinating disc are Villa-Lobos' transcriptions of various Bach preludes and fugues.

The second CD is a showcase for the composer's music for flute, and for the talents of flautist William Bennett. If you don't find this an attractive array of music, you're not going to get on with Villa-Lobos.

ANTONIO VIVALDI

(1678–1741)

"The same concerto four hundred times" is how Stravinsky dismissed him, but no reputation has mushroomed more in recent times than that of Antonio Vivaldi. Early this century he was an unknown name whose works were turned into salon-pieces by the violinist Fritz Kreisler; now his *Four Seasons* are bought by people who have never listened to any other piece of classical music.

The life behind the music is elusive. His father was a musician at Saint Mark's in Venice, and Antonio – the youngest of six children – is said to have studied at the church under the maestro di cappella, Giovanni Legrenzi. Vivaldi was ordained as a priest of a minor order in 1703 (he was later known as the "Red Priest", on account of his distinctive russet hair), and entered the service of the Conservatorio della Pietà, an orphanage for girls which placed special emphasis on musical education. In addition to teaching the violin, Vivaldi composed music for the Pietà's excellent choir and orchestra, and made himself well liked by the governors, who in 1713 granted him leave of absence to supervise the performance of his first opera, *Ottone in Villa*, in Vicenza.

By now his fame was beginning to spread as a result of the publication of *L'estro armonico* in Amsterdam in 1711. These twelve concertos were greatly admired, especially in Germany, where Bach copied and arranged six of them. Much of Vivaldi's time was soon devoted to opera, acting as impresario on his travels throughout Italy: although he continued to work in Venice, from 1718 he was also in the service of Mantua and then spent several years based in Rome. The governors of the Pietà, trying to rein in their increasingly errant maestro, contracted him to provide two concertos per month, and for a while the scheme paid off. Shortly before Christmas 1725 he produced his last works for them – *Il cimento dell'armonica e dell'inventione* (Contest between harmony and invention), another series of twelve concertos,

MARY EVANS PICTURE LIBRARY/EXPLORER

of which the first four were *Le quattro stagioni* (The Four Seasons).

He was invited to Amsterdam, where *Il cimento* had been published, and proved a major attraction there, but when he returned to Venice in 1739, to supervise a festival in honour of a visit from the son of the King of Poland, he found his reputation beginning to wane in his native city. The following year Vivaldi departed for Vienna in the hopes of gaining patronage from the Emperor, but this plan came to nothing. At his death in 1741 he was almost a forgotten man, and he was buried a pauper outside the Vienna city walls. One of six choristers at his funeral was the young Joseph Haydn.

Characterized by dramatic contrasts of dynamics and harmony, Vivaldi's music was often criticized by his contemporaries as eccentric, and after his death it lay forgotten until the 1930s. Yet as a violin virtuoso he was fascinated by the range of possibilities in string sound, and he greatly extended the boundaries of instrumental technique: the slow movement of his B minor concerto for four violins, for example, is an exploration of different methods of spreading a chord and bowing it. Moreover, Vivaldi's contribution to the development of the solo concerto was immense, chiefly in that the structure of his concertos anticipated the three-movement plan of the classical concerto. His first movements are notable for their taut economy and the rhythmic drive of opening themes; his slow movements have the eloquence of operatic arias; and his finales anticipate those of the classical symphony in their buoyancy and pace.

GLORIA IN D

Vivaldi wrote two settings of the Gloria, both in D major. The one catalogued as RV 589 is the most accessible of all Vivaldi's sacred music, and has been in the repertory since it was revived in 1939 by Alfredo Casella, a pupil of Fauré. Notable for its fusion of festive brilliance with moments of profound sadness, it was composed in Venice some time between 1713 and 1717. Musical life in Venice at this time was centred on St Mark's, whose acoustics gave rise to the distinctively Venetian technique of writing for multiple choirs. Although the lack of male soloists might suggest that the Pietà was the venue Vivaldi had in mind, the *Gloria*'s bold contrasts and striking sonorities acknowledge this Venetian polychoral tradition to as splendid effect as the music of Monteverdi or Schütz.

⦿ Nelson, Kirkby; Choir of Christ Church Oxford; Academy of Ancient Music; Preston (L'Oiseau-Lyre 414 678-2).
◗ Vaughan, Baker; Choir of King's College, Cambridge; Academy of St Martin-in-the-Fields; Willcocks (Decca 421 146-2).

The freshest account of the *Gloria* comes from Simon Preston, whose use of authentic instruments and techniques opens up a wider range of colour and tempo. David Willcocks' old-fashioned version is good value, though, with buoyant singing from soloists and choir alike.

L'ESTRO ARMONICO

Of one of Vivaldi's concerts a contemporary wrote, "At the end he improvised a fantasy which quite confounded me, for such playing has not been heard before and can never be equalled. He played with his fingers but a

hair's breadth from the bridge, so that there was hardly room for the bow. He played thus on all four strings, and at unbelievable speed." The stupendous technique is confirmed by the concertos of *L'estro armonico*, yet there is much more than mere virtuosity to what has been called perhaps the most influential collection of instrumental music from the eighteenth century. The title is the key, for *l'estro* means "inspiration", and indeed the impersonal stateliness of Corelli's Opus 6, the precedent for these concertos, pales beside Vivaldi's music. The scholar H. C. Robbins Landon tallied the qualities of *L'estro armonico* when he wrote of the music's "freshness, the vigour, the variety and – in the slow movements – the mysterious tenderness". It was, he concluded, "unlike anything published before."

⦿ Standage; English Concert; Pinnock (Deutsche Grammophon Archiv 423 094-2; 2 CDs).

Where this account scores over its rivals is in its acknowledgement that a certain brusqueness is essential to Vivaldi's masterpiece. It was the metrical abruptness and crispness of *L'estro armonico* that lifted the composer above his predecessors, as Pinnock makes clear in this agile and exhilaratingly alert performance.

LA STRAVANGANZA

The *Capriccio stravagante* of Carlo Farina, published in 1626, was crammed with every trick of current violin technique. To the virtuosic Vivaldi the challenge must have been irresistible, and he rose to it in his Opus 4 set, *La stravaganza*, which he dedicated to Vettor Delfino, a former pupil and member of a celebrated Venetian noble family. "I cannot wish for a better protection of my feeble works," the composer wrote, "than that of Your Excellency." They have been neglected by comparison with *L'estro armonico*, but the concertos of *La stravaganza* are anything but "feeble". They display a winning flair throughout, with slow movements every bit as lyrical as their predecessors', and their astringent modulations, so bewildering to Vivaldi's contemporaries, make them vibrantly fresh for modern audiences.

◗ Kaine, Loveday; Academy of St Martin-in-the-Fields; Marriner (Decca 430 566-2; 2 CDs).

Marriner's vintage recording still leads the field. The soaring contributions of his soloists and the verve of the Academy in its heyday create an account which the authentic movement has yet to match.

LE QUATTRO STAGIONI – THE FOUR SEASONS

Once a potent enough force to influence Haydn, *Le quattro stagioni* was not republished until 1950 but is now the most recorded piece of classical music, with over one hundred and fifty versions issued to date. Each of the four concertos depicts a season, beginning with spring, and takes its structure from sonnets written by Vivaldi himself – it is thus an early example of programme music. A bravura showpiece for its violin soloist, *Le quattro stagioni* is one of the most dazzling examples of musical scene-painting, evoking buzzing flies, drunkards and goatherds dozing in the sun, dripping rain and so on. The imagination with which Vivaldi manipulates rhythm and timbre to achieve each effect are crucial to its success, and the opening motif (a bouncy alternation of quavers and semiquavers) gives the work a sense of forward movement which is never lost.

- ◉ Drottningholm Baroque Ensemble; Sparf (BIS CD-275).
- ◉ Standage; English Concert; Pinnock (Deutsche Grammophon 400 045-2).
- ◉ Moscow Virtuosi; Spivakov (RCA RD 60369; with other Vivaldi concertos).
- ◉ I Solisti delle Settimane Internazionali di Napoli; Accardo (Philips 422 065-2; with other Vivaldi concertos).
- ◉ English Chamber Orchestra; Garcia (ASV Quicksilver CDQS148; with other Vivaldi concertos).

As an example of the authentic movement's capacity to strip away preconceptions, the brilliantly exuberant playing of the Drottningholm Baroque Ensemble is second to none. The sheer weight of ornamentation in Spring means that a little of the music's directness is lost and there should be a greater sense of fragility here, but overall this is bracing, challenging stuff. Tamer, yet just as perceptive and almost as well recorded, is the English Concert's performance. The drawback with both these authentic accounts is that they offer no fill-up items. Amongst modern-instrument versions, Spivakov directs a sleek, deftly sprung and light-textured performance that is atmospheric and graceful rather than opulent. Salvatore Accardo's voluptuous interpretation is distinguished by masterly command of timbre, and if he doesn't match Spivakov's individuality, Accardo rarely allows the momentum to flag. At rock-bottom price, Garcia's recording is as elegant as any. Whatever you do, don't choose Nigel Kennedy's over-blown and overhyped recording, which has more to do with the Nige personality cult than it does with Vivaldi.

FLUTE CONCERTOS

In 1726 Venice played host to the virtuoso flautist Johann Joachim Quartz, and immediately afterwards the flute enjoyed an unprecedented vogue in the city. Vivaldi promptly wrote an ornate flute part in his opera Orlando, which was premiered in 1727, the year before an Amsterdam publisher commissioned the Opus 10 flute concertos from him. In a few cases Vivaldi was able to recycle music from existing movements, but the instrument also drew from him some of his freshest feats of imagination, and as a compedium of flute technique it had no rival at the time. The concertos' haunting evocations of night and birdsong compare with any of the onomatopoeic effects in *The Four Seasons*.

- ◉ Beznosiuk; The English Concert; Pinnock (Deutsche Grammophon Archiv 423702-2).

Liza Beznosiuk's fluidity of phrasing and articulation draws the best from this music, and minimizes any sense of routine in Vivaldi's less inspired patches.

RICHARD WAGNER

(1813–1883)

No composer ever polarized opinion as violently as Richard Wagner. Nowadays, as in his lifetime, he attracts a cult following, and every year thousands of people make a pilgrimage to the small Bavarian town of Bayreuth, where in 1876 he inaugurated a festival devoted to his own music. For many others, Bayreuth is the

ROYAL COLLEGE OF MUSIC

Wagner was the archetypal Romantic artist, with a life story as fantastic as his plots. His true parentage has never been fully established: his father was either his mother's husband, Carl Friedrich Wagner, or her lover, the actor and painter Ludwig Geyer. (This uncertainty surely has some connection with the number of characters in his operas whose fathers were equally unknown to them – Siegmund, Siegfried, Parsifal.) Whatever the truth, Carl Friedrich died a year after Richard's birth, and his widow married Geyer. Wagner thus grew up in a theatrical milieu, and he was already writing plays in his early teens. His need for incidental music for these dramas sent him in search of composition teachers, and his first musical works (now lost) date from 1829, when he was sixteen. His first completed opera, *Die Feen*, dates from only four years later, a period when he was gaining his first experiences of working in the theatre as chorus master.

By 1843 his reputation had been firmly established with the premieres of *Rienzi* and *Der fliegende Holländer* (The Flying Dutchman) in Dresden, where, as a result of these successes, he was appointed Kapellmeister to the Saxon court. There he worked on *Tannhäuser* and *Lohengrin*, and made preliminary drafts for the *Ring* and *Die Meistersinger*, at the same time becoming involved in the republican movement that swept across Europe in the late 1840s. In 1849 a warrant was issued for his arrest. With the help of Liszt, who was to be a devoted ally throughout his life, he fled to Zürich, where he wrote many of his most influential essays, among them *The Artwork of the Future* and *Opera and Drama*, in which he set out his theories of the *Gesamtkunstwerk*.

During this period of exile he finalized the libretto for the four dramas of *The Ring* and began composing their music, but he found himself distracted by his infatuation with Mathilde Wesendonck, the wife of one of his wealthy Swiss patrons. Showing his customary propensity for self-mythologizing, Wagner's thoughts now turned towards the Tristan legend, and soon he had interrupted work on his colossal operatic cycle to concentrate on *Tristan und Isolde*, a work he hoped would finance the building of the theatre he

embodiment of the composer's megalomania, and the adoption of Wagner's music as a cultural and political icon by the Nazis is seen not as a propagandist perversion of his art but as the apotheosis of a man who prefigured the Teutonic, anti-Semitic triumphalism of the Third Reich. To his admirers, Wagner's vision of the *Gesamtkunstwerk*, the "total work of art" in which music, poetry, drama and the visual arts were synthesized, is one of the mightiest achievements of European culture, on a par with the drama of ancient Greece. To the sceptics, the four-part *Ring of the Nibelung* is a boring tale of dwarfs and giants, while *Tristan und Isolde* is an impossibly long-winded love story with pseudo-medieval trappings. Yet none of Wagner's contemporaries was untouched by his music, even if they felt his influence to be malign, and to ignore his music is to turn away from a figure as seminal as Beethoven. You might never find Wagner appealing; it is equally likely that you'll hear the prelude to *Tristan* and be hooked for life.

had realized would be necessary to stage *The Ring* as he had conceived it. The Wesendonck affair was but the most damaging in a succession of infidelities that his wife, the actress Minna Planer, had been forced to endure since their marriage in 1836. Suffering from a heart condition, Minna spent much of her time in the 1850s either seeking cures or following Wagner around his various lodgings, with a dog and parrot in tow, trying to lure him back. But before long he was obsessed with yet another woman: Cosima von Bülow, Liszt's daughter and wife of the renowned conductor Hans von Bülow. Minna died in 1866, by which time Cosima and Wagner had been living together for a couple of years; in 1869 the Bülows' marriage was annulled, and the following year Cosima married Wagner, having already produced three children with him.

In the meantime, Wagner had found a new patron in King Ludwig II of Bavaria, the "mad King Ludwig", whose enthusiasm for Wagner's music was such that his fairytale castles in the Bavarian alps had interiors based on images from *Lohengrin*. It was through Ludwig's limitless largesse that Wagner could at last realize his planned theatre, though political intrigue made it impossible to build it in the first-choice location, Munich. In 1872 the foundation stone was laid in the backwater town of Bayreuth and four years later the inaugural Bayreuth Festival opened with the first complete performances of *The Ring*. The ensuing financial loss, like most of Wagner's debts in his later years, were borne by Ludwig. The premiere of his last music-drama, *Parsifal*, took place at Bayreuth in 1882, a little over six months before Wagner died of a heart attack in Venice.

THE OPERAS

Wagner's reputation rests on the sequence of ten operas beginning with *Der fliegende Holländer*. These were preceded by a trio of works, each of which explored a different aspect of the operatic tradition as it stood in the 1830s. The first, *Die Feen* (The Fairies; 1833–44) is in the manner of the German Romantic operas of Weber; its successor, *Das Liebesverbot* (The Ban on Love; 1834–46) is a comic opera in the style of Bellini and his Italian contemporaries; and the third, *Rienzi* (1837–40), is an extravagant Meyerbeer-like historical tragedy. *Rienzi* occasionally receives a production, but none of these three apprentice works is anything like a match for what followed.

Der fliegende Holländer (The Flying Dutchman; 1840–44), is the work which marks the emergence of Wagner's distinctive stagecraft and musical style, a style that evolved through *Tannhäuser* (1843–45) and *Lohengrin* (1845–48), to achieve maturity in *Der Ring des Nibelungen* (text 1848–1853, music 1853–74). Even though the same thematic material extends through the whole of this four-part epic, a growing sophistication of technique is manifest within the *Ring* cycle, as you'd expect of a work that was written over some twenty years. In the third episode, *Siegfried*, there is a stylistic shift between the second and third acts, for it was here that Wagner broke off composition of *The Ring* to compose *Tristan und Isolde* (1856–59) and *Die Meistersinger von Nürnberg* (1862–67), both of which are vast, single-evening works. His final drama, the "sacred stage festival play" *Parsifal*, occupied him from 1877 to 1882.

Superficially, the chief characteristic of Wagner's major operas is their length: ranging from three to five hours in duration, they require an unprecedented concentration on both music and text. However, Puccini's witticism that Wagner contains "wonderful moments but terrible quarters of an hour" is wide of the mark, for these massive creations are emphatically not composed as a succession of highlights padded out with narrative material. Containing very few arias, Wagner's works are not so much operas as vocal dramas structured symphonically. By the time he came to write *The Ring*, Wagner had mastered a means of weaving long spans of music into a continuous fabric, chiefly by the use of thematic leitmotifs ("leading motifs"), short phrases associated with either a character, an object or a dramatic idea. Debussy dismissed these leitmotifs as "musical calling cards", and at their most basic they are indeed little more than this – thus character X mentions character Y, and the leitmotif of character Y duly appears in the music. However, Wagner's technique became far more subtle than this. For example, in *The Ring*, the river Rhine has a swelling theme of arpeggios from which, ultimately, all the opera's other leitmotifs are derived – a horn call for Siegfried, a fanfare-like theme for his sword, an ominous motif for Alberich's curse of death on future holders of the ring, and so on. Furthermore, these leitmotifs are not static: each is modified by its contact with other motifs, thus mirroring and qualifying the action of the opera. The climactic destruction of Valhalla at the end of *Götterdämmerung* takes place against a sort of symphonic recapitulation into which some ninety leitmotifs are blended.

So you shouldn't be daunted by Wagner's epic scale. That said, it is perhaps better to start with his most concise mature work, *The Flying Dutchman*, before moving on to *The Ring* and the late works. *Tannhäuser* and *Lohengrin*, though once the most popular of his operas, are best appreciated once you have come to grips with Wagner at his best, as they do contain dull patches that may discourage further exploration.

> ◗ **Der fliegende Holländer; Tannhäuser; Lohengrin; Der Ring des Nibelung; Tristan und Isolde; Die Meistersinger von Nürnberg; Parsifal**: Bayreuth Festival (Philips 434 420–2; 32 CDs).
> ◗ **Preludes & other orchestral excerpts**: New Philharmonia, London Philharmonic Orchestra, London Symphony Orchestra; Boult (EMI CZS 7 62539 2; 2 CDs).
> ◗ **Siegfried Idyll & orchestral excerpts**: Concertgebouw; Haitink (Philips 420 886-2).

Of all operas, Wagner's are best heard in live performances. Few conductors have managed to sustain the long spans of this music through the mosaic-like procedures of studio recording, and Wagner singers usually require the adrenalin of the stage to really get going. Hence a large proportion of our recommended recordings come from Bayreuth. Boasting the best Wagner orchestra in the world, as well as theatre acoustics specifically designed for this music, Bayreuth performances have for decades set the standards for others to follow.

The Bayreuth 32-CD bumper set features all ten mature operas in live Bayreuth performances of varying quality, ranging from an unsatisfactory *Ring* from Boulez (best experienced on video) to the best available *Holländer*, *Tristan* and *Parsifal*. This huge set offers a simple and relatively inexpensive way to get hold of Wagner's masterpieces, though for anyone new to Wagner, his operas are probably best approached one at a time.

More than any other composer, Wagner is misrepresented by so-called "bleeding chunks" torn out of the operas, but you might nonetheless want to sample extracts before committing yourself. Adrian Boult's two-disc collection of the best-known preludes and orchestral passages contains performances of drama and passion, while Bernard Haitink's similarly strong single-disc selection features a warm account of the *Siegfried Idyll*, Wagner's lyrical reworking for chamber orchestra of themes from *Siegfried*. It was written as a birthday present for Cosima, and as a celebration of their belated marriage, while Wagner was completing the last act of the opera, and was first performed outside Cosima's bedroom window on Christmas Day 1870 by a gathering of their friends – including the conductor Hans Richter, who learned the trumpet specially for the occasion.

DER FLIEGENDE HOLLÄNDER

The idea of salvation through love is a common theme in Wagner's work, and it first emerges in *Der fliegende Holländer*, a work inspired by the legend of a Dutch sea captain whose blasphemy led to his being condemned to sail the seas for eternity, unless he could be redeemed by a faithful woman. The action begins in a Norwegian fjord, where a sailor named Daland is sheltering his vessel from a storm. A ghostly ship pulls in alongside and its captain, the Dutchman, offers Daland vast wealth in exchange for a single night's hospitality. Daland's daughter, Senta, is revealed to be obsessed by the tales she has heard of the Dutchman's fate and vows to be his salvation, forsaking her lover, Erik, in the process. When the Dutchman overhears Erik complain to Senta that she had once pledged to be true to him, the sailor believes he has lost her, but reasserting her fidelity, she throws herself into the sea after him. In a climax that foreshadows the end of *Tristan*, the lovers are finally seen transfigured, rising above the waves.

Der fliegende Holländer is in three acts, but is often performed as a continuous two-and-a-half-hour whole. It is Wagner's most compact drama, though there is an imbalance between the rather leisurely first half and the swift pattern of events in the second. There is a certain imbalance too in the musical treatment, which ranges from strophic ballads and arias with definite Italianate overtones to more Germanically dramatic choruses and arias, something that was not helped by

Wagner's piecemeal revisions in 1860, when parts of the opera were reworked in his more advanced *Tristan* style.

> ❶ Estes, Salminen, Balslev; Bayreuth Festival Orchestra & Chorus; Nelsson (Philips 434 599–2; 2 CDs).
> ❷ Hale, Rydl, Behrens; Vienna Philharmonic Orchestra & Opera Chorus; Dohnányi (Decca 436 418–2; 2 CDs).

The catalogue is now overwhelmed with recordings of this opera, but there still isn't one that can boast a completely satisfactory Dutchman. Simon Estes on the live Bayreuth set is gruff and uningratiating, but Matti Salminen is a wonderfully sonorous Daland and taken as a whole this is the most exciting account on disc.

Dohnányi's 1994 recording is the best studio account. Robert Hale is not an ideal Dutchman, but he's more pleasant than Estes, and Hildegard Behrens makes up in characterization what she lacks in vocal allure. The Vienna Philharmonic plays magnificently.

TANNHÄUSER

At the heart of Wagner's next opera is another theme to which he was to return – the conflict between the sacred and profane, the spiritual and the sensual. Furthermore its main protagonist, the minstrel-knight Tannhäuser, is saved by the love of a woman. He is condemned for having succumbed to the carnal temptations of Venus on the Venusberg, when supposedly in love with the pure Elisabeth, and is sent to Rome to seek the pope's forgiveness, which is refused. Meanwhile, Elisabeth has prayed for him and gone to heaven to intercede with God on his behalf, thus saving Tannhäuser's soul. It is not one of Wagner's most gripping plots, though it provides him with a number of marvellous musical opportunities, from the orgiastic opening scene through the drama of the central song contest (when Tannhäuser boasts of his experiences on the Venusberg) to the forward-looking narration of his experiences in Rome.

Tannhäuser exists in two versions. The so-called Dresden version is basically the form in which it received its premiere in that city in 1845, with a few later revisions, and is the one invariably performed at Bayreuth. When the opportunity for a production in Paris came up in 1861, Wagner expanded the opening bacchanal (pandering to the Parisian liking for operas full of ballets) and extensively revised

Placido Domingo ventures into Wagner

other passages in the style of his recent *Tristan*, creating a work that's stylistically hybrid yet more potently brings out the conflict between the erotic and the spiritual.

> ❶ **Tannhäuser (Dresden version)**: Windgassen, Silja, Bumbry; Bayreuth Festival Orchestra & Chorus; Sawallisch (Philips 434 607–2; 3 CDs).
> ❷ **Tannhäuser (Paris version)**: Domingo, Studer, Baltsa; Royal Opera House Chorus, Philharmonia; Sinopoli (Deutsche Grammophon 427 625-2; 3 CDs).

The Bayreuth performance of the Dresden version dates from 1962 and the era of classic, stylized productions by Wieland Wagner, the composer's grandson. Sawallisch directs a fervent account and has the advantage of a vintage cast, including Wolfgang Windgassen and Grace Bumbry, as well as the unsurpassed singing of the Bayreuth chorus. Sinopoli's studio recording of the Paris revision is more spacious in concept though no less dramatic. With his Latinate timbre and slightly insecure German, Placido Domingo takes a little getting used to in Wagner, but he is joined by more characteristically Wagnerian colleagues in Agnes Baltsa (a rich-toned Venus), Cheryl Studer (sometimes a little wan as Elisabeth – but it's that sort of role) and Matti Salminen's wonderfully resonant Landgraf. The Philharmonia is on top form and the recording is spectacular, particularly in the *Entry of the Guests*, with its twelve off-stage trumpets.

LOHENGRIN

Lohengrin, a tale of a Christian saviour overcoming the powers of darkness, has one of Wagner's more dubious plots. Lohengrin is Parsifal's son and a knight of the Grail, who arrives on a swan when called by Elsa of

Brabant to defend her honour against Telramund, who has accused her of murdering her brother, Gottfried. Lohengrin promises to marry Elsa, on the condition that she never asks him his name or origin. Telramund's wife Ortrud fuels Elsa's curiosity and, after the wedding (featuring the famous *Bridal March*), the bride fatefully pops the forbidden question. Lohengrin has to fulfil his vow and leave forever, but not before miraculously restoring Gottfried to life, transforming him from the swan – a form to which the wicked Telramund and Ortrud had consigned him.

Whereas *Der fliegende Holländer* moves rather uneasily between the old-fashioned set-piece opera and through-composed drama, while *Tannhäuser* has protracted periods of inertia, *Lohengrin* marks a move on from both in the way each act is cast in a continual dramatic sweep. It's rather too one-paced, but it contains music of great range and lyricism, featuring some marvellously powerful choral work and expanses of orchestral splendour.

⦿ Thomas, Grümmer, Ludwig, Fischer-Dieskau; Vienna State Opera Chorus; Vienna Philharmonic Orchestra; Kempe (EMI CDS 7 49017 8; 3 CDs).
◗ Frey, Studer, Schnaut, Wlaschiha; Bayreuth Festival Chorus & Orchestra; Schneider (Philips 434 602-2; 4 CDs).

Kempe's is a classic recording, a supremely lyrical interpetation, with a cast that has no weak link. Schneider's highly accomplished Bayreuth account from the early 1990s is not so lucky in its casting: Paul Frey is a sometimes strained Lohengrin and Gabriele Schnaut is a wayward Ortrud, but the orchestral playing and choral singing more than make up for them.

DER RING DES NIBELUNGEN

Nothing in Wagner's output prefigures the sheer scale of *Der Ring des Nibelungen*, and indeed it was not initially envisaged on anything like the scale it ultimately attained. In 1848 Wagner began searching for a subject that could express the political fervour engendered by the Europe-wide uprisings of that year. He wanted a theme that would possess the power of ancient Greek theatre, with its emphasis on myth and communal experience, and he found it in the Norse-Germanic myth of the hero Siegfried, through whom an old, corrupt world was destroyed and replaced by one of hope.

Soon he had sketched the libretto for an opera called *Siegfrieds Tod* (Siegfried's Death), but then realized he needed to elaborate upon the events that led up to the hero's demise, and thus wrote a "prequel" called *Der junge Siegfried* (The Young Siegfried). Even that was not enough, so he drafted a scenario that added two more dramas, *Das Rheingold* (The Rhinegold) and *Die Walküre* (The Valkyries). Having written the libretti for the four dramas in reverse order he began composing the music in sequence, beginning with *Rheingold*, the shortest part of the cycle, described merely as a prelude to the main drama (though it's longer than many full-length operas). Having completed *Walküre* and much of *Siegfried* (formerly *Der junge Siegfried*), in 1857 he broke off composition of *The Ring* to write *Tristan* and *Die Meistersinger*. Resuming *Siegfried* in 1865, he then composed the gargantuan finale, *Götterdämmerung* (Twilight of the Gods), as *Siegfrieds Tod* had now become. From a single opera, his project had grown to a length of some fifteen hours, spread over four evenings.

Obviously enough, the plot is impossible to convey in a few sentences, though one wit summarized it as a moral tale about what happens when a god defaults on the repayments on his house. This might well sum up *Das Rheingold*, in which the ruler of the gods, Wotan, tricks a power-wielding ring from the Nibelung dwarf Alberich (who in turn has stolen gold from the Rhinemaidens), then is obliged to use it to pay the giants Fafner and Fasolt for building his fortress, Valhalla. In a nutshell, the rest of the cycle depicts the attempts of both Wotan and Alberich to retrieve the ring from Fafner (who guards it in the form of a dragon) by fathering off-spring to do the deed for them. Wotan's grandson Siegfried kills the dragon and then, with Brünnhilde (his betrothed, and Wotan's daughter) foils Alberich's son Hagen's plan to gain the ring, which is returned to the Rhinemaidens as the old world is cleansed by fire and water.

In outline *The Ring* sounds a bit like a Dungeons and Dragons yarn, but it's in fact a drama so complex that it can bear – and has borne – scores of different interpretations. At

Bayreuth, where they don't take kindly to frivolous cleverness, it has been presented both as a ritualistic exploration of such eternal verities as Love and Death, and as a quasi-Marxist study in power relations. The musical structure of *The Ring* is even more rich than its text, and includes some of the most powerful scenes in all opera: the very opening, for example, which conjures up the Rhine in a single, extended and elaborated chord; or the entry of the gods into Valhalla at the end of *Rheingold*; or the *Ride of the Valkyries* and *Magic Fire Music* in the third act of *Die Walküre*; or Siegfried's Funeral March from *Götterdämmerung*. But these are just moments of extreme intensity in an epic that is highly charged from start to finish. Take the plunge – this is one of the great musical journeys.

Part one of Barenboim's hi-tech Ring

◖ **Der Ring des Nibelungen – complete**: Franz, Mödl, Suthaus, Windgassen, Konetzni, Pernerstorfer, Greindl; RAI Rome Chorus & Orchestra; Furtwängler (EMI CCZS7 67123–2; 13 CDs).

Das Rheingold:
◕ Tomlinson, Finnie, Kannen, Clarke; Bayreuth Festival Orchestra; Barenboim (Teldec 4509-91185–2; 2 CDs).
◕ Adam, Burmeister, Neidlinger, Windgassen; Bayreuth Festival Orchestra; Böhm (Philips 412 475–2; 2 CDs).

Die Walküre:
◕ Tomlinson, Evans, Elmung, Secunde, Hölle; Bayreuth Festival Orchestra; Barenboim (Teldec 4509-91186–2; 4 CDs).
◕ Adam, Nilsson, King, Rysanek, Nienstedt; Bayreuth Festival Orchestra; Böhm (Philips 412 478–2; 4 CDs.

Siegfried:
◕ Windgassen, Adam, Nilsson, Wohlfart; Bayreuth Festival Orchestra; Böhm (Philips 412 483–2; 4 CDs).

Götterdämmerung:
◕ Windgassen, Nilsson, Neidlinger, Greindl; Bayreuth Festival Orchestra; Böhm (Philips 412 488–2; 4 CDs).

A perfect *Ring* cycle on CD is an elusive thing. Early recordings tend to suffer from unsatisfactory sound, while more recent ones are weaker in purely vocal terms, as singers capable of *The Ring*'s considerable demands seem in ever diminishing supply – particularly in the case of the dramatic Heldentenor ("heroic tenor") required for the role of Siegfried.

Of all recorded *Ring* cycles, none has the same prestige as Furtwängler's recording from the early 1950s. It's only available as a single set, the orchestra is frankly poor, and the recording quality isn't brilliant, but Furtwängler has the cream of the Wagnerian singers of the time, and his interpretation is incandescently intense. Karl Böhm's Bayreuth cycle from the mid-1960s is very nearly as fervent, and boasts the outstanding Birgit Nilsson as Brünnhilde and Wolfgang Windgassen as

Siegfried. Its sound quality is vastly superior to the Furtwängler Ring, and it has the advantage of being available in four separate sets.

The top recommendation for a modern cycle is the one from Daniel Barenboim. His account of *The Ring* at Bayreuth was heavily criticized by many who saw the production live, but these performances – recorded in the theatre for a video of Harry Kupfer's highly physical staging – contain the most gripping Wagner to have appeared on CD for many a year. The great Bayreuth orchestra is recorded more vividly than ever before and the performances are dominated by the towering vocal presence of bass John Tomlinson as Wotan. Anne Evans is a lighter Brünnhilde than others on disc, but few have equalled her musicality and vocal beauty: here, for once in this role, there is not a hint of a screech or an uncontrollable wobble. The rest of the cast in these two operas is almost uniformly fine. At the time of going to press only the first two instalments have been issued, but *Siegfried* and *Götterdämerung* are imminent; they have a lot to live up to.

TRISTAN UND ISOLDE

Arthurian legend provided the raw material for Wagner's greatest opera, but his treatment of the story was inspired by the philosophy of Schopenhauer, specifically its contention that bliss can only be found through the negation of the will and of desire. Schopenhauer is certainly a presence in the completed opera, which ends in blissful annihilation, but desire is its governing force. *Tristan und Isolde* is in essence a five-hour love song.

The plot is refreshingly simple. Tristan has been sent to Ireland to bring back the Irish princess Isolde as bride for his uncle, King

Mark of Cornwall. But Tristan has fallen passionately in love with Isolde himself and she reciprocates. They conclude that death is the only way out and on the voyage to Cornwall they take a potion they believe to be poison, but Isolde's maid Brangäne has substituted a love draught and their passion is only reconfirmed. They continue their affair until caught in the act, when Tristan is wounded by one of Mark's knights. He is taken back to his castle in Brittany, where he dies just as Isolde arrives. Mark forgives them for their love and Isolde sinks onto Tristan's body, united with him in death.

Right from the prelude, with its sinuous melodic lines and suspended harmonies, a sense of heady sensuality and physical longing saturates *Tristan und Isolde*. The long love duet of the second act is as explicitly sexual as any piece of music ever written, complete with a musical *coitus interruptus* when the two lovers are discovered. The ever-present unfulfilled yearning is only satisfied in the closing bars of the whole opera, as Isolde's famous *Liebestod* ("love-death"), in which she sings herself into ecstatic oblivion, finally achieves harmonic fulfilment. *Tristan* is revolutionary in its chromatic language, which stretches tonal harmony to its very limits, casting the listener adrift in a world that has no reliable markers. When you listen to the overture of a Mozart opera, its harmonic structure tells you how long the piece will last; with *Tristan* you don't have any idea which way the music is heading. The atonalism of Schoenberg is just around the corner.

Karl Böhm – one of the greatest Wagner conductors

classic status. The sound quality doesn't match the Böhm set, the cast isn't ideal (even the legendary Kirsten Flagstad is past her best here), and the orchestra isn't in the same league as the Bayreuth players, but such is the cohesion and passion of this performance that these considerations really don't matter. You'll get to the end of this recording and be amazed at how quickly the time has passed.

The Kleiber recording is one to listen to after you've got to know the opera through Böhm or Furtwängler. The Isolde of Margaret Price is perhaps the finest technical performance of the role on record, but doesn't pack the emotional punch of Flagstad or Nilsson, while René Kollo is just about the most wimpish Tristan ever heard. Kleiber's conducting, however, wrings extraordinary intensities out of the score by pulling the tempi about all over the place, and the orchestral playing is sublime. If Kleiber's account of the opening of Act Three doesn't reduce you to a quivering wreck, you must have a heart of stone.

DIE MEISTERSINGER VON NÜRNBERG

As if to cleanse his system of the excesses of *Tristan*, Wagner next turned to comedy and the purer world of C major. *Die Meistersinger von Nürnberg* is not, however, a simple comedy: it is a hymn to German art and a celebration of progressiveness in culture.

The setting is medieval Nuremberg and its society of trade guilds. The most revered of these is the guild of Mastersingers, one of whom, Pogner, has decided to offer his daughter Eva to the winner of the Midsummer Day song contest. Eva is already in love with an itinerant knight, Walther von Stolzing, who

○ Windgassen, Nilsson, Ludwig, Talvela, Waechter; Bayreuth Festival Orchestra; Böhm (Philips 434 425–2; 3 CDs).

◉ Flagstad, Suthaus, Thebom, Greindl, Fischer-Dieskau; Philharmonia; Furtwängler (EMI CDS 7 47322 8; 4 CDs).

◉ Price, Kollo; Leipzig Radio Chorus; Staatskapelle Dresden; Kleiber (Deutsche Grammophon 413 315-2GH4; 4 CDs).

Tristan's hot-house atmosphere is ideally caught in Böhm's live 1966 Bayreuth performance, featuring Wolfgang Windgassen and Birgit Nilsson at the height of their powers. Böhm directs the performance of his life: tempos are swift and the orchestra plays at white heat, never allowing the tension to flag. Not a recording for the faint-hearted.

For many people the greatest of all Wagner conductors was Wilhelm Furtwängler, and his 1952 account of *Tristan* has attempts to gain admittance into the guild. Only the cobbler-poet Hans Sachs, a widower who himself is not immune to Eva's charms, sees the potential in his modern style of song and promises to help him. Walther has a rival in the shape of the fussy, carping town clerk Beckmesser – a caricature of Wagner's arch critic in Vienna, Eduard Hanslick. At the contest, Beckmesser is laughed off after his catastrophic performance of a song he believes to be by Sachs, but is actually by Walther, who sings it properly and, of course, wins Eva's hand.

Although less musically extreme than *Tristan*, it is nonetheless a sublime work, particularly in its characterization – Sachs is Wagner's most sympathetic creation, and the pomposity of the Mastersingers is wonderfully delineated. There are several magnificent set pieces in this most social of Wagner's works: the nocturnal comedy of Act II, where Beckmesser tries to lure Eva with a serenade, is a bewitching piece of scene-setting; the first scene of Act III, in which Sachs relinquishes his claim on Eva, is an extremely moving episode; and the final song contest is genuinely funny.

◗ Edelmann, Hopf, Schwarzkopf, Dalberg; Bayreuth Festival Chorus & Orchestra; Karajan (EMI CHS 7 63500 2; 4 CDs).
◗ Adam, Kollo, Donath, Ridderbusch; Dresden State Opera Choir, Leipzig Radio Chorus; Dresden Staatskapelle; Karajan (EMI CDS 7 49683 2; 4 CDs).

Successful recordings of this opera are not thick on the ground. Karajan's 1951 Bayreuth set from the first post-war festival is regarded as a classic, but the warmth of his approach is perhaps better caught in his Dresden studio recording from twenty years later, where the cast has an authoritative Sachs in Theo Adam and a finely characterized Beckmesser in Geraint Evans (René Kollo's unattractive Walther is the only weakness). The Dresden Staatskapelle is one of the great Wagnerian orchestras.

PARSIFAL

Wagner's last opera has always divided even the composer's admirers. Some think *Parsifal* Wagner's masterpiece, others find it depraved in its celebration of ascetic virtue through music of sometimes overwhelming sensuality. The climactic scene of this Arthurian moral-ity drama takes place on Good Friday, and the opera is replete with Christian imagery such as the Grail, baptism, Holy Communion and the Crucifixion. Into this scheme Wagner mixes Buddhist notions of self-denial and elements of Schopenhauer's grim philosophy, to produce a distinctively Wagnerian exploration of the theme of enlightenment through sacrifice.

As with Wagner's previous Arthurian opera, the action is more straightforward than the music. Amfortas, one of the senior knights guarding the Holy Grail, has succumbed to the temptation of lust and has thereby lost the sacred spear that pierced Christ's body on the cross. The spear has fallen into the possession of the magician Klingsor, who has inflicted on Amfortas a wound that can only be healed by a man "made wise through compassion". Parsifal at the start of the opera witnesses Amfortas's plight but doesn't understand it; eventually, having been similarly tempted by Kundry, he renounces sexuality in order to recover the spear and bring salvation to Amfortas and his knights.

Parsifal takes the harmonic experiments of *Tristan* one step further, dissipating the energies of tonal music to such an extent that the opera sometimes approaches the very verge of stasis. Though *Parsifal*'s slow-building crescendoes and languid cadences express the seductiveness of spiritual goals and the duration of suffering, rather than the sexual ecstacy of *Tristan*, the overall dynamics of the two operas are very similar. In each opera a long prelude creates a state of suspension which lasts all the way through to the last moments – in the case of *Parsifal*, until the heavenward-reaching choral writing as the hero conducts Communion for the Knights of the Grail.

◗ Bayreuth Festival Orchestra, Thomas, Hotter, London, Dalis, Neidlinger, Talvela; Knappertsbusch (Philips 416 390-2; 4 CDs).

With *Parsifal* there is only one set really worth considering. Knappertsbusch's 1962 account (there is also an earlier one from 1951 on Teldec) is arguably the most beautiful, the most spiritually truthful and the most sonically rich recording to have come from Bayreuth.

WILLIAM WALTON
(1902–1983)

Although he dabbled briefly with atonality in his early *String Quartet*, William Walton was an unrepentant neo-Romantic for most of his life. By his late twenties he had settled on a style that reconciled the essentially lyrical Englishness of Elgar with the pungency of Prokofiev and Stravinsky, a style characterized by earthy rhythms, wide intervallic writing, colourful and unstable harmonies, and a predilection for melancholy. Walton's music isn't the most challenging of the twentieth century, but it's extremely well made, and his output features a handful of pieces that are worth anyone's attention.

The son of a choirmaster and singing teacher, Walton spent his formative years in Oxford where he was a chorister at Christ Church Cathedral. It was in Oxford that he began to compose, and in 1918 he was taken up by the upper-class bohemian Sitwell family, with whom he lived in London and Italy. Three years later he composed *Façade*, a superficially modernist "Entertainment" for six players and narrator, using poems by Edith Sitwell. The first public performance of *Façade* in 1926 gave Walton's name widespread currency, and his reputation was enhanced by his *Viola Concerto*, which Hindemith premiered in 1929.

His style reached maturity in 1931 with *Belshazzar's Feast*, a dramatic cantata which was acclaimed as the finest in English choral work since Elgar's *Dream of Gerontius*, while attracting accusations of modernistic and eclectic tendencies from some quarters. His next success came with the *Symphony No. 1* and the *Violin Concerto*, commissioned by Heifetz in 1939. During World War II he composed a number of patriotic film scores, including the music to Olivier's *Henry V*. After the war, Walton moved to Italy where he remained for the rest of his life, producing less and less music as his brand of Romantic traditionalism became ever more unfashionable.

THE MUSIC

Walton's reputation depends primarily upon *Belshazzar's Feast*, a fine piece of Biblical Gothic, scored for baritone solo, full choir and large orchestra. In his handling of these vast forces Walton displays remarkable abilities for orchestration and ensemble writing, and his music is typified by ardent, sometimes violent, thematic material. Indeed its pulsating quasi-paganism upset many of those present at the first performance in 1931, and the Three Choirs Festival wouldn't touch the piece until 1957.

Walton's next major score after *Belshazzar*, the *Symphony No. 1*, gave him such difficulties that it took three years to complete, and the work conveys a strong sense of personal victory and fulfilment. Opening with a gorgeous extended flute solo, the symphony builds its ideas in a way similar to the symphonies of Sibelius, and it also owes much to Elgar and Hindemith – the fugal passage in the finale is almost a homage to his German friend. With its broad emotional horizons, Walton's first symphony stands in the front rank of English symphonies alongside those of Elgar and Vaughan Williams.

Most attractive of all Walton's music is the *Violin Concerto*, a work designed to display the virtuosity and beautiful tone of Jascha Heifetz. The soloist's opening theme, a lyrical idea which sets the emotional tone of the work, leads to a staccato section in which the violinist battles with the orchestra for dominance; having won, the violinist is rewarded with yet another captivating solo episode. This movement's sensuousness is carried through into the Scherzo, while the Finale makes much of the composer's facility for orchestral writing.

Finally, if you've acquired a taste for Walton, you should investigate *Henry V*, the best of numerous film scores in which he rivalled Prokofiev's talent for characterization and illustration. Ranging from bombastic battle scenes to moments of delicate tenderness, this is one of Walton's outstanding achievements.

◉ **Belshazzar's Feast**: Luxon, London Philharmonic Choir & Orchestra, Solti (Decca 4251542LM).
◉ **Symphony No. I**: London Philharmonic Orchestra, B. Thomson (Chandos CHAN 8862; with Varii caprici).
◑ **Violin Concerto**: Heifetz; Philharmonia Orchestra, Walton (RCA GD87966; with Elgar, Violin Concerto).
◉ **Henry V**: Westminster Cathedral Choir, Academy of St Martin's-in-the-Field; Plummer; Marriner (Chandos CHAN 8892).

Solti's unrestrained recording of *Belshazzar's Feast* is at times astonishingly brutal but he maintains a fabulously clear balance and his handling of the chorus is superb. Benjamin Luxon is a fine narrator, and the recorded sound is very immediate. Bryden Thomson's account of the *Symphony No. 1*, part of the Chandos label's grand retrospective of Walton's work, is efficient rather than inspired, but he allows the music to unfold in a way that reveals the architecture of the piece. Heifetz's recording of the concerto, made in 1950 with the composer conducting, is an extraordinary performance, exploiting its intense romanticism to the fullest; it's coupled with a playing of the Elgar concerto that is similarly little short of ideal. The complete *Henry V*, conducted by Neville Marriner with Christopher Plummer narrating excerpts from Shakespeare's play, is not the place to begin your Walton collection, but fans will find it a fascinating disc.

CARL MARIA VON WEBER
(1786–1826)

If any single person can be credited with the creation of German Romantic opera, it is Carl Maria von Weber. His *Der Freischütz*, with its magical orchestral atmospherics and its use of Germanic folklore, established a lineage that would lead ultimately to Wagner. Weber was also in his time a highly regarded music critic, a pianist of international renown and one of the first to establish the importance of the role of the conductor.

He was born near Lübeck in northern Germany, into a musical and theatrical family. He soon learned to play the piano and his subsequent training included a period with Joseph Haydn's brother Michael in Salzburg, where, aged twelve, he wrote his first compositions. The following year he composed his first opera, the manuscript of which was destroyed by fire shortly after is completion. As a seventeen-year-old he secured the post of Kapellmeister at the theatre in Breslau, where he stayed for a couple of years until falling ill after accidentally swallowing some engraver's acid. His career as a travelling virtuoso pianist then took up most of his time until 1813, when he was put in charge of the Prague opera house. Here, resuming the efforts he had made at Breslau, he set about reforming the repertory, placing the emphasis on Mozart and contemporary French opera, in opposition to the prevalent taste for Italian opera.

This principle was taken further in his next major appointment, as Royal Saxon Kapellmeister in Dresden, a post he took up in 1817. Weber's endeavours to develop a German national opera company led to years of antagonism within the court, where the music of Rossini was greatly preferred. Until, that is, *Der Freischütz* was performed in Berlin in 1821. Its success was instant: it received dozens of productions throughout Germany within a year of its premiere, then was played throughout Europe. *Der Freischütz* was to remain the most popular German opera throughout the first half of the century.

Weber made two attempts to follow up his success with *Euryanthe* (1823) and *Oberon* (1826), but neither lived up to the promise of their predecessor, chiefly because of their terrible libretti. While in London to conduct the premiere of *Oberon*, his years of ill health caught up with him and he died the day before he was due to return home to his family. He was buried in Moorfields Chapel but in 1844 Richard Wagner, his successor in Dresden, arranged for his body to be returned to that city.

DER FREISCHÜTZ

The structure of *Der Freischütz* (The Marksman), in which the musical numbers are linked by spoken dialogue, derives from the Germanic genre of music-theatre known as *Singspiel*, of which Mozart's *Magic Flute* is the best known example. However, Weber's opera is an advance on its predecessors in its use of recurrent motifs to achieve musical continuity, notably in the use of horns to underline the huntsman theme. Furthermore, in its fusion of the supernatural, the folkloric and the rustic, *Der Freischütz* brought together some of the dominant strands of German Romanticism for the first time in the history of opera.

The hero of the piece is the huntsman Max, who makes a pact with the forces of darkness to gain some magic bullets that will allow him to win a shooting contest, and thus gain the hand of his sweetheart, Agathe. At the heart of the opera is the scene in which the magic bullets are forged in a gloomy, inhospitable mountain valley called the Wolf's Glen. This wonderful musical evocation of evil is Weber's most impressive creation, but his command of orchestral colouring is deft throughout the opera, especially in his use of folk-like melodies for his choruses.

● **Der Freischütz**: Schreier, Janowitz, Weikl, Adam, Vogel, Mathis; Leipzig Radio Chorus; Dresden Staatskapelle; Kleiber (Deutsche Grammophon 415 432-2; 2 CDs).

Buy this record – Kleiber's Freischütz brooks no argument

● **Overture to Der Freischütz and other operas**: Karajan; Berlin PO (Deutsche Grammophon 419 070-2; with *Invitation to the Dance*).

Carlos Kleiber adopts some extreme speeds in his recording of *Der Freischütz*, but he conveys the dramatic energy of the score like no other conductor. He gets sumptuous playing out of the Dresden Staatskapelle (from Weber's home territory), and his cast is splendid, including Peter Schreier as Max and Gundula Janowitz as Agathe. The theatricality of the spoken dialogue can take a bit of getting used to, but it is all done in the best possible taste.

If you want to sample Weber's music first, get Karajan's CD of the overtures *Der Freischütz*, *Der Beherrecher der Geister*, *Euryanthe*, *Oberon* and *Peter Schmoll*; he distils the mood of each opera to perfection, and also includes Berlioz's exuberant orchestration of Weber's piano waltz, *Invitation to the Dance*.

CLARINET MUSIC

Next to his work in opera, Weber's principal claim to fame is as a composer of clarinet music. He wrote two concertos, a concertino, a set of variations (all 1811), a quintet (1814), and a showpiece for piano and clarinet called *Grand Duo Concertant* (1816), thereby extending the instrument's repertoire in a way comparable to the work of Mozart and Brahms. And just as Mozart and Brahms were inspired by a particular musician – the former by Anton Stadler, the latter by Richard Mühlfeld – Weber's clarinet music was composed for his friend Heinrich Bärmann, the principal clarinet of the Munich court orchestra.

Weber's instrumental music is theatrically virtuosic on the whole, though the central movements of the concertos are beautiful slow episodes in which Weber highlights the vocal sonority of the clarinet's timbre. In the concerto finales, however, everything is subservient to display, while the *Grand Duo* – the most important work for solo clarinet and piano – is notable for its operatic brilliance and the extreme difficulty of the two evenly balanced roles. The finale is a sensational battle for supremacy.

● **Clarinet Concertos Nos. 1 & 2; Concertino Op. 26**: Pay; Orchestra of the Age of Enlightenment (Virgin VC 7 90720-2).
● **Clarinet Concertos Nos. 1 & 2; Concertino Op. 26; Grand Duo Concertant**: Johnson, Back; English Chamber Orchestra; Tortelier (ASV DCA 747).

Antony Pay plays a copy of an instrument of Weber's day and is accompanied by the period instruments of the Orchestra of the Age of Enlightenment. Weber's writing sounds even more fiendish than usual in this context, but everyone involved brings it off with great style and wit. Emma Johnson's modern-instrument accounts of the same pieces are also extremely beguiling, and are combined with a fine rendition of the *Grand Duo Concertant*.

ANTON WEBERN

(1883–1945)

Like Alban Berg, Anton Webern became a disciple of Arnold Schoenberg and then proceeded to take a path of his own creation. The path that Webern followed, however, went in an entirely different direction from his colleague's. Berg went on to write large-scale works in which the dictates of modernism were reconciled with the Romantic tradition of Wagner and Mahler; Webern worked relentlessly towards a state of absolute economy, compressing a vast range of emotions into a few bars of music. An assiduous, self-critical perfectionist, he assigned opus numbers to only thirty-one compositions, the great majority of which last for less than ten minutes, and some of which seem on first hearing like mere splinters or tissues of sound. Yet these are among the most important works of the twentieth century. Webern once finished a lecture with the words "There is no other way", and for the generation of Boulez and Stockhausen the music of Webern was indeed the truth.

Webern was born in Vienna and his studies began with his mother, who oversaw his first attempts at composition when he was only five. In 1902 he entered Vienna University, where he studied with Hans Pfitzner (see p.267), but before graduating from the university he began to work with Schoenberg, with

LEBRECHT COLLECTION

whom he was to remain until 1908. As with Schoenberg and Berg, Webern's early work bore plentiful signs of the influence of Brahms, Mahler and Strauss, but within weeks of embarking upon his studies with Schoenberg he had begun to revise his ideas on tonality. By the time he moved out from under Schoenberg's wing, he was wholly committed to atonality, and had formed what was to be a lifelong friendship with Alban Berg. Webern's first major atonal work, the *Five Movements for String Quartet*, appeared in 1909, the same year as Schoenberg's trailblazing *Three Pieces* for piano.

For the next nine years he devoted himself to conducting and composing, and after World War I he rekindled his association with Schoenberg, with whom he and Berg formed the Society for Private Musical Performances, a group for the promotion of new music. When the society ceased operating in 1922, Webern continued to devote most of his energies to conducting: for twelve years he was the conductor of the Vienna Workers' Symphony Orchestra and Chorus, and he gave numerous concerts for the BBC between 1929 and 1936. During this period he found time to produce an intermittent flow of music and followed Schoenberg in the development of serial techniques, abandoning free-floating atonalism in favour of a method that defined exactly which notes were at the composer's disposal. Always obsessed with structural precision (his works include the formal applications of fugues, canons and passacaglias), Webern established a more complete form of serialism, applying rigorous principles not just to the intervals between the notes, but to aspects of timbre, rhythm and dynamics, thereby laying the foundations for the "total serialism" of the post-war modernist vanguard.

His work was banned by the Nazis as an example of "cultural Bolshevism", but he stayed in Austria throughout the war, earning his money by proof-reading other composers' scores. A terrible accident made him one of the war's last casualties. On September 15, 1945, he stepped out of his daughters' house to take the night air, lit a cigarette beneath a tree and was shot dead by an American sentry, who mistook the composer for his son-in-law, a notorious black marketeer.

THE MUSIC

The ten-minute *Passacaglia* of 1908, Webern's first published score, marked an enormous advance on the quasi-Romanticism of his early tone poem, *Im Sommerwind*. One of his few pieces for a full orchestra, it is a highly individual interpretation of the variation form, consisting of a simple Handelian theme that Webern builds upon some twenty-three times, before closing the whole piece with a dauntingly complex coda. Even in this early work there's an impressive concentration on the quality of each note and on the music's architecture, but it's a positively lush creation compared to what was to come.

Webern attached the abstract labels "Pieces" or "Movements" to most of his atonal and serial compositions, thereby declaring his antipathy to all extra-musical connotations. These works are conceived as self-sufficient expressive entities, in which emotion is transmitted by a fanatically focused attention to the essence of sounds and the minutiae of the relationships between notes. Schoenberg's dissonance is present here, but Webern's style is distinguished above all by its fastidiousness, its clarity of texture, and its speed of transition, ranging in seconds from the edge of silence to vast momentary climaxes. The *Six Pieces for Orchestra* Op. 6, written little more than a year after the *Passacaglia*, exemplifies Webern's ability to pack a symphonic span into the duration of a prelude. Veering from hallucinogenic violence to dream-like calm, the *Six Pieces* can be a devastating experience if you approach it with an open mind, and if anything there's an even greater intensity to chamber works such as the *Five Movements for String Quartet* Op. 5 (later reworked as *Five Pieces for Orchestra*). Written in response to his mother's death, *Five Movements* is a soundscape of desolation, where fragmentary melodies and fragile sounds dart out from silence and disappear in an instant. This is as tragic a work as Berg's *Wozzeck*, but – like all Webern's music – it demands unswerving attention. Don't, however, be deterred by talk of "difficulty", for modern music offers few more enriching experiences than Webern's hyper-refined miniatures.

The Sony three-disc set is a landmark: boasting performances of everything worth hearing by the likes of Isaac Stern, Pierre Boulez, Heather Harper, John Williams and Webern himself, this is the best possible survey of the composer's output. You may, however, prefer to approach Webern via a single CD, in which case you should go either for the Karajan or the Abbado collection of orchestral pieces. The Karajan disc first appeared as part of a revelatory set of LPs given over to works from the Second Viennese School, and won converts to Webern by revealing the sheer beauty of these strange sounds. (This disc is also available as part of the original set, now grouped on three mid-price CDs.) Abbado's similar anthology is even more lush and immediate. Getting at the best of the chamber music is an expensive business, as there are no good single-CD accounts. The best recommendations are the Sony set or the superb La Salle survey of the quartet music of Schoenberg, Berg and Webern.

KURT WEILL

(1900–1950)

On the night of August 31, 1928, an extraordinary piece of music theatre called *Die Dreigroschenoper* (The Threepenny Opera) was presented to a shocked and titillated Berlin audience. *Die Dreigroschenoper* thronged the stage with prostitutes, pimps and thieves who rejoiced in their low-life existence, and it was a huge hit, comparable to the success of Lehár's *Merry Widow* (see p.193). Within months European theatres were clamouring to stage productions of the work, and by January 1933 it had received an astonishing ten thousand performances, while popular entertainers were covering show-stopping numbers like *Mack the Knife*. The text was written by Bertolt Brecht and Elisabeth Hauptmann, the score by the twenty-eight-year-old Kurt Weill.

A prodigously talented musician, Weill received an impeccable training from such brilliant pedagogues as Humperdinck and Busoni. As a student he flirted with the atonalism of Schoenberg and the neo-classicism of Hindemith, but Weill was by nature drawn to less esoteric principles. Despite the artistic and commercial success of his operas *Der Protagonist* and *Der Zar lässt sich photographieren* (The Tsar has his photograph taken), Weill felt restricted by the protocols of the opera house, and began, as he put it, "to dream of a special brand of musical theatre which would completely integrate drama and music, spoken word, song and movement". *Die Dreigroschenoper* marked the first great leap towards its realization.

Weill's reputation was cemented by stage works such as *Happy End* and *Aufstieg und Fall der Stadt Mahagonny* (The Rise and Fall of the City of Mahagonny), but his life, like that of so many German artists in the 1930s, was shattered when the Nazis came to power in 1933. That same year the Jewish-born Weill and his wife, the singer Lotte Lenya, went into exile. The Weills first settled in Paris, where pieces such as *Die sieben Todsünden* (The Seven Deadly Sins) met with mixed fortunes, despite the support of influential friends like Milhaud and Honneger. Then in 1935 Weill went to New York to complete a work for the Manhattan Opera House, and recognized immediately that the USA offered a way out of what he saw as the dead end of the European avant-garde. He determined to make it as a Broadway composer: "When I arrived in this country . . . another dream began to get hold of me – the dream of an American opera."

It was an uphill struggle, for Weill was not used to the demands of the American commercial theatre, where producers tended to put marketing considerations above artistic ones. Nonetheless, Weill and his collaborators achieved a workable compromise with the ethics of Broadway, and managed to introduce risky new musical and dramatic elements to American music-theatre. Investors might have felt uncomfortable with the plots of works such as *Love Life* (1948), a critique of marriage in the context of industrial society, or *Lost in the Stars* (1949), which was based on Alan Paton's anti-apartheid novel *Cry the Beloved Country*, but there could be no doubt that they were getting a high-class product. Weill gave extra sophistication to the genre in many ways: by drawing American folk and dance music into well-integrated orchestral scores; by creating pungent new timbres through the use of jazz instrumentation; and above all by bringing to the New York stage a sense of musical characterization and theatrical form that had lost none of its bite since his Berlin days.

In the eyes of some of his former admirers, however, Weill was a former socialist firebrand who had sold out to the pursuit of wealth. For Weill there was no discontinuity in his life, for he had always seen himself as a composer commentating on society in the most direct way possible. As he told an interviewer in 1940 – "Schoenberg has said that he is writing for a time fifty years after his death . . . For myself, I write for today. I don't give a damn about writing for posterity."

THE MUSIC

The finest of Weill's large-scale pieces of music-theatre is the early *Die Dreigroschenoper*, which is based substantially on Elisabeth Hauptmann's translation of John Gay's *Beggar's Opera*. Hauptmann and Brecht transposed the action from eighteenth-century London to modern Soho, and its exultant seediness is typical of the Weimar cabaret scene. The anti-bourgeois satire of *Die Dreigroschenoper* still packs a strong punch, thanks chiefly to the way in which Weill wraps the most savage and subversive sentiments in the sweetest and

most insinuating music: songs such as *Mack the Knife* and *The Song of Sexual Dependency* are almost as shocking now as they were when new.

The same goes for *Die sieben Todsünden* (The Seven Deadly Sins), another decadent piece in which Weill deploys a full armoury of spicy harmonic ambiguities, spiky instrumentation and witty dance rhythms – notably waltzes and foxtrots. This was the last substantial collaboration between Kurt Weill and Bertolt Brecht, who ultimately fell out because, in the words of Lotte Lenya, Weill wasn't interested in setting the Communist Manifesto to music. Premiered in 1933, *Die sieben Todsünden* is a mordant attack on the hypocrisies of capitalist morality, revealed in the dilemmas faced by two sisters named Anna. The first is a realist and is represented by the singer, the other is an endlessly compromised idealist, whose part is taken by a dancer; Anna I sings a commentary on the predicaments of Anna II, who by the end of the piece has been all but ruined.

Weill regarded *Street Scene* (1946) as the work in which he first achieved "a real blending of drama and music, in which the singing continues naturally where the speaking stops, and the spoken word as well as the dramatic action are embedded in overall musical structure". Based on a socialist-realist study of life in a New York tenement, it is consistent with *Die Dreigroschenoper* in its focus on "the poorest of the poor", but quite unlike it in tone. Where *Die Dreigroschenoper* excoriated and ridiculed the oppressors of the underclass, *Street Scene* is a compassionate depiction of the oppressed.

◉ **Die Dreigroschenoper**: Lenya, Schellow, Trenk-Trebitsch; Radio Free Berlin Orchestra; Brückner-Rüggeberg (CBS CD42637).
◉ **Die sieben Todsünden**: Fassbaender, Brandt, Sojer, Komatsu, Urbas; Radio-Philharmonie Hannover des NDR; Garben (Harmonia Mundi 901420; with other songs).
◉ **Street Scene**: Ciesinski, Kelly, Bottone, Van Allen; English National Opera Chorus and Orchestra; Davis (TER CDTER2 1185; 2 CDs).

With Weill's widow Lotte Lenya in the lead female role – as in the first performance – the 1958 recording of *Die Dreigroschenoper* comes as close to complete authenticity as is possible. Most recordings cut out a song or two, but this superb set gives you the caustic brew undiluted. This is the essential Weill CD. There are now several recordings of *Die sieben Todsünden* in the catalogue, but none to beat this inspired performance, headed by the ferocious and seductive Brigitte Fassbaender. Carl Davis may be best known as a composer of film scores, but as his recording of *Street Scene* demonstrates he is also a first-class conductor of theatre music. The ENO stalwarts are in exceptionally fine voice, turning in nicely judged and idiomatic performances.

JUDITH WEIR

(1954–   )

Judith Weir is one of Britain's rising stars, and has the rare distinction of being as popular with audiences as with critics. Her music, which uses modal or tonal techniques, is as accessible as that of John Tavener (see p.371) with whom she trained, and like Tavener she makes frequent gestures towards the music of the distant past. Her interest in medieval culture has led to two works based on the music of thirteenth-century composer Pérotin (see p.266): *Sederunt Principes* for chamber ensemble; and *Lovers, Learners and Libations – Scenes from Thirteenth-Century Parisian Life*, for singers and early music consort. Homage of an even more direct kind is found in her reworkings of Mozart (*Scipio's Dream*, 1991) and Monteverdi (*Combattimento II*, 1992). But Weir's music is distinguished above all by her talent for lucid narrative structure, a talent most apparent in her operatic and music-theatre works.

Her first full-length adult opera, *A Night at the Chinese Opera*, was premiered in 1987 and was the first of her works to reach a wide audience. Weir wrote her own libretto from a thirteenth-century Chinese play about a collaborator with the Mongolian regime, and the music – which is mostly based around the fundamental intervals of the octave and the fifth – has a clear and open texture, showing Weir's abiding concern that her texts should be heard and understood. In 1990 came another opera, *The Vanishing Bridegroom*, retelling three traditional Scottish tales in which the supernatural obtrudes into everyday life. It's a work in which Weir's attachment to her Scottish heritage is especially noticeable, both in her use of Celtic folklore and literature, and in her quotations of fragments of Scottish music. Weir's third full-length adult opera, *Blonde Eckbert*, was first performed in April 1994; once again she wrote her own libretto, deriving it from an enigmatic German tale of incest, deception and betrayal.

MUSIC DRAMAS

As yet, none of Weir's lengthier pieces has been recorded, but some of her smaller dramatic works are readily available, and they have the same qualities of clarity and concision as her full-length operas.

King Harald's Saga (1979), billed as a "Grand Opera in Three Acts" for solo soprano, compacts the story of King Harald's unsuccessful invasion of Britain in 1066 into less than ten minutes. The soprano sings eight clearly differentiated solo roles as well as that of Harald's entire Norwegian army, a technique which – combined with the matter-of-fact quality of Weir's text – emphasizes the absurdity of the violence depicted. The *Consolations of Scholarship* (1985) is a music drama for mezzo-soprano and nine instruments, and is based on the same source as *A Night at the Chinese Opera*. Like that later work, it carries much of the narrative through rhythmically notated speech, a style that recreates the transparent formality of classical Chinese theatre. In *Missa del Cid* (1988), a work for ten singers, Weir's text combines the medieval Spanish epic of El Cid with the liturgy of the Mass, each section being introduced by a speaker who tells the story of El Cid's bloodthirsty campaign against the Moors. Offsetting rich music for unaccompanied voices against the stark facts of slaughter, *Missa del Cid* shows Weir's predilection for simple, eloquent dramatic devices.

This CD provides the listener with a fascinating introduction to Weir's vocal music. The excellent performances are all given by the performers for whom the works were originally written.

HUGO WOLF

(1860–1903)

Hugo Wolf was the archetypal Romantic artist: manically driven, misunderstood, impoverished, mad and short-lived. He was also, after Schubert, the finest of all composers of German art songs. As a musician he was not in the same league as his great precursor, but where he surpassed everyone was in his sensitivity to words. Wolf conceived the music of his songs as exact translations of the poems that provided their texts: thus, unlike Schubert's songs, in which the music follows the mood of the text rather than the seman-

tics, Wolf's make no sense without a complete grasp of what is being sung. He reconciled the dramatic and theatrical intensity of opera with the discipline of song, employing a Wagner-influenced style that took the form as far as tonality would allow. In short, Wolf's songs are highly wrought and complex creations, which deserve a far wider audience than they currently enjoy.

Born in Slovenia, Wolf was taught by his father until 1875, when he entered the Vienna conservatory, where one of his contemporaries was Gustav Mahler. In December of the same year he met Richard Wagner, who encouraged him to concentrate on orchestral music, thereby condemning him to struggle at compositions for which his abilities did not equip him. He was a fractious student and in 1877 – the year he contracted the syphilis that was to kill him – he was expelled from the conservatory, although Wolf maintained he had resigned over the college's inflexible conservatism. For the next decade he made his money chiefly from teaching, but in 1884 his songs aroused the interest of the greatly influential critic Eduard Hanlisck, who recommended Wolf to two publishers, neither of whom was prepared to back the young composer. In emulation of Hanslick he began writing criticism, but as he sided with the recently deceased Wagner against the very much alive Brahms he made many enemies in Vienna.

In 1888 he composed dozens of songs, including much of the *Spanisches Liederbuch* (Spanish Song Book), a work that established him in certain quarters as the finest songwriter of his time. By the mid-1890s a Hugo Wolf Society had been established in Berlin and even the Viennese were beginning to

LEBRECHT COLLECTION

acknowledge his talent. In 1896 he completed his greatest body of songs, the *Italianisches Liederbuch* (Italian Song Book), but in the same year his mind began to collapse. The following year he fell into syphilitic dementia – he announced, for example, that he, and not Mahler, was director of the Vienna State Opera, and that the opera house would perform nothing but his music in future. He was committed to an asylum and remained incarcerated until his death, except for a brief period in 1898, when he was deemed to be cured, only to attempt suicide as soon as he was released. In belated recognition of his achievement, he was buried next to Schubert and Beethoven in the city's central cemetery.

SONGS

For the first twenty-eight years of his life, Wolf composed extensively for chamber groups, solo piano and orchestra. Most of these pieces were left unfinished, and the few that Wolf did complete met with little or no success. He submitted his string quartet to the Rosé Quartet, who sent it back covered with derisory comments, and the Vienna Philharmonic were reduced to tears of laughter at the rehearsal for his tone poem *Penthiselea*. Wolf began to realize that, contrary to the advice given to him by Wagner, Brahms and Liszt, he was better suited to songs than to orchestral or instrumental music.

His most important work dates from the years between 1888 and 1898 and fall into several large groups. His preferred working method was to immerse himself in the works of a particular poet and produce nothing but settings of that writer's work until he had exhausted the material. Thus the clusters of Eichendorff, Mörike, Goethe, Michelangelo and Keller settings dominate his output, alongside two books of songs inspired by poetry from Italy and from Spain. Finest of all his songs are those of the *Italienisches Liederbuch*, the first twenty-two of which were composed in 1890–91, with the remaining twenty-four being completed five years later. The texts were taken from a translation of anonymous Italian poems published in the year of Wolf's birth, and the obscurity of the verses evidently liberated him. Because these poems came with no burden of previous interpretation, Wolf was free to read himself into them and thereby produce his most profoundly personal music. Generally terse and very dense, they are not the most immediately engaging songs, but concentration brings great rewards.

◗ **Selected Songs**: Schwarzkopf, Moore (EMI CDH 7 64905 2).

◉ **Italienisches Liederbuch**: Schwarzkopf, Fischer-Dieskau; Moore (EMI CDM7 63732-2).

Elisabeth Schwarzkopf championed Wolf's music throughout her career, and her Salzburg recital from 1958 – when both she and her accompanist Gerald Moore were at the height of their powers – is a highly moving homage. Their selection consists mainly of Goethe and Mörike songs, plus some fine Keller pieces and excerpts from the Italian and Spanish books. Schwarzkopf's word characterization is as sensitive as any to be heard on disc, and she encompasses every gradation of tone between declamation and extreme tenderness without overstressing. As an introduction to Wolf, there is nothing finer.

Schwarzkopf and Moore are again at their best on their milestone recording of the *Italienisches Liederbuch* with Dietrich Fischer-Dieskau. The delivery of both singers is incredibly subtle, and the nurturing of the often fractured melodic lines is unimaginably beautiful.

IANNIS XENAKIS

(1922–   )

I annis Xenakis is known for three things: he's the only famous composer whose name begins with the letter X, he's the only Greek composer who's famous outside Greece, and, most importantly, he's one of the crucial figures in the development of electronic music. Rejecting the straitjacket of serialism, Xenakis aimed to liberate sound from all *a priori* rules. His inspirations were the mythologies of Greek culture and natural phenomena such as the sounds of rain or the slow movement of shifting sand on a beach. His tools were chance operations, computer technologies and mathematical procedures, and at its best his music combines organic yet meticulously thought-out design with intense emotion.

Born into a wealthy Greek family in Romania, Xenakis went to school in Greece and then studied architecture and engineering in Athens. The next phase of his life reads like a parable of triumph over adversity. Deeply involved with the anti-Nazi resistance, he had half his face blown away in a street battle. After the war, his involvement in the Greek nationalist movement in British-occupied Athens led to a death sentence. In 1947 he escaped under a false passport to Paris, where he took a job with Le Corbusier, for whom he worked for twelve years. For the 1958 Brussels World's Fair he co-designed the futuristic Philips Pavilion, the venue for Varèse's ground-breaking *Poème Electronique* for tape machines and four hundred loudspeakers.

After creating the orchestral sound-blast of *Mestastaseis* in the mid-1950s, Xenakis took up composing full-time, and set about applying probability theories and computer programmes to the processes of composition. The pieces produced during the 1960s were often characterized by dense clusters and explosions of sound, and revealed a dazzling talent for stretching timbres to their limits. In 1966 he founded the centre for Automatic and Mathematical music in Paris and subsequently set up a similar unit at Indiana University, turning out work that impressed Pierre Boulez and led to his association with both IRCAM and the Ensemble Intercontemporain. Subsequent sound-and-light works such as *Hibiki-Hana-Ma* (1970), for twelve tapes and eight hundred speakers, displayed Xenakis's unparalleled technical virtuosity, but in later years the mythic and spiritual element of his music has come to the fore, expressing the composer's Christian faith and his profound feelings about his homeland, to which he returned after twenty years of exile.

THE MUSIC

Since Xenakis's larger-scale works demand a lot of work from the uninitiated, the best place to start is with his smaller instrumental creations. *Nomos Alpha* (1965) for solo cello is a breathtaking sound continuum which pushes the instrument and its player to their limits through the use of simultaneous scales and the overlaying of low notes with high-pitched harmonics; the throbbing effect might recall the Bach suites for unaccompanied cello, yet the sound has an electrifying modern edge. *Pleiades* is a beautiful quartet of pieces for percussion which in places evokes the richness of the Balinese gamelan – *Claviers* is particularly fine, utilizing Indonesian scales and the bright timbres of vibraphone, xylophone and marimba to produce a fascinating ethno-Minimalist concoction. *Phlegra* (1975) and *Jalons* (1986), two string-and-brass works of saturated sound and mythic feeling, are perhaps the most accessible of the compositions written since Xenakis went back to Greece.

⊙ **Jalons; Keren; Nomos Alpha; Phlegra; Thallein**: Boulez, Tabachnik; Ensemble Intercontemporain; Sluchin; Strauch (Erato 2292-45770-2).
⊙ **Pleiades**: Dhalmann; Percussion Orchestra of Strasbourg (Harmonia Mundi HMC 905 185).
⊙ **Pleiades; Idmen**: Gualda; Ensemble Pleiades (Erato 2292-45771-2).

The Boulez CD, supervised by Xenakis himself, is the perfect introductory recording. In addition to *Nomos Alpha*, it contains plenty of fine (and often abrasive) music, from the dense polyphony of *Jalons* to the melodic richness of *Keren*, one of the few works in the repertoire for solo trombone. The Harmonia Mundi disc features the ensemble for which *Pleiades* was written and was recorded in the presence of the composer, who contributes a sleevenote analysis of the piece. The primitiveness of the music is underplayed on the Erato disc, but the latter has a clearer sound and also comes with *Idmen*, an hallucinogenic reminiscence of Greek tragedy for chorus and percussion.

ALEXANDER ZEMLINSKY

(1871–1942)

Arnold Schoenberg once wrote – "I owe almost everything I know about composing and its problems to Alexander Zemlinsky . . . I always thought he was a great composer". Yet until the 1980s Zemlinsky was likely to feature in an A–Z of music only in order to justify its title, or in his secondary role as Schoenberg's mentor. Zemlinsky's essential problem was that he was too advanced for his conservative contemporaries, but not interesting enough for the radicals. To make matters worse, he was physically unprepossessing (Alma Mahler uncharitably described him as a "horrid little gnome – chinless, toothless and stinking of the coffee-houses"), and was uncomfortable pushing his own work. The result was relegation to the margins of history until the last decade, which has seen a re-assessment of Zemlinsky's sumptuous *fin de siècle* Romanticism.

Zemlinsky was a typical example of Viennese multi-culturalism. His father was Slovakian, his mother from a Bosnian Jewish family in Sarajevo, and Zemlinsky went on to become one of the cabal of Viennese musicians who formed around Gustav Mahler, the reforming force in the city's musical life. When Zemlinsky left the conservatoire in the 1890s, he became a member of the *Wiener Tonkünstlerverein* (Viennese Society of Composers), whose honorary president, Johannes Brahms, encouraged the young composer.

Opera and song were to comprise the greater part of his output: *Sarema*, the first of his eight completed operas, was performed in Munich in 1897, and his second, *Es war einmal* (Once Upon a Time), was premiered by Mahler at the Court Opera in Vienna in 1900. His career as a conductor developed in parallel: from 1899 he was conductor at the Carltheater in Vienna, then he moved on to the Volksoper and was invited by Mahler to the Court Opera. He and Schoenberg founded a society to promote new music in Vienna, and his star seemed to be rising under the patronage of Mahler, who was going to present his next opera, *Der Traumgörge* (Görge the Dreamer). However, after numerous disagreements Mahler was forced out of the Court Opera in 1907, prompting Zemlinsky to walk out in protest. *Der Traumgörge* wasn't performed until 1980.

After another spell at the Volksoper, Zemlinsky went to work in the Deutsches Landestheater in Prague, where he was to remain for sixteen years. Under his direction it became one of the most important opera houses in Europe – Stravinsky, though usually begrudging in his praise, once described Zemlinsky conducting Mozart as one of the most satisfying experiences of his life. This was the most successful period of Zemlinsky's life as a composer too – it was in Prague that he wrote his best operas and the *Lyric Symphony*, his most famous work. In 1927 he went to work with Otto Klemperer at the Kroll Opera in Berlin, where his last completed opera, *Der Kreidekries* (The Chalk Circle), was given a performance in 1934, before being suppressed by the Nazis. Zemlinsky fled first to Vienna and then, in 1938, to America, where he died a forgotten man.

DER GEBURTSTAG DER INFANTIN

The most remarkable of Zemlinsky's eight operas is the one-act *Der Zwerg* (The Dwarf), first given under Otto Klemperer in 1922 and the work most frequently performed in Zemlinsky's lifetime. Based on *The Birthday of the Infanta*, a short story by Oscar Wilde, it was revived in Hamburg in 1981 with a revised libretto that's closer to Wilde's original text – this version, renamed *Der Geburtstag der Infantin* (The Birthday of the Infanta), is the one you're likeliest to see on stage. The opera tells of a dwarf given as a birthday present to a spoilt young girl. She adores him and he falls in love with her, but she eventually forsakes him, and he dies of a broken heart. *Der Geburtstag* brings out all

Zemlinsky's strengths in orchestral colour, lyricism and highly charged emotion – the dwarf's achingly beautiful music no doubt gains some of its power from Zemlinsky's own feelings at his rejection by Alma Mahler.

◉ **Der Geburtstag der Infantin**: Nielsen; Riegel; Radio-Symphonie-Orchester Berlin; Albrecht (Schwann CD 11626).

Sung by the cast of the Hamburg revival, this is the best introduction to Zemlinsky's operatic world. Kenneth Reigel has just the right qualities of innocence and vulnerability for the role of the dwarf, while the contrast between his luscious music and that of the social whirl around him is finely drawn.

ORCHESTRAL MUSIC

Like Mahler's *Das Lied von der Erde*, Zemlinsky's *Lyrische Symphonie* (1923) is a cross between an orchestral song cycle and a symphony. A setting of seven love poems by the Indian poet Rabindranath Tagore, it's typically Viennese in its fascination with yearning, parting and death, and clearly illustrates Zemlinsky's place between the classical Austro-German tradition and the innovative Second Viennese School. Alban Berg, one of the key figures of that school, underlined the work's importance by quoting it in his *Lyric Suite*, which he dedicated to Zemlinsky. Of Zemlinsky's other orchestral works, the best is the wonderful tone poem *Die Seejungfrau* (The Mermaid), which had the misfortune to be performed on the same programme as Schoenberg's *Pelleas and Melisande* in 1905. Zemlinsky's piece was overshadowed and the composer lost interest in its future – it was not heard again until 1984. Also worth investigation are the masterly *Six Maeterlinck Songs* (1913), which display shimmering and unusual orchestrations and, once again, a strong preoccupation with death.

◉ **Lyric Symphony; Six Maeterlinck Songs**: Söderström, Duesing; Berlin Radio Symphony Orchestra; Klee (Schwann, CD 311 053 H1).
◉ **Die Seejungfrau**: Berlin Radio Symphony Orchestra; Chailly (Decca 417 450-2).

The soloists in the recording of the *Lyric Symphony* bring off its wide-ranging vocal lines very well, and the orchestra produces some colourful outbursts – notably in the fanfare that launches this symbolist meditation. Even better is Riccardo Chailly's glorious recording of *Die Seejungfrau*, a CD which completely justifies the current re-assessment of Zemlinsky. The shimmering woodwind and strings of this Mahlerian showpiece perfectly evoke the undersea world of its source – Hans Christian Andersen's The Little Mermaid.

A DIRECTORY OF ARTISTS

What follows is a brief run-down on some of the performers whose work has featured prominently in this book. We've indicated the areas in which each artist is strongest, and we've marked with an asterisk the composer entries in which you'll find recommended recordings by the artist in question. In the case of soloists and singers, we've also recommended several recital or compilation discs not listed elsewhere in the book. Note that many recital discs have extremely unwieldly titles, which we've summarized with descriptive titles. Thus, for example, a CD listed in the catalogue as *Arias by Donizetti, Bellini, Verdi, Leoncavallo and Rossini* would appear below just as *Italian Arias*.

As with all the rest of our CD recommendations, we've included full serial numbers to avoid any confusion.

CLAUDIO ABBADO (1933–   )

Italian conductor. Now principal of Berlin Philharmonic (in succession to Karajan) but has also headed the London Symphony, Vienna Philharmonic and Vienna Symphony orchestras. Very versatile conductor. Has made excellent recordings of Verdi* and Mussorgsky*, but his work in the opera house is generally less successful than his expansive performances of Schubert, Mahler, Brahms* and Beethoven*.

MARTHA ARGERICH (1941–   )

Argentinian pianist. Studied with Benedetti Michelangeli; won Busoni and Chopin piano competitions. Renowned for the fiery virtuosity of her playing of Chopin*, Liszt* and Prokofiev*. Rarely appears in solo recitals; frequently performs chamber music with Gidon Kremer and Micha Maisky. Recorded by Deutsche Grammophon.

CLAUDIO ARRAU (1903–1992)

Chilean pianist. Made his debut in 1908 and appeared with the Berlin Philharmonic in 1920. Famed in the 1930s for his promotion of J.S. Bach's keyboard music but was most successful in the Viennese classics and Chopin, Schumann, Brahms and Liszt. A highly intellectual, reflective musician, but his later recordings do him scant justice. Recorded by Philips.

❿ **Chopin, Sonata No. 3; Schumann, Carnaval** (EMI CDH7 64025-2).

A monumental performance of Chopin's third sonata.

VLADIMIR ASHKENAZY (1937–   )

Russian pianist and conductor. Won the 1962 Tchaikovsky competition jointly with British pianist John Ogdon (1937–1989). Perhaps the most recorded pianist in history, with a phenomenally wide repertoire. Now devoted to conducting, and as principal conductor of Royal Philharmonic Orchestra has recorded a vast catalogue. Especially successful in Scriabin* and Sibelius*. Recorded chiefly by EMI and Decca, but there are some amazing recordings of the young Ashkenazy on Saga.

❿ **Prokofiev, Piano Sonatas Nos. 7 & 8; Liszt, Mephisto Waltz** (Decca 425 046-2).

Blistering Prokofiev and poetic Liszt; a fine introduction to the music and the pianist.

WILHELM BACKHAUS (1884–1969)

German pianist. Made his first concert tour in 1900 and later toured the world. Hailed as a master of Beethoven*, although he did not record all the sonatas until the 1960s. Also superlative in Schumann and Brahms. Recorded by Decca.

❿ **Schubert, Moments Musicaux & Impromptus; works by Mendelssohn and Schumann** (Decca 433 902-2).

Excellent recital disk, notable for a haunting live performance of Schumann's *Warum*.

JOHN BARBIROLLI (1899–1970)

English conductor of Italian-French parentage. Conducted dozens of orchestras throughout his long career, but most famed for his work with the Hallé, for whom he was principal conductor from 1943 until his death. One of the few English conductors to find acceptance with the Berlin Philharmonic. Excellent in Brahms*, Mahler, Sibelius, Puccini and especially Elgar* and Vaughan Williams. Recorded by EMI.

DANIEL BARENBOIM (1942–   )

Israeli pianist and conductor. A child prodigy, he caused a sensation in the 1950s and 1960s for his performances of Beethoven and Mozart. Married Jacqueline du Pré (see below) in 1967. Very fine in chamber music and, since 1966, as a conductor – his Bruckner* and Wagner* recordings have been notably successful. Since 1991 has been principal of Chicago Symphony, with whom he has recorded extensively. One of the world's most powerful and influential musicians. Recorded by EMI, Deutsche Grammophon and Erato.

◗ Romantic Works for Piano (Deutsche Grammophon 415 118-2GH).

Superb playing of Liszt's *Liebesträum*, Schubert's *Moments Musicaux* and excerpts from Mendlessohn's *Songs without Words*.

CECILIA BARTOLI (1966–   )

Italian mezzo-soprano. Has a wonderfully dark and smoothly cultured tone, and excels in Rossini. Just about the most glamorous singer around, she could become as famous as Maria Callas. Recorded by Decca.

◗ Rossini Operatic Arias (Decca 425 430-2).

Fabulous virtuoso singing of some of the best of Rossini's mezzo arias.

YURI BASHMET (1953–   )

Russian violist. Possessing supreme technical ability and a marvellous sense of lyricism, he has done more for the viola as a solo instrument than anyone else in the post-war era. Recorded by RCA.

◗ Works by Schubert, Schumann, Bruch and Enescu (RCA RD60112).

Brilliant recital, notable especially for a beautifully rich performance of Schubert's *Arpeggione Sonata*.

THOMAS BEECHAM (1879–1971)

English conductor. Promoted the early work of Strauss and worked closely with Sibelius and Delius. Formed the London Philharmonic Orchestra and Royal Philharmonic Orchestra, and did much to revitalize pre-war Covent Garden. Particularly fine interpreter of Mozart and Haydn. Recorded by EMI.

ARTURO BENEDETTI MICHELANGELI (1920–   )

Italian pianist. Won the Geneva competition in 1939, and since then has made few records or live appearances. Nonetheless is revered as one of the greatest pianists ever. An obsessive perfectionist, he has a formidable technique, with unsurpassed delicacy of fingerwork and sensitivity to instrumental tone. Has possibly the smallest repertoire of any virtuoso, as he tends to spend years preparing a piece before playing it. Supreme in the music of Chopin and Debussy*, but also magnificent in Mozart, Beethoven and Grieg. Recorded by EMI and Deutsche Grammophon; various live performances also available on Italian imports of doubtful legality.

◗ Early Recordings (EMI CDH 7 64490-2).

Scarlatti, Brahms, Beethoven, Grieg and some lesser-known Spanish pieces, recorded at various times and locales, but all displaying the preternatural Benedetti Michelangeli control. Essential to any collection of piano music.

CARLO BERGONZI (1924–   )

Italian lyric tenor. A master of Puccini*, Verdi and bel canto, with a grand, sonorous and beautifully produced sound. He spent his early years as a baritone but became a tenor in 1951, later memorizing some 75 roles. During the 1960s was regarded by many as the heir to Enrico Caruso, but his later work has done his reputation harm. Recorded by Decca, EMI and RCA.

◗ Operatic Arias (Decca 421 328-2DA).

His earliest Decca recording, with a staggering performance of Alvaro's Act One aria from Verdi's *La Forza del destino*.

LEONARD BERNSTEIN (1918–1991)

American conductor and composer. One of the most extensively recorded conductors, he was principal of the New York Philharmonic from 1958 – the first American to be offered the position – and went on to work closely with the Vienna Philharmonic and London Symphony orchestras. His tastes were extremely catholic, but he was most highly regarded for his flamboyant and highly emotional performances of Mahler's symphonies*. Recorded by Deutsche Grammophon, CBS and Sony – Sony have produced a Bernstein Edition, running to over a hundred CDs, all available as single, double or treble CDs.

JUSSI BJÖRLING (1911–1960)

Swedish tenor. Had a strong but effortless and incredibly smooth voice, with one of the largest ranges of any modern tenor. Always displayed immaculate phrasing. Notable in the music of Verdi and Puccini, he was also highly suited to Lieder, although he made very few song recordings after the 1930s. Recorded by EMI.

◗ Operatic Arias (Decca 421 316-2).

A fine introductory disc with a sensational performance of *Ch'ella mi creda* from *La Fanciulla del West*.

KARL BÖHM (1894–1981)

Austrian conductor. Great friend of Richard Strauss*, who dedicated his opera *Daphne* to him. As well as being perhaps Strauss's pre-eminent post-war interpreter, he was one of the greatest Mozart* conductors of the century, did much to promote Berg's *Wozzeck*, and recorded performances of Wagner's* *Tristan* and the *Ring* that continue to dominate the catalogue. Recorded by Decca and Deutsche Grammophon.

JORGE BOLET (1914–1990)

Cuban-born American pianist. A formidable and thoughtful virtuoso, he was principally famed for his performances of Liszt. Recordings from his later years are often disappointing. Recorded by Decca.

◉ Liszt/Schubert song transcriptions (Decca 414 575-2DH).

Sublime performances of Liszt's wonderful Schubert transcriptions. This is one of the finest examples of Bolet's art.

INGE BORKH (1921–   )

Swiss soprano. One of the greatest lyric-dramatic sopranos of the century, she was renowned in the title roles of Strauss's *Salome* and *Elektra**, and as Verdi's Lady Macbeth. At first her voice was light and frequently uneven, but with age her tone quality darkened and her capacity for characterization deepened. Recorded by RCA and Deutsche Grammophon.

◗ Scenes from Elektra and Salome (RCA GD60874).

Recorded with Reiner in the 1950s, when her voice was lighter than when she came to record Elektra for Böhm – nonetheless, the atmosphere is palpable.

PIERRE BOULEZ (1925–   )

French composer and conductor. One of the most influential composers of the post-war years, he began to devote substantial amounts of time to conducting in the 1960s, working with the Vienna Philharmonic Orchestra and at Salzburg. He came to international prominence when the Wagner family engaged him to conduct the centenary *Ring* cycle at Bayreuth in 1976. Especially revealing as a conductor of twentieth-century music, from Stravinsky's* work to his own*. Recorded by CBS, Sony and Deutsche Grammophon.

ADRIAN BOULT (1889–1983)

English conductor. A friend of Elgar, he came to be regarded as the quintessential English musician, developing a restrained style that produced the greatest effect from the least amount of show. He gave the first performance of Holst's *The Planets* and championed the music of Vaughan Williams* and Elgar*, whose symphonies he recorded with unrivalled success. He was also particularly successful in Brahms's music. Did not retire until his ninetieth year. Recorded by EMI.

DENNIS BRAIN (1921–1957)

English player of the French horn, widely regarded as the finest of his generation. Principal horn with the Royal Philharmonic

Orchestra and the Philharmonia; celebrated for his beautiful, even tone, as shown on recordings of concertos by Mozart, Strauss and Hindemith. Died after falling asleep at the wheel of his car. Recorded by EMI.

⏺ **Strauss and Hindemith Horn Concertos** (EMI CDC747834-2).

Hindemith conducts Brain in his own concerto while Sawallisch conducts performances of both the Strauss concertos.

ALFRED BRENDEL (1931–)

Austrian pianist. In many respects the heir to Schnabel (see below), Brendel is noted for his cerebral approach to the Viennese classics; his disciplined approach has resulted in some fine recordings, but his analytical mentality is not so well suited to the music of Liszt and the Romantics. A fine classicist, he is best in the works of Mozart, Haydn and Schubert. Recorded by Philips – they have issued a ten-CD Brendel Collection that covers almost every aspect of Brendel's repertoire (also available as separate CDs).

JULIAN BREAM (1933–)

English guitarist and lutenist. Protegé of the great Andrés Segovia, who remained Bream's mentor until his death in 1987. Though an expert in English lute music, he is still best known for his performances of Spanish guitar music. Britten, Walton and many other composers have written for his intense and brilliant talents. RCA have released a twenty-five-CD Bream Edition that gathers most of his recorded work; the discs are all available separately.

MONTSERRAT CABALLÉ (1933–)

Spanish coloratura soprano. Has perfect technique, a widely coloured voice and amazing breath control, and has sung in every major opera house and for every major conductor since the 1960s. Like Callas, she made some early appearances in Wagner's music, but soon devoted herself to the bel canto repertoire, in particular the operas of Bellini, Rossini and Donizetti. She has also produced fine performances in Verdi (eg Violetta in *La Traviata*) but her work in verismo operas (eg *Tosca*) and German dramatic works (eg *Salome*) has been less than successful. Still appears on stage, even if she is now past her prime. Recorded by RCA.

⏺ **Operatic Arias by Bellini and Donizetti** (RCA 09026 614582).

The young Caballé at her best, in repertoire for which she is perfect.

MARIA CALLAS (1923–1977)

Greek-American dramatic coloratura soprano. "Discovered" and trained by Tullio Serafin, Callas effectively revitalized bel canto opera, and she dominated the world's opera houses as the greatest singing actress of her time. Her highly distinctive vocal timbre was not to everyone's taste, but in her prime she was indisputably a thrillingly convincing dramatic soprano, superb in a repertoire that ran from Bellini* to Puccini*. Her voice began to decline in the 1960s and by the 1970s she was singing beyond her means. Recorded by EMI.

⏺ **La Divina – Operatic Arias** (EMI CDC 754702-2).

There are many highlights discs on the market, but this is the best, containing excerpts from her EMI opera recordings from every stage of her career.

GUIDO CANTELLI (1920–1956)

Italian conductor. A protégé of Toscanini, he was hailed as one of the most exciting conductors to emerge in the post-war years and made a number of exceptional recordings. He inherited Toscanini's philosophy of logic, clarity and energy, but brought his own sense of romantic idealism to his performances, which were characterized by an intense attention to details of colour and balance – qualities heard at their finest in his Debussy* recordings. He died in a plane crash shortly after being appointed music director of La Scala. Recorded by EMI and Testament.

⏺ **Artist Profile – Guido Cantelli** (EMI 7243 5 68217 2 9; 2 CDs).

Stereo recordings of Mozart, Beethoven, Schubert and Franck, from the last two years of Cantelli's tragically short life.

JOSÉ CARRERAS (1946–)

Spanish lyric tenor. Made his debut in 1970 and soon established himself as the heir to di Stefano, with his effortlessly resonant, full and high-ranged voice. Unhappy with the essentially one-dimensional tenor roles in bel canto opera, he began to look to the latter half of the nineteenth century for fresh challenges. The strain of verismo roles and his battle with leukemia have left his voice a shadow of what it was. Recorded by Philips.

🌓 **Operatic Arias** (Philips 426 371-2).

Most of the recordings on this disc are from before Carreras's illness, and explain what inspired the adulation.

ENRICO CARUSO (1873–1921)

Italian lyric tenor. The first tenor to make records and probably the greatest Italian tenor of the recording era. His uncommonly sonorous and resonant voice had the strength of a baritone and was notable for its lyrical projection. Puccini found him lazy and composed only one role for him (in *La Fanciulla del West*); he also described him as a gift from God. Recorded by RCA and Nimbus.

● **Operatic Arias** (Nimbus N17803).

Not all Caruso's recordings did him justice but Nimbus have chosen only the very finest examples, from his earliest sessions to his last in 1921. Notable for a staggeringly perfect *Una furtiva lagrima* from Donizetti's *L'Elizir d'amore*.

PABLO CASALS (1876–1973)

Spanish cellist, conductor and composer. Born the year of the first *Ring* cycle, made his first American tour in 1901 and gave his last concerts some seventy years later. Produced a uniquely dark, sensuous sound, and played with an extraordinary passion. Did more to establish the cello as a solo instrument than any other musician. Recorded by Sony and EMI.

🌓 **Bach Cello Suites** (EMI CHS7 61027-2; 2 CDs).

These performances restored the Bach suites to the repertoire – others since have played them more cleanly, but nobody makes this music sound so vital.

SERGIU CELIBIDACHE (1912–)

Romanian conductor and composer. Made principal conductor of the Berlin Philharmonic Orchestra in 1945, shortly after completing his musical studies, and remained

with the orchestra until Furtwängler returned in 1952. His work is characterized by spacious, often very slow tempi and an intense concentration on architecture. Hates recording, but his accounts of the Bruckner symphonies are available on laserdisc from Sony.

SHURA CHERKASSKY (1911–)

Russian-born American pianist. Since the death of Horowitz, Cherkassky has been championed as the last great Russian romantic. He studied with Josef Hofmann as a boy and inherited his teacher's unpredictability; this sense of the unexpected is best heard in the Romantic repertoire, for which he is rightly famous. Even in his eighties, Cherkassky remains in complete control of his stupendous technique, and at his best he is one of the century's most exciting pianists. Recorded by Decca.

● **Encores** (Decca CD433 651-2).

A collection culled from various concerts, including his own *Boogy-woogy Étude*.

FRANCO CORELLI (1923–)

Italian tenor. Corelli's massive, thrilling voice and handsome stage presence made him the world's most popular tenor in the 1960s. He was capable of overkill, especially in the verismo operas of Puccini* and Leoncavallo, but in the bel canto roles of Donizetti and Bellini* and the spinto roles of Verdi he was unrivalled. Recorded by EMI.

🌓 **Live Operatic Excerpts** (Memories HR4204-05; 2 CDs).

A retrospective of his best years, this two-disc set offers some of his greatest moments – the excerpts from *Poliuto* and *Les Hugenots* are like nothing else on earth.

LISA DELLA CASA (1919–)

Swiss soprano. Blessed with a staggeringly flexible voice of exquisite, lyrical radiance, Lisa della Casa is best remembered for her singing of Richard Strauss's music* – above all the *Four Last Songs* and the title role in *Arabella*. Although she retired before her prime, she did make a small number of legendary recordings. Recorded by Deutsche Grammophon and Decca.

A marvellous release, featuring substantial excerpts from *Ariadne auf Naxos*, together with previously unreleased performances of Strauss songs.

MARIO DEL MONACO (1915–1982)

Italian tenor. Commonly believed to be the loudest tenor in history, del Monaco boasted an extraordinary stamina and vocal strength that made him highly popular in the verismo operas of Puccini*, Leoncavallo and Giordano*, as well as in the lead role in Verdi's *Otello*, for which he was especially celebrated. A stupendously entertaining and committed singer, he was immensely popular during the 1950s and 1960s, but as he revelled rather too enthusiastically in his enormous voice, he was much less successful on record than in the theatre. Recorded by Decca.

◗ **Operatic Arias** (Decca 440 407-2).

Full throttle all the way, showing del Monaco at his best and his worst.

VICTOR DE SABATA (1892–1967)

Italian conductor and composer. Began as a composer and did not turn to conducting until 1918. Within the year he was appointed conductor at Monte Carlo Opera, where he gave the first performance of Ravel's *L'Enfant et les sortilèges*. Became renowned for his blistering interpretations of *Tristan* and for his conducting of music by Ravel*, Puccini, Strauss and Giordano. Such was his command and understanding of the orchestra that even Toscanini publicly admired him, and those who heard him live claim he was without equal. Recorded by EMI, Decca and Music & Arts.

GIUSEPPE DI STEFANO (1921–   )

Italian lyric tenor. Found early success in America singing genuine lyric roles. However, after 1953 he placed his voice under terrible pressure when he abandoned the bel canto repertoire in favour of heavier, more romantic roles; attempting to compete with Corelli, del Monaco and Bergonzi, he severely damaged his elegant, velvety sound.

By the late 1960s, after his ill-advised work with Callas, his voice was ruined. He is best heard in bel canto repertoire pre-1955. Recorded by EMI.

◗ **Operatic Arias** (EMI CDM 7 63105-2).

Although this disc contains none of the brilliant earliest recordings, it still boasts some beautiful singing.

PLACIDO DOMINGO (1941–   )

Spanish tenor. The most recorded tenor in history, Domingo has amassed an enormous catalogue of roles, many of which are not suited to a voice that is strictly speaking a pushed-up baritone. However, he is very strong in Verdi* – he's unquestionably the finest *Otello* of his time – and his move towards the lighter of Wagner's* tenor roles has resulted in some refreshingly immediate performances. Recorded by EMI, Deutsche Grammophon and RCA.

◗ **The Placido Domingo Album** (RCA GD 60866; 2 CDs).

Arias from Bizet, Donizetti, Leoncavallo and numerous others in this fine two-disc collection; the second CD is entirely given over to Verdi arias, showing Domingo at his strongest.

ANTAL DORATI (1906–1988)

Hungarian conductor. One of the century's finest conductors, excelling in early twentieth-century music – his relationship with the record company Mercury resulted in a series of great recordings of Bartók* and Stravinsky*. He was also the first conductor to record all Haydn's* symphonies. Recorded by Decca and Mercury.

JACQUELINE DU PRÉ (1945–1987)

English cellist. From the time of her London debut in 1961 she was acclaimed for her warm and flexible sound, her technical proficiency, and above all her emotional openness – she gave everything in every single performance. Her repertoire was very wide, but she was best known for her playing of Elgar's concerto*. In 1973 multiple sclerosis forced her into retirement. Recorded chiefly by EMI.

◗ **Favourite Cello Concertos** (EMI CMS 763283-2; 3 CDs).

A three-disc set of most of her concerto recordings for EMI (including Elgar, Haydn and Dvořák), the majority of which are glorious. Emotional stuff.

BRIGITTE FASSBAENDER (1939–)

German mezzo-soprano. The natural successor to Christa Ludwig. Fassbaender's rich, resonant and well-disciplined voice is not as beautiful as Ludwig's, but she brings a real insight to everything she sings. Very successful in the theatre (especially in comic operas by Strauss and Mozart), she is also an excellent song recitalist, and has made superb recordings of songs by such diverse composers as Schubert*, Mahler* and Weill*. Recorded by EMI, Decca and Deutsche Grammophon.

🔘 **Wolf, Möricke-lieder** (Decca 440 208-2).

A fine recording with Jean Yves Thibaudet, showing Fassbaender at her most instinctive.

KATHLEEN FERRIER (1922–1953)

English contralto. Worked as a switchboard operator before winning a singing competition in 1937. Rose to fame through her performances of Elgar's *Gerontius* and Bach's *Matthew Passion*, and in 1946 made her operatic debut in Britten's *Rape of Lucretia*. Most celebrated in Mahler's *Das Lied von der Erde*, Gluck's *Orfeo* and Brahms's *Alto Rhapsody*. She was one of the most popular singers of the post-war years, and her early death from cancer was internationally mourned. Recorded by Decca.

🔘 **Lieder by Schubert, Schumann and Brahms** (Decca 433 476-2).

A legendary recording, with Bruno Walter at the piano. One of a series of Decca CDs dedicated to Ferrier.

DIETRICH FISCHER-DIESKAU (1925–)

German baritone. An extremely perceptive musician, he is perhaps the most successful baritone since the war – certainly the most versatile, though he has attempted music that suits neither his smooth, cultured voice nor his rather serious personality. He is best heard in German operatic roles, and above all in songs by Wolf*, Beethoven and Schubert*. Recorded chiefly by Deutsche Grammophon and EMI.

🔘 **Live at Salzburg** (Orfeo C140501A).

Fischer-Dieskau singing Beethoven; good sound, superb performances.

KIRSTEN FLAGSTAD (1895–1962)

Norwegian soprano. Flagstad's range, power and extraordinary stamina made her one of the greatest Wagner* sopranos, but she allowed her voice to mature before placing it at the mercy of Isolde and Brünnhilde. Her voice was warm but it had a ring and a brilliance that distinguished it from almost every other – only Birgit Nilsson is comparable. Recorded by Decca, Nimbus and EMI.

🔘 **Operatic Arias** (Nimbus NI7847).

Fine recordings of Flagstad in her prime, with a superb remastered 78 of her singing the *Liebestod* from *Tristan*. Many live recordings are also now available.

MIRELLA FRENI (1935–)

Italian soprano. In the 1960s became established as one of the world's best lyric sopranos, working a lot with Karajan and Pavarotti. A fine vocal actress, she is outstanding in Verdi*, Donizetti, Mozart, Tchaikovsky* and verismo opera. Recorded by EMI and Decca.

🔘 **Verismo Arias** (Decca 433 316-2).

A splendid studio recital of highlights from Puccini and others.

FERENC FRICSAY (1914–1963)

Hungarian conductor. Although principally known for his work in the opera house, he spent many years with the RIAS Orchestra in Berlin (from 1948) and made a number of sensational recordings, especially of music by Bartók and Mozart. Both Kodály and Bartók thought very highly of him, and his death at the age of forty-nine robbed the world of a great interpretive talent. Recorded by Deutsche Grammophon.

WILHELM FURTWÄNGLER (1886–1954)

German conductor and composer. Dominant within Berlin and Vienna (whose orchestras he conducted for most of his working life), Furtwängler represented the antithesis to the "objectivity" of Toscanini – his interpretations were the expressions of a mind that never ceased re-appraising what it knew. His controversial decision to remain in Nazi Germany clouded his reputation, but he has legions of admirers, for whom his performances of Beethoven*, Brahms* and Wagner* are without equal. Recorded by Deutsche Grammophon and EMI, and there are many live recordings from small labels, some of dubious legality.

JAMES GALWAY (1939–)

Irish flautist. The most famous flautist of recent years. He began as principal flute for the London Symphony, London Philharmonic and, under Karajan, the Berlin Philharmonic. After six years in Berlin he pursued a solo career in which he showed an amazing talent for self-marketing. His tone is especially sweet and his technique fabulous, but he is notoriously unselective when it comes to repertoire. Recorded by RCA.

● **Galway plays Bach** (RCA GD86517).

Galway in repertoire he clearly enjoys. A relaxed introduction to this mercurial performer.

JOHN ELIOT GARDINER (1943–)

English conductor. Highly popular promoter of the early music and period performance cause, whose expressive approach to this potentially arid field has resulted in some highly revealing performances. Notable especially for his well-researched recordings of Handel*, Purcell* and Mozart*. His foray into Romantic repertoire has been much less successful and he remains at his best in music from the sixteenth to the eighteenth century. Recorded by Philips, Deutsche Grammophon and Erato.

WALTER GIESEKING (1895–1956)

German pianist. Gieseking played with a smooth, even touch and an old-fashioned facility for phrasing, seen to great effect in the music of Schumann, Beethoven and Brahms, while his recordings of Debussy* and Ravel* show a rare mastery of colour. His career was overshadowed by Nazi affiliations. Recorded by EMI.

● **Beethoven Sonatas Nos. 9, 10, 13 & 14** (EMI CDZ 762857-2).

A budget-price issue of Gieseking playing the *Pathétique* and *Moonlight* sonatas, plus two others.

BENIAMINO GIGLI (1890–1957)

Italian tenor. Although Gigli's voice was not as expressive or as elegant as Caruso's, it was nonetheless a marvellous instrument, and after Caruso's death in 1921, Gigli was acclaimed his successor. His range (to an easy high C) and emotional exuberance were highly prized in the operas of Puccini, Donizetti and Verdi. Gigli was one of the first to make complete opera recordings, and he carried on singing with great success until shortly before his death. Recorded by HMV and EMI.

● **Operatic Arias** (Nimbus NI7807 & 7817).

Two good selections: the first is from 1918–24 and the second from 1925–40.

EMIL GILELS (1916–1985)

Russian pianist. Extremely successful powerhouse pianist, celebrated for his formidable "New Russian school" technique, intense concentration and wide-ranging tonal palette. Together with Richter, Gilels was the most prominent of the Russian pianists to remain at home during the communist years. His recordings of music by Brahms* and Beethoven* are highly prized. Recorded chiefly by Deutsche Grammophon.

● **Live Recordings 1930–1984** (Olympia OCD166).

A fascinating disc, including music by Scriabin, Debussy and Ravel.

CARLO MARIA GIULINI (1914–)

Italian conductor. Giulini first made his name in the opera house and, in particular, through his work with Maria Callas, then in 1967 announced his intention to concentrate on concert music. His early performances were characterized by a blend of lyricism and dynamism, but his performances since the end of the 1970s have been dogged by impossibly slow speeds and a weak sense of architecture. Recorded by EMI, Deutsche Grammophon and Sony.

TITO GOBBI (1913–1984)

Italian baritone. One of the greatest operatic character actors, Gobbi mirrored Callas in his concentration on the theatricality of performance. His rich and resonant voice was far from perfect but he used it with unparalleled skill and imagination. Although his repertoire was vast, he shone as Berg's Wozzeck and Verdi's* Rigoletto, Falstaff and Iago, but he was at his best as the evil Scarpia in Puccini's *Tosca**, a role he recorded twice with Callas. Recorded by EMI.

Opera Arias (EMI CDM7 63109-2).

A selection of arias from his various EMI studio recordings, including *Andrea Chénier*, *Otello* and *Le Nozze di Figaro*.

GLENN GOULD (1932–1982)

Canadian pianist. Shot to fame with debut recording of Bach's* *Goldberg Variations* in 1956; retired from the concert platform in early 1960s to concentrate on recordings. A reclusive and eccentric character, Gould was consciously provocative in his approach to tempi and phrasing, and many of his performances and recordings caused outrage. Had a vast knowledge of the repertoire, but detested all Romantic piano music – a notable omission in a vast catalogue that stretches from Gibbons* to Schoenberg. Recorded by CBS/Sony – Sony's mid-price Glenn Gould Edition, repackaging virtually all his recordings, is well under way.

BERNARD HAITINK (1929–   )

Dutch conductor. Famous for his work with the Concertgebouw, London Philharmonic Orchestra and Covent Garden opera house. Haitink's repertoire is refreshingly narrow, and he is best heard in the music of Mahler, Bruckner, Strauss and the German-Viennese classics. Recorded by Philips.

NIKOLAUS HARNONCOURT (1929–   )

German conductor. One of the principal influences on the revival of period-instrument performances, Harnoncourt made his name with recordings of Bach's choral works. In recent years has moved away from period performance, and has made many well-received orchestral recordings, notably Beethoven and Schubert* symphony cycles. Recorded by Teldec.

JASCHA HEIFETZ (1901–1987)

Russian violinist. The most complete violinist of the century. A child prodigy, he gave his debut at Carnegie Hall in 1917. Some found his detached platform manner off-putting, but there was no argument about the perfection of his pure-toned technique nor the passion of his interpretations. He recorded almost everything of note but he is best heard in Romantic repertoire. Recorded by RCA, whose colossal Heifetz Collection gathers together all his RCA recordings plus several others. The complete 65-CD survey is being repackaged in some 46 smaller units over the course of the next few years. Live Heifetz recordings are also available on smaller labels – Music & Arts produce a stunning double-CD including the Beethoven* and Brahms concertos.

Heifetz plays . . . (Biddulph LAB025).

Music by Franck, Saint-Saëns and Vieuxtemps. Staggering virtuosity and musicianship.

VLADIMIR HOROWITZ (1903–1991)

Russian pianist. Horowitz was to the piano what Heifetz was to the violin. His attention-grabbing tricks were not to everyone's liking, and later in life he took impossible liberties with the score but, as was the case with Liszt, Horowitz was incapable of performing a score the same way twice. At his best in Schumann* and Russian music – especially Tchaikovsky*, Rachmaninov* and Scriabin. Recorded chiefly by RCA and Sony – both labels have issued boxed sets of his performances, also available in smaller units. The RCA set (22 CDs) concentrates on the first two-thirds of his career, the Sony edition (13 CDs) picks up the story in 1962, and includes an amazing live recording of his Carnegie Hall comeback concert in 1965. Together, these two surveys constitute one of the greatest legacies of recorded piano music, comparable to those of Gould, Richter, Schnabel, Lipatti and Rachmaninov (see p.282 for Rachmaninov's own recordings).

GUNDULA JANOWITZ (1937–)

German soprano. "Discovered" by Karajan and promptly employed at the Vienna Statsoper, heralding the opera house's finest decade. Particularly suited to Strauss* and Mozart* but the purity of her tone, allied to an inflexible stylistic approach, can make what she is singing seem less important than the manner in which she is singing it. At her best she has one of the most beautiful voices on record. Recorded by Deutsche Grammophon.

◉ Strauss Orchestral Lieder (Virgin VC7 90794-2).

Nine of Strauss's orchestral songs, together with a good *Metamorphosen*. Effortlessly beautiful.

EUGEN JOCHUM (1902–1987)

German conductor. Known for his spacious tempi and highly tuned sense of pulse, he was best in German and Austrian symphonic music, especially Bruckner*. His performances were always imaginative, even if he was not the most exciting conductor around. Recorded by Deutsche Grammophon.

HERBERT VON KARAJAN (1908–1989)

Austrian conductor. The last of the autocratic maestros, Karajan ruled with a fist of iron but was highly respected, if not loved, by nearly all those who worked with him. He was especially fine with singers, and conducted some stunning productions of Mozart and Strauss. In the concert hall, his life was dominated by his relationship with the Berlin Philharmonic, by whom he was made principal conductor for life in 1957. His best recordings are from the 1960s (notably Beethoven*, Haydn* and Mozart*), before he developed the homogenous, slick orchestral sound with which he became associated. Recorded by EMI and Deutsche Grammophon.

NIGEL KENNEDY (1956–)

English violinist. Trained by Menuhin, Kennedy became the great white hope of English violin playing, thanks to a clutch of fine recordings. In recent years has remoulded himself as football-obsessed, streetwise lad, to great commercial effect. Recorded by EMI.

◖ Elgar, Violin Concerto (EMI EMX2058).

The recording that made Nige a star, and better than anything he's produced since the image-makers went to work on him.

EVGENY KISSIN (1971–)

Russian pianist. A sensational prodigy, Kissin recorded both Chopin concertos in one evening when only twelve years old, and has produced some of the most remarkable piano discs of recent years. Some have detected signs that his pressurized childhood is now beginning to take its toll, but he's still a breathtaking performer. Recorded by Sony and RCA.

◉ In Tokyo (Sony SK 45931).

Astounding recital from the fifteen-year-old, making his debut in Japan. Chopin, Liszt, Scriabin, Rachmaninov – and a performance of Prokofiev's sixth sonata that is simply the best in the catalogue.

CARLOS KLEIBER (1930–)

German conductor. The son of Erich Kleiber, Carlos is widely esteemed as the greatest living conductor. His work is characterized by a balletic, flowing sense of style and a piercing interpretive insight that he clearly learned from his father. Harshly self-critical, he has now all but retired from public life, but everything he has recorded remains in the catalogue – his performances of Beethoven*, Brahms*, Weber*, Wagner*, Verdi* and Johann Strauss* are astounding. Recorded by Deutsche Grammophon, Orfeo and Sony.

ERICH KLEIBER (1890–1956)

Austrian conductor. Oversaw one of the golden periods of operatic life in Berlin as director of the State Opera (1924–34); gave the first performance of Berg's *Wozzeck* in 1925, for which he took 137 rehearsals. Left Nazi Germany in 1934, returned to the post twenty years later, then resigned over political interference. A profound intellect, with a marvellous feel for musical structure, Kleiber was a masterful conductor of Mozart*, Beethoven and Strauss. Recorded by Decca.

OTTO KLEMPERER (1885–1973)

German conductor. Klemperer led an extraordinary life in which he worked with an astonishing number of the century's seminal musicians, including Mahler, Korngold (whose *Die tote Stadt* he premiered in 1920) and Caruso. He spent many years battling with hardship and ill health and did not really attain international fame until the 1950s when he began to work with the Philharmonia in London. Undoubtedly one of the greatest conductors, his performances were characterized above all by slow tempi that allowed the music to unfold in a dauntingly intense manner. His recorded work is dominated by German-Austrian music of the nineteenth century – Beethoven*, Brahms* and Mahler in particular. Recorded by EMI.

HANS KNAPPERTSBUSCH (1888–1965)

German conductor. He studied with Steinbach, a friend of Wagner*, and went on to become one of the great Wagnerians. He was a particularly fine interpreter of *Parsifal* and his recordings of the opera have never been surpassed. Also a fine interpreter of Strauss. Recorded by Philips and Teldec.

SERGE KOUSSEVITSKY (1874–1951)

Russian conductor. A remarkable character, whose life brought him into contact with many of the greatest musicians of his period. Close friend of Scriabin, Sibelius, Prokofiev, Stravinsky and Bartók. Originally a double-bassist, he began conducting in 1907, but is best known for his work with the Boston Symphony Orchestra from 1924 to 1949. Founded the Koussevitsky Foundation in 1943, to promote and commission new work – including Bartók's *Concerto for Orchestra*.

STEPHEN KOVACEVICH (1940–

American pianist. A child prodigy, Kovacevich (then known as Stephen Bishop) studied with Myra Hess, who clearly influenced his feeling for pacing and colour. Known especially for his playing of Schumann*, Brahms and Beethoven*. Recorded by Philips and EMI.

ALFREDO KRAUS (1927–   )

Spanish tenor. Kraus is a genuine lyric tenor who has been denied his rightful acclaim because of his decision to remain true to the bel canto repertoire for which his voice was trained. His fluency does sometimes decline into blandness but, at his best, he is one of the finest singers of his period. Recorded chiefly by EMI and RCA.

> ◗ **Public Performances** (Memories HR 4233/4; 2 CDs).

There are ludicrously few Krauss recital discs in the catalogue; this compilation of live performances is the best of those that are readily available.

CLEMENS KRAUSS (1893–1954)

German conductor. One of the outstanding figures in the history of twentieth-century music, Krauss raised the standards of almost every musical centre he worked in. While assistant at Vienna Opera, he became close friends with Richard Strauss*, for whom he gave the first performances of *Arabella*, *Friedenstag* and *Die Liebe der Danae*. His performances were famously exciting, and his perfect ear and remarkable feel for internal balance made him one of the most complete conductors of the day. Recorded chiefly by Decca, but his stupendous live *Ring* cycle was issued by a small company called Foyer – you may still be able to find copies lying around.

JOSEF KRIPS (1902–1974)

Austrian conductor. Krips was appointed conductor at the Vienna Volksoper aged just nineteen. Banned by the Nazis, he returned in 1945 and played a major part in restoring the Vienna Opera's reputation. Particularly famed for his performances of Mozart* – his lucid realizations of the late operas are regarded by some as unsurpassable. Recorded by Decca.

LOTTE LEHMANN (1888–1976)

German soprano. One of the great figures in modern opera, possessed of exceptional interpretive qualities. Created the roles of the Composer (*Ariadne*), Dyer's Wife (*Die Frau ohne Schatten*) and Christine (*Intermezzo*) for

Strauss – and was one of the few sopranos to have successfully sung all three of the leading roles in *Der Rosenkavalier*. Her singing did not transfer well onto record but, even so, her available recordings testify to a rare talent. Recorded by EMI.

❸ Der Rosenkavalier (EMI CHS 7 64487-2; 2 CDs).

A legendary (abridged) recording of Lehmann in her greatest role, the Marschallin, with the equally wonderful Elizabeth Schumann as Octavian and Richard Mayr as Baron Ochs.

ERIC LEINSDORF (1912–1992)

Austrian-born American conductor. After assisting Walter and Toscanini at the Salzburg Festival, Leinsdorf moved to America in the late 1930s, and rarely performed outside America after that. His many recordings reflect a highly individual, driven personality; at his best in German music. Recorded by RCA.

JAMES LEVINE (1943–)

American conductor. For many people he epitomizes the sentimental indulgences legitimized by Bernstein, but aged just twenty-eight, he was made principal conductor of the Met in New York, with whom he has remained ever since. He has conducted an enormous amount of music on record, though he's best when dealing with singers, as in his recording of Verdi's *La Forza del Destino**. Recorded by Deutsche Grammophon.

DINU LIPATTI (1917–1950)

Romanian pianist. A much-loved pianist and phenomenally gifted musician, once nicknamed "God's chosen instrument". Noted above all for the patrician poise of his playing, and for the precision and delicacy of his technique. Superb in Chopin*, but also highly suited to the disciplines of Mozart. Made few recordings before his death from leukemia. Recorded by EMI.

❸ Dinu Lipatti – the complete recordings (EMI CZS 767163-2; 5 CDs).

This boxed set features sublime performances of music by Scarlatti, Mozart, Grieg, Schumann and many others – Lipatti's Chopin waltzes have never been surpassed. The five CDs are also available separately.

CHRISTA LUDWIG (1928–)

German mezzo-soprano. Perhaps the greatest post-war German mezzo, Ludwig excelled in almost every area of repertoire. Her striking, beautifully produced voice is a mixture of mezzo and dramatic soprano, and she has exploited this flexibility in performances of extraordinary originality. Best known for her Leonora (Beethoven's *Fidelio**), Cherubino (Mozart's *Nozze di Figaro*) and Octavian (Strauss's *Rosenkavalier**), but was also a superb Adalgisa (Bellini's *Norma**) and Brangäne (Wagner's *Tristan**). Also celebrated as a Lieder recitalist. Recorded by EMI and RCA.

❸ Mahler, Das Lied von der Erde (EMI CDC 747231-2).

One of Ludwig's greatest performances, conducted by Klemperer, with Fritz Wunderlich singing the tenor part.

YO YO MA (1955–)

American cellist. One of the world's leading cellists, Ma has approached just about every strand of the instrument's repertoire and has worked extensively in a trio with Isaac Stern and Emanuel Ax. He makes a wonderful, concentrated sound but is best when working with a disciplined conductor. Recorded by CBS/Sony.

◉ Made in America (Sony SK 53126).

Fine compilation of music by Bernstein, Gershwin, Kirchner and Ives – the Ives *Piano Trio* is the highlight.

LORIN MAAZEL (1930–)

American conductor. Began conducting the New York Philharmonic. Has held many posts but is best known for his work with the Vienna Philharmonic, with whom he recorded an excellent cycle of Mahler symphonies. Always brings a lot of character to his performances, and even if they are not always successful, they are entirely his own. Recorded by CBS/Sony.

KURT MASUR (1928–)

German conductor. Principal of Leipzig Gewandhaus and New York Philharmonic. Self-proclaimed traditionalist, working extensively in the Viennese classics and German

Romantics such as Mendelssohn*. Recorded by Philips.

ZUBIN MEHTA (1936–)

Indian conductor. One of the most popular of his generation, he has developed a very wide repertoire but has specialized in the German Romantics. A good technician, his performances are characterized by a fierce, almost brutal stick technique – he attacks every performance as if it were his last. Conductor of the "Three Tenors" concerts. Recorded by CBS/Sony.

LAURITZ MELCHIOR (1890–1973)

Danish tenor. Possessed a huge voice that was ideally suited to Wagner's most heroic roles, including Tristan, Siegmund and Siegfried. A ringing top and a resonant lower register made his voice instantly recognizable, and although he took liberties with the rhythmic character of Wagner's music and was incapable of anything approaching acting, he remains one of the few genuine Wagner tenors to have made records. Many live recordings on small independent labels.

⊙ **Opera Arias** (Nimbus NI7816).

Leoncavallo, Verdi and Meyerbeer are featured on this superb disc, but Wagner dominates the proceedings. Seismic singing.

WILLEM MENGELBERG (1871–1951)

Dutch conductor. Highly regarded by Mahler and Strauss (who dedicated his *Heldenleben* to him), he was appointed principal of the Concertgebouw in 1895 and remained with the orchestra until 1941. Mengelberg was the first to champion Mahler's music and his few recordings are fascinating historical documents. Because of his Nazi collaboration, he was banned from conducting by the Dutch government in 1945, and he died in exile six years later.

YEHUDI MENUHIN (1916–)

American-born violinist and conductor. A child prodigy, Menuhin first became famous for his association with Elgar, whose concerto he recorded with the composer conducting in 1932. Bartók* later composed his solo violin sonata for him. His pure and refined technique had begun to decline by the 1960s, but he carried on playing. He is now a full-time conductor and musical ambassador. Recorded by EMI.

⊙ **The Young Yehudi Menuhin** (Biddulph LAB031).

These recordings were made while Menuhin was still a boy, but the performances of the Bruch *Concerto* and Mozart *Concerto No. 3* reflect an awesome maturity. Miraculous playing.

PIERRE MONTEUX (1875–1964)

French conductor. As a young man he played in a string quartet, giving concerts for the likes of Brahms, Tchaikovsky and Grieg. During the early years of the twentieth century he began conducting for Diaghilev's Ballets Russes, for whom he gave the first performances of Stravinsky's *Petrushka* and *Rite of Spring*, Debussy's *Jeux* and Ravel's *Daphnis et Chloë*. Moved to the USA in 1917, based in San Francisco; continued conducting to the end of his life. He is the most important French conductor of the century, outstanding in French music and the work of Stravinsky, but also excellent in Brahms. Recorded by RCA – the company has issued a boxed Monteux Edition, also available as single CDs.

CHARLES MUNCH (1891–1968)

French conductor. Moved to America in 1946, becoming conductor of Boston Symphony Orchestra in 1949. For the next thirty years he raised the orchestra's standards to unprecedented heights and made a string of extraordinary recordings. Had an excellent feeling for tone colour, and is best heard in Ravel* and other French music, although he did a lot to promote contemporary American composers. Recorded by RCA.

RICCARDO MUTI (1941–)

Italian conductor. Highly regarded as an opera conductor (he's currently in charge at La Scala), he has been almost as successful in the concert hall, where he introduces a rare vitality and sense of occasion. His recordings of Verdi* are widely acclaimed for their power and immediacy. Recorded by EMI.

ANNE-SOPHIE MUTTER (1963–)

German violinist. A Karajan discovery, she is notable not just for her prodigious technique but also for her commitment to new music. Generally brings a greater sense of intellectual weight to her performances than you get with many of the more recent prodigies. Recorded by Deutsche Grammophon.

◉ Berg, Violin Concerto; Rihm, Gesunge Zeit: Mutter; Chicago Symphony Orchestra; Levine (Deutsche Grammophon 437 093-2GH).

Superb account of the Berg concerto, coupled with a fascinating example of post-war expressionism.

BIRGIT NILSSON (1918–)

Swedish soprano. A magnificent Wagner* singer, Nilsson was blessed with one of the most sensational voices ever recorded, notable for its power, flexibility, technique and stamina. The finest Isolde and Brünnhilde since the war, she was also supreme as Strauss's Salome* and Puccini's Turandot*. Recorded by Deutsche Grammophon and Philips.

◉ Operatic Arias (Deutsche Grammophon 431 107-2).

A budget issue that includes a sensational live concert performance of the closing scene from *Salome* at the Met, conducted by Böhm.

JESSYE NORMAN (1945–)

American soprano. Her spectacularly ample voice has a dark and resonant lower register and a thrilling, dynamic top. She has been criticized for her excessive volume but she possesses a fine technique and uses it with great imagination. Mightily impressive in Strauss, Schoenberg*, Mahler, Berlioz and Wagner; also an excellent if infrequent Lieder singer. Recorded by Philips.

◉ Songs by Handel, Schubert, Schumann (Philips 422 048-2).

A splendid live Lieder recording, including Schubert's *Erlkönig* and *Gretchen am Spinnrade*.

ROGER NORRINGTON (1934–)

English conductor. Music director of Kent Opera before forming and conducting the London Classical Players, an orchestra devoted to period performances of eighteenth- and nineteenth-century music. This radical change of direction has brought him much success, but many find his performances dry and expressionless. Recorded by EMI.

DAVID OISTRAKH (1908–1974)

Russian violinist. Came to international prominence after winning the Brussels Competition in 1937. Although he toured extensively, he never left Russia. Dedicatee and first performer of both of Shostakovich's concertos and recorded them to great acclaim. A beautifully full tone and lyrical sense of line made him one of the finest violinists of his time. Recorded chiefly by Deutsche Grammophon and Philips.

◗ Nineteenth-Century Violin Works (Deutsche Grammophon 413 844-2GW2-2; 2 CDs).

Concertos by Brahms, Bruch and Dvořák, plus the *Romances* by Beethoven*.

LUCIANO PAVAROTTI (1935–)

Italian tenor. Made his debut in 1961 and specialized in bel canto roles, in which, with his thrilling extended register, he was exceptional. In the 1970s he began to extend his sights towards verismo roles, and by the 1980s his voice had lost much of the warm quality so common in his earlier work. Since then his timbre has thinned and his expressive range has narrowed. Superb in Rossini*, Bellini*, Donizetti* and early Verdi* but to be avoided in late Verdi, Puccini, Giordano and verismo opera in general. Recorded by Decca.

◗ Donizetti Arias (Decca CD417 638-2).

Pavarotti at his lyrical best.

PETER PEARS (1910–1986)

English tenor. Partner of Benjamin Britten*, he gave the first performances of many of Britten's works, creating roles in *Peter Grimes*, *Albert Herring*, *The Rape of Lucretia*, *Billy Budd*, *Gloriana*, *The Turn of the Screw* and *Death in Venice*. Also a noted singer of Lieder (especially Schubert) and oratorio (especially the Evangelist in Bach's *Matthew Passion*). His voice was slightly nasal but very distinctive, and all his performances were well thought-out. Recorded by Decca and EMI.

◗ Britten, Works for Tenor (Decca 417 153-2DH).

A marvellous recital, with Britten conducting.

ITZHAK PERLMAN (1945–   )

Israeli violinist. His generous and uncompromisingly emotional tone is particularly suited to the Romantic repertoire and his recordings of Brahms, Beethoven and Bruch are essential listening. He is less suited to the disciplines of Mozart and Bach, but he has shown himself to be a master of some of the more accessible twentieth-century concertos, especially those by Elgar and Berg. Though a generally intense performer, he sometimes sounds like a man who has done it all, twice. Recorded by EMI and Deutsche Grammophon.

> ◗ **Great Romantic Concertos** (EMI 7 64922 2 3; 3 CDs).
>
> A fine collection of the repertoire Perlman plays best, featuring the concertos of Beethoven, Brahms, Bruch, Mendelssohn, Paganini and Tchaikovsky. Good value.

MAURIZIO POLLINI (1942–   )

Italian pianist. Winner of Chopin Competition in 1960, Pollini then studied with Benedetti Michelangeli before resuming his career. A supreme technician, he is regarded by many as the greatest living pianist, but is often criticized for an excessive preoccupation with accuracy and structure. Has made benchmark recordings of Beethoven*, Schubert*, Schumann*, Chopin*, Schoenberg* and Stravinsky*, among others. Now recorded exclusively by Deutsche Grammophon.

> ◗ **Chopin Recital** (EMI CDM7 64354-2).
>
> Pollini's debut recording – a breathtaking account of Chopin's *Piano Concerto No. 1*, and a wondrous selection of shorter pieces.

LEONTYNE PRICE (1927–   )

American soprano. Made her debut at the Met in 1961, singing *Il Trovatore* with Franco Corelli (a recording of which exists), and went on to shine in most of Verdi's* major roles, dominating the American operatic stage for twenty years. A favourite of Samuel Barber's, she sang in the first performance of his *Antony and Cleopatra* in 1966; also magnificent as Bizet's* Carmen. Recorded by RCA.

> ◉ **Price sings Barber** (RCA 09026 61983-2).
>
> The first performance of the *Hermit Songs* and a fine selection from *Antony and Cleopatra*.

MARGARET PRICE (1941–   )

Welsh soprano. Has a beautiful, evenly produced lyric soprano voice, always used to tasteful effect. Made her name singing Mozart but graduated to Verdi* and, more famously, Wagner*. She is perhaps at her best in Lieder – in the songs of Brahms she is a supreme interpreter. Recorded by Philips and RCA.

> ◉ **Brahms songs** (RCA 09026 60901-2).
>
> A fine recital of some of Brahms's most beautiful songs.

SAMUEL RAMEY (1942–   )

American bass. A magnetic performer with an unusually powerful voice, he has achieved enormous success as Figaro (Mozart) and Attila (Verdi). However, he is at his best as Bartók's Bluebeard* and Gounod's Mephistopheles. Recorded by Deutsche Grammophon and CBS/Sony.

> ◉ **Rossini Arias and Duets** (Sony SMK 48399).
>
> A marvellous disc, with Ramey joined by Ricciarelli, Horne and Baltsa.

SIMON RATTLE (1955–   )

English conductor. One of the few English conductors to achieve international acceptance, he has now worked with the Philharmonics of both Berlin and Vienna and has scored great successes at Salzburg. An exciting and enthusiastic performer, with a fine ear for ensemble and characterization, he has built the City of Birmingham Symphony Orchestra into a first-class unit. Though best known for his Mahler*, he is equally illuminating with Sibelius* or Szymanowski*. Recorded by EMI.

FRITZ REINER (1888–1963)

Hungarian conductor. A good friend of Richard Strauss and Bartók, Reiner moved to the USA in 1922 and had a lasting impact upon musical life. Was most productive with the Chicago Symphony Orchestra (1953–63), which he made into one of the world's greatest. His fierce, often belligerent manner resulted in some sensationally exciting performances, especially of Strauss*, Bartók, Wagner and Beethoven*. Recorded by RCA.

SVIATOSLAV RICHTER (1914–)

Russian pianist. One of the most exceptional virtuosos of the century. A friend of Prokofiev, he gave the first performances of the sixth, seventh and ninth Prokofiev sonatas. He came late to the West, not making his debut in London until 1961, and his subsequent performances outside Russia have been limited by his hatred of flying. He has a wide-ranging mind, and there is nothing beyond his technical capabilities – he has made stunning recordings of Bach, Haydn, Beethoven, Schumann and Prokofiev. Recorded by RCA, Olympia, Decca and Philips. The Richter Authorized Edition, a 22-CD boxed set from Philips, is an extraordinary body of work, showing an unrivalled consistency of achievement across a vast range of music. The set is also available as smaller boxes dedicated to single composers or small groups of composers – they are all superb, but the best starting place is the double-CD of Beethoven sonatas.

ARTUR RUBINSTEIN (1887–1982)

Polish pianist. Rubinstein led an exceptionally colourful life. As a boy he was sent to Brahms's friend Joachim, who helped pay for his musical training, and he began touring in 1897, the start of an eighty-year career. As he spoke eight languages fluently, he acted as an interpreter during World War I, and also gave charity recitals. Carried on playing until his ninetieth birthday. His imaginative, powerful playing was soaked in the nineteenth-century traditions that formed him, and he was especially outstanding in the music of Chopin*, as well as Stravinsky and Falla (both of whom wrote for him). Recorded by EMI and RCA.

◗ **Recital** (RCA RD85670).

Marvellous performances of music by Prokofiev, Schumann, Ravel, Debussy, Albéniz and Villa-Lobos.

WOLFGANG SAWALLISCH (1923–)

German conductor. Learned his craft carefully: he was thirty before gaining his first position, at Aachen Opera (Karajan's early stamping ground). In 1971 he moved to the Bavarian State Opera where his success was consistent. A sound rather than an inspiring conductor, he is famed for his performances of Schumann*, Mozart, Wagner and Strauss. Also a fine Lieder pianist. Recorded by EMI.

ARTUR SCHNABEL (1882–1951)

Austrian pianist. A pupil of Liszt's friend Leschetizky, he made his debut in 1890. From then on he was famous throughout the world for his performances of Beethoven (whose complete sonatas he was the first to record) and Schubert. Playing the piano to Albert Einstein's violin, he was heard to ask in exasperation "My dear Albert, can't you count?". Recorded by EMI.

◗ **Beethoven, Complete Sonatas** (EMI CHS 763765-2; 8 CDs).

A legendary set which has greatly influenced the way modern pianists approach Beethoven.

ELISABETH SCHWARZKOPF (1915–)

German soprano. One of the most influential German musicians of the post-war era. Gifted with a hauntingly beautiful voice, she was originally a coloratura soprano but developed into a lyric soprano of remarkable quality, specializing in the music of Mozart and Strauss* – though her repertoire was huge. She has also won wide acclaim as a Lieder recitalist, especially as an interpeter of Schubert and Wolf*. Recorded by Deutsche Grammophon and EMI.

◗ **Romantic Opera Arias** (EMI CDM 769501-2).

A fine recording, showing her voice at its most sumptuous; includes arias from *Der Freischütz* and *Eugene Onegin*.

IRMGARD SEEFRIED (1919–1988)

German soprano. One of the outstanding lyrical sopranos of the post-war years, superb in Mozart and, in particular, Strauss. Her few recordings are treasured as the finest in their repertoire. Recorded by EMI.

◗ **Song Recital** (Testament SBT 1018).

A wonderful collection of Lieder by Brahms, Schubert, Wolf and Mozart.

TULLIO SERAFIN (1878–1968)

Italian conductor. He "discovered" Callas, Bergonzi and Gobbi, and tutored dozens of other great names, and there has been no greater master of the bel canto repertoire – in particular Bellini* and Donizetti, whose music he did much to revive. Less suited to the passions of verismo, but nonetheless a fine interpeter of Puccini's* *La Bohème* and *Madama Butterfly*. Made his debut in 1898, conducted the first *Turandot* in America, and the first *Der Rosenkavalier* and *Peter Grimes* in Italy. Recorded by Decca and EMI.

GIUSEPPE SINOPOLI (1946–   )

Italian conductor. Sinopoli favours grand, Romantic repertoire and very slow tempi – his recordings of Bruckner, Wagner, Strauss and Mahler attract as much condemnation as praise. However, he believes firmly in what he does and displays a consistency that, in itself, deserves respect. Recorded by Deutsche Grammophon.

GEORG SOLTI (1912–   )

Hungarian conductor. Studied with Bartók and Kodály before working with Toscanini in Salzburg. Appointed principal at Munich Opera in 1946 and helped re-establish the company's high standards. Began making records as a pianist (having won the Geneva competition in 1942), then in 1949 conducted the music at Richard Strauss's funeral. Went on to become one of the most influential conductors of the century, turning Covent Garden into one of the greatest opera houses. Made the first-ever recording of the *Ring* cycle and has since made thousands of records. An exciting, frequently violent conductor, Solti continues to conduct with the energy of a man half his age. Best heard in Bruckner, Bartók, Mahler* and Strauss*. Recorded by Decca.

GÉRARD SOUZAY (1918–   )

French baritone. His superbly mellow, extended and flexible voice was only rarely heard in opera – he excelled as singer of French and German songs, making several outstanding recordings, notably of Schubert* Lieder. Recorded by Philips and Decca.

 Songs by Chausson and Fauré (Decca 425 975-2).

A classic recital of French songs.

ISSAC STERN (1920–   )

American violinist. Made his debut aged only fourteen, and hit his peak during the ten years after the war. Excelled in the concertos by Brahms, Sibelius and Prokofiev, but was very good in almost all Romantic repertoire. A fine chamber musician, he spent many years playing in a piano trio with Istomin and Rose but for the past ten years he has worked almost exclusively (but less successfully) with Ma and Ax. Recorded by CBS/Sony.

 The Early Concerto Recordings (Sony SM3K 45956; 3 CDs).

Fabulous playing of concertos by Sibelius, Prokofiev, Bruch and Saint-Saëns.

LEOPOLD STOKOWSKI (1882–1977)

British-born conductor. Born to a Polish father, moved in 1909 to the USA, where he introduced a huge amount of new music, including Mahler's *Symphony No. 8* and Schoenberg's *Gurrelieder*. Enthusiastically championed the work of Charles Ives; conducted the film score of *Fantasia*. Returned to England in 1972, where he established a good relationhip with the London Symphony Orchestra. Was at his best in music that demanded a fine understanding of orchestral texture, and although he took outrageous liberties with the scores he was a fascinating interpretive artist. Recorded chiefly by RCA.

JOAN SUTHERLAND (1926–   )

Australian soprano. Made her debut in 1947 but achieved major fame after singing the title role in *Lucia di Lammermoor* at Covent Garden in 1959. Went on to tackle a string of hugely demanding coloratura roles (many of which were revived especially for her) but was also a wonderful Violetta in *Traviata*. Very identifiable sound, which in later life lost much of its original firmness and linear beauty, but at her best Sutherland was the most complete bel canto soprano of the post-war years. Bellini* and Donizetti* were her particular strengths. Recorded by Decca.

 Italian Operatic Arias (Decca 440 404-2).

Her finest bel canto repertoire. A staggering recital.

GEORGE SZELL (1897–1970)

Hungarian conductor. Archetypal prodigy – as a boy he played his transcription of Strauss's *Till Eulenspiegel* to the composer, who was highly impressed. In 1917 he conducted the Berlin Philharmonic Orchestra in a concert of his own works. Strauss's recommendation took him to Strasbourg Theatre where he became conductor before his twentieth birthday. Went on to take over the Cleveland Orchestra in 1946 and during the next twenty-four years he made it one of the best. Excellent for Strauss, Mahler*, Wagner and Russian twentieth-century music – in particular, Prokofiev*. Recorded by CBS/Sony.

RENATA TEBALDI (1922–   )

Italian soprano. Engaged by Toscanini to sing at the re-opening of La Scala in 1946, she shot to fame as a rival to Callas for the accolade of finest dramatic soprano. Tebaldi was the finer musician and her enormously powerful and colourful voice comes over far better on record. She excelled in verismo roles and, in particular, as Puccini's* Butterfly and Mimi. Established a long partnership with del Monaco. Recorded by Decca.

◗ **Italian Operatic Arias** (Decca 440 408-2).

A beautiful selection from *Bohème*, *Butterfly*, *Otello* and others.

KIRI TE KANAWA (1944–   )

New Zealand soprano. Made her name as the Countess in Mozart's *Le Nozze di Figaro*, and became one of the finest lyric sopranos of the present generation. Has a lusciously beautiful voice, which she does not always use with the greatest thought. Wonderful in Strauss, and also a fine Desdemona in Verdi's *Otello*. Recorded by EMI.

◉ **French Operatic Arias** (EMI CDC 749863-2).

Te Kanawa on top form.

KLAUS TENNSTEDT (1926–   )

German conductor. Tennstedt has only come to international prominence during the last twenty years, largely as a result of his performances of Mahler*, in particular of the last three symphonies. One of the few conductors widely respected by his orchestral players. Recorded by EMI.

ARTURO TOSCANINI (1964–1957)

Italian conductor. Perhaps the most influential conductor of the twentieth century. Made his debut in 1886, when at the last minute he stepped in to conduct *Aida* from memory. Was a cellist at the first performance of Verdi's *Otello* in 1887. Conducted first performances of *I Pagliacci* (1892), *La Bohème* (1896), *La Fanciulla del West* (1910) and *Turandot* (1926). Gave the first Italian performances of hundreds of new operas including the first *Ring* cycle and he generally revolutionized performance standards at La Scala, and throughout Italy as a whole. He insisted on fidelity to the composer's intentions – the first ever to do so – and did everything he could to destroy the star system, forbidding encores and unwritten extensions. Wielded unprecedented power in almost every musical centre, including Bayreuth and New York, where he headed the Met for many years. Opposed the fascists, refusing to conduct under their aegis. He had a perfect musical memory, never forgetting a single note of a full score once he had studied it. Recorded by RCA, who have packaged nearly all his recordings in an 82-disc set, also available separately.

MITSUKU UCHIDA (1948–   )

Japanese pianist. Famous above all for her performances of Mozart's keyboard music (she has recorded all of the sonatas and concertos), but also excellent in Debussy*. A delicate, subtle musician, she has a brilliantly smooth technique and is an immensely intelligent interpreter. Recorded by Philips.

◉ **Mozart Concertos No. 20 and No. 23** (Philips 434 164-2).

An excellently priced sample of Uchida playing Mozart.

MAXIM VENGEROV (1974 –   )

Russian violinist. Probably the most formidable violinist since Heifetz, with an interpretive maturity that lifts him some way above

the production-line virtuosos of his generation. Like Heifetz, he possesses an immediately identifiable sound, with a very flexible
vibrato and a sweeping, sensual projection of
line. Virtually everything he plays is worth
hearing. Now recorded by Teldec.

⊙ **Recital** (Biddulph LAW 001).

Debut recorded recital from the fifteen-year old Vengerov,
including awesome performances of works by Ravel, Schubert
and Ysaye. Defies belief.

EBERHARD WÄCHTER (1929–1990)

Austrian baritone. Gifted with an exceptional,
smoothly produced voice – if ever a voice
merited the description "honeyed", it would
be Wächter's. Outstanding in Strauss* (especially as Jokanaan in *Salome*) and in Berg's
*Wozzeck**; also shone in Wagner* and Mozart
(as Don Giovanni), and in Beethoven's *Missa
Solemnis*.

⊙ **Schumann Lieder** (Decca 425 949-2).

Wächter displaying abundant talent in the non-operatic
repertoire.

BRUNO WALTER (1876–1962)

German conductor. As Toscanini is
associated with Puccini, so Walter is linked
with Mahler, with whom he worked from 1894
to 1911. He gave the first performances of his
Symphony No. 9 and *Das Lied von der Erde*,
and also premiered Pfitzner's *Palestrina*. His
knowledge of the orchestra was astonishing,
and he had an uncanny ability to make the
orchestra sing – in a sense he represented the
antithesis of Klemperer's hard-faced
idealism. Outstanding in Beethoven, Brahms*
and Mozart*. Recorded by EMI and
CBS/Sony.

FELIX WEINGARTNER (1863–1942)

Austrian conductor. After studying philosophy, he became a pupil of Liszt and began
conducting in 1884. Is best known for his
performances of Beethoven's symphonies – he
wrote a book on their interpretation and was
the first to record them all. His performance of
the ninth had a unique stamp of authenticity,
in that Weingartner based his interpretation
partly upon the reminiscences of a woman who
had sung at the first performance, with the
composer conducting. Recorded by EMI.

WOLFGANG WINDGASSEN (1914–   )

German tenor. One of the last great Wagner*
tenors. He did not possess the vocal weight to
be classed a true heldentenor, but he was a
fine dramatic musician and, most importantly, had the stamina to keep going. His
voice is beautifully controlled with a wide
expressive range and his high notes ring as
almost no other German tenor's. Best heard in
the live Wagner recordings from the 1950s, in
which his voice is at its richest. Recorded by
Deutsche Grammophon and Philips.

FRITZ WUNDERLICH (1930–1966)

German tenor. A perfect German lyric tenor,
he had an exceptionally beautiful voice, capable of balletic flexibility. Perfect in Strauss
and Mozart*, and although he recorded only
one Wagnerian role, great things were
expected of him. Also a fine Lieder singer,
happiest in Schumann* and Beethoven.

◗ **Wunderlich sings arias, songs and operetta**
(Deutsche Grammophon 435 145-2; 5 CDs).

Almost all his Deutsche Grammophon recordings in one set –
a must for anyone with an interest in singing.

GLOSSARY

Absolute music
Music that makes no references to events, paintings, literature and so forth; purely abstract art.

A cappella
Literally "In the church style". Unaccompanied choral singing.

Accelerando
Gradually increasing speed.

Accent
A stress on a particular note or beat, highlighting its place within a musical phrase.

Adagio
Slow and drawn-out tempo.

Alberti bass
In keyboard music, a running figure for the left hand that arpeggiates (see "Arpeggio") a simple series of chords, allowing the right hand to concentrate on melody. Highly popular in the eighteenth century.

Aleatory music
Derived from *alea*, the Latin word for "game of dice". Music composed by random procedures, often computerized. Very popular in the 1960s.

Allegro
Fast and lively tempo. The customary marking for the opening movement of a symphony.

Alto
1. The highest of the male voices.
2. The lowest of the female voices.
3. Prefix to an instrument that is lower in pitch and darker in tone than a treble instrument – eg alto saxophone, alto flute.

Andante
Moderate tempo. Slightly faster than Adagio – literally "walking pace".

Anthem
Brief, solemn composition for church choir; Protestant equivalent of the Latin Motet. Masters of the form include Purcell. Also used to define a patriotic vocal composition.

Aria
Term used since time of Alessandro Scarlatti to describe an independent solo vocal piece within an opera, frequently created to display the artist's vocal facility.

Arpeggio
A chord performed as a broken run of notes.

Atonal
Music that is not in any key. With atonal music the traditional harmonic language no longer applies and the twelve notes of the octave function independently of any key centre. Atonality is associated above all with Schoenberg and his chief followers, Berg and Webern.

Ballade
Term used by Chopin to describe an extended single-movement piano piece in which narrative is suggested, without reference to any extra-musical source. Later adopted by Grieg, Brahms, Liszt and Fauré.

Ballet
Dance form in which a story is told through the unification of music and dance. Originated in the French court of the sixteenth century. Used by Lully as an interlude in his operas, then evolved into hybrid opera-ballet. Later became an independent art form, dominated by the French until Tchaikovsky's emergence. Since the end of the nineteenth century many composers have written for the ballet, notably Prokofiev and Stravinsky.

Barcarolle
A composition (usually a song) that was originally associated with Venetian gondoliers' songs; usually has a gentle swaying motion, imitating the movement of the gondola.

Baritone
The male voice between tenor and bass.

Baroque
Music composed between 1600 and 1750, spanning the period from Monteverdi and Gabrieli to Bach and Handel. The period before Classical.

Bass
1. The lowest of the male voices.
2. The lowest part of a chord or piece of music.
3. The lowest of all instrument groups – eg double-bass, bass clarinet etc.

Bel canto
Literally "beautiful song". An eighteenth- and early nineteenth-century school of singing, characterized by a concentration on beauty of tone, virtuosic agility and breath control. Bellini, Rossini and Donizetti are the main bel canto composers.

Berceuse
A lullaby – the most famous instrumental example is by Chopin.

Binary form
A short work in two evenly balanced sections. Infrequently used since the death of Handel. Pre-dated sonata form.

Bitonal
Music that uses two keys at the same time. Favoured by Stravinsky.

Cabaletta
An heroic but brief aria (or end to an aria) built upon an unchanging rhythm. The most famous example is *Di quella pira* (for tenor) from Verdi's *Il Trovatore*.

Cadence
The closing sequence of a musical phrase or composition. The "perfect cadence" gives a sense of completion; the "imperfect cadence" leaves the music hanging in mid-air.

Cadenza
A solo passage designed to show off the soloist's abilities, occuring at the end of a concerto movement (generally the first), using material based upon the movement's main themes. Originally improvised, but composers began writing them out in the eighteenth century.

Canon
The strictest of contrapuntal forms. A work in which the same melody is played or sung by two or more voices, each beginning slightly after the preceding one. The most famous examples are *London's Burning* and *Frère Jacques*.

Cantabile
A "singing" style. Generally applied to instrumental and orchestral music.

Cantata
Literally "sung piece". An extended vocal work with an instrumental accompaniment that tells a story through the use of arias, recitative and choruses. Distant relative of opera. First composed in the seventeenth century and mastered by Bach and Handel; Elgar, Bartók, Britten and Stravinsky – among others – created their own versions.

Cantus firmus
Literally "fixed song". A melody borrowed from a religious or secular source as the basis to a polyphonic composition in which other melodies are set in counterpoint against it. Popular between the fourteenth and seventeenth centuries.

Castrato
A male singer castrated as a child, developing a soprano or contralto voice. Very popular during the seventeenth and eighteenth centuries; the last castrato died in the twentieth century.

Cavatina
A lyrical operatic song or aria in one section, or an instrumental work in imitation of such a song – eg the fifth movement from Beethoven's *Quartet No. 13*.

Chaconne
A dance-piece in a slow three-beat time, consisting of variations upon a repeated theme in the bass part. Finest examples are the final movement of Bach's *Violin Partita No. 2* and Purcell's *When I am laid in earth*, from *Dido and Aeneas*.

Chamber music
Instrumental music composed for a small number of players. Sometimes applied to solo instrumental pieces, but more commonly used for duos, trios, quartets etc.

Chanson
French song form of the fourteenth to sixteenth centuries; generally polyphonic.

Chorale
Metrical hymn-tune, with its foundations in the Lutheran Church of sixteenth-century

Germany. Originally sung in unison, but Bach extended the form into separate parts for soprano, alto, tenor and bass.

Chord
Any simultaneous combination of notes.

Chromaticism
Use of notes not belonging to the diatonic scale – ie using sharps, flats or naturals alien to the key. The chromatic scale comprises twelve ascending or descending semitones. Chromaticism is a strong element of Romantic music – Wagner in particular.

Classical
The post-Baroque period, roughly between 1750 and 1830. Pre-eminent Classical composers were Haydn, Mozart and Beethoven, who refined the sonata, symphony and concerto forms.

Coda
The closing section to a movement. Originally made a basic summary of what had gone before, but Mozart and Beethoven developed the coda into a substantial sub-section, some-times introducing new ideas.

Coloratura
Soprano voice capable of great agility and delicacy. Most famous coloratura role is the Queen of the Night in Mozart's *Magic Flute.*.

Concerto
Originally an orchestral work in several movements, with or without soloists, but in the eighteenth centuries it developed into a large-scale work in which a solo instrument is contrasted with an orchestral ensemble. The form was refined by Mozart, whose three-movement concertos became the model for the genre.

Concerto grosso
An orchestral work in which two bodies of instruments (one large and one small) play off against each other. Popular in the seventeenth and eighteenth centuries, and with twentieth-century neo-classicists.

Continuo
The same as figured bass (see below). Generally performed by a harpsichord, organ or any other chordal instrument.

Contralto
The lowest of the female voices – same as an alto, but alto is associated with sacred and choral music, whereas contralto is applied to opera singers.

Contrapuntal
Adjective derived from "counterpoint".

Counterpoint
The placing of two or more parts against each other.

Counter-tenor
The highest male voice.

Cyclic form
The repetition or modification of a single theme in two or more of a work's movements. The most perfect use of cyclic form can be found in Franck's *D minor Symphony*; Berlioz's *idée fixe* and Wagner's leitmotif are related concepts.

Da capo
Means "repeat from the beginning".

Diatonic
Music using the major and minor scales; music constructed exclusively of the notes defined by the key.

Dissonance
A combination of notes that jars the ear, requiring swift resolution.

Divertimento
A light and entertaining suite or movement. Mozart's are supreme examples; popular also with neo-classicists.

Dodecaphonic music
See "serial music".

Double stopping
Simultaneous playing of two strings on a bowed instrument.

Dynamics
The qualities and degrees of softness and loudness.

Étude
A "study", or essay in technique. Paganini, Chopin, Liszt and Debussy – among others – developed the étude into an expressive form rather than a merely technical exercise.

Expressionism
As in the visual arts, a term used to describe works in which the artist's state of mind is the primary subject; similarly applied above all to German music of the early twentieth century – above all, the work of Schoenberg and Berg. The antithesis of Impressionism, but just as imprecise a label.

Fantasia (or Fantasie or Fantaisie)
A loosely structured composition, allowing more freedom of expression than the classical forms. Mozart employed the term, but it is more closely associated with Schubert, Chopin and Schumann.

Figured bass
A bass part played on a keyboard or other chordal instrument, with detailed figures specifying the harmonies to be played above it. Extensively used during the Baroque period.

Fugue
A highly complicated contrapuntal form in which two or more voices are built around a single theme. Their entries are in direct imitation of the theme's opening but each voice is developed independently, so that ultimately the two or more voices are complete melodies in themselves. Bach was the greatest master of the form, which he characterized as resembling "people engaged in rational conversation".

Gavotte
An old French dance in 4/4 time, but beginning on the third beat of the bar. Popularized by Lully.

Gesamtkunstwerk
Literally "unified work of art". Wagner's term for his dramatic ideal in which music, drama and poetry would unite to create an unprecedented art form.

Gigue
A sprightly dance in binary form. Much used by Bach and other eighteenth-century composers as a finale to a dance suite.

Glissando
Principally applied to string instruments. The sliding of a finger over a number of consecutive notes, thus creating an extended slither of sound. Best used by Ravel and Strauss.

Gregorian chant
A type of solo and unison plainsong codified during the papacy of Gregory I (590–604).

Ground bass
A brief, constantly repeated thematic bass pattern that serves as the foundation for the melody, counterpoint and harmony in the upper parts. The basis of Passacaglias and Chaconnes.

Harmony
The simultanous grouping of notes to form a musically significant whole; the basic unit of harmony is the chord. Harmony can colour any single melodic line in innumerable different ways and a composer's harmonic language is one of his or her most immediately identifiable characteristics.

Homophony
Music in which the parts move as one, in grouped chordal patterns, with no independent movement. The opposite of polyphony.

Hymn
A congregational work of praise in which the structure is invariably strophic and the words specially written.

Idée fixe
Berlioz's term for the motto theme that recurs throughout his *Symphonie Fantastique*. Led towards the formulation of leitmotif.

Impressionism
Term taken from painting, to describe music in which suggestion and atmosphere were dominant considerations; typified by Debussy and his followers.

Impromptu
A short, improvisatory piece of song-like piano music – Schubert's are the best examples.

Instrumentation
The scoring of music for particular instruments – not the same as orchestration, which refers to a composer's skill in writing for groups of instruments. Thus Schubert's *Octet*, which shows a remarkable awareness of the qualities of each component, is a superb example of instrumentation.

Intermezzo

1. A brief instrumental or orchestral diversion performed during an opera's scene changes, to denote the passing of time. The intermezzo in Mascagni's *Cavalleria rusticana* is perhaps the best known.

2. A single-movement concert piece, usually for piano – Brahms wrote many.

Interval

The distance between two notes. Intervals are expressed numerically – thirds, fourths etc (though "octave" is used rather than "eighth"). Composers' preferred intervals are highly recognizable aspects of style – perhaps the most immediate are those of Puccini and Richard Strauss.

Key

The basis of tonal music. The keynote is the foundation of the key, which classifies the notes lying at specified intervals from that keynote – thus the key of C major specifies the notes of the major scale, whereas C minor specifies the notes of the minor scale, which has different intervals from the major. As there are twelve notes in the chromatic scale, it follows that there are twenty-four keys. Each key has a certain number of flats and sharps, signified by the key signature. Notes other than those belonging to a work's key are referred to as "accidentals" – accidentals are the basis of chromaticism.

Klavier

German word for "keyboard" – can apply to harpsichord, piano or any domestic keyboard instrument.

Largo

Slow and broad tempo.

Legato

Instruction to play smoothly.

Leitmotif (or leitmotiv)

Literally "leading motif". First used with reference to Weber, to describe a short, constantly recurring musical phrase that relates to a character, emotion or object. Associated above all with Wagner, who turned the leitmotif into a means of blending numerous associations and making structural connections across vast spans of time.

Libretto

The text of an opera.

Lied

German word for song, commonly applied to the songs of Schubert, Schumann, Brahms and Wolf.

Madrigal

A secular, polyphonic composition, frequently unaccompanied; at its height in sixteenth- and seventeenth-century Italy – Monteverdi and Gesualdo wrote outstanding examples.

Mass

The main service of the Roman Catholic Church. Most Mass settings use the so-called "Ordinary" of the Mass, the unchanging five-part core of Kyrie, Gloria, Credo, Sanctus and Agnus Dei. Settings of the "Proper" of the Mass have additional sections required by special circumstances – the best-known example being the Requiem.

Mezzo

The lowest of the soprano voices. One grade above contralto.

Minimalism

First used to describe a school of American music which rejected the complexities of nineteenth-century Romanticism and the twentieth-century avant-garde. Associated most famously with Steve Reich, Philip Glass and John Adams, the term usually denotes music which uses repeating cycles or additions of small phrases to achieve an hypnotic effect. It is now also applied to European composers such as Arvo Pärt, John Tavener and Henryk Górecki, whose music has affinities with the religious music of pre-Renaissance Europe.

Minuet

A brisk French dance in triple time, developed by Lully then highly popular during the eighteenth century. Became the standard third movement in classical sonata form, where it is coupled with a Trio. It later grew into the Scherzo, as mastered by Beethoven.

Modes

In essence, the scales used in European music prior to the seventeenth century, when they were reduced to the major and minor scales known today.

Monody

Term used to describe the style of writing in which a single line or melody is given a continuo accompaniment. Developed around 1600, in reaction to the complexities of polyphonic composition.

Monothematic

Having only one theme.

Motet

Sacred unaccompanied choral composition; the text is usually in Latin, but is never taken from the liturgy.

Motif (or motiv or motive)

A brief, recognizable musical idea, usually melodic but sometimes rhythmic.

Movement

A self-contained section of a larger work; so called because each section had a different, autonomous tempo indication.

Nationalism

The expression of distinctive national characteristics in music, usually through the adaptation of folk material. A prevalent tendency all over Europe in the latter half of the nineteenth century; associated with such diverse figures as Glinka, Liszt, Smetana, Dvořák, Bartók, Kodály, Grieg, Vaughan Williams, Janáček and Sibelius.

Neo-classicism

A trend that became particularly strong during the 1920s, in reaction to the indulgences of late Romanticism. Typified by the adoption of Baroque and Classical forms, and the use of heavily contrapuntal writing. Much of Stravinsky's output can be classified as neo-classical.

Nocturne

1. In eighteenth-century music, a short serenade in several movements for a small group of instruments.
2. A brief, lyrical piano piece; associated especially with Chopin.

Note-row

The foundation of serialism; the order in which a composer choses to arrange the composition's basic twelve notes, none of which can be repeated until the other eleven have been deployed. See "Serialism".

Octave

The interval that divides two notes of the same written pitch – eg C to C.

Opera buffa

A form of opera in which everyday characters are placed in comic situations. Mastered by Mozart in *Le Nozze di Figaro*, by Rossini in *Il Barbiere di Siviglia* and Donizetti in *Don Pasquale*.

Opera seria

The dominant operatic genre during the seventeenth and eighteenth centuries. Characterized by heroic or mythological scenarios, often with extensive florid writing for castrati. The last and greatest example of the highly disciplined form was Mozart's *La clemenza di Tito*.

Oratorio

A dramatic musical setting of a religious text, usually for solo voices, chorus and orchestra. Originated in Rome around 1600; later examples are Handel's *Messiah*, Mendelssohn's *Elija* and Elgar's *The Dream of Gerontius*.

Orchestra

The first regular orchestras appeared in the Baroque era, and consisted of strings, oboes and bassoons, plus a widely changing list of solo instruments. The layout became standardized during the Classical period, when Mozart and Haydn made specific demands regarding the number and quality of players for their symphonies. This Classical orchestra established the basic division of the players into four sections: strings; woodwind (flutes, oboes, bassoons and clarinets); brass (horns and trumpets); and percussion (kettledrums). Beethoven's symphonies demanded more (and better) players, and Berlioz, Wagner and Mahler required yet further expansions of the orchestra's resources. Though the instruments have changed over the years, the orchestra of today is not much different from the sort of array that sat before Mahler.

Orchestration

1. The art of writing for an orchestra, demanding an understanding of the qualities of each instrumental section, and an ability to manage and combine them.

2. The scoring of a work not originally intended for the orchestra – eg Mussorgsky's *Pictures from an Exhibition*, which was orchestrated by Ravel.

Ornaments (or Embellishments)

Notes added to the printed score in performance by a singer or instrumentalist. In the seventeenth and eighteenth centuries composers generally indicated where such additions were required; by the start of the nineteenth century this improvisatory element had been virtually quashed.

Overture

1. An orchestral introduction to an opera, oratorio or play.
2. A single-movement orchestral piece composed for the concert hall, otherwise known as a "Concert Overture". Examples include Mendelssohn's *Hebrides Overture* and Brahm's *Tragic* and *Academic Festival* overtures.

Passacaglia

Instrumental work (originally a dance) with a continually repeated theme – not necessarily in the bass, and thus not the same as a Chaconne.

Pizzicato

The plucking of bowed string instruments.

Plainchant (or Plainsong)

Medieval unaccompanied sacred music in which a single vocal line is notated in free rhythm, like speech. The ancestor of Gregorian chant.

Polyphony

Music in which a group of voices are combined contrapuntally. The heyday of polyphonic music was from the thirteenth to the late sixteenth century – Palestrina, Lassus and Byrd are among the major polyphonists. However, Bach's music can also be described as polyphonic, even though it is governed by different harmonic principles from those of the Renaissance polyphonists.

Polytonality

The use of two or more keys at the same time. Stravinsky's music is full of examples.

Programme music

Music that relates to a specific story, painting, text, character or experience. Most often used in connection with "symphonic poems" or "tone poems" of Romantic composers such as Liszt, Berlioz, Tchaikovsky and Strauss.

Recitative

Semi-sung dialogue and narrative in opera and oratorio. In its rhythmic freedom it is closer to dramatic speech than to song.

Rhapsody

A Romantic term, applied to compositions suggestive of heroic endeavour or overwhelming emotion. Best-known examples are Brahms's *Alto Rhapsody*, Rachmaninov's *Rhapsody on a Theme of Paganini*, and Gershwin's *Rhapsody in Blue*.

Romanticism

The cultural epoch heralded by Beethoven and Schubert, and dominated by Chopin, Schumann, Liszt, Berlioz and Wagner. Characterized by the abandonment of traditional forms and structures, a predilection for extra-musical subjects, an increase in the scale of composition, and an affection for chromaticism.

Rondo

A structural form in which one section recurs at certain times throughout a work – thus (A) B (A) C (A) D (A).

Rubato

A subtle flexibility of pace that alters the shape of a phrase but does not affect its pulse, tempo or structure. A necessity in Chopin's music. Summarized by Liszt as being like the collective motion of the leaves of a tree.

Scherzo

Literally a "joke". Began as a lively movement derived from the Minuet, but developed into an autonomous genre in which the original humour is replaced by a free-ranging, rather tempestuous expressiveness – Chopin's piano *Scherzi* are the most famous examples.

Serenade

1. A love song.
2. In the eighteenth century, an evening entertainment for orchestra – eg Mozart's *Eine kleine Nachtmusik*.

Serialism

Also known as twelve-tone or dodecaphonic music, serialism was developed by Schoenberg as a replacement for traditional harmonic and tonal languages. A serial composition is based on a twelve-note theme (the tone-row or note-row), which can then be used in different ways: forwards, backwards, upside down, upside down and backwards, or superimposed to create chords. Its most extreme form, in which predetermined rules govern every aspect of the piece, including volume and speed, is known as total serialism, and is associated primarily with the post-war work of Messiaen and Boulez.

Singspiel

Germanic genre – in essence comic opera with spoken dialogue instead of recitative. A good example is *The Magic Flute*.

Sonata

1. From around 1600 to the mid-eighteenth century, a solo instrumental composition not in any strict form – literally "sounded" rather than sung.
2. From the era of Haydn, an instrumental work in three or four movements for solo instrument and keyboard or for solo keyboard. The form of the first movement became known as sonata form.

Sonata form

The crucial invention of the Classical era, sonata form was used in most instrumental and symphonic music until the Romantic era, and even then the likes of Brahms kept it alive, as did the great symphonists of the twentieth century. Sonata form is divided into the following three sections:
A. The exposition: here a first subject, the work's main theme, leads to a second subject in another key, in which fresh material is introduced.
B. The development: this consists of material already heard in the exposition, but develops it considerably.
C. The recapitulation: this presents a varied repetition of the material first heard in the exposition. Ends with a coda.

Soprano

The highest female voice.

Spinto

Urgent, heroic Italian tenor voice.

Sprechgesang

Literally "speechsong", a singing style midway between song and speech. Invented by Schoenberg, the technique requires the singer to approximate the pitch of the note and deliver it with the right amount of colour. Used by Schoenberg in his *Pierrot Lunaire* but the finest example is Berg's *Wozzeck*.

Staccato

The opposite of legato. A direction for a note to be played shorter than is marked, detaching it from the note that follows.

Strophic

Term used to describe a song which uses the same music for each new verse.

Study

See "Étude".

Symphonic Poem (or Tone Poem)

Orchestral programme music, a genre devised by Liszt and perfected by Strauss.

Symphony

First used to designate an orchestral interlude or overture to a vocal work, but since the mid-eighteenth century the term has been used for a large-scale orchestral work, generally in four movements, sometimes in three or five. The Classical symphony was developed by Haydn, Mozart and Beethoven, and many of the greatest subsequent composers have added to the repertoire – Schubert, Brahms, Mahler, Bruckner, Sibelius, Nielsen and Shostakovich being notable masters of the form.

Syncopation

Emphasis on the off-beat; characteristic of jazz, much used in jazz-influenced early twentieth-century music.

Tempo

The pace of a work.

Tenor

The second highest male voice.

Ternary form

An instrumental or orchestral composition in three sections, in which the first section is repeated – ie (A) B (A).

Tessitura

The natural range of a voice, or the range within which lie most of the notes of a role.

Timbre

The quality of a sound – literally its "stamp".

Time signature

The numbers at the beginning of a composition, movement or section (or, indeed, midway through a phrase in some twentieth-century scores) to indicate the number and kind of beats in a bar – 4/4, 3/4, 9/16 etc.

Tonality

Adherence to a single key.

Trio

1. Combination of three performers.

2. Work for such a combination.

3. Central section of a Minuet, so-called because originally written in three-part harmony.

Twelve-tone

See "Serialism".

Vibrato

Rapid but small vibration in pitch – most often used in reference to string players, singers and wind players.

Waltz

A dance in triple time. Especially popular throughout the nineteenth century in Austria – most famously, through the music of the Strauss family.

INDEX OF COMPOSERS

INDEX OF TITLES & GENRES